ETHICAL PROBLEMS
IN THE
PRACTICE OF LAW

ASPEN CASEBOOK SERIES

ETHICAL PROBLEMS IN THE PRACTICE OF LAW

CONCISE THIRD EDITION FOR TWO-CREDIT COURSES

Lisa G. Lerman
Professor of Law and Coordinator of Clinical Programs
The Catholic University of America, Columbus School of Law

Philip G. Schrag
Delaney Family Professor of Public Interest Law
Director, Center for Applied Legal Studies
Georgetown University Law Center

Wolters Kluwer
Law & Business

Library of Congress Cataloging-in-Publication Data

Lerman, Lisa G.
   Ethical problems in the practice of law / Lisa G. Lerman, Professor of Law and Coordinator of Clinical Programs. The Catholic University of America, Columbus School of Law; Philip G. Schrag, Delaney Family Professor of Public Interest Law, Director, Center for Applied Legal Studies, Georgetown University Law Center. — Concise third edition for two-credit courses.
      pages cm.—(Aspen casebook series)
   Includes index.
   ISBN 978-1-4548-3070-2
   1. Legal ethics—United States. I. Schrag, Philip G., 1943- II. Title.

KF306.L47 2013
174′.3—dc23

2013005457

SUSTAINABLE FORESTRY INITIATIVE

Certified Sourcing
www.sfiprogram.org
SFI-01234

SFI label applies to the text stock

About Wolters Kluwer Law & Business

Wolters Kluwer Law & Business is a leading global provider of intelligent information and digital solutions for legal and business professionals in key specialty areas, and respected educational resources for professors and law students. Wolters Kluwer Law & Business connects legal and business professionals as well as those in the education market with timely, specialized authoritative content and information-enabled solutions to support success through productivity, accuracy and mobility.

Serving customers worldwide, Wolters Kluwer Law & Business products include those under the Aspen Publishers, CCH, Kluwer Law International, Loislaw, Best Case, ftwilliam. com and MediRegs family of products.

CCH products have been a trusted resource since 1913, and are highly regarded resources for legal, securities, antitrust and trade regulation, government contracting, banking, pension, payroll, employment and labor, and healthcare reimbursement and compliance professionals.

Aspen Publishers products provide essential information to attorneys, business professionals and law students. Written by preeminent authorities, the product line offers analytical and practical information in a range of specialty practice areas from securities law and intellectual property to mergers and acquisitions and pension/benefits. Aspen's trusted legal education resources provide professors and students with high-quality, up-to-date and effective resources for successful instruction and study in all areas of the law.

Kluwer Law International products provide the global business community with reliable international legal information in English. Legal practitioners, corporate counsel and business executives around the world rely on Kluwer Law journals, looseleafs, books, and electronic products for comprehensive information in many areas of international legal practice.

Loislaw is a comprehensive online legal research product providing legal content to law firm practitioners of various specializations. Loislaw provides attorneys with the ability to quickly and efficiently find the necessary legal information they need, when and where they need it, by facilitating access to primary law as well as state-specific law, records, forms and treatises.

Best Case Solutions is the leading bankruptcy software product to the bankruptcy industry. It provides software and workflow tools to flawlessly streamline petition preparation and the electronic filing process, while timely incorporating ever-changing court requirements.

ftwilliam.com offers employee benefits professionals the highest quality plan documents (retirement, welfare and non-qualified) and government forms (5500/PBGC, 1099 and IRS) software at highly competitive prices.

MediRegs products provide integrated health care compliance content and software solutions for professionals in healthcare, higher education and life sciences, including professionals in accounting, law and consulting.

Wolters Kluwer Law & Business, a division of Wolters Kluwer, is headquartered in New York. Wolters Kluwer is a market-leading global information services company focused on professionals.

To Sam and Sarah,
who continue to light up our lives

Summary of Contents

CONTENTS

About the Authors 601

TABLE OF PROBLEMS

PREFACE FOR TEACHERS AND STUDENTS

Our goals

This book introduces the law that governs lawyers. Our principal goals in writing it were to offer an overview of the law governing lawyers and to provide materials through which law students may explore some of the ethical problems that lawyers encounter in practice. We also sought to provide opportunities for law students to consider the various professional roles that lawyers occupy and the moral quandaries that students will struggle with when they begin to practice law. For example, in negotiating a settlement for a client, a lawyer might say that his client would refuse to accept less than $100,000, even though the client has told the lawyer that she would be delighted to receive $50,000. This is deceptive, but lawyers commonly use this tactic to obtain favorable outcomes for their clients. Does the pervasiveness of this type of deception make it acceptable? Is a lawyer's only duty to get the best result for his client, or does he also owe his opposing counsel a duty of honesty?

This book introduces students to many aspects of the law that governs lawyers. The book does not include an encyclopedic analysis of every ethical rule, much less the entire body of law governing the legal profession. We focus primarily on the subjects that are most likely to arise during the first years of an individual's law practice. For example, many new lawyers become associates in law firms, so this book explores what an associate should do when a more senior associate or a partner asks the associate to do something that seems improper. Also, most new lawyers in private practice make frequent decisions about how to record their time for billing purposes. This book includes many problems that arise from everyday practice issues. Most of the examples and problems in this book involve lawyers who represent individuals or businesses in matters

"*Ms. Burney, do we have anything on right and wrong?*"

involving contracts, torts, criminal prosecution and defense, civil litigation, real estate, and family law. We have sought to develop problems and to select cases in which a student can understand the facts and the ethical issues regardless of whether the student has taken advanced courses in law school.

The problem-based approach

This book offers opportunities to explore ethical dilemmas that have actually arisen in practice, some of which have resulted in published judicial decisions. While we have excerpted numerous important judicial opinions in the book, we have transformed a larger number of cases into problems for class discussion. Instead of reprinting the appellate opinions, we have presented the essential facts of these cases as one of the lawyers saw them, walking the cases backward in time to the moment at which the lawyer had to make a difficult choice based on both ethical and strategic considerations. Rather than building the book primarily around predigested legal analyses by appellate judges, we invite students to put themselves in the shoes of lawyers who face difficult choices among possible actions. The dilemmas in most of our problems are based on tough situations that have confronted real lawyers.

Evaluating ethical dilemmas in class will help students to handle similar quandaries when they encounter them in practice. A student who has worked through the problems assigned in this course will know where in the law a particular issue might be addressed, how to begin to analyze the relevant rules, and what questions to ask. Grappling with these problems also will increase students' awareness of ethical issues that otherwise might have gone unnoticed.[1]

We set out to write an introduction to the law governing lawyers that students would enjoy reading. Studies show that by the third year of law school, the class attendance rate is only about 60 percent and that a majority of those students who do attend class read the assignments for half or fewer than half of the classes they attend.[2] Increasingly, law students use their computers to play solitaire or write e-mails during class.[3] Law schools seem to be failing in their efforts to retain the interest and attention of their students, particularly third-year law students. We have sought to write a book whose content and methodology capture and sustain the reader's interest. This aspiration is reflected in our choice of topics and materials, our concise summaries of the law, our challenging problems, and our use of graphic materials.

Defining features of this book

We built a number of unique features into this book based on our experience teaching professional responsibility classes:

- ▪ Almost every section of the book begins by summarizing the relevant doctrine that provides the legal background students need to analyze the problems that follow.

---

1. See Steven Hartwell, Promoting Moral Development Through Experiential Teaching, 1 Clin. L. Rev. 505, 527 (1995) (reporting on his empirical research, which shows that professional responsibility students' moral reasoning skills made significant advances during a course in which students discussed simulated ethical dilemmas); and Lisa G. Lerman, Teaching Moral Perception and Moral Judgment in Legal Ethics Courses: A Dialogue About Goals, 39 Wm. & Mary L. Rev. 457, 459 (1998) (explaining the reasons to use experiential methodology in professional responsibility classes).

2. Mitu Gulati, Richard Sander & Robert Sockloskie, The Happy Charade: An Empirical Examination of the Third Year of Law School, 51 J. Leg. Educ. 235, 244-245 (2001).

3. Ian Ayres, Lectures vs. Laptops, N.Y. Times A25 (Mar. 20, 2001) (available at http://www.nytimes.com/2001/03/20/opinion/20AYRE.html); David Cole, Laptops vs. Learning, Wash. Post A13 (Apr. 7, 2007) (available at http://www.washingtonpost.com/wp-dyn/content/article/2007/04/06/AR2007040601544.html).

- Most summarized rules and doctrines appear in question-and-answer format. This structure provides an ongoing roadmap, anticipating readers' questions and forecasting the content of the next subtopic.
- Numerous concrete examples, set off from the text, further illustrate the general doctrinal principles.
- A few judicial opinions appear in the book; they have been edited carefully to present only the most relevant sections. Several other opinions are summarized rather than reprinted so that students can move quickly to the book's challenging application problems.
- The 44 problems that appear in the book are designed to focus class discussion and immediately engage students by describing real-life ethical dilemmas.
- The problems present facts from real cases in narrative form to allow students to analyze the issues as if they were the lawyers facing those dilemmas. This structure tends to produce livelier discussion than does the autopsy method traditionally used in law classes, in which teachers invite post hoc dissection of court opinions.
- Pertinent rules of professional conduct are included in the book so that students do not need to flip constantly back and forth between this text and a statutory supplement. When studying a particular rule, students will find it worthwhile to review the entire rule and comments in another published source or on the Internet.[4] However, this text is structured so that it can be read without constant reference to a supplement.
- The book's many bulleted lists and tables clarify legal doctrines and other conceptual material in easily reviewable sections.
- Photographs, diagrams, and cartoons break up the text. Some of these, like the photographs of some of the lawyers, parties, judges, and scholars, add important context. Others, like the cartoons, offer a change of pace from the textual narrative.

We hope that you enjoy this book. We welcome your reactions and suggestions, small or large, for the next edition. Please send any comments or questions to lerman@law.edu.

Lisa G. Lerman
Philip G. Schrag

---

4. For example, students will find the full text of the Model Rules of Professional Conduct and the explanatory comments interpreting each rule at http://www.americanbar.org/groups/professional_responsibility/publications/model_rules_of_professional_conduct/model_rules_of_professional_conduct_table_of_contents.html (accessed Nov. 29, 2012).

ACKNOWLEDGMENTS

Hundreds of law professors, practitioners, and judges have worked to regulate the practice of law, to study its regulation, and to publish their ideas. Decades of effort have gone into the drafting of successive model codes for lawyers, rules of state bars, and the Restatement. Academics have made countless contributions in the form of books and law review articles on the legal profession and papers delivered to conferences convened under the auspices of the American Bar Association, the Association of American Law Schools, the Keck Foundation, and other organizations. This book is in part a summary of many of those efforts.

We particularly want to acknowledge our intellectual debt to the authors of the Restatement and of the other treatises and textbooks that are used in courses on legal ethics and the American legal profession. We have consulted these books frequently in the course of writing this volume, and some of the materials we have used were called to our attention by other casebook authors.

We have received invaluable encouragement and assistance from our editors at Aspen, especially Susan Boulanger, Melody Davies, John Devins, Troy Froebe, Richard Mixter, Barbara Roth, and Mei Wang. We are particularly grateful to Lisa Wehrle, who has copy-edited every edition of this book and significantly improved its readability. Several colleagues have reviewed various drafts of the book and have given us amazingly insightful and detailed comments and suggestions. These include Tom Andrews, Carrie Griffin Basas, Paul Chill, Russell Engler, Susan Saab Fortney, William Freivogel, Steve Goldman, Mark Harrison, Peter Joy, Ann Juergens, Arlene Kanter, Donald Lundberg, Judith Maute, Ben Mintz, Jane Moriarty, Rob Rubinson, Ted Schneyer, and Brad Wendell. Many other people assisted us by answering questions and providing needed information. These include Frank Armani, Carl Bogus, Kathleen Clark, Nathan Crystal, Scott Cummings, Richard Dieter, Sarah Duggin, Susanna Fischer, Lawrence Fordham, David Frakt, Alex Garnick, Art Garwin,

Lisa Wehrle

Stephen Gillers, John Gleason, Bruce Green, Denise Greskowiak, James Grogan, Alexandra Lahav, David Luban, Deborah Luxenberg, Peter Margulies, Michael Mello, Carrie Menkel-Meadow, Ellen Messing, Nancy Moore, Wendy Muchman, Charles Oates, Mark Pautler, Lucian Pera, Joan Peterson, Paul Reingold, Jennifer Renne, John Rooney, Stephen Saltzburg, Mitchell Simon, Roy Simon, William Simon, John Taylor, Rebecca Tushnet, David Vladeck, Leah Wortham, and Ellen Yaroshefsky. We also benefited from excellent research assistance by Dori Antonetti, Noel DeSantos, Jessica Kendall, Connie Lynch, Keith Palfin, Jason Parish, and Michael Provost.

Special thanks go to Jason Parish, who cite-checked the entire manuscript of the first edition of this book and drafted the tables of cases, rules, and articles. He did all of this work with amazing precision and care. For contributions to the second edition, we would like to thank Erica Pencak, Ruth Harper, and Taylor Strickling. For the third edition, we are particularly grateful to Patrick Kane and to our extraordinary research assistant Bria DiSalvo.

We note with sorrow the passing in 2010 of Leo Cullum, who drew most of the *New Yorker* cartoons in this book. Mr. Cullum was an extraordinary cartoonist and a perceptive and acerbic observer of the legal profession.

We appreciate the support given us (in the form of leaves of absence from teaching and summer writing grants) by our employers, Catholic University and Georgetown University, and we appreciate the hospitality shown us by Gail Saliterman during our work on Chapters 2 and 3 of this edition.

We would like to thank our children, Samuel Schrag Lerman and Sarah Lerman Schrag (to whom the book is dedicated). Both of them are exquisitely sensitive to moral and ethical issues. Our understanding of ethical problems has been much advanced by our many conversations with them about the dilemmas that they have confronted. These conversations have informed our analysis of several problems in this book.[1] Besides being our ethics tutors, Sam and Sarah sat through an untold number of

---

1. The ethical problems that lawyers encounter are often similar to those faced by non-lawyers, including adolescents; both kinds of problems involve issues such as loyalty, confidentiality, truthfulness, and conflicts of interest. For example, suppose that you are a teenager and that your friend tells you in confidence about a serious problem that she is having (e.g., with drugs or depression). Should you consult your parents despite your promise of confidence? What if your parents might inform your friend's parents who do not yet know about the problem? If your friend might pose a danger to others, should you tell the administration at your school or talk directly to your friend's parents?

conversations about the book at dinner, on vacations, and elsewhere. They continue to provide us with many good ideas about teaching and learning.

We thank these owners of literary and photographic rights for granting permission to reprint copyrighted material, including excerpts from articles and books, photographs, and cartoons:

Textual material

American Law Institute, Restatement of the Law Governing Lawyers. Copyright 2000 by the American Law Institute. Reproduced with permission. All rights reserved.

Ken Armstrong & Maurice Possley, Trial and Error, Part 1: Verdict: Dishonor. Reprinted with permission of the Chicago Tribune; copyright Chicago Tribune; all rights reserved.

Stephen Gillers, Can a Good Lawyer Be a Bad Person? 84 Mich. L. Rev. 1011 (1986), revised and reprinted in 2 J. Inst. Study Leg. Ethics 131 (1999). Reprinted with permission.

Patrick J. Schiltz, On Being a Happy, Healthy, and Ethical Member of an Unhappy, Unhealthy, and Unethical Profession, 52 Vand. L. Rev. 871 (1999). Reprinted with permission of the Vanderbilt Law Review.

Ted Schneyer, Moral Philosophy's Standard Misconception of Legal Ethics, 1984 Wis. L. Rev. 1529 (1985). Copyright 1984 by the Board of Regents of the University of Wisconsin System. Reprinted by permission of the Wisconsin Law Review and the Board of Regents of the University of Wisconsin System.

Susan Shapiro, Tangled Loyalties: Conflict of Interest in Legal Practice (2002). Reprinted with permission of the University of Michigan Press.

William Simon, Virtuous Lying: A Critique of Quasi-Categorical Moralism, 12 Geo. J. Leg. Ethics 433 (1999). Reprinted with permission of the Georgetown Journal of Legal Ethics.

Harry Subin, The Criminal Defense Lawyer's "Different Mission": Reflections on the "Right" to Present a False Case, 1 Geo. J. Leg. Ethics 129 (1987). Reprinted with permission of the Georgetown Journal of Legal Ethics.

Ellen Yaroshefsky, Wrongful Convictions: It is Time to Take Prosecution Discipline Seriously, 8 D.C. L. Rev. 275 (2004). Reprinted with permission of the D.C. Law Review.

Images

Frank H. Armani, photograph. Reproduced with permission of Frank H. Armani.

"Attention, please." Cartoon. Copyright The New Yorker Collection 1984 Leo Cullum from cartoonbank.com. All rights reserved. Reproduced with permission.

Michele DeStefano Beardslee, photograph. Reproduced with permission of the University of Miami School of Law

Francis Richard Belge, photograph. Reproduced with permission of Frances M. Belge.

"Can we talk . . . ?" Cartoon. Copyright The New Yorker Collection Mick Stevens from cartoonbank.com. All rights reserved. Reproduced with permission.

Nora Freeman Engstrom, photograph. Photo credit: Joe Neto, Jr.

"First we discuss my percentage." Cartoon. Copyright The New Yorker Collection 2009 Leo Cullum from cartoonbank.com. All rights reserved. Reproduced with permission.

Susan Saab Fortney, photograph. Reproduced with permission of Frank Ramos Jr. and Texas Tech University.

William Freivogel, photograph. Reproduced with permission of Caroline Freivogel.

Robert Garrow, photograph. Reprinted from the Post-Standard (Syracuse, N.Y.). Reproduced with permission.

Daniel J. Gatti, photograph. Reproduced with permission of Gatti, Gatti, Maier, Krueger, Sayer & Associates.

Dominic Gentile, photograph. Reproduced with permission of Dominic Gentile.

Stephen Gillers, photograph. Reproduced with permission of Stephen Gillers.

"God help me, Henry. . . ." Cartoon. Copyright The New Yorker Collection Jack Ziegler from cartoonbank.com. All rights reserved. Reproduced with permission.

Bruce Green, photograph. Reproduced with permission of Chris Taggart.

James J. Grogan, photograph. Reproduced with permission of James J. Grogan.

"He's talking. . . ." Cartoon. Copyright The New Yorker Collection 1999 Liza Donnelly from cartoonbank.com. All rights reserved. Reproduced with permission.

"Hey, Conroy, your lawyer is here." Cartoon. Copyright The New Yorker Collection 2007 Arnie Levin from cartoonbank.com. All rights reserved. Reproduced with permission.

"Hi. I'm your court appointed lawyer." Cartoon. Copyright The New Yorker Collection 2000 J. B. Handelsman from cartoonbank.com. All rights reserved. Reproduced with permission.

Webster Hubbell, photograph. Reproduced with permission of the Arkansas Democrat-Gazette.

"I'd like to tell you. . . ." Cartoon. Copyright The New Yorker Collection 2007 Mick Stevens from cartoonbank.com. All rights reserved. Reproduced with permission.

"If we're being honest, it was your decision. . . ." Cartoon. Copyright The New Yorker Collection 1999 Leo Cullum from cartoonbank.com. All rights reserved. Reproduced with permission.

"I love my testimony. . . ." Cartoon. Copyright The New Yorker Collection 2004 Leo Cullum from cartoonbank.com. All rights reserved. Reproduced with permission.

"I'm going to get you acquitted, . . ." Cartoon. Copyright The New Yorker Collection 2000 Leo Cullum from cartoonbank.com. All rights reserved. Reproduced with permission.

"I never discuss. . . ." Cartoon. Copyright The New Yorker Collection 2004 Danny Shanahan from cartoonbank.com. All rights reserved. Reproduced with permission.

"I shot a man in Reno. . . ." Cartoon. Copyright The New Yorker Collection 1998 Danny Shanahan from cartoonbank.com. All rights reserved. Reproduced with permission.

"Is it right?" Cartoon. Copyright The New Yorker Collection 2006 Leo Cullum from cartoonbank.com. All rights reserved. Reproduced with permission.

Kimberly Kirkland, photograph. Reproduced with permission of the University of New Hampshire School of Law.

Lawyer-assisted suicide. Cartoon. Copyright The New Yorker Collection 1997 Roz Chast from cartoonbank.com. All rights reserved. Reproduced with permission.

Leslie Levin, photograph. Reproduced with permission of the University of Connecticut School of Law.

David Luban, photograph. Reproduced by permission of Georgetown University Law Center.

Kenneth Mann, photograph. Reproduced by permission of Kenneth Mann.

Carrie Menkel-Meadow, photograph. Photo credit: Alan Levenson. Reproduced by permission.

Jane Moriarty, photograph. Reproduced by permission of Jane Moriarty.

Ethical Problems
in the
Practice of Law

INTRODUCTION

A. Ethics, morals, and professionalism

Why study the law governing lawyers?

The law governing lawyers is worth studying for two reasons. First, knowledge of this subject is an important element of your professional security. (That is, it will help you to stay out of trouble.) Second, you need to know the boundaries imposed by law on the conduct of the other lawyers you encounter so that you will recognize improper conduct and not allow your clients to be harmed by it.

This course is somewhat different from other courses in the curriculum because it has a very practical goal — to assist you in avoiding professional discipline, civil liability, and criminal charges. Some lawyers get into serious trouble, and others experience near-misses, at some point during their careers. Many lawyers who have gotten into trouble made simple and avoidable mistakes. Some of the ethical and legal rules that govern lawyers are counterintuitive, so an educated guess about what a rule provides is sometimes incorrect. An empirical study in New York concluded that "[v]ery few lawyers ever looked at the New York [professional responsibility] Code to resolve ethical issues they encountered in practice" and, in fact, "had not consulted it since law school."[1]

> **FOR EXAMPLE:** Suppose that you are representing a plaintiff and are in the middle of a civil lawsuit. The other side offers to pay a preposterously low settlement. You are tempted to turn it down on the spot to demonstrate your contempt for the offer and to increase the pressure on your adversary to come up with a better one. But if you reject this offer without consulting your client, you are inadvertently violating an ethical rule. You could be disciplined, or your client might sue you for malpractice.

Why study the history and sociology of the legal profession?

One reason to study the profession as well as its ethical rules is to acquire useful background knowledge about the various organizations that make and enforce the rules for lawyers.

> **FOR EXAMPLE:** The American Bar Association writes many rules and opinions. What is this entity? Does it have some kind of governmental authority? What is its relationship to the bars of the 50 states?

Also, as a lawyer you need to be familiar with the various policy issues relating to the structure and regulation of the profession so that, through your state or local bar association or otherwise, you can participate in the improvement of the profession and the justice system.

> **FOR EXAMPLE:** Should legal assistants be allowed to provide some services to clients without being supervised by lawyers? Should lawyers

---

1. Leslie C. Levin, The Ethical World of Solo and Small Law Firm Practitioners, 41 Hous. L. Rev. 309, 368-369 (2004).

be required to offer some services to clients who cannot afford to pay them? If you believe the answer to either of these questions is yes, you might become involved in advocacy to license such assistants or to mandate pro bono work.

Even as a new lawyer, you will have opportunities to affect the ever-changing law of the legal profession. You may become a law clerk to a judge. You might be asked to draft an opinion on an appeal of a lawyer disciplinary matter or to advise your judge about proposed ethical rules. You could become involved in legislative policymaking as a staff member to a state or federal legislator, or even as an elected representative. Many recent law graduates serve on committees of state and local bar associations that initiate or comment on changes in the rules that govern lawyers. Much of the impetus for law reform comes from the fresh perceptions of new-comers to a particular field of law who have not yet become fully accustomed to "business as usual."

What is the difference between ethics and morals?

That depends on whom and in what context you ask. These two terms are sometimes used synonymously[2] and sometimes distinguished, but in varying ways. One scholar defines "morals" as

> values that we attribute to a system of beliefs that help the individual define right versus wrong, good versus bad. These typically get their authority from something outside the individual — a higher being or higher authority (e.g. government, society). Moral concepts, judgments and practices may vary from one society to another.[3]

We use the word "moral" to refer to the broad question of whether an act is right or wrong.

"Ethics" as a general concept is "also called moral philosophy, the discipline concerned with what is morally good and bad, right and wrong. The term is also applied to any system or theory of moral values or principles."[4] We use the term "ethics" or "ethical," however, to refer not to the field of moral philosophy, but to the field of legal ethics. The term "legal ethics" is defined as "principles of conduct that members of the profession

---

2. See, e.g., Merriam-Webster On-Line Dictionary, http://www.m-w.com/cgi-bin/dictionary?book = Dictionary&va = moral (accessed Dec. 4, 2012), which lists "moral" and "ethical" as synonyms.

3. Frank Navran, What Is the Difference Between Ethics, Morals and Values? Ethics Resource Center, Ethics Glossary, http://www.ethics.org/resource/ethics-glossary (accessed Dec. 4, 2012).

4. "Ethics," Encyclopædia Britannica, http://www.britannica.com/eb/article-9106054/ethics (accessed Dec. 4, 2012).

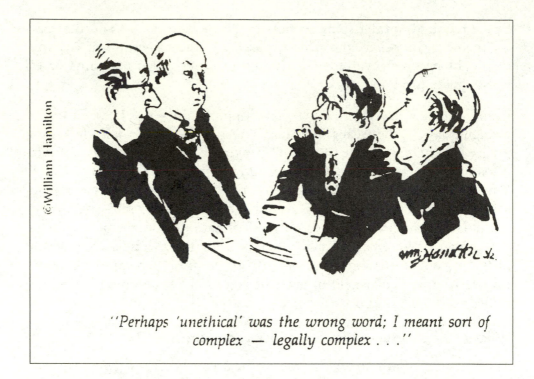

"Perhaps 'unethical' was the wrong word; I meant sort of complex — legally complex . . ."

are expected to observe in the practice of law. These principles are an outgrowth of the development of the legal profession itself."[5] When we ask whether a particular act is "unethical," usually we are asking whether the act would violate the ethics codes that govern lawyers. We also invite readers to consider whether a particular response to a problem is moral or immoral. Often, but not always, the "right thing to do" in a particular situation also would comply with the ethical rules. Even so, it is important to ask both questions. Of course, lawyers often disagree both about the best interpretation of ethical rules and about what is "the right thing to do."

The ethics codes reflect a fairly strong consensus within the legal profession about what lawyers should do when faced with certain kinds of pressures and dilemmas. Most lawyers would say that it is immoral as well as professionally improper to violate a state's code of ethics for lawyers. But many lawyers could identify some rules whose mandates do not correspond with their individual moral judgment.

FOR EXAMPLE: One rule bars litigating lawyers from helping indigent clients to pay their rent. While providing such assistance would violate the rule and could get a lawyer in trouble, few people would say that it would be immoral to do so.

---

5. "Legal Ethics," Encyclopædia Britannica, http://www.britannica.com/eb/article-9106474 (accessed Dec. 4, 2012).

The critical point here is that in evaluating any question in legal ethics, you must ask whether the conduct in question violates the ethics codes. (For the protection of both the lawyer and the client, you also must ask whether the conduct violates other law, such as criminal law or regulatory law.) Quite apart from the question of compliance with law, you should add a final question: "What is the right thing to do?"

What difference does it make that lawyers are "professionals"?

The words "profession" and "professional," like the words "ethics" and "ethical," have multiple meanings. Some fields, such as medicine, law, and architecture, are considered "professions," while others are not. Members of most professions are permitted to do work that is forbidden to non-members. They must be licensed before they are allowed to ply their trades. To obtain licenses, they must receive extensive technical training. Governing bodies of professional associations develop standards for licensing professionals and for disciplining licensees who fail to meet the standards.

Second, a critical aspect of what it means to be a professional is a commitment to serving others. The training and licensing of lawyers is intended to promote the delivery of high-quality services, to expand the opportunities for people to have access to justice, and to foster support throughout society for the rule of law. Because the profession is essential to the protection of democratic government, and because lawyers, through the licensing process, have a monopoly on the service they provide, lawyers are expected to provide some service to clients who cannot afford to pay. They are also expected to participate in the improvement of the legal system.

Third, to be "professional," or do something in a professional way, means to do an unusually careful job. This sense of the word does not require advanced training, but it does imply a high degree of skill and care. One can do a professional job of any work, not just the work required of members of the "professions." Most people who consider themselves "professionals" have their own internal standards of performance. They want to perform at high levels at all times, even when no one is watching. They derive internal satisfaction as well as external rewards for doing excellent work.

A fourth aspect of becoming a professional is that a person joining a profession adopts a defined role and agrees to comply with articulated standards of conduct. This may lead the individual to make moral choices about his conduct that are justified by reference to the defined role.[6]

---

6. There are many fine books and articles discussing professionalism among lawyers. See, e.g., ABA Commn. on Professionalism, In the Spirit of Public Service: A Blueprint for the Rekindling of Lawyer Professionalism (ABA 1986); ABA Section of Leg. Educ. & Admissions to the Bar, Teaching and Learning Professionalism 6 (ABA 1996).

> **FOR EXAMPLE:** A criminal defense lawyer might urge that it is proper to seek to exclude from evidence an exhibit that shows his client's guilt because the police obtained the evidence improperly. Even if the court's ability to discern the true facts is compromised by the exclusion of the evidence, the criminal defense lawyer would argue that it is consistent with his role.

Some scholars have questioned whether this "role differentiation" is a justification for conduct that otherwise might be viewed as immoral.[7]

Most students are very excited by the prospect of joining a profession. Membership offers the opportunity to develop your skills and to evolve internal standards of performance, to challenge yourself to lifelong learning and improvement, and to serve others. And at least in law, after the first few years of training, no one but you will know the details of much of what you do. The external standards play an important role, but they often lie in the background. You must set most of your professional standards internally, especially those that relate to your treatment of clients and the quality of your work product.

Joining the legal profession[8] requires mastery of a large and complex body of externally imposed ethical and legal standards. Many decisions are left to the professional discretion of the lawyer who is handling a particular matter, but the lawyer is expected to know which standards are discretionary and which are not. In this course, you will become acquainted with many external standards, and you will have opportunities to cultivate and refine your own internal standards.

Lawyers and law students usually think of themselves as members of an honorable and prestigious profession whose members devote themselves to client service and to our system of justice. However, public opinion polls show that most people view lawyers as dishonest and unethical. For example:

- In a 2010 Gallup poll, lawyers ranked 16th among 22 professions in terms of the public's view of their honesty and ethical standards.

---

7. Richard Wasserstrom, Lawyers as Professionals: Some Moral Issues, 5 Hum. Rts. 1, 7-8 (1975).

8. In this book, we use the phrase "the legal profession." But neither the fact that lawyers aspire to become "professionals" nor the fact that the United States has about a million lawyers necessarily prove that lawyers are part of a profession. Indeed, Professor Thomas Morgan has cogently argued that law is merely a business like many others and that "American lawyers are not part of a profession." He suggests that lawyers are like many other people in business and that the idea of a "legal profession" is a clever fiction perpetuated by the American Bar Association to confer prestige on lawyers and to prevent competition from nonlawyers. Thomas D. Morgan, The Vanishing American Lawyer 19-69 (Oxford U. Press 2010).

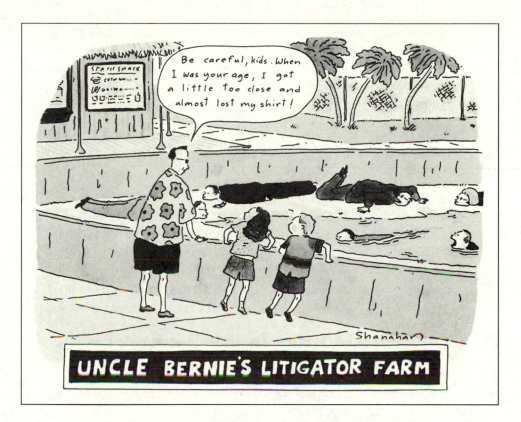

Only 17 percent of the public rated lawyers "high" or "very high" for honesty, while 35 percent gave lawyers a low or very low rating. Lawyers beat out car salespeople but ranked below auto mechanics (28 percent of auto mechanics were rated "high" or "very high" for honesty vs. 16 percent rated "low" or "very low") and far below pharmacists (71 percent vs. 4 percent, same).[9]

- The prestige of lawyers fell dramatically over a 30-year period, with the percentage of people who thought they had very great prestige falling from 36 percent in 1977 to 26 percent in 2009. No other profession experienced such a dramatic drop in prestige during the period surveyed by Harris.[10]

- A 2006 Harris poll found that only a quarter of the public would trust lawyers to tell the truth, far lower than the percentage who would

---

9. Gallup's 2010 Ethics Poll: Little Trust Where We Need It Most (Dec. 9, 2010) (available at http://ethicsalarms.com/2010/12/09/gallups-2010-ethics-poll-little-trust-where-we-need-it-most).

10. Harris Interactive, Firefighters, Scientists and Doctors Seen as Most Prestigious Occupations (Aug. 4, 2009) (available at http://www.harrisinteractive.com/vault/Harris-Interactive-Poll-Research-Pres-Occupations-2009-08.pdf).

trust ordinary people (66 percent), and the lowest percentage for any profession except actors.[11]

■ A 2011 Harris poll found that leaders of law firms inspired a great deal of confidence in only 11 percent of Americans. Only leaders of Congress and Wall Street scored lower.[12]

The public's perception of lawyers is also reflected in the many cartoons (like some of those reproduced in this book) depicting lawyers as avaricious and unethical, and in oft-told jokes such as this one:

> An ancient, nearly blind old woman retained the local lawyer to draft her last will and testament, for which he charged her $200. As she rose to leave, she took the money out of her purse and handed it over, enclosing a third $100 bill by mistake. Immediately, the attorney realized he was faced with a crushing ethical decision: Should he tell his partner?[13]

B. Some central themes in this book

Several themes come up repeatedly in this book. Perhaps they represent fundamental questions about the practice of law.

1. Conflicts of interest

One common thread is that many ethical problems present conflicts of interest. One might define an ethical dilemma as a situation in which a person notices conflicting obligations to two or more people, one of whom may be herself. Chapters 5 through 9 deal with the body of law that lawyers usually refer to when they are talking about "conflicts of interest," but many of the other topics could also involve conflicts between competing interests or obligations.

---

11. The Public Thinks Lawyers Lie, Justice Denied 6 (Summer 2007) (available at http://justicedenied.org/issue/issue_37/jd_issue_37.pdf), quoting Harris Interactive, Doctors and Teachers Most Trusted Among 22 Occupations and Professions, Harris Poll No. 61 (Aug. 8, 2006).

12. Harris Interactive, Confidence in Congress and Supreme Court Drops to Lowest Level in Many Years (May 18, 2011) (available at http://www.harrisinteractive.com/NewsRoom/HarrisPolls/tabid/447/ctl/ReadCustom%20Default/mid/1508/ArticleId/780/Default.aspx).

13. Marc Galanter, The Faces of Mistrust: The Image of Lawyers in Public Opinion, Jokes and Political Discourse, 66 U. Cin. L. Rev. 805, 819 (1998).

FOR EXAMPLE: Suppose a client informs you that he was arrested in the course of planning a terrorist attack. The other conspirators have not been apprehended. You have a duty to protect the confidences shared with you by your client, but you also have a duty to your community to do your part to prevent the terrorist attack from taking place.

FOR EXAMPLE: Your firm will pay you a bonus of $25,000 if your annual billings exceed 2,300 hours.[14] You are working on one major memo, billing by the hour. You can achieve a very good result for the client in 30 hours, or you could do the "dissertation" version of the memo and bill 100 hours.

Examine each of the topics covered in this course through this "conflict of interest" lens. Sometimes you can see the issues more clearly by articulating the nature of the conflict.

2. Truthfulness

Another central theme is the question of whether and to what extent a lawyer is obliged to be truthful. Rule 8.4 prohibits "dishonesty, fraud, deceit [and] misrepresentation." At first blush, this might seem like a very simple issue. In fact, however, very many ethical dilemmas involve a conflict about truthfulness. Some of the issues about truth and deception turn out to involve a conflict between a lawyer's personal interests and an obligation to a client, or a conflict between her duty to a client and to another person. These are two of the other recurrent themes.

FOR EXAMPLE: Suppose you are conducting a direct examination of a client in court. Your client surprises you with a statement that you know is false. You have a duty to advance your client's interests, or at least not to harm them, and a duty to be truthful in dealing with the tribunal. If you tell the judge that your client lied on the stand (or if you persuade your client to correct his testimony), you are being fully truthful. If you conceal the information, however, you might better advance your client's interests.

FOR EXAMPLE: A prospective client is considering hiring you to handle a large (that is, lucrative) matter involving toxic waste disposal. You

---

14. Many law firms tie the amount they pay in bonuses to the number of hours worked and the number of years an associate has been with a firm. At Baker Botts, for example, senior associates who billed 2,300 or more hours in 2004 were eligible for bonuses of up to $25,000. Brenda Sapino Jeffreys, Big-Billables Bonus, Tex. Law. A3 (Apr. 26, 2004).

once did a very modest amount of work on a matter involving similar facts. The client asks, "Do you have a lot of experience in this area?" A truthful answer probably will result in the client seeking representation elsewhere.

Many problems raise questions about whether a lawyer can lie or mislead someone, withhold information, shade the truth, or sit quietly and watch a client mislead someone. In an ideal world, we might aspire to unvarnished truthfulness in dealings with others, but the obligations of an advocate present many situations in which at least withholding information seems desirable.

3. Lawyers' duties to clients versus their duties to the justice system

Lawyers differ in their perceptions of their role in society. Some lawyers see themselves as important cogs in the "adversary system" machine. These lawyers see their role almost exclusively to be the protection and advancement of client interests. As we discuss later in the text, the justification for this narrow view of lawyers' duties is strongest for criminal defense lawyers who represent indigent defendants. If there are substantial resources available for prosecution and few for defense, lawyers might properly focus their energies on the protection of their clients. Criminal defense lawyers in particular often urge that, by focusing on the representation of their clients, they *are* contributing to the improvement of the justice system.

At the other end of the spectrum are lawyers who believe their primary responsibility is to protect our system of justice, to ensure that proceedings are fair, that participants play by the rules, and so on. Lawyers who become judges or who work for judges are in this group. To a lesser degree, so are lawyers who work for government agencies, including prosecutors. In addition, some lawyers in private practice and in nonprofit organizations have a broad view of their public responsibilities. Sometimes lawyers' conceptions of their roles affect the fields in which they work. Some spend their lives, for example, trying to improve access to justice for disadvantaged groups. Sometimes this sense of responsibility affects lawyers' choice of types of work. A "public interest" lawyer might pursue class action litigation rather than individual cases or might work on legislation rather than litigation to produce broader results.

Although some lawyers define their roles in a way that places them closer to one end of the "client-centered" than the "public-centered" spectrum, most lawyers reside somewhere between those poles. Most lawyers take very seriously their duties to their clients, and simultaneously notice aspects of their work that might impact a broader group of people. Very many ethical dilemmas involve some conflict between the interests of a client and the interests of a larger community.

> **FOR EXAMPLE:** Suppose you are representing a client in a products liability suit involving a child's car seat that failed to restrain a child during a car accident because the straps came loose. You know that the defect that your client discovered in the car seat could endanger many other children. If you take the matter to trial, you will have the opportunity to publicize the problem and possibly to obtain an injunction requiring the manufacturer to correct the defect. However, the manufacturer has offered your client an attractive settlement, and your client prefers to accept the offer and put the episode behind her.

In this situation, a lawyer might advise the client of the other interests and considerations that point toward turning down the settlement. But the lawyer should defer to the client's wishes if she wants to accept the settlement. Even if the client wants to settle, there may be other steps that the lawyer could take independent of the work on the client's matter that would assist others who have purchased the same car seat. The perennial problem for many lawyers is that other clients' work awaits, and the possible law reform work is unlikely to generate fees.

This theme of the public interest versus a client's individual interest pops up throughout the text. Chapter 2, for example, describes a lawyer who did not fulfill his duty to report the misconduct of another lawyer because his client did not want him to make a report.[15] In Chapters 3 and 10, we discuss some circumstances in which a lawyer might have confidential information that, if revealed, could prevent or mitigate harm to others or could help to ensure a just outcome in litigation.

4. Lawyers' personal and professional interests versus their fiduciary obligations

Throughout the book are examples of situations in which a lawyer's own interests conflict in some way with her duties to a client. Chapter 8 addresses such conflicts directly, but they arise elsewhere also. In Chapter 3, for example, we discuss the tension between the duty to protect confidences and a lawyer's felt need to share aspects of her working life with her friends.

---

15. In re Himmel, 533 N.E. 2d 790 (Ill. 1988). This case is described in Daryl van Duch, Best Snitches: Land of Lincoln Leads the Nation in Attorneys Turning In Their Peers, Natl. L.J. (Jan. 27, 1997).

In Chapter 12, we discuss the duty to provide services to clients who cannot afford to pay fees, which is in the public interest but may not be in the lawyer's financial self-interest.

5. Self-interest as a theme in regulation of lawyers

In the study of the rules that govern lawyers, especially the ethics codes, one often sees reflections of the drafters' concern for their own or other lawyers' interests. These concerns tend to predominate over attention to the interests of clients, adversaries, the public, or those who cannot afford to hire lawyers. For example, look at ABA Model Rule 1.5(b), which explains lawyers' duty to inform clients about the basis of fees based on time spent.

> The scope of the representation and the *basis or rate* of the fee and expenses for which the client will be responsible shall be communicated to the client, *preferably* in writing, before or *within a reasonable time* after commencing the representation, *except* when the lawyer will charge a regularly represented client on the same basis or rate. Any changes in the basis or rate of the fee or expenses shall also be communicated to the client.

We italicize the various qualifiers in this rule. A client-centered rule might require disclosure of the amount to be charged before the client hires the lawyer. But this rule requires only disclosure of the "basis or rate" of the fee and expenses. The rule does not specify what must be disclosed, although the comments offer some details on disclosure of what expenses will be separately billed. This rule usually is understood to require disclosure of how much a lawyer plans to charge for each hour worked. It does not require disclosure of whether the lawyer plans to bill only for high-quality research and advocacy time, or whether the lawyer also intends to bill at that rate or some other rate for time spent doing administrative work, "thinking" time, airplane time, or time spent chatting with the client about their children's sporting events. Nor need the lawyer disclose how many hours the lawyer thinks the new matter might require. So a lawyer might comply with the rule but leave the client knowing almost nothing about the fees to be charged.

But there are more hedges. Need the lawyer make this paltry disclosure before the client hires the lawyer? No. The rule requires a lawyer only to inform the client of his hourly rate "before or within a reasonable time after" the lawyer begins the work. Need the lawyer make the disclosure in writing, so that the client has a record of what was said? The rule says no. Writing is preferred, but not required. Does the lawyer have to make a fee rate disclosure at the beginning of each matter undertaken for a client? No, this disclosure is required only if the lawyer has not regularly represented the client on the same basis.

The rule also requires a lawyer to tell the client if the basis or rate of the fee changes. But notice that the rule does not require the lawyer to consult with the client to get permission to raise his rates. Nor does the rule even require notice of an increase in the rate in advance of beginning to bill at a higher rate. A more consumer-oriented rule would disallow changes in the price of the service without the consent of the person charged. But not so for lawyers.

Why is this rule so hedged? One part of the answer is that it was drafted mainly by lawyers and then, in the states that adopted it, approved through a process in which most or all of the participants were lawyers. Perhaps we should not be surprised that many lawyers want maximum latitude and minimum regulation of their financial relationships with their clients.

This rule provides a vivid example of how lawyers' self-interest is expressed in the law governing lawyers. When reading rules and opinions, watch for other examples of rules that give primary attention to the interests of lawyers rather than of clients.

6. Lawyers as employees: Institutional pressures on ethical judgments

Professor Kimberly Kirkland

One last theme that comes up often in the text involves lawyers as employees. Many ethical dilemmas are caused or exacerbated by conflicts between a lawyer's obligations under ethics rules or other law and the lawyer's felt duties to her employer. Lawyers often feel duty-bound to follow instructions from more senior lawyers, even if what they are asked to do seems wrong. In addition, lawyers tend to absorb the ethical norms of the institutions that employ them, even if what is going on around them is inconsistent with published or official professional norms.

Professor Kimberly Kirkland did an empirical study in which she interviewed 22 large-firm lawyers about the structure of large firms and the influence of these structures on the ethical awareness of their associates. She concluded that as lawyers "climb case hierarchies and negotiate their firms' management bureaucracies . . . they look to the lawyers they are working for and with, and those who matter to them at the time, as the source of norms," including ethical norms. The individuals from whom the associates absorb professional norms are not the "elite partners" but those who really matter, such as their immediate supervisors and the firms' managers.[16]

Lawyers who are employees may also feel obliged to keep private information about the misconduct of others in their firms or agencies, information that the rules require to be reported. New lawyers often have good familiarity with the ethics rules. They may know what the rules say, and they may notice aspects of the work that seem to be inconsistent with what the rules require. But new lawyers often have little authority within the institutions where they work, and they have strong incentives to be diligent and loyal and not to criticize the conduct of their superiors. If they do raise questions about ethical problems, they may face retaliation through loss of raises, bonuses, attractive assignments, or promotions. They may even get fired.

In evaluating many problems in this text, you will encounter ethical dilemmas that require action. In considering what to do, you will often find yourself caught between your duties as a member of the profession and your obligations to your employer institution. By exploring a large number of these problems, you will become more adept at distinguishing those that are serious enough to require action, even when that action might be considered disloyal. You will also develop a repertoire of methods by which you might fulfill your duties to the profession without placing yourself at risk of retaliation.

C. The structure of this book

Our primary focus in organizing this book is on the interests and needs of the law students who will read it.[17] We have ordered the topics based on

---

16. Kimberly Kirkland, Ethics in Large Firms: The Principle of Pragmatism, 35 U. Mem. L. Rev. 631, 710-711 (2005).

17. One could organize a textbook on legal ethics with a discussion of the formation of a lawyer-client relationship and then take up issues chronologically, according to when they arise in the course of the relationship. One could organize a text (following the structure of the Model Rules) according to who are the parties to a particular set of issues — lawyers dealing with clients, former clients, courts, adversaries, and so on. We have used the "who are the actors" question as one organizing principle, but not the only one.

Another organizing principle for this book is pedagogical. Professional responsibility is not an easy course to teach; establishing open communication and ongoing student engagement can be an uphill battle. We offer an organized, logical outline of the law governing lawyers, but some choices about topic order is affected by judgments about the interests and needs of our student readers and about what will make for a good course. For example, it's important at the beginning to get some basic information across, but it's even more important to offer an interesting problem for discussion on the first day of class. Also, it is desirable to cover the what we believe law students need to learn first about the law governing lawyers. We put early in the book issues that are of pressing concern to law students or that may arise in the course of externships, clinics, or part-time work. We begin Chapter 1 by discussing the basic structure of the legal profession and the law that governs lawyers because absent that background, the rest of the book might not make sense. Then we take up admission to the bar, a topic of great urgency for many students. We proceed in Chapter 2 through an overview on lawyer liability, looking at the disciplinary system, at legal malpractice liability, and at legal protections for subordinate lawyers. These topics appear early so that as students proceed to study the ethics codes, they will understand the consequences of violating these rules.[18]

In Chapter 3 we turn to the duty to protect confidences and the attorney-client privilege. Chapter 3 opens with a set of questions that confront many law students every day. "If I'm working on a client matter, can I talk about it outside the office? How much can I say? What if I'm in a public place?" Law students do not create autonomous lawyer-client relationships, but most law students do work on client matters, so these are some of the first ethical questions that students encounter.

Chapter 4 explains the law of lawyer-client relationships. It covers the rules on how lawyers and clients begin and end their work together and lawyers' duties to clients, including the duties of competence, candor, and diligence. This chapter also examines the allocation of decision-making authority between lawyers and clients.

Chapters 5 through 9 explore the law on conflicts of interest, which involves questions of confidentiality and of loyalty. The law of conflicts, which is probably the most complex material in the book, includes ethical rules, liability rules, and disqualification rules. Chapter 5 describes the different types of conflicts and introduces the subject of concurrent conflicts between the interests of two or more present clients. Chapter 6 discusses examples of concurrent conflicts in particular practice settings. Chapter 7 examines conflicts between the interests of present clients and past clients. Chapter 8 addresses conflicts between the interests of lawyers and their own clients, most of which involve money. It covers issues relating to fee arrangements and billing practices, the rules governing care of client money and property, and other issues that raise conflicts between the interests of lawyers and clients. Chapter 9 discusses conflicts issues for

---

chapters on conflicts of interest before the point in the semester at which many students take the MPRE. But because the conflicts material is difficult, it's important not to reach it too early in the semester. These and other pedagogical ideas guided our decisions.

18. This is a bit like starting a contracts course with a study of remedies for breach of contract.

present and former government lawyers and the ethical responsibilities of judges.

Chapters 10 and 11 look at lawyers' duties to people who are not their clients. They explain the obligations of truthfulness to courts, adversaries, witnesses, and others. They consider the conflicts that arise between (a) protecting confidences and advocating for a client's interests, and (b) dealing honestly and fairly with everyone else.

Chapter 12 examines the responsibility of lawyers to serve the public, particularly to provide service to low-income individuals who cannot afford to pay for legal representation. It also looks at ways in which the legal profession has limited the availability of legal services to persons who might benefit from them.

D. The rules quoted in this book: A note on sources

This book quotes the text of numerous "rules of professional conduct" and their "comments." The American Bar Association (ABA) drafts and issues Model Rules of Professional Conduct and recommends that state courts adopt them as law. Most state courts have adopted the ABA's Model Rules, often with several variations reflecting local policy. Most law students study the Model Rules, not a particular state's variations, because most law schools are populated by students who will practice in many different states. The Model Rules are taught as a proxy for the state rules. Another reason why courses in professional responsibility focus on the Model Rules is that the states require applicants for admission to the bar to take the Multistate Professional Responsibility Examination (MPRE), which tests students on the Model Rules, not on the state variations.[19] One goal of many professional responsibility courses is to prepare the students for the MPRE.

Most law school textbooks on professional responsibility cite the ABA's Model Rules but do not quote them. The practice of not quoting the rules in the texts requires students to use two thick books while preparing for and attending class, the textbook and a supplement containing the text of the rules. A conscientious student often must refer back and forth between the

---

19. The correct answers on the MPRE are "governed by the current ABA Model Rules of Professional Conduct." National Conference of Bar Examiners, Multistate Professional Responsibility Examination (MPRE), http://www.ncbex.org/multistate-tests/mpre (accessed Dec. 4, 2012).

two books while reading a case or a problem. This is cumbersome. You should possess and consult a copy of the full text of the Model Rules of Professional Conduct, but it should be possible to read a textbook without constantly consulting the supplement. In this text, we quote the language of many of the rules that we discuss.

We asked the ABA for permission to reprint some of the Model Rules and some of the comments in this text.[20] The ABA replied that it "cannot grant [the] request. It is the policy of the ABA and its Center for Professional Responsibility not to permit the reproduction of more than 25% of publications it is selling itself. Moreover, it is the policy of the ABA . . . not to permit reproduction of the Model Rules without the applicable Comments."[21]

The ABA indicated that if we submitted a request to use fewer rules, it might allow us to do so if we also would (a) pay a substantial fee and (b) agree to "reprint all the Comments contained in each Rule."

Veasey does it

Law is not so easily privatized.[22] Soon after the ABA revised its Model Rules in 2002, Delaware adopted the Model Rules and their official comments as its own rules and comments, with the identical numbering system and with

---

20. Federal, state, and local law is not copyrightable but is considered to be in the public domain. The ABA claims a proprietary interest in the Model Rules, even though these rules have official status and are more than mere models in three senses. First, most states have adopted them (with a few variations). Second, as noted above, state governments make study of the Model Rules a legal requirement in that their MPREs, which students must pass to become licensed, test students on the ABA's Model Rules (not on state variations). Third, the U.S. Department of Education has made the ABA's Section of Legal Education and Admissions to the Bar the accrediting body for law schools, and nearly all states require graduation from an ABA-accredited law school as a condition for becoming licensed to practice law. Exercising its federally delegated governmental authority, the ABA requires all law students to study its Model Rules. ABA, Section of Leg. Educ. & Admissions to the Bar, Standards for Approval of Law Schools and Interpretations, Chapter 3, Program of Legal Education, Standard 302, Curriculum, subsection (a), and Interpretation 302-9, http://www.americanbar.org/content/dam/aba/publications/misc/legal_education/Standards/standardsarchive/2011_ 2012_standards_and_rules_complete_book.pdf (accessed Dec. 4, 2012).

21. Ltr. from Nicole M. Maggio, Manager, Copyrights & Licensing, ABA, to Lisa Lerman (Apr. 7, 2004). Ironically, the ABA posts this same document on the Internet for free public examination. We doubt that our textbook, which discusses only some of the rules and reproduces very few of the drafters' comments, actually competes with sales of ABA publications.

22. Veeck v. S. Bldg. Code Congress Intl., Inc., 293 F.3d 791 (5th Cir. 2002) (en banc) (reproduction of a jurisdiction's code, identifying it as the code of that jurisdiction, does not infringe the copyright of the organization that drafted a Model Code that the jurisdiction enacted).

very few variations. Delaware moved more rapidly than the other states not because it is known as the "First State" (having been the first to ratify the Constitution), but probably because its chief justice at the time, E. Norman Veasey, chaired the ABA's Ethics 2000 Commission, which drafted the 2002 revision of the rules. Many other states have more recently adopted the revised Model Rules and the ABA's comments as their own rules and official comments, again with minor variations. Since the Delaware and other state-adopted rules are in the public domain, we have in most cases quoted and cited state rules that match the Model Rules instead of citing the Model Rules.

Our citation to the rules should be understood as follows. When we reproduce particular rules, we are quoting the *Delaware Lawyers' Rules of Professional Conduct*, not the Model Rules. However, the rules and the comments that we quote from Delaware are identical in numbering and wording to the ABA Model Rules and comments. So, for example, where we provide the text of "Rule 1.2" without further elaboration of the citation, we are giving you Delaware Rule 1.2, which happens to be identical to the ABA's Model Rule 1.2.

In a few instances, we quote a rule for which Delaware did not adopt the ABA Model Rule verbatim. In those cases, we quote the Delaware rule and explain how it differs or specify the rule from another state that uses text identical to the corresponding Model Rule. In a few instances, we quote and compare two states' versions of a rule.

E. Stylistic decisions

We use the following stylistic conventions:

- We indicate in the text which problems are based on real cases. In those problems, we change the names of the lawyers, clients, and other actors.
- In problems and examples, we refer to the lawyers, judges, clients, and other actors as "him," "her," or "him or her." In most cases, the male or female referent is chosen randomly. This is less cumbersome than to use the phrase "him or her" consistently.
- In excerpts from court opinions and articles, we eliminate citations and footnotes without inserting ellipses. We use ellipses where we omit text.
- In evaluating each problem, assume that the relevant jurisdictions have adopted the Model Rules. We do not repeat this point before each problem.

- When we refer to the "Restatement" without specifying a different Restatement (such as the *Restatement of Contracts*), we mean the American Law Institute's *Restatement of the Law Governing Lawyers (Third)* (2000).
- In cases, headings in brackets are those that we supply. The headings without brackets appear in the court's opinion.
- In tables that provide the language and brief explanations of ethical rules, the explanations are those of the authors, not of any official source.
- Our citations follow the format of the Association of Legal Writing Directors & Darby Dickerson, *ALWD Citation Manual: A Professional System of Citation* (4th ed., Wolters Kluwers 2010), rather than the format of the Bluebook. We have diverged from the ALWD format by putting all references in Roman type and by using the full word "comment" rather than "cmt." in our citations.

1 THE REGULATION OF LAWYERS

A. Institutions that regulate lawyers
1. The highest state courts
2. State and local bar associations
3. Lawyer disciplinary agencies
4. American Bar Association
5. American Law Institute
6. Federal and state courts
7. Legislatures
8. Administrative agencies
9. Prosecutors
10. Malpractice insurers
11. Law firms and other employers
12. Clients

B. State ethics codes

C. Admission to practice
1. A short history of bar admission
2. Contemporary bar admission requirements
3. The bar examination
4. The character and fitness inquiry

The legal profession is formally governed by the highest court in each state, but many other institutions also play roles in the governance of lawyers. This chapter provides a brief guided tour of the primary institutions that govern lawyers, describes the primary sources of law that govern lawyers, and reviews the requirements for admission to the bar.

A. Institutions that regulate lawyers

The law governing lawyers is complex and multifaceted, and is created by a panoply of federal, state, and local legislatures, courts, and agencies. Professor Fred Zacharias explains:

> Law in the United States is a heavily regulated industry. Lawyers are licensed in each state. They are governed by professional rules, usually adopted and enforced by state supreme courts. The courts regulate lawyers separately as well, through supervisory decisions in the course of litigation and by implementing common law civil liability rules that govern legal practice. These include malpractice, breach of fiduciary duty, and other causes of action. Administrative agencies — particularly federal agencies — also establish and implement rules governing lawyers who practice before them. Federal and state legislatures play a further role in regulating the bar, providing statutory regulations and criminal penalties that apply to lawyers.[1]

Despite the reality that Zacharias describes, lawyers, judges, and scholars assert often and with great confidence that law is a self-regulated profession, governed primarily by its members because of their respected status and their unique role in society. Each lawyer is urged to have the responsibility to participate in the governance of and the improvement of the profession. The Preamble of the Model Rules of Professional Conduct explains it this way:

> The legal profession is largely self-governing. . . . The legal profession is unique in this respect because of the close relationship between the profession and the processes of government and law enforcement. This connection is manifested in the fact that ultimate authority over the legal profession is vested largely in the courts.

---

1. Fred Zacharias, The Myth of Self-Regulation, 93 Minn. L. Rev. 1147, 1147-1148 (2009); see also John Leubsdorf, Legal Ethics Falls Apart, 57 Buff. L. Rev. 959 (2009) (discussing the fragmented nature of governmental regulation of lawyers).

To the extent that lawyers meet the obligations of their professional calling, the occasion for government regulation is obviated.[2]

Ideas about self-governance have been used to inspire lawyers to take active roles in improving the legal profession and the justice system. But these same ideas have been used to support self-interested arguments that lawyers should be exempt from regulation by legislatures and administrative agencies. In recent decades, the reality that the legal profession is a heavily regulated industry renders assertions of self-regulation charming but anachronistic. Lawyers do play an important part in devising many of the standards that apply to them, whether those standards are embodied in the formal ethics codes that are ultimately promulgated by state supreme courts or in laws that are created by legislators or administrators and made applicable to all of society. But they are also governed by a complex web of statutory and regulatory law.

1. The highest state courts

a. The responsibility of "self-regulation"

Most law is made by legislatures, courts, and administrative agencies. Is this also true of "lawyer law"?

In most states, the highest court of the state,[3] not the legislature, is responsible for adopting the rules of conduct that govern lawyers.[4] In this respect, the high court performs a role usually played by a legislature. Most of the rules are based on a model that was written (and is occasionally amended) by the American Bar Association (ABA), and much of the drafting of the rules and amendments is done by a committee of practicing lawyers, judges, and law professors. When considering the adoption of ethics rules for their own jurisdictions, state courts often rely heavily on committees of lawyers at the state bar associations. These committees produce drafts of new or amended rules and usually seek public comment.

---

2. ABA, Model R. Prof. Conduct, Preamble, Comments 10 & 11 (available at http://www.abanet.org/cpr/mrpc/preamble.html).

3. The highest court in most states is called the supreme court. In some states, however, the highest court has a different name. In New York and Maryland, for example, the highest court is called the court of appeals.

4. See the discussion below of the inherent powers doctrine. The notable exception is California, where many of the ethical rules for lawyers have historically been embodied in statutes enacted by the state legislature.

Typically, most of the comments come from lawyers. Most of the people involved in the writing of the ethical rules, then, are licensed lawyers, though judges (who are themselves lawyers) have the ultimate responsibility for adopting them.

The highest court in each state is ultimately responsible for enforcing its rules by disciplining lawyers who violate them. As with the rulemaking function, state supreme courts often delegate primary responsibility for seeing that rules are enforced to disciplinary agencies run by lawyers. In addition, the ethical rules require lawyers to report certain misconduct (their own or that of another lawyer) to these disciplinary agencies, so every lawyer has a duty to help enforce the ethics codes.[5]

Is the legal profession unique in the role it plays in writing many of its standards of conduct?

In many regulated industries, from the medical profession to the insurance industry, trade associations of those who are regulated have a considerable degree of influence over the regulations. Often, lawyers or lawyer-lobbyists for those groups advocate for or against proposed regulatory laws or administrative rules. But lawyers have an unusual degree of influence when it comes to regulating their own industry. Even the judges who promulgate the rules are legally trained and, in most cases, practiced law before becoming judges.

Is it a good idea to give lawyers such a major role in regulating their profession?

Maybe. Many scholars and consumer advocates observe that the rules governing lawyers are more protective of lawyers and impose less regulatory constraint than they would if state legislatures wrote them.[6] But insulating lawyers, to some degree, from regulation by the executive and legislative branches of government can benefit society because lawyers often challenge governmental actions in the course of representing clients. Lawyers raise questions about the validity of statutes and regulations and defend people charged with crimes by the state. If lawyers were subject to greater state control, they might be restricted in their representation of clients whose interests conflicted with those of the government.

---

5. Rule 8.3. The duty to report misconduct is explained in Chapter 2.
6. Restatement § 1, comment d.

FOR EXAMPLE: According to one report, 50 Chinese lawyers who advocated for human rights or the rule of law were effectively disbarred in 2009; others were arrested, held incommunicado, or beaten by unidentified persons.[7] Among those penalized for their advocacy were Chinese lawyers Tang Jiatan and Liu Wei, who

Tang Jiatan and Liu Wei

represented a follower of the Falun Gong spiritual movement, which is banned in China. Their law licenses, which were subject to annual approval, were not renewed,[8] and they were permanently disbarred.[9]

How do state courts regulate lawyers?

The highest court in each state usually performs the following roles, though it sometimes delegates one or more to other government agencies. It

- adopts ethics codes and court procedural rules that govern lawyers;
- sets and implements standards for licensing lawyers, including educational and moral character requirements (covered in more detail later in the chapter);
- supervises agencies that investigate and prosecute complaints of unethical conduct by lawyers; and
- supervises administrative judicial bodies that impose sanctions on lawyers who violate the ethics codes.

A license to practice law in one state does not entitle a lawyer to practice law across the border in the next state. Also, the ethical and procedural rules that govern lawyers vary from one state to another. So a lawyer who is licensed in both Wyoming and South Dakota is expected to know the rules

---

7. Michael Wines, Public Interest Lawyer Is Held in China, N.Y. Times (Aug. 19, 2009) (available at http://www.nytimes.com/2009/08/19/world/asia/19china.html).

8. Edward Wong, 2 Chinese Lawyers Are Facing Disbarment for Defending Falun Gong, N.Y. Times (Apr. 21, 2010) (available at http://www.nytimes.com/2010/04/22/world/asia/22beijing.html).

9. China Digital Times, 2 Chinese Rights Lawyers Slapped with Permanent Ban, http://china-digitaltimes.net/2010/05/2-china-rights-lawyers-slapped-with-lifetime-ban (May 8, 2010). Tang and five other Chinese human rights lawyers were subsequently "'disappeared' by the police for periods of time ranging from several weeks to several months"; some described being tortured in custody. Ltr. from Lotte Leicht, EU Director, and Sophie Richardson, China Director, Human Rights Watch, to Herman von Rompoy, President of the European Council (Feb. 10, 2012) (available at http://www.hrw.org/news/2012/02/10/letter-european-council-and-european-commission-regarding-european-union-china-summi).

of both jurisdictions. She is also expected to know when she is subject to the rules of one jurisdiction and when the other.[10]

b. The inherent powers doctrine

The regulation of lawyers by courts is an exception to the usual principle that rules of law should be made by democratically elected representatives of the people. Under a traditional view of separation of powers, legislatures make the law, the executive branch implements the law, and the courts interpret the law. At least with respect to ethical and procedural rules that govern lawyers, the courts make most of the rules, implement the rules, interpret the rules, enforce the rules, and hear challenges to the validity of those rules.

Why are the courts mainly responsible for regulation of lawyers?

Courts claim authority to regulate lawyers as an aspect of their authority to administer the courts. In a few states, the state constitution expressly assigns to the courts authority to regulate the conduct of lawyers.[11] In other states, courts claim inherent authority to regulate lawyers' conduct as a matter of common law, reasoning that they need to be able to govern the conduct of those who appear before them. This is called the inherent powers doctrine.[12] Some state courts have asserted that their regulatory authority over lawyers is exclusive of other branches of government. This version of the inherent powers doctrine is called the negative inherent powers doctrine. Based on this rationale, some courts have invalidated legislation regulating lawyers.[13] The cases in this arena most often strike down laws that allow nonlawyers to engage in some activity that overlaps with the practice of law, such as drafting documents for the sale of real estate or handling hearings before administrative agencies.[14]

---

10. It isn't always possible to know which of two conflicting state rules applies. The first step is to look at each state's version of Rule 8.5, which provides guidance for lawyers who are licensed in one state but undertake permitted activities in a state that has different ethical rules.

11. Restatement § 1, comment c, reporter's note.

12. For discussions of the inherent powers doctrine, see, e.g., Benjamin H. Barton, An Institutional Analysis of Lawyer Regulation: Who Should Control Lawyer Regulation — Courts, Legislatures, or the Market?, 37 Ga. L. Rev. 1167 (2003); Charles W. Wolfram, Toward a History of the Legalization of American Legal Ethics — II The Modern Era, 15 Geo. J. Leg. Ethics 205 (2002); Charles W. Wolfram, Lawyer Turf and Lawyer Regulation — The Role of the Inherent-Powers Doctrine, 12 UALR L.J. 1 (1989-1990).

13. Charles W. Wolfram, Modern Legal Ethics 27-28 (West 1986).

14. See the examples discussed in Nathan M. Crystal, Core Values: False and True, 70 Fordham L. Rev. 747 (2001) (urging that the negative inherent powers doctrine impedes the ability of legislatures to act to improve the availability of legal services to those who are not affluent).

FOR EXAMPLE: The legislature of Kentucky passed a statute that authorized nonlawyers to represent workers' compensation claimants in administrative hearings. The state supreme court held that the law violated the state constitution, which gave the supreme court exclusive power to regulate the practice of law.[15]

Some state court decisions, however, acknowledge that, in fact, all three branches of government play roles in the regulation of lawyers.[16] Also, many statutes regulating lawyers have been adopted and implemented without objection.

FOR EXAMPLE: Most states have passed statutes authorizing law firms to reorganize as limited liability partnerships (LLPs). These statutes protect lawyers from vicarious liability for some acts of their partners.[17] None of these statutes has been invalidated because of the negative inherent powers doctrine.[18]

2. State and local bar associations

Most state bar associations are organized as private nonprofit organizations, but some courts delegate lawyer regulatory functions to state bar associations. State bars often administer bar exams and review candidates for admission. Historically, state bar associations had an important role in establishing lawyer disciplinary systems.[19] A state bar that accepts delegated functions from the state's highest court is called an integrated or unified bar rather than a voluntary bar. In unified state bars, membership is a condition of obtaining a license to practice law.[20] Most bar associations have numerous

---

15. Turner v. Ky. B. Assn., 980 S.W.2d 560 (Ky. 1998), discussed in Crystal, supra n. 14, at 766-767.

16. Restatement § 1, comment c, reporter's note.

17. See generally Charles W. Wolfram, Inherent Powers in the Crucible of Lawyer Self-Protection: Reflections on the LLP Campaign, 39 S. Tex. L. Rev. 359 (1998).

18. For decades, bar associations supported the negative inherent powers doctrine to prevent regulation of the legal profession by state legislatures. But when they perceived that leaders of law firms might achieve limited liability for their partners' negligence through the passage of legislation to authorize the organization of firms as LLPs, bar associations and prominent lawyers led the lobbying efforts to pass this legislation. Wolfram, supra n. 17, at 381-382.

19. See Wolfram, History of Legalization, supra n. 12, at 217.

20. This requirement was challenged as a violation of the constitutional right to free association, but the requirement was upheld in *Lathrop v. Donohue*, 367 U.S. 820 (1961). Another more recent challenge was rejected in *Levine v. Heffernan*, 864 F.2d 457 (7th Cir. 1988), *cert. denied*, 493 U.S. 873 (1989) (finding no constitutional violation where lawyers licensed in a state were required to belong to a bar association). Thirty-two states have unified bars. ABA, State and Local Bar Associations, http://www.americanbar.org/groups/bar_services/resources/state_local_bar_associations.html (accessed Oct. 30, 2012).

committees that draft ethical rules, write advisory opinions interpreting the rules, and undertake law reform activities in many different fields of law. Bar associations do not require their members to participate in association activities (except for continuing legal education), but many members choose to participate because they want to be involved in law reform work. Some lawyers participate in bar association activities for other reasons — to meet people, to keep up in their fields, or to obtain client referrals.

Does each state have only one bar association?

No. In addition to the state organizations, there are many voluntary bar associations — city and county bar associations, bar associations for women and minorities, bar associations for lawyers in particular fields, and so on. With the exception of the patent bar, which has a separate licensing exam, a lawyer is not required to join any voluntary bar association to practice in a particular field. A lawyer admitted to practice in a state may appear in any of that state's courts. However, the lawyer may need separate admission to appear in the federal courts located in that state.

3. Lawyer disciplinary agencies

Lawyer disciplinary agencies (often called bar counsel's offices or disciplinary counsels) bear the responsibility for investigating and prosecuting misconduct that violates the state ethics code. Possible sanctions include disbarment, suspension, and public or private reprimand. These agencies usually are run by the highest court in the state, by the state bar association, or jointly by the court and the state bar. The disciplinary process is explained in Chapter 2. A large body of published opinions in disciplinary cases is available on Lexis and Westlaw.

4. American Bar Association

The American Bar Association (ABA) is a private nonprofit membership organization founded in 1878.[21] The state bar associations are independent of, not subordinate to, the ABA, although a majority of the membership of the ABA House of Delegates (the main governing unit) is selected by state and local bar associations.[22] Each ABA member pays an annual member-

---

21. Wolfram, supra n. 13, at 34.

22. ABA, ABA Groups, ABA Leadership, House of Delegates — General Information, http://www.americanbar.org/groups/leadership/delegates.html (accessed Oct. 29, 2012).

ship fee.[23] The ABA has more than 400,000 lawyer members; this means that more than half the lawyers in the United States are *not* members of the ABA.[24] Although it is the primary drafter of lawyer ethics codes, the ABA has only limited governmental authority.[25] That's why the ABA ethics rules are called the Model Rules of Professional Conduct.[26] These rules have no legal force unless they are adopted by the relevant governmental authority, usually a state's highest court.[27]

How are ethics rules written and adopted?

Usually, an ABA committee drafts a model rule or a set of revisions to the existing rules. Next, the model rule is debated and approved by the ABA as a whole through its House of Delegates at one of its twice-yearly national meetings. Committees of the state bar associations then review these model rules, sometimes at the request of their state's highest court. The state bar committee or the court may solicit comments from members of the bar and from the public. Ultimately, the state's highest court accepts, rejects, or amends the rule. The court is under no duty to consider a rule just because it was proposed by the ABA or analyzed by a state bar association. However, the ABA's work strongly influences the views of most state bar associations and courts.

Some ABA decisions about ethical rules are controversial, particularly when the Association appears to protect lawyers at clients' expense. In fact, on some occasions when the ABA's House of Delegates has considered proposals by its committees to change the rules to better protect client

---

23. As of 2012, the ABA asks lawyer members with ten or more years of experience to pay annual dues of $399. Lawyers with fewer years of experience, as well as government lawyers, judges, legal aid lawyers, and public defenders, are charged a reduced amount. For the first year after a lawyer is admitted to the bar, ABA membership is free. ABA, Membership, http://www.americanbar.org/membership/dues_eligibility/dues_aba_membership.html (accessed Oct. 29, 2012).

24. ABA, Membership, http://www.americanbar.org/membership.html (accessed Oct. 29, 2012).

25. For example, the ABA's Section of Legal Education is recognized by the U.S. Department of Education as the organization that provides accreditation to law schools. ABA, The American Bar Association Law School Approval Process 3, http://www.americanbar.org/content/dam/aba/publications/misc/legal_education/2010_aba_accreditation_brochure.authcheckdam.pdf (accessed Oct. 29, 2012).

26. Wolfram, supra n. 13, at 57. Wolfram explains that the word "Model" was added to the earlier version of the ABA rules as one term of a settlement of a lawsuit brought by the U.S. Department of Justice against the ABA. The Department of Justice had charged the ABA with attempting to regulate lawyers in a manner that violated the federal antitrust laws.

27. It is asserted sometimes that state ethics codes do not have the force of law. See, e.g., Niesig v. Team I, 76 N.Y.2d 363, 369 (1990) ("While unquestionably important, and respected by the courts, the [N.Y. Code of Professional Responsibility] does not have the force of law."). Despite the tradition of regarding ethical rules as "guidelines to be applied with due regard for the broad range of interests at stake," id. at 369-370, it is undeniable that compliance with ethical rules is mandatory for lawyers and that noncompliance leads in many cases to suspension or disbarment.

interests, the House has rejected the proposals as being unnecessarily intrusive on lawyer discretion.[28]

5. American Law Institute

The American Law Institute (ALI) is a private organization of 3,000 judges, lawyers, and law teachers that produces summaries of the law called Restatements. During the 1990s, the ALI wrote the *Restatement (Third) of the Law Governing Lawyers*, which summarizes the rules of law that govern lawyers. The Restatement includes rules governing malpractice liability to clients and third parties; rules governing disqualification of lawyers for conflicts of interest; and ethical rules that, when violated, may subject a lawyer to discipline. The Restatement also covers the evidentiary rules on attorney-client privilege, the criminal law governing lawyers, the law of unauthorized practice, and many other topics.

The Restatement includes black-letter rules, which often summarize the rule followed in a majority of jurisdictions.[29] The black-letter rules are followed by textual comments that explain them and by Reporter's Notes, which provide citations to court decisions, statutes, books, and articles on each topic addressed. A practicing lawyer is well advised to keep a copy of the *Restatement of the Law Governing Lawyers* for reference. The Restatement is not law, but it is the best available synthesis of information about "lawyer law," and it includes information about a much broader range of legal authority than the ABA Model Rules or the state ethics codes.

Is the Restatement consistent with the Model Rules?

Not always. In some instances, the Restatement's summary of the law appears at odds with a Model Rule or with a rule adopted by some states. In these instances, the comments in the Restatement usually note the discrepancy and explain why the authors of the Restatement take a different position. Sometimes the Restatement diverges from the ethical rules because the liability rules differ from the ethical rules, because the authors of

---

28. One example is the rejection by the House of Delegates of the ABA Ethics 2000 Commission's proposal that lawyers should be required to communicate the basis or rate of their fees to clients in writing. See ABA, Center for Professional Responsibility, Summary of House of Delegates Action on Ethics 2000 Commission Report, http://www.americanbar.org/groups/professional_responsibility/policy/ethics_2000_commission/e2k_summary_2002.html (accessed Oct. 29, 2012) (reporting House of Delegates August 2001 adoption of an amendment to remove the writing requirement proposed by the Ethics 2000 Commission from Model Rule 1.5 on fees).

29. See Geoffrey C. Hazard Jr. & W. William Hodes, The Law of Lawyering § 1.19 (3d ed., Aspen Publishers 2001). The mission of the ALI is "to promote the clarification and simplification of the law and its better adaptation to social needs." ALI, About the American Law Institute, http://ali.org/doc/thisisALI.pdf (accessed Oct. 29, 2012).

the Restatement do not agree with the ABA about what the rule should be, or because the Restatement is more specific than the Model Rules.

When a state ethics rule and the Restatement are inconsistent, shouldn't a lawyer always follow the state rule?

It's not so simple. Many ethical questions are not addressed by the ethical rules or are addressed only in general terms. If a state ethics rule clearly requires or prohibits certain conduct, in most cases a lawyer should follow the rule. On rare occasions, a lawyer might decide not to follow a rule because compliance seems inconsistent with the lawyer's own ethical judgment. More often, a lawyer will find that the text of the state's ethical rule does not provide clear guidance on the specific problem that the lawyer is facing. Then the lawyer must seek additional guidance from sources such as the commentary in the Restatement.

6. Federal and state courts

State and federal courts play important roles in the regulation of lawyers by setting rules for the conduct of lawyers in litigation, by sanctioning lawyers who violate those rules, by ruling in malpractice and other cases, and by hearing and deciding motions to disqualify lawyers who may have conflicts of interest that preclude their representation of particular clients.

A judge who becomes aware of lawyer misconduct in a matter before the court may sanction the lawyer directly under the federal or state civil procedure rules. For example, the court may hold a lawyer in contempt or may impose sanctions for obstructive behavior during discovery. Sanctions include fines, fee forfeiture, or other penalties. The judge must report the misconduct to the lawyer disciplinary agency if the misconduct violates an ethical rule that "raises a substantial question regarding the lawyer's honesty, trustworthiness or fitness as a lawyer in other respects."[30] Despite this requirement, many judges tend not to report lawyer misconduct to disciplinary agencies.[31]

---

30. Model Code Jud. Conduct canon 2 (as amended, 2007). This language is in the rules that govern judges in most states. The rule requires judges to take "appropriate action" upon receiving information "indicating a substantial likelihood" that a lawyer has violated the rules of professional conduct. An accompanying comment states that "appropriate action" may include reporting the lawyer to disciplinary authorities.

31. ABA Standing Comm. on Prof. Discipline, The Judicial Response to Lawyer Misconduct (ABA 1984).

Federal courts in each jurisdiction adopt their own standards for bar admission, and some adopt their own ethical rules.[32] Many federal courts adopt the same ethical rules that are in force in the states in which they are located. Some adopt additional rules of practice. Federal courts impose sanctions on lawyers who engage in misconduct in the course of federal litigation.[33]

Appellate courts also contribute to the regulation of lawyers. State appellate courts review malpractice and disqualification decisions of lower state courts, and the federal appellate courts play the same role with respect to federal trial decisions. The U.S. Supreme Court has increasingly become involved in regulation of the legal profession through decisions protecting lawyer advertising under the First Amendment, construing statutes that sometimes require one litigating party to pay the legal fees of another party, and reviewing convictions when defendants assert ineffective assistance of counsel.[34]

Is a member of a state bar automatically allowed to practice in the federal courts of that state?

No. Each federal district court and court of appeals requires lawyers to be admitted to practice before it. Applicants for admission to practice in the federal courts are not required to take another bar exam. Usually any licensed lawyer who applies and pays a fee is admitted to practice before the federal court.[35]

7. Legislatures

Despite the inherent powers doctrine, Congress and the state legislatures play a major role in the regulation of lawyers. Legislatures adopt constitutions and statutes, including criminal laws, banking laws, securities laws, and so on, that apply to everyone doing business in the state, including lawyers.[36] Some state consumer protection laws explicitly govern

---

32. Judith A. McMorrow & Daniel R. Coquillette, Moore's Federal Practice: The Federal Law of Attorney Conduct § 801 (3d ed., Matthew Bender 2001).

33. For a discussion of the sources of the federal courts' authority to regulate lawyers, see Fred C. Zacharias & Bruce A. Green, Federal Court Authority to Regulate Lawyers: A Practice in Search of a Theory, 56 Vand. L. Rev. 1303 (2003).

34. Renee Newman Knake, The Supreme Court's Increased Attention to the Law of Lawyering: Mere Coincidence or Something More?, 59 Am. U. L. Rev. 1499, 1571 (2010).

35. Some federal courts condition admission to practice before them on admission to the bar in the states in which the courts are located. Others condition admission to practice on admission before some other state or federal court. McMorrow & Coquillette, supra n. 32, at § 801.20[3].

36. Restatement § 8 (pointing out that with the exception of "traditional and appropriate activities of a lawyer in representing a client in accordance with the requirements of the applicable

lawyers, while others exempt lawyers.[37] In California, statutory law governing lawyers is extensive and addresses some topics that are covered by
the ethics codes in other states. Nearly every state has a statute that makes it
a criminal offense to engage in the unauthorized practice of law (UPL), and
at least four impose felony sanctions for some UPL offenses.[38]

**Are lawyers who testify at legislative hearings or meet with legislators
on behalf of clients required to comply with additional statutes and
regulations?**

Yes, in some cases. Usually a lawyer may appear at a legislative hearing
without any "admission" process, but federal and some state laws require
lawyers who engage in legislative advocacy for profit to register as lobbyists
and to report financial and other information about their activities.[39]
Federal law imposes additional conflict of interest rules on those who
engage in lobbying and requires a separate registration process for lobbyists
who represent foreign nations.

8. Administrative agencies

**Do lawyers need separate admission to practice before an
administrative agency?**

Lawyers often represent clients in administrative adjudication (such as
social security or immigration hearings) or in agency rulemaking proceedings. In general, lawyers admitted to practice in any state may appear

---

lawyer code," lawyers are subject to criminal law to the same extent as nonlawyers). See Bruce A.
Green, The Criminal Regulation of Lawyers, 67 Fordham L. Rev. 327 (1998); Ted Schneyer, Legal
Process Scholarship and the Regulation of Lawyers, 65 Fordham L. Rev. 33 (1996); Charles W.
Wolfram, Lawyer Crime: Beyond the Law, 36 Val. U. L. Rev. 73 (2001).

37. See Manuel R. Ramos, Legal Malpractice: Reforming Lawyers and Law Professors, 70 Tul. L.
Rev. 2583, 2599 (1996) (noting that most state consumer protection laws exempt lawyers because
"the lawyers are supposedly regulating themselves"); cf. Stewart Macaulay, Lawyers and Consumer
Protection Laws, 4 L. & Socy. Rev. 115 (1979).

38. George C. Leef, Lawyer Fees Too High? The Case for Repealing Unauthorized Practice of
Law Statutes, http://www.cato.org/pubs/regulation/regv20n1/reg20n1c.html (accessed Oct. 29,
2012). One example of a criminal UPL statute is Cal. Bus. & Prof. Code § 6126 (2011) ("Any person
advertising or holding himself or herself out as practicing or entitled to practice law or otherwise
practicing law who is not an active member of the State Bar, or otherwise authorized pursuant to
statute or court rule to practice law in this state at the time of doing so, is guilty of a misdemeanor
punishable by up to one year in a county jail or by a fine of up to one thousand dollars ($1,000), or by
both that fine and imprisonment."). In a few states, UPL may be prosecuted as a felony. See, e.g., S.C.
Code Ann. § 40-5-310 (1991 & Supp. 2003). However, criminal prosecution for UPL is uncommon.
See ABA/BNA Laws.' Man. on Prof. Conduct 21:8008 (1984).

39. See, e.g., Office of the Clerk, U.S. House of Representatives, Lobbying Disclosure, http://
lobbyingdisclosure.house.gov/register.html (accessed Oct. 29, 2012).

before an agency of that state, and before any federal agency, without a separate admission to practice before the agency.[40]

Do administrative agencies impose additional ethical or procedural rules on lawyers who appear before them?

Many agencies have special ethical or procedural rules.[41] Such rules may impose disclosure or other duties that are more stringent than those imposed by other law.[42] Lawyers who engage in misconduct in practice before these agencies may be subject to civil or criminal penalties.[43]

> **FOR EXAMPLE:** The law firm of Kaye, Scholer, Fierman, Hays & Handler was the object of a 1992 administrative action by the Office of Thrift Supervision (OTS), a federal banking agency. The firm had assisted one savings and loan bank in reports to bank examiners. The OTS alleged that those reports included some misleading information and omitted some material information. OTS sought $275 million in compensation from the firm. When the administrative action was initiated, an order was issued freezing all of the firm's assets to prevent their transfer until the matter was resolved. The law firm settled the matter within a week after the charges were filed by agreeing to pay $41 million to the OTS.[44]

9. Prosecutors

An increasing number of lawyers are indicted and prosecuted each year for crimes, some of which were committed in the course of practicing law.[45] Prosecutors have enormous discretion as to whether to file charges against a particular defendant. Prosecutors may once have been reluctant to charge lawyers as defendants, but any reservations about prosecuting lawyers evaporated in the last quarter of the twentieth century.

This cultural change began with the 1972 Watergate scandal, a series of events in which President Nixon used government officials and other associates to commit and cover up various crimes, including breaking into the office of the psychiatrist of a Department of Defense official who leaked

---

40. 5 U.S.C. § 500 (2004); see Wolfram, History of Legalization, supra n. 12, at 219 n. 48.

41. See, e.g., 8 C.F.R. § 1003.101-.109 (2004) (Executive Office for Immigration Review's ethical rules for practitioners).

42. See, e.g., 17 C.F.R. § 205.3 (2004) (requiring lawyers to assure that material information is not omitted from papers filed before the agency).

43. Id.

44. Sharon Walsh, Law Firm Settles S & L Complaint, Wash. Post A5 (Mar. 9, 1992).

45. See generally Green, supra n. 36.

Vietnam War documents to the press. The conspiracy unraveled when five burglars who were part of the conspiracy were caught while breaking into the Watergate building offices of the Democratic National Committee. One of them was carrying the business card of a White House official to whom the burglars were reporting. Eventually the president, himself a lawyer, was forced to resign to avoid imminent impeachment. For their participation in Watergate, 29 lawyers — including two U.S. attorneys general, the president's White House counsel, and other high government officials — were convicted of crimes, named as unindicted co-conspirators, or otherwise disciplined for misconduct related to efforts to reelect President Nixon.[46]

John Mitchell, President Nixon's attorney general

Ten years later, several prominent savings and loan associations collapsed, and lawyers were found to have participated in some fashion in the perpetration of massive financial frauds. The federal banking agencies, seeking to recoup some of the losses resulting from these frauds, indicted scores of lawyers and accountants who had served the savings and loan associations.[47]

These events shattered public assumptions that lawyers would never be involved in criminal activity. At the same time, the disciplinary agencies were becoming better staffed and more effective, and some of the disciplinary investigations sparked criminal investigations. During the 1990s, prosecutors indicted a rising number of lawyers, including several affluent partners of large law firms.[48]

---

46. N.O.B.C. Reports on Results of Watergate-Related Charges Against Twenty-Nine Lawyers, 62 ABA J. 1337 (1976).

47. For an exploration of the roles of lawyers in the savings and loan scandal, see Symposium, The Attorney-Client Relationship in a Regulated Society, 35 S. Tex. L. Rev. 571 (1994); James O. Johnson Jr. & Daniel Scott Schecter, In the Matter of Kaye, Scholer, Fierman, Hays & Handler: A Symposium on Government Regulation, Lawyers' Ethics, and the Rule of Law, 66 S. Cal. L. Rev. 977 (1993); Susan P. Koniak, When the Hurlyburly's Done: The Bar's Struggle with the SEC, 103 Colum. L. Rev. 1236 (2003).

48. Some examples of such cases are discussed in Lisa G. Lerman, Blue-Chip Bilking: Regulation of Billing and Expense Fraud by Lawyers, 12 Geo. J. Leg. Ethics 205 (1999).

10. Malpractice insurers

Insurance companies sell malpractice insurance policies to lawyers and law firms, but these companies also "regulate" the lawyers they insure. A malpractice insurer may require a law firm that it insures to adopt a system to evaluate potential conflicts of interest, or it may insist that senior partners review all opinion letters that the firm sends to its clients. It may require a firm to have a "tickler" system to help prevent lawyers from missing deadlines. These "risk management" and "loss prevention" measures are designed to reduce the likelihood that a lawyer or a law firm will be held liable for malpractice. Many of these policies also promote compliance with ethical rules. These rules form a body of "private law" that governs lawyers who contract with those companies.

Some malpractice insurers provide advice to lawyers at the firms they insure about ethical or professional dilemmas that could mushroom into lawsuits or disciplinary proceedings. With careful management, these crises are often prevented or resolved. Some insurers conduct audits to verify compliance with conditions of the insurance contracts. This guidance to and supervision of law firms by insurers is an important, though nongovernmental, form of regulation. The regulatory behavior of malpractice insurers may have more impact on practicing lawyers than the prospect of discipline by a public agency.[49]

11. Law firms and other employers

While one responsibility of every organization that employs lawyers is to ensure compliance with ethical rules and other law, many employers have their own additional rules of practice. Some larger law firms have developed a comprehensive "ethical infrastructure" to provide lawyers and nonlawyers with training, offer expert advice about ethics and liability questions, and prevent conflicts of interest. Many such firms designate one or more lawyers to be "ethics counsel" or "loss prevention counsel," or both.

Law firms and government agencies sometimes have stricter confidentiality rules than those imposed by the state ethics code.[50] Likewise,

---

49. See, e.g., Anthony E. Davis, Professional Liability Insurers as Regulators of Law Practice, 65 Fordham L. Rev. 209 (1996); John Leubsdorf, Legal Malpractice and Professional Responsibility, 48 Rutgers L. Rev. 101 (1995); Ramos, supra n. 37, at 2591-2599; David B. Wilkins, Who Should Regulate Lawyers?, 105 Harv. L. Rev. 799 (1992).

50. Students who work as externs at government agencies, for example, are sometimes prohibited from carrying texts out of the office or from talking with anyone about the substance of the matters that they are working on. See generally Alexis Anderson, Arlene Kanter & Cindy Slane, Ethics

many firms have policies on file maintenance, consultation with other lawyers, timekeeping, and other issues. Like the "rules" made by malpractice insurers, law firm rules constrain lawyer employees as do rules of law, but they are imposed by a contract rather than by a licensing authority or legislature.

12. Clients

Institutional clients have a quasi-regulatory role in relation to the law firms that they employ. While many individual clients have very little ability to "regulate" their lawyers, large corporations and government agencies are major consumers of legal services. Government agencies and corporations, of course, have their own lawyers, but they sometimes hire outside counsel to provide a variety of services. Both governmental and corporate clients have a great deal of bargaining power in dealing with law firms.

A federal agency, for example, might make a policy prohibiting lawyers from doing "block billing," in which a lawyer records time worked on a matter in eight-hour blocks without specifying what tasks were performed during each block. An insurance company might impose a policy prohibiting its outside counsel from billing more than ten hours of paralegal time on each case. Many institutional clients have lengthy and detailed policies. Institutional clients also may insist on some oversight of the lawyers who represent them. For example, some hire outside auditors to review the work performed and the bills submitted.[51] Law firms that represent those corporations must agree to comply with these policies and to submit to client oversight as a condition of their employment.

B. State ethics codes

While many institutions govern lawyers, applying many different bodies of law, perhaps the most important sources guiding lawyers about their ethical obligations are the state ethics codes. In this section, we briefly summarize how these codes developed.

---

in Externships: Confidentiality, Conflicts, and Competence Issues in the Field and in the Classroom, 10 Clin. L. Rev. 473 (2004).

51. See generally Roy Simon, Conference on Gross Profits: Gross Profits? An Introduction to a Program on Legal Fees, 22 Hofstra L. Rev. 625 (1994).

The ABA adopted its first set of Canons of Ethics in 1908.[52] These were mostly exhortations to lawyers of "best practices," based in large part on an ethics code that had been adopted in Alabama.[53] In the 1960s, Justice Lewis F. Powell, then in private practice, led an initiative within the ABA to rewrite the canons. This produced the ABA Model Code of Professional Responsibility, adopted by the ABA in 1969. This code was quickly adopted by courts in the vast majority of states, superseding the 1908 Canons.[54] Suddenly, the standards for lawyers became a lot more like binding "law."

Justice Lewis F. Powell

The codification of the law governing lawyers in the 1960s marked a major change in the structure and content of the ethical rules, but there was little regulatory infrastructure to implement the rules.

When was the old ABA Model Code replaced by the current ABA Model Rules?

Some observers criticized the Model Code for focusing too much on litigation-related issues and ignoring other important problems that practitioners encounter. In 1977 the ABA appointed a committee called the Kutak Commission to rewrite the rules. The ABA adopted a much-amended version of the Commission's proposal in 1983. The states did not rush to adopt the Model Rules as they had done with the Model Code. Most states made significant amendments to the ABA Model Rules before they adopted them.

In 1997 the ABA undertook another revision of the Model Rules. Dramatic changes in the legal profession during the 1980s and 1990s had made this new revision necessary. One such change was that law practice increasingly involved interstate and international issues or parties. One aspiration of the revision was to promote greater uniformity among the state ethics codes to reduce conflicts of law and confusion about how particular situations should be handled.[55] The revision committee, called the Ethics 2000 Commission, proposed significant amendments to the

---

52. The 1908 code included 32 canons. Fourteen more canons were added between 1908 and 1969. Professional Responsibility: Standards, Rules and Statutes 649 (John S. Dzienkowski ed., 2002-2003 ed., West 2002).

53. Wolfram, supra n. 13, at 54 n. 21. By the time the ABA undertook to write the Canons of Ethics, ten states had adopted such codes. Most of the state codes also were modeled on the Alabama code. Id.

54. Wolfram, supra n. 13, at 56.

55. See Lucian T. Pera, Grading ABA Leadership on Legal Ethics Leadership: State Adoption of the Revised ABA Model Rules of Professional Conduct, 30 O.K.C.U. L. Rev. 637, 639 (2005).

Model Rules. Between 2001 and 2003, the ABA House of Delegates accepted most, but not all, of the Commission's recommendations.[56] By 2012, nearly every state had adopted some version of the Model Rules, as revised, as well as some version of its numbering system.[57] However, the state ethics codes that govern lawyers contain substantial variations from the ABA Model Rules,[58] so practitioners must rely on the pertinent state rules, not the Model Rules.

In 2012, at the recommendation of an ABA "Ethics 20/20 Commission" appointed in 2009, the ABA amended some of its Model Rules once again, primarily to take account of lawyers' widespread use of the Internet and the increasing globalization of legal advice and transactions. It may take several years before the highest courts in most of the states fully consider the proposed changes.[59]

What are the functions of the state ethics codes?

The primary functions of all state ethics codes are (1) to guide lawyers in evaluating what conduct is proper in various situations and (2) to provide a basis for disciplining lawyers who violate the rules. Courts also consult the ethics codes for guidance in determining whether a lawyer has engaged in malpractice, has charged an unreasonable fee, or should be disqualified from representation of a client because of a conflict of interest.[60] The ethics codes are a primary source of guidance for lawyers and judges about standards of conduct for lawyers. Also, many of the rules in the ethics codes are drawn from rules of tort law, contract law, agency law, and criminal law.[61]

---

56. ABA, Center for Professional Responsibility, Summary of House of Delegates Action on Ethics 2000 Commission Report, http://www.americanbar.org/groups/professional_responsibility/policy/ethics_2000_commission/e2k_summary_2002.html (accessed Oct. 29, 2012).

57. See ABA, Center for Professional Responsibility, Status of State Review of Professional Conduct Rules, http://www.abanet.org/cpr/pic/ethics_2000_status_chart.pdf (Sept. 14, 2011).

58. Every state posts its rules of professional conduct on the World Wide Web. The Cornell Legal Ethics Library, http://www.law.cornell.edu/ethics/ (accessed Oct. 29, 2012), has links to all of them. For a detailed survey of the state rules that examines the degree of collective divergence from the Model Rules, see Pera, supra n. 55. For a statutory supplement that includes the Model Rules and a good survey of the principal state variations, see the latest edition of Stephen Gillers, Roy D. Simon & Andrew M. Perlman, Regulation of Lawyers: Statutes and Standards (Wolters Kluwer 2012).

59. Several of the 2012 changes are discussed in this book. For the full set of changes, see ABA, Center for Professional Responsibility, Ethics 20/20 News, http://www.americanbar.org/groups/professional_responsibility/aba_commission_on_ethics_20_20.html (accessed Oct. 29, 2012).

60. Restatement § 1, comment b.

61. Id.

Does the ethics code in each state apply to every lawyer admitted in the state?

Yes. Every lawyer admitted to practice in a state must comply with the ethics code of that state. (If the lawyer litigates or practices elsewhere, some of the lawyer's conduct may be governed by a different state code.) The drafters of the rules attempted to write one-size-fits-all rules to guide the conduct of every lawyer admitted to practice in the state, whether a solo practitioner or a partner in a large law firm, and regardless of practice area. Within the codes, some rules apply more narrowly. For example, because of the constitutional protections afforded to criminal defendants, certain provisions in the codes include special rules for prosecutors and for lawyers representing people who are charged with crimes.

Do judges also have ethical rules?

Another important code drafted by the ABA is the Model Code of Judicial Conduct, which sets out ethical rules for judges. The development of the judicial ethics code has followed a course similar to the lawyer codes. The ABA adopted Canons of Judicial Ethics in 1924. The ABA adopted a much-expanded Code of Judicial Conduct in 1972 and updated it in 2007.[62] The Code has been adopted in some form in most states.[63]

Do other ethics codes apply to lawyers in specialized practice areas?

Yes. Various bar organizations have recommend standards of conduct for lawyers in particular practice areas. Perhaps the most influential are the ABA Standards for Criminal Justice, which include standards of conduct for prosecutors and criminal defense lawyers. The current version of the standards (extensively amended in the early 1990s) include separate sets of guidance for "The Prosecution Function" and "The Defense Function." Like other ABA recommendations, these standards do not have the force of law, but more than 40 states have made changes in their criminal codes to incorporate some of these standards.[64]

Do the ethics codes explain most of what a lawyer needs to know about his ethical obligations?

No. The ethics codes do not anticipate or provide answers to most of the ethical problems that lawyers encounter. Although they contain a few clear prohibitions, they mostly provide general guidelines only. The codes

---

62. See ABA, Model Code of Jud. Conduct (Feb. 2007) (available at http://www.abanet.org/judicialethics/ABA_MCJC_approved.pdf).

63. Some issues of judicial ethics are discussed in Chapter 9.

64. Gillers, Simon & Perlman, supra n. 58.

contain some specific prohibitions and mandates, but many ethical dilemmas are not addressed by the rules. It is the essence of professionalism that a lawyer faced with an ethical issue should exercise judgment, which should be informed by the ethics codes. But the ethics codes are not the final word. Some of the problems in this book present circumstances in which a lawyer might make a well-considered decision that deliberately violates an ethical rule.

Does a lawyer need to read more than the ethics code to understand her obligations?

Yes. Many lawyers believe that, to understand their ethical obligations, they need only read the ethical rules adopted by the highest court of their state and perhaps the official comments. This belief is mistaken. A large body of disciplinary case law and advisory ethics opinions interprets the ethics codes.

What is the difference between a court opinion in a lawyer discipline case and an advisory ethics opinion?

As we explain in Chapter 2, a lawyer may be sanctioned for violating the state ethics code. A case in which a lawyer is charged with ethical violations is a discipline case, and the analysis of the case may be reported in an administrative or a judicial court opinion.

An advisory opinion is not a decision in a case but is written by a bar committee, sometimes in response to an inquiry from a lawyer. These opinions interpret the ethics codes and provide guidance to lawyers as to the meaning of the rules. The ABA, the state bar associations, and the bar associations of some cities and counties have ethics committees that write advisory opinions for lawyers seeking guidance on ethical questions. The committees are comprised of both lawyers and nonlawyers. Courts are relying on advisory opinions with increasing frequency.[65]

What should a lawyer do when, after reading the ethics rules and cases, she still doesn't know whether a contemplated course of action is permissible?

The lawyer might call the bar counsel or the bar's ethics committee. Sometimes off-the-cuff, nonbinding guidance is available from either the disciplinary counsel or from a staff lawyer from the ethics committee. A lawyer may write a formal inquiry to the ethics committee, giving a factual

---

65. Peter A. Joy, Making Ethics Opinions Meaningful: Toward More Effective Regulation of Lawyers' Conduct, 15 Geo. J. Leg. Ethics 313, 319 (2002).

scenario in hypothetical form, but it can take months between submission of an inquiry and issuance of an opinion.

Besides the ethics codes, the disciplinary cases, and the advisory ethics opinions, what other bodies of law govern lawyers?

The ethics codes are just one branch of the law governing lawyers. There is a large body of case law involving legal malpractice, motions to disqualify lawyers from representing particular clients, appeals by criminal defendants who claim that they didn't receive competent representation, motions to sanction lawyers for violating court rules, challenges to lawyers' fees, and so on. In addition, a large number of statutes applicable to lawyers have been enacted by federal, state, and local legislative bodies. Some of the other "lawyer law" is explained further in Chapter 2.

C. Admission to practice

1. A short history of bar admission

The requirements to become a lawyer have changed a lot over the last century. In the colonial era, there were no law schools. A man who wished to become a lawyer first had to be an apprentice to another lawyer. In the middle of the nineteenth century, many law schools were established or reestablished, and legal education took root in American legal culture.[66] By 1860, all but 2 states had established bar examinations, but the questions were administered orally and the process was fairly informal.[67] No state required law school attendance as a precondition of admission to the bar, and only 9 of 39 states required a defined period of apprenticeship before admission.[68]

In the late nineteenth and early twentieth centuries, law school training was optional but not mandatory to practice law. During this period, many states began to require applicants to take written bar examinations.[69] As of 1900, 80 to 90 percent of lawyers had never attended college or law school.[70] Neither was college a prerequisite to law school. Some law students never

---

66. Robert Stevens, Law School: Legal Education in America from the 1850s to the 1980s, at 20-22 (U.N.C. Press 1983).

67. Id. at 25.

68. Id.

69. Id.

70. Robert Stevens, Democracy and the Legal Profession: Cautionary Notes, Learning & L. 15 (Fall 1976)

even finished high school.[71] The majority of lawyers qualified for bar admission simply by completing a three-year apprenticeship.[72] Between 1870 and 1920, the legal education curriculum expanded in many universities from one year to three years. Only later did law become a course of graduate study.[73]

In the first half of the twentieth century, law school overtook apprenticeship as the primary, and later nearly exclusive, path of entry into the profession. By 1930, there were three times as many law schools as there had been in 1890.[74] The ABA urged state bars to make attendance at law school mandatory for admission.[75] By 1941, graduation from an ABA-accredited law school was a prerequisite to sitting for the bar exam in all but a few states. This requirement is now imposed by nearly every state.[76]

2. Contemporary bar admission requirements

In most states, the rules for admission to the bar are established by the state's highest court. The licensing process is organized by state, so that a lawyer who wishes to practice law in New York and New Jersey must seek two separate bar admissions. In most states, the basic requirements for bar admission are

- graduation from an accredited undergraduate college (usually required for admission to law school);
- graduation from a law school that meets the state's educational standards (this usually means one accredited by the ABA);
- submission of an application for admission to the bar;
- a finding that the applicant is of good moral character and is fit for the practice of law;[77] and
- a passing score on the bar examination administered by the state.

---

71. Stevens, supra n. 66, at 38.

72. Lawrence M. Friedman, A History of American Law 606 (2d ed., Simon & Schuster 1985).

73. Stevens, supra n. 66, at 36-37.

74. Herb D. Vest, Felling the Giant: Breaking the ABA's Stranglehold on Legal Education in America, 50 J. Leg. Educ. 494, 496 (2000).

75. The ABA pushed the states to require attendance at law school as a prerequisite to bar membership. Records of their discussions show that their goals were (1) to raise standards; (2) to restrict numbers of lawyers; and (3) to keep out blacks, Jews, and other immigrants. Stevens, supra n. 70, at 16.

76. The few states that do not require graduation from an ABA-accredited law school in order to take the bar exam usually have additional, difficult-to-meet requirements, such as prior passage of another state's bar exam combined with practice as a lawyer in that other state for a number of years. See Vest, supra n. 74, at 497.

77. See ABA, Section on Legal Education and Admissions to the Bar, Overview on Bar Admissions, http://www.abanet.org/legaled/baradmissions/basicoverview.html (accessed Oct. 29, 2012).

Once admitted to the bar of a state, a lawyer must comply with various requirements to maintain his admission. These may include completion of a certain number of hours of continuing legal education every year, payment of annual dues, membership in a state bar association, and compliance with any requirements to maintain or submit records relating to the operation of a law office. Some states require that each member maintain an office in the state.[78]

If a lawyer is admitted to practice in one state, he may gain admission in some other states without taking the bar examination, sometimes only after a specified number of years of practice. If a lawyer seeks admission to litigate only one case, he may be admitted *pro hac vice* by association with a lawyer admitted in the state. Most federal courts admit any licensed lawyers who apply for admission to appear before them.[79]

3. The bar examination

Every state administers a bar examination to its applicants for admission, though some states allow candidates to "waive in" to the bar if they pay a fee, have practiced for a specified number of years in another state, and satisfy character and fitness requirements.[80]

The state bar exams generally include a set of essay questions on identified subjects, the Multistate Bar Examination (MBE), and the Multistate Professional Responsibility Examination (MPRE). The MBE and the MPRE consist of multiple-choice questions. As of 2010, 48 states and the District of Columbia used the MBE and 47 states and the District of Columbia used the MPRE as part of the bar examination. Each state decides what score is required to pass the multistate sections of the exam.[81] Most candidates prepare for the bar exam by taking a six-week cram course from one of several private companies.

Critics charge that the bar examination favors those who can afford the time and money for the bar review course, tests nothing that has not already been tested by the law schools, and discriminates against minorities and

---

78. Restatement § 2, comment f.

79. Id. at comment b.

80. National Conference of Bar Examiners & ABA, Comprehensive Guide to Bar Admission Requirements 25-27 (2004). Graduates of the University of Wisconsin law school are granted a "diploma privilege" and are admitted to the Wisconsin bar without examination.

81. Information about the multistate exams, including lists of which jurisdictions administer each one, is available at the National Conference of Bar Examiners, http://www.ncbex.org (accessed Oct. 29, 2012). Many jurisdictions also use the Multistate Performance Test, an essay test that measures performance skills, and some use the Multistate Essay Examination.

"Attention, please. At 8:45 A.M. on Tuesday, July 29, 2008, you are all scheduled to take the New York State Bar Exam."

disabled persons.[82] One critic argues that "whether the bar exam tests for legal skills or abilities related to lawyering is highly questionable."[83] Nevertheless, states continue to administer the examination because "no one has advanced a persuasive substitute."[84]

4. The character and fitness inquiry

How does a bar admissions authority evaluate the character and fitness of an applicant for admission to the bar? The point, obviously, is to try to

---

82. Daniel R. Hansen, Do We Need the Bar Examination? A Critical Evaluation of the Justifications for the Bar Examination and Proposed Alternatives, 45 Case W. Res. L. Rev. 1191 (1995) (bar examinations do not test what lawyers must do); Society of American Law Teachers Statement on the Bar Exam, 52 J. Leg. Educ. 446, 449-451 (2002) (bar exams disproportionately exclude people of color from the practice of law); see Bartlett v. N.Y. Bd. of L. Examiners, 156 F.3d 321 (2d Cir. 1998) (New York bar exam administered without accommodations to reading-disabled applicant violated Americans with Disabilities Act).

83. Hansen, supra n. 82, at 1206.

84. Stephen Gillers, Regulation of Lawyers: Problems of Law and Ethics 552 (7th ed., Aspen Publishers 2005).

assess whether the applicant will practice law in an honest and competent manner. This is a difficult exercise in prediction. If someone did something dishonest last year, will she do something dishonest next year? What should be the scope of the inquiry? What is relevant to the assessment of the "moral character" of a lawyer? Suppose the person has radical political views, an unusual lifestyle, or peculiar personal habits? What if the applicant has had trouble repaying debts, plagiarized an article while in college, was arrested in a political protest, pled guilty to shoplifting, or has a history of mental illness? The character committee members' political or moral biases might unfairly deny admission to an applicant. An overly broad question could demand that an applicant disclose highly sensitive personal information that may not be relevant to the individual's qualifications for admission to the bar.

a. Criteria for evaluation

Most states require each bar applicant to fill out an application. This may require assembly and submission of a wide range of information, including residence and employment history, criminal records, traffic records, credit history, records of any litigation in which the applicant has been a party, and other information. The National Conference of Bar Examiners' standard moral character application form, which is used in many states and which runs 31 pages, asks for the following information, among many other things.

> List every permanent and temporary physical address where you resided for a period of one month or longer [for the last ten years]:
> Have you ever been dropped, suspended, warned, placed on scholastic or disciplinary probation, expelled, requested to resign, or allowed to resign in lieu of discipline from any college or university (including law school), or otherwise subjected to discipline by any such institution or requested or advised by any such institution to discontinue your studies there? . . .
> List your employment and unemployment information [for the last ten years]. . . . Employment encompasses all part-time and full-time employment, including self-employment, externships, internships (paid and unpaid), clerkships, military service, volunteer work, and temporary employment. . . . Account for any unemployment period of more than three months. . . .
> Have you ever been a named party to any civil action? . . . Note: Family law matters (including continuing orders for child support) should be included here. . . .
> Have you ever been cited for, arrested for, charged with, or convicted of any moving traffic violation during the past ten years? . . . Include

> matters that have been dismissed, expunged, subject to a deferred prosecution program, or otherwise set aside. . . .
>
> Have you ever been cited for, charged with, or convicted of any violation of law other than a case that was resolved in juvenile court? Include matters that have been dismissed, expunged, subject to a deferred prosecution program, or otherwise set aside. . . .
>
> Have you had any debts of $500 or more (including credit cards, charge accounts, and student loans) that have been more than 90 days past due within the past three years? . . .[85]

Most states ask some questions about abuse of drugs or alcohol and/or treatment for substance abuse.[86] All states ask questions about past criminal conduct. Some states ask not only about criminal convictions but also about arrests or citations.[87] Some states include broad requests to reveal any moral indiscretions. The South Carolina questionnaire, for example, asks:

> Are there any other facts not disclosed . . . concerning your background, history, experience, or activities which in your opinion may have a bearing on your character, moral fitness, or eligibility to practice law in South Carolina and which should be placed at the disposal or brought to the attention of the examining authorities? If yes, explain fully.[88]

Often applicants are asked to have lawyers write letters of recommendation for their admission. Most states require that the dean of the law school attest to the moral character of applicants for the bar. Some state bars conduct personal interviews with every applicant, while others interview only those whose applications raise questions. An application that raises significant problems of moral character may trigger an investigation by the bar and a formal hearing on the applicant's qualifications for admission.

---

85. National Conference of Bar Examiners, Request for Preparation of a Character Report (June 11, 2012) (available at http://www.ncbex.org/assets/media_files/CandF/StandardNCBE.pdf).

86. Stephanie Denzel, Second-Class Licensure: The Use of Conditional Admission Programs for Bar Applicants with Mental Health and Substance Abuse Histories, 43 Conn. L. Rev. 889, 908 & n. 27 (2011) ("thirty-nine states ask specifically about a diagnosis of or treatment for substance abuse," but many of those limit the inquiry about substance abuse currently affecting the applicant).

87. The Florida Bar, for example, asks applicants for "information about arrests, charges or accusations (including traffic violations) reporting dates, law enforcement agency, explanation of event and final disposition. If your arrest records are sealed, you must petition the appropriate court to unseal those records." Florida Board of Bar Examiners, Checklist to File a Bar Application, http://www.floridabarexam.org/public/main.nsf/checklistnoreg.html?OpenPage (accessed Oct. 29, 2012).

88. South Carolina Judicial Department, Bar Application, http://www.sccourts.org/bar [link to Bar Application] (accessed Oct. 29, 2012).

Does it make any sense for the bar examiners to ask every applicant to compile so much information about his or her personal history?

The moral character inquiry seems to critics an overly broad fishing expedition into the background of applicants. In most states, there is no published list of what conduct gives rise to an inquiry and no consistency in practice. The nature of the inquiry allows unfettered discretion to the biases of the examiners. The bar admissions authorities are asked to assess applicants' mental health even though they have no training in the mental health professions.[89] The questionnaires tend to ask many questions that do not lead to investigation, such as where an applicant has lived for the last ten years. Do examiners really contact landlords to verify these residences or question applicants' past neighbors, as the FBI does when conducting security investigations?

The lack of clear standards for fitness to practice results in a strikingly idiosyncratic body of case law. There is an unusually high rate of court reversals and remands of bar determinations on admission cases.[90] Much scholarship criticizes the character and fitness evaluation process as subjective, sometimes discriminatory, and very unpredictable.[91]

The following table gives examples of actual cases deciding whether particular applicants satisfied the moral character requirement. Facts most relevant to the court's decision appear in italics, and judgments are shown in boldface. The table provides a sample of the range of issues that come up in moral character inquiries. This is not a random or a representative sample, but a selection of interesting cases.[92] Most of the cases summarized resulted in denial of admission; all of those cases are exceptional. The vast majority of bar admission cases, even cases in which the application presents some issue — a criminal conviction, a credit history issue, a law school discipline incident — result in the admission of the applicant to the bar. However, bar committees sometimes delay for many months a decision on an application that raises such issues, and they may require the applicant to submit additional documentation to prove good character or rehabilitation.

---

89. See Deborah L. Rhode, Moral Character as a Professional Credential, 94 Yale L.J. 491 (1985) (empirical study of the moral character evaluation process). Rhode concludes that "[a]s currently implemented, the moral fitness requirement both subverts and trivializes the professional ideals it purports to sustain." Id. at 592.

90. Id. at 534.

91. See, e.g., Jon Bauer, The Character of the Questions and the Fitness of the Process: Mental Health, Bar Admissions and the Americans with Disabilities Act, 49 UCLA L. Rev. 93, 95 (2001); Carol M. Langford, Barbarians at the Bar: Regulation of the Legal Profession through the Admissions Process, 36 Hofstra L. Rev. 1193 (2008).

92. Even a random sample of litigated cases would be unrepresentative because in most cases in which an application raises issues, either a bar committee eventually admits the applicant or the applicant gives up on her effort to be admitted. Those unlitigated cases are not reported anywhere and therefore are unavailable for study by scholars.

The cases that are litigated are the exceptional cases. Although they are atypical, they are informative as to some bar examiners' ideas about what kinds of conduct raise questions about character and fitness.

Bar admission issue and citation	Synopsis
Manslaughter: In re Manville, 538 A.2d 1128 (D.C. 1988)	While in college, Manville *"agreed to assist another student in recovering drugs and money believed to have been stolen* by [another student named Edgar. They entered Edgar's apartment and] threatened him with a gun and a knife. When two visitors arrived unexpectedly, Manville *used chloroform to render Edgar and the visitors unconscious. One of the visitors died* from an unusual reaction to the chloroform." Manville evaded arrest for four months. Charged with murder, *he pled to manslaughter and was sentenced to serve from 54 months to 15 years in prison*. "He became a 'jailhouse lawyer,' completed his college education, and helped other inmates as [a tutor]. After his release on parole [he] . . . went to Antioch Law School [and later was] . . . employed by the American Civil Liberties Union's National Prison Project." He also published a prisoner's litigation manual. The court **granted admission to the bar**, finding that he had sufficiently rehabilitated himself.
Sexual relations with minors: Vaughn v. Bd. of B. Examiners, 759 P.2d 1026 (Okla. 1988)	Vaughn had been dismissed as a public school teacher after an allegation that he had had *sexual and/or romantic relationships with two 14-year-old students*. The criminal charges against him were dismissed. **Admission was denied.** The court wrote, "[W]e find his ethical value system deplorable. Vaughn has failed to demonstrate personal as well as professional ethics which are both imperative for bar admission."
Shoplifting and misrepresentation of debt: In re Tobiga, 791 P.2d 830 (Or. 1990)	Tobiga, a graduate of the law school at Lewis and Clark College, was arrested for shoplifting after leaving a store with a *package of meat in his coat pocket*. The charge was dismissed upon his agreement to pay $100. Tobiga also *had failed to disclose unpaid loans on his bar application*; he claimed confusion. There were many positive character witnesses. **He was admitted**, found to have proven moral character. Tobiga said he didn't know how much he owed. Several debts were owed to the bar itself for educational loans. The court wrote, "[T]he Bar's records are unclear; the collection agency's are worse."
Declaration of bankruptcy: Fla. Bd. of B. Examiners re S.M.D.,	S.M.D. lived on student loans and charged a wedding, a move, and other expenses to credit cards during law school. She filed for bankruptcy during her last semester of law school because of *$109,000 of*

Bar admission issue and citation	Synopsis
609 So. 2d 1309 (Fla. 1992)	*accumulated debt, most of which was nondischargeable student loans*. The state supreme court overturned a recommendation by the board to deny admission; **she was admitted**. The court stated, "The Board is rightly concerned over the morality of a person who continues to incur large debts with little or no prospect of repayment." But "we cannot agree that the evidence sufficiently demonstrates financial irresponsibility. . . ."
Pattern of hostile and disruptive conduct: In re Converse, 602 N.W.2d 500 (Neb. 1999)	While a law student at the University of South Dakota, Converse engaged in a series of provocative acts, including writing a letter to an assistant dean that read, "Hope you get a full body tan in Costa Rica," displaying a *photo of a nude female's backside in his study carrel, and producing a T-shirt showing a nude caricature of the dean sitting astride a hot dog (described by the student as "Deanie on a Weanie")*. He also showed a tendency to launch personal attacks in response to disputes. **Admission was denied.** The court found "such a pattern of acting in a hostile and disruptive manner as to render him unfit." The First Amendment did not preclude consideration of conduct relevant to moral character, even if the conduct might be protected by the First Amendment.
Cheating on law school exam: Friedman v. Conn. B. Examining Comm., 77 Conn. App. 526 (2003)	Two other students at Quinnipiac reported that Friedman had *concealed a one-page outline on his desk during a closed-book exam*. Before a student disciplinary committee, Friedman denied he cheated and claimed he wrote the outline during the exam. The students gave very specific testimony that they had seen Friedman retain a written page on his desk under a blank sheet before the exam was distributed. The committee proposed to reduce Friedman's grade and to reprimand him. The law dean reversed the committee's reprimand because of delays in the school's adjudication of the charge. **The court denied admission.** The court noted that in a dispute of fact, the bar examining committee could decide that the student who complained of cheating was more credible than the applicant, and that cheating on a law school exam was sufficient evidence that the applicant lacked good moral character.
Criticism of the bar: Lawrence v. Welch, 531 F.3d 364 (6th Cir. 2008) (denying review of Mich. Supreme Court decision)	Lawrence, who attended an accredited law school in Michigan, had *unsuccessfully sued the Board of Law Examiners and the state bar, alleging that some state bar rules were unconstitutional.* He also operated a website called StateBarWatch criticizing those bodies for alleged dishonesty in the lawyer licensing system. He reaffirmed his opinions in his interview with the

Bar admission issue and citation	Synopsis
	character committee, which concluded that "[w]e are concerned about providing a law license to someone who, even before he has handled his first case as a member of the bar, has effectively written off such a huge component of the justice system." **Admission was denied.**
Posing naked in a *Playboy* video: See Dina Epstein, Have I Been Googled? Character and Fitness in the Age of Google, Facebook, and YouTube, 21 Geo. J. Leg. Ethics 715 (2008); Dominguez Law Office, http://www.dominguezlawoffice.com/profile.html (accessed Oct. 29, 2012).	While a student at Brooklyn Law School, Dominguez reportedly *posed naked in a* Playboy *TV video* that was posted on the Internet. A spokesman for New York's character committee said, "It's a possibility in the worst-case scenario that the person does not get admitted." Dominguez did not apply for admission to the New York bar, but applied to the bar of California, her home state, and **was admitted**.
Debt: In re Application of Griffin, 128 Ohio St. 3d 300, 2011-Ohio-20 (2010)	After he graduated from law school at Ohio State University, Griffin had *$170,000 of student loan debt*, $20,000 from college and $150,000 from law school. He also had $16,500 of credit card debt. *He earned $12/hour working 24 to 32 hours a week for the public defender's office.* He lived with his nine-year-old daughter and the child's mother in her home. He contributed as he could to their living expenses. He had not been able to begin loan repayment in a year since graduating from law school. **Admission was denied.** The court concluded that Griffin had "neglected his personal financial obligations by electing to maintain his part-time employment with the Public Defender's Office in the hope that it will lead to a full-time position upon passage of the bar exam, rather than seeking full-time employment." It permitted him to start over with a new bar examination.[93]

---

93. This case has been criticized on the ground that the debt incurred by the applicant is actually not unusual for current law school graduates. See Susanna Kim, Ohio Supreme Court Denies Law License for Grad with $170,000 in Student Loans, ABC News, http://abcnews.go.com/Business/ohio-supreme-court-denies-law-license-law-grad/story?id = 12632984 (Jan. 18, 2011). The court did not discuss the extent to which full-time jobs were actually available for new lawyers in Ohio during the recession.

b. Filling out the character questionnaire

Once you become a member of the bar, you might seek to participate in much-needed reform of the moral character inquiry process. In the coming year or two, however, your interest in this arena may focus on your own admission to the bar. Completing the character and fitness questionnaire can be a complex and time-consuming process, so it is helpful to start early. Obtain a copy of the application forms and make a list of the information and records that you need to collect. Especially if you anticipate any possible problems, it is worthwhile to begin work on this process during your second year of law school.

Is it risky to be too candid with the bar examiners? If you tell them too much, are you setting yourself up for rejection?

Bar admissions committees, courts, and the Model Rules take the position that, in filling out the questionnaire, you should be scrupulously honest in everything you write, even if your disclosures could delay or prevent your admission to the bar.[94] Bar examiners particularly dislike having applicants lie or conceal information.

What if you have something in your personal history that you think might raise the eyebrow of a bar examiner?

You would be surprised how many law students have skeletons in their closets — minor brushes with the criminal justice system, academic or disciplinary problems during college, or other such life events. Such facts must be disclosed if the questionnaire or the relevant bar officials ask questions that call for the information at issue. Most of these disclosures do not lead to character and fitness inquiries. If you are worried about something, get a copy of the character questionnaire from the state where you will apply for admission and read the questions carefully to see whether the questionnaire requires you to disclose the past event. If the issue is potentially serious, you might seek expert advice well in advance about how serious the problem is and how to handle it. In some jurisdictions, you can initiate the moral character part of the review during your second year of law school. If you anticipate that your history may lead to an inquiry, you can avoid a delay in your ultimate bar admission by starting this process early.

---

94. Rule 8.1 requires that applicants for admission to the bar be honest and forthright with bar admissions authorities.

How would you know whether a particular past event might be serious enough to warrant getting legal advice?

Many law students get very worried about fairly trivial past problems. Use your common sense. A speeding ticket will not hold up your bar admission, but a whole series of DUIs might. A minor misdemeanor charge during college or earlier is unlikely to raise serious eyebrows, but if you have a felony conviction on your record, you would be well advised to seek legal advice. Bar examiners tend to be more concerned about events that took place in the last several years and less concerned about events that took place longer ago. And patterns of misconduct usually matter more than single instances. If you are not sure about whether you need legal advice, ask your professional responsibility teacher about whether he or she will give you informal advice. Some professors prefer not to give such advice to students, but many are willing to do so.

Do bar admission officials look at applicants' Facebook pages?

They might, since everyone else does.[95] Some law firms and other employers look at Facebook information about applicants. Some trial lawyers peruse the Facebook pages of people called for jury duty. Some law professors look at Facebook to help them recognize their students in class. (One of Professor Lerman's students listed among her favorite activities "shopping on the Internet during class while pretending to pay attention.") Law students should be cautious about putting potentially embarrassing material on public Facebook pages, even in jest. In fact, bar applicants should be careful about their *private* Facebook pages as well, because bar examiners may require applicants to give them access. In Florida, as a matter of policy, the Board of Bar Examiners checks the social networking sites of certain applicants, such as those who have histories of substance abuse or "significant candor concerns."[96]

What if the issue that might trouble the bar examiners is something you should have disclosed on your law school application?

The information you disclose on your bar application must be consistent with the information you disclosed on your law school application. The law school dean's office is asked to fill out a questionnaire on each applicant for admission to the bar. The questionnaire asks various questions, such as

---

95. See Dina Epstein, Have I Been Googled? Character and Fitness in the Age of Google, Facebook, and YouTube, 21 Geo. J. Leg. Ethics 715 (2008).

96. Jan Pudlow, On Facebook? FBBE May Be Planning a Visit, Fla. B. News (Sept. 1, 2009) (available by searching at https://www.floridabar.org).

*"I shot a man in Reno, just to watch him die. After that,
law school was pretty much a given.*

whether the student has a criminal record, so an omission on your law school application could lead the dean's office to provide information that is inconsistent with the information that you provide.

If there is something that you need to disclose on your character questionnaire, review your law school application to see whether the law school asked a question that should have elicited the information at issue. Examine your answer. (If you don't have a copy of your law school application, you should be able to obtain a copy for review from your law school registrar.) If your earlier answer was incomplete, consider making a belated disclosure to the law school of the same information. You can write a letter to the relevant administrator explaining that in preparing your application for admission to the bar, you realized that you had omitted a piece of information on your law school application. If the information is so serious that it would have led to your being denied admission to the law school (such as a homicide conviction), the law school might take disciplinary action as a result of your disclosure. If, as is more common, the disclosure is of something minor (such as a citation for a college dorm party), the late disclosure probably won't lead to disciplinary action. Even so, dealing with law school application omissions can be daunting. Even if the late disclosure to the law school might raise eyebrows, it is probably less professionally hazardous to correct the record than not to do so.

PROBLEM 1-1 WEED

This problem includes an actual question from the application form for admission to the Iowa state bar.[97]

You are a third-year law student. In a few months, you plan to apply for admission to the Iowa bar. You have just received a copy of the application form, which begins with this statement:

OFFICE OF PROFESSIONAL REGULATION, APPLICATION FOR THE IOWA BAR EXAMINATION

The contents of this application will be public information subject to the limitations of Iowa Code section 602.10141 [which provides that a member of the five-person Board of Law Examiners shall not disclose information relating to the criminal history or prior misconduct of the applicant].

[Question 41 reads as follows:]

41. _____ Are you currently, or have you been in the last three years, engaged in the illegal use of drugs? If Yes, give complete details below (or on an attached sheet).

_____

"Illegal Use of Drugs" means the use of controlled substances obtained illegally as well as the use of controlled substances which are not obtained pursuant to a valid prescription or taken in the accordance [sic] with the directions of a licensed health care practitioner. "Currently" does not mean on the day of, or even the weeks or months preceding the completion of this application. Rather, it means recently enough so that the condition or impairment may have an ongoing impact.

You have a right to elect not to answer those portions of the above questions which inquire as to the illegal use of controlled substances or activity if you have reasonable cause to believe that answering may expose you to the possibility of criminal prosecution. In that event, you may assert the Fifth Amendment privilege against self-incrimination. . . . If you choose to assert the Fifth Amendment privilege, you must do so in writing. . . . Your application for licensure will be processed if you claim the Fifth Amendment privilege against self incrimination. . . .

---

97. Office of Professional Regulation of the Supreme Court, Application for the Iowa Bar Examination, http://www.iowacourtsonline.org/wfdata/frame14033-1600/Bar_Application.pdf (accessed Oct. 29, 2012).

RELEASE

> ... I ... authorize and request every person ... having ... information pertaining to me ... to furnish to the Iowa Board of Law Examiners or their agents or representatives, any such information. ...
>
> I, _____, being first duly sworn, deposes and states [sic]: ... my answers to the foregoing questions are full, true, and correct to the best of my knowledge and belief. [Applicant's signature must be notarized.]

Several times during each of your three years of law school, you and a few law school friends have smoked marijuana at parties. The last time you did this was three weeks ago. Now that you have read this question, you certainly won't smoke any more pot, at least not before you are admitted to the bar.

There is a rumor on campus that, a few years ago, a member of the bar admissions committee was asked what would happen to applicants who answered the question affirmatively, and he said that they would be denied admission to the bar. How will you answer the question?

---

c. Mental health of applicants

Should bar admissions authorities ask questions about the mental health of applicants?

Perhaps some people who suffer from serious mental illness would disserve their clients because of their illnesses. Perhaps some applicants actually pose a danger to others. Such concerns have led bar examiners to ask a variety of questions. Until the 1980s and 1990s, many states asked very detailed and intrusive questions. Most states have now narrowed their questions to ask about mental illnesses that require hospitalization or that involve psychotic disorders. Which ones are those, you might ask? Is this the right place to draw the line?

The National Conference of Bar Examiners publishes a model character and fitness questionnaire that many states use. The mental health questions on this form are reprinted below, along with their explanatory preamble.

> PREAMBLE TO QUESTIONS 25, 26, and 27
>
> Through this application, the National Conference of Bar Examiners makes inquiry about recent mental health and addiction matters. This information, along with all other information, is treated confidentially by the National Conference and will be disclosed only to the jurisdiction(s)

to which a report is submitted. The purpose of such inquiries is to determine the current fitness of an applicant to practice law. The mere fact of treatment for mental health problems or addictions is not, in itself, a basis on which an applicant is ordinarily denied admission in most jurisdictions, and boards of bar examiners routinely certify for admission individuals who have demonstrated personal responsibility and maturity in dealing with mental health and addiction issues. The National Conference encourages applicants who may benefit from treatment to seek it.

Boards do, on occasion, deny certification to applicants whose ability to function is impaired in a manner relevant to the practice of law at the time that the licensing decision is made, or to applicants who demonstrate a lack of candor by their responses. This is consistent with the public purpose that underlies the licensing responsibilities assigned to bar admission agencies; further, the responsibility for demonstrating qualification to practice law is ordinarily assigned to the applicant in most jurisdictions.

The National Conference does not ordinarily seek medical records, although the jurisdiction in which the applicant is seeking admission may do so.

The National Conference does not, by its questions, seek information that is fairly characterized as situational counseling. Examples of situational counseling include stress counseling, domestic counseling, grief counseling, and counseling for eating or sleeping disorders. Generally, the National Conference and the various boards of bar examiners do not view these types of counseling as germane to the issue of whether an applicant is qualified to practice law.

25. Within the last five years, have you been diagnosed with or have you been treated for bipolar disorder, schizophrenia, paranoia, or any other psychotic disorder? ☐ Yes ☐ No If you answered yes, complete FORMS 7 & 8. Duplicate FORMS 7 & 8 as needed.

26. A. Do you currently have any condition or impairment (including, but not limited to, substance abuse, alcohol abuse, or a mental, emotional or nervous disorder or condition) which in any way currently affects, or if untreated could affect, your ability to practice law in a competent and professional manner?
☐ Yes ☐ No

B. If your answer to Question 26(A) is yes, are the limitations caused by your mental health condition or substance abuse problem reduced or ameliorated because you receive ongoing treatment (with or without medication) or because you participate in a monitoring program?
☐ Yes ☐ No

If your answer to Question 26(A) or (B) is yes, complete FORMS 7 & 8. Duplicate FORMS 7 & 8 as needed. As used in Question 26, "currently" means recently enough so that the condition could reasonably have an impact on your ability to function as a lawyer.

27. Within the past five years, have you ever raised the issue of consumption of drugs or alcohol or the issue of a mental, emotional, nervous, or behavioral disorder or condition as a defense, mitigation, or explanation for your actions in the course of any administrative or judicial proceeding or investigation; any inquiry or other proceeding; or any proposed termination by an educational institution, employer, government agency, professional organization, or licensing authority?

☐ Yes ☐ No If you answered yes, furnish a thorough explanation below:[98]

_____

_____

What is your reaction to this form? Do you believe that all of its questions have a legitimate basis? How might a person who suffers from depression or an anxiety disorder view these questions? Keep in mind that one study of depression among law students (a study of students in Arizona) showed that 32 percent were depressed by the end of the first year, 40 percent were depressed by the end of the third year, and 17 percent were depressed two years after graduation.[99]

In recent years, at least 18 states have created systems through which applicants with a history of emotional trouble or substance abuse can be admitted to the bar conditionally for a probationary period, during which the applicant would have to comply with specified conditions, such as participating in mental health care, mentoring, or random drug tests.[100] The purpose of these rules is to encourage law students who have such problems to seek counseling without fear that doing so would make it impossible for them to be admitted to a bar. In 2009, the ABA adopted a Model Rule on Conditional Admission to Practice Law, which can be used as a template by states that have not yet created a conditional admission procedure.[101] At least one article has criticized conditional admission on the ground that it permits bar admission committees to ask improper and possibly illegal questions.[102]

_____

98. National Conference of Bar Examiners, Request for Preparation of a Character Report (June 11, 2012) (available at http://www.ncbex.org/assets/media_files/CandF/StandardNCBE.pdf).

99. G. Andrew H. Benjamin, Elaine J. Darling & Bruce Sales, The Prevalence of Depression, Alcohol Abuse, and Cocaine Abuse Among United States Lawyers, 13 Intl. J. L. & Psych. 233, 234 (1990).

100. Rule Would Allow Conditional Admission of Bar Applicants with Troubled History, 76 U.S.L.W. 2356 (Dec. 18, 2007).

101. ABA, Model Rule on Conditional Admission to Practice Law (Aug. 2009) (available at http://www.abanet.org/legalservices/colap/downloads/model_rule_on_conditional_admission_aug 2009.pdf).

102. Denzel, supra n. 86.

d. Law school discipline: A preliminary screening process

Most law schools have established internal disciplinary processes to evaluate student misconduct allegations and to impose sanctions. Sanctions range from asking the offending student to write a letter of apology to suspension or expulsion from law school. Sometimes the law school's sanctions include a transcript notation that bar examiners are certain to see. In other cases, the sanction is noted only in the student's confidential record, which may or may not be reported to the bar by the law school. But bar examiners often ask applicants to disclose any sanctions imposed by a law school, whether or not the law school considered them "confidential."

Some law school disciplinary boards are staffed entirely by students, others by students and faculty, and still others by faculty only. Likewise, some schools ask student or faculty volunteers to prosecute these cases, while a few have professional staff handle the prosecution of students. Student respondents are permitted to have counsel in these proceedings. Some schools allow nonlawyer advocates to assist respondents, and some allow or require faculty to represent the respondents. A student respondent may be represented by an outside lawyer of his choosing, but generally must pay the lawyer's fee himself.[103] The law school disciplinary systems tend to be structured like microcosms of the lawyer disciplinary system. The law schools perform a prescreening process for the bar examiners with respect to students who engage in misconduct while in law school.

PROBLEM 1-2 **THE DOCTORED RESUME**

The following problem is based on a true story, though some facts have been changed to protect the identity of the individual involved.

You are a member of your law school Honor Board, a judicial body that does fact-finding and recommends disposition of allegations of misconduct by law students. The Board has the authority to recommend reprimand, suspension from law school, expulsion from law school, community service, or other sanctions. The law school administration generally adopts recommendations by the Honor Board. Any finding of violation of the law school Honor Code is reported to the bar to which a respondent applies for admission. The following matter has been presented to the Board for review.

Erica Kass, a third-year law student, is charged with violation of the Honor Code because she included false information on her

---

103. See generally Elizabeth Gepford McCulley, Note, School of Sharks, Bar Fitness Requirements of Good Moral Character and the Role of Law Schools, 14 Geo. J. Leg. Ethics 839 (2001).

resume and then submitted the resume to law firms recruiting through the law school placement office. The law school Honor Code specifically prohibits students from "providing false or misleading information about their academic credentials, employment history, or other matters, to the law school, to prospective employers, or to anyone else."

Erica came to the United States from Estonia a year before she began law school; her father is a diplomat and was sent to the United States. Her undergraduate degree is from Tartu University. Erica listed her undergraduate degree as having been awarded "magna cum laude." Upon investigation, the Honor Board learned that Tartu University has never conferred Latin honors upon graduation — to Erica or to anyone else. Also, Erica was in the bottom quarter of her law school class. On her resume, she listed her law school class rank as "top third." Erica used Photoshop to make some corresponding changes in her actual law school transcript. Finally, during the year before she enrolled in law school, Erica worked at the Estonian embassy in Washington. On her resume, she listed her position as cultural attaché. Her former employer informed an Honor Board investigator that Erica's position at the embassy was as receptionist.

A hearing was held, at which Erica admitted that all three of the alleged falsehoods on her resume were in fact false and that she had added this information to her resume in the hope of obtaining a good job in a law firm.

"I was new to the U.S., so even though I studied very hard, I didn't do very well on my exams. It seemed unfair to me that my grades were not good even though I worked harder than most of the other students. My normal English was pretty good by the time I started law school, but the technical language was very difficult for me.

"I have very high student loans — by the time I finish, it will be above $200,000. My family is not wealthy — they cannot help me pay for this. Also the family is watching me to see whether I will succeed in the U.S. — I felt I must get a good position or else they would be ashamed of me.

"I tried applying for jobs but I wasn't getting any interviews. I talked with one of my American friends. He's another law student, I'd rather not say his name. He looked at my resume for me, and said I just needed to fix it up a little bit. He made some suggestions — I think the changes were all his ideas.

"At first I thought he was crazy — he was telling me to lie. He said they were just little white lies, and that if I wanted to succeed in

America, I had to stop being so prissy. He said at his college, no one ever wrote their own papers — they just copied over someone else's paper from the year before or downloaded one from the Internet. It's a free country, he said. I knew it wasn't right, but also I knew I needed to get a job, so I decided to take his advice. Obviously it was a mistake."

What sanction, if any, should the law school impose on this student? Should the alleged conduct preclude Erica from admission to the bar?

2 | LAWYER LIABILITY

A. **Professional discipline**
1. The process of lawyer discipline
2. Grounds for discipline
3. Reporting misconduct by other lawyers

B. **Civil liability of lawyers**
1. Legal malpractice
2. Malpractice insurance
3. Other civil liability of lawyers
4. Disqualification for conflicts of interest

C. **Criminal liability of lawyers**

The potential claims against lawyers can be divided into disciplinary claims, civil claims, and criminal claims. The first section of this chapter explores the lawyer disciplinary system, the administrative process through which lawyers may be charged with violation of the state ethics codes. The disciplinary system is the process by which the rules of professional ethics are enforced. A lawyer found to have violated one or more provisions of the state ethics code may lose her license to practice law, may be ordered to cease practice for a period of time, or may receive a reprimand or some other lesser sanction.

As part of this discussion, we examine the ethical duty imposed on lawyers to report misconduct by other lawyers. Every lawyer is responsible to help maintain high standards of professional conduct for himself and to report serious misconduct by other lawyers, even lawyers who work in the same firm. The reporting duty is a key feature of the system of professional self-regulation. After the section on reporting misconduct, we explore the rights and duties of supervisory and subordinate lawyers, including the conditions under which a lawyer may face disciplinary liability for the conduct of a subordinate lawyer. Less experienced lawyers are often directed by more senior lawyers, so it is important to know what to do if a conflict arises between a supervisor's directions and what the ethical rules seem to require.

The second section of the chapter explains the bases for civil liability of lawyers. We discuss legal malpractice, breach of fiduciary duty, and other civil liability that arises from tort law, contract law, and agency law. In this section, we offer some examples of potential lawyer liability for violation of statutes, agency regulations, and court rules. This section includes a discussion of cases in which lawyers are disqualified from representation of clients because of conflicts of interest. A conflict of interest may lead to a disciplinary or malpractice action, but it may also be the basis of a disqualification motion.

The third section of the chapter explains that lawyers may also be prosecuted for criminal conduct that relates to the practice of law. It has become surprisingly common for lawyers to be indicted, prosecuted, and imprisoned for crimes such as tax fraud, mail fraud, and securities fraud, as well as theft from clients or from their firms and other serious offenses.

A. Professional discipline

1. The process of lawyer discipline

How does a disciplinary proceeding work?

In most states, the highest court runs the disciplinary system. An independent office set up by the court uses paid staff attorneys to investigate and prosecute charges against lawyers. Some disciplinary offices are administered by state bar associations, but a majority are independent of the bar associations.[1] When a complaint against a lawyer appears warranted,

---

1. Thirty-two states and the District of Columbia require lawyers to be members of the bar association as a condition of receiving a license to practice law. ABA, State & Local Bar Associations, http://www.americanbar.org/groups/bar_services/resources/state_local_bar_associations.html (accessed Oct. 31, 2012). Of those jurisdictions, 22 state bar associations run the lawyer disciplinary agencies under the supervision of the states' highest courts. The other 11 have independent disciplinary agencies. In the 18 states in which bar membership is not mandatory, lawyers pay registration fees each year to agencies of the states' highest courts. Those agencies handle admission and discipline of lawyers. Mary M. Devlin, The Development of Lawyer Disciplinary Procedures in the United States, 7 Geo. J. Leg. Ethics 911, 933-934 (1994).

the disciplinary agency first presents it to an adjudicator, who may be a judge, a single volunteer lawyer adjudicator, or a three-person volunteer hearing committee (which often includes two lawyers and a nonlawyer).[2] The adjudicators hear evidence, make findings of fact, and recommend sanctions.[3] According to the model disciplinary procedures recommended by the American Bar Association (ABA), the adjudicators' recommendations are then reviewed by an administrative board. Decisions of the administrative board may be appealed to the state's highest court.[4]

Are most of the complaints made to the lawyer disciplinary agencies investigated? Are all of the serious complaints prosecuted?

Probably not. As far back as 1992, a ABA commission report on lawyer discipline wrote that although there had been improvements in disciplinary process since the 1970s, "[t]he disciplinary system does not address . . . tens of thousands of complaints annually." It found that "[s]ome jurisdictions dismiss up to ninety percent of all complaints." The commission looked at a sample of complaints and found that many that were dismissed alleged serious problems. The report concluded that the current system

> does not usually address complaints that the lawyer's service was over-priced or unreasonably slow. The system does not address complaints of incompetence or negligence except where the conduct was egregious or repeated. It does not address complaints that the lawyer promised services that were not performed or billed for services that were not authorized.[5]

More recent reports suggest that this problem has not yet been solved. A scathing evaluation of the District of Columbia's disciplinary system by

---

2. David Summers, Adjudicating Attorney Discipline: Are Panels Necessary? 20(2) Prof. Law. 30 (2010) (referring to an uncited survey, perhaps by the author or his research assistant, indicating that about one-third of the states use a single adjudicator, who may be a professional judge or a volunteer lawyer, and that about two-thirds of the states use volunteer hearing committees).

3. See Restatement, ch. 1, tit. C, introductory note. Disciplinary proceedings used to be more heavily controlled by bar associations, but partly in response to the ABA's Model Rules for Lawyer Disciplinary Enforcement, these proceedings have become more independent of bar association influence. See Charles W. Wolfram, Toward a History of the Legalization of American Legal Ethics — II The Modern Era, 15 Geo. J. Leg. Ethics 205, 206 (2002).

4. ABA, Model Rules for Disciplinary Enforcement, http://www.americanbar.org/groups/professional_responsibility/resources/lawyer_ethics_regulation/model_rules_for_lawyer_disciplinary_enforcement.html (accessed Oct. 31, 2012).

5. ABA Center for Professional Responsibility, Commission on Evaluation of Disciplinary Enforcement, Lawyer Regulation for a New Century xv (1992). An earlier ABA investigation had found that when a client complained that a lawyer had stolen money from the client, the prosecutor would often offer to dismiss the complaint if the lawyer paid the client back. ABA Special Committee on Evaluation of Disciplinary Enforcement, Problems and Recommendations in Disciplinary Enforcement 78 (1970). The 1992 report indicated that these problems persisted.

Professor Michael Frisch, a former senior assistant bar counsel, concluded that

> routine cases drag on for years with little indication that interminable delay is in any manner frowned upon. The fact-finding and legal conclusions of both the hearing committees and the Board [on Professional Responsibility] far too often reflect an institutional hostility to both Bar Counsel and the victims of lawyer misconduct. Most lamentably, the Board has shown a notable tendency to create under the rubric of due process more rights for accused lawyers than would be granted to a criminal defendant facing loss of liberty. Further, the Board has reached interpretations of the rules of conduct that too often further the parochial and self-interested concerns of the legal profession.[6]

Professor Leslie Levin reports that

> [m]any disciplinary agencies will not docket charges of incompetence against criminal defense attorneys, legal malpractice, complaints arising out of ongoing litigation, or many allegations of incivility. . . . In Virginia, . . . fee disputes are routinely dismissed by disciplinary authorities [even though] the billing of excessive fees is an ethical violation. . . . Similarly, in New Jersey, grievances concerning fee disputes are typically referred to the district fee arbitration committee.[7]

> **FOR EXAMPLE:** In 2004, the Virginia Bar made public disciplinary charges against one William P. Robinson, a former state legislator, who had been reprimanded four times by the bar and then held in contempt three times for not showing up in court. Twice the courts imposed suspended jail sentences. In addition, a court found that he had defaulted on four appeals. Robinson also was found to have lied to two clients. He told one client that his case was still pending even though it had been dismissed because of Robinson's negligence. He falsely told the other client that the Virginia Supreme Court had dismissed his appeal.[8] Despite this parade of misconduct, a court considering the state bar's complaint against him suspended his law license for only 90

---

6. Michael S. Frisch, No Stone Left Unturned: The Failure of Attorney Self-Regulation in the District of Columbia, 18 Geo. J. Leg. Ethics 325 (2005).

7. Leslie C. Levin, The Case for Less Secrecy in Lawyer Discipline, 20 Geo. J. Leg. Ethics 1, 18 & n. 115 (2007).

8. Wash. Post, Editorial, A Lawyer's Tale (Aug. 6, 2004) (available at http://www.washingtonpost.com/wp-dyn/articles/A44150-2004Aug5.html) (reporting that Robinson had defaulted on eight other appeals and asking, "What exactly does it take to get disbarred in Virginia? Mr. Robinson is an extreme example, but as our study has shown, he is far from the state's only defense lawyer who frequently tosses a client's rights away.").

days.[9] The *Washington Post* reported that "[o]ne of the judges commented in open court that he'd played golf with Mr. Robinson. Another said that 'if I was in trouble, I wouldn't hesitate to hire Mr. Robinson if I could just get him to court on time.'"[10] The Virginia Supreme Court affirmed the light sanction[11] over the objection of the state bar, which wanted to disbar Robinson.[12]

Professor Leslie Levin

Professor Leslie Levin reports that "horror stories abound about clients who were defrauded by their lawyers while those same lawyers were under investigation by disciplinary counsel in other discipline cases."[13] In addition, she writes,

the sanctions imposed on lawyers are often light and inconsistent. . . . [P]rivate sanctions — the lightest form of discipline — are imposed almost twice as often as any other type of sanction.

Lawyers often receive several private admonitions before they receive any public discipline. If a lawyer is suspended from practice, the period of suspension is frequently so brief that it does not interrupt a lawyer's practice. In many of these cases, sanctions fail to achieve the primary goal of lawyer discipline, which is protection of the public.[14]

There are other problems too:

■ Although serious misconduct occurs in large firms and small firms, in government agencies and in corporate general counsel's offices, most of the people disciplined are sole practitioners. For example, the 2003 report of the Illinois Attorney Registration and Disciplinary Commission stated that 67 percent of the lawyers sanctioned were sole practitioners, even though only 19 percent of the licensed lawyers are sole practitioners.[15]

---

9. Va. St. B. ex rel. Second Dist. Comm. v. Robinson, Case CL-04-2184 (Cir. Ct. Norfolk, Va. 2004) (available at http://www.vsb.org/disciplinary_orders/robinson_opinion060905.pdf) (suspension by three-judge panel of circuit court).

10. Wash. Post, Editorial, Another Slap on the Wrist (May 11, 2005) (available at http://www.washingtonpost.com/wp-dyn/content/article/2005/05/10/AR2005051001292.html).

11. Va. St. B., Disciplinary Actions Taken by the Virginia State Bar (Jan.-June 2005) (available at http://www.vsb.org/profguides/actions_jan05-jun05.html) (taking notice that the Supreme Court of Virginia had affirmed the suspension on Oct. 6, 2005).

12. Wash. Post, supra n. 8 (reporting e-mail to the *Post* from Bar Counsel Barbara Williams).

13. Leslie C. Levin, The Case for Less Secrecy in Lawyer Discipline, 20 Geo. J. Leg. Ethics 1, 8 (2007).

14. Leslie C. Levin, The Emperor's Clothes and Other Tales About the Standards for Imposing Lawyer Discipline, 48 Am. U. L. Rev. 1, 9 (1998).

15. Patricia Manson, Solo Practitioners Draw Majority of Sanctions, Chi. Daily L. Bull. 1 (May 3, 2004). This pattern is observed throughout the United States. Ted Schneyer, Professional

- Formal discipline is disproportionately imposed on members of minority groups.[16]
- Most disciplinary complaints come from clients. Much lawyer misconduct is unknown to clients, so the types of misconduct that lead to discipline are skewed toward the problems that clients discover. (See the discussion of reporting misconduct below.[17])
- In many states, the lawyer disciplinary systems remain underfunded and overwhelmed. In Minnesota, the average number of cases per staff attorney in the disciplinary system is only 37, but in Pennsylvania, it is 209, and in Alabama it is 740.[18]
- The purposes of a disciplinary system have not been analyzed with care in most jurisdictions. It is often said that a disciplinary system exists to "protect the public," but this shorthand conceals tensions among punitive, deterrent, and rehabilitative goals.[19]

Are some states making significant improvements in their disciplinary systems?

Yes. Many states are engaged in an ongoing process of review and implementation of improvements in their disciplinary systems. For example:

- California now posts to the Internet the names of attorneys who have been charged with violations of the state's ethics rules, even when those charges have not yet been adjudicated.[20] Attorneys who opposed public posting of pending charges had argued that

---

Discipline for Law Firms?, 77 Cornell L. Rev. 1 (1992); but see Julie Rose O'Sullivan, Professional Discipline for Law Firms? A Response to Professor Schneyer's Proposal, 16 Geo. J. Leg. Ethics 1 (2002) (arguing that sole practitioners are not disproportionately disciplined).

16. Manson, supra n. 15 (reporting that the Illinois disciplinary data showed that "[b]lack lawyers were disciplined in disproportionately larger numbers than their white counterparts." Eleven percent of the lawyers disciplined were black, but only about 4.9 percent of the lawyers who are admitted in Illinois are black).

17. See William T. Gallagher, Ideologies of Professionalism and the Politics of Self-Regulation in the California State Bar, 22 Pepp. L. Rev. 485, 612-614 (1995).

18. ABA, Center for Professional Responsibility, Disciplinary Agency Caseload Statistics 2009 (Nov. 2010), http://www.americanbar.org/content/dam/aba/migrated/cpr/discipline/09-ch4.pdf. In Louisiana, the disciplinary system takes almost four years, on average, after receiving a complaint, before it even files a formal complaint against a lawyer. Eighteen states reportedly refuse to release to the ABA data on how promptly complaints are resolved. HALT, 2006 Lawyer Discipline Report Card, http://halt.org/news-a-publications/report-cards/2006-lawyer-discipline-report-card (accessed Oct. 31, 2012).

19. Fred C. Zacharias, The Purpose of Lawyer Discipline, 45 Wm. & Mary L. Rev. 675 (2003) (identifying nine possible purposes for lawyer discipline and the conflicts among them, and noting that disciplinary agencies tend to structure their priorities haphazardly).

20. See State Bar of California, Proposed State Bar Policy Re Posting of Notices of Disciplinary Charges on the State Bar's Website, http://bog.calbar.org/docs/agendaItem/Public/agendaitem 1000002442.pdf (accessed Oct. 31, 2012) (text of proposal); California State Bar to Post Notice of Disciplinary Charges on Web Site, 77 U.S.L.W. 2069 (Aug. 5, 2008) (approval).

prosecutors routinely charged lawyers not only with violating specific rules but also with being guilty of "moral turpitude," that litigation opponents of lawyers thus charged would quote that charge routinely in court papers, and that innocent lawyers who are charged with moral turpitude would lose clients even though they might ultimately be vindicated.[21]

- The Arizona bar has a well-developed diversion program that considers client complaints involving neglect, lack of diligence, inadequate communication by lawyers to their clients, and problems of poor law office management; it trains lawyers to improve their skills so they can prevent similar incidents.[22]

If the disciplinary agencies tend to underenforce the rules, does that mean that lawyers need not worry about compliance with the ethics rules?

No. All lawyers must take seriously their duty to comply with the ethics rules. One reason is that disciplinary agencies may not prosecute every violation, but they do prosecute a large number of cases every year, and even being accused of unethical conduct is professionally damaging. Another reason is that noncompliance with the ethics code can be a basis for legal malpractice liability if the violation causes harm to a client or a third party. The ethics codes tend to be viewed as a statement of the collective views of the profession on standards of practice. A third issue is that noncompliance with the ethics code could have employment consequences; a violation might lead an employer to fire a lawyer or to decline to hire a candidate. In any event, lawyers, as professionals, should in most circumstances seek to comply with ethics codes and other law, regardless of whether they are likely to be caught or punished for a violation.

2. Grounds for discipline

What kinds of professional conduct can result in discipline?

Lawyers are disciplined for a wide variety of conduct in and out of practice. Among the most common conduct that leads to discipline are misappropriating client funds, comingling law firm and client funds, missing court filing deadlines, failing to respond to client communications,

---

21. California State Bar Eyes Proposal to Post Notice of Disciplinary Charges on Web Site, 77 U.S.L.W. 2035 (July 15, 2008).

22. See Ariz. S. Ct., Arizona Attorney Diversion Guidelines (Jan. 1, 2011), http://www.azbar.org/media/66357/diversion%20guidelines%20effective%2001-01-11.pdf; Diane M. Ellis, A Decade of Diversion: Empirical Evidence that Alternative Discipline Is Working for Arizona Lawyers, 52 Emory L.J. 1221 (2003).

committing mail fraud and tax evasion, and neglecting client cases (often because of substance abuse problems).[23]

Can a lawyer be disciplined for conduct that has nothing to do with the practice of law?

Yes. A lawyer may be disciplined for violation of the applicable ethics code whether or not the violation occurs in the course of law practice. Most ethical rules impose requirements on the conduct of law practice, but a lawyer also may be disciplined for any conduct that is dishonest or prejudicial to the administration of justice or that reflects lack of fitness to practice. Lawyers are often disciplined for conduct that was not part of their work as lawyers. Lawyers have been disciplined for domestic violence,[24] failure to pay child support,[25] drunk driving,[26] and even for putting slugs in parking meters.[27] One lawyer was disciplined because he sent flowers and a note offering legal assistance to the family of a deceased person, both of which were delivered to a funeral home.[28]

> **FOR EXAMPLE:** Stanley Protokowicz, a Maryland lawyer, helped a former client (who was one of his buddies) to break into the home of the former client's wife. They ransacked the house, clogged the toilet, and stole some jewelry and other items. Most disturbing, the lawyer and his former client killed Max, the family kitten, in the microwave oven. The wife and her children found Max dead on the kitchen floor, smelling of champagne. The lawyer was indefinitely suspended from law practice with leave to

---

23. In Illinois 2009, the most common problems that led to lawyer discipline were fraudulent activity (70 of 137 cases that led to discipline); failure to communicate with a client, including failure to communicate the basis for a fee (51 cases); neglect of client cases (46 cases); criminal conduct by the lawyer (37 cases); improper management of client or third party funds (35 cases); and fee violations, including failure to refund unearned fees (28 cases). The individual numbers exceed 137 because some cases of discipline involved more than one type of violation. Ill. Atty. Registration & Disc. Comm., Annual Report 2009, Chart 23, at 27 (available at https://www.iardc.org/Annual Report2009.pdf).

24. See In re Grella, 777 N.E.2d 167 (Mass. 2002) (lawyer suspended for two months after criminal conviction for domestic violence).

25. In 1996, Congress enacted a law requiring the states to suspend professional licenses of persons who failed to pay child support. 42 U.S.C. § 666(a)(16) (1997); Restatement § 5, comment b, reporter's note. But even before this federal law was passed, some lawyers were disciplined for nonpayment of child support. See, e.g., In re Wolfrom, 681 N.E.2d 1336 (Ohio 1997).

26. In re Conduct of McDonough, 77 P.3d 306 (Or. 2003) (lawyer suspended for 18 months for driving while intoxicated and other offenses).

27. Fellner v. B. Assn. of Baltimore City, 131 A.2d 729 (Md. 1957).

28. Norris v. Ala. St. B., 582 So. 2d 1034 (Ala.), *cert. denied*, 502 U.S. 957 (1991).

apply for reinstatement after a year.[29] Protocowicz was reinstated four years later.[30] His website indicates an active law practice.[31]

FOR EXAMPLE: George Goldsborough Jr., a Maryland lawyer, was suspended from practice after he was found to have spanked his secretaries and his clients at the office, sometimes putting them over his knees and baring their bottoms.[32]

FOR EXAMPLE: As a prank, lawyer Jim Carpenter set up an account on Classmates.com in the name of one of his former high school classmates, who had become a teacher at the school. Pretending to be the teacher, he posted a message that said, "I am married to an incredibly beautiful woman, AND I get to hang out with high school chicks all day (and some evenings too). I have even been lucky with a few. It just doesn't get better than this." The school investigated the teacher, who denied posting the message and filed a complaint with the police. In response to a police subpoena, Classmates.com revealed that Carpenter had established the account. After Carpenter apologized, the school, the teacher, and the police closed the matter. But the state bar filed a complaint, and the Supreme Court of Oregon publicly reprimanded Carpenter for engaging in dishonesty, adding that it believed that his conduct indicated that he lacked "aspects of trustworthiness and integrity that are relevant to the practice of law."[33]

Can a lawyer be disciplined for committing a crime?

Yes. A lawyer may be disciplined for the commission of any criminal act that violates an ethical rule or that reflects dishonesty, untrustworthiness, or lack of fitness to practice.

---

29. Atty. Grievance Commn. of Md. v. Protokowicz, 619 A.2d 100 (Md. 1993); see Stanley E. Protokowicz, Jr., P.A., http://www.stanprolaw.net/home.html (accessed Oct. 31, 2012). (His website says, "Hire them before your spouse does!")

30. Anju Kaur, Bad Lawyers Get Worse with Easy Punishment, Wash. Examr. (Dec. 29, 2007) (available at http://halt.org/news-a-publications/report-cards/2006-lawyer-discipline-report-card).

31. Stanley E. Protokowicz, Jr., P.A. See the URL at n. 29, supra.

32. Atty. Grievance Commn. of Md. v. Goldsborough, 624 A.2d 503 (Md. 1993). In another spanking case, Milo J. Altschuler, a Connecticut lawyer received only a reprimand from the lawyer disciplinary agency in a case involving an alleged spanking of a client, but he was criminally charged and received a suspended sentence and three years' probation based on this incident. Altschuler claimed that he threatened to spank his clients as part of his preparing them to testify, to make them "more afraid of him than they would be of the prosecutor." Scott Brede, Spanking Client Not Legitimate Trial Prep Tactic, Conn. L. Trib. (July 15, 2002).

33. In re Complaint as to the Conduct of Jim Carpenter, 95 P.3d 203 (Or. 2004).

"Hey, Conroy, your lawyer is here."

FOR EXAMPLE: A part-time prosecutor was suspended from practice because he physically assaulted his girlfriend (who was also his client). After she asked him to leave her house, he followed her into her bedroom, told her to "go and have sex" with a woman with whom he'd earlier had cocktails, straddled her, and hit her in the face with his fist, cutting her lip. He claimed that the incident was a "private matter," but the state supreme court concluded that it raised concerns about his fitness to practice in light of his responsibilities as a prosecutor to the system of justice.[34]

What if the lawyer has not been convicted of or even charged with the crime?

A lawyer may be disciplined for committing a criminal act even when no criminal charge is filed or the lawyer is acquitted of a charge in a criminal proceeding. The purpose of criminal prosecution is to vindicate the interest

---

34. In re Walker, 597 N.E.2d 1271, *modified*, 601 N.E.2d 327 (Ind. 1992).

of the state in prohibiting the act. The purpose of the disciplinary proceeding is to protect the public and the profession by disallowing practice by unfit lawyers. However, if a disciplinary action is filed based on conduct that is the subject of a pending criminal charge, the disciplinary action usually is stayed until the criminal proceeding is concluded.[35]

Can a lawyer be disciplined based on the actions of an employee?

Yes. Suppose a lawyer tells a paralegal to shred a document that opposing counsel has requested in discovery. This lawyer may be disciplined for inducing or assisting another person to do something that would violate the rules if done by the lawyer.

> **FOR EXAMPLE:** For years, Dennis Whelan and his wife Heide had taken care of an elderly neighbor. In gratitude, the neighbor wanted to leave money to Whelan. When he became a lawyer, she asked him to draft a codicil to her will, leaving him a legacy. He said he could not ethically draft the codicil and suggested that she ask her own lawyer, who was his law partner, to do the drafting. She followed the suggestion. He was publicly censured for circumventing the rule that bars lawyers from drafting legal documents for clients that transfer the client's property to themselves. (The partner who drafted the codicil was also censured.)[36]

Can a lawyer be disciplined for something she does outside the state in which she is licensed to practice?

Yes. The lawyer may be disciplined for violation of the rules regardless of whether the violation occurs in the state in which the lawyer is admitted. So, for example, if a lawyer admitted in Idaho commits a crime in Nevada, she could be disciplined in Idaho for the criminal act in Nevada.[37]

If a lawyer violates a rule in a state in which he is not licensed, can he be disciplined by the authorities in that state?

It depends. Most ethics codes subject only lawyers admitted to practice in that state to discipline for violation of the rules. However, the ethics rules of California, the District of Columbia, and Maryland allow discipline of any lawyer who violates a rule of the jurisdiction, regardless of whether the person is licensed to practice in that state.[38]

---

35. Restatement § 5, comment g.
36. In re Whelan, 619 A.2d 571 (N.H. 1992).
37. See Rule 8.5, which explains choice of law rules in such situations.
38. Restatement § 5, comment h.

What if a lawyer is admitted to practice in several states but is suspended or disbarred in one of those states? Can the lawyer continue her practice in the other states?

A lawyer disbarred in one state could continue to practice in another state unless or until the other state imposes reciprocal or other discipline. A lawyer who is admitted in more than one state must report to the other states where she is admitted if discipline is imposed in one of the states. If she does not comply with that obligation, she might get caught. The ABA maintains a National Regulatory Data Bank[39] that compiles information about discipline imposed around the country. Bar counsels periodically consult this data bank to see whether any of their members have been disciplined in other states. Once a bar counsel learns of a sanction imposed on a member of the bar by another jurisdiction, the bar counsel may initiate a proceeding to impose "reciprocal discipline." A lawyer who is sanctioned in one jurisdiction often receives the same sanction in any other jurisdictions where she is admitted.[40]

Can a lawyer be disciplined for engaging in discriminatory behavior?

Yes. The ABA Model Rules do not explicitly prohibit discriminatory behavior, but several states do through their disciplinary rules.[41] Others interpret more general rules to prohibit such conduct, some of them including a comment after Rule 8.4 explaining that some discrimination violates Rule 8.4(d). A comment to the rule states that a lawyer who manifests bias or prejudice in the course of representing a client would violate Rule 8.4(d) if the conduct is prejudicial to the administration of justice.[42]

To what extent can disciplinary violations be traced to substance abuse and other addictive behavior by lawyers?

Between 50 and 75 percent of major disciplinary cases involve lawyers with substance abuse problems.[43] As this statistic suggests, alcohol and drug

---

39. ABA, Center for Professional Responsibility, National Lawyer Regulatory Data Bank, http://www.americanbar.org/groups/professional_responsibility/services/databank.html (accessed Oct. 31, 2012).

40. Telephone interview with John Rooney, D.C. Asst. B. Counsel (Mar. 4, 2004).

41. N.J. R. Prof. Conduct 8.4(g) (1984); Ohio R. Prof. Conduct 8.4(g) (2007). For states that have done so and the variations in wording, see ABA, Center for Professional Responsibility, Variations of the ABA Model Rules of Professional Conduct, Rule 8.4, http://www.americanbar.org/content/dam/aba/migrated/cpr/pic/8_4.authcheckdam.pdf (accessed Oct. 31, 2012).

42. Rule 8.4, Comment 3.

43. Linda Himelstein, Defense for Misconduct: Addiction to Legal Drugs, Leg. Times 1 (Jan. 15, 1990) (60 percent); Report of the AALS Special Committee on Problems of Substance Abuse in the Law Schools, 44 J. Leg. Educ. 35, 36 (1994) (50 to 75 percent).

dependence is a very serious problem for the legal profession. About 20 percent of lawyers abuse alcohol,[44] and other lawyers are addicted to unlawful narcotics, prescription drugs, and other substances.[45] This human tragedy also has heavy ethical implications. Lawyers who suffer from alcohol addiction often have trouble providing competent representation to clients. Other addicted lawyers "borrow" from their trust accounts to pay for their habits. Some lawyers accept representation of many more clients than they have time to serve. They ask each client for a retainer (perhaps several thousand dollars) when the client hires the lawyer. The lawyer cashes the checks but — in part because of the impairment caused by addiction — never manages to follow through on many of the matters she has taken on. Lawyers with addiction problems miss deadlines, lose files, and fail to return phone calls. Any lawyer might do one of those things from time to time, but lawyers with addiction problems usually make these mistakes repeatedly.

Alcoholism is also a serious problem for many law students. In 1993, a study by the Association of American Law Schools asked law students whether they had abused alcohol, defining abuse to mean "in a manner that does physical, psychological, or emotional harm to yourself and/or others." Thirty-one percent of law students responded that they had done so, including 12 percent who had abused alcohol while in law school. Three percent of the students reported that they "often" drove under the influence of alcohol.[46]

Alcoholism or drug addiction is a disease, not a moral failing, as people once believed. Lawyers need help to overcome their addictions. Most state bar associations sponsor programs that offer free evaluation and counseling to lawyers and law students who have substance abuse problems (as well as challenges stemming from other diseases such as depression or bipolar

---

44. Seventeen percent of lawyers in a North Carolina study admitted to drinking three to five alcoholic beverages a day. N.C. B. Assn., Report of the Quality of Life Task Force and Recommendations 4 (June 1991); Patrick J. Schiltz, On Being a Happy, Healthy, and Ethical Member of an Unhappy, Unhealthy, and Unethical Profession, 52 Vand. L. Rev. 871, 876-877 (1999), collects other sources with similar findings. In Massachusetts, lawyer assistance programs have seen a shift in recent years in their clients' presenting problems from substance abuse to depression. In 2005, 26 percent of all lawyers who sought counseling needed help with depression or anxiety, compared with 21 percent who were struggling with alcohol or drugs. Sacha Pfeiffer, Law and a Disorder, Boston Globe (June 27, 2007) (available at http://www.boston.com/business/articles/2007/06/27/law_and_a_disorder).

45. See G. Andrew H. Benjamin, Elaine J. Darling & Bruce Sales, The Prevalence of Depression, Alcohol Abuse, and Cocaine Abuse Among United States Lawyers, 13 Intl. J. L. & Psych. 233 (1990).

46. Report of the AALS, supra n. 43, at 43. Ten years later, the ABA saw "no firm evidence of improved sobriety." Thomas Adcock, Substance Abuse Persists at Law Schools, N.Y.L.J. (June 27, 2003).

disorder). The services provided are strictly confidential. The counseling programs do not share information with bar admissions, disciplinary authorities, or anyone else.

3. Reporting misconduct by other lawyers

A cornerstone of the disciplinary system is the duty of lawyers to report serious misconduct by other lawyers. The issue of whether an act must be reported arises often in connection with the analysis of other ethical issues. Consequently, it is useful to explore this aspect of the system at an early stage of the study of professional responsibility.

This section examines the duty to report misconduct and the degree of legal protection available to subordinate lawyers (such as law firm associates) who refuse to commit misconduct or who complain of the misconduct of others. We consider when a subordinate lawyer should or should not follow orders. We also look at the developing body of law that provides relief for lawyers who are fired for insisting on compliance with the ethical rules. If you encounter lawyer misconduct committed by your colleagues or superiors, and you take the reporting duty seriously, you run some risk of retaliation. If you are familiar with the law of wrongful discharge of lawyers, you will be better able to protect yourself should such a situation arise.

Many lawyers observe misconduct by other lawyers from time to time. Here are a few examples.

- A lawyer might notice that another lawyer in her law firm is neglecting his work because of substance abuse, a personal crisis, or some other problem.
- A lawyer might encounter an opposing counsel who is deliberately obstructing the discovery process.
- A judge or a lawyer might observe another lawyer in court who is unprepared for a hearing.
- A lawyer might be asked by a supervising lawyer to falsify time records.

These situations present various problems and dilemmas. Should the observing lawyer report the other lawyer? If so, to whom? To the firm management, a judge (if the matter is in litigation), a disciplinary agency, or the prosecutor's office? A second issue is whether the observing lawyer may be responsible (that is, subject to discipline or liability) for the other lawyer's actions. A third question is what the lawyer should do if another lawyer asks him to do something improper. And finally, what happens if the observing lawyer reports the other lawyer's misconduct and is fired as a result?

a. The duty to report misconduct

One of the most important aspects of the lawyer self-regulatory system is that, in nearly all states, lawyers are obliged to report other lawyers' serious misconduct to the disciplinary authorities. Rule 8.3 articulates this duty.

Rule 8.3   Professional Misconduct Reporting

Rule language*	Authors' explanation**
(a) A lawyer who **knows** that another lawyer has **committed a violation of the Rules** of Professional Conduct that **raises a substantial question as to that lawyer's honesty, trustworthiness or fitness as a lawyer in other respects, shall inform the appropriate professional authority**. . . . [(b) Requires reporting misconduct by judges.] (c) This Rule **does not require disclosure of information otherwise protected by Rule 1.6** or information gained by a lawyer or judge while participating in an approved lawyers assistance program.	A lawyer who "knows" of a violation by any other lawyer (an adversary, a public official, or a lawyer in own firm) must report it to the bar disciplinary agency. Exceptions: (1) Not all violations must be reported — only those raising a "substantial question" of the lawyer's "honesty, trustworthiness or fitness." (2) A report need not be made if it would reveal information *required* to be kept in confidence under Rule 1.6. But a lawyer should encourage a client to waive confidentiality and permit reporting if that would not substantially prejudice the client. Comment 2. (3) A lawyer who learns information about misconduct while participating in an "approved lawyers' assistance program" is exempted from the requirement to report that information. Comment 5.

*All emphasis added.

**This and other authors' explanations draw from the comments to the rules and from other sources. They are not comprehensive but highlight some important interpretive points.

At least 48 states and the District of Columbia have adopted language that is similar or identical to Rule 8.3.[47]

Must every lawyer in a state with a reporting rule report serious ethical violations by other lawyers?

Yes as to those that raise "a substantial question as to that lawyer's honesty, trustworthiness or fitness as a lawyer in other respects,"[48] if the lawyer "knows" of another lawyer's misconduct. Knowledge must be more than a

---

47. ABA, Center for Professional Responsibility, Variations of the ABA Model Rules of Professional Conduct, Rule 8.3 (Oct. 21, 2010), http://www.americanbar.org/content/dam/aba/migrated/cpr/pic/8_3.authcheckdam.pdf.

48. Rule 8.3(a).

mere suspicion that misconduct has occurred. The question is whether "a reasonable lawyer in the circumstances would have a firm opinion that the conduct in question more likely than not occurred."[49]

Reporting on a member of your own profession is usually unpleasant, but it is necessary for the protection of the public because co-professionals are often the only people who become aware of misconduct. Suppose, for example, that your surgeon was drunk while he was operating on you. Wouldn't you want other doctors in the operating room to report him to the authorities?[50]

Does this mean I have to blow the whistle on my boss if he does something unethical?

Yes, if the conduct raises a "substantial question" about the "honesty, trustworthiness or fitness" of your boss. The reporting rule requires every lawyer to report serious misconduct by any other lawyer, whether the other lawyer is an adversary, a partner, a boss, or in some other relationship. Associates have a duty to report misconduct by partners. A lawyer can't get off the hook by informing senior lawyers in a firm about the misconduct of another lawyer.

Is a lawyer required to report lawyer misconduct if the report would require disclosure of confidential information?

No. A lawyer is not required to report (1) information protected by the confidentiality rules and (2) information learned while participating in a lawyers' assistance program.[51] The confidentiality exception does not require a lawyer to get client approval before reporting the misconduct of another.[52] Neither does it allow a client to veto a lawyer's reporting of misconduct. The rule simply shields lawyers from reporting confidential client information.[53] The Restatement takes the position that if a lawyer learns of misconduct during an adversary proceeding and reporting would harm the client's interests, the lawyer should defer reporting until the

---

49. Restatement § 5, comment i.

50. Ninety-six percent of doctors think that physicians should report incompetent or impaired doctors to the authorities, but 45 percent of them don't always do so. Christopher Lee, Study Finds Gaps Between Doctors' Standards and Actions, Wash. Post (Dec. 4, 2007) (available at http://www.washingtonpost.com/wp-dyn/content/article/2007/12/03/AR2007120301771.html).

51. Rule 8.3(c).

52. The exemption of lawyers from being required to report confidential information, if read broadly, could swallow a substantial part of what is otherwise required by the rule. For discussion of this issue, see Peter K. Rofes, Another Misunderstood Relation: Confidentiality and the Duty to Report, 14 Geo. J. Leg. Ethics 621 (2001).

53. Consider how important it is to be clear about what is confidential. Suppose, for example, that a lawyer is overbilling a client. Can this be reported without revealing confidences about the subject matter of the work at issue? Usually it is possible to report allegations of lawyer misconduct without revealing a client's secrets.

client's interests can be safeguarded and the client consents to waive confidentiality.[54]

Illinois Attorney Registration and Disciplinary Commission administrator James Grogan

A lawyer who fails to report serious misconduct by another lawyer may be subject to discipline. While nearly every state has adopted a rule requiring lawyers to report misconduct of other lawyers, there are relatively few public reports of discipline of lawyers for not reporting. However, in a groundbreaking case prosecuted by James Grogan, the Illinois disciplinary agency suspended attorney James H. Himmel for his failure to report misconduct. Himmel represented an accident victim whose previous lawyer had settled a case and stolen $23,000 of the client's settlement money. The previous lawyer agreed to pay $75,000 in return for a promise not to prosecute, but the lawyer didn't pay. Himmel got a judgment against the lawyer, but only a fraction of the funds were paid to the client. Himmel's client asked Himmel not to report the opposing lawyer for fear that doing so would hamper further efforts to collect the money. Himmel did as his client requested, but his license was suspended for failure to report the misconduct.[55] As a result of this case, the number of reports by Illinois attorneys on other attorneys jumped from 154 the year *Himmel* was decided to 922 the following year.[56]

In the years since the *Himmel* decision, a number of attorneys have been charged with violation of Rule 8.3 or disciplined for failure to report the misconduct of another lawyer.[57] In most cases where a violation is found of Rule 8.3 or the state's counterpart, other misconduct is alleged as well. Although imposition of sanctions for violation of Rule 8.3 is still rare, the duty to report misconduct remains a mandatory duty under most states'

---

54. Restatement § 5, comment i.

55. In re Himmel, 533 N.E.2d 790 (Ill. 1988).

56. Daryl van Duch, Best Snitches: Land of Lincoln Leads the Nation in Attorneys Turning In Their Peers, Natl. L.J. (Jan. 27, 1997). The article also reports a "downside" to *Himmel*; some lawyers were reportedly "using the pretense of reporting unethical behavior just to trash another partner [in their own firm] and take over their business."

57. During a conference program in 2007, James Grogan, then the chief counsel of the Illinois Attorney Registration and Disciplinary Commission, noted that violations of Rule 8.3 are reported far more often than they are prosecuted. In Illinois, he said that since the *Himmel* case in 1988, there had been four other cases in which lawyers were charged with violation of Rule 8.3. Misconduct: Conference Panelists Call for Clarification of Obligation to Report Peer Misconduct, ABA/BNA Laws.' Man. on Prof. Conduct 23:297 (June 13, 2007). Illinois Circuit Court Judge Thomas R. Mulroy Jr., another participant in the discussion, explained that many lawyers report alleged violations of Rule 8.3 as a tactical ploy, even when the conduct at issue does not present a serious ethical problem. This, he said, explains why so many 8.3 reports do not lead to disciplinary charges against lawyers. Id.

ethics codes.[58] And in states that enforce it, even occasionally, attorneys regularly report misconduct by other lawyers.[59]

PROBLEM 2-1 EXCULPATORY EVIDENCE

This problem is based on events that occurred in the 1990s.

You and Bobby Harris were law school classmates and have stayed close friends. Both of you worked as assistant district attorneys in Chicago for a few years and then moved on to become solo practitioners doing criminal defense work. One spring evening five years ago, you met Harris at a bar near the courthouse. During your conversation in the bar, Harris told you that he had just come from a doctor's appointment in which he was diagnosed with advanced colon cancer and told that he had only months to live. Later that same evening, Harris told you that a few years ago, while he was prosecuting a murder case, he had suppressed blood evidence that would have cast doubt on the guilt of his defendant. The defendant was sentenced to death, but his execution was not likely to take place for several years. You found this revelation astonishing, since both you and Harris had prided yourselves on being ethical prosecutors. You both understood that prosecutors must reveal exculpatory evidence to criminal defendants. You urged Harris to tell you the name of the defendant and to disclose this information so that the arguably wrongful conviction could be reevaluated. Harris said he would think about it. You did not tell anyone what Harris had told you. Two months later, Harris died without having revealed his misfeasance.

---

58. See generally Nicki A. Ott & Heather F. Newton, A Current Look at Model Rule 8.3: How Is It Used and What Are Courts Doing About It?, 16 Geo. J. Leg. Ethics 747 (2003) (discussing *Himmel* and subsequent cases in which lawyers were sanctioned for failure to report the misconduct of another lawyer). The Illinois Supreme Court reaffirmed its view that the duty to report under Rule 8.3 is mandatory. Skolnick v. Altheimer & Gray, 730 N.E.2d 4 (Ill. 2000) (holding that a trial court's refusal to modify a protective order to allow a lawyer to report evidence of misconduct to the disciplinary authorities was not a reasonable exercise of discretion). James Grogan, the administrator of the Illinois lawyer disciplinary system, reports that "several other states have [sanctioned lawyers for failures to report] but not many boast any published opinions. Even in Illinois, we are talking about a handful of reported matters after *Himmel* [such as In re Thomas Michael Daley, https://www.iardc.org/rd_database/rulesdecisions.html (search for "Daley, Thomas Michael"), *aff'd*, https://www.iardc.org/rd_database/rulesdecisions.html (search for "M.R. 17023")]." E-mail from James Grogan to Lisa Lerman (Aug. 22, 2011).

59. In Illinois, as of 2011, 26.9 percent of the formal charges lodged by that state's disciplinary commission arise from reports from other lawyers or from judges. E-mail from James Grogan, supra n. 58.

Nearly five years after your friend Harris died, a man named Maurice LaVoie was scheduled to be executed for robbing and killing a man. LaVoie had already spent more than a decade in prison after he was convicted of the crime. Several weeks before the execution date, you read a series of newspaper articles about the case. The first cited a confidential source who claimed that before LaVoie's trial, a crime lab had tested blood found on the victim's pants. The reporter noted that this lab report was never introduced at trial and wondered whether it concluded that the blood did not match either the victim's or LaVoie's. If so, LaVoie's lawyers should have received the report during pretrial discovery, pursuant to the Supreme Court's *Brady* doctrine. When the reporter asked the district attorney's office about the lab report, he was told that nothing was known about it because the prosecutor in the case, Robert Harris, had since died. In a follow-up story, the reporter quoted LaVoie's current lawyers as saying that Harris had never turned over any such evidence. The district attorney's office declined a request from LaVoie's lawyers to recall all of the archived case records from the warehouse in which they were located, saying that the case was closed unless a court ordered it reopened.

When you read these stories, you immediately realized that this was the case to which Harris had referred in the conversation in the bar.

What should you do now? Consider first what obligations you may have under the ethics code and then consider the risks presented by each possible course of action.

---

b. Lawyers' responsibility for ethical misconduct by colleagues and superiors

Ethical misconduct in legal organizations is not merely a problem for the individual transgressor. The ethics codes impose a limited degree of collective responsibility on other lawyers in the firm or other organizations for the conduct of other lawyers and of nonlawyer employees. Rules 5.1, 5.2, and 5.3 address these issues.

- **Rule 5.1** establishes the responsibility of a partner or supervising lawyer for ensuring compliance with the ethical rules by subordinate lawyers, and explains when a senior lawyer may be subject to discipline for the conduct of a subordinate lawyer.
- **Rule 5.2** states when a subordinate lawyer is responsible for her own conduct, and under what circumstances she may follow orders without fear of discipline.

■ **Rule 5.3**, using language nearly identical to that of Rule 5.1, explains the responsibilities of lawyers who supervise nonlawyer employees for ensuring that the employees comply with the rules of professional conduct, and explains when a lawyer may be subject to discipline based on the conduct of a nonlawyer employee.

We reprint Rules 5.1 and 5.2 below. We do not include Rule 5.3 because it is substantively so similar to Rule 5.1.

5.1   Rule Responsibilities of Partners, Managers, and Supervisory Lawyers

Rule language*	Authors' explanation**
(a) **A partner in a law firm**, and a lawyer who individually or together with other lawyers possesses comparable managerial authority in a law firm, **shall make reasonable efforts to ensure that** the firm has in effect measures giving reasonable assurance that **all lawyers in the firm conform to the Rules of Professional Conduct**.	Lawyer managers must set up systems to prevent ethical problems. These include procedures to check for conflicts of interest and to manage client funds. They must provide continuing education in legal ethics. In small firms of experienced lawyers, "informal supervision and periodic review" may suffice, while "more elaborate measures" may be needed in large firms. Comments 2 and 3. On its face, this rule applies only to partners and other managers "in a law firm," but Rule 1.0(c) and its Comment 3 define "law firm" to include legal services organizations or the legal departments of corporations, government agencies, and other organizations.
(b) **A lawyer having direct supervisory authority** over another lawyer **shall make reasonable efforts** to ensure that the other lawyer conforms to the Rules of Professional Conduct.	If a subordinate lawyer commits an ethical violation, the supervising lawyer is not responsible for that violation as long as the supervisor did not direct or know about it. But the violation could reveal a breach of the supervisor's duty under Rule 5.1(b) to make reasonable efforts to prevent violations. Comments 6 and 7.
(c) **A lawyer shall be responsible for another lawyer's violation** of the Rules of Professional Conduct **if**:	A lawyer may be responsible for the conduct of a partner, associate, or subordinate. Partners have "at least indirect responsibility" for all work being done by the firm, as well as supervisory responsibility for work being done by subordinate lawyers on matters for which they are responsible. Comment 5.
(1) **the lawyer orders** or, with knowledge of the specific conduct, ratifies **the conduct** involved; or	A lawyer cannot avoid responsibility for violation of an ethical rule by ordering

Continued

Rule language[*]	Authors' explanation[**]
	another lawyer to do the prohibited act. Comment 4 and Rule 8.4(a).
(2) the **lawyer is a partner** or has comparable managerial authority in the law firm in which the other lawyer practices, **or has direct supervisory authority** over the other lawyer, **and knows of the conduct** at a time when its consequences can be avoided or mitigated **but fails to take remedial action**.	The directly supervising partner is not the only partner who may be responsible for a violation. Any partner in the firm who knows of the improper conduct and fails to take action to reduce or prevent the harm also commits a violation. In organizations that do not have partners, other lawyers with "comparable managerial authority" are equally responsible.

[*]All emphasis added.

[**]This and other authors' explanations draw from the comments to the rules and from other sources. They are not comprehensive but highlight some important interpretive points.

5.2   Rule Responsibilities of a Subordinate Lawyer

Rule language[*]	Authors' explanation[**]
(a) A lawyer is bound by the Rules of Professional Conduct **notwithstanding that the lawyer acted at the direction of another person**.	Like the foot soldier accused of committing a war crime, a lawyer is not excused from responsibility on the ground that she was just "following orders." However, if a supervisor directed the action, the subordinate lawyer may be able to prove that she did not actually know that the action was improper. Comment 1.
(b) A subordinate lawyer **does not violate the Rules** of Professional Conduct **if that lawyer acts in accordance with a supervisory lawyer's reasonable resolution of an arguable question of professional duty.**	Lawyers often disagree about whether proposed conduct would violate a rule. If the supervisor reasonably thinks the conduct is proper, the subordinate may undertake the action even when she believes otherwise. If the supervisor turns out to be wrong, however, the supervisor could be disciplined. Comment 2. If the supervisor was so wrong that her belief that the action was proper was not reasonable, the subordinate may also be disciplined.

[*]All emphasis added.

[**]This and other authors' explanations draw from the comments to the rules and from other sources. They are not comprehensive but highlight some important interpretive points.

Are lawyers, then, only partially responsible for their colleagues' ethical violations?

In terms of disciplinary enforcement, these rules do make lawyers only partially responsible for one another's actions. The law does not allow discipline of all of the lawyers in a firm, or even of all of the partners, if one of the firm's associates violates a disciplinary rule. Supervising lawyers are liable for the unethical acts of lawyers they are supervising if they direct the act or know of the proposed act and do not prevent it. Other managers of the organization are also responsible if they know of the proposed actions.

Under Rule 5.2(b), subordinate lawyers may be held accountable for unethical actions that they were ordered to undertake if the supervisor's instruction was not based on a "reasonable resolution of an arguable question of professional duty."

How can a lawyer know whether a supervising lawyer's decision is reasonable?

Suppose a partner tells an associate not to produce a particular document in discovery. The partner says it's not covered by the request. The associate thinks it is covered and that concealing it is unethical. The associate needs to assess whether the supervisor's instruction is a "reasonable resolution of an arguable question of professional duty." To answer that question, the associate should (a) do some research, and (b) seek advice from someone more experienced. The research might include study of the case law and commentary interpreting the ethical or procedural rules involved. The associate should look for authority that supports or refutes the supervisor's interpretation or his own. The associate might seek guidance from a trusted mentor within the firm or from the firm's ethics advisor, or the associate might seek confidential advice from a former professor or another lawyer outside the firm. If the associate seeks advice outside the firm, he should endeavor not to disclose client confidences, or should do so only to the extent allowed by Rule 1.6. (See Chapter 3.)

The limitations imposed by the ethical rules on one lawyer's responsibility for the conduct of others apply in the context of professional discipline. State tort law and judges who impose sanctions in litigation may not recognize them. For example, in a malpractice suit, an entire partnership may be held liable for the malpractice of any lawyer in the firm.[60]

---

60. See, e.g., Dresser Indus. v. Digges, 1989 WL 139234 (D. Md. Aug. 30, 1989) (holding that Edward Digges's partners were jointly and severally liable with him for misconduct he committed within the scope of the partnership). The extent of the partners' liability for the actions of other partners is affected by the organizational structure of the firm. Many firms reorganized as limited liability partnerships (LLPs) during the 1990s in an attempt to protect themselves from joint and several liability. See Chapter 8 for discussion of LLPs. Firms organized as LLPs may as a whole be

Can discipline be imposed on a whole law firm?

In most states, only individual lawyers can be disciplined for violating ethical rules. Two exceptions are New York and New Jersey, which discipline law firms for certain misconduct, such as failure to supervise employees or failure to maintain a system for checking new matters to identify conflicts of interest.[61] This approach aligns with the views of Professor Ted Schneyer and others, who believe that misconduct is sometimes the result of structural or cultural pressures within a firm, or at least could be prevented by better training and oversight within a firm.[62] Schneyer argues that it should be possible to impose disciplinary sanctions, such as fines and suspension, on entire law firms. The Ethics 2000 Commission initially embraced this idea but ultimately rejected it because it feared that imposing firm-wide responsibility for ethical violations would diminish individual accountability.[63] Many scholars, however, believe that disciplining law firms would help the profession.

In a number of widely publicized cases, a law firm partner was engaged in a pattern of flagrant financial misconduct and other partners in the firm were aware of the misconduct but did nothing to stop it. Sometimes the other partners were being loyal. In other cases, they failed to act because they, too, were making money from their partner's wrongdoing.[64] These cases point to a need to allow disciplinary authorities to hold firms accountable for the misconduct of lawyers in certain circumstances.

Could a law student get in trouble for violating an ethics rule?

Law students are not subject to professional discipline for violating the ethics rules,[65] except for Rule 8.1, which governs disclosures by applicants for admission to the bar.[66] However, if a character and fitness committee became aware that a law student, working as a part-time law clerk, doing an externship, or working in a law school clinic, had violated a provision of the rules, the

---

liable for the malpractice of one partner, but the other partners would not be liable individually. Thus the victim of the malpractice could reach the assets of the lawyer or lawyers who were individually responsible and the assets of the firm, but not the individually held assets of the other partners. State statutes usually require firms organized as LLPs to have malpractice insurance, but "typically the required policy limits are quite modest." Geoffrey C. Hazard Jr. & W. William Hodes, The Law of Lawyering §§ 12.18, 12.56 (3d ed., Aspen Publishers Supp. 2004).

61. N.J. R. Gen. Application 1:20-1(a); N.J. R. Prof. Conduct 5.3(a) (1984), 5.4; N.Y. Code Prof. Resp. 5.1, 1.7 (2009); see also Schneyer, supra n. 15.

62. Schneyer, supra n. 15.

63. Margaret Colgate Love, The Revised ABA Model Rules of Professional Conduct: Summary of the Work of Ethics 2000, 15 Geo. J. Leg. Ethics 441, 470-471 (2002).

64. Some of these cases are described in Lisa G. Lerman, Blue-Chip Bilking: Regulation of Billing and Expense Fraud by Lawyers, 12 Geo. J. Leg. Ethics 205 (1999).

65. See Rule 5.3, Comment 1.

66. Rule 8.1 prohibits both applicants and lawyers from making false statements and from withholding material information from bar admissions authorities and from disciplinary authorities.

committee might well inquire into the events and delay or deny the admission of the student into the state bar.[67] As noted above, the lawyer responsible for supervising the student also might be disciplined if the lawyer knew of the student's conduct and did not take prompt remedial action. If harm resulted, the student might be sued by a client or even by the supervising lawyer.

> **FOR EXAMPLE:** Alexandria Marzano-Lesnevich, a Harvard law student, was a summer intern at the Louisiana Capital Assistance Center. She published an essay about her work there in which she stated that one of the Center's clients, who had confessed to a murder and had been convicted, "knew he'd killed a boy." She described details of the murder, including the "red ligature mark ringing the boy's neck from where the man had used a piece of wire he'd found in the house." She also wrote that "I knew he had done this only after suffocating the boy with a sock stuffed down his throat, piling one method upon the other, killing the already dead."
>
> At the time Marzano-Lesnevich wrote the essay, the conviction was being appealed. She planned to write a book about the prosecution of the case. The Center sued her to prevent the publication of the book, claiming that she was breaching a client's confidentiality and using information about a client to his disadvantage by characterizing him as guilty.[68] At this writing, the outcome of the suit is unknown.

PROBLEM 2-2   THE LITTLE HEARING

This problem is based on the experiences of a recent law school graduate. She accepted her first job as an associate of a sole practitioner of immigration law. After her second day on the job, she called Professor Lerman, who had been one of her law professors. The problem is based on what she told Lerman that evening.

I started work this week at the law firm of Solomon Helman. He's a solo practitioner who does mostly immigration work. It looks like a

---

67. Related issues are discussed in Chapter 1, in the section on the character and fitness part of the bar admission process.

68. Michael Kunzelman, Law Office Sues to Block Info in Ex-Clerk's Book, Associated Press (Aug. 28, 2011) (available at http://seattletimes.com/html/localnews/2016040752_aplalawclerk lawsuit1stldwritethru.html). Model Rule 1.6, discussed in the next chapter, prohibits divulging information relating to the representation of a client, with certain exceptions. Model Rule 1.8(b) prohibits using information relating to the representation of a client to the disadvantage of the client without the client's informed consent.

very challenging position. He has so much more work than he can do that he's expecting me to take on the responsibilities of an experienced lawyer. I feel very fortunate to have gotten this job, given how bad the job market is. The only problem is, I'm not sure I can hack it.

Yesterday Helman told me that this morning, we'd take the train together and each handle separate cases in Newark and New York. I said that was impossible — I'd never done immigration work and had never appeared at any kind of court proceeding. He said he had to conduct a trial in federal court, so there was no way he could go to Newark with me, and one of us had to show up. "It's just a little hearing," he said. I guess it seemed like I didn't have any choice but to go.

Needless to say, I was completely petrified since I knew nothing about immigration law or immigration hearings. I tried to get Helman to explain the case to me, but he said he had to leave. He said, "Don't worry, we can talk about it on the train tomorrow." So I met him at the train station this morning. I was all keyed up, and looking forward to getting some guidance about what the heck I was supposed to do. We got on the train, and he handed me the file and then sat across the aisle from me, putting his feet up on the empty seat next to him. I said, "Aren't we going to talk about the case?" He said, "Sorry, I need to sleep." He passed me an immigration law textbook and said, "Read the file. The hearing isn't until two. Anything you need to know about the law you will find in that book." I read the file on the train and skimmed through what I thought were the relevant parts of the book, but frankly, it didn't help much.

I got to the hearing office, and I had to ask the receptionist which of the people waiting there was my client. The client's English wasn't good, but she was happy to see me. Almost as soon as I got there, she started crying and begging me not to let them send her back to Rwanda. I was sweating; I didn't have a clue what to do. I tried to get her to explain the story, but it was hard to understand her.

The hearing started; the judge started asking questions to the client. We really needed an interpreter, but we didn't have one. I asked if we could get an interpreter, but the judge said no. We did the best we could. I felt really bad that I couldn't do more for her. The hearing was a disaster. I don't know which was worse, my insecurity or my lack of preparation. I kept wondering how much Mr. Helman was charging the client for my brilliant assistance. The judge said he would issue a decision in the next month. I took the train back, feeling really bad about the whole situation. I had thought it would be worse for me not to show up at all, but now I'm not so sure.

When I got back to the office, Mr. Helman's secretary gave me two more files and told me Mr. Helman wanted me to handle the hearings on those matters. Both hearings are scheduled for tomorrow, one in the morning, one in the afternoon. I asked her why he is dumping all this work on me. She told me he has 1,500 active cases. There are more hearings scheduled each workday than Helman can attend.

I am troubled by the lack of prehearing preparation that seems to be the norm in this firm. Rule 1.1 requires competent representation, and I don't think I am really competent to do this work. I went into Mr. Helman's office to ask him about this problem. He tried to reassure me. He said it makes a big difference for the clients to have someone at the hearing, even if the person is not fully prepared. He says in his kind of practice, it is not financially feasible to prepare carefully for each hearing. He said that because his clients can only afford modest legal fees, he can only afford to give them modest service. If he took twice as long to work up each case, he would have to close the doors and go out of business. He said that he appreciated my concern, but now it was time to get on with the work. There were clients scheduled for hearings tomorrow.

What should this lawyer do? Show up and do a bad job at two more hearings tomorrow? Quit her job tonight? Aside from her decision about staying in or leaving her job, is there anything else that she should or must do?

---

c. Legal protections for subordinate lawyers

Most associates in law firms are employees at will. That means they do not have contracts for terms of years but may resign at any time for any reason or may be fired at any time for any reason. Well, almost any reason. Associates also are members of the bar. As such, they have independent obligations to comply with the law, including the ethical rules. Sometimes a lawyer's duties to his firm may conflict with his duties to the profession. Suppose an associate in a law firm sees a partner engage in behavior that "raises a substantial question as to that lawyer's honesty, trustworthiness or fitness as a lawyer in other respects." Under Rule 8.3 or its equivalent, the lawyer is obliged to "inform the appropriate professional authority." If the misconduct is serious, an associate is ethically obliged to blow the whistle on his boss or on another partner in the law firm. This, needless to say, puts the associate in an awkward position. Suppose instead that a partner instructs an associate to destroy a document that has been requested in discovery. If the partner's instruction is unethical and is not "a reasonable resolution of an arguable question of professional duty" (Rule 5.2(b)), then the associate would be subject to discipline for following orders.

A lawyer who is told to do something that the lawyer thinks is unethical has several options.

- Accept the directions of the superior.
- Argue with the superior.
- Discuss the problem with another superior.
- Do more research or investigation to try to clarify the problem.
- Ask to be relieved from work on the matter.
- Resign (or be fired) from employment.

Which of these options are available as a practical matter depends on the situation and the players. From time to time, an associate resigns or is fired because of his or her ethical qualms about something going on at work.

> **FOR EXAMPLE:** One of our students had a friend who had accepted a six-figure salary as an associate at a New York law firm. In one case, he was helping to represent a doctor accused of malpractice for failure to make a timely diagnosis of cancer. The x-rays of the plaintiff's decedent showed a cancerous growth that the doctor had missed. The partner on the case told the associate to destroy the x-ray plate, saying "I'd rather have a missing documents case than have that picture come out at the trial." The associate resigned from his job.

Does the law provide any protection for lawyers who are fired because they refuse to participate in unethical conduct or because they report misconduct of other lawyers?

Howard Wieder

Until the 1990s, the law provided no such protection. Associates in law firms could be fired for any reason other than one expressly prohibited by law (for example, race). However, starting with the *Wieder* case in New York State, some courts have developed doctrines to protect attorneys who insist on ethical conduct or report breaches. Howard Wieder, an associate at a New York law firm, complained to the firm's partners that another associate had failed to do promised work on a matter on which the associate was representing Wieder and that he had forged firm checks. He asked them to report the alleged misconduct to the state bar. The partners initially refused, apparently believing that no misconduct had occurred. Eventually, after incessant prodding by Wieder, the partners did report the lawyer to the disciplinary authorities. A few months later, they fired Wieder, who then sued the firm for wrongful discharge. The firm argued that Wieder was an at-will employee and therefore could be fired for any reason. In a precedent-setting decision, the New York Court of Appeals held that the right to fire employees at will did not include the right to fire lawyers who complained of unethical conduct by another lawyer, because lawyers have professional duties not only to their employers but to a "broader public."[69] Some other jurisdictions have adopted similar rules,[70] but others have rejected the principle.[71]

B. Civil liability of lawyers

Suppose a client hires a lawyer to represent her in a matter that is scheduled to be heard in court in a week. The lawyer misses the court appearance, and as a result, a default judgment is entered against the client, ordering her to pay damages. This client, having been damaged by the lawyer's mistake, might sue the lawyer for negligence, intentional misconduct, breach of contract, or breach of fiduciary duty.[72] The client might, in addition, file a complaint with a disciplinary agency, but a disciplinary action would not provide the client with compensation for the harm she suffered.

1. Legal malpractice

The term "legal malpractice" refers to a claim brought against a lawyer for professional misconduct that is alleged to have caused harm to another person.[73] The claim may involve a tort claim for negligence or intentional misconduct, an asserted breach of the contract[74] between lawyer and client,

---

69. Wieder v. Skala, 593 N.Y.S.2d 752 (N.Y. 1992).

70. See Gen. Dynamics Corp. v. Super. Ct., 876 P.2d 487 (Cal. 1994).

71. Jacobson v. Knepper & Moga, P.C., 706 N.E.2d 491 (Ill. 1998); see Douglas R. Richmond, Professional Responsibilities of Law Firm Associates, 45 Brandeis L.J. 199 (2007).

72. See Restatement § 48, comment c; § 49; John Leubsdorf, Legal Malpractice and Professional Responsibility, 48 Rutgers L. Rev. 101 (1995).

73. For more comprehensive explication of these issues, see Susan S. Fortney & Vincent R. Johnson, Legal Malpractice Law: Problems and Prevention (West 2007).

74. Thomas D. Morgan, Sanctions and Remedies for Attorney Misconduct, 19 S. Ill. U. L.J. 343, 349-350 (1995) (explaining that legal malpractice often has been characterized as a tort claim, but urging that the claim is more appropriately premised on the lawyer-client contract, which spells out the lawyer's duties).

or an allegation that the lawyer violated her fiduciary responsibility to the client. A single lawsuit may assert more than one of these theories of liability. The term "legal malpractice" is an umbrella term that covers all of these types of causes of action.[75]

What are the elements of a tort claim of legal malpractice?

A tort claim of legal malpractice may involve either a claim of negligence or one of intentional misconduct. The client must assert

- that the lawyer owed a duty to the plaintiff,
- that the lawyer failed to exercise "the competence and diligence normally exercised by lawyers in similar circumstances,"[76] and
- that the breach of duty caused harm to the plaintiff.[77]

Why do people say it is so hard to win a malpractice case?

One of the difficulties in proving legal malpractice is that, in order to show that the lawyer's conduct "caused" the harm, one must establish that "but for" the lawyer's conduct, the harm would not have occurred. This requires the plaintiff in a legal malpractice matter to try "a case within a case." Not only must he demonstrate that the lawyer's conduct was below par, but he must prove that but for the lawyer's mistake, the client would have prevailed in the matter in which the lawyer represented him.

It used to be that an aggrieved client had a hard time finding a lawyer who was willing to sue another lawyer. This may still be a problem for some clients, especially in small communities in which all the lawyers know one another, but this problem is largely a thing of the past. There has been enormous growth in the last few decades in claims against lawyers and in judgments against lawyers. Consequently, there are many lawyers, and even entire law firms, that specialize in representing lawyers or clients or both in matters involving professional liability.

Why is legal malpractice sometimes characterized as a tort and sometimes as a breach of contract?

Although many malpractice claims are framed as tort claims, the lawyer-client relationship is contractual in nature, so a client seeking redress against a lawyer may also allege breach of contract. There are differences in what must be proven to establish a cause of action and in the rules for calculation of damages. State law is inconsistent on whether legal malpractice is a tort claim, a contract claim, or both. Some jurisdictions allow

---

75. See Restatement § 48, introductory note.
76. Restatement § 52(1).
77. Restatement § 48; see also Ronald E. Mallen & Jeffrey M. Smith, Legal Malpractice vol. 5, § 35.13, at 1227-1228 (2009 ed., Thomson Reuters/West).

only tort claims. Others allow only contract claims. A third group allows both types of claims but differentiates based on the facts alleged or on the relief sought.[78]

What are some of the most common mistakes made by lawyers that lead to malpractice liability?

A client may sue a lawyer for malpractice on the basis of any mistake by a lawyer that would not have been made by an ordinarily competent and diligent lawyer in the same circumstances. For example, a lawyer who allows a statute of limitations to run without filing suit on behalf of a client may incur malpractice liability.[79] A lawyer who represents two clients with conflicting interests may be liable for malpractice if harm results.[80]

Many malpractice claims have common origins. One experienced practitioner in Seattle offered the following "top ten" list of professional practices that risk triggering claims of professional liability.

1. Ignore conflicts of interest.
2. Sue your former client for an unpaid fee.
3. Accept any client and any matter that comes along.
4. "Do business" with your client.
5. Practice outside your area of expertise.
6. Go overboard in opening branch offices and making lateral hires.
7. Leave partner peer review to the other firms.
8. Ignore a potential claim and represent yourself in a professional liability dispute.
9. Settle a matter without written authorization from your client.
10. Fail to communicate with your client.[81]

What remedies are available to a client who sues for legal malpractice?

A court may order the lawyer to pay damages for harm caused by malpractice, but it also could order compliance with an injunction, return of property, alteration or cancellation of a legal document, or other remedies.[82]

---

78. Restatement § 48, comment c.

79. See, e.g., Dixon Ticonderoga Co. v. Est. of O'Connor, 248 F.3d 151 (3d Cir. 2001).

80. See, e.g., Streber v. Hunter, 221 F.3d 701 (5th Cir. 2000).

81. Harry H. Schneider Jr., See You in Court: Follow These Ten Rules and You, Too, Can Be Sued for Malpractice, ABA J. (Mar. 1994) (available at http://apps.americanbar.org/legalservices/lpl/downloads/journalmar94.pdf). Harry Schneider is a partner at Perkins, Coie in Seattle.

82. Restatement § 6.

How frequent are legal malpractice suits, and what is the range of damage awards that lawyers are required to pay?

The ABA reported in 2007 that between 2004 and 2007, more than 40,000 claims of legal malpractice were made against lawyers' insurance companies. In most of the cases, no money was paid to the claimant, but about 6,200 of the claims concluded with a payment of more than $10,000, and in 124 cases, more than a million dollars was paid. The most common practice areas in which malpractice claims occur are personal injury (claims against plaintiffs' lawyers) (22 percent); real estate (20 percent); domestic relations (10 percent); and estate, trust, and probate cases (10 percent). The most common types of claims were for the attorney's failure to know or apply the law (12 percent), failure to file documents (11 percent), procedural and planning errors (9 percent), and inadequate investigation (8 percent).[83]

Is a claim for breach of fiduciary duty different from a negligence-based malpractice claim?

Yes and no. It is a separate cause of action that originates in the common law of fiduciary duty, which applies not only to lawyers but also to other kinds of fiduciaries. A fiduciary is someone who assumes a position of trust in relation to another; examples include stockbrokers and financial advisors as well as lawyers. Fiduciaries owe special duties not to misuse property or information that has been entrusted to them,[84] must place the interests of the other above their own interests, and must act in good faith on the other's behalf.[85] Many claims against lawyers allege more than one cause of action: negligence, breach of contract, breach of fiduciary duty, or a combination of two or three.[86]

A client who sues her lawyer for malpractice will sometimes include a claim of breach of fiduciary duty because in some states, there are procedural advantages to doing so, such as a longer statute of limitations or a shift in the burden of proof. But the differences between the two types of

---

83. ABA Standing Comm. on Lawyers' Professional Liability, Profile of Legal Malpractice Claims 2004-2007 (ABA 2008). Because the study covered only claims against insurance companies, the magnitude of claims against uninsured lawyers is unknown.

84. A person can become a fiduciary as a matter of law, such as in attorney-client or principal-agent relationships, or a fiduciary relationship can arise because one person justifiably places trust in another so that the other assumes a position of superiority and influence in relation to the first. Chou v. U. of Chicago, 254 F.3d 1347 (Fed. Cir. 2001).

85. See Restatement § 7, comment b, explaining that "[t]he relationship between lawyer and client is one in which the lawyer generally owes the client rigorously enforced fiduciary duties, including duties of utmost good faith and fair dealing." Id. at § 49 (explaining that breach of the fiduciary duty articulated in § 16(3) would render a lawyer civilly liable to a client if the breach causes injury to the client). The tort of breach of fiduciary duty is also discussed in Chapter 4.

86. Restatement § 49, comment c.

claims is not very great; in both cases, the plaintiff must prove that a duty was breached and that the breach caused financial or other injury.[87]

What fiduciary duties does a lawyer owe a client?

The Restatement provides the following list of the fiduciary duties owed by lawyers to their clients.

- Safeguarding the client's confidences and property
- Avoiding impermissible conflicting interests
- Adequately informing the client
- Following instructions of the client
- Not employing adversely to the client powers arising from the client-lawyer relationship[88]

What are the elements of a claim of breach of fiduciary duty?

As in a negligence action, a plaintiff must prove that but for the lawyer's misconduct, the plaintiff would have obtained a favorable judgment or settlement in the case in which the lawyer originally represented the client or that the plaintiff suffered some other compensable harm.[89]

Do some lawyers owe fiduciary duties based on something other than a lawyer-client relationship?

Yes. Lawyers often take on fiduciary roles other than that of legal representative. A lawyer may serve as a broker, an escrow agent, an expert witness, an executor, a mediator, or a trustee. Such lawyers may owe fiduciary duties to clients and/or to nonclients as a result of these assumed duties. For example, a lawyer who serves as an escrow agent might have obligations to disclose information about the escrow to an opposing party.[90] But even a lawyer who does not take on a special fiduciary role has fiduciary obligations that arise out of the duties undertaken in representing a client.

Could a lawyer be disciplined, sued for malpractice, and criminally prosecuted, all for one act of misconduct?

Yes, a lawyer who violates criminal law in the course of practicing law or who helps a client violate criminal law can be prosecuted in addition to being disciplined and sued for legal malpractice. As in other types of cases,

---

87. Panelists Review Practicality of Inserting Breach of Fiduciary Duty Counts into Suit, 79 U.S.L.W. 2208 (Mar. 15, 2011).

88. Restatement § 49, comment b (references omitted).

89. Restatement § 53, comment b.

90. Restatement § 48, comment d and reporter's note.

defendants can be held both criminally and civilly liable. It is not common for lawyers to go to jail, but it does occasionally happen.

> **FOR EXAMPLE:** Former associate attorney general Webster Hubbell was prosecuted for mail fraud and tax evasion because he engaged in billing and expense fraud while in private practice in Arkansas.[91] He was disbarred for the same misconduct and also sued by his law firm for fraud, larceny, and embezzlement.[92]

Webster Hubbell

Could a lawyer be liable to a person who was not a client?

Lawyers do various work on behalf of clients that, if done improperly, could cause harm to someone other than a client. If the lawyer is found to have owed a duty to the third person, and if it is shown that harm was caused by improper conduct by the lawyer, the lawyer might be found liable to the third person. Among the third parties to whom a lawyer owes duties are prospective clients and people who are the intended beneficiaries of the lawyer's work for a client, such as those who will inherit assets under a will drafted by a lawyer.[93]

> **FOR EXAMPLE:** Seeking to help his brother-in-law get a loan with the borrower's farm equipment as collateral, a lawyer falsely represented to the lender that he had searched and ascertained that there were no liens on the equipment. The borrower defaulted on the loan and committed suicide. The lender sued the lawyer for negligent misrepresentation. The court held that the lawyer was liable to the lender despite the lawyer's argument that the lender was not his client.[94]

2. Malpractice insurance

In the last several decades, an increasing number of lawyers have been held civilly and criminally liable for misconduct. Some forms of civil liability are covered by malpractice insurance. All large firms are covered by

---

91. See U.S. v. Hubbell, 530 U.S. 27 (2000).

92. Rose Law Firm v. Hubbell, No. LR-C-96-212, Consent Judgment and Order (E.D. Ark. Oct. 28, 1996). For some other cases of theft by lawyers, see Lerman, supra n. 64.

93. Restatement § 51 inventories duties owed by lawyers to nonclients and discusses the scope of these duties in comments b through g.

94. Greycas, Inc. v. Proud, 826 F.2d 1560 (7th Cir. 1987), *cert. denied*, 484 U.S. 1043 (1988).

malpractice insurance policies, and most small firms and solo practitioners carry insurance also.

Are lawyers required to carry malpractice insurance?

Lawyers are not required to purchase malpractice insurance, except in Oregon.[95] Even so, most lawyers purchase policies.[96] Uninsured firms tend to explain their lack of coverage either by asserting that insurance was not necessary to their practice or that they believed that purchasing malpractice insurance would increase the likelihood that they would be sued.[97]

Can prospective clients find out whether the lawyers they seek to hire have malpractice insurance?

Yes, in many states. About half the states now require that lawyers disclose whether they have malpractice insurance, either to the bar or directly to clients. In most states in which lawyers are required to disclose coverage to the bar, this information is made available to the public.[98] The idea is that if lawyers are required to disclose whether they have malpractice insurance, lawyers will have a business incentive to obtain coverage.[99]

The ABA has issued a Model Court Rule on Insurance Disclosure. States that have adopted the Model Rule may suspend a lawyer who fails to state whether she is insured or provides false information about coverage.[100]

What kinds of mistakes are unlikely to be covered by a malpractice insurance policy?

If you go to work for a law firm that has malpractice insurance, you should not get a false sense of security from having a policy. Although malpractice

95. Or. Rev. Stat. § 9.080(2)(a) (2003).

96. By one estimate, about 60 percent of practicing lawyers *do* have malpractice insurance. Lance Christopher Kassab, Impact of Malpractice Insurance, http://www.texaslegalmalpractice.com/impact.htm (accessed Oct. 31, 2012).

97. David Hechler, Malpractice Policies Going Up, Natl. L.J. A1 (June 3, 2002).

98. For a state-by-state survey, see ABA, Standing Comm. on Client Protection, State Implementation of ABA Model Court Rule on Insurance Disclosure as of Jan. 3, 2011, http://www.americanbar.org/content/dam/aba/administrative/professional_responsibility/chart_implementation_of_mcrid_080911.pdf (Apr. 25, 2011).

99. Sheri Qualters, No Malpractice Insurance? You Must Tell, Natl. L.J. (Aug. 3, 2006). Among the states that require lawyers to disclose whether they carry insurance are Illinois, Massachusetts, North Carolina, Ohio, and Pennsylvania. Id.

100. ABA, Standing Comm. on Client Protection, ABA Model Court Rule on Insurance Disclosure (adopted by the American Bar Association House of Delegates on Aug. 10, 2004) (2005) (available at http://www.americanbar.org/content/dam/aba/migrated/cpr/clientpro/Model_Rule_InsuranceDisclosure.authcheckdam.pdf). Despite the provision in the rule that allows discipline of a lawyer who fails to comply, the rule was not adopted as an amendment to the Model Rules of Professional Conduct but as a model court rule.

insurance policies do provide coverage for some lawyer negligence, they exclude many types of problems from coverage.

Here is a list of some types of liability that are not covered in many malpractice insurance policies.

- Intentional acts, including fraud or other dishonest conduct (like billing or expense fraud)[101]
- Orders of restitution of legal fees, fines, or penalties
- Orders to pay punitive damages (though in some states, lawyers can purchase separate coverage for these)
- Conduct of lawyers in other roles, such as notary public, title agent, fiduciary, or trustee
- Conduct of lawyers who represent businesses of which they are also part owners
- Intra-firm disputes, such as liability to former partners or former employees[102]

If you work in a small firm and have to purchase malpractice insurance, how do you decide what policy to buy?

Malpractice insurance can be expensive.[103] Pamela Bresnahan, an expert on legal malpractice insurance, advises that "you should spend at least as much time picking out malpractice insurance as you do picking out a new suit. After all, the suit is probably less than the deductible on one claim."[104]

3. Other civil liability of lawyers

Lawyers may be responsible for conduct that nonlawyers engage in as well.[105] For example, a lawyer could be liable for

- advising or assisting unlawful client conduct,
- stealing,
- lying,

---

101. Some policies pay for attorneys' fees whenever an insured lawyer is sued for fraud or other dishonest behavior; others provide coverage only when the lawyer wins.

102. Pamela A. Bresnahan, Tips on Taking Coverage: Learn What Malpractice Insurance Can and Cannot Do for You Before Choosing, ABA J. (July 2002) (available at http://apps.americanbar.org/legalservices/lpl/downloads/journaljuly02.pdf).

103. Hechler, supra n. 97 (noting that malpractice insurance policies can increase in cost from 10 to 40 percent per year). According to one report, the average cost per lawyer is $5,000 to $8,000 per year, but the rates are higher for lawyers with certain specialties, such as divorce and personal injury cases. Maggie Gebremichael, The Average Cost of Legal Malpractice Insurance, http://www.ehow.com/about_5390403_average-cost-legal-malpractice-insurance.html (accessed Oct. 31, 2012).

104. Bresnahan, supra n. 102.

105. Restatement § 56.

- intentional infliction of emotional distress,
- violation of regulatory statutes,[106] or
- breach of contract.

a. Liability for breach of contract

Another set of cases that create "lawyer law" are cases in which courts nullify contracts to which lawyers were parties or contracts negotiated by lawyers. If a lawyer negotiates an unfair fee agreement with a client through misrepresentation or overreaching, the fee agreement is voidable, just as is any contract so negotiated.[107] If a lawyer negotiates a settlement based on false representations, the settlement agreement may be voidable even if it is embodied in a judgment.[108] Similarly, if a lawyer enters into a business transaction with a client without complete disclosure of the lawyer's interest in the transaction and her consequent inability to give disinterested advice, the transaction may be invalidated.[109]

b. Liability for violation of regulatory statutes

Even though the courts claim the exclusive authority to regulate lawyers, lawyers are bound by law as are ordinary citizens. In the twenty-first century, every professional (and many other people) must be aware of a wide range of federal, state, and local statutes and regulations that require or prohibit certain conduct. For example, if you have clients who are required to file documents with banking or securities regulatory agencies, you as the lawyer may be directly subject to certain regulatory requirements. Many administrative agencies have special rules that govern lawyers who practice before or file documents with those agencies. If you engage in lobbying before federal or state legislative bodies, you must comply with registration and disclosure requirements. Lawyers are subject to laws on employment discrimination, debt collection, and to some consumer protection laws. We do not offer a comprehensive review of the "other law" that governs lawyers. Some examples are mentioned in the section on criminal liability of lawyers. We suggest that in whatever field of practice you pursue, you should familiarize yourself not just with the relevant law that particularly governs lawyers, but with other applicable law as well.

---

106. Restatement § 56, comments c-i.
107. See, e.g., Restatement (Second) of Contracts, §§ 2, 162, 164 (1981).
108. Fed. R. Civ. P. 60(b).
109. See, e.g., Abstract & Title Corp. v. Cochran, 414 So. 2d 284 (Fla. Dist. Ct. App. 1982).

4. Disqualification for conflicts of interest

Another substantial body of "lawyer law" consists of the judicial opinions resulting from motions to disqualify lawyers because of conflicts of interest. These motions are often made by opposing counsel rather than by the lawyer's own clients.[110]

In deciding motions to disqualify lawyers because of alleged conflicts of interest, do the courts simply interpret the state's ethical codes?

No. In deciding these cases, the courts are influenced by the ethics rules on conflicts of interest, but the ethics rules articulate standards for discipline, not disqualification. Many courts follow their own common law standards, which may not be the same as those in the ethics rules. This issue is explored in Chapters 5, 6, and 7.

C. Criminal liability of lawyers

Lawyers are supposed to be "officers of the court" and guardians of our legal system. One might suppose, then, that members of the legal profession would be scrupulously attentive to the law that governs them and that few lawyers would ever be charged with or convicted of serious crimes.

If there ever was a time when lawyers were somewhat protected from criminal prosecution for white-collar crime, that time has passed. In recent years, numerous lawyers, including many elite or high-profile lawyers, have been indicted, convicted, sentenced, and disbarred for dishonest professional conduct that might not have had significant professional consequences 20 years ago.[111]

A recent development is a rising number of indictments of corporate general counsels. In 2007, for example, 10 general counsels faced federal indictments for civil or criminal fraud, most relating to the backdating of stock options.[112] Indictments of lawyers for securities fraud are also increasing. David W. Porteous, a Chicago lawyer, reports that between 1999 and 2005, the SEC brought cases against 125 lawyers.[113] Some people claim that the SEC has been too aggressive. But Linda Chatman Thomsen, the director of the Enforcement Division at the SEC from 2005 until 2009, disagrees. She noted that recent cases against companies involved "secret

---

110. Restatement § 6, comment i.
111. Lerman, supra n. 64.
112. Pamela A. MacLean, The Year of Living Dangerously for GCs, Natl. L.J. 1 (Oct. 1, 2007).
113. Id. Few of the SEC lawyer defendants before 2007 were general counsels.

slush funds, forgery, grants to fictitious employees, falsified corporate documents, self-dealing, self-enrichment and lying" to auditors. "Are we overreaching?" she asked a reporter. "You tell me."[114]

---

114. Id.

3 THE DUTY TO PROTECT CLIENT CONFIDENCES

A. **The basic principle of confidentiality**
   1. Protection of "information relating to the representation of a client"
   2. Protection of information if there is a reasonable prospect of harm to a client's interests
   3. The bottom line on informal communications
   4. Additional cautions about protecting client confidences

B. **Exceptions to the duty to protect confidences**
   1. Revelation of past criminal conduct
   2. The risk of future injury or death
   3. Client frauds and crimes that cause financial harm
   4. Revealing confidences to obtain advice about legal ethics
   5. Using a client's confidential information to protect the lawyer's interests
   6. Revealing confidences to comply with a court order or other law
   7. Revealing confidences to prevent certain conflicts of interest

C. **Use or disclosure of confidential information for personal gain or to benefit another client**

D. **Talking to clients about confidentiality**

E. **The attorney-client privilege**
   1. Confidentiality and attorney-client privilege compared

A. The basic principle of confidentiality

One of the basic rules of client representation is that lawyers are obliged to keep clients' secrets. In fact, lawyers are required to keep confidential much of what they learn in the course of representing clients. This duty is expressed in the ethical rules; in the law of agency, which requires all agents to keep the confidences of their principals; and in the law of evidence, which protects lawyers and clients from being compelled to testify about confidential communications. This chapter explains the ethical and legal rules concerning the lawyer's obligation to protect client confidences, exploring what information must be kept confidential and under what circumstances a lawyer may or must reveal confidential information. It also discusses the related rules of evidence protecting attorney-client communications and the doctrine protecting the lawyer's work product.

1. Protection of "information relating to the representation of a client"

Rule 1.6(a) Confidentiality of Information
A lawyer shall not reveal information relating to representation of a client unless the client gives informed consent, the disclosure is impliedly authorized in order to carry out the representation, or the disclosure is permitted by paragraph (b) [which lays out some exceptions that are discussed later in the chapter].[1]

---

1. In Rule 1.6(a), the Delaware version has a comma after the second use of the word "representation," as shown here, and the ABA version does not, but the difference between the Delaware version and the ABA version is purely stylistic.

Comment 4

Paragraph (a) prohibits a lawyer from revealing information relating to the representation of a client. This prohibition also applies to disclosures by a lawyer that do not in themselves reveal protected information but could reasonably lead to the discovery of such information by a third person. A lawyer's use of a hypothetical to discuss issues relating to the representation is permissible so long as there is no reasonable likelihood that the listener will be able to ascertain the identity of the client or the situation involved.

Rule 1.6 requires lawyers to protect as confidential all information "relating to representation of a client."[2] This standard covers any information a lawyer learns in connection with a matter the lawyer is handling for a client's case, regardless of whether the lawyer receives the information from the client or from another source.[3] Here is a summary of what qualifies as confidential information.[4]

Information that must be protected as confidential
- All information relating to the matter on which the lawyer is representing the client, except information that is "generally known"
- Personal information relating to the client that the client would not want disclosed
- Information learned from the client, and information learned from interviews, documents, photographs, observation, or other sources
- Information relating to the representation acquired before the representation begins (such as during a preliminary consultation) and after the representation terminates
- Notes or memoranda that the lawyer creates relating to the matter

---

What could happen if a lawyer fails to protect confidences?

If a lawyer improperly reveals confidences, her client might be harmed. For example, if a client who was in a car accident tells his lawyer that he believes

---

2. The Restatement uses the same phrase, but exempts from protection "information that is generally known." Restatement § 59.

3. Restatement § 59, comment b.

4. The information in the box is drawn from Restatement § 59, comments.

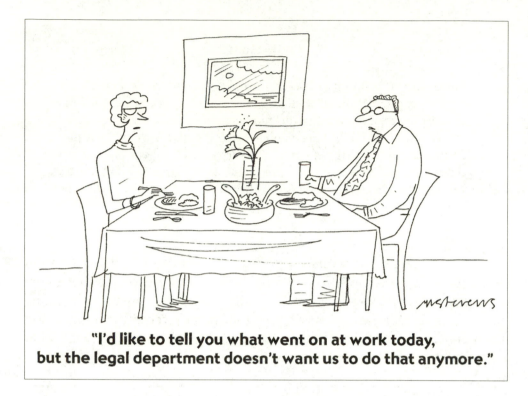

"I'd like to tell you what went on at work today,
but the legal department doesn't want us to do that anymore."

he was at fault and the lawyer tells her opposing counsel, the opposing lawyer might use this information to win a lawsuit against the client.

A lawyer who improperly reveals client confidences might suffer various legal or other consequences. The client might fire the lawyer or refuse to pay the fee. The lawyer might be

- subject to professional discipline,
- liable in tort or contract for negligent or intentional breach of duty,
- disqualified from representation of one or more clients, or
- enjoined by a court from further revelation.

What is the policy behind the confidentiality rule?

The primary purpose of the confidentiality rule is to facilitate open communication between lawyers and clients. Lawyers need to get accurate and complete information from their clients to represent them well. If lawyers were not bound to protect clients' secrets, clients might be more reluctant to share their secrets with their lawyers.

FOR EXAMPLE: A former client of Professor Lerman's got fired from his job as a hospital janitor because he broke a faucet on a sink with a two-by-four. He wanted to bring a lawsuit against the hospital because he believed that he was wrongfully fired. He explained to Lerman that he had become agitated because he had not taken his prescription medication for an anxiety problem. The reason he hadn't taken his medication is that the hospital changed the location where employees were to pick up prescriptions, and he didn't know where to get it. He also told Lerman about other episodes of violence that had occurred when he was not medicated. Once he had hijacked a plane. He had not had a weapon, but he had bitten the pilot.

If the client thought that his lawyer might reveal his violent history to the hospital's lawyer without his permission, he might not have shared this sensitive information.

Isn't the recitation of those facts itself a violation of the rule on confidentiality?

It could be. Even though Professor Lerman is now a law professor and not a practicing lawyer, she must still comply with the rules of confidentiality as to former clients. She has had no contact with this client in ages. He has not given her permission to talk about his story. But in recounting this tale, she hasn't mentioned his name, where he worked, when she represented him, or many other details that might enable the reader to identify him. Is that enough? We explore this question later in this chapter.

Is the fact that a lawyer is representing a particular client confidential?

Sometimes. Some clients don't care whether other people know that they are represented by counsel. Every large corporation, for example, has ongoing relationships with various lawyers who assist with transactional, regulatory, and other matters. However, if a lawyer (with a certain client's permission) reveals that he is representing that client, he must then avoid disclosing confidential information about that client's matter.

Some clients do not want anyone to know that they have consulted an attorney. In such cases, the fact of consultation or representation is confidential.[5] For example, if a client is considering seeking a divorce but has not yet decided what to do, revelation of the fact that the client has consulted a lawyer could make reconciliation impossible. Or suppose a politician consults a lawyer after he learns that he is the target of a criminal investigation. If it became known that the politician had hired a lawyer, people might infer that he had committed a crime.

Many of the problems involving the principle of client confidentiality arise out of its several exceptions. But before we turn to those exceptions, let's look at a very common problem involving the scope of the duty to protect confidences.

---

5. Lawyers may be able to avoid being compelled to reveal client identity under the attorney-client privilege.

PROBLEM 3-1   YOUR DINNER WITH ANNA

It is mid-August. You graduated from law school in May and took the bar exam in July. You have just finished your first day as a lawyer in a law firm, Porter & Quarles.[6]

You reach Chez Francois before Anna gets there. You settle down at an empty sidewalk table where you will see her when she arrives. You have known Anna since you were in a freshman seminar together in college. Your career paths have diverged, but today was Anna's first day at her first professional job too. She has become a social worker on the children's ward of the city hospital. When you discovered last month that you would be starting work on the same day, you arranged to celebrate with Chez Francois's famous lobster thermidor and a bottle of good wine.

You order a sparkling water with lime while you keep a lookout for Anna. You feel pretty good about your new firm. Some of your classmates will earn higher salaries than you, but probably they will have to work much longer hours. Everyone at Porter & Quarles seems pretty relaxed. Maybe that's because it's summer. But maybe a firm with just 15 lawyers isn't as high-pressure as the bigger firms in town.

"Hey there," Anna calls. You get up and give her a hug. "You look great in your lawyer suit," she says.

"Well, it turns out I didn't have to dress up like this. The lawyers only dress up for clients and meetings, I gather. But heck, the first day, who knew? You look good too."

"So what's it like? Get any murderers off today?"

In fact you spent the day working on a civil suit against the local police department on behalf of a client whose wrist was broken by a police officer.

Before continuing with this problem, consider whether you can even tell her that much about your first day at work.

Anna catches the waiter's eye and orders a bottle of wine. She tells you about her first day at work. She is part of a team that counsels parents of children with serious or terminal illnesses. Anna spent much of the day with the mother of an 11-year-old girl, Estella, who has cystic fibrosis. Anna's team knows that Estella probably will die

---

6. You have not yet learned whether you passed the bar, so you are technically a law clerk and not yet a member of the bar. Even so, assume that you are required to comply with the ethics rules. Although the rules may not formally bind lawyers not yet admitted, new lawyers are well advised to comply with them because violations could impair their prospects for bar admission.

within a few years. Her team is trying to help Estella to cope with her illness and with the possibility of death, and to prepare the family so that Estella's death will not devastate them.

Anna's story makes you feel relieved that you decided to be a lawyer. It is hard to imagine having to deal with problems like Estella's every day.

"So what about your first day?" Anna asks.

"I am working on a case against the police, police brutality, I guess. Our client is this guy named Joey. I better not say his last name. Not that it would mean anything to you, but you know, it's confidential. Late one night last fall, Joey was in a bar downtown, a place called The Alley. He'd had quite a lot to drink. There was a fight between some other guys in the bar. The bartender called the cops, and Joey got arrested."

"Wait a minute. If Joey wasn't involved in the fight, why did he get arrested?"

"Well, Joey says he wasn't fighting. But my boss, Arthur, thinks he may have been the instigator. You see, one of the other guys who was arrested for fighting is the live-in boyfriend of Joey's ex-wife.

"Anyway, when it was all over, Joey had a broken arm. Joey says a police officer named Mallory broke the bone by twisting his arm.

Mallory's report says Joey's arm got broken during the fight. It also says that he was resisting arrest. Joey denies it."

"Are there criminal charges?"

"Joey was charged with assault and with resisting arrest. But the charges were thrown out when Mallory didn't show up in court either the first time the case was called or the second."

"But," Anna asks, "if the charges were thrown out, why does Joey need a lawyer?"

"Joey wants to sue the police department for using excessive force. That is a reasonable thing to do, if the officer really broke his arm. I have to find out more about what happened.

"Starting tomorrow, I'm supposed to read all the recent police brutality decisions in the state and write a memo on the legal standards for police liability. Then I'll go with Mason, our investigator, to talk to the bartender. We will try to find some of the other men who were involved in the fight. They all got arrested, so we should be able to locate them from the police records."

Anna leans back in her chair. "Sounds interesting."

"Yeah. Pretty good for day one, don't you think?"

The wine arrives. As the waiter pours, you start to wonder: Have I told Anna too much? Have I just violated my duty to protect client confidences on my first day as a lawyer?

Notes and Questions

1. **Why talk?** If you were having dinner with Anna, why might you want to talk to her about your new case?

2. **Rule 1.6(a).** Do you think that any of the disclosures you made to Anna violated Rule 1.6(a)? (Also look at Comment 4.) In the conversation with Anna, you did not reveal Joey's last name. Does this solve the possible problem about revealing confidential information? If not, which statements about your case might you have omitted to better protect your client's identity?

3. **Did Anna disclose too much?** Social workers, like lawyers, are supposed to follow an ethics code. The Code of Ethics of the National Association of Social Workers provides, in relevant part, that

> [s]ocial workers should protect the confidentiality of all information obtained in the course of professional service, except for compelling professional reasons. The general expectation that social workers will keep information confidential does not apply when disclosure is necessary to prevent serious, foreseeable, and imminent harm to a client or other identifiable person. In all instances, social workers should disclose the least amount of

confidential information necessary to achieve the desired purpose; only information that is directly relevant to the purpose for which the disclosure is made should be revealed.[7]

4. **Swearing Anna to secrecy.** You have known Anna for a long time and you know that she is very discreet. Could you solve the confidentiality problem by obtaining her agreement to keep confidential the information you tell her about your case?

5. **The walls have ears.** What about the fact that you are in a public place? Suppose you conclude that you can talk to Anna without stepping over the line. What about the people at the next table? Is your subjective assessment of the noise screen provided by the other diners' conversations an adequate basis for discussing sensitive information in a public place?

6. **Blowing off steam.** Suppose that your firm eventually assigns you to meet with Joey and you become the firm's primary contact with him. Suppose you find Joey to be demanding, somewhat mentally unstable, and even slightly paranoid. In a subsequent conversation with Anna, you say: "Joey is such a pain. He called me three times today, each time with another piece of neurotic minutia. I wouldn't be surprised if he wound up in a mental hospital. But if he keeps pestering me, I'm going to wind up in a mental hospital too." Apart from compliance with the duty to protect confidences, is it problematic to talk this way about a client? If so, why?

---

2. Protection of information if there is a reasonable prospect of harm to a client's interests

The *Restatement (Third) of the Law Governing Lawyers* describes the category of protected information as "confidential client information," which is defined to include "information relating to the representation of a client, other than information that is generally known."[8] This definition is similar to that in Rule 1.6, but while 1.6 prohibits the revelation of any such

---

7. National Assn. of Social Workers, Code of Ethics (2008) (available at http://www.naswdc.org/pubs/code/code.asp). Members of the Academy of Licensed Social Workers must hold a membership in NASW and must agree as a condition of their ACSW membership to comply with the NASW Code of Ethics and to satisfy other requirements. The regulatory system to sanction violators of the ethics code is less developed than in the legal profession. See National Assn. of Social Workers, Academy of Certified Social Workers, New Applicants Only, http://www.naswdc.org/credentials/credentials/acsw.asp (accessed Nov. 1, 2012).

8. Restatement § 59.

information except as permitted by the rules, the Restatement prohibits revelation of confidential information only if "there is a reasonable prospect that doing so will adversely affect a material interest of the client or if the client has instructed the lawyer not to use or disclose such information."[9] Under this standard, you could discuss Joey's case with Anna if you didn't reveal any information from which his identity could be ascertained.[10] Even if his identity could be ascertained, you could reveal the information if there was no "reasonable prospect" that your discussion with Anna would adversely affect Joey's material interests, unless Joey had told you not to talk about it.

The Restatement defines "adverse effects" to include frustration of the client's objectives in the representation; material misfortune, disadvantage, or other prejudice to the client; financial or physical harm to the client; or personal embarrassment to the client.[11] So the Restatement version of the rule articulates a lower standard of secrecy than do the ethical rules. While Rule 1.6 appears to favor a bright line test barring almost all disclosure, the Restatement distinguishes between disclosures that could harm a client and those that are very unlikely to cause harm.

How do you know whether there is a "reasonable prospect" of harm to a client's interests?

The Restatement says that a reasonable prospect of harm to a client depends on "whether a lawyer of reasonable caution, considering only the client's objectives, would regard use or disclosure in the circumstances as creating an unreasonable risk of adverse effect either to those objectives or to other interests of the client."[12] This is a little circular, but the point is that a lawyer must make a judgment about whether a careful lawyer in his position would foresee a problem with the disclosure.

3. The bottom line on informal communications

Unfortunately, there isn't a simple bottom line to explain when a lawyer may or may not have an informal discussion about a client matter. Rule 1.6 does not seem to take into account the reality that most lawyers, like most

---

9. Restatement § 60(1)(a).

10. A comment to § 60 defines "disclosure" as revealing information "in a form that identifies the client or the client matter either expressly or through reasonably ascertainable inference." It adds that "revealing information in a way that cannot be linked to the client involved is not a disclosure." Restatement § 60, comment c(i).

11. Id.

12. Id.

"I never discuss my clients with their mothers."

other people, talk to friends and family about their work. Some lawyers are more discreet than others, of course. The rule does not mention a "reasonable prospect of harm" test, though Comment 4 acknowledges that at least in some circumstances, a lawyer may talk hypothetically about a case so long as the identity of the client is protected.

A lawyer who wants to "play it safe" might decide never to discuss a client's case with anyone who is not at the lawyer's firm or otherwise involved in the matter (such as an opposing counsel). This might have adverse personal or social consequences, but the lawyer would comply with the literal language of the rule.

A careful lawyer probably doesn't need to draw the line quite that sharply. The (relatively) permissive standard of the Restatement bars revelation of client information whenever there is a "reasonable prospect" of harm to the client. This, although it is simply a description of the law rather than an actual legal standard, is probably closer to the norm of the profession than the language of Rule 1.6. However, it is difficult to apply the "reasonable prospect" standard in any particular case.

Two ethics gurus, Professors Hazard and Hodes, offer the following advice about protecting client confidences.

> In functional terms, the line between permissible and impermissible disclosure should probably be drawn at the point of anonymity: a lawyer may talk shop if she is virtually certain that the listeners could not ascertain the identity of the client or the situation involved. . . . To honor the rule of confidentiality, however, and to maintain its strength, lawyers

should exercise self-restraint and resolve marginal cases in favor of non-disclosure.[13]

We add only that talking about cases with friends or family members involves some degree of risk. All lawyers must learn habits of discretion, avoid being casual about such conversations, consider the risks, and avoid or minimize them.

4. Additional cautions about protecting client confidences

The duty to protect information relating to representation of clients is not limited to keeping their secrets. Lawyers also must take care to protect such information from inadvertent or unauthorized disclosure (for example, by leaving information on a laptop screen while using the restroom in a Starbucks). Model Rule 1.6(c) provides:

> A lawyer shall make reasonable efforts to prevent the inadvertent or unauthorized disclosure of, or unauthorized access to, information relating to the representation of a client.

Comment 16 to Model Rule 1.6 states that allowing unauthorized access or disclosure is not a violation of the rule if the lawyer made reasonable efforts to prevent it. The comment does not describe the steps that a lawyer must take but lists factors to consider:

- The sensitivity of the information
- The likelihood of disclosure in the absence of additional safeguards
- The cost of additional safeguards
- The difficulty of implementing such safeguards
- The extent to which the safeguards adversely affect the lawyer's ability to represent clients (e.g., by making a device or important piece of software excessively difficult to use)

May a lawyer communicate with clients by e-mail without breaching the confidentiality rule?

E-mail communication is fairly private, but sometimes third parties can access e-mail. Is this type of communication sufficiently confidential? An ABA opinion concluded that methods of communication that offer a reasonable expectation of privacy are permissible and that unencrypted

---

13. Geoffrey C. Hazard Jr. & W. William Hodes, The Law of Lawyering § 9.15 (3d ed., Aspen Publishers 2004-2 Supp.).

e-mail ordinarily affords sufficient privacy.[14] However, in recent years, many employers have been reading employees' e-mails that are sent over company servers to discourage employees from doing personal tasks at work. As a result, the ABA recommended in a subsequent opinion that "as soon as practical after a client-lawyer relationship is established, a lawyer typically should instruct the employee-client to avoid using a workplace device or system for sensitive or substantive communications, and perhaps for any attorney-client communications."[15]

B. Exceptions to the duty to protect confidences

The duty to protect "information relating to the representation of a client" is very broad, but it is not absolute. The ethical rules identify several situations in which — depending on the rules of a particular jurisdiction — a lawyer *may* or, under certain circumstances, *must* reveal confidential information.

Rule 1.6   Confidentiality of Information

Rule language[*]	Authors' explanation of exceptions[**]
(a) A lawyer shall not reveal information relating to the representation of a client unless	
the client gives **informed consent**,	
the disclosure is **impliedly authorized** in order to carry out the representation	
or the disclosure is permitted by paragraph (b).	
(b) A lawyer **may reveal** information relating to the representation of a client to **the extent the lawyer reasonably believes necessary**:	Rule 1.6(b) explains when a lawyer is permitted to disclose confidential information even if the disclosure is contrary to the client's interest. Before making a disclosure authorized by 1.6(b), a lawyer should try to persuade a client to take action that will "obviate the need for disclosure." If a lawyer reveals information based on 1.6(b), the

---

14. ABA Standing Comm. on Ethics & Prof. Resp., Formal Op. 99-413 (edited version available at http://www.tomwbell.com/NetLaw/Ch12/EmailEthics.html).

15. ABA Standing Comm. on Ethics & Prof. Resp., Formal Op. 11-459 (available at http://www.americanbar.org/content/dam/aba/administrative/professional_responsibility/11_459_nm_formal_opinion.authcheckdam.pdf).

Rule language[*]	Authors' explanation of exceptions[**]
	disclosure should be as narrow in content as possible and should be made to as few other people as possible.[16]
(1) **to prevent reasonably certain death or substantial bodily harm;**	"Such harm is reasonably certain to occur if it will be suffered imminently or if there is a present and substantial threat that a person will suffer such harm at a later date if the lawyer fails to take action necessary to eliminate the threat."[17]
(2) **to prevent** the client from committing **a crime or fraud** that is **reasonably certain to result in substantial injury to the financial interests or property of another** and in furtherance of which the **client has used or is using the lawyer's services;**	"The client can . . . prevent such disclosure by refraining from the wrongful conduct." Also, the rule does not require revelation, but other rules bar the lawyer from counseling or assisting the conduct in question, and may require the lawyer to withdraw from representation.[18]
(3) to **prevent, mitigate, or rectify substantial injury to the financial interests or property** of another that is reasonably certain to result or has resulted from the **client's commission of a crime or fraud in furtherance of which the client has used the lawyer's services;**[19]	This paragraph "addresses the situation in which the lawyer does not learn of the client's crime or fraud until after" the act occurred, and in which the loss can be prevented, rectified, or mitigated. This paragraph does not apply when a person who has committed a crime or fraud "thereafter employs a lawyer for representation concerning that offense."[20]
(4) to **secure legal advice** about the lawyer's compliance with these rules;	This provision allows a lawyer to reveal otherwise confidential information to secure legal advice relating to compliance with the rules.
(5) to establish a claim or defense on behalf of the lawyer in a controversy between the lawyer and the client, to establish a defense to a criminal charge or civil claim against the lawyer based on conduct in which the client was involved, or to respond to allegations in	A lawyer may reveal confidences to the extent needed to collect a fee. Also, a client or a third party may allege that a lawyer has committed some wrongful act. In that event, a lawyer may reveal confidences to the extent necessary to respond to such an allegation. The lawyer

16. Rule 1.6, Comment 14.

17. Id. at Comment 6.

18. Id. at Comment 7.

19. The ABA version of this section omits the comma after the word "mitigate," but this is only a stylistic difference.

20. Rule 1.6, Comment 8. Delaware adds to its version of the comment an explicit statement that disclosure is permitted if the lawyer's services are used to commit a further crime or fraud such as obstruction of justice.

Rule language[*]	Authors' explanation of exceptions[**]
any proceeding concerning the lawyer's representation of the client; or	need not wait for a complaint to be filed before the right to defend applies.[21]
(6) to comply with other law or a court order.	A court order or other law may require a lawyer to reveal a confidence. If so, that other law trumps the ethics rules, and the lawyer may reveal the information.[22]
(7) to detect and resolve conflicts of interest arising from the lawyer's change of employment or from changes in the composition or ownership of a firm, but only if the revealed information would not compromise the attorney-client privilege or otherwise prejudice the client. . . .	This exception allows lawyers to reveal information to other lawyers, under certain circumstances, to avoid conflicts of interest.

[*]All emphasis added.

[**]This and other authors' explanations draw from the comments to the rules and from other sources. They are not comprehensive but highlight some important interpretive points.

If a client consents to a lawyer's revelation of confidences, does the client waive the protection of this rule?

Yes, but only to the extent that the lawyer has given the client full information about the potential risks. A client's willing consent to reveal otherwise confidential information always releases a lawyer to reveal it. Clients often consent to reveal information they have told lawyers. For example, a plaintiff might confidentially inform his lawyer about his claim and later authorize the lawyer to present that claim in court. Likewise, the client may authorize the lawyer to inform the press about his claim.

A special situation arises when a lawyer is representing two co-clients. The clients may agree that they will have no secrets from each other, so the lawyer may tell each of them everything the lawyer learns from the other. Or they may reach the opposite agreement: that each may tell the lawyer confidences that the lawyer will not share with the other. Under the latter arrangement, the lawyer may have to withdraw if he learns something from one that could have adverse consequences for the other. What if they make neither agreement? May the lawyer tell each client what the other said? The authorities seem divided, but, as we explain in Chapter 6, the Model Rules encourage lawyers who represent two parties in the same matter to seek an agreement from both of them that there will be no confidentiality as between them.[23]

---

21. Rule 1.6, Comments 10 and 11.

22. See id. at Comments 12 and 13.

23. See Rule 1.7, Comment 31; Thomas E. Spahn, Keeping Secrets or Telling Tales in Joint Representations, Part I, 79 U.S.L.W. 2571 (May 24, 2011).

The next part of the chapter explores these exceptions to the duty to protect confidences. First, we take up the question of crime by a client. What if a client confesses to a lawyer that she has committed a murder? Is the lawyer supposed to keep that a secret? What if the client confesses that she is about to commit a murder, and the lawyer might be able to prevent it? Does it make a difference whether the intended crime is a violent crime or a financial crime? These situations present a conflict between the lawyer's duty to protect his client and the lawyer's duty as a citizen or an officer of the court.

1. Revelation of past criminal conduct

A client who has committed a crime needs legal advice. To get good advice, the client may need to tell the lawyer all about the crime. This means the client needs to be able to talk to the lawyer in confidence. If the crime is over, the lawyer cannot prevent the harm by revealing it. Society, on the other hand, benefits by the fair administration of justice and by clients having unobstructed access to counsel.[24] This analysis has led to a broad consensus in the legal profession that lawyers should protect as confidential most information about past criminal activity by clients.

The missing persons case: The defense of Robert Garrow

In the 1970s in the Adirondack mountains of upstate New York, Frank Armani and Francis Belge, two local lawyers, were assigned by a judge to represent Robert Garrow, who was accused of murdering a teenager. In the course of representing this client, the lawyers became embroiled in an agonizing test of their commitment to protect client confidences. In this section, we put you in the shoes of those lawyers so that you may explore the difficult choices they faced. The following account is entirely based on the facts of the real case, except that you are written into the story as Armani's co-counsel and the story is told in the present tense.[25]

Francis R. Belge

---

24. See Rule 1.6, Comment 2.

25. The facts about the actual case, other than those in reported opinions, are drawn primarily from Tom Alibrandi with Frank Armani, Privileged Information (Dodd Mead 1984), and from the authors' correspondence and interviews with Mr. Armani.

PROBLEM 3-2 THE MISSING PERSONS, SCENE 1

Several teenagers have disappeared recently in your county. An 18-year-old boy named Philip Domblewski was murdered during a camping trip with three friends. The young people were ambushed in the woods by a psychopath with a rifle who tied them to trees and then killed Domblewski. One of the other boys escaped and summoned the police, who found Domblewski's body and rescued the other kids. After a massive eleven-day manhunt in the mountains, the police arrested a man named Robert Gar-

Robert Garrow

row. He was hiding at his sister's house in Vermont. When the police arrived, Garrow tried to run and was shot in the foot, arm, and back by police trying to stop him.

The police charged Garrow with the murder of Domblewski. They suspected that Garrow had committed a string of other unsolved murders in the area. One of them involved a young couple, Daniel Porter and Susan Petz, who had been camping 50 miles from the site where Philip Domblewski was murdered. Nine days before Domblewski was murdered, the police had found the body of Dan Porter, who had been stabbed to death. Susan Petz, a student at Boston College, has been missing since then, for about three weeks now. Another of the missing teenagers was Alicia Hauck, a teenager from Syracuse who disappeared on her way home from school a few weeks before the Domblewski murder.

A Syracuse lawyer named Frank Armani had represented Garrow on several occasions before the Domblewski murder. Twelve years earlier, Armani had represented Garrow in a criminal case in which Garrow was charged with having sexually assaulted a teenage girl and attacked her boyfriend. Garrow was convicted and spent eight years in prison but was then paroled. After his release from prison, he resumed life with his wife and children and worked as a master mechanic at a bakery.

About a year before the Domblewski murder, Garrow had come to Armani for advice about an auto accident. A few months later, Garrow faced criminal charges again. He was alleged to have kidnapped two students at Syracuse University, Karen Lutz and Leonard Garner, and held them hostage at gunpoint. These charges were dismissed. Two months later, Garrow was arrested and charged with having abducted and sexually assaulted two girls aged 10 and 11. Garrow was arraigned and released on bail, but then he disappeared. Armani knew nothing of Garrow's whereabouts until his arrest for the Domblewski murder.

Armani had never before represented a defendant in a murder case, so when the judge asked him to represent Garrow in the Domblewski matter, he was hesitant. He wasn't sure he knew enough to handle the case. Also, the allegations were uncomfortably close to home. One of the disappeared teenagers, Alicia Hauck, went to the same school as Frank Armani's daughter Dorina; Alicia's sister was Dorina's classmate. There were lots of reasons for Armani to stay out of this matter.

The "current" situation (assuming that you are to become co-counsel with Armani) The judge insisted that Armani accept the appointment, saying "I've been advised that he won't talk with any lawyer but you." The judge noted that because Garrow trusts Armani, he is the best person for the job. Garrow has no money to pay a lawyer, so the judge ordered Armani to serve as a court-appointed lawyer. His legal fees are to be paid by the state. Armani was reluctant to handle this matter alone, so he asked you to be his co-counsel. You and Armani are old friends, and you have more trial experience than he does. You agree to assist.

Initially, Garrow denied that he murdered Domblewski and said he couldn't remember what happened. He remembered having had a terrible headache at around the time Domblewski was murdered.

As you and Armani investigate the case, you discover that Garrow was severely abused by his parents as a child. At age 7, he was sent to work on a neighbor's farm, where he stayed for eight years. During that period, he began having sex with animals and drinking animal blood. At 15, after a fight with his father, Garrow was sent to live at a state industrial school. Two years later he joined the Air Force, but he wound up in a military prison and eventually got a medical discharge. Soon after that, he got married, but he continued to have legal problems. All this background convinces you that Garrow's best defense is likely to be to plead not guilty by reason of insanity. If the insanity defense is successful, Garrow would go to a mental hospital instead of to prison.

Armani goes to the prison hospital where Garrow is recuperating from gunshot wounds in his foot. Armani advises Garrow that the prosecutor has solid evidence that Garrow killed Domblewski. If the case goes to trial, Garrow is likely to be convicted. He urges Garrow to plead not guilty by reason of insanity. Garrow concurs, fearing that he would never survive in prison.

Armani tells Garrow that the best strategy would be to persuade the prosecutor to accept a plea of guilty by reason of insanity in exchange for Garrow providing information about the whereabouts of the other missing teenagers. Garrow responds that he doesn't know anything about the other murders. Armani had been trained in hypnosis some years earlier. He is convinced that Garrow is repressing memories about the other murders, so he persuades Garrow to allow Armani to hypnotize him. Once he is hypnotized, Armani instructs Garrow that after he wakes up, he will remember and be able to answer questions about some events that took place earlier that year.

Armani doesn't tell you that he has hypnotized Garrow, but he asks you to go see the client alone that afternoon. During your conversation, Garrow begins to share information about the un-solved cases.

Garrow says he picked up Alicia Hauck, who was hitchhiking, took her to a secluded place, and raped her. Then, he says, "I made her walk with me into Oakwood Cemetery. . . . All of a sudden . . . she tried to run away. When I tried to talk her into staying with me for a little while more, she got hysterical. I got scared and hit her with my knife."

"You mean you stabbed her?"

"Yeah, I hit her with my knife."

"Did you kill her?"

"I think so."

"You *think* so?"

"Yeah, she was dead."

"What did you do with her body?"

"I stashed it in a deserted corner of the cemetery. In the under-brush behind the maintenance shack."

Then you move on to ask about Susan Petz. Garrow tells a story about stopping for a nap during a road trip and being awakened by a young man yelling at him to move his car. He had one of his bad headaches. He got out of the car and got into a fight with the guy who had yelled at him. "When we fell into the ditch alongside the road," Garrow recalls, "he got stabbed."

You assume that this was Dan Porter and tell Garrow that the body was found tied to a tree. He doesn't remember this, but he does know that the guy "was dead."

"So what did you do with the girl?" you ask.

"I took her with me."

He was on his way to visit his father, who had just had a heart attack. When he got to his parents' house, he pitched a tent nearby in a heavily wooded area. He said, "I kept the girl up there in the tent with me."

He admits that he raped her, but also mentions that they had some "great conversations. She told me about the college she went to. Stuff like that."

Garrow says he did not stay with Petz all the time, but slept at his sister's house. You ask how he kept her there.

"I tied her up at night with hose clamps and ropes. I left her food and water."

On the fourth day, Garrow reports that he took Susan Petz down the hill for a swim.

"I put my knife on the ground, and she grabbed it. We had a fight. She cut my hand. I finally got my knife away from her, and she got stabbed."

"You mean you killed her?"

"She was dead."

"What did you do with her body?"

"I shoved it down the airshaft of the mine." He says he covered it with old tires and timbers from the mine.[26]

You are dumbfounded by these confessions, but you pull yourself together and ask Garrow for exact information about the location of the bodies of Hauck and Petz. After you get this information, you tell him you will be back to visit in a few days.

Garrow has not yet given you permission to share any of this information with the prosecutor. You reassure him that, for the moment, your lips are sealed.

You are not certain whether Garrow is telling you the truth. It is possible that he is making up these stories to seem more insane, to tantalize the prosecutor, or just to waste your time. For all you actually know, Petz and Hauck might still be alive somewhere.

Questions

1. **What to do?** What would you do at this point? To help you think about this question, here is a menu of choices, but you may also suggest choices that are not listed here.

   Option one: Alert the police, the prosecutor, or the press of the location of the bodies.

   ■ If you are going to alert someone, whom will you alert?
   ■ Would you reveal that you are Garrow's lawyer, or would you send an anonymous tip?

---

26. Alibrandi with Armani, supra n. 25, at 107-113. The quoted language is excerpted from the dialogue reported in the book.

- If you lean toward alerting someone, would you try to get Garrow to consent to the revelation of this information, or would you make the disclosure without consulting him?
- If you ask for his permission to reveal the information and he says no, then what would you do?

Option two: Do a site investigation. Check on your client's tale by visiting the supposed sites of the bodies to see whether they are really there.

- If you find the bodies where Garrow says he put them, how would that help you to decide what to do?

Option three: Do nothing about the missing girls. Just defend your client against the charge he is facing.

2. **Rule 1.6(b)(1).** Assume that this scenario is taking place in the present and is governed by the contemporary rules of professional conduct. Does Rule 1.6(b)(1) provide an argument that you could ethically reveal the location of the bodies?

3. **Rule 1.6(b)(6).** A state health law requires reporting the discovery of bodies (so that they can be given a proper burial). Does Rule 1.6(b)(6) permit disclosure of the location of the bodies because such disclosure is necessary "to comply with other law or a court order"?

PROBLEM 3-3 THE MISSING PERSONS, SCENE 2

In the real case, Belge and Armani chose to check out their client's story.

Suppose, like Belge and Armani, you conduct your own investigation. Garrow gives you instructions about where to find the hidden remains of the two girls. With great difficulty, because they are in fact well hidden, you find and photograph the remains without disturbing them.

A couple of weeks later, you are sitting in your office, and your secretary calls to say "Mr. Petz is here to see you." You sit down to meet with Susan Petz's father. He says, "I've traveled from Chicago to inquire about my daughter. I'd like to know if you have any information." He asks if Garrow has "told you what he's done with my daughter."

You equivocate, explaining that your client is only a suspect, that charges have not even been filed.

"Can you tell me anything?" Petz pleads. "My wife and I have exhausted every other possible source of information." He dabs his eyes with his handkerchief. "Should we keep hoping and praying?"[27] he asks.

What should you do now? Again, you consider options:

Option one: Tell Petz's parents (or the authorities, who will tell them) that she is dead.

Option two: Refuse to give Petz's father any information and go to trial, pleading insanity. (If you choose this option or the previous one, Garrow is likely to be convicted of the Domblewski murder and go to prison for life (rather than to a mental institution), because the chance of prevailing with an insanity defense is not great unless the prosecutor agrees to accept the plea. If you choose the second option, the bodies of Petz and Hauck might never be found because the police have been searching fruitlessly for those bodies for a long time.)

Option three: Decline to share information with Mr. Petz, but instead offer to give the prosecutor information that will help solve the two missing persons cases in exchange for a plea-bargained acceptance of Garrow's insanity defense.

Perhaps you can think of other options. Before you read on, pause here to think about what you would actually do.

The real case

In the actual case, Belge and Armani initially decided not to reveal anything to the parents or to the authorities. They feared that if they led the authorities to the bodies, they would betray their client because the prosecutors would know that Garrow was guilty of additional murders. Also, evidence on the bodies might tie Garrow to the crimes. The prosecutors would almost certainly seek additional indictments, and the lawyers would lose all possible leverage for a plea bargain.

As the trial was approaching and Garrow's prospects seemed poor, the lawyers changed course and tried to bargain with the prosecutor, suggesting that they had information about some other unsolved homicides, which they would reveal if the prosecutor accepted the insanity defense (meaning that Garrow would be confined in a mental institution).

The prosecutor rejected the lawyers' offer and got really angry. "I have to say that we are outraged that you would even consider trading information on the bodies of Alicia Hauck and Susan Petz to extract a deal for a cold-blooded killer." Armani and Belge insisted that they had not ac-

---

27. Alibrandi with Armani, supra n. 25, at 146-148.

knowledged possession of any such information. The prosecutor, furious, said, "If you know the locations of those bodies and haven't informed the police, I'll seek criminal charges against you for withholding evidence and obstructing justice."

During the following month, Armani's law office was broken into three times. Nothing was stolen. The file cabinet was searched. The intruders found nothing, however, because Armani had hidden the photographs of the girls' bodies and the tape recordings of the interviews with Garrow in the basement of his father's house.

Garrow went to trial, and his lawyers tried to establish his insanity. During the trial, as part of his insanity defense, the lawyers put Garrow on the stand. He confessed under oath to the murders of Philip Domblewski, Alicia Hauck, Susan Petz, and Daniel Porter, and to sexual assault of seven girls including the ones he killed. The jury did not buy the insanity defense. Garrow was convicted of the murder of Domblewski and sentenced to prison.

After Garrow confessed on the witness stand to the multiple murders, the prosecutor realized that the lawyers had known for months that Petz and Hauck were dead and where their bodies were located. The lawyers admitted as much in a public statement; they felt compelled to respond to public indignation about their long silence and to explain why they had not revealed the information earlier in the case. The community was furious with them. Armani's law practice withered. He received death threats and a stream of hate letters. He carried a gun for self-defense. His wife received obscene phone calls. She found a Molotov cocktail (an incendiary bomb) in the bushes next to her house. She and the Armani children moved to her parents' house.

The *Belge* case

Some people urged the prosecutor to indict Belge and Armani for obstruction of justice. The prosecutor did not do that but did charge Belge with violation of a New York State public health statute that required anyone who knew that a person had died without receiving medical attention to report that fact to the authorities. What follows is an excerpt of the county court opinion in that case.

People v. Belge

372 N.Y.S.2d 798 (County Ct., Onondaga Co. 1975)

ORMAND N. GALE, J. . . .

[Belge's claim]

Defense counsel moves for a dismissal of the Indictment on the grounds that a confidential, privileged communication existed between him and Mr.

Garrow, which should excuse the attorney from making full disclosure to the authorities. The National Association of Criminal Defense Lawyers, as Amicus Curiae succinctly state the issue in the following language: If this indictment stands, "the attorney-client privilege will be effectively destroyed." No defendant will be able to freely discuss the facts of his case with his attorney. No attorney will be able to listen to those facts without being faced with the Hobson's choice of violating the law or violating his professional code of Ethics.[28]

[The importance of confidentiality]

The effectiveness of counsel is only as great as the confidentiality of its client-attorney relationship. If the lawyer cannot get all the facts about the case, he can only give his client half of a defense. This, of necessity, involves the client telling his attorney everything remotely connected with the crime.

Apparently, in the instant case, after analyzing all the evidence, and after hearing of the bizarre episodes in the life of their client, they decided that the only possibility of salvation was in a defense of insanity. For the client to disclose not only everything about this particular crime but also everything about other crimes which might have a bearing upon his defense, requires the strictest confidence in, and on the part of, the attorney. . . .

[The Fifth Amendment privilege against self-incrimination]

A hue and cry went up from the press and other news media suggesting that the attorneys should be found guilty of such crimes as obstruction of justice or becoming an accomplice after the fact. From a layman's standpoint, this certainly was a logical conclusion. However, the constitution of the United States of America attempts to preserve the dignity of the individual and to do that guarantees him the services of an attorney who will bring to the bar and to the bench every conceivable protection from the inroads of the state against such rights as are vested in the constitution for one accused of crime. Among those substantial constitutional rights is that a defendant does not have to incriminate himself. His attorneys were bound to uphold

---

28. [Authors' footnote.] The National Association of Criminal Defense Lawyers apparently argued that Garrow's revelations were both "confidential" (the subject of this chapter) and "privileged" (a concept discussed later in this chapter). The attorney-client privilege protects lawyers and clients from being compelled to reveal private lawyer-client communications in which legal advice was sought or given. Lawyers usually don't invoke the privilege unless the government or a party to litigation asks for information about a lawyer-client communication. Here, no one had asked Belge for information about the missing persons, but a public health statute required revelation of the location of bodies without any official request. Belge claimed that he had no duty to report information protected by privilege. So the questions in this case were whether Belge was excused from reporting the location of the bodies by either the ethical duty of confidentiality or the attorney-client privilege.

that concept and maintain what has been called a sacred trust of confidentiality.

The following language from the brief of the Amicus Curiae further points up the statements just made:

> The client's Fifth Amendment rights cannot be violated by his attorney. . . . Because the discovery of the body of Alicia Hauck would have presented a significant link in a chain of evidence tending to establish his guilt, Garrow was constitutionally exempt from any statutory requirement to disclose the location of the body. And Attorney Belge, as Garrow's attorney, was not only equally exempt, but under a positive stricture precluding such disclosure. . . . The criminal defendant's self-incrimination rights become completely nugatory if compulsory disclosure can be exacted through his attorney. . . .

[Balancing Belge's duty to Garrow and his duty under the health law]

If the Grand Jury had returned an indictment charging Mr. Belge with obstruction of justice under a proper statute, the work of this Court would have been much more difficult than it is. . . . [But here] we have the Fifth Amendment right, derived from the constitution, on the one hand, as against the trivia of a pseudo-criminal statute on the other, which has seldom been brought into play. Clearly the latter is completely out of focus when placed alongside the client-attorney privilege. An examination of the Grand Jury testimony sheds little light on their reasoning. The testimony of Mr. Armani added nothing new to the facts as already presented to the Grand Jury. He and Mr. Belge were co-counsel. Both were answerable to the Canons of professional ethics. The Grand Jury chose to indict one and not the other. It appears as if that body were grasping at straws. . . . Both on the grounds of a privileged communication and in the interests of justice the Indictment is dismissed.

After the trial court dismissed the indictment, the prosecutor appealed to the intermediate appellate court.

People v. Belge

376 N.Y.S.2d 771 (App. Div. 1975)

MEMORANDUM:

We affirm the Order of the Trial Court which properly dismissed the indictments laid against defendant for alleged violations of section 4200 (duty of a decent burial) and section 4143 (requirement to report death occurring without medical attendance) of the Public Health Law. We believe that the attorney-client privilege . . . effectively shielded the defendant-attorney from his actions which would otherwise have violated the Public Health Law. . . .

We note that the privilege is not all-encompassing and that in a given case there may be conflicting considerations. We believe that an attorney must protect his client's interests, but also must observe basic human standards of decency, having due regard to the need that the legal system accord justice to the interests of society and its individual members.

We write to emphasize our serious concern regarding the consequences which emanate from a claim of an absolute attorney-client privilege. Because the only question presented, briefed and argued on this appeal was a legal one with respect to the sufficiency of the indictments, we limit our determination to that issue and do not reach the ethical questions underlying this case.

Questions about *People v. Belge*

1. **Should Belge have been indicted?** Was it a proper exercise of prosecutorial discretion for the prosecutor to ask a grand jury to indict Belge for violation of the health law? Even if Belge committed a technical violation of law, did Belge do something wrong for which he deserved to be punished criminally?

2. **Obstruction of justice?** The courts dismissed the indictment. But suppose the statute had been more clearly applicable to these facts. For example, suppose that New York's obstruction of justice law declared that corpses are essential evidence in homicide investigations and made it a crime for any person with knowledge of the location of a dead body not to report that location to the police within four hours. Should the courts hold that such a statute overrides any obligations of confidentiality that a lawyer might otherwise have under Rule 1.6?

PROBLEM 3-4   THE MISSING PERSONS, SCENE 3

This problem, like those in scenes 1 and 2, is based on the events of the real case.

Co-counsel Frank Armani's daughters Debbie and Dorina went to watch one day of Garrow's trial. In the courtroom, "Garrow dropped his hand from his face and turned toward [Dorina]. Their eyes locked for a moment, Garrow's hard penetrating stare frightening Dorina. His lips turned upward in a smile. 'Nice to see you again, Dorina.' The young woman's face froze in horror. She had to force herself to look away from Garrow's hypnotic stare. When she did, Dorina found herself looking into her sister's eyes. 'I didn't realize you knew Garrow,' Debbie said softly. 'I don't know him,' Dorina answered. Debbie's eyes widened. There was only one way Garrow could have known who Dorina was. He had to have been stalking her."[29]

Frank Armani

After Garrow's conviction, he was sentenced to prison for twenty-five years to life. He was sent to a maximum security prison. While in prison, he sued the state of New York for $10 million. As we explained above, in the course of capturing Garrow, the police had shot him. In the lawsuit, Garrow alleged that the state's doctors had been negligent in the treatment of his gunshot wounds and had caused him to become partially paralyzed. In exchange for his dropping the suit, the State transferred him to a medium security prison. State officials believed that he was unable to rise from a wheelchair because of his gunshot wounds. It turns out, however, that Garrow had been faking his paralysis.

Imagine, again, that you are Garrow's lawyer. It is now a year after Garrow has been convicted. The police come to see you. They tell you (as in real life they told Belge and Armani) that Garrow had scaled a 14-foot fence topped with barbed wire and made his escape. When they searched Garrow's cell, corrections officials had found a hit list. Armani's name was on the list — and so was yours. The police ask you whether you have any idea where he might be hiding. Your first thought is to wonder whether, now that he's on the loose, Garrow will try to kill you or a member of your family.

You recall that Garrow once told you, in confidence, about where he used to hide when the police were searching for him. Will you tell the police where he might be?

Notes and Questions

1. **Duration of the duty to protect confidences.** Assume that after his conviction, Garrow ceases to be your client. Does the termination of the representation free you up to share information with the police?

---

29. Alibrandi with Armani, supra n. 25, at 230.

2. **May you tell?** Under Rule 1.6, are you permitted to tell the police where Garrow sometimes hides?

3. **Will you?** In any event, what will you do?

---

2. The risk of future injury or death

In the case that Armani and Belge handled, the lawyers became aware of deaths that had already occurred. Sometimes, lawyers learn about serious risks of future physical harm to others.

Under Rule 1.6, if the information relates to the representation of a client, the lawyer has a duty to protect the confidence, unless an exception applies. This is true whether the lawyer learns the information from a client or from another source.[30]

However, the rule allows a lawyer to reveal confidential information "to prevent reasonably certain death or substantial bodily harm." Under this standard, it doesn't matter whether the possible harm will be perpetrated by the client or by another person. What matters is what the lawyer believes to be the degree of possible harm and how likely the lawyer believes it is that the harm will occur. A comment explains that the purpose of the rule is to recognize "the overriding value of life and physical integrity." It explains that death or substantial bodily harm is "reasonably certain to occur if it will be suffered imminently or if there is a present and substantial threat that a person will suffer harm at a later date if the lawyer fails to take action necessary to eliminate the threat."[31]

The language discussed in the preceding paragraph is the product of an amendment of the Model Rules by the American Bar Association (ABA) in 2002; as of January 2011, 26 states have adopted the exception allowing revelation of confidences "to prevent reasonably certain death or substantial bodily harm."[32] American lawyers have debated for decades how broad or narrow this exception should be, so other states include many different variations on this language. Some states have selected language

---

30. Rule 1.6, Comment 3.

31. Id.

32. Alaska, Arizona, Colorado, Delaware, Idaho, Indiana, Iowa, Kentucky, Louisiana, Maine, Maryland, Minnesota, Mississippi, Missouri, Montana, Nebraska, New Hampshire, New Mexico, New York, North Carolina, Ohio, Oklahoma, Oregon, Pennsylvania, South Carolina, and Utah. This and subsequent notes on which state ethics codes contain language similar to that under discussion were developed by electronic searches of the state codes presented at ABA, Center for Professional Responsibility, Links to Other Legal Ethics and Professional Responsibility Pages, http://www.americanbar.org/groups/professional_responsibility/resources/links_of_interest.html#States (accessed Nov. 1, 2012).

that is closer to the formulation of this exception in one of the previous ABA model codes. DR 4-101 of the Model Code of Professional Responsibility, which was first adopted in 1970 and preceded the Model Rules, allowed a lawyer to reveal "the intention of his client to commit a crime and the information necessary to prevent the crime." This language was adapted from the 1908 ABA Canons of Professional Ethics. Four states retain this language, allowing a lawyer broad discretion in the face of *any* future criminal act by a client.[33]

After the ABA jettisoned the Model Code, but before the 2002 amendment of Rule 1.6, the Model Rules provided that a lawyer may reveal confidences "to prevent the client from committing a criminal act that the lawyer believes is likely to result in imminent death or substantial bodily harm." That language allows revelation only when the harmful act is criminal in nature, the crime would be perpetrated by the lawyer's own client, the lawyer believes the crime is likely to kill or seriously harm another person, and the death or harm that would be caused by the crime is "imminent." That rule, which remains in force in at least six jurisdictions,[34] is narrower than either the previous Model Code language or the current Model Rules language. The current Model Rules language permits disclosure under the specified conditions regardless of whether the imminent conduct is that of a client or of another person, and regardless of whether the conduct would be a crime. Suppose a client told you that a friend of hers was about to commit suicide and you practice in a state in which suicide is *not* a crime. The Model Rules language would permit the lawyer to reveal information to prevent this suicide, but the Model Code language would not permit it.

Finally, some state ethics rules impose an *affirmative duty* on lawyers to reveal information about a threat of harm by a client to another person.[35] Illinois Rule 1.6(c), for example, states that "a lawyer *shall reveal* information relating to the representation of a client to the extent the lawyer reasonably believes necessary to prevent reasonably certain death or substantial bodily harm" (emphasis added).

The following chart summarizes the major variations in the model codes discussed above. In studying these variations, think about the potentially dramatic consequences that result from choosing one or another version of a rule. Not every state is listed because some use variations that don't fit neatly

---

33. Colorado, Michigan, Oregon, and Virginia.

34. The following ethics codes include language similar to the 1983 Model Rules' language on revelation of a future crime by a client: Alabama, California, District of Columbia, Hawaii, Rhode Island, and South Dakota.

35. States that specifically require revelation of confidences to prevent a client from committing certain crimes include Arizona, Illinois, Nevada, New Jersey, North Dakota, Tennessee, Texas, Vermont, and Wisconsin.

into these three categories. Colorado and Oregon appear more than once. Their rules contain language drawn from two of the sources.

Origin of language	Language used in each model code	States currently using similar language
Model Code 1970	A lawyer may reveal "the intention of his client to commit a crime and the information necessary to prevent the crime."	Colorado, Michigan, Oregon, Virginia
Model Rules 1983	A lawyer may reveal confidences "to prevent the client from committing a criminal act that the lawyer believes is likely to result in imminent death or substantial bodily harm."	Alabama, California, District of Columbia, Hawaii, Rhode Island, South Dakota
Model Rules 2003	A lawyer may reveal information related to the representation of a client "to the extent the lawyer reasonably believes necessary to prevent reasonably certain death or substantial bodily harm."	Alaska, Arizona, Colorado, Delaware, Idaho, Indiana, Iowa, Kentucky, Louisiana, Maine, Maryland, Minnesota, Mississippi, Missouri, Montana, Nebraska, New Hampshire, New Mexico, New York, North Carolina, Ohio, Oklahoma, Oregon, Pennsylvania, South Carolina, Utah

Because the state rules use such a wide range of language on when a lawyer may or must reveal confidences relating to possible future physical harm, it is essential to study the rule in the state in which you are admitted to practice.

PROBLEM 3-5 RAT POISON

The following problem is based on a true story that was related to one of the authors by a lawyer. He was pleased to share the problem with you. He said that although more than a decade has passed, he still worries about what he should have done.

You are a criminal defense lawyer. Your client, Harry Norton, operated a small extermination business from the back of his truck. Harry mostly treated homes for termites, cockroaches, and rodent infestation. He has been charged with involuntary manslaughter based on the death of a four-year-old boy who died after eating rat poison that Harry had placed in the basement of the boy's home. The powerful rat poison that Harry had used in the home was intended only for industrial use because of the danger to humans who might ingest it. Harry is out on bail while the charge is pending.

You noticed that Harry seemed kind and well intentioned, but not very smart. Since he graduated from high school, you assume that his IQ is normal.

During the first interview, now three months ago, you asked Harry whether he had put rat poison into other homes besides the one in which the child had died. Harry said he had. He wasn't sure how many other homes — perhaps 30 or 40. He said he had a file box with records of the services he had provided to each customer. You urged Harry to go through the box and find all of the other homes where he had put that type of rat poison, and then to revisit those homes and remove it. Harry has not gotten around to doing this. You have offered several times to help Harry go through the files, but Harry insisted that he would do it himself.

You considered approaching the prosecutor to arrange an exchange of the information about the location of the other rat poison for a promise that the prosecutor would not file additional charges against Harry based on that information or any further harm discovered as a result of the revelation. Harry has been unwilling to allow you even to broach the subject with the prosecutor. He keeps saying he will revisit his former customers and get the rat poison out of there.

The prosecutor has not sought a warrant for Harry's records on services provided to other customers. You do not understand why he has not. You are worried that Harry may try to "solve" this problem by destroying his records.

A criminal law in your state provides that "any person who recklessly engages in conduct that creates a substantial risk of death or serious physical injury to another person is guilty of the misdemeanor of reckless endangerment."

What should you do? Would you actually do what you think you should do? Why or why not? Consider not only Rule 1.6, but also Rule 4.1.

3. Client frauds and crimes that cause financial harm

Thus far, we've been concerned with physical harm — either past harm, as in the case of the missing persons, or future harm, as in a case like the one in the rat poison problem. What if the harm to others is only to their property, for instance, in the form of stealing or property destruction?

The ethics rules and other laws permit lawyers, under certain circumstances, to reveal a client's frauds and other financial crimes. These rules evolved from the principle that lawyers should not advise or assist their clients to commit crimes or frauds. Before we explore the exceptions to the confidentiality rule that relate to client frauds, we examine the duty of lawyers not to help their clients to break the law.

a. Lawyers prohibited from advising or assisting clients' crimes and frauds

Rule 1.2(d) provides: "A lawyer shall not counsel a client to engage, or assist a client, in conduct that the lawyer knows is criminal or fraudulent." Comment 10 after Rule 1.2 explains:

> The lawyer is required to avoid assisting the client, for example, by drafting or delivering documents that the lawyer knows are fraudulent or by suggesting how the wrongdoing might be concealed. A lawyer may not continue assisting a client in conduct that the lawyer originally supposed was legally proper but then discovers is criminal or fraudulent. The lawyer must, therefore, withdraw from the representation of the client in the matter. See Rule 1.16(a). In some cases, withdrawal alone might be insufficient. It may be necessary for the lawyer to give notice of the fact of withdrawal and to disaffirm any opinion, document, affirmation or the like.

A lawyer who assists a client fraud or participates in making material misrepresentations could face civil, criminal, or disciplinary liability.[36] The lawyer may be liable if the lawyer participates in the client's wrongful act as a co-principal or an accessory.[37]

Consider an extreme example. Suppose a lawyer tutors a client in federal tax law so that the client can pass herself off (falsely) as an accountant. If the lawyer knows that the client plans to misrepresent her credentials, the lawyer might be criminally charged for abetting the client's fraud.[38]

---

36. Restatement § 66, comment g.

37. See Restatement § 8, comment e, outlining a lawyer's potential criminal liability as an accomplice.

38. For a discussion of lawyers' liability for *assisting* client fraud, see Donald C. Langevoort, Where Were the Lawyers? A Behavioral Inquiry into Lawyers' Responsibility for Clients' Fraud, 46 Vand. L. Rev. 75 (1993).

What is fraud?

To comply with the rules that prohibit lawyers from assisting fraud by a client, and to reduce the risk of liability for assisting fraud, a lawyer must understand what conduct is fraudulent. Fraud refers to *deliberate deception*, but the term is defined somewhat differently in the rules of legal ethics, tort law, criminal law, and contract law.

The ethics codes   Rule 1.0(d) defines fraud as "conduct that is fraudulent under the substantive or procedural law of the applicable jurisdiction and has a purpose to deceive." A comment explains that the drafters did not intend to include in this definition "merely negligent misrepresentation or negligent failure to apprise another of relevant information. For purposes of these rules, it is not necessary that anyone has suffered damages or relied on the misrepresentation or failure to inform."[39] Since the rules do not explain whether one should refer to criminal law, tort law, securities law, consumer law, or contract law, nor whether one should refer to state law or federal law, perhaps a lawyer should make a conservative judgment and assume that an act would be fraudulent under any substantive or procedural legal standard relevant to the act in question in the applicable jurisdiction. In other words, one might refer to securities law for a definition of securities fraud and to consumer law for a definition of consumer fraud. We offer a bit of guidance about some of the legal standards.

Torts   To prove that another person committed a fraud for the purpose of civil liability, one must demonstrate that the other person (1) intentionally (2) made a misrepresentation of a fact, an intention, or a law (3) with the intention of inducing the other person to act or to refrain from acting in reliance on the misrepresentation, and (4) that the plaintiff suffered financial loss (5) as a result of reliance on the misrepresentation.[40]

Criminal law   Certain federal and state statutes make particular types of fraudulent actions criminal. Among these are laws on mail fraud, wire fraud, bank fraud, health care fraud, consumer fraud, securities fraud, and bankruptcy fraud.[41] State law is variable. In California, a person commits fraud when the person "knowingly and designedly, by any false or fraudulent representation or pretense, defrauds any other person of money,

---

39. Rule 1.0, Comment 5.
40. See Restatement (Second) of Torts § 525 (1977).
41. See Courts Refine Elements of Federal Fraud Crimes, 7(3) Bus. Crimes Bull. 3 (2000).

labor, or property."[42] Florida's penal code includes 89 different and very specific fraud laws,[43] one for almost every conceivable context, such as fraud in urine testing.[44] Unlike tort law, criminal law does not require a showing of harm to find an act fraudulent.

Contracts   A contract may be voidable if one party was induced to sign it by a fraudulent (intentional) misrepresentation.[45] A contract may be voided also for a *material* misrepresentation even if it was not *intentional*.[46] While tort law and criminal law require that the misrepresentation was deliberate, contract law recognizes an action for rescission based on a material misrepresentation even if there was no intent to deceive. A "misrepresentation" that would be a basis for rescission of a contract may be a false statement, but it could be a nondisclosure of a fact.[47] A contract could be voidable for "fraud" even though the same "fraud" would not subject the actor to tort liability or to criminal sanctions.

What lawyer conduct constitutes "assisting a fraudulent act"?

In 1987, the ABA Ethics Committee explained the meaning of "assisting client fraud" in an opinion interpreting Rule 3.3, which deals with candor to tribunals. The committee said that if a lawyer had offered false testimony, failure to disclose that fact to the court would constitute "assisting fraud." The committee noted that

> the language "assisting a criminal or fraudulent act by the client" is not limited to the criminal law concepts of aiding and abetting or suborna-tion. Rather, it seems clear that this language is intended to guide the

---

42. Cal. Penal Code § 532 (2007). California also provides that "[w]henever, by any of the provisions of this Code, an intent to defraud is required in order to constitute any offense, it is sufficient if an intent appears to defraud any person, association, or body politic or corporate, whatever." Id. § 8.

43. Fla. Stat. tit. 46, ch. 817 (2007).

44. It is a crime "willfully to defraud or attempt to defraud any lawfully administered urine test designed to detect the presence of chemical substances or controlled substances." Id. § 817.565(1)(a).

45. To be fraudulent, the person making the representation must (1) know or believe that it is false, or (2) must lack confidence that what he says is true, or (3) must know that he does not have a good basis for the stated facts. Restatement (Second) of Contracts § 162(1) (1981). A contract is voidable if a material misrepresentation (a misrepresentation important to the agreement) was made by the party who wants to enforce the agreement, if the party who wants to void the agreement was justified in relying on the misrepresentation. Id. § 164.

46. Id. § 162(2).

47. A nondisclosure could be "equivalent to an assertion that the fact does not exist" if the person who is withholding information "knows that the disclosure of the fact is necessary to prevent some previous assertion from being a misrepresentation or from being fraudulent or material . . . [or] knows that disclosure of the fact would correct a mistake of the other party as to a basic assumption on which that party is making the contract" and if nondisclosure of the fact amounts to a failure to act in good faith and in accordance with reasonable standards of fair dealing. Id. § 161.

conduct of the lawyer as an officer of the court as a prophylactic measure to protect against client perjury contaminating the judicial process.[48]

How can a lawyer know whether he is assisting a client fraud?

A shady client won't tell her lawyer that the client wants help in defrauding someone. Rule 1.2 only prohibits assisting a client in conduct that the lawyer "knows" is fraudulent (which seems to exclude a lawyer's negligent and perhaps even reckless conduct). But a lawyer could be accused of fraud if he prepared a fraudulent document, even if the lawyer did not know that some of the information in the document was false. Disciplinary authorities might infer from the circumstances that a lawyer did know that the legal assistance would be used for fraudulent purposes.[49] Also, law other than the ethics rules might require a lawyer to verify the information that the client provides. If a lawyer does not exercise the prevailing standard of care to discern client fraud, the lawyer might be liable for negligence to those injured by the fraud. In addition, a lawyer could be subject to discipline or criminal charges merely for advising a client to engage in criminal or fraudulent action, or for advising the client how to evade detection or prosecution.

The Restatement offers examples of "assisting fraud." In one case, a lawyer was charged with obstruction of justice because he had advised a client to destroy documents. In a second case, a lawyer was disciplined for advising a client to conceal the identity of the owners of a business when applying for a liquor license. The third example involves a lawyer who was disciplined for advising his client to leave the state to avoid prosecution.[50]

---

48. ABA Standing Comm. on Ethics & Prof. Resp., Formal Op. 87-353. The formal opinion interpreted the recently deleted language that used to be Rule 3.3(a)(2), which stated that a lawyer shall not "fail to disclose a material fact to a tribunal when disclosure is necessary to avoid assisting a criminal or fraudulent act by a client." Although this language was deleted in the 2002 revision, the interpretation in the formal opinion probably is still valid. The reason why the ABA deleted Rule 3.3(a)(2) is that it replaced that subsection with the broader language of Rule 3.3(b), which requires "reasonable remedial measures, including, if necessary, disclosure to the tribunal" in a situation in which a lawyer is representing a client in an adjudicative proceeding and learns that *someone* (not just the client) "is engaging or has engaged in criminal or fraudulent conduct related to the proceeding." The previous language required action by the lawyer only upon learning of criminal or fraudulent conduct by a client. See ABA, Center for Professional Responsibility, Reporter's Explanation of Changes to Rule 3.3 (2003) (available at http://www.americanbar.org/content/dam/aba/migrated/leadership/2003/journal/119a.authcheckdam.pdf).

49. Rule 1.0(f). According to the Restatement, "a lawyer's intent to facilitate or encourage wrongful action may be inferred if in the circumstances it should have been apparent to the lawyer that the client would employ the assistance to further the client's wrongful conduct, and the lawyer nonetheless provided the assistance." Restatement § 94, comment c.

50. Restatement § 94, comment c, reporter's note. Just as you could be charged with a tort or a crime for conduct that would not be assisting a fraud under the ethical rules, you could be subject to ethics discipline even if your conduct is not tortious or criminal. For example, civil liability for fraud

A good rule of thumb is that a lawyer should be wary if a client's past or contemplated conduct appears to involve an intentional or knowing misrepresentation to another person. Legal consequences are more likely if the false statement concerns something important, if it is made to induce another person to act, if the other person acts in reliance on the statement, and if harm results.

Under what circumstances might a lawyer commit or assist a fraud by failure to act or by omission?

Omissions and half-truths can constitute fraud. In many legal contexts, such as the sale of securities, material omissions, or "half-truths," are regarded as fraudulent. Under the Model Rules, a lawyer's omission may be fraudulent if the lawyer intended to deceive another person. For example, Rule 4.1(b) bars a lawyer from knowingly failing to disclose a nonconfidential material fact when disclosure is necessary to avoid assisting a client's fraudulent act. Comment 1 after Rule 4.1 explains that "[m]isrepresentations can also occur by partially true but misleading statements or omissions that are the equivalent of affirmative false statements."[51]

b. Ethics rules allowing revelation of client crimes or frauds to prevent, mitigate, or remedy harm to others

Few lawyers deliberately set out to counsel clients on how to commit crimes, but they often encounter situations in which their clients have committed or are committing frauds.

Such a situation might develop like this:

1. A lawyer helps a client to prepare documents that include false information, not knowing that the information is false.
2. The recipients of the documents rely on the statements in the documents and on the fact that the documents were prepared in part by a reputable lawyer or law firm.
3. The lawyer later discovers that the documents include false statements or that the client plans to use or has used the documents in a misleading way.

---

requires a showing of reliance on the fraud and damage resulting from the reliance. Neither reliance nor damages need be shown in a disciplinary proceeding. Id. § 94, comment c.

51. As noted in text at infra n. 81, Rule 4.1 imposes important disclosure obligations in many states that have confidentiality provisions allowing disclosures of frauds. The Restatement also takes the view that there is not much difference between false statements and deliberate deception by half-truths and omissions. It explains that "inaction (through nondisclosure) as well as action may constitute fraud under applicable law." Restatement § 67, comment d.

In this type of situation, Rules 1.6(b)(2) and (3) sometimes allow the lawyer to reveal information about the client fraud despite the lawyer's obligation to protect confidences. Here is the language of those rules:

> **(b) A lawyer may reveal information relating to the representation of a client to the extent the lawyer reasonably believes necessary: . . .**
>
> > **(2) to prevent the client from committing a crime or fraud that is reasonably certain to result in substantial injury to the financial interests or property of another and in furtherance of which the client has used or is using the lawyer's services;**
> >
> > **(3) to prevent, mitigate or rectify substantial injury to the financial interests or property of another that is reasonably certain to result or has resulted from the client's commission of a crime or fraud in furtherance of which the client has used the lawyer's services.**[52]

The two subsections are similar, but subsection (b)(2) applies if the client *plans to commit or is committing* the crime or fraud, and (b)(3) refers to a *past crime or fraud*. Under these rules, a lawyer may reveal client criminal or fraudulent conduct whether it is past, ongoing, or future, if

- there is a reasonable certainty that the client's conduct will result in substantial financial injury or substantial injury to the property of another person,
- the client is using or has used the lawyer's services in committing the act(s), and
- the purpose of revealing confidences is to prevent the criminal or fraudulent act or to prevent, mitigate, or rectify the harm resulting from the act(s).

If the criminal or fraudulent conduct is past, the client did not use the lawyer's services to assist in that conduct, and the client has hired the lawyer for representation relating to the conduct, the lawyer may not reveal information under Rule 1.6(b)(3).[53]

FOR EXAMPLE: Suppose a lawyer learns that her client intends to burn down a newly built (but not yet occupied) home that belongs to the client's former boss. (The client is angry because he feels that he was fired unfairly.) Even if the lawyer could prevent the crime from occurring by revealing the information, she would not be permitted to do

---

52. The counterpart to Rules 1.6(b)(2) and (3) in the Restatement is at § 67. The standard articulated in the Restatement is similar to that in Rule 1.6, though organized differently.
53. Rule 1.6, Comment 8.

so under Rule 1.6(b)(2). The client has not used the lawyer's services to commit the crime.

FOR EXAMPLE: Suppose a lawyer unwittingly assists a client in preparing documents to demand compensation from his former employer for a work-related injury. The lawyer then learns that the client invented the injury. The lawyer would have discretion to reveal the intended financial fraud under Rule 1.6(b)(2) if revelation is necessary to prevent substantial financial injury to the employer.[54]

What if the lawyer has transmitted the papers to the client's former employer, and the employer has agreed to pay the claim? Still, the lawyer would have the discretion to reveal the fraud to the employer under Rule 1.6(b)(3), if revelation is necessary to assist in mitigation or rectification of the resulting substantial financial injury.

In defining a lawyer's discretion to reveal confidences to prevent *physical* harm, the rules focus on whether the act that would cause the harm is past or future and on the severity of the harm that might result if the lawyer remains silent. In dealing with threats of financial harm, the distinction between past and future acts is a much harder line to draw. For example, if a lawyer tells a lie about the financial status of a company, a stock purchaser might rely on the misrepresentation a month or a year later. Such reliance is speculative.[55] Therefore the rules allow revelation of confidences about past, present, or future client fraud that has caused or is reasonably certain to cause financial harm to another person.

A lawyer is allowed to reveal information about client crimes and frauds only if the lawyer's services were used in the perpetration of the criminal or fraudulent act. If lawyers were allowed to reveal all past or future criminal or fraudulent behavior, clients could have no confidence that they could safely talk to their lawyers about past wrongdoings. In the case of crimes and frauds that cause financial harm, however, lawyers whose services were used to commit the crimes or frauds do have some discretion. Perhaps these qualifications and uncertainties make it unlikely that a client could

---

54. The question of what "substantial" means in this context has not yet been resolved. Is a fraud in which an employer or other person loses a million dollars automatically one causing a "substantial" injury? Does it depend on the wealth of the victim? If the victim is a large corporation with billions of dollars of assets, is the loss of a million dollars not a "substantial" injury? Could a tax fraud cause a "substantial" injury even though the federal government's revenues are so large that the loss of funds from any individual or corporate taxpayer would be insubstantial?

55. There are instances in which a past act might cause physical harm in the future, such as situations in which a company has dumped carcinogenic material into a landfill or, as in the *Garrow* case, where an uncertainty about whether crime victims are living or dead causes their families severe anguish and perhaps accompanying physical harm. But in most cases involving physical harm, the line between past and future harm is "brighter" than in cases of fraud.

know whether a particular fact, if revealed, would or would not be confidential.

The drafters of the new exceptions allowing revelation of financial crimes and frauds tried to balance three policies:

- To encourage frank communication between clients and lawyers
- To prevent harm to the public
- To protect the "integrity of the profession" by allowing lawyers to blow the whistle if their own work is being used to commit crimes or frauds[56]

In the balance struck by the rule as currently drafted, prevention of harm to the public from client wrongdoing is not alone sufficient to overcome the policy favoring protection of confidences. But when a lawyer's services have been used to assist a client's crime or fraud, the balance tips in favor of permissive disclosure.[57]

Do the ethics rules permit a lawyer to reveal information about a client's crime or fraud if the lawyer had nothing to do with it?

Suppose a client tells her lawyer in confidence about a crime or fraud that she has committed or is contemplating. The lawyer has had absolutely no role in the commission of this act. Suppose, for example, that a lawyer is representing a criminal defendant on a charge of armed robbery. The defendant tells the lawyer that she has a little business, unrelated to the pending charge, in which she helps people with their taxes, falsely passing herself off as a certified public accountant.

Rule 1.6 does not allow a lawyer who has not assisted a client's financial crime or fraud to make a disclosure to protect another person from injury.[58] A lawyer may reveal confidences "to prevent reasonably certain death or substantial bodily harm"[59] regardless of whether the lawyer's work may have contributed to the harm. However, if the client has not used and is not

---

56. ABA, Task Force on Corporate Responsibility, Recommendation to Amend Rule 1.6(b) of the ABA Model Rules of Professional Responsibility 16-17 (2003) (available at http://www.americanbar.org/content/dam/aba/migrated/leadership/2003/journal/119a.authcheckdam.pdf).

57. Rule 1.13, discussed below, comes into play when a lawyer represents an organization such as a corporation, and it strikes a similar balance. It permits (but does not require) a lawyer to disclose confidences if despite the lawyer's efforts, the organization is violating a law, the highest authority in the organization acts or fails to act appropriately, and the violation of law is reasonably certain to result in substantial injury to the organization. Also, Rule 3.3, discussed in Chapter 10, may require a lawyer to disclose to a tribunal the fact that the lawyer's client or other witness has provided false testimony.

58. If a lawyer is employed or retained by an organization, however, the lawyer might have a duty to reveal information about economic crime or fraud by a client even if the lawyer's services had not been used in the commission of the crime or fraud. See Rule 1.13, discussed in Chapter 6.

59. Rule 1.6(b)(1).

using the lawyer's services to commit a fraud, the lawyer may not warn the intended victim of the fraud.[60]

The rules that allow lawyers to reveal confidences to prevent or rectify client fraud have been adopted by the ABA and by many states in recent years. These rules were highly controversial. Before the Enron scandal, the ABA rejected this language from inclusion in the Model Rules. After Enron, the ABA changed its mind. Here is what happened.

c. Enron and the Sarbanes-Oxley Act

Enron was a major energy corporation based in Houston. In October 2001, it was discovered that the company's officers, lawyers, and accountants had massively overstated its earnings, pocketed billions of dollars, and caused massive losses to the company's stockholders. To prevent discovery of the fraud, the company's accounting firm, Arthur Andersen LLP, one of the largest accounting firms in the nation, destroyed documents to prevent Securities and Exchange Commission (SEC) investigators from finding them. It did so on the advice of Nancy Temple, its in-house lawyer. Andersen was convicted of obstruction of justice. The company went bankrupt, even though the Supreme Court later overturned the conviction because of errors in the instructions to the jury.[61] Nancy Temple is now in private practice in Chicago.[62]

During the same period, several other large corporations—Imclone, Tyco, WorldCom, and HealthSouth, for example—had similar financial collapses that also involved financial fraud.

In the aftermath of these scandals, Congress passed the Sarbanes-Oxley Act to prevent further episodes of massive corporate fraud.[63] Section 307 of the new law authorized the SEC to promulgate tough new disclosure rules for professionals, including lawyers, who practice before the Commission and who become aware of clients' frauds.

---

60. Therefore, a client who commits an economic crime or fraud and then consults a lawyer (for example, for purposes of criminal defense) may do so with assurance that the lawyer will not disclose confidences, even to warn victims. Such a lawyer could not possibly have contributed to the client's offense because the client consulted the lawyer after the client completed the acts in question (though the effects of the fraud may be ongoing). See Rule 1.6, Comment 8.

61. Charles Lane, Justices Overturn Andersen Conviction; Advice to Enron Jury on Accountants' Intent Is Faulted, Wash. Post (June 1, 2005) (available at http://www.washingtonpost.com/wp-dyn/content/article/2005/05/31/AR2005053100491.html). The Enron story is told in detail in Stephen Gillers & Roy D. Simon, Regulation of Lawyers: Statutes and Standards 1049-1072 (Aspen Publishers 2003).

62. Katten & Temple, LLP, Nancy A. Temple, Partner, http://kattentemple.com/nan.html (accessed Nov. 1, 2012).

63. Public Company Accounting Reform and Investor Protection (Sarbanes-Oxley) Act of 2002, Pub. L. No. 107-204, 116 Stat. 745 (codified as amended in scattered sections of 18 U.S.C., 15 U.S.C., and 28 U.S.C.).

In introducing an amendment to add § 307, Senator John Edwards, its chief sponsor, said:

> If executives and/or accountants are breaking the law, you can be sure that part of the problem is that the lawyers who are there are involved and not doing their jobs. . . . What this amendment does [is to require that] [i]f you are a lawyer for a corporation, . . . you work for the corporation and . . . the shareholders. . . . This amendment is about making sure those lawyers . . . don't violate the law and . . . ensur[ing] that the law is being followed. . . . If you find out that the managers are breaking the law, you must tell them to stop. If they won't stop, you go to the board of directors, . . . and tell them what is going on.[64]

The amendment to add § 307 passed, and the SEC promptly issued a rule that requires lawyers who practice before the Commission or who advise companies regulated by the Commission to report any information about securities fraud to the highest officials of the corporation.[65] If the fraud is likely to harm investors, the reporting lawyer may (but is not required to) report the matter to the SEC.[66]

The Commission proposed a more stringent rule and published it for public comment, but it held that proposal in abeyance. Under that proposed rule, if a lawyer reported securities fraud to senior officials in a corporation, and those officials did not act promptly on the lawyer's internal report, the lawyer would be obliged to withdraw from representing the client and to notify the SEC that the lawyer was no longer representing the company "based on professional considerations." This "noisy withdrawal" would blow the whistle on the company and trigger a government investigation.[67]

The chairman of the SEC suggested that the Commission might refrain from imposing this more drastic reporting obligation if the legal profession changed its official position on the disclosure of client fraud. Specifically, he suggested that further rulemaking would be influenced by action taken by the ABA.[68] In other words, if the ABA amended its Model Rules to permit lawyers to blow the whistle on their clients' frauds, the SEC might refrain from imposing even more stringent reporting obligations on lawyers.

---

64. Senator Edwards's statement is excerpted in Special Section: Sarbanes-Oxley Before the SEC, Stephen Gillers & Roy D. Simon, Regulation of Lawyers: Statutes and Standards 1002 (Aspen Publishers 2004).

65. Public Company Accounting Reform and Investor Protection Act of 2002 § 307 (codified at 15 U.S.C. § 7245) (requiring the SEC to issue rules requiring securities lawyers to report violations of securities laws by company agents up the chain of command); 17 C.F.R. § 205 (2007) (implementing regulation).

66. 17 C.F.R. § 205.3(d)(2) (2007).

67. The regulation, proposed regulation, and related history are reported in depth in Gillers & Simon, supra n. 64, at 1001-1023.

68. This history is described in ABA, Task Force on Corporate Responsibility, supra n. 56.

Even before Enron, most states had adopted ethical rules permitting or requiring lawyers to report clients' use of their services to commit fraud. The Model Rules, however, gave lawyers no discretion to reveal confidential information to prevent or mitigate the harm from client fraud. The Ethics 2000 Commission proposed to add language allowing lawyers to make such revelations, but the ABA House of Delegates rejected this proposal in August 2001.[69]

In the months that followed, the Enron scandal unraveled. By November 29, 2001, the company was on the brink of bankruptcy.[70] A public outcry about lawyers' participation in the Enron and other corporate scandals of the period prompted the ABA to reconsider its position on lawyers' responsibility to blow the whistle on client fraud. An ABA Task Force on Corporate Responsibility initially recommended mandatory disclosure of client crimes and frauds in which the lawyer's work was being used. But the task force later withdrew that proposal in the face of "strong criticism" from lawyers. The task force feared that if the rule made disclosure of client fraud mandatory, clients might be deterred from consulting lawyers "regarding close issues" that were in reality "a matter of business judgment."[71] The task force substituted disclosure exceptions to confidentiality that allowed lawyers discretion to reveal those crimes and frauds. In 2003, the House of Delegates adopted the very same language (1.6(b)(2) and (3)) that it had rejected two years earlier. The House of Delegates also changed Model Rule 1.13 (which is discussed in Chapter 6). That rule requires lawyers to report fraud by the employees of a client organization to more senior officials of the organization.

Recent developments in the implementation of Sarbanes-Oxley

The ABA's action appears to have quieted the SEC initiative to require lawyers to blow the whistle on client fraud. In June 2007, the press commented that "more than four years have passed [but] the SEC has not introduced a final rule requiring noisy withdrawal and, in fact, has given no indication that it will anytime soon. . . ."[72]

---

69. ABA, Center for Professional Responsibility, A Legislative History: The Development of the Model Rules of Professional Conduct, 1982-2005, at 118-132 (ABA 2006) (documenting the proposal of the Ethics 2000 Commission to amend Rule 1.6 to add language identical to the language eventually adopted by the ABA, and the 2001 rejection of this proposed language by the House of Delegates).

70. Peter Behr, Deal to Take Over Enron Unravels; Once Proud Energy Trading Firm Left Near Bankruptcy; Market Impact Feared, Wash. Post E1 (Nov. 29, 2001) (available at http://www.highbeam.com/doc/1P2-479909.html).

71. ABA, Task Force on Corporate Responsibility, supra n. 56, at 16 n. 38.

72. Shawn Harpen, Eric Landan & Kathryn Lohmeyer, Ethically Speaking: The SEC's Proposed Noisy Withdrawal Rule: Intended and Unintended Consequences, 49 Orange Co. Law. 42 (2007).

Since 2003, the reported opinions suggest that the SEC does not seem to have done much to enforce § 307 against lawyers.[73] The only prominent case appears to have been an action against John Isselmann Jr., who was general counsel (and the only lawyer) at Electro Scientific Industries, Inc. When Isselmann discovered that his company was overstating its income, he tried to report that fact at a company audit committee meeting. He was cut off by the chief financial officer, who had developed the scheme to inflate the books. Fearing for his job, Isselmann kept quiet for five months and then resigned, rather than informing the audit committee promptly.[74] Isselmann settled with the SEC for a $50,000 fine.[75] Isselmann later explained that he didn't realize at the time of his inaction that he'd done anything wrong. He was "just eight years out of law school and had no accounting experience, and only a limited securities law background. 'Like many general counsel, I was a generalist — my job was a mile wide and an inch deep. I relied heavily on accounting people like . . . outside auditors to flag those issues for me. . . . ' He says he probably spent an hour and a half in total on the . . . matter."[76]

What is the relationship between § 307 of Sarbanes-Oxley and Rule 1.6(b)?

One thing to notice is that the ethics codes apply more broadly than does the Sarbanes-Oxley Act. The exceptions in 1.6(b)(2) and (3) apply to all lawyers in states that adopt the ABA's proposal;[77] they are not restricted to the disclosure of frauds by publicly held companies, nor to lawyers who practice before the SEC.[78]

Some lawyers are subject to the "fraud" exceptions of the ethics code and to Sarbanes-Oxley. A lawyer practicing before the SEC in a state that

---

73. A July 2009 article reports that "the SEC has not brought any enforcement actions under these [§ 307] rules." Bowne Securities Connect, Attorneys Facing Vigorous Enforcement Stance from the SEC (July 2009).

74. Kim T. Vu, Conscripting Attorneys to Battle Corporate Fraud Without Shields or Armor? Reconsidering Retaliatory Discharge in Light of Sarbanes-Oxley, 105 Mich. L. Rev. 209, 213-214 (2006).

75. Cathleen Flahardy, Chutes and Ladders, Corp. Leg. Times (Jan. 2005).

76. Tamara Loomis, SEC Gores GC in Sarbanes-Oxley Dustup, Leg. Times (Jan. 24, 2005).

77. By 2010, at least 26 states had adopted rule changes incorporating the substance of subsections (b)(2) and (b)(3) in whole or part. Susan R. Martyn, Lawrence J. Fox & W. Bradley Wendel, The Law Governing Lawyers (2010-2011 ed.) 112-119 (Wolters Kluwer 2010).

78. As noted in Chapter 1, there are many instances when the ethics rules of particular states diverge from the Model Rules. On this topic, the divergence is particularly dramatic. For example, several states require (rather than permit) disclosure to rectify substantial loss from client crimes or frauds involving a lawyer's services. ABA, Task Force on Corporate Responsibility, supra n. 56, at 14-15 n. 33. There are many variations among the states in the language used to authorize or require revelation of client fraud, so it is especially important for practicing lawyers to be familiar with the rules of their own jurisdictions.

has adopted Rules 1.6(b)(2) and (b)(3) must observe all of the applicable rules. The lawyer must report securities frauds to management as required by Sarbanes-Oxley, even when the lawyer's services had not been used to commit the fraud. Similarly, even if the lawyer is prohibited by state law from revealing information about a fraud (e.g., because it was committed without the assistance of the lawyer's services), the lawyer may report the fraud to the SEC under Sarbanes-Oxley because federal law preempts contrary state law.[79] Therefore, a lawyer may be allowed to reveal evidence of a client's fraud even if revelation is not permitted by Rule 1.6.

Are some lawyers blowing the whistle on their clients under the Sarbanes-Oxley law?

Some are, though the degree of compliance is hard to measure. In one major incident, Thomas Sjoblom, a lawyer at the Proskauer Rose law firm, publicly disavowed information he had given to the SEC regarding his client, an Antiguan investment firm affiliated with the billionaire Robert Allen Stanford. A few days later, the SEC charged Stanford with selling $8 billion worth of certificates of deposit, based on unsubstantiated claims that the certificates were producing substantial returns.[80]

Is a lawyer really free under the rules to decide not to reveal a client crime or fraud that will cause financial harm to another person?

Sometimes the answer is no. The new exceptions to Rule 1.6 give the impression that a lawyer may choose not to reveal a client crime or fraud, even if her services have been used in its commission and even if it will cause financial harm to another person. However, another rule *mandates* revelation in some circumstances. Rule 4.1(b) states:

> In the course of representing a client a lawyer shall not knowingly . . . fail to disclose a material fact when disclosure is necessary to avoid assisting a criminal or fraudulent act, unless disclosure is *prohibited* by Rule 1.6.[81]

Comment 3 after Rule 4.1 explains:

---

79. N.C. Bar Ethics Comm., Formal Op. 2005-9 (Jan. 20, 2006) (available at http://www.ncbar.com/ethics/ethics.asp?page = 2&from = 1/2006&to = 6/2006).

80. Debra Cassens Weiss, Sarbanes-Oxley Governed Lawyer's "Noisy Withdrawal" in Stanford Case, ABA J. (Feb. 19, 2009) (available at http://www.abajournal.com/news/article/sarbanes-oxley_governed_lawyers_noisy_withdrawal_in_stanford_case/). (Note that the "withdrawal" in the title of the article refers to withdrawal of the lawyer's connection to the documents he had prepared, not withdrawal from representation.) Stanford ended up in prison. Anthony Lake, Sir Robert Allen Stanford's Congressional Ties and Prison Blues, Federal Criminal Defense Blog, http://www.federalcriminaldefenseblog.com/2010/01/articles/high-profile-cases/sir-robert-allen-stanfords-congressional-ties-and-prison-blues/ (Jan. 19, 2010).

81. This is the text of Delaware Rule 4.1(b) (emphasis added). The ABA Model Rule includes the phrase "to a third person" after the words "material fact."

Ordinarily, a lawyer can avoid assisting a client's crime or fraud by withdrawing from the representation. Sometimes it may be necessary for the lawyer to give notice of the fact of withdrawal and to disaffirm an opinion, document, affirmation or the like. In extreme cases, substantive law may require a lawyer to disclose information relating to the representation to avoid being deemed to have assisted the client's crime or fraud. If the lawyer can avoid assisting a client's crime or fraud only by disclosing this information, then under paragraph (b) the lawyer is required to do so, unless the disclosure is prohibited by Rule 1.6.

Rule 1.6 now permits revelation of confidential information to prevent, mitigate, or remedy some criminal and fraudulent client conduct. This means that in any situation in which a lawyer's *failure to reveal* would constitute "assisting a criminal or fraudulent act," Rule 4.1 now *requires* a lawyer to reveal the information.[82]

Obviously, this is confusing. Why would the drafters write Rule 1.6 to give lawyers discretion to disclose or not, and then not mention in 1.6 that the discretion conferred by Rule 1.6 is restricted in situations covered by Rule 4.1? We are not sure.

What other ethics rules besides Rules 1.2, 1.6, and 4.1 allow or require revelation of criminal or fraudulent conduct?

In addition to Rule 1.6, several other ethics rules define lawyers' duties in relation to client crimes and frauds. We explore these rules later in the book; here we simply identify them.

Dishonesty   Rule 8.4(c) prohibits lawyers from engaging in any "dishonesty, fraud, deceit or misrepresentation."

Duty of a lawyer representing an organization to call attention to crimes and frauds   Rule 1.13, discussed in Chapter 6, addresses the duties of a lawyer representing an organization if the lawyer learns that someone associated with the organization is acting or intends to violate the law. The rule requires the lawyer to call the attention of corporate management to the wrongful conduct. If the senior corporate officials do not address the conduct, the rule permits the lawyer to reveal the information to the extent necessary to prevent substantial injury to the organization.

---

82. Keep in mind that we are speaking only of the Model Rule and the rule in states that have used identical or similar language. When New York promulgated a new set of rules in 2009, it simply omitted Rule 4.1(b). See New York Unified Court System, Rules of Professional Conduct (2009) (available at http://www.nysba.org/Content/NavigationMenu/ForAttorneys/Professional StandardsforAttorneys/NYRulesofProfessionalConduct4109.pdf).

Duty to reveal client crimes or frauds to tribunals   Rule 3.3, discussed in Chapter 10, explains under what circumstances a lawyer must disclose to a tribunal that the lawyer's client or another witness has provided false testimony.

Duty to withdraw rather than assist client crime or fraud; discretion to withdraw if client persists in crimes or frauds   Rule 1.16(a) requires a lawyer to withdraw from representing a client if continued representation would result in a violation of the rules. Rule 1.16(b) permits a lawyer to withdraw from representing a client who persists in criminal or fraudulent conduct. Under some circumstances, withdrawal could be a form of revelation because it could suggest to a judge or an adversary that the lawyer has discovered serious wrongdoing. We discuss this rule in Chapter 4.

To the extent that the ethics rules give lawyers discretion to reveal client fraud, are lawyers protected from civil or criminal liability if they elect not to reveal?

No. The ethics rules articulate a standard of conduct that may result in discipline if violated by a lawyer. The ethics rules do not provide a separate basis for civil or criminal liability,[83] but neither do they protect a lawyer from liability.

PROBLEM 3-6   REESE'S LEASES

This problem is based on a series of events that took place in New York City.

After you finished law school, you started a law firm with three classmates who are now your partners. The firm has done well, thanks largely to the work you do for one client, Executive Leasing Services. This company was founded by two of your childhood friends, Charlie Reese and Paula Suarez. Their company now does $17 million worth of business each year, and your legal work for them accounts for 60 percent of your law firm's monthly receipts. As they have prospered, so have you. Your firm now has three associates, a paralegal, and three secretaries. This pattern of growth is likely to continue if Executive Leasing continues to do well. If Executive Leasing Services were to fail, however, your law firm

---

83. In the Scope note at the beginning of the Rules, Comment 20 explains: "The Rules are designed to provide guidance to lawyers and to provide a structure for regulating conduct through disciplinary agencies. They are not designed to be a basis for civil liability."

would have to lay off some staff immediately, and the firm would be unable to pay you or the other partners. The law firm probably would go out of business within a matter of months.

Executive Leasing Services leases luxury cars to corporations for use by corporate managers. It started out by borrowing money from a bank to buy a few cars. Then it leased out those cars to its first corporate customers, using the promise of income under the leases as collateral to borrow more money and buy more cars to lease out.

Your firm's role was to draw up the paperwork for each lease and to supply legal opinions (for the benefit of the bank) affirming that Executive Leasing Services owned the cars that it was leasing. Occasionally, the firm negotiated leases between the company and its corporate customers. At some point, you noticed that Executive Leasing Services was charging customers 15 percent less than other firms were charging to lease comparable cars. Also, you noticed that the income from the leases often was less than repayments on the bank loans. You wondered why the bank kept giving your client larger and larger loans when the company seemed to be losing money.

Eventually, you learned the answer to your question. Executive Leasing's accountant asked whether she could tell you something in confidence. You agreed. She said that the firm's owners were leasing some cars, but in addition, they were creating some counterfeit leases for fictitious transactions. The counterfeit leases, each covering several cars, included both the vehicle identification numbers of some cars that the firm owned, and some vehicle identification numbers of cars that Executive Leasing had leased previously to the same customer and later sold or was currently leasing to other customers.

"Why would they do that?" you inquired.

"Well," she said, "Charlie and Paula want to borrow more money, so that they can expand their business by purchasing and leasing out additional cars. Also, you know, both of them live pretty high. (Last year, Charlie bought a mansion overlooking the river and Paula bought a house in Barbados.) To get the loans, they need collateral to give the bank. The higher volume of business they show, the larger the loans they can get. The phony leases make their business look much bigger than it is."

"Wow," you said, not sure how else to respond to this astonishing news.

Today, you met with Charlie Reese privately. You shared your concern that the numbers didn't add up. You asked him straight out whether he had been cooking the books or inflating the firm's value when requesting new loans. After some hemming and hawing, he admitted that the firm had submitted forged leases to the bank.

"How did you do it?" you asked, wondering whether Charlie or Paula would be facing criminal charges in the near future.

"It's pretty easy," Charlie said, with just a hint of pride in his voice. "Once a month, Paula and I stay late to go over the books. After the rest of the folks go home, we settle down in my office, modify the numbers on some existing leases, and generate some new leases."

"What do you mean, 'modify the numbers'?" you asked.

"Well, sometimes, we just add digits to the numbers in genuine leases to create what appear to be new leases."

"Okay. But don't you need customer signatures for those?" you asked, starting to sweat.

Charlie smiled. "We always make it appear that the new leases are coming from existing customers. We just copy their signatures onto the new leases."

"That's not so easy," you observed.

"It's not so hard. I have a glass desktop. We turn off the lights, and I get down on the floor and shine a flashlight up. Paula covers the last page of a real lease with a fresh lease form. Then she traces the customer's signature onto the new lease form. We fill out the lease and send it to the bank."

"Wow," you repeated.

"Don't worry," Charlie responded. "The banks just add up the numbers. They don't check the signatures, call the customers for verification, or compare vehicle identification numbers in various leases. The money keeps rolling in."

Charlie noticed the sweat rolling down the side of your face. "Hey, pal," he said, "this is paying your mortgage as well as mine. Of course I'm telling you all this in the strictest confidence."

"I can't believe you have been doing this!" you retorted. "I wrote opinion letters attesting to the validity of all the leases you submitted as collateral for your bank loans."

"No, actually your letters didn't say that the leases that we used as collateral were genuine, just that we had title to the cars that we bought with the money that we borrowed, which was true. Your nose is clean."

"Look, Charlie, this scheme is just too risky," you said. "It has got to stop, or all three of us could wind up in prison for a very long time."

Charlie stopped looking smug. "I know it's risky. Paula and I have been worried all along. Last month after we got that last loan we decided it was enough. We won't fiddle with any more leases, I promise."

You thought for a moment. "I guess that might be the best we can do for right now."

Questions

1. **Our little secret?** Consider the following possible actions. Which of them are permitted or required by the rules?
   - Reveal the fraud to the bank or the district attorney if Reese refuses to do so.
   - Do not reveal the fraud but stop representing Executive Leasing Services.
   - Do not reveal the fraud and continue to represent Executive Leasing Services, taking more care that the company does not engage in future fraud.
2. **Economic realities.** Keeping in mind that your own livelihood and the livelihoods of your partners and staff members depend on keeping Executive Leasing Services afloat, what would you actually do in this situation?

---

4. Revealing confidences to obtain advice about legal ethics

Rule 1.6(b)(4) permits a lawyer to reveal confidences to the extent necessary for the lawyer to obtain advice about complying with the rules of professional conduct. A lawyer may invoke this exception to consult another lawyer for advice. The other lawyer might be in another firm, or a law professor, or a bar official. This exception makes clear that lawyers seeking advice about their ethical duties may reveal client confidences to the extent necessary to get the advice they need.[84]

A lawyer may seek advice about ethical duties from others in his firm or organization, but lawyers facing ethical dilemmas often feel constrained not to consult with supervisors or co-workers because in many cases the other lawyers are directing or participating in conduct that raises ethical questions. A lawyer might call the bar counsel's office, an ethics hotline sponsored by the bar, a former professor, or another practicing lawyer. It might take more than one phone call to find a willing advisor. But to obtain

---

84. Rule 1.6, Comment 9.

disinterested advice in such a situation is very important and is permitted by the rules. Obtaining ethical guidance is not a shield against liability, but having proof that a lawyer sought such advice, such as memo written to the file, will show that the lawyer took the problem seriously and tried to find the best solution if later his actions are questioned.

5. Using a client's confidential information to protect the lawyer's interests

Rule 1.6(b)(5) allows a lawyer to reveal confidential information to the extent necessary to authenticate a claim for legal fees, to defend herself against any civil claim or any criminal charge that involves the lawyer's work on behalf of a client, or to respond to any allegations that the lawyer has engaged in professional misconduct. Revelation of confidences is allowed if needed to defend the lawyer against any allegation of misconduct. It might be difficult for a lawyer to show that she acted properly unless she is allowed to reveal the substance of her work.

> **FOR EXAMPLE:**   Imagine a client who falsely says that his lawyer didn't do any work at all. The work at issue consisted of writing a document based on confidential information. If the lawyer can't produce the document as part of her defense, the lawyer cannot prove that she did any work.

A comment to Rule 1.6 limits how much a lawyer can reveal in her own defense or in other circumstances:

> Where practicable the lawyer should first seek to persuade the client to take suitable action to obviate the need for disclosure. In any case, a disclosure adverse to the client's interest should be no greater than the lawyer reasonably believes necessary to accomplish the purpose. If the disclosure will be made in connection with a judicial proceeding, the disclosure should be made in a manner that limits access to the information to the tribunal or other persons having a need to know it and appropriate protective orders or other arrangements should be sought by the lawyer to the fullest extent practicable.[85]

So if a lawyer needs to reveal confidences to protect her own interests, she must take steps to avoid the need for revelation, to limit its scope, or to limit the dissemination of the information.

---

85. Id. at Comment 14.

If a lawyer is about to be sued for malpractice, must he wait until the lawsuit is filed before he may reveal information to defend himself?

No. The lawyer is allowed to respond to an assertion that he has engaged in wrongdoing by revealing information necessary to defend himself:

> The lawyer's right to respond arises when an assertion of such complicity [in wrongdoing] has been made. Paragraph (b)(5) does not require the lawyer to await the commencement of an action or proceeding that charges such complicity, so that the defense may be established by responding directly to a third party who has made such an assertion. The right to defend also applies, of course, where a proceeding has been commenced.[86]

Similarly, the Sarbanes-Oxley Act permits a lawyer practicing before the SEC who has reported a fraud to a client company's officials to use that report in connection with any investigation concerning the lawyer's compliance with the SEC's rules.[87]

Does the self-defense exception apply if a third party makes a claim against a client and the lawyer is accused of some minor role in a client's misconduct?

The lawyer may be allowed to reveal confidences even if he is not alleged to be the primary wrongdoer:

> A charge [of wrongdoing that justifies revelation of confidences] can arise in a civil, criminal, disciplinary or other proceeding and can be based on a wrong allegedly committed by the lawyer against the client or on a wrong alleged by a third person, for example, a person claiming to have been defrauded by the lawyer and client acting together.[88]

This means that a lawyer may reveal confidences even if the "allegation" is made by an injured third party rather than by a client, and even if the lawyer is not the primary target of the allegation.

Under what conditions may a lawyer reveal confidential information in self-defense?

To establish a claim against a client for unpaid fees

To defend against a claim of malpractice or other claim of civil liability against the lawyer

To defend against a disciplinary proceeding

To defend against a criminal charge

---

86. Id. at Comment 10.
87. 17 C.F.R. § 205.3(d)(1) (2007).
88. Rule 1.6, Comment 10.

When is revelation allowed?

The lawyer need not wait for formal proceedings to be instituted but may reveal information to prevent such action.

When authorized, how much can a lawyer reveal?

No more than necessary to vindicate the lawyer. The lawyer should minimize the number of people who learn the confidential information revealed, should seek a protective order, and should take other available steps to avoid the dissemination of the information.

Should the lawyer inform the client before revealing confidential information?

Yes. The lawyer should notify the client before using confidential information in self-defense and should seek solutions that do not require the lawyer to make the revelation, but the lawyer may use the information even if the client does not consent.

6. Revealing confidences to comply with a court order or other law

Rule 1.6(b)(6) permits a lawyer to disclose confidential information to comply with a court order or with other law. If a court order or "other law" requires a lawyer to disclose information, the court order trumps the obligation to protect confidences.[89] For example, most states require anyone who knows of ongoing child abuse to report it to welfare agencies. Some states exempt lawyers from the reporting requirement; others do not. Whether a law really requires such reporting by lawyers requires interpretation of that law, not of the rules of professional conduct.[90]

> **FOR EXAMPLE:** In the "Missing Persons" case discussed earlier in this chapter, it was not self-evident that the health law (requiring members of the public to report knowledge of bodies that had not been buried properly) was intended to override the usual rules of attorney-client confidentiality and privilege.

---

89. However, a comment to Rule 1.6 urges lawyers to assert all nonfrivolous objections to the order and to consult with the client about the possibility of appealing the order. Rule 1.6, Comment 13.

90. Rule 1.6, Comment 12.

7. Revealing confidences to prevent certain conflicts of interest

As the text discusses in Chapter 7, when a lawyer moves to another firm, or when firms merge, the new firm must check for conflicts. For example, new firm X should not assign recently hired lawyer Y to work on behalf of an X client who is adverse to someone Y represented in the prior matter at Y's old firm. To prevent such conflicts, the new firm usually needs to know at least the identities of the lawyer's clients at his old firm. Rule 1.6(b)(7) permits a limited disclosure to "detect and resolve" conflicts of interest. Comment 13 adds that a disclosure pursuant to this exception "should ordinarily include no more than the identity of the persons and entities involved in a matter, a brief summary of the general issues involved, and information about whether the matter has been terminated." The last clause in the new exception prohibits disclosure where it would prejudice a client unless that client gives consent. The comment provides examples of situations in which this limited disclosure is prohibited, such as where a person has consulted a lawyer about a criminal investigation that has not led to a public charge.

C. Use or disclosure of confidential information for personal gain or to benefit another client

If a lawyer acquires confidential information in the course of her legal work, she needs to be concerned not only about improper revelation but also about improper use of the information.

> **Rule 1.8(b) Conflict of Interest: Current Clients: Specific Rules**
> **A lawyer shall not use information relating to representation of a client to the disadvantage of the client unless the client gives informed consent, except as permitted or required by these Rules.**

Comment 5 explains:

> Paragraph (b) applies when the information is used to benefit either the lawyer or a third person, such as another client or business associate of the lawyer. . . . The Rule does not prohibit uses that do not disadvantage the client. For example, a lawyer who learns a government agency's interpretation of trade legislation during the representation of one client may properly use that information to benefit other clients. Paragraph (b) prohibits disadvantageous use of client information unless the client gives informed consent, except as permitted or required by these Rules. . . .

When is a lawyer permitted to use confidential information for personal gain?

Occasionally, a lawyer may have the opportunity to use confidential information that the lawyer obtains from a client for personal gain. Some — but not all — uses of confidential information from clients are considered improper.

> **FOR EXAMPLE:**   Suppose a lawyer represents a publicly traded Internet start-up. The lawyer learns confidential information that suggests that this company's stock will escalate in value very dramatically over the next year. May the lawyer purchase stock based on this knowledge? No, because the purchase probably would be illegal insider trading, and the lawyer might be criminally prosecuted.

The following problem raises a similar issue that does not implicate the securities laws.

PROBLEM 3-7   AN INVESTMENT PROJECT

> You represent a company that is investigating possible sites for a new plant. Because you are privy to your client company's research, you learn that developers are acquiring contiguous parcels of land in a suburb called Lakeshore where they probably will build a shopping mall. One parcel of land remains to be sold. Your client has decided not to buy land in Lakeshore. The value of the Lakeshore property probably will rise either because the developers will want to buy it or as a result of its better proximity to shopping.
>
> You would like to buy this parcel of land. Are you permitted to do so under Rule 1.8(b)? Does your answer change if your client has not yet decided whether to purchase the land?

May a lawyer use confidential information to benefit another one of his clients?

Rule 1.8(b) does not prohibit a lawyer from using confidential information obtained from one client to benefit another client, so long as the first client gives informed consent or is not disadvantaged by the use of the information. The Restatement recognizes that it is not always clear whether one use of confidential information will disadvantage the client on whose behalf the information was obtained. The Restatement prohibits use of confidences "if there is a reasonable prospect that [the use] will adversely affect a material interest of a client or if the client has instructed the lawyer not to use or disclose such information."[91] It offers an example of a permissible use of confidences on behalf of another client:

> [A] lawyer representing a plaintiff who has acquired extensive confidential information about the manner in which a defendant manufactured a product may employ that information for the benefit of another client with a claim against the same defendant arising out of a defect in the same product.[92]

D. Talking to clients about confidentiality

Professor Fred Zacharias

A cornerstone of lawyer-client relationships is the lawyer's duty to keep client information confidential. But as we have seen, there are some circumstances in which a lawyer is permitted to reveal confidential information. There are also some situations in which a lawyer must reveal client confidences — if ordered to do so by a judge or if required to do so by a statute or by an ethical rule. Should a lawyer explain these exceptions to a client so that the client will not expect that the duty to protect confidences is absolute? What might be the adverse consequences of making such disclosures? Of not doing so?

The late Professor Fred C. Zacharias surveyed the lawyers in one county in New York State in the 1980s and reported that most of the lawyers he surveyed say little or nothing to their clients about confidentiality. If they say anything at all, they just reassure their clients that whatever the clients tell them will be confidential. None of the lawyers interviewed told clients that the protection is not absolute or identified situations in which confidences would be revealed.

Zacharias also interviewed a set of clients in the same county to find out what they knew about the confidentiality rules. Most of the clients he interviewed had learned whatever they knew about lawyers' duties to keep confidences from watching television shows. They didn't know that there were situations in which lawyers were permitted or required to reveal confidential information.[93]

---

91. Restatement § 60.
92. Id. at comment j.
93. Fred C. Zacharias, Rethinking Confidentiality, 74 Iowa L. Rev. 351, 379-392 (1989).

Zacharias studied lawyers in only one county in upstate New York. Perhaps other clients are better advised than the ones he interviewed. It seems clear, however, that if a lawyer might need to reveal confidential information in a particular matter, a client should know that. Most clients would prefer to have that information at the beginning of the relationship, before they reveal a great deal of sensitive, confidential information. On the other hand, a well-counseled client might be less open with her lawyer. Even if the lawyer wants to make such an advance disclosure, it's not so easy. The exceptions to the basic confidentiality rule are numerous, complex, and sometimes ambiguous.

E. The attorney-client privilege

The duty of confidentiality to clients is similar to the attorney-client privilege in that the purpose of each is to encourage open and honest communication between lawyers and clients. But the privilege is, in many ways, a more limited protection for clients. The privilege gives lawyers and clients a right not to divulge what they say to each other, provided that the lawyer and client communicate in confidence outside of the presence of third parties for the purpose of delivery of legal services to the client.

1. Confidentiality and attorney-client privilege compared

The most basic difference between confidentiality and privilege is that the duty to protect confidences is imposed by the ethical rules, violation of which can result in discipline. Privilege is "evidence law," which governs what kinds of evidence can be admitted in court. Privilege rules provide that neither lawyer nor client may be compelled to testify in court about protected communications. The ethical rules are more demanding because they require lawyers to protect confidential information whether or not someone is trying to compel the disclosure of information.

How does attorney-client privilege protect the right to be represented by counsel?

Both confidentiality and privilege are based on the idea that the legal system will work best if clients can speak openly to their attorneys. The privilege encourages open communication and helps protect lawyers and clients from lawyers being called as witnesses against their own clients.

FOR EXAMPLE: Suppose a civil defendant told a certain secret to her lawyer. The lawyer is a "witness" to the defendant's revelation. Now suppose that the plaintiff subpoenaed the lawyer to testify about what the defendant said to the lawyer. The lawyer would say that his duty of confidentiality precluded the lawyer from revealing the secret. However, the court might override that duty. Rule 1.6(b)(6) allows revelation of confidences if necessary to comply with a court order. If the information is also covered by the attorney-client privilege, the court should not issue such an order. The privilege requires courts to refrain from ordering lawyers or clients to reveal the contents of certain conversations that they have with each other.

If a communication is protected by attorney-client privilege, is it fully protected, or can the claim of privilege be overcome by a showing of need for the information?

The privilege is pretty close to absolute. Occasionally courts talk about balancing the privilege against the need for a party to obtain a fair trial, but it is exceedingly difficult to find cases in which the court balances even a compelling need against the importance of the privilege and actually overrides the privilege. The Supreme Court has noted that the Sixth Amendment right of a criminal defendant to confront adverse witnesses can come into conflict with certain privileges, such as the marital privilege and the privilege against self-incrimination. But in the cases involving those privileges, the result has been to reverse convictions based on the prosecutor's introduction of some of the privileged information (without having made the privileged provider available for cross-examination), not to require the privileged person (such as the spouse) to testify. In addition, the Supreme Court has expressly declined to decide whether the Sixth Amendment can trump the attorney-client privilege.

The duty of confidentiality is very broad, as we saw earlier in the chapter. It has some important exceptions, to be sure. But it covers all information "relating to the representation" that a lawyer obtains. By contrast, the privilege covers only a relatively small part of that information: the part that involves communications between lawyer and client in which the client is seeking legal advice or other legal services.[94]

---

94. Other information (besides lawyer-client communications) that is not privileged but is protected by confidentiality rules includes, for example, much of the information a lawyer learns through interviews, discovery, and research, and information produced by experts hired by the lawyer. The obligation to protect confidences does not prohibit disclosure of information gathered by a lawyer that is drawn from public sources or is otherwise "generally known." Restatement § 59 and comment d.

> **FOR EXAMPLE:** If a lawyer interviews a witness to an accident that is the subject of a lawsuit, the information is confidential but not covered by the attorney-client privilege because the communication is not between attorney and client.

The confidentiality and privilege rules are implemented or enforced in different ways. If a lawyer violates a confidentiality rule, the lawyer might be subject to discipline. If a lawyer seeks information that an opposing lawyer claims is privileged, that lawyer claiming privilege might move to quash a subpoena or object to compliance with a discovery request.

Are the attorney-client privilege rules laid out somewhere?

Only unofficially. The drafters of the Federal Rules of Evidence attempted to create a uniform statement of the privilege, at least for the federal courts, when they proposed Rule 503. This rule was not formally adopted, but even so, it provides a good summary of the general rule. You may find it in your statutory supplement. Also, the American Law Institute has summarized the rules on attorney-client privilege in Restatement §§ 68 to 86. We focus on the Restatement version to explain this set of rules.

2. The elements of attorney-client privilege

a. Communication

The first element needed to claim attorney-client privilege is "communication" between lawyer and client. The privilege may be claimed for a face-to-face conversation or for a telephone call, a memorandum, a letter, a fax, an e-mail, a text message, or any other mode of exchanging information. However, as we explain below, the privilege protects only against disclosure of the communication itself, not against disclosure of the underlying facts that might have been communicated.

b. Privileged persons

Most lawyers work closely with secretaries, paralegals, and investigators, and sometimes with interpreters, parents of minor children, and experts such as the client's psychologist. Communications with these agents of a lawyer or client are privileged. Also, a lawyer's or secretary's notes of a privileged conversation are privileged.[95]

---

95. Restatement § 69 at comment f.

Communications with a prospective client or lawyer also are privileged. Not having such a privilege would make it very hard for a client to tell a lawyer enough information, in confidence, to enable the lawyer and the client to decide whether they would work on the matter together.

c. Communication in confidence

The client must reasonably believe that the communication is confidential. Conversations in elevators of the lawyer's office building, when strangers are also present, are not privileged. Perhaps you've seen signs in hospital elevators cautioning doctors not to discuss patient matters in public places. Lawyers are well advised to be equally careful, to protect confidences, to comply with their ethical obligations, to respect the privacy of their clients, and to avoid inadvertent waiver of attorney-client privilege.

d. Communication for the purpose of seeking legal assistance

The last element is that communication is privileged only if the purpose was obtaining legal assistance. If a client asks for "business" advice (such as an investment tip), the conversation is not privileged.

> FOR EXAMPLE: Suppose that a lawyer's friend confesses to him that she caused an automobile accident and fled the scene. She tells him about this event because she needs his advice and support as a friend, not because she wants his legal help. The fact that he happens to be a lawyer does not render her admission privileged. He could be required to testify about what she told him.[96]

If a conversation with a lawyer is partly for the purpose of seeking legal advice and partly to obtain personal advice, only the part of the conversation that relates to the legal advice is privileged.

Does the privilege protect only what the client tells the lawyer, or does it protect also what the lawyer tells the client?

The privilege protects communications from the client to the lawyer and from the lawyer to the client.[97] The privilege also protects a confidential memo a lawyer writes for his files or for a co-counsel that includes a record of a privileged communication with the client.

---

96. Restatement § 72, comment c.
97. See Kobluk v. U. of Minn., 574 N.W.2d 436 (Minn. 1998) (drafts of documents by lawyer sent to client for review found privileged).

If a client tells a lawyer some factual information during a privileged conversation, can the client claim privilege to avoid testifying about those facts?

No. The communication with the lawyer is privileged, but the underlying facts are not. The facts might be protected by a different privilege, such as the privilege against self-incrimination. But if other privileges don't apply (for example, if the prosecutor gives the client immunity and thus nullifies the privilege against self-incrimination), and the prosecutor then calls the client to testify, she must tell the truth about the facts.

> **FOR EXAMPLE:**   A client meets with the lawyer who is defending her in a civil automobile accident case. The client confesses to the lawyer that she had taken more than the prescribed dose of a pain-killing drug that causes drowsiness before starting to drive on the day of the accident. Neither the lawyer nor the client could be compelled to testify about what the client told the lawyer. However, if asked whether she had taken the drug that day, and if so, how much she had taken, the client could not invoke the attorney-client privilege to avoid revealing those facts.

If the underlying information isn't privileged, of what use is the privilege to someone who doesn't want to disclose?

It matters a great deal, in many circumstances. First, there are many aspects of lawyer-client communications that involve theories and tactics, not simply facts, so much information is in fact protected. Second, obtaining disclosure of underlying facts isn't so simple. In criminal cases, prosecutors have no right to take depositions from defendants or to force them to take the stand. Therefore they may not obtain information from defendants without granting them immunity from prosecution. If there were no attorney-client privilege, however, a prosecutor might be able to call a defendant's lawyer as a witness and ask what the defendant and the defense counsel said to each other about certain aspects of the case. In civil cases, the parties can use discovery to require each other to testify about the underlying facts, but discovery is expensive and is not always employed. If there were no privilege or work product doctrine (described later in this chapter), a lawyer could simply take the deposition of the other side's lawyer to learn all about the facts, strengths, and weaknesses of an opponent's case.

If a client gives a lawyer a document (say, a copy of a contract) related to the matter on which the client seeks legal advice, the document does not thereby become privileged. The document is a piece of evidence. The lawyer or the client could be compelled to provide a copy of the document to an adverse party.

Does the attorney-client privilege protect any documents?

Yes. Some papers are privileged, but only if the papers themselves are lawyer-client communications for the purpose of obtaining legal advice.

3. Waiver

a. Waiver by the client

The attorney-client privilege can be waived by the client's voluntary revelation of the privileged information to a non-privileged person.

> **FOR EXAMPLE:** A woman named Stephanie Lenz made a 29-second video of her toddler dancing to "Let's Go Crazy" by Prince and posted it on YouTube. Universal Music, which held the copyright, demanded that YouTube remove the video from its website. Lenz sued Universal, claiming that her video was a "fair use" under the copyright law. During the litigation, Lenz sent an e-mail to her mother saying that her lawyer was planning a publicity blitz related to the suit and that any legal fees would come out of the settlement. She sent an e-mail to a friend saying that her lawyer was "salivating" about suing Universal Music. Also, in an online chat with a friend, she said that her lawyer had advised her to sue under federal rather than California law to avoid a retaliatory suit by Universal. At a deposition, she refused to answer questions about her motives for suing and the strategy of the case, but a federal district court held that she had waived the privilege through these social conversations with non-privileged persons.[98]

b. Waiver by the lawyer

Privilege can be waived by the client's lawyer if the client has authorized the waiver. The client could authorize the lawyer to waive privilege by telling the lawyer that he may do so (express authority), by giving the lawyer authority that impliedly includes the authority to waive (implied author-

---

98. See Lenz v. Universal Music Corp., Case C-07-03783JF (N.D. Cal. 2010) (magistrate judge); Plaintiff's Blog, Chats About Case Strategy Destroyed Privilege for Related Information, Lenz v. Universal Music Corp., http://lawprofessors.typepad.com/files/07cv3783_102210-1.pdf (accessed Oct. 16, 2011), 79 U.S.L.W 1670 (2010) (order affirmed by district judge). For the video, see Edenza, "Let's Go Crazy," YouTube (Stephanie Lenz posted Feb. 7, 2007) (available at http://www.youtube.com/user/edenza#p/a/u/1/N1KfJHFWlhQ).

ity), or by making a statement to a third party that the lawyer has the authority to waive privilege (apparent authority). If the lawyer deliberately reveals the information without having express, implied, or apparent authority, the revelation does not effect a waiver of privilege.[99]

During a trial, a lawyer can waive the privilege by failing to invoke it. Suppose that a lawyer's client is examined on the witness stand by opposing counsel, who asks the client a question about a privileged communication. The lawyer could and should claim the privilege unless the client has authorized the lawyer to waive it. A waiver by inaction occurs if the lawyer fails to object and the client answers the question.[100]

c. Waiver by putting privileged communication into issue

The privilege is also waived if the client puts the privileged communication into issue in a case.

> FOR EXAMPLE: If a client sues a lawyer for malpractice and asserts that the lawyer gave her certain incorrect advice, the lawyer may reveal the details of the relevant conversations for the purpose of self-defense.

d. Waiver as to a conversation by disclosure of part of it

If a lawyer or client discloses part of an otherwise privileged lawyer-client communication, a judge might find that the partial disclosure was a waiver of the privilege as to the part of the conversation that relates to the subject matter on which the client volunteered testimony. The reason for this subject matter test is to prevent the client from offering misleading testimony by revealing only a half-truth.

e. Compliance with court orders

If the lawyer thinks that her notes on a conversation with her client are privileged, but a judge says that the communication was never privileged or that the privilege was waived, the judge might order the lawyer to turn over the notes. At that point, the lawyer may turn over the information rather than withhold it because the lawyer's only alternative may be to go to jail for contempt of court. (The same principle applies if a judge orders disclosure of information protected by the ethical rule on confidentiality.) Turning the information over in response to a court order does not waive the issue for purposes of appeal or of other litigation.

---

99. Restatement § 78 and 79.
100. Restatement § 63, comment b, and § 78(3) and comment e.

4. The crime-fraud exception

Does the privilege cover a conversation in which a client asks a lawyer for advice or help in committing a crime or fraud?

No. Even if a lawyer-client conversation satisfies all the criteria above for privilege, no privilege attaches if the client consults a lawyer for assistance in committing a crime or a fraud. Likewise, there is no privilege for a conversation if the client later uses the advice he received from the lawyer during the conversation to commit a crime or a fraud.

> **FOR EXAMPLE:** Suppose a husband consults a lawyer after he shoots his wife and asks what countries he might escape to without risk that he will later be extradited to the United States. This question is a request for legal advice (Which countries do not have extradition treaties with the United States?), so this communication might be privileged. This conversation is not privileged, however, because the client is asking for advice about how to commit the federal crime of flight to avoid prosecution. No privilege attaches even if the client didn't realize that flight to avoid prosecution was criminal.

What if a client asks for advice about a crime she plans to commit but does not ask the lawyer to give advice that assists her in the act?

Clients need to be able to talk in confidence with their lawyers before they commit crimes as well as afterward. Otherwise, lawyers would not have the opportunity to dissuade the clients from committing the crimes. Consequently, a distinction is made between a request for advice that would help a client to commit a crime or to avoid apprehension, and a request for advice about whether a certain act is permitted under the law. In the latter case, the communication is privileged, at least in most states.[101]

If a client asks his lawyer for advice about a past act that was criminal or fraudulent, is that communication privileged?

Yes, such communication is privileged so long as the past act is really past. If there is a continuing crime or fraud that results from a past act, there is no privilege. The crime-fraud exception does not apply to past crimes or frauds.

---

101. There are important state variations in the law of attorney-client privilege, just as there are in the state rules governing confidentiality. For example, in 2003, California amended its law of attorney-client privilege to provide that the privilege does not protect otherwise confidential communications if the lawyer reasonably believes that disclosure is necessary to prevent a criminal act (by the client or anyone else) that is likely to result in death or substantial bodily harm. Cal. Evid. Code § 956.5 (2010).

What if a client consults a lawyer about a plan that she knows involves a crime or fraud but conceals facts from the lawyer that would reveal the illegality of the scheme?

The lawyer's knowledge or intentions are irrelevant. Only the client's intentions are relevant. Such a conversation is not privileged because the client's planned transactions violate the law. If, on the other hand, the lawyer has criminal intent and the client does not, the conversation is privileged. Only the client's intentions are relevant to the privilege.

> FOR EXAMPLE: Suppose the client plans to sell merchandise legally, and the lawyer advises him about how to evade taxes on the transaction illegally. The lawyer does not tell the client that following his tax advice will violate the law. This conversation is privileged because the client has no intent to commit a crime or fraud.

The attorney-client privilege sometimes plays a central role in major litigation. During the 1990s, for example, many states sued companies that made tobacco products to recover the health care costs they had expended over the years for their residents' smoking-related illnesses. In the suits, they sought to discover the research that the companies had done over a period of decades, hoping to learn that the companies knew decades earlier that their products caused heart disease and cancer, and that they suppressed the research. Anticipating that adversary parties would try to pry open their secret research, tobacco companies had put their general counsels in charge of the studies, so that all of the research would consist of employee or contractor reports to a tobacco company's lawyer. Then the companies resisted discovery by invoking the attorney-client privilege.

After extensive litigation of the issue, the tobacco companies' strategy failed. Courts found that the companies had used their attorneys and their privilege claims to defraud the public — essentially by releasing any studies that seemed to show little harm from smoking while burying in the lawyers' offices, perhaps forever, studies showing that tobacco products caused disease and death. The courts found either that the studies were not protected by the privilege to begin with or that they were covered by the crime-fraud exception. As a result, the tobacco companies were forced into settlements under which they agreed to pay more than $200 billion to the states.[102]

---

102. Haines v. Liggett Group, Inc., 140 F.R.D. 681, 695 (D.N.J.), *rev'd on other grounds*, 975 F.2d 81 (3d Cir. 1992); Michael V. Ciresi, Roberta B. Walburn & Tara D. Sutton, Decades of Deceit: Document Discovery in the Minnesota Tobacco Litigation, 25 Wm. Mitchell L. Rev. 477 (1999) (reprinting excerpts from unpublished decisions by courts and special masters in the Minnesota tobacco litigation); Milo Geyelin, Forty-Six States Agree to Accept $206 Billion Tobacco Settlement, Wall St. J. (Nov. 23, 1998).

5. The death of the client

Traditionally, the attorney-client privilege remains in force even if revelation would prevent the wrongful incarceration or execution of an innocent person, and it remains in effect after the client dies. But if the right to waive the privilege belongs to a client who, as a result of death, is no longer able to exercise it, may the client's lawyer choose to reveal the information? Lawyers sometimes believe that they have good reason to do so.

The issue sometimes arises when a client (a criminal defendant or convicted criminal) reveals to his lawyer that he committed a crime of which someone else has been accused, but the client is unwilling to make that confession public. This situation implicates both the duty of confidentiality and the attorney-client privilege. The problem for the lawyer who knows the secret becomes even more difficult if her client dies.[103]

PROBLEM 3-8 **A SECRET CONFESSION**

This problem is based on events that occurred in a mid-Atlantic state in 2007.

You are a criminal defense lawyer representing James Chester. Your client has been charged, along with Martin Parnett, with the murder of Hans and Inez Sosa. Chester and Parnett were part of a marijuana distribution ring; Parnett was the leader. The Sosas were found in their rural home, accessible only by dirt road; they had been shot and had their throats slit. Parnett and Chester were put on trial separately, and Parnett was already tried. He was represented by another lawyer.

There were no eyewitnesses to the murders, but after he received immunity, Tom Willis, another member of the marijuana ring, testified for the prosecution at Parnett's trial. Willis claimed that Parnett had told him, before the murders took place, that Parnett planned to "teach Hans Sosa a lesson" for stealing marijuana from

---

103. The ABA Ethics Committee explored whether a lawyer accused by a former client of having provided ineffective assistance of counsel may defend herself by revealing a client's secret confession to the prosecutor. Although an attack on the former lawyer usually waives the attorney-client privilege for information relevant to the claim, the committee concluded that revelation to a prosecutor is not justified by Rule 1.6(b)(5) unless it is necessary to respond to the former client's allegations. This is true even if the prosecutor asks for the information. The ABA would make an exception for revelation during a court-supervised hearing, during which the former client could object to the disclosure. ABA Standing Comm. on Ethics & Prof. Resp., Formal Op. 10-456 (2010) (available at http://www.americanbar.org/content/dam/aba/migrated/2011_build/professional_responsibility/ethics_opinion_10_456.authcheckdam.pdf).

Parnett's ring. Willis also testified that on the night of the murders, he had dropped Parnett off at the Sosas' house and later picked up Chester and Parnett, both of whom were wearing bloody clothing.

Parnett admitted to his lawyer that he ran the marijuana ring, but insisted that he had never killed anyone. Parnett's mother and aunt testified that Parnett was with them and his infant son the entire evening on the date of the murder. Before the trial ended, though, Parnett entered into a plea agreement with the prosecutor; he pleaded guilty in exchange for the prosecutor's agreement to request a life sentence rather than the death penalty. His sentencing is scheduled for next week.

When you first met with Chester, you explained attorney-client confidentiality and the attorney-client privilege to him. Yesterday, you met again with him to discuss whether you should seek a plea agreement for him. He said that he did not want to confess publicly, but he confessed to you that he alone had killed the Sosas and that Parnett had nothing to do with it. He asked you what he should do. If you advise Chester to reveal that he alone committed the murder, the prosecutor may refuse any plea agreement in which Chester is sentenced to life in prison and may instead seek the death penalty.

Questions

1. May you reveal to the prosecutor, before Parnett is sentenced to life in prison, that Chester has confessed to the killing and exonerated Parnett?
2. Would you have greater discretion to reveal the secret confession if Parnett is going to be sentenced to death rather than to life in prison?
3. Fast-forward 21 years and assume that Parnett has been in prison for that period of time and that you have never revealed what Chester told you. Last week, Chester committed suicide in prison, leaving no family behind. May you now reveal Chester's admission and testify about it if you are asked to do so?
4. Assume that you decide to reveal Chester's confession to Parnett's lawyer. He asks for a new trial for Parnett and, as you expected, subpoenas you to testify at the hearing on the motion for a new trial. During the hearing, you are about to tell the judge about Chester's confession. The judge says, "Stop right there. If you testify, I will be compelled to report you to the state bar for violating your former client's attorney-client privilege, which outlasts his death." (In the real case on which this problem is based, this is what the judge warned.)

a. Is the judge correct in thinking that the state bar would have reason to discipline you for your revelation?

b. What will you do?

F. The work product doctrine

The work product doctrine (which you may have encountered in your civil procedure course) is related to, but quite separate from, the attorney-client privilege. It protects notes and other material that a lawyer prepares "in anticipation of litigation" from discovery in pretrial civil proceedings. The work product doctrine applies to documents that a lawyer prepares or collects while working on pending litigation or on a matter in which the lawyer knows that a lawsuit is about to be filed. For example, the doctrine usually protects statements that a lawyer obtains from witnesses. It protects some types of documents that are not covered by the attorney-client privilege because they do not relate to communications between lawyer and client. Professor Charles Wolfram explains:

> Work product extends to information prepared by a lawyer without regard to whether it was communicated to the lawyer in confidence and without regard to whether the lawyer's client or some other person was its source. The critical element for work product is possession of lawyer-generated information in the lawyer's mind or private files.[104]

Protection of work product is not absolute. Courts are more likely to enforce it in the case of a witness statement, for example, if the lawyer asks questions and takes notes that reflect her strategic thinking in asking the questions rather than merely asking the witness to mail her a statement.

The work product doctrine does not protect materials that a lawyer creates or collects for reasons other than to prepare for litigation. Suppose the general counsel of a corporation routinely keeps records of the reasons for hiring or firing all employees. If one of those employees later sues for wrongful discharge, these records are not protected by this doctrine. On the other hand, if the lawyer does not routinely keep records of the reasons for all employee discharges but collects information only after discharged employees threaten to sue the corporation, the doctrine applies. In other words, it is only the lawyer's need to use the information in litigation that creates a degree of protection.

---

104. Charles W. Wolfram, Modern Legal Ethics § 6.6.3, at 296 (West 1986).

Lawyers who work in the office of a corporate general counsel often collect information for more than one purpose. If certain information would have been collected routinely but was also collected because litigation was anticipated, most courts will deny protection to the information.

A judge can order disclosure of written or oral information otherwise protected by this doctrine when the opposing party can show "substantial need" for the material and is "unable without undue hardship to obtain the substantial equivalent" of the material by other means.[105] This is a rather vague standard, so an attorney can never be certain that particular work product will, in the end, be protected. In practice, an opponent may try to prove "undue hardship" by showing that a witness from whom an opposing attorney obtained information (for example, a witness statement) is unavailable (for example, dead) or hostile, or that through no fault of the seeking attorney, records of the event, other than those in the hands of the attorney asserting the protection of the work product doctrine, no longer exist.

The doctrine gives stronger protection to work product that reveals the lawyer's thoughts, strategies, or mental impressions than it does to other forms of work product. A lawyer's notes of his own opinions, theories, observations, or feelings are immune from discovery.

The protection offered by the work product doctrine is not as powerful as it might seem at first blush. A lawyer often can get the information contained in protected documents from the original witnesses or sources. If an opposing counsel collects questionnaires from a group of witnesses, a lawyer can develop her own questionnaire and contact the same witnesses (so long as contact is allowed under Rule 4.2 or the lawyer uses permitted discovery techniques). The doctrine prevents freeloading on an opponent's work, but it does not enable the opponent to close off a lawyer's sources of information by getting there first.

The Federal Rules of Civil Procedure require experts who will testify at trial to provide to opposing counsel, in advance, summaries of the facts and opinions they will discuss. However, work product protection is given to their working drafts and to many of their communications with the attorneys who hired them. Experts who are merely consultants and not expected to testify are given even greater work product protection for their communications with attorneys.[106]

---

105. Fed. R. Civ. P. 26(b)(3).
106. Fed. R. Civ. P. 26(a)(2)(B) and (b)(4)(B), (C), and (D).

G. The attorney-client privilege for corporations

1. The *Upjohn* case

Corporate clients, like individual clients, may invoke an attorney-client privilege. Lawyers rarely question whether corporations should be able to invoke this privilege, but the scope of the privilege for corporate clients has been controversial. For a long time, only the communications between the senior officers who controlled a corporation (the so-called control group) and the corporation's lawyers were thought to be privileged. In the early 1980s, in *Upjohn Co. v. United States*, the U.S. Supreme Court decided that — in federal proceedings applying federal law — the scope of the privilege should depend on the subject matter of the communication, not on who was doing the communicating.[107] Senior officers of Upjohn, a drug manufacturer, had discovered that a company subsidiary had paid bribes to foreign government officials to obtain government business. Upjohn's General Counsel's office conducted an internal investigation. Its lawyers sent a questionnaire to many employees and also interviewed 33 of them. Subsequently, the SEC issued a subpoena requesting the completed questionnaires and interview notes. Upjohn claimed privilege, though the prevailing rule at the time was that only communications between lawyers and senior officials of a corporation — those who controlled its policies — were privileged. The Supreme Court reasoned that

> [i]n the corporate context . . . it will frequently be employees beyond the control group . . . who will possess the information needed by the corporation's lawyers. Middle-level — and indeed lower-level — employees can . . . embroil the corporation in serious legal difficulties, and it is only natural that these employees would have the relevant information needed by corporate counsel if he is adequately to advise the client with respect to such actual or potential difficulties.

It therefore ruled that the communications between lawyers and the lower-level employees who had knowledge of the bribery were privileged. It noted that the government could repeat Upjohn's internal investigation by taking depositions of each of the employees, as the underlying information was not privileged. The Court seemed unconcerned with the fact that the SEC operated on a limited budget and that its new rule would as a practical matter prevent many investigations and prosecutions from going forward.

---

107. Upjohn Co. v. U.S., 449 U.S. 383, 386 (1981). Although the decision has widely been acknowledged to have decided this question, the Court expressed some hesitancy in its opinion about whether it was actually ruling on the scope of the privilege. Id at 383, 386 (1981).

The Supreme Court did not spell out in detail what communications are privileged. But the Eighth Circuit's *Diversified Industries* case, which the Court cited with apparent approval, held that the privilege applies when these conditions are met: (1) the communication is made for the purpose of securing legal advice; (2) the employee making the communication does so at the direction of his corporate superior; (3) the superior makes the request so that the corporation could secure legal advice; (4) the subject matter of the communication is within the scope of the employee's corporate duties; and (5) the communication is not disseminated beyond those persons who, because of the corporate structure, need to know its contents.[108]

2. Governmental requests for waiver of privilege

The *Upjohn* opinion allowed corporations a fairly broad privilege to facilitate open communication between employees and their employers' lawyers. In the years after the decision, however, federal prosecutors investigating corporations strongly encouraged corporations under investigation to waive the privilege, disclose the products of their internal investigation, and be rewarded with lesser penalties for doing so. This practice circumvented *Upjohn* and posed ethical problems for corporate lawyers conducting internal investigations and practical difficulties for the employees whose conduct is being investigated. If the FBI questions an employee who may have participated in a crime such as bribery or fraud, the employee is likely to be on guard and hire a lawyer. But if the employer's lawyer does the questioning, the employee may be more trusting; she may know the lawyer or may not understand that the lawyer serves the corporation rather than its employees. She may not realize that the corporation could waive its protections and provide her disclosures to prosecutors. Alternatively, she may cooperate simply because she could be fired for refusing to do so. As a result, the employee may unwittingly provide information that she could have kept from the government by invoking her Fifth Amendment privileges against self-incrimination. She may also end up becoming "a corporate scapegoat" while a more senior management official manages to keep quiet and stay out of trouble. An investigating lawyer needs to know how and when to disclose that he represents the corporation (which might waive the attorney-client privilege) and when to advise an employee of the possible need to retain her own attorney.[109]

---

108. Diversified Indus. v. Meredith, 572 F.2d 596, 609 (8th Cir. 1977).

109. Sarah Helene Duggin, Internal Corporate Investigations: Legal Ethics, Professionalism, and the Employee Interview, 2003 Colum. Bus. L. Rev. 859, 862-865, 899-902, 907-912.

The ABA and many members of Congress complained bitterly about governmental requests to corporations that they waive the privilege and turn over the results of their internal investigations in exchange for possible lenient treatment. After several years of controversy, the Bush administration backed down. In 2008, it announced that federal prosecutors would no longer consider whether a corporation waived the attorney-client privilege in their decisions on whether to be lenient when charging the corporation with criminal conduct:

> [C]redit for cooperation will not depend on whether a corporation has waived attorney-client privilege or work product protection, or produced materials protected by attorney-client or work product protections. It will depend on the disclosure of facts. Corporations that timely disclose relevant facts may receive due credit for cooperation, regardless of whether they waive attorney-client privilege or work product protection in the process. Corporations that do not disclose relevant facts typically may not receive such credit, just like any other defendant.[110]

Federal prosecutors also would no longer take into account whether a corporation paid attorneys' fees for employees who were caught up in an investigation, whether the corporation had entered into a joint defense agreement with them, or whether the corporation had disciplined the employees.[111]

Even after this retreat, the ABA and others have continued to press for legislation to restrict the government permanently from seeking waivers of corporate privilege and to bind all federal agencies, not just the Department of Justice.[112] Meanwhile, the advisability of and impact of the 2008 policy change remain unclear. Professor Michael Ariens bemoans the policy change, claiming that Americans have too soon forgotten the Enron and other corporate scandals that led to increased prosecution of corporate crime:

> The ABA continues to claim, with the slimmest evidence, that nearly all of the government has created a "culture of waiver." . . . [It has] used claims of public interest to protect the interests of corporations, most of them large and publicly traded.[113]

---

110. Press statement of Deputy Attorney General Mark R. Filip (Aug. 28, 2008) (*available at* http://www.justice.gov/archive/dag/speeches/2008/dag-speech-0808286.html).

111. Id.

112. Justice Department Eases Policy on Waiver of Privileges by Corporations, 77 U.S.L.W. 2133 (Sept. 9, 2008).

113. Michael Ariens, "Playing Chicken": An Instant History of the Battle over Exceptions to Client Confidences, 33 J. Leg. Prof. 239, 294 (2009).

Professor Katrice Copeland, on the other hand, argues that the new policy does not go far enough and echoes the cry for new legislation, urging that the Department of Justice's policy change will prove to be illusory:

> If facts are understood to . . . include interview memoranda, factual chronologies created by counsel, and reports containing investigative facts, then providing those facts would probably lead to a full waiver of the attorney-client privilege.[114]

PROBLEM 3-9 WORLDWIDE BRIBERY

This problem presents facts similar to those of the Upjohn *case but asks you to consider how the analysis would be affected by current Justice Department policy.*

You are the general counsel of the Horizon Corp., a publicly traded company that manufactures cell phones and sells them worldwide. An employee told you that some officers of the corporation had been directing bribes to officials of foreign governments in violation of U.S. law. You directed the lawyers on your staff to interview officers and employees throughout the company. They verified that officers of the company had engaged in rampant bribery. Your staff interviewed the officers who had engaged in the bribery (most of whom claimed that Valerie Patel, the president of the company, knew about the bribes and silently condoned them). They wrote memoranda to you describing those interviews. They also made copies of records that were created while the bribery was taking place. The records showed which company officials paid bribes, along with the dates, amounts, and recipients of each bribe.

You wrote a report about your investigation and sent it to Patel. Your report began with the words, "This report is covered by the attorney-client privilege and is attorney work product." The report summarized all of the facts that you learned and concluded that the corporation had probably committed several felonies, for which severe penalties might be imposed if it were prosecuted. Corporate officers such as Patel might be prosecuted as well. The report also warned that if Patel turned it over to prosecutors, stockholders who sued the company could probably obtain it as well because the attorney-client privilege could not be waived selectively. Attachments to the report included all of the interview summaries that

---

114. Katrice Bridges Copeland, Preserving the Corporate Attorney-Client Privilege, 78 U. Cin. L. Rev. 1199, 1231 (2010).

your staff made and the corporate records that they collected. Then you and Patel jointly sent a memo to all corporate employees directing them not to participate in bribery, even in countries where it is accepted as a routine business practice. You and Patel also agreed that you would contact the U.S. attorney, admit in general terms that bribery had occurred, and offer to pay a civil fine to avoid criminal prosecution.

The U.S. attorney responded that he could not consider plea bargaining unless you first gave him "all the facts" uncovered in your internal investigation, including summaries of any interviews conducted during the internal investigation and all of the relevant documents that had been located. He was confident that Horizon would want to cooperate with his investigation, he said, so that it would receive favorable consideration. He explained that he was not asking the corporation to waive attorney-client privilege or to reveal any document covered by work product protection, such as your covering memorandum to Patel, because such a request was forbidden under current Department of Justice policy. But he added, "If you decline to provide the interview summaries and records of bribery, we will open our own investigation, and you can expect to receive a grand jury subpoena. We will take the corporation's lack of full disclosure into account, just as we would with any criminal defendant."

After tearing out some of her hair, Patel asks you to advise her about what she should do.

————————————————

4 Relationships Between Lawyers and Clients

     E. Terminating a lawyer-client relationship
        1. Duties to the client at the conclusion of the relationship
        2. Grounds for termination before the work is completed

This chapter explores the basic elements of the lawyer-client relationship. We begin by describing how the lawyer-client relationship is established. Then we explain the application of agency law to the lawyer-client relationship. The chapter next reviews the duties of competence, candor, communication, and diligence, which are among the most important responsibilities of lawyers to their clients. (Recall that we explored the duty to protect confidences in Chapter 3. Chapters 5 through 9 examine the duty of loyalty.)

In any lawyer-client relationship, some decisions are made by the lawyer and some are made by the client. This chapter explores when a lawyer must consult with a client or defer to a client's wishes. If the client has a mental impairment or is a juvenile, the question of how much a lawyer should defer to a client is more complex. This chapter examines these questions as well. We conclude with consideration of the rules that govern termination of lawyer-client relationships and the duties of lawyers toward clients at the end of those relationships.

A. Formation of the lawyer-client relationship

1. Choosing clients

Many lawyer-client relationships begin in a very straightforward manner. A client comes to a lawyer's office, explains the problem, signs an agreement, and pays a fee; the lawyer then goes to work. But sometimes complications occur. A lawyer may be precluded from taking on the work because of a conflict of interest, a lack of expertise, or another problem. The lawyer may prefer not to represent the client because he dislikes the prospective client or disagrees with the goal of the representation. What happens then? The issues are discussed below.

Is a lawyer permitted to accept legal work that requires knowledge of an area of law in which the lawyer has no experience?

Yes, if the lawyer compensates for inexperience through study or affiliation with another lawyer. Rule 1.1 of the ethics codes, which is discussed later in this chapter, requires lawyers to provide competent representation. The question is whether a lawyer who has never handled a particular type of matter before can fulfill this duty. Comment 2 to Rule 1.1 explains that a lawyer can take on a matter in an unfamiliar field if the lawyer has the time and resources to get up to speed.

> A lawyer need not necessarily have special training or prior experience to handle legal problems of a type with which the lawyer is unfamiliar. A newly admitted lawyer can be as competent as a practitioner with long experience. . . . A lawyer can provide adequate representation in a wholly novel field through necessary study. Competent representation can also be provided through the association of a lawyer of established competence in the field in question.

Must a lawyer turn down a request for legal assistance if he lacks time, expertise, or interest in the matter?

A lawyer may take on work in a new field only if he does the necessary study.

> **FOR EXAMPLE:** After Hurricane Katrina devastated much of New Orleans and the Mississippi Delta, Louisiana lawyers sought to set up a victims' hotline and to staff a booth to provide free legal assistance to people who had been forced to flee from their homes and businesses. The Louisiana Bar ethics committee wrote an advisory opinion cautioning that lawyers should not participate unless they had the knowledge, skill, and preparation necessary to provide competent advice on the subjects in which advice was being sought. The ethics committee urged participating lawyers to decline to offer advice on matters outside their competence "compassionately but firmly."[1]

May a lawyer who does extensive self-education to prepare to represent a client in a new field bill a client for that study time?

Lawyers who bill by the hour routinely charge for time spent on research, but a lawyer may be subject to discipline if the lawyer bills the client for spending an unreasonable amount of time on research, especially if the research does not lead to worthwhile progress in the matter.

A lawyer who takes on a matter in an unfamiliar field would be well advised to discuss with the client that the lawyer will need to spend time "getting up to speed," and to reach an explicit agreement with the client about whether and how much the client will be billed for that time. Clear

---

1. La. State B. Assn. R. of Prof. Conduct Comm., Op. 05-RPCC-005 (available at http://www.lsba.org/DocumentIndex/EthicOpinions/05-005RPCC.pdf).

and regular communication (including monthly billing statements) can avoid many conflicts with clients.

Can an inexperienced associate assume that her firm is providing competent service if she is keeping a partner informed about her work on the matter?

Not necessarily. It may depend on how assiduously she insists on genuine supervision.

> **FOR EXAMPLE:** A company hired a Connecticut law firm to assist it in selling health club franchises in Connecticut. A partner in the firm assured an officer of the company that the firm was expert in this area of law. The partner then assigned the matter to an inexperienced associate. The associate sent the partner copies of her work product and assumed, incorrectly, that the partner was reading and evaluating it. The firm never advised the company that it had to register with the state; its failure to register eventually destroyed its business. It sued the law firm and the lawyers for malpractice. Referring to Rule 1.1, a court held that the associate as well as the partner had committed malpractice.[2] The associate escaped a $16 million damage award, however, because the appellate court ruled that the company's claim for lost profits was too speculative.

Is a lawyer obliged to help a client who wants to hire him?

In general, lawyers are allowed the discretion to decide whom to represent. They don't have to accept any particular clients and may craft their practices according to their interests and aspirations. Likewise, a lawyer may represent a client but limit the scope of the work according to the lawyer's wishes and abilities.[3] However, there are several caveats to these propositions.

Rule 6.1, which is discussed in Chapter 12, addresses lawyers' duty to provide legal assistance to people who are not able to pay for it. The rule says that lawyers should "aspire" to provide at least 50 hours per year of pro bono representation. This rule does not compel a lawyer to represent or assist any particular indigent person but urges lawyers to assist some clients in this category. A comment after Rule 6.1 mentions the desirability of representing unpopular clients:

---

2. Beverly Hills Concepts, Inc. v. Schatz & Schatz, Ribicoff & Kotkin, 717 A.2d 724, 730, 734-740 (Conn. 1988). The case is discussed in Douglas R. Richmond, Professional Responsibilities of Law Firm Associates, 45 Brandeis L.J. 199 (2007).

3. Rule 1.2(c).

> All lawyers have a responsibility to assist in providing pro bono publico service. See Rule 6.1. An individual lawyer fulfills this responsibility by accepting a fair share of unpopular matters or indigent or unpopular clients.[4]

No lawyer is obliged to accept representation of a client "whose character or cause the lawyer regards as repugnant," even if a judge asks the lawyer to accept a particular matter.[5] If a lawyer undertakes representation of an unpopular or disagreeable client, Rule 1.2(b) explains that the lawyer's representation of that client "does not constitute an endorsement of the client's political, economic, social or moral views or activities."[6]

Lawyers are seldom criticized for declining to represent unpopular clients because such decisions are made behind closed doors. Occasionally, public discussion ensues when a lawyer accepts representation of an unpopular client and then backs out of the representation because of reputational or business concerns.

> **FOR EXAMPLE:** In 2011, the Obama administration, although believing the Defense of Marriage Act (which barred the federal government from recognizing the validity of gay marriages) to be unconstitutional, declined to defend the law in court. The House of Representatives then enlisted the respected law firm of King & Spalding to defend the law. After gay rights groups protested, King & Spalding withdrew from handling the matter. One partner who had been working on the matter then resigned from the firm and joined a different firm that would allow him to complete the work. Professor Stephen Gillers criticized the firm's decision to back away from a client because of public pressure, saying that the "firm's timidity here will hurt weak clients, poor clients and despised clients."[7]

A court may assign a lawyer to represent an indigent criminal defendant, even if the court does not have the resources to pay the lawyer for the work. Rule 6.2 directs lawyers to accept such assignments except for "good cause." Rule 6.2 and court appointment also are discussed in Chapter 12.

A second constraint on a lawyer's freedom arises from Rules 1.2 and 1.16. A lawyer may not agree to represent a client if the assistance sought by the client would involve the lawyer in a violation of law or of the professional ethics rules.[8] If a lawyer takes on representation of a client, the lawyer may not "counsel a client to engage, or assist a client, in conduct that the

---

4. Rule 6.1, Comment 1.

5. Rule 6.2, Comment 1.

6. Rule 1.2(b)

7. Michael D. Shear & John Schwartz, Law Firm Won't Defend Marriage Act, N.Y. Times (Apr. 25, 2011) (available at http://www.nytimes.com/2011/04/26/us/politics/26marriage.html?_ r = 1& ref = us).

8. Rule 1.16(a)(1).

lawyer knows is criminal or fraudulent."[9] If the client insists on advice or action by the lawyer that would constitute assistance with a criminal or fraudulent act or a violation of the ethics code, the lawyer must withdraw from representation of the client.[10]

Finally, lawyers providing legal services may be bound not to reject clients for discriminatory reasons. At least one court has held that a lawyer may not discriminate on the basis of race, religion, nationality, sex, age, disability, or another protected category in her decisions about which clients to represent.[11]

What should a lawyer tell a prospective client about the possible downsides of hiring the lawyer before agreeing to do legal work for the client?

Professor Fred Zacharias notes that the Model Rules have little to say about lawyers' pre-employment discussions with clients. He argues that more guidance is needed because at this stage, in particular, lawyers and clients have conflicting interests. Lawyers generally are eager to be retained and to earn fees, while clients might be best served by shopping around or refraining from using legal services. Zacharias quite reasonably queries whether a lawyer should be obliged to reveal to a prospective client his belief that the client might obtain similar services elsewhere for a lower price, that she could resolve her problem without using legal services at all, that she should consider hiring a different lawyer with more experience in the relevant area of law, or that she has a hopeless case and should settle immediately rather than wasting money on legal fees.[12]

2. Offering advice as the basis for a lawyer-client relationship

To form a lawyer-client relationship, must the client sign an agreement or pay a fee?

No. An agreement to pay a fee is not a necessary aspect of a lawyer-client relationship. Many lawyers represent clients without charging fees. Lawyers have the same duties to pro bono clients as they do to paying clients. Also, a

---

9. Rule 1.2(d). The lawyer may discuss a potentially unlawful course of conduct with a client, but may not counsel or assist that conduct unless the client is seeking to test the validity or meaning of the law in question. Id. and Comment 12.

10. Rule 1.16(a)(1).

11. See Nathanson v. Mass. Commn. Against Discrimination, 16 Mass. L. Rptr. 761 (Super. Ct. 2003) (affirming an administrative order to female divorce attorney to "cease and desist from engaging in discriminatory conduct" by refusing to accept male clients).

12. Fred C. Zacharias, The Preemployment Ethical Role of Lawyers: Are Lawyers Really Fiduciaries?, 49 Wm. & Mary L. Rev. 569 (2007).

person can become a client of a lawyer without signing a written agreement. When a person seeks legal advice or legal services from a lawyer, and the lawyer receives confidences, gives legal advice, or provides legal services, the lawyer may owe some professional duties to the other person. A lawyer, therefore, must be careful about what casual advice or assistance she provides to others.

The ethics codes express this in terms of "duties to prospective clients." They make clear that once a lawyer begins a conversation with a prospective client, some professional duties attach.

Consider the following case.

Togstad v. Vesely, Otto, Miller & Keefe

291 N.W.2d 686 (Minn. 1980)

PER CURIAM . . .

In August 1971, John Togstad began to experience severe headaches and on August 16, 1971, was admitted to Methodist Hospital where tests disclosed that the headaches were caused by a large aneurism on the left internal carotid artery. The attending physician, Dr. Paul Blake, a neurological surgeon, treated the problem by applying a Selverstone clamp to the left common carotid artery. The clamp was surgically implanted on August 27, 1971, in Togstad's neck to allow the gradual closure of the artery over a period of days.

The treatment was designed to eventually cut off the blood supply through the artery and thus relieve the pressure on the aneurism, allowing the aneurism to heal. It was anticipated that other arteries, as well as the brain's collateral or cross-arterial system would supply the required blood to the portion of the brain which would ordinarily have been provided by the left carotid artery. The greatest risk associated with this procedure is that the patient may become paralyzed if the brain does not receive an adequate flow of blood. In the event the supply of blood becomes so low as to endanger the health of the patient, the adjustable clamp can be opened to establish the proper blood circulation.

In the early morning hours of August 29, 1971, a nurse observed that Togstad was unable to speak or move. At the time, the clamp was one-half (50%) closed. Upon discovering Togstad's condition, the nurse called a resident physician, who did not adjust the clamp. Dr. Blake was also immediately informed of Togstad's condition and arrived about an hour later, at which time he opened the clamp. Togstad is now severely paralyzed in his right arm and leg, and is unable to speak.

Plaintiffs' expert, Dr. Ward Woods, testified that Togstad's paralysis and loss of speech was due to a lack of blood supply to his brain. Dr. Woods stated that the inadequate blood flow resulted from the clamp being 50%

closed and that the negligence of Dr. Blake and the hospital precluded the clamp's being opened in time to avoid permanent brain damage. . . .

Dr. Blake and defendants' expert witness, Dr. Shelly Chou, testified that Togstad's condition was caused by blood clots going up the carotid artery to the brain. They both alleged that the blood clots were not a result of the Selverstone clamp procedure. . . .

[The legal consultation]

About 14 months after her husband's hospitalization began, plaintiff Joan Togstad met with attorney Jerre Miller regarding her husband's condition. Neither she nor her husband was personally acquainted with Miller or his law firm prior to that time. John Togstad's former work supervisor, Ted Bucholz, made the appointment and accompanied Mrs. Togstad to Miller's office. Bucholz was present when Mrs. Togstad and Miller discussed the case.

Mrs. Togstad had become suspicious of the circumstances surrounding her husband's tragic condition due to the conduct and statements of the hospital nurses shortly after the paralysis occurred. One nurse told Mrs. Togstad that she had checked Mr. Togstad at 2 A.M. and he was fine; that when she returned at 3 A.M., by mistake, to give him someone else's medication, he was unable to move or speak; and that if she hadn't accidentally entered the room no one would have discovered his condition until morning. Mrs. Togstad also noticed that the other nurses were upset and crying, and that Mr. Togstad's condition was a topic of conversation.

Mrs. Togstad testified that she told Miller "everything that happened at the hospital," including the nurses' statements and conduct which had raised a question in her mind. She stated that she "believed" she had told Miller "about the procedure and what was undertaken, what was done, and what happened." She brought no records with her.

Miller took notes and asked questions during the meeting, which lasted 45 minutes to an hour. At its conclusion, according to Mrs. Togstad, Miller said that "he did not think we had a legal case, however, he was going to discuss this with his partner." She understood that if Miller changed his mind after talking to his partner, he would call her. Mrs. Togstad "gave it" a few days and, since she did not hear from Miller, decided "that they had come to the conclusion that there wasn't a case." No fee arrangements were discussed, no medical authorizations were requested, nor was Mrs. Togstad billed for the interview.

Mrs. Togstad . . . did not consult another attorney until one year after she talked to Miller. Mrs. Togstad indicated that she did not confer with another attorney [until a year later] because of her reliance on Miller's "legal advice" that they "did not have a case." [But by the time she saw another lawyer, the two-year statute of limitations for a suit against Dr. Blake and the hospital had run. Mr. and Mrs. Togstad sued Miller's law firm for malpractice.]

[The suit against Miller's law firm]

On cross-examination, Mrs. Togstad was asked whether she went to Miller's office "to see if he would take the case of (her) husband. . . ." She replied, "Well, I guess it was to go for legal advice, what to do, where shall we go from here? That is what we went for." Again in response to defense counsel's questions, Mrs. Togstad testified as follows:

Q: And it was clear to you, was it not, that what was taking place was a preliminary discussion between a prospective client and lawyer as to whether or not they wanted to enter into an attorney-client relationship?

A: I am not sure how to answer that. It was for legal advice as to what to do.

Q: And Mr. Miller was discussing with you your problem and indicating whether he, as a lawyer, wished to take the case, isn't that true?

A: Yes.

On re-direct examination, Mrs. Togstad acknowledged that when she left Miller's office she understood that she had been given a "qualified, quality legal opinion that (she and her husband) did not have a malpractice case." . . .

Miller's testimony was different in some respects from that of Mrs. Togstad. . . . According to Miller, Mrs. Togstad described the hospital incident, including the conduct of the nurses. He asked her questions, to which she responded. Miller testified that "[t]he only thing I told her [Mrs. Togstad] after we had pretty much finished the conversation was that there was nothing related in her factual circumstances that told me that she had a case that our firm would be interested in undertaking." . . . Miller stated that at the end of the conference he told Mrs. Togstad that he would consult with Charles Hvass and if Hvass's opinion differed from his, Miller would so inform her. Miller recollected that he called Hvass a "couple days" later and discussed the case with him. It was Miller's impression that Hvass thought there was no liability for malpractice in the case. Consequently, Miller did not communicate with Mrs. Togstad further.

On cross-examination, Miller testified . . . :

Q: You understood that . . . she was seeking legal advice from a professional attorney licensed to practice in this state and in this community?

A: I think you and I did have another interpretation or use of the term "Advice." She was there to see whether or not she had a case and whether the firm would accept it.

Q: We have two aspects; number one, your legal opinion concerning liability of a case for malpractice; number two, whether there was or wasn't liability, whether you would accept it, your firm, two separate elements, right?

A: I would say so.

Q: Were you asked on page 6 in the deposition, folio 14, "And you understood that she was seeking legal advice at the time that she was in your office, that is correct also, isn't it?" And did you give this answer, "I don't want to engage in semantics with you, but my impression was that she and Mr. Bucholz were asking my opinion after having related the incident that I referred to." The next question, "Your legal opinion?" Your answer, "Yes." Were those questions asked and were they given?

MR. COLLINS: Objection to this, Your Honor. It is not impeachment.

THE COURT: Overruled.

THE WITNESS: Yes, I gave those answers. Certainly, she was seeking my opinion as an attorney in the sense of whether or not there was a case that the firm would be interested in undertaking.

Kenneth Green, a Minneapolis attorney, was called as an expert by plaintiffs. He stated that in rendering legal advice regarding a claim of medical malpractice, the "minimum" an attorney should do would be to request medical authorizations from the client, review the hospital records, and consult with an expert in the field. John McNulty, a Minneapolis attorney, and Charles Hvass testified as experts on behalf of the defendants. McNulty stated that when an attorney is consulted as to whether he will take a case, the lawyer's only responsibility in refusing it is to so inform the party. He testified, however, that when a lawyer is asked his legal opinion on the merits of a medical malpractice claim, community standards require that the attorney check hospital records and consult with an expert before rendering his opinion.

Hvass stated that he had no recollection of Miller's calling him in October 1972 relative to the Togstad matter. He testified that

when a person comes in to me about a medical malpractice action, based upon what the individual has told me, I have to make a decision as to whether or not there probably is or probably is not, based upon that information, medical malpractice. And if, in my judgment, based upon what the client has told me, there is not medical malpractice, I will so inform the client.

Hvass stated, however, that he would never render a "categorical" opinion. In addition, Hvass acknowledged that if he were consulted for a "legal opinion" regarding medical malpractice and 14 months had expired since the incident in question, "ordinary care and diligence" would require him to inform the party of the two-year statute of limitations applicable to that type of action. . . .

The jury found that Dr. Blake's negligence . . . was a direct cause of the injuries sustained by John Togstad; that there was an attorney-client contractual relationship between Mrs. Togstad and Miller; that Miller was negligent in rendering advice regarding the possible claims of Mr. and Mrs. Togstad; that, but for Miller's negligence, plaintiffs would have been successful in the prosecution of a legal action against Dr. Blake; and that neither Mr. nor Mrs. Togstad was negligent in pursuing their claims against Dr. Blake. The jury awarded damages to Mr. Togstad of $610,500 and to Mrs. Togstad of $39,000 [for loss of consortium]. . . .

[The legal standard]

In a legal malpractice action of the type involved here, four elements must be shown: (1) that an attorney-client relationship existed; (2) that defendant acted negligently or in breach of contract; (3) that such acts were the proximate cause of the plaintiffs' damages; (4) that but for defendant's conduct the plaintiffs would have been successful in the prosecution of their medical malpractice claim. . . . *elements*

We believe it is unnecessary to decide whether a tort or contract theory is preferable for resolving the attorney-client relationship question raised by this appeal. The tort and contract analyses are very similar in a case such as the instant one,[13] and we conclude that under either theory the evidence shows that a lawyer-client relationship is present here. The thrust of Mrs. Togstad's testimony is that she went to Miller for legal advice, was told there wasn't a case, and relied upon this advice in failing to pursue the claim for medical malpractice. In addition, according to Mrs. Togstad, Miller did not qualify his legal opinion by urging her to seek advice from another attorney, nor did Miller inform her that he lacked expertise in the medical malpractice area. Assuming this testimony is true, as this court must do,[14]

---

13. [Court's footnote 4.] Under a negligence approach it must essentially be shown that defendant rendered legal advice (not necessarily at someone's request) under circumstances which made it reasonably foreseeable to the attorney that if such advice was rendered negligently, the individual receiving the advice might be injured thereby. See, e.g., Palsgraf v. Long Island R. Co., 248 N.Y. 339, 162 N.E. 99, 59 A.L.R. 1253 (1928). Or, stated another way, under a tort theory, "[a]n attorney-client relationship is created whenever an individual seeks and receives legal advice from an attorney in circumstances in which a reasonable person would rely on such advice." 63 Minn. L. Rev. 751, 759 (1979). A contract analysis requires the rendering of legal advice pursuant to another's request and the reliance factor, in this case, where the advice was not paid for, need be shown in the form of promissory estoppel. See 7 C.J.S., Attorney and Client, §65; Restatement (Second) of Contracts, §90.

14. [Court's footnote 5.] . . . [I]n determining whether the jury's verdict is reasonably supported by the record a court must view the credibility of evidence and every inference which may fairly be drawn therefrom in a light most favorable to the prevailing party.

we believe a jury could properly find that Mrs. Togstad sought and received legal advice from Miller under circumstances which made it reasonably foreseeable to Miller that Mrs. Togstad would be injured if the advice were negligently given. Thus, under either a tort or contract analysis, there is sufficient evidence in the record to support the existence of an attorney-client relationship. . . .

Defendants argue that even if an attorney-client relationship was established the evidence fails to show that Miller acted negligently in assessing the merits of the Togstads' case. They appear to contend that, at most, Miller was guilty of an error in judgment which does not give rise to legal malpractice. However, this case does not involve a mere error of judgment. The gist of plaintiffs' claim is that Miller failed to perform the minimal research that an ordinarily prudent attorney would do before rendering legal advice in a case of this nature. The record, through the testimony of Kenneth Green and John McNulty, contains sufficient evidence to support plaintiffs' position. . . .

It was reasonable for a jury to determine that Miller acted negligently in failing to inform Mrs. Togstad of the applicable limitations period. . . . There is also sufficient evidence in the record establishing that, but for Miller's negligence, plaintiffs would have been successful in prosecuting their medical malpractice claim. Dr. Woods, in no uncertain terms, concluded that Mr. Togstad's injuries were caused by the medical malpractice of Dr. Blake. Defendants' expert testimony to the contrary was obviously not believed by the jury. Thus, the jury reasonably found that had plaintiff's medical malpractice action been properly brought, plaintiffs would have recovered.

Based on the foregoing, we hold that the jury's findings are adequately supported by the record. . . .

Affirmed.

Notes and Questions about *Togstad*

1. **The court says, "a lawyer-client relationship is present here" and it spends some time justifying that conclusion. Why was it important that there was "a lawyer-client relationship"?** The Togstads could have sued Miller for negligence if he'd run over them with his car, even if there had been no such relationship. Why couldn't the Togstads win their case against Miller for his negligent advice if the court had concluded that there was no lawyer-client relationship?

    State negligence law usually asks whether the defendant had a duty to the plaintiff, whether the defendant breached the duty, whether the breach proximately caused the injury, and whether the plaintiff was damaged. In the case of automobile accidents or other events causing physical injury, the defendant is said to have had a duty to the plaintiff because people have a duty to use ordinary care so that they do not negligently kill or injure strangers on the street. However, if the harm is solely economic (such as the harm caused by providing faulty information), the law of most states requires a relationship between the parties closer than that of strangers before it imposes liability for conduct that is merely negligent and not deliberate or willful.[15]

2. **Fair to Miller?** Mrs. Togstad asked Miller whether she had a case. He gave her his honest opinion that she did not. He never said he was her lawyer or was willing to become her lawyer, never signed any agreement with her, and never charged her a dime. Yet his firm ended up having to pay $649,500. Is this a fair decision?

3. **Mr. Togstad's claim.** Miller met Mrs. Togstad in his office. He never laid eyes on or spoke to her paralyzed husband. Yet apparently Mr. Togstad also became his client, and in fact, most of the judgment was awarded to him. When Mrs. Togstad consulted Miller, she was doing so on behalf of her paralyzed husband as well as on her own behalf. Miller had reason to know that Mrs. Togstad would communicate his advice to her husband, or that if she had been appointed her husband's legal guardian, she would act on the advice on his behalf. Miller's advice to Mrs. Togstad was advice to Mr. Togstad as well.

4. **What's the test of a lawyer-client relationship?** If someone can become your client (and can sue you for malpractice) even though you don't even discuss the terms of the representation, much less sign a written agreement, it is important to know exactly what conduct triggers the creation of a lawyer-client relationship. Where does this opinion draw the line?

5. **What could Miller have done?** How could Miller have avoided this liability?

6. **The possible relevance of Rule 1.18.** This case was decided before the issuance of Rule 1.18, under which certain persons who discuss their potential cases with lawyers become "prospective clients." Rule 1.18 (discussed in Chapter 5) provides that lawyers have some duties to prospective clients, though not all the duties that they owe to clients. The rule imposes certain duties to keep prospective clients' confidences and certain duties not to represent clients — specifically, a duty of confidentiality and to avoid certain conflicts of interest

---

15. See generally Restatement (Second) of Torts § 282, annotations (1965).

with the prospective client by representing persons with adverse interests. But Rule 1.18 does not mention a duty to give competent advice to the prospective client, and like other rules, it does not purport to impose malpractice liability if incompetent advice is given. How, if at all, would Rule 1.18 affect a case like *Togstad* if such a case arose today?

B. Lawyers' responsibilities as agents

Lawyers are the "agents" of their clients who, in turn, are considered "principals" (the people in charge). Therefore, with very rare exceptions, a client is bound by what the lawyer does or fails to do, regardless of the client's own actions or culpability. The principles of the law of agency, which are much older than the modern legal profession, apply to clients, lawyers, and third parties.[16]

> **FOR EXAMPLE:** If a lawyer fails to file a client's lawsuit within the statute of limitations period, the client loses her right to sue the defendant. This is true even if the client directed the lawyer to file the case on time and even if the lawyer falsely told the client that she had done so.[17] The client might sue her lawyer for malpractice if the lawyer misses a deadline. This imposes a terrible burden on a client and may not produce an adequate remedy if, for example, the lawyer does not have good malpractice insurance and has less money than the original defendant.

These principles apply to lawyers' dealings on behalf of clients, in court and out of court. For example, a client in litigation is bound by a lawyer's decisions to waive a defense in an original or amended answer to a complaint (even though such a decision should be made by the client). Out of court, a client is bound by a lawyer's agency agreement to buy or sell property.

---

16. Usually state agency law applies to lawyers and their clients because the lawyer-client relationship is a contractual relationship governed by state law. However, some federal courts have applied federal principles of agency law to cases arising under federal law. See, e.g., Kinan v. Cohen, 268 F.3d 27 (1st Cir. 2001).

17. See In re Crocket, 912 P.2d 176 (Kan. 1996) (lawyer suspended for a year, but appeal he filed too late was nevertheless untimely).

The law of agency recognizes three different ways that a person can become an agent of another: express authority, implied authority, and apparent authority.

1. Express and implied authority

A client may explicitly give a lawyer "express" authority to act on the client's behalf. For example, a client could tell a lawyer directly to sign a contract or to settle a case. Alternatively, a client may give a lawyer a general instruction that implicitly allows the lawyer to take certain actions on the client's behalf. In fact, just by asking a lawyer to represent him in a matter, a client impliedly authorizes the lawyer to take action that is reasonable and calculated to advance the client's interest.[18] Express authority and implied authority are both considered "actual" authority. In many cases, either type of authority binds a client to a lawyer's actions.[19] However, certain actions taken by lawyers may not be valid unless the lawyers have express rather than implied authority. For example, in most jurisdictions, as discussed below, lawyers need express authority to settle disputes on behalf of their clients. But some jurisdictions presume that if a client authorizes a lawyer to negotiate, the lawyer is also authorized to settle.[20]

2. Apparent authority

Even if an agent has neither express nor implied authority, she may have "apparent" authority. When a client tells a third party (such as the opposing party in a case) that the client's lawyer has the authority to settle a claim on his behalf, the third party may rely on the lawyer's subsequent actions, even if the client did not actually authorize those actions. Apparent authority also is sometimes found if a principal places an agent in a position that causes a third person reasonably to believe that the principal had given the

---

18. Restatement (Second) of Agency § 7, comment c (1958); Restatement (Third) of Agency § 2.03, comment b (2006). In addition, the "appearance of an attorney for one of the parties is generally deemed sufficient proof of his or her authority for the opposite party and for the court." State ex rel. Nixon v. Overmyer, 189 S.W.3d 711 (Mo. App. W. Dist. 2006).

19. Restatement § 26(1).

20. Geoffrey C. Hazard Jr., Susan P. Koniak & Roger C. Cramton, The Law and Ethics of Lawyering 823 (4d ed., Found. Press 2005). Because most jurisdictions do not presume that authority to negotiate implies the authority to settle, lawyers usually insist that settlement agreements be signed by the clients for both sides as well as by their attorneys. Id. In some jurisdictions, however, a lawyer may settle a case based on implied authority. See, e.g., Natare v. Acquatic Renovation Sys., 987 F. Supp. 695 (S.D. Ind. 1997). Even in such jurisdictions, however, actual authority to settle is not implied from the mere fact that a client retains a lawyer to handle the litigation. Koval v. Simon Telelect, 693 N.E.2d 1299 (Ind. 1998).

agent express authority.[21] Retaining a lawyer may confer apparent authority for many actions by lawyers, both in transactions and in litigation. But notice that a *lawyer's* statement to a third party that she is authorized to act does *not* constitute apparent authority. Only the acts or statements of a client (or another principal) can justify reliance by the third party.[22]

> **FOR EXAMPLE:** Suppose a client authorizes her lawyer to negotiate terms for the purchase of a building but privately instructs the lawyer not to enter into an agreement without her explicit approval. Suppose further that the client informs the seller that her lawyer is acting on her behalf and that the seller should deal with the lawyer, not the client. If the lawyer violates the instructions and agrees that the client will buy the building for $1 million, the client would be held to have bought the building.

3. Authority to settle litigation

A few states conclude that merely by hiring lawyers to represent them in litigation, clients authorize their lawyers to settle cases.[23] In most states, however, the mere fact that a lawyer represents a client in litigation does not provide implied or apparent authority to allow the lawyer to *settle* the case. In those states, however, to protect adversaries, a settlement agreed to by an attorney in open court is considered binding on the basis of apparent authority or of the attorney's "inherent agency power."[24] A client also may be bound by the lawyer's out-of-court settlement on the basis of implied authority discerned from an extensive course of conduct.[25]

> **FOR EXAMPLE:** An employee claimed that he had been wrongfully fired by a state agency. A hearing officer of the State Personnel Commission agreed that the termination was wrongful. The State appealed, and the

---

21. See Feltman v. Sarbov, 366 A.2d 137, 139 (D.C. 1976), citing Drazin v. Jack Pry, Inc., 154 A.2d 553, 554 (D.C. 1959).

22. Restatement § 27 and comment c.

23. In these states, the mere fact that a client retains a lawyer for purposes of litigation imbues the lawyer with apparent authority to settle. Pembroke St. Bank v. Warnell, 471 S.E.2d 187 (Ga. 1996).

24. *Koval,* 693 N.E.2d 1299; Nelson v. Consumers Power Co., 497 N.W.2d 205 (Mich. App. 1993). Some courts state, usually in dicta, that an attorney may not settle a case without *express* authority. See, e.g., Bradford Exch. v. Trein's Exch., 600 F.2d 99 (7th Cir. 1979) (applying Illinois law).

25. See, e.g., *Natare,* 987 F. Supp. 695 (applying Indiana law) (lawyer has implied authority to settle a case where, over a period of years, the client authorized the lawyer to participate in settlement negotiations and did not express reservations about a proposed settlement).

parties agreed to mediation, which took place in the mediator's office in the courthouse. The parties agreed to the mediator's ground rule that each party had to have someone with settlement authority present at all times. After several hours, the parties and their lawyers agreed that the State would pay damages to the employee but would not rehire him. The employee's lawyer asked for $450,000, and the State counter-proposed $150,000. After more hours of haggling, however, the difference was narrowed to about $7,500. At that point, the employee picked up his briefcase and left the room, saying to his lawyer, "I'm leaving, you handle it." The two lawyers then reached agreement on a $208,000 settlement. The lawyers also agreed that the State's lawyer would draft the agreement. A month later, the employee, who had decided that he wanted reinstatement more than the settlement money, rejected the agreement and refused to sign it. The State sued for specific performance to enforce the agreement, and it prevailed. The court held that apparent authority would not have warranted enforcement of the settlement that was reached without the actual agreement of the employee. However, the employee's departure, after he had agreed to the ground rule that someone with settlement authority had to be present throughout the negotiation, together with the words "you handle it," imbued his attorney with actual authority to settle the case in his absence.[26]

C. Lawyers' duties of competence, diligence, honesty, and communication

This section explores lawyers' duties to act competently, deal honestly, keep clients informed, and perform work diligently in the interests of the client. Lawyers owe other duties to clients as well, such as the duty to protect confidences, the duty to avoid conflicts of interest, and the duty to charge reasonable fees. Some of these other duties are treated in depth elsewhere in this book. The duties discussed in this section are clustered together because they are critically important, interrelated obligations.

---

26. Caballero v. Wikse, 92 P.3d 1076 (Idaho 2004).

1. Competence

Rule 1.1 Competence
A lawyer shall provide competent representation to a client. Competent representation requires the legal knowledge, skill, thoroughness and preparation reasonably necessary for the representation.

Comment 2 elaborates:

> Some important legal skills, such as the analysis of precedent, the evaluation of evidence, and legal drafting, are required in all legal problems. Perhaps the most fundamental legal skill consists of determining what kinds of legal problems a situation may involve. . . .

Additional comments identify various other features of competent lawyering. Competent representation is in some part a question of study and training, but competent performance also requires diligence, thoroughness, preparation, and analysis of the factual and legal elements of the problem.[27]

FOR EXAMPLE: Irwin Jay Katz was retained by several individual clients to prepare documents through which they would obtain loans to buy real estate. He arranged for his clients to sign loan forms that he had previously used, without problems, for commercial loans. Katz had a J.D. and two advanced degrees in tax law, had practiced law for seven years, and had taught in a law school. Despite his education and experience, Katz did not know that the use of these commercial forms to make loans to consumers violated federal law because of the forms' payment terms. Even though Katz's mistake was unintentional, he was found to have violated Rule 1.1, and his license was suspended. His extensive prior experience as a lawyer was considered an "aggravating factor."[28]

Some scholars have pointed out that the definition of competence in the ethics rules offers only "limited guidance."[29]

---

27. See Rule 1.1, Comments 1 & 5.

28. Ky. B. Assn. v. Katz, 317 S.W.3d 592 (Ky. 2010) (applying reciprocal discipline following Katz's suspension in Delaware). Katz was also charged with a conflict of interest because he had represented the lender and had not obtained the necessary informed consent.

29. Alexis Anderson, Arlene Kanter & Cindy Slane, Externships and Ethics: A Primer on Confidentiality, Conflicts and Competency Issues in the Field and in the Classroom, 10 Clin. L. Rev. 473 (2004). A more rigorous definition of competent lawyering was developed by an ABA task force that explored some of the shortcomings of legal education as preparation for practice. This task force recommended that law school curricula give more attention to the development of lawyering skills, such as problem solving, fact investigation, counseling, and work management; and values, such as justice, fairness, and the elimination of bias in the profession. ABA, Section of Legal Education &

"You seem to know something about law. I like that in an attorney."

When lawyers are charged by disciplinary agencies with lack of competence, they often face other charges as well—neglect of client matters, failure to communicate, and others. Often such cases come to the attention of the disciplinary authorities because of a string of complaints by clients. In some cases, the problem originates because the lawyer accepts more cases than she can handle well. In other instances, the lawyer's failure of performance is related to alcohol or drug abuse, depression, or some other serious personal problem.

FOR EXAMPLE: Drew Alan Neal was a successful criminal lawyer and former public defender in New Mexico. He had practiced for eight years but had never handled an appeal to the State Supreme Court. His client, a convicted murderer, was entitled to an "automatic" appeal. Neal did not file a notice of appeal within the 30-day limit, believing (correctly) that since the client could not be denied his appeal, the client would not lose his right to appeal if Neal did not file the necessary documents on time. After the court clerk directed him to file the appeal, he sent a copy to the

---

Admissions to the Bar, Report of the Task Force on Law Schools and the Profession: Narrowing the Gap (Robert MacCrate ed., ABA 1992) (available at http://www.americanbar.org/groups/legal_education/publications/maccrate.html).

district attorney but not to the trial judge and other officials as required by the rules. The appeal was therefore delayed by several months. Neal was brought up on disciplinary charges by the bar counsel. He was charged with violation of the rule requiring competent representation. Like many lawyers who neglect cases, he suffered from depression and alcohol abuse. He was suspended for two years but allowed to practice while participating in a drug and alcohol program and in psychotherapy.[30] He did not comply with the conditions of his discipline and was later disbarred.[31]

FOR EXAMPLE: In many states, the office of the public defender is seriously understaffed compared to the number of defendants who need its services. Public defender offices with high caseloads may assign each lawyer 200 or more cases. The ABA ethics committee, however, issued an advisory opinion urging that public defenders should not dilute the representation they give to existing clients to meet the needs of other, equally needy clients clamoring for assistance. They must instead refuse new cases, shift work to colleagues, and even move to withdraw from their cases if they are unable to provide competent representation to current clients.[32]

PROBLEM 4-1 THE WASHING MACHINE

The facts of this problem are adapted from a case that Professor Lerman supervised in a law school clinic.

You are a general practitioner in a small town in your state. A new client, Nasser Kamath, comes to your office because he is being sued by Hallmart, a reputable chain of retail stores. He had bought a new washing machine on an installment contract. After he had made two of his twelve $60 monthly payments (that is, $120 of the $720), Kamath was laid off from his job and could no longer afford to make payments. The store called him at home several times, saying that his credit record would be spoiled if he did not pay. But he was simply unable to make the third payment, so the store sued him. Kamath can't afford to pay your fee, but you agreed to represent

---

30. Matter of Neal, 20 P.3d 121 (N.M. 2001).

31. Matter of Neal, 81 P.3d 47 (N.M. 2003); see Isabel Sanchez, State High Court Disbars Lawyer, Albuquerque J. (Jan. 26, 2004) (available at http://www.abqjournal.com/news/state/137823nm01-26-04.htm).

32. ABA Standing Comm. on Ethics & Prof. Resp., Formal Op. 06-441.

him anyway. Kamath's daughter is on the same soccer team as your daughter, and he's the coach, so you feel you owe him a favor. You thought you could handle this matter without spending a lot of time.

A term in the contract provided that if the buyer missed a payment, the buyer was in "default" and the seller was entitled to sue for the entire remaining balance (in this case, $600 minus a bit of interest that hadn't yet accrued), plus the seller's attorneys' fees. So Hallmart sued for about $600 plus its attorneys' fees.

When he learned about the lawsuit, Kamath called the store and offered to return the washing machine. The store's credit department said that the store had no use for a used machine and that he should pay the money.

A week ago, you filed papers informing Hallmart's lawyer and the court that you are representing Kamath. This morning, Hallmart's lawyer called to ask whether your client wanted to set up a "payment plan." The lawyer offered to settle the case for an agreement under which your client would pay $25 per month for 26 more months. Under this plan, your client would pay the store an additional $650. This means he would end up paying a total of $770 for the washing machine ($50 more than under the original contract), but each payment would be much smaller.

You called Kamath. He said that he could probably pay $25 per month, but not $60 per month. He said that the proposed payment plan seems like a good solution.

What should you do?

---

2. Competence in criminal cases

Dissatisfied clients seek recourse against lawyers in various ways. Some complain to their lawyers and object to paying the legal fee. Some complain to bar disciplinary authorities. Some file malpractice suits against their former lawyers. Some clients who are convicted in criminal cases file appeals urging that the conviction should be reversed because the trial lawyer was incompetent. Such a defendant would claim that he was denied the "effective assistance of counsel." The Sixth Amendment requires that a

"Hi, I'm your court-appointed lawyer—whoa!
Don't tell me you've been executed already."

criminal defendant be provided with a lawyer whose work meets at least the minimum standard of being "effective." A state could provide a higher degree of protection to its criminal defendants than the constitutional minimum, but this constitutional right may be claimed in every state regardless of any variation in state law or state ethics rules.

Many judges are very reluctant to overturn a criminal conviction because a different lawyer might have done a better job for a defendant. Therefore, it is unlikely that a defendant can win an ineffective assistance appeal unless his lawyer's performance was really awful. Furthermore, a defendant appealing a conviction must prove not only that the assistance was unusually poor, but also (as in civil malpractice cases) that better representation would have made a difference. The leading case is *Strickland v. Washington*.[33]

---

33. 466 U.S. 668 (1984).

Strickland v. Washington: The standard for proving ineffective assistance of counsel

In *Strickland*, Washington committed several crimes, including three gruesome murders. After his accomplices were apprehended, he surrendered. The state appointed William Tunkey, an experienced criminal lawyer, to represent him in a capital case. Against Tunkey's advice, Washington confessed to having committed murder, and he pleaded guilty. Also he agreed to testify against a co-defendant. Thus there was no trial, but Washington was entitled to a hearing on whether he would receive the death penalty or life imprisonment. At the hearing, he had the right to present "mitigation" evidence, including a psychiatric report, to justify a life sentence. Tunkey did not meet with Washington's wife or mother, did not seek out character witnesses, did not obtain a psychiatric evaluation of Washington, and did not introduce evidence about Washington's prior criminal record. Tunkey hoped that the judge would be merciful because Washington had expressed remorse, had stated on the record that he had been under great stress, accepted that he accepted responsibility for his crimes, had no significant criminal record, and had surrendered, confessed, and agreed to testify against a co-defendant. In addition, Tunkey knew that the judge had a reputation for dealing fairly with people who took responsibility for their crimes.

Nevertheless, the judge sentenced Washington to death, relying on several aggravating factors such as the cruelty of the crimes. Washington appealed to the Supreme Court. He claimed that Tunkey had not provided effective assistance because he had not requested a psychiatric report or a presentence investigation report and had not interviewed possible character witnesses. His appellate lawyer submitted 14 affidavits from friends and neighbors who stated that they would have testified for him and two psychological reports stating that he was chronically depressed at the time of the crimes. In an opinion by Justice O'Connor, the Court analyzed the duty of counsel under the Sixth Amendment. It said that lawyers for a criminal defendant must avoid conflicts of interest, must advocate the defendant's cause, must consult with the defendant on important decisions, and must keep the defendant informed of important developments in the case. The lawyer must also "bring to bear such skill and knowledge as will render the trial a reliable adversarial testing process"[34] and must "make reasonable investigations or to make a reasonable decision that makes particular investigations unnecessary."[35] Before a Sixth Amendment violation occurs, the errors of counsel must be very serious — so serious that

---

34. Id. at 688.
35. Id. at 691.

"counsel was not functioning as the 'counsel' guaranteed the defendant" by that Amendment.[36]

However, the Court continued, there remained a second hurdle for a person claiming ineffective assistance of counsel. Even if a defense lawyer made a serious error, the conviction should not be reversed unless the defendant had been prejudiced by the lawyer's conduct; that is, the conviction should stand unless the defendant could somehow prove that the error affected the outcome. "The defendant must show that there is a reasonable probability that, but for counsel's unprofessional errors, the result of the proceeding would have been different."[37]

Tunkey's conduct, the Court concluded, was not unreasonable. Tunkey reasonably relied on what he knew of the judge's reputation regarding remorseful defendants. By not introducing psychological reports, Tunkey had prevented the prosecutor from introducing his own, contrary psychological evidence. The Court added that even assuming that Tunkey's conduct was unreasonable, Washington had not shown that a more assiduous effort by Tunkey would have changed the result. The psychological report and character witnesses "would barely have altered the sentencing profile presented to the sentencing judge."[38]

Justice Marshall dissented[39] and would have remanded for a new sentencing hearing. He argued that the Court had provided no standard by which to assess whether a lawyer had acted reasonably, and that in fact Tunkey had not acted reasonably because he never interviewed the potential character witnesses to find out what they would have said on Washington's behalf. In Marshall's view, if Tunkey had done so and had presented testimony from character witnesses, there was a "significant chance" that Washington would have received a life sentence rather than the death penalty. As for the Court's requirement that "prejudice" be proven before a conviction could be reversed for ineffective assistance of counsel, Marshall argued that when a lawyer acts incompetently, it is nearly impossible for a defendant to show that the result would have been different if the lawyer had acted in a different way.

Notes and Questions on *Strickland*

1. **Who's right?** Do you agree with the majority or with Justice Marshall as to the standards to be applied and their application to the actual *Strickland* case? Should Washington have been given another

---

36. Id. at 687.
37. Id. at 694.
38. Id. at 700.
39. Id. at 706.

chance to avoid execution by being granted a resentencing hearing at which his new lawyer could present to the sentencing judge some evidence about his character and his psychological state at the time he committed the crimes?

2. **Standards and reality.** The ABA has promulgated a set of practice standards for criminal defense lawyers. These are "intended to be used as a guide to professional conduct and performance [and] not as criteria for the judicial evaluation of alleged misconduct of defense counsel to determine the validity of a conviction." However, the standards "may or may not be relevant in such judicial evaluation, depending upon all the circumstances."[40]

These standards provide, among other things, that:

- As soon as practicable, defense counsel should seek to determine all relevant facts known to the accused.
- Defense counsel should keep the client informed of the developments in the case and the progress of preparing the defense and should promptly comply with reasonable requests for information.
- Defense counsel should inform the accused of his or her rights at the earliest opportunity and take all necessary action to vindicate such rights. Defense counsel should consider all procedural steps which in good faith may be taken, including, for example, motions seeking pretrial release of the accused, obtaining psychiatric examination of the accused when a need appears . . . [and] moving to suppress illegally obtained evidence. . . .
- Defense counsel should conduct a prompt investigation of the circumstances of the case and explore all avenues leading to facts relevant to the merits of the case and the penalty in the event of conviction. The investigation should include efforts to secure information in the possession of the prosecution and law enforcement authorities. The duty to investigate exists regardless of the accused's admissions or statements to defense counsel of facts constituting guilt or the accused's stated desire to plead guilty.[41]

There is apparently no national survey documenting how often lawyers adhere to these standards, but numerous smaller-scale studies suggest that many lawyers do not meet promptly with their

---

40. ABA, Standards for Criminal Justice: Prosecution Function and Defense Function 119 (3d ed., ABA 1993) (available at http://www.americanbar.org/content/dam/aba/publications/criminal_justice_standards/prosecution_defense_function.authcheckdam.pdf).

41. Id. at 152, 170, 176, 181.

clients, keep them informed, investigate all the facts, or pursue defenses aggressively:

■ In New York, only 36 percent of court-appointed lawyers in homicide cases visited their clients in prison, and only 31 percent visited the scene of the homicide. The investigation of these cases continued for at least five weeks in only 12 percent of cases.[42]

■ Even though the success of a defendant often depends on the availability of investigators, most public defenders in Pennsylvania were unable to recall having used an investigator.[43]

■ The office of the public defender in Calcasieu Parish, Louisiana, used an expert in only 1 of 171 cases. The criminal defense lawyers in that parish visited their clients in jail in only 1 out of 14 cases.[44]

■ New York City defense lawyers talked to their client's families before sentencing to learn about the defendant's character and background and to explore whether the defendant might qualify for a treatment program rather than incarceration in only 12 percent of cases.[45]

■ According to the Innocence Project, "a review of convictions overturned by DNA testing reveals a trail of sleeping, drunk, incompetent and overburdened defense attorneys, at the trial level and on appeal."[46] Nevertheless, in the five years after the *Strickland* decision, defendants prevailed in their claims of ineffective assistance of counsel in only 4 percent of the 702 reported cases.[47]

■ In Chippewa County, Michigan, defense attorneys routinely had their first meetings with their clients at the courthouse just before their arraignments. The lawyers were not able to meet their clients at the public defender's office because there is not enough space.[48]

---

42. Jane Fritsch & David Rohde, Lawyers Often Fail New York's Poor, N.Y. Times (Apr. 8, 2001) (available at http://www.nytimes.com/2001/04/08/nyregion/lawyers-often-fail-new-york-s-poor.html?pagewanted = all&src = pm).

43. Mary Sue Backus & Paul Marcus, The Right to Counsel in Criminal Cases, A National Crisis, 57 Hastings L.J. 1031, 1098 (2006).

44. Michael M. Kurth & Daryl V. Burckel, Defending the Indigent in Southwest Louisiana (July 2003) (available at http://lpdb.la.gov/Serving%20The%20Public/Reports/txtfiles/pdf/Defending%20the%20Indigent%20in%20Southwest%20Louisiana.pdf).

45. Michael McConville & Chester L. Mirsky, Criminal Defense of the Poor in New York City, 15 N.Y.U. Rev. L. & Soc. Change 581, 773 (1987).

46. Innocence Project, Understand the Causes: Bad Lawyering, http://www.innocenceproject.org/understand/Bad-Lawyering.php (accessed Nov. 2, 2012).

47. Martin C. Calhoun, Note, How to Thread the Needle: Toward a Checklist-Based Standard for Evaluating Ineffective Assistance of Counsel Claims, 77 Geo. L.J. 413, 458 (1988).

48. Natl. Legal Aid & Defender Assn., A Race to the Bottom: Speed & Savings over Due Process — A Constitutional Crisis (June 2008) (available at http://www.nlada.net/library/documents/mi_racetothebottomjseri06-2008_report).

■ In some Florida counties, defense lawyers were routinely absent from hearings to determine whether juvenile defendants will be detained. Although indigent juvenile defendants are entitled to appointed counsel,[49] in at least two counties the court clerks determined that "if the parent has $5.00 in his bank account, he is not indigent."

When juveniles are represented, the lawyers often meet their clients "for the first time in the hallway or in the courtroom at the time of the hearing." This pattern occurs in other states as well. For example, in Maryland, juvenile defenders "provide virtually no advocacy for their clients at detention hearings . . . , usually conduct no investigation of the facts of the case, and rarely meet with their client before the adjudicatory hearing."[50]

■ In Hamilton County, Ohio, staff attorneys handling misdemeanor cases in the public defender's office "never interview witnesses before trial, almost never subpoena witnesses, never investigate cases, and never go to crime scenes." Staff members who represent juveniles receive no training before they begin to do so.[51]

These studies have implications for how the *Strickland* doctrine should be applied. If most criminal defense attorneys do an excellent job of investigating the law and facts, a strong degree of deference to the decisions of trial counsel is warranted. If inadequate representation is rare, the cost, in time and other resources, of holding hearings on ineffective assistance claims and of reversing convictions based on those claims might be disproportionate to the social value of allowing challenges based on poor representation. But if many criminal defense lawyers are so overworked that they must give short shrift to some clients, perhaps courts should be less deferential to their decisions and should more often reverse convictions for ineffective assistance. This policy question turns on whether, on the whole, criminal defense lawyers represent their clients with the kind of energy that we expect of competent lawyers.

3. **Standards of practice.** The studies cited above suggest that in at least some cities and counties, defense lawyers do not live up to the ABA standards. Do the standards impose unrealistic demands on lawyers? If not, what should be done to raise the standards of practice of

---

49. In re Gault, 387 U.S. 1 (1967).

50. Jerry R. Foxhoven, Effective Assistance of Counsel: Quality of Representation for Juveniles Is Still Illusory, 9 Barry L. Rev. 99, 101, 112, 115 (2007).

51. Natl. Legal Aid & Defender Assn., Taking Gideon's Pulse: An Assessment of the Right to Counsel in Hamilton County, Ohio (July 2008) (available at http://www.nlada.net/library/documents/oh_takinggideonspulsejseri07-2008_report).

criminal defense lawyers? Should the criminal justice standards be added to state disciplinary codes as mandatory rules and be enforced? Are there other steps that could be taken to improve the quality of representation of criminal defendants?

4. **Relationship to standards of professional responsibility.** Assume that you are a member of the disciplinary committee of the Florida State Bar. Assume that from his cell, Washington has filed a complaint accusing his lawyer of having violated the state version of Rule 1.1. What discipline, if any, should you impose on the lawyer? Does it matter to you, as it did to the Supreme Court, whether different tactics might have led to a different result?

5. **Criminal cases with immigration consequences.** In 2010, the Supreme Court added a new element to the *Strickland* doctrine for criminal cases in which the defendant is not a U.S. citizen. Convictions for many types of crimes, including certain misdemeanors, can subject the defendant to mandatory deportation after a sentence is served. Immigration law is very complex and technical, and many experienced criminal defense lawyers do not know it well enough to explain to their clients the risk that accepting a proffered plea bargain poses to their ability to remain in the United States. The Court concluded that the Sixth Amendment is violated if the attorney for such a defendant does not warn the client of the possibly serious immigration consequences of a guilty plea. The noncitizen in *Padilla v. Kentucky* was a Vietnam War veteran who had lived in the United States lawfully for more than 40 years. He pleaded guilty to a state charge of transporting marijuana in his tractor-trailer. This was a deportable offense under federal law, but his lawyer didn't tell him that before advising him to plead guilty. In fact, his lawyer told him that he "did not have to worry about immigration status since he had been in the country so long." The Supreme Court held that the failure to provide accurate advice to noncitizens about the immigration consequences of possible conviction renders the representation incompetent for purposes of the Sixth Amendment.[52] A noncitizen defendant must still prove that the lawyer's inadequate advice had a prejudicial impact on the outcome of the case.

---

52. Padilla v. Ky., 130 S. Ct. 1473 (2010). Having found that Padilla's lawyer's advice was incompetent, the Court remanded for a determination of whether Padilla could demonstrate that accepting the prosecutor's plea bargain prejudiced him, as required by the second prong of *Strickland*. For a discussion of the application of the *Strickland* standard in cases that were resolved by a plea bargain, see Jenny Roberts, Proving Prejudice, Post-*Padilla*, 54 How. L.J. 693, 698 (2011).

A new Sixth Amendment duty: Defense lawyers must communicate plea offers and advise clients effectively about plea offers.

In 2012, the Supreme Court again addressed issues raised by defendants who claimed ineffective assistance by their lawyers after prosecutors offered plea bargains.[53] Galin Frye was charged with driving while his license was revoked, which under the circumstances was a felony with a four-year maximum sentence. The prosecutor informed Frye's lawyer, in writing, that if Frye would plead guilty to a misdemeanor, carrying at most a one-year sentence, the prosecutor would recommend a 90-day sentence. The lawyer never told Frye of the offer, a clear violation of Rule 1.4.[54] After the offer expired, Frye pleaded guilty, but it was too late, and the judge sentenced him to three years in prison.

Justice Kennedy, writing for the majority, explained that criminal defendants are entitled under the Sixth Amendment "'to have counsel present at all "critical" stages of the criminal proceedings,'" including "arraignments, postindictment interrogations, postindictment lineups, and the entry of a guilty plea."[55] In *Padilla*, discussed above, the Court "made clear that the negotiation of a plea bargain is a critical phase of litigation for purposes of the Sixth Amendment." The Court also "rejected the argument . . . that a knowing and voluntary plea supersedes errors by defense counsel."[56] While *Padilla* involved the advice of counsel as to a *plea offer that was then accepted*, *Frye* and its companion case explore whether a defendant may claim ineffective assistance based on advice (or lack of advice) that led to the *rejection or lapse of a plea offer*. The Court concluded that such a claim may involve a violation of the defendant's Sixth Amendment rights.

Justice Kennedy noted that 97 percent of federal and 94 percent of state criminal cases are resolved by plea bargaining. In our contemporary system of criminal justice, he wrote, "the negotiation of a plea bargain, rather than the unfolding of a trial, is almost always the critical point for a

---

53. Missouri v. Frye, 132 S. Ct. 1399 (2012); Lafler v. Cooper, 132 S. Ct. 1376 (2012). The decisions in both cases were five to four. Justice Kennedy, writing for the majority, was joined by Justices Ginsburg, Breyer, Sotomayor, and Kagan. Justice Scalia wrote dissenting opinions in both cases, and Justice Alito wrote a separate dissent in the *Cooper* case. For an overview of these opinions, see Adam Liptak, Justices' Ruling Expands Rights of Accused in Plea Bargains, N.Y. Times (Mar. 21, 2012) (available at http://www.nytimes.com/2012/03/22/us/supreme-court-says-defendants-have-right-to-good-lawyers.html?pagewanted = all).

54. See Rule 1.4, Comment 2.

55. *Frye*, 132 S. Ct. at 1405.

56. Id. at 1406.

defendant."[57] The Court held in *Frye* that "defense counsel has the duty to communicate formal offers from the prosecution to accept a plea on terms and conditions that may be favorable to the accused," and that "[w]hen defense counsel allowed the offer to expire without advising the defendant or allowing him to consider it, defense counsel did not render the effective assistance the Constitution requires."[58] This decision constitutionalizes the existing ethical duty of a defense lawyer to communicate an offer of a plea bargain to his client.

Since defense counsel had failed to communicate the offer to Frye, the Court found that the first element of the *Strickland* standard had been met. The Court went on to ask whether prejudice resulted from the lawyer's breach of duty. The Court said that to prove prejudice in this context, a defendant must show "a reasonable probability that [the defendant] would have accepted the lapsed plea [and] a reasonable probability that the prosecution would have adhered to the agreement and that it would have been accepted by the trial court."[59] In this case, the Court found that there was a reasonable probability that Frye would have accepted the offer. However, the Missouri Court of Appeals failed to require a showing that the offer would have been adhered to by the prosecutor or accepted by the trial court. The Court noted that there was reason to doubt that these elements would have been present because Frye was once again arrested for driving without a license before the hearing at which the plea agreement would have been presented to the court. The Court vacated the judgment and remanded the case to the Missouri Court of Appeals for determination of the remaining issues.

In a companion case, Anthony Cooper had shot a woman and was charged with assault with intent to murder. The prosecutor offered Cooper's lawyer a plea bargain in which he could serve a sentence of four to seven years in exchange for pleading guilty. His lawyer told him — erroneously, and probably in violation of Rule 1.1 — that he could not be convicted of the charged offense because the four bullets had struck his victim below the waist. Relying on his lawyer's incorrect counseling, Cooper rejected the plea bargain, went to trial, was found guilty, and was sentenced to 15 to 30 years in prison. Like Frye, Cooper claimed that his lawyer's incompetence constituted ineffective assistance within the meaning of the Sixth Amendment.

The Court found that both cases presented conduct that fell below the standard required by the Sixth Amendment. In *Frye*, defense counsel failed to communicate a plea offer, which led to its lapse. In *Cooper*, defense counsel offered incorrect legal advice that led the defendant to reject a favorable plea offer. The Court held in *Cooper*, as in *Frye*, that a lawyer's failure to provide

---

57. Id. at 1407.
58. Id. at 1408.
59. Id. at 1410-1411.

effective assistance of counsel in relation to an offered plea bargain presents a basis for relief if the defendant can show that he suffered prejudice as a result and that, but for the ineffective advice, there is a reasonable probability that the plea offer would have been adhered to by the prosecutor and accepted by the court. In *Cooper*, the Court ordered the state to reoffer the plea; if the defendant accepted, the state could exercise its discretion whether to vacate the convictions and resentence the defendant, to vacate some of the convictions and resentence, or to leave the conviction and sentence undisturbed.

Justice Scalia, in dissent, suggested that the expansion of the Sixth Amendment to cover representation in plea bargaining would create "a whole new boutique of constitutional jurisprudence."[60]

Steven Banks, of the Legal Aid Society in New York, offered one example of a practice that might be called into question because of this decision. In New York and in 15 other states, prosecutors need not turn over evidence or lists of witnesses until just before the trial date. In these jurisdictions, it is hard for defense attorneys to help their clients to evaluate plea offers.[61] For the defense lawyer to offer effective assistance, does the prosecutor need to share information about evidence and witnesses at the time a plea offer is made?

Justice Kennedy acknowledged the possibility that the outcome in many criminal cases might be challenged on the basis of these decisions. He suggested that courts would develop procedures to protect against frivolous or fabricated claims, including possibly requiring that plea offers be made in writing or that they be presented to the court for review.

3. Diligence

One fundamental duty of lawyers toward clients is to do the work that they have been hired to do, and to do it without undue delay. Rule 1.3 puts it this way: "A lawyer shall act with reasonable diligence and promptness in representing a client." Many disciplinary cases include charges that lawyers have neglected client matters. They may have failed to return phone calls or to file court papers on time. These are charged as violations of Rule 1.3. Comment 1 states that a lawyer should pursue a matter for a client despite opposition or personal inconvenience and take "whatever measures are required" to vindicate a client's cause. The lawyer must act "with zeal in advocacy upon the client's behalf." Comment 3 notes that "perhaps no professional shortcoming is more widely resented than procrastination."

---

60. *Cooper*, 132 S. Ct. at 1398.

61. Erica Goode, Stronger Hand for Judges in the "Bazaar" of Plea Deals, N.Y. Times (Mar. 22, 2012) (available at http://www.nytimes.com/2012/03/23/us/stronger-hand-for-judges-after-rulings-on-plea-deals.html).

The Model Code of Professional Responsibility (which preceded the Model Rules) included a canon stating that a lawyer should represent a client "zealously within the bounds of the law."[62] This exhortation was dropped from the black letter rule in the Model Rules and most of the state rules because of a concern that it encouraged unethical behavior.[63] Even though the Model Code directed lawyers to treat opponents and opposing counsel with courtesy and consideration,[64] some lawyers used and still use the requirement of zealous advocacy to justify pursuing every possible argument or advantage in litigation. The use of "scorched earth" litigation tactics dragged out lawsuits, ran up costs, and contributed to negative public opinion about lawyers. The Model Rules replaced the requirement of zeal with one of "diligence" and demoted the language on zeal to the comments.

The present formulation of the comment reflects ambivalence about aggressive lawyering. Comment 1 urges zealous advocacy, but it states that a lawyer is "not bound . . . to press for every advantage that might be realized." It says that the rule does not "require" the use of offensive tactics or "preclude" a lawyer from treating all persons with courtesy and respect. (This locution is really peculiar. It would make more sense for the comment to *prohibit* offensive tactics and *require* respectful treatment.)

The opposite of diligent representation is total neglect of clients' cases. Any search of recent lawyer disciplinary decisions turns up examples in which lawyers ignored their clients' cases. In some of these decisions, the lawyer never filed the case, and the statute of limitations had passed. In others, the lawyer filed a case but allowed it to languish. Often, neglect of client matters is caused or compounded by substance abuse, as in *Matter of Neal*, discussed above.

Lawyers are responsible for paying attention to all matters for which they accept responsibility by making agreements with clients or filing appearances with courts. In cases they initiate, they are not excused from the duty of diligence if they leave a law firm unless they formally withdraw from representation.

FOR EXAMPLE: In one case, a client hired a firm to bring an employment discrimination case. One of the firm's partners signed the com-

---

62. Model Code Prof. Resp. canon 7 (as amended, 1980). "Canons" were "statements of axiomatic norms, expressing in general terms the standards of professional conduct expected of lawyers." Id.

63. Some jurisdictions retain the requirement of zealous representation in their rules. D.C. Rule 1.3, for example, states that "a lawyer shall represent a client zealously and diligently within the bounds of the law." Mass. Rule 1.3 provides that a lawyer shall act with reasonable diligence and promptness but adds that the lawyer "should represent a client zealously within the bounds of the law."

64. Model Code Prof. Resp. DR 7-101(A)(1) (as amended through 1980).

plaint as an accommodation to his partner who was actually handling the case, but he never met the client or worked on the case. The secretaries routed all documents to the partner who was supposed to be handling the case, but he neglected the matter, and the complaint was dismissed. The partner who had signed the complaint as an accommodation was not aware of the dismissal, and he eventually left the firm. Years later, he was formally (though privately) reprimanded for having neglected the case; he was found to have had responsibility for it because he'd signed the complaint.[65]

4. Candor and communication

a. Lying versus deception: Is there a moral distinction?

Some philosophers say that in evaluating the morality of a statement, the important question is not whether there is a false statement but whether the speaker intends to deceive the other person.[66] If the speaker intends to deceive, an evasive statement that withholds information is arguably morally identical to a false statement. Each accomplishes the same deceptive purpose. But perhaps it is not as bad to deceive another person if one does it without saying anything false or misleading. If the deceiver manages just to keep silent, is the withholding of information immoral? This question is pretty complicated because so much depends on the circumstances. Like lies, some deceptions may be justifiable, while other deceptions are just as morally reprehensible as telling an overt lie.

> **FOR EXAMPLE:** Suppose you are representing the wife in a divorce. She fills out a financial statement disclosing her assets, but she confesses to you privately that she has not listed in her assets one bank account where she deposits most of her very substantial consulting fees. If you transmit the financial statement to your opposing counsel without saying a word, you have not told a lie, but by transmitting a document that purports to be a complete financial statement, you are perpetrating a deception. If your opposing counsel asks, "Are there any assets not listed on the financial statement?" and you say, "No, they are all listed," have you done anything more morally culpable than you did by simply transmitting the financial statement without comment?

---

65. Matter of Anonymous, 724 N.E.2d 1101 (Ind. 2000).

66. Moral philosopher Sissela Bok defines a lie as "any intentionally deceptive message which is stated." She defines deception more broadly, as encompassing "messages meant to mislead others . . . through gesture, through disguise, by means of action or inaction, even through silence." Sissela Bok, Lying: Moral Choice in Public and Private Life 14 (Pantheon 1978).

As we explore the ethical rules on deception here and in Chapters 10 and 11, you will notice that many rules (e.g., Rules 3.3 and 4.1) more categorically prohibit lying by commission than deceiving by omission. An advocate's role often requires him to withhold information or to present information selectively or in the best light. Because of this, many lawyers believe that deception is problematic only if it is accomplished by making a false statement. As you study this section of the chapter, consider your views on this question.

b. Truth versus truthfulness

Another important distinction in considering questions about dishonesty is the one between "truth" and "truthfulness." Truth is factual, but truthfulness involves intent. Is it dishonest to make a false statement that you believe to be true? We think not, unless you had some reason to know that you might have been mistaken. Similarly, if a lawyer is competent and does diligent research or investigation, she might still miss some information or obtain some incorrect information, which she might then report to her client. But if she is diligent and is honest with her client about what she does learn, she is being truthful even if she makes a mistake.

c. Honesty and communication under the ethics rules

Do the ethical rules ever allow lawyers to lie to or deceive their clients?

The ethics rules explicitly direct lawyers not to lie to tribunals or to persons other than clients.[67] Curiously, the portion of the rules dealing with the "Client-Lawyer Relationship" does not explicitly require lawyers to be honest with their clients. Probably the reason for the failure to impose a specific duty of truthfulness to clients is that most lawyers assume that lawyers will be truthful with clients, and that a lawyer is more likely to deceive someone else on a client's behalf. However, a careful reading of the rules makes it clear that the drafters intended that lawyers should generally be truthful, and this intention extends to clients as well as to others.

Rule 8.4(c) prohibits a lawyer from engaging "in conduct involving dishonesty, fraud, deceit, or misrepresentation." A lie to a client might or might not amount to "fraud" because the ethics rules limit "fraud" to conduct that is fraudulent under the state's substantive or procedural law.[68] As noted in Chapter 3, however, definitions of fraud vary from state to state and also depend on whether the fraud is being asserted as part of a claim in

---

67. Rules 3.3(a) (tribunals) and 4.1 (third persons). Rule 4.1 does not bar lying to clients because clients are not "third" persons. Rules 3.3 and 4.1 are discussed in Chapters 10 and 11.

68. Rule 1.0(d).

tort or contract or in a criminal case. Even if a lie is not "fraud," however, it may amount to deceit or misrepresentation and therefore be a ground for professional discipline under Rule 8.4(c).[69]

In addition, Rule 1.4 requires that a lawyer shall provide information to a client about matters that require informed consent, about which a client must make a decision, about the status of a matter, and about matters on which the client has requested information. Perhaps the duty to keep clients informed implies the duty to give accurate rather than false information. Comment 1 notes that "reasonable communication between the lawyer and the client is necessary for the client effectively to participate in the representation." It would be a stretch to think that "reasonable communication" could include lies by lawyers to their clients. On the other hand, Rule 1.4 does not deal with every type of communication between lawyer and client, nor does it require lawyers to communicate every minor event that occurs during the course of a representation.[70]

Whether or not Rule 1.4 prohibits lying to clients, it certainly requires a lawyer to inform clients about important developments in their cases.

Rule 1.4   Communication

Rule language*	Authors' explanation**
(a) A lawyer shall: (1) promptly **inform the client** of any **decision or circumstance** with respect to which the client's **informed consent**, as defined in Rule 1.0(e), is required by these Rules;	• Requires communication with clients when another rule requires the lawyer to obtain "informed consent." • Example: Another rule prohibits lawyers from representing two clients concurrently if the clients have adverse interests, but permits the representation if several conditions are met, including the informed consent of both clients.[71]
(2) **reasonably consult** with the client **about the means** by which the client's objectives are to be accomplished;	Rule 1.2 gives lawyers some discretion about the "means" used to carry out the representation (as opposed to the "objectives," which clients are entitled to decide). But lawyers must consult with clients about these means.

---

69. See Iowa Sup. Ct. Bd. Prof. Ethics & Conduct v. Jones, 606 N.W.2d 5 (Iowa 2000) (lawyer's unintentionally false statement persuading a former client to make a loan to a current client did not amount to "fraud" but resulted in suspension for misrepresentation).

70. Rule 7.1 may also be relevant. It prohibits lawyers from making false or misleading communications about themselves or their services. While Rule 7.1 was drafted with an eye to lawyer advertising, the language of this rule is broad enough to apply to all communications about legal services.

71. Rule 1.7, discussed in Chapter 5.

Rule language*	Authors' explanation**
(3) **keep the client reasonably informed** about the status of the matter;	• "Status" includes "significant developments affecting the timing or substance of the representation." Comment 3. • Example: If the court's schedule delays resolution of a case for six months, the lawyer should inform the client.
(4) promptly **comply with reasonable requests** for information; and	• If the lawyer cannot respond promptly, he should explain when a response may be expected. Comment 4. • Client telephone calls "should be promptly returned or acknowledged." Comment 4.
(5) **consult** with the client about any relevant **limitation on the lawyer's conduct** when the lawyer knows that the client expects **assistance not permitted** by the Rules of Professional Conduct or other law.	Example: If client asks lawyer to claim a tax deduction that the client is not entitled to claim, the lawyer should explain that he cannot do that.
(b) A lawyer shall **explain a matter to the extent reasonably necessary** to permit the client to make **informed decisions** regarding the representation.	The lawyer should give the client enough information "to participate intelligently" in decisions about objectives and means. But a lawyer "ordinarily will not be expected to describe trial or negotiation strategy in detail." Comment 5.

*All emphasis added.

**This and other authors' explanations draw from the comments to the rules and from other sources. They are not comprehensive but highlight some important interpretive points.

d. Civil liability for dishonesty to clients

The prohibition on lying to clients is not limited to exhortations that are stated or implied in the ethical rules. A client injured by a dishonest lawyer may sue the lawyer in tort for fraud or for breach of the lawyer's fiduciary responsibilities to the client. To fulfill his fiduciary duties to a client, a lawyer must comply with obligations concerning the client's confidences and property, avoid impermissible conflicting interests, deal honestly with the client, and not employ advantages arising from the client-lawyer relationship in a manner adverse to the client.[72]

Breach of fiduciary duty, in the context of a lawyer-client relationship, is the lawyer's failure to act consistently with the trust that a client reposes in a lawyer because the lawyer has special skills and knowledge. Professors

---

72. Restatement § 16(3). Restatement § 49, comment b, explains that the duties specified in the quoted section constitute a lawyer's fiduciary duties to a client.

Roy Anderson and Walter Steele explain the fiduciary nature of the lawyer-client relationship as follows:[73]

> Although definitions of an attorney's fiduciary duty to her client abound, they are framed in quite general terms. The following is typical: "[T]he relationship between attorney and client has been described as one of uberrima fides, which means, 'most abundant good faith,' requiring absolute and perfect candor, openness and honesty, and the absence of any concealment or deception."[74] Fiduciary obligation is shaped by the discretionary control that an attorney usually has over a significant aspect of the client's life or assets, and by the fact that very often the interests of the lawyer are not always the same as, and may be in conflict with, those of the client. One court explained the special nature of a relationship that gives rise to fiduciary obligation in this way:
>
> > There is no invariable rule which determines the existence of a fiduciary relationship, but it is manifest in all the decisions that there must be not only confidence of the one in the other, but there must exist a certain inequality, dependence, weakness of age, of mental strength, business intelligence, knowledge of the facts involved, or other conditions, giving to one advantage over the other.[75]

Most cases of breach of fiduciary duty result from disloyalty (for example, undisclosed conflicts of interest), which are treated as "constructive frauds," but the tort can result from actual fraud as well.

FOR EXAMPLE: A male lawyer representing a female client in a divorce told her that he wanted to have a sexual relationship with her and stated that he was divorced. In response to her request, he told her that he was willing to have a monogamous relationship with her. Later, he conceded that he was only separated, not divorced. The client then called her lawyer's wife and learned that the lawyer had been married for 20 years, had been living with his wife the entire time, and was still living with her. The court held that the client's complaint stated a valid claim for breach of fiduciary duty.[76] Similarly, an attorney who "willfully and deliberately lied to, misled, and stole from his clients" could be sued for punitive as well as compensatory damages,[77] although punitive damages are not available for the ordinary negligence-based tort of malpractice.

---

73. Roy Ryden Anderson & Walter W. Steele Jr., Fiduciary Duty, Tort, and Contract: A Primer on the Legal Malpractice Puzzle, 47 SMU L. Rev. 235 (1994).

74. [Article's footnote 26.] Perez v. Kirk & Carrigan, 822 S.W.2d 261, 265 (Tex. App.–Corpus Christi 1991, *writ denied*).

75. [Article's citation.] Garrett v. BankWest, 459 N.W.2d 833, 838 (quoting Yuster v. Keefe, 90 N.E. 920 (Ind. App. 1910)).

76. Walter v. Stewart, 67 P.3d 1042 (Utah App. 2003).

77. Anand v. Allison, 55 Va. Cir. 261 (2001).

In some states, a plaintiff who adds a claim of breach of fiduciary duty to a malpractice suit against a lawyer may gain certain procedural advantages, such as a longer statute of limitations, a shift in some burdens of proof, the right to recover her legal fee without proving actual loss, or the right to recover punitive damages.[78]

5. Candor in counseling

Rule 2.1 describes the role of a lawyer as counselor:

> **In representing a client, a lawyer shall exercise independent professional judgment and render candid advice. In rendering advice, a lawyer may refer not only to law but to other considerations such as moral, economic, social and political factors, that may be relevant to the client's situation.**

Comment 1 explains that "legal advice often involves unpleasant facts and alternatives" and that "a lawyer should not be deterred . . . by the prospect that the advice will be unpalatable to the client."[79]

The rule seems intended to caution lawyers against simply giving clients the advice they want to hear. As Professor David Luban has noted,

Professor David Luban

> often, clients come to lawyers because they want the lawyer to bless their endeavors — sometimes, with maximum cynicism, in order to create an advice-of-counsel defense for themselves — or to write an opinion letter stating that a dubious transaction is entirely proper. The temptation for the lawyer to play ball with the client is great; as Elihu Root said, "The client never wants to be told he can't do what he wants to do; he wants to be told how to do it, and it is the lawyer's business to tell him how." . . . [Nevertheless] lawyers must [sometimes] assume the (admittedly distasteful) gatekeeper's role.[80]

---

78. Panelists Review Practicality of Inserting Breach of Fiduciary Duty Counts into Suit, 79 U.S.L.W. 2208 (Mar. 15, 2011).

79. Both the rule and Comment 2, which states that "it is proper for a lawyer to refer to relevant moral and ethical considerations," seem to distinguish between the lawyer's obligation to render candid advice and the permission that the rule confers on a lawyer to refer to nonlegal considerations while providing legal counsel. One commentator argues, however, that the second sentence of the rule also is of a mandatory nature. Larry O. Natt Gantt II, More Than Lawyers: The Legal and Ethical Implications of Counseling Clients on Nonlegal Considerations, 18 Geo. J. Leg. Ethics 365 (2006).

80. David Luban, Legal Ethics and Human Dignity (Cambridge U. Press 2007).

Lawyers are seldom disciplined for violation of Rule 2.1, perhaps because lawyer-client counseling almost always takes place in private. In fact, we have not located a single case in which a lawyer was disciplined for violating this rule. Not only is enforcement rare, but there is scant authority discussing what the rule requires of lawyers.

6. Duties imposed by contract in addition to those imposed by the ethics codes

May a lawyer and a client agree that the lawyer will comply with higher standards of performance than those set by the ethics codes?

Yes, of course. The ethics codes articulate minimum standards of performance for lawyers, so a lawyer may agree to meet higher standards. In addition to duties imposed by the law (such as the rules of professional responsibility and tort law), lawyers undertake contractual duties to their clients. Some of these set more demanding standards of performance than those required by the rules. For example, Rule 1.4 requires that a lawyer keep a client "reasonably informed," but a lawyer and client might agree that the lawyer would give the client weekly reports on the lawyer's progress. Similarly, Rule 1.5 requires that fees be "reasonable" and that a lawyer should inform a client, "preferably in writing," as to the basis on which the fee will be determined. By contract, however, a lawyer may agree to provide detailed billing statements on a specified schedule.

A lawyer may not agree to a "higher" contractual standard if the duty might cause the lawyer to violate another ethical rule.

> **FOR EXAMPLE:** As is noted above in the discussion of the duty of diligence, zealous advocacy was strongly encouraged under the now obsolete Model Code of Professional Responsibility.[81] Although the idea of "zealous advocacy" was a touchstone of traditional notions of professionalism, the drafters of the Model Rules of Professional Conduct were concerned that lawyers used this standard to justify aggressive and uncivil litigation tactics. Therefore they moved the exhortation to zealous advocacy from the canon to a comment, and qualified it. Rule 1.3 requires a lawyer to act with "reasonable diligence and promptness." The comment following the rule mentions that a lawyer must also act "with zeal in advocacy upon the client's behalf. A lawyer is not bound, however, to press for every advantage that might be realized for a client."

---

81. Canon 7 of the Model Code of Professional Responsibility stated that "a lawyer should represent a client zealously within the bounds of the law."

Suppose a lawyer wants his lawyer to be not just diligent but zealous? A lawyer and a client could agree to this, but not to the extent that the lawyer would violate duties imposed by other rules, such as the duty not to deceive a judge or the duty not to unlawfully alter, destroy, or conceal a document relevant to a case.

If a lawyer violates duties that are imposed only by contract, the lawyer may be subject to discipline for those contractual violations, even though the duties violated are not mandated by the ethics code. A lawyer arguably has an ethical duty to fulfill promises made to a client.[82]

7. Contractual reduction of a lawyer's duties: Client waiver of certain lawyer duties and "unbundled legal services"

May a lawyer and a client agree that the lawyer will be exempted from compliance with some of the standards of performance imposed by the ethics codes?

Yes, under certain conditions a lawyer and a client may contract to *lower* the expectations on the lawyer below those the ethical rules impose in exchange for an agreement that the fee charged to the client will be discounted. The purpose of such an agreement would be to make legal services available to clients who cannot afford the fees that would be charged for top-quality legal services. If car dealers sold only Lexuses, few people could have cars.

Suppose a client wants some legal advice about the requirements to set up a corporation in your state. As a soon-to-be small business owner, she wants to know the basics of what she has to do, but she cannot afford to pay for the thorough research that would explore every detail of her obligations. May the lawyer provide discount service for a discount price?

Rule 1.2(c) allows a lawyer to "limit the scope of the representation if the limitation is reasonable under the circumstances and the client gives informed consent."[83] A lawyer may agree to undertake legislative advocacy but not litigation on behalf of a client. Or the lawyer might agree to attempt to negotiate a settlement but not to file a lawsuit. However, such limitations could result in an impermissible conflict of interest. Comment 8 following

---

82. Restatement § 16, comment f. The cases cited by the Restatement impose discipline for violations of Model Code DR 7-101 (an earlier version of Rule 1.3).

83. As in other bodies of law, some of the ethical rules are default rules, meaning they are imposed unless the parties agree otherwise. For example, some of the rules prohibiting representation of a client in the face of a conflict of interest or prohibiting using information to the detriment of a client may be waived if a client gives informed consent. See, e.g., Rules 1.7(b) and 1.8(b). Other rules are mandatory and may not be waived or altered by contract.

Rule 1.7 cautions lawyers evaluating conflicts to consider "the likelihood that a difference in interests will eventuate, and, if it does, whether it will materially interfere with the lawyer's independent professional judgment in considering alternatives or foreclose courses of action that reasonably should be pursued on behalf of the client." Perhaps this suggests that the lawyer may limit what she agrees to *do* on a client's behalf, but the lawyer must provide *disinterested advice* if the lawyer believes that the client needs service that the lawyer has not agreed to provide.

Certain limitations are not permissible. A lawyer may not enter into an agreement waiving the duty of competent representation. However, a limitation on the scope of the representation "is a factor to be considered when determining the legal knowledge, skill, thoroughness and preparation reasonably necessary for the representation."[84] If a client asks a lawyer to perform a limited service, the lawyer would not be found incompetent for having failed to do work that he was not asked to do. A lawyer also is barred from making "an agreement prospectively limiting the lawyer's liability for malpractice unless the client is independently represented in making the agreement."[85]

May a client waive his rights to be kept informed or to be consulted about settlement offers?

In ordinary representation, a lawyer must keep a client apprised of important developments in a matter and absolutely must consult the client before responding to settlement offers. But what about in lawsuits designed to challenge institutional practices or to develop new law? In many such cases, the lawyer is really the driving force behind the case and the client is just a nominal plaintiff.

> **FOR EXAMPLE:** Some of the school desegregation cases filed in the 1950s and 1960s dragged on for a decade or more. Parents whose young children were the named plaintiffs didn't expect to hear from the civil rights lawyers handling the cases until the cases were over. By the time the cases were finally won, some of the children who had been in elementary school when the suits were filed were eligible to be hired as teachers in the newly desegregated school systems.[86]

---

84. Rule 1.2, Comment 7.

85. Rule 1.8(h)(1).

86. One desegregation case, *Briggs v. Elliot*, 98 F. Supp. 529 (D.S.C. 1951), which was argued together with and reversed by the famous case of *Brown v. Board of Education*, 349 U.S. 294 (1955), wasn't fully resolved until a costs and fees proceeding was upheld in *Brown v. Unified School District No. 501*, 56 F. Supp. 2d 1212 (D. Kan. 1999), more than four decades later. *Flax v. Potts*, 204 F. Supp. 458 (N.D. Tex. 1962), filed well after *Brown* was decided, was not resolved until *Flax v. Potts*, 915 F.2d 155 (5th Cir. 1990).

FOR EXAMPLE: In contemporary fair housing litigation, African American "testers" are employed by fair housing organizations to see whether landlords will rent them vacant apartments. If the landlord refuses to rent, civil rights lawyers may sue the landlord in the name of the tester, but the real instigator of the litigation is the civil rights organization. The testers often have very little personal interest in the cases.[87]

The ethical rules were written with a broad range of lawyers and clients in mind. Although in a few places the drafters made special rules for criminal defense lawyers, they may not always have considered the special issues that arise in law reform cases or in class actions. It is not clear whether or when lawyers and their clients in such cases may knowingly agree to unusual arrangements (such as less consultation). One looks in vain for case law resolving these issues.

Despite Rule 1.2(c) and a growing trend in favor of limited representation, some lawyers believe that whenever a lawyer agrees to represent a client, he must provide the best-quality services that he can. They fear that if a lawyer offers brief, off-the-cuff advice, without thorough research, to a client who can afford only an hour's consultation, the lawyer might do poor work and face disciplinary charges of incompetence or malpractice liability.[88] Several cases and ethics opinions suggest that a lawyer might get in trouble for offering discounted legal services.

- In *Nichols v. Keller*,[89] a lawyer filed a workers' compensation claim for a client but neglected to advise the client that he might be able to sue someone other than his employer to obtain compensation for his injuries. A California court held that this lawyer could be sued for malpractice, "even when [the] retention is expressly limited," at least if the lawyer did not "make such limitations in representation very clear to his client."[90]

- Several state bar ethics opinions have stated that although a lawyer may offer some assistance to a pro se litigant and help the litigant to prepare pleadings, the lawyer may be acting unethically if she offers a

---

87. See Leroy D. Clark, Employment Discrimination Testing: Theories of Standing and a Reply to Professor Yelnosky, 28 U. Mich. J.L. Reform 1, 19 (1994).

88. Margaret Graham Tebo, Loosening Ties: Unbundling of Legal Services Can Open Door to New Clients, ABA J. 35 (Aug. 2003); see also Mary Helen McNeal, Redefining Attorney-Client Roles: Unbundling and Moderate-Income Elderly Clients, 32 Wake Forest L. Rev. 295 (1997). Professor McNeal suggests that at least when representing elderly clients, lawyers should tread cautiously before offering limited services. She suggests several guidelines that they should follow before considering offering less than full-service representation. For example, she urges that "to avoid ethical breaches for the lack of competency and diligence, the lawyer must engage in sufficient factual investigation to identify relevant legal issues, such as potential counterclaims." Id. at 336.

89. 15 Cal. App. 4th 1672 (1993).

90. Id. at 1687.

litigant "active and extensive" help before and during a trial without disclosing that fact to the court.[91]

■ In a few cases, judges have admonished lawyers for "improper" conduct after they wrote portions of briefs for pro se litigants.[92]

A related issue involves lawyers who do not want to take on all the burdens and responsibilities of participating in litigation but are willing to help indigent clients with one phase of a case, such as filing a complaint. Court rules provide that once a lawyer enters an appearance in a case, the lawyer may not withdraw without court approval.[93] But if a lawyer and a client reach a clear agreement at the outset that the lawyer will provide only limited assistance, it seems unlikely that a judge would compel the lawyer to represent the client in litigation.

Defenders of a Lexus-only rule of full-service representation of clients might respond that no automobile can be driven unless it meets minimum safety requirements, enforced through state vehicle inspections. The ethical rules protect the public by requiring basic levels of competence, diligence, conflict avoidance, and so on.

In 2003, an ABA task force recommended greater use of "limited scope legal assistance" because "in the great majority of situations some legal help is better than none. An informed pro se litigant is more capable than an uninformed one."[94] The task force noted with approval two modest changes in the 2002 Model Rules amendments that would facilitate limited representation.

---

91. See the state bar opinions collected in Maryland Legal Assistance Network, Informal National Survey of Ethical Opinions Related to "Discrete Task Lawyering" (Nov. 2003) (available at http://www.courts.ca.gov/partners/documents/ethicalopinions.pdf) (collecting opinions that declare it to be unethical for lawyers to write pleadings for pro se clients, to sell do-it-yourself divorce forms, or to advise clients while disclaiming the creation of an attorney-client relationship).

92. See, e.g., Duran v. Carris, 238 F.3d 1268 (10th Cir. 2001) (observing that a lawyer who helps a pro se litigant without revealing the lawyer's involvement misleads a court into giving "liberal treatment" to the litigant); Ricotta v. Cal., 4 F. Supp. 2d 961, 974-977 (S.D. Cal. 1998) (reviewing prior cases and agreeing that (a) ghostwriting a pleading is an evasion of a lawyer's responsibility under Fed. R. Civ. P. 11 to sign pleadings and personally represent that there are grounds to support them, and (b) such behavior implicates the ethical prohibitions against dishonesty, fraud, deceit, and misrepresentation). But in 2007, the ABA ethics committee concluded that the practice was not inherently dishonest. ABA Standing Comm. on Ethics & Prof. Resp., Formal Op. 07-446 (available at http://www.americanbar. org/content/dam/aba/migrated/media/youraba/200707/07_446_2007.authcheckdam.pdf). State bars are divided in their views on this issue. For a review of those that have expressed opinions, see Ala. State B. Disciplinary Commn. Op. 2010-01 (available at http://www.alabar.org/ogc/PDF/2010-01.pdf).

93. See, e.g., Mich. Ct. R. 2.117(c)(2). Washington State, however, now permits a lawyer to represent a client for one stage of a case and to withdraw without court permission when that limited representation has been completed. Wash. Ct. R. 70.1.

94. ABA Section of Litigation, Modest Means Task Force, Handbook on Limited Scope Legal Assistance 12 (ABA 2003) (available at http://www.ftp.abanet.org/litigation/taskforces/modest/report.pdf).

- Comment 6 to Rule 1.2 was amended to make clear that a lawyer could legitimately offer limited service to a client to "exclude actions that the client thinks are too costly."[95]
- New Rule 6.5 allows a lawyer providing short-term services such as advice or form completion "under the auspices of a program sponsored by a nonprofit organization or court" to do so without having to perform an extensive check for conflicts of interest with other clients.

The task force also recommended amending court rules to allow lawyers to draft pleadings anonymously for pro se clients.[96]

Since then, several states have changed their ethics rules and court rules to permit lawyers to provide "unbundled" services.[97] (Full-scale legal services would be a complete "bundle.") For example, some states allow lawyers to enter limited appearances for particular purposes in their courts and make it easier for lawyers who enter such appearances to withdraw when their limited representation has been completed.[98] In addition, at least 12 states now allow lawyers to ghostwrite pleadings for pro se litigants,[99] although some of them require lawyers who do so to be identified in the papers that the litigants file.[100]

8. Contractual modification of a lawyer's duties: Collaborative law practice

The ethics codes are premised primarily on an adversarial model of representation of parties in conflict. Lawyers may seek amicable settlement of disputes, but if efforts to settle fail, they may resort to litigation or arbitration.[101]

---

95. The new text in Rule 1.2 and in Comment 7 is qualified by the statement in Comment 6 that the "limitation must be reasonable under the circumstances."

96. Modest Means Task Force, supra n. 94, at 144-145.

97. The changes are summarized in ABA Standing Comm. on the Delivery of Legal Services, An Analysis of Rules That Enable Lawyers to Serve Pro Se Litigants (Nov. 2009) (available at http://www.americanbar.org/content/dam/aba/migrated/legalservices/delivery/downloads/prose_white_paper.authcheckdam.pdf).

98. Id. at 18 et seq.

99. Chad Acello, Seeing Ghosts, ABA J. (Sept. 2010) (available at http://www.abajournal.com/magazine/article/seeing_ghosts/).

100. See, e.g., Colo. C.R.C.P. 11(b). In 2011, the U.S. Court of Appeals for the Second Circuit held that ghostwriting pleadings or briefs was permissible in federal cases so long as the lawyer did not cause the litigant to represent that no attorney had helped prepare the documents. In re Liu, 2011 U.S. App. LEXIS 23326 (2d Cir. Nov. 22, 2011).

101. Corporations frequently insert clauses into contracts with consumers and employees that require arbitration and prohibit litigation of disputes. One study found that already at least 75

Suppose that a divorcing couple who have children are keen to avoid litigation. May they contract with counsel to seek a collaborative rather than an adversarial outcome?

Some family law practitioners offer clients the opportunity to pursue divorces using a collaborative system. Each client has his or her own lawyer, but all agree to work in a problem-solving, nonadversarial mode in which each party takes account of the interests of the others and works to avoid damage to the network of family relationships. This has come to be known as "collaborative law practice," but it has been used mainly in divorce cases.[102] The two parties and their lawyers make a contract at the outset in which they agree to work toward these goals and, if litigation becomes necessary, to have both lawyers resign and have the clients proceed pro se or engage new counsel. This arrangement helps to motivate both lawyers and clients to work collaboratively.

The state bar ethics committees that have examined this set of contractual limitations on provision of legal services have found, in general, that these restrictions are permissible so long as the clients are informed of the potential risks.[103] The sticking point, in some jurisdictions, is whether a lawyer may agree in advance to resign if litigation becomes necessary. The bar ethics committee in Colorado issued an opinion in which it found such an agreement to violate a lawyer's fundamental duties.[104] Then the ABA ethics committee published an opinion affirming this process as a permissible one, if the client gives truly informed consent.[105] Some clients seek to avoid an adversarial process because it does not serve their interests, because they cannot afford the legal fees, or both. Collaborative law practice

---

percent of agreements with consumers include mandatory arbitration clauses, although the same corporations that write such clauses into agreements with their customers almost never require arbitration of disputes in their contracts with each other. Jonathan D. Glater, Companies Unlikely to Use Arbitration with Each Other, N.Y. Times (Oct. 5, 2008) (available at http://www.nytimes.com/2008/10/06/business/06arbitrate.html). The use of mandatory arbitration clauses in contracts with employees and consumers is likely to increase markedly as a result of the Supreme Court's decision in *AT&T Mobility v. Concepcion*, 131 S. Ct. 1740 (2011) (Federal Arbitration Act overrides state law declaring invalid and unconscionable certain types of mandatory arbitration clauses imposed on consumers).

102. Pauline H. Tesler, Collaborative Law: Achieving Effective Resolution in Divorce Without Litigation (2d ed., ABA 2008).

103. See, e.g., S.C. B. Ethics Advisory Comm., Op. 10-01 (available at http://ww2.scbar.org/member_resources/ethics_advisory_opinions/&id = 683); see generally Ted Schneyer, The Organized Bar and the Collaborative Law Movement: A Study in Professional Change, 50 Ariz. L. Rev. 289, 305-310 (2008) (available at http://www.collaborativelawflorida.com/Articles/The-Collaborative-Law-Movement.html).

104. See Colo. B. Assn. Ethics Comm., Ethics Op. 115 (2007) (available at http://www.cobar.org/group/display.cfm?GenID = 10159&EntityID = CETH).

105. ABA Standing Comm. on Ethics & Prof. Resp., Formal Op. 07-447, at 3 (available at http://www.collaborativelaw.us/articles/Ethics_Opinion_ABA.pdf).

is one example of how the profession is evolving to provide legal services that meet the needs of clients.

In 2009, after three years of drafting and deliberation, the National Conference of Commissioners on Uniform State Laws (NCCUSL) issued a uniform state law on the collaborative practice of law that presents collaborative lawyering as a form of alternative dispute resolution and standardizes the primary features of collaborative lawyering with an eye to the ethical issues and the privilege issues raised by this type of practice.[106] As of November 2012, this Collaborative Law Act has been adopted by the state legislatures in Nevada, Utah, Hawaii, Texas, and the District of Columbia, and has been introduced in the legislatures of Maryland, Washington, and Massachusetts.[107]

Collaborative lawyering remains controversial, at least in the ABA House of Delegates. The ABA debated endorsing the NCCUSL Collaborative Law Act in 2011. Endorsement was defeated in the House of Delegates by a vote of 154 to 208. Two objections were raised. First, echoing the archaic controversy about who should govern the legal profession (discussed in Chapter 1), former ABA president Carolyn Lamm argued that only state bar associations, not state legislatures, should decide how law should be practiced. Lamm urged that state regulation is "not lawyers regulating themselves." She maintained this objection, even though the NCCUSL had amended its act in 2010 to permit states to adopt the uniform provisions by court rule rather than legislation. Second, Lawrence J. Fox of Philadelphia argued that collaborative practice is objectionable because it allows either party to direct that the other party's lawyer be removed from the matter. This would interfere with clients' choice of counsel.[108] The negative vote on endorsement of the Collaborative Law Act suggests that many delegates agreed with these objections. Despite the ABA's failure to endorse the measure, state legislatures may enact the NCCUSL proposal.

D. Who calls the shots?

1. The competent adult client

Which decisions may a lawyer make without consulting a client, and which decisions require client consultation? To resolve a legal matter, whether in

---

106. NCCUSL, Collaborative Law Act, http://www.uniformlaws.org/Act.aspx?title = Collaborative Law Act (accessed Nov. 2, 2012). The act was amended by NCCUSL in 2010. Id.

107. Id.

108. ABA Nixes Model Collaborative Practice Law, Wants Law Graduations to be "Practice Ready," 80 U.S.L.W. 217 (Aug. 16, 2011).

*"If we're being honest, it was your decision to follow my
recommendations that cost you money."*

court or privately, a lawyer often must make hundreds of decisions. They
range in significance from the obviously momentous (e.g., the decision
whether to file suit or to sign a contract) to the apparently trivial (such as
whether, in order to seek an extension of time within which to file a brief,
the lawyer should telephone opposing counsel, write a letter, or send a fax).
Even apparently unimportant choices can have a significant impact on the
outcome of a case. For example, a lawyer asking for a filing deadline extension often telephones opposing counsel rather than writing a letter. This
saves time, but what happens if later a dispute arises about whether opposing counsel agreed to the extension? A phone conversation carries no
written record. Also, it opens the door for opposing counsel to make a
counter-request (perhaps for information about the case) and to negotiate
about both requests. In either case, a small decision could have substantive
consequences.

Suppose a lawyer consults a client about a particular decision and they
then disagree about what should be done. Who gets to call the shots? Does
it depend on what the issue is?

Because a lawyer is his client's agent, one might argue that *all* decisions
should be a matter of consultation and ultimately should be left to the
client. However, this is impractical. Some decisions, such as the decision
whether to make an objection to a question during a hearing, must be made

instantly. In addition, legal work involves so many decisions that for the client to be involved in all of them, the client would practically have to live in the lawyer's office while the lawyer was working on the case.[109]

On the other hand, lawyers must consult with clients about some decisions about how to proceed in the clients' cases. Some decisions that lawyers make have profound consequences for clients. Also, agency law imputes most lawyers' decisions to clients, so a client could face liability for a decision made by his lawyer. Rule 1.2 offers guidance on which decisions a lawyer must make after consultation with the client. The standard is necessarily somewhat vague because of the enormous variety of types of decisions that lawyers and clients make during the course of representation.

Rule 1.2 Scope of Representation and Allocation of Authority Between Client and Lawyer

Rule language*	Authors' explanation**

(a) Subject to paragraphs (c) and (d), a lawyer **shall abide by a client's decisions** concerning the **objectives** of representation and, as required by Rule 1.4, **shall consult** with the client as to the **means** by which they are to be pursued. A lawyer may take such action on behalf of the client as is impliedly authorized to carry out the representation. **A lawyer shall abide by a client's decision whether to settle** a matter. In a **criminal** case, the lawyer **shall abide by the client's decision**, after consultation with the lawyer, as to a **plea to be entered**, whether to **waive jury trial** and whether the **client will testify**.	• Client decides objectives of representation (usually with advice and guidance by the lawyer).
	• Lawyer must consult client as to means used to pursue objectives.
	• Civil case: Client decides whether to settle.
	• Criminal case: Client decides whether
	  ○ to plead guilty,
	  ○ to waive jury trial,
	  ○ to testify.

(b) A lawyer's **representation** of a client, including representation by appointment, does **not constitute an endorsement** of the client's political, economic, social or moral views or activities.	Example: A lawyer might represent the American Nazi Party even though he thought its goals were objectionable.

---

109. Many published descriptions of civil litigation capture the quality of the constant decision making in which lawyers engage. See, e.g., Jonathan Harr, A Civil Action (Random House 1995).

Rule language*	Authors' explanation**
(c) A lawyer may **limit the scope of the representation** if the limitation is reasonable under the circumstances and the client gives informed consent.	A lawyer and a client may agree that the lawyer will provide less than the full range of services. The client may prefer this arrangement to reduce costs or for other reasons.
(d) A lawyer **shall not counsel a client to engage, or assist a client, in conduct that the lawyer knows is criminal or fraudulent**, but a lawyer may discuss the legal consequences of any proposed course of conduct with a client and may counsel or assist a client to make a good faith effort to determine the validity, scope, meaning or application of the law.	This provision bars lawyers from advising or assisting clients in illegal or fraudulent activity.[110]

*All emphasis added.

**This and other authors' explanations draw from the comments to the rules and from other sources. They are not comprehensive but highlight some important interpretive points.

Both Rule 1.2 and the communication requirements of Rule 1.4, discussed above, allocate decision making between lawyers and clients. A lawyer must keep the client "reasonably" informed about the "status" of a matter.[111] The lawyer must also explain the work to the extent "reasonably necessary" to permit the client to make "informed decisions" regarding the representation.[112] Once consulted and advised, the client has the right to make decisions concerning the "objectives" of the representation and the explicit right to make four particular decisions: in a civil dispute, whether to settle; and in a criminal case, what plea to enter, whether to waive a jury trial, and whether to testify.[113]

Rule 1.2 does not define "objectives," nor does it say much about what decisions the lawyer may make, except the obvious point that the lawyer may take actions that are "impliedly authorized." The rule does not explain what types of decisions a client impliedly authorizes the lawyer to make. Comment 2 states that "clients normally defer to the special knowledge and skill of their lawyer with respect to the means to be used to accomplish their objectives, particularly with respect to technical, legal, and tactical matters." The comment explains also that lawyers usually defer to clients with respect to "questions such as the expense to be incurred and concern for third persons who might be adversely affected." The rule does not prescribe how

---

110. See the discussion in connection with the problem on Reese's Leases in Chapter 3.

111. Rule 1.4(a)(3).

112. Rule 1.4(b).

113. Rule 1.2(a).

disagreements between lawyers and clients about the means to be employed are to be resolved.

The Restatement provides more guidance than the ethics rules. It states that except for decisions reserved for clients and in the absence of an agreement on these matters, a lawyer may take "any lawful measure within the scope of representation that is reasonably calculated to advance a client's objective."[114] For example, the lawyer may decide whether

- to move to dismiss a complaint and what discovery to pursue or resist, to accommodate reasonable requests of opposing counsel,
- to object or waive objections to questions during hearings, or
- to decide what questions to ask a witness.[115]

The Restatement suggests that unless a lawyer and client have agreed otherwise, the lawyer, not the client, should make decisions that "involve technical legal and strategic considerations difficult for a client to assess."[116]

Both the ethics rules and the Restatement leave unanswered many questions about what lawyers can do in the absence of specific authorization from their clients or in the face of specific opposition from their clients.

- May a lawyer transfer a case to another lawyer in his law firm without the client's consent?
- Although a lawyer may not settle a case without the client's permission, may she make a settlement offer to see how the other side responds? If she does this, must she disclose that she has not yet discussed the offer with the client?
- May a lawyer decide without consulting a client or over a client's objection to waive a technical defense or a jury trial in a civil case?
- May a lawyer decline to press a weak legal argument that he thinks will not prevail but instead will signal the court that his whole case is very weak?

Jones v. Barnes: May a lawyer decide what issues to pass on appeal?

The Supreme Court decision in *Jones v. Barnes*[117] explored the scope of a criminal defense lawyer's authority in representing a client. As you have seen in other cases, when the issue arises in a criminal context, the ordinary issues of legal ethics are overlaid with a set of issues relating to the con-

---

114. Restatement § 21, comment e.
115. Id.
116. Id.
117. 463 U.S. 745 (1983).

stitutional rights of criminal defendants. In *Jones*, a man named Butts had been robbed at knifepoint. Butts told a detective that he knew that one of his assailants was a person he knew as "Froggy," and he described the man. The police arrested Barnes, who was known as "Froggy." The prosecution case was based mainly on Butts's testimony. On cross-examination, Barnes's lawyer asked Butts whether he had ever undergone psychiatric examination, but the judge directed Butts not to answer the question. Barnes was convicted. The appellate court assigned Michael Melinger to represent him. Barnes wrote to Melinger, asking him to argue in his appellate brief that Butts's identification testimony should have been suppressed, that the trial judge improperly excluded psychiatric evidence, and that respondent's trial counsel was ineffective. Barnes enclosed a copy of an appellate brief that he had written. In a return letter, Melinger rejected most of the arguments that Barnes wanted him to make. He said that they would not help Barnes and that they could not be raised on appeal because they were not based on evidence in the record. Melinger listed seven claims of error that he was considering including in his brief. He invited Barnes to react to them, but Barnes did not respond.

Melinger's brief included some but not all of the arguments that Barnes wanted him to make. Melinger also submitted the brief that Barnes had written. At the oral argument, Melinger argued the points in his own brief but not Barnes's additional arguments. After Barnes's conviction was affirmed, Barnes filed a writ of habeas corpus claiming that Melinger's assistance on appeal had been unconstitutionally ineffective because it did not assert all the arguments that Barnes wanted Melinger to use. That constitutional claim was eventually analyzed by the Supreme Court.

In an opinion written by Chief Justice Burger, the Court acknowledged that under its precedents, Barnes could have acted as his own representative.[118] But the Court held that an indigent defendant has no

> right to compel appointed counsel to press nonfrivolous points [he] requested . . . , if counsel, as a matter of professional judgment, decides not to present those points. . . . This Court, in holding that a state must provide counsel for an indigent appellant on his first appeal as of right, recognized the superior ability of trained counsel in the "examination into the record, research of the law, and marshaling of arguments on [the appellant's] behalf. . . . [O]ne of the first tests of a discriminating advocate is to select the question, or questions, that he will present orally [because] "most cases present only one, two, or three significant questions. . . . Usually, . . . if you cannot win on a few major points, the others are not likely to help, and to attempt to deal with a great many in the limited number of pages allowed for briefs will mean that none may receive

---

118. Faretta v. Cal., 422 U.S. 806 (1975).

adequate attention. The effect of adding weak arguments will be to dilute the force of the stronger ones." R. Stern, Appellate Practice in the United States 266 (1981). . . . A brief that raises every colorable issue runs the risk of burying good arguments — those that, in the words of the great advocate John W. Davis, "go for the jugular." Davis, The Argument of an Appeal, 26 A.B.A.J. 895, 897 (1940)[119] — in a verbal mound made up of strong and weak contentions. . . . [Except for decisions allocated to the client in the ethical rules,] an attorney's duty is to take professional responsibility for the conduct of the case, after consulting with his client. . . .[120]

The Court upheld the conviction.

Justice Blackmun concurred, stating that "as an ethical matter, an attorney should argue on appeal all nonfrivolous claims upon which his client insists,"[121] but the lawyer's refusal to do so does not violate the Sixth Amendment when the lawyer's conduct is "'within the range of competence demanded of attorneys in criminal cases'"[122] and "'assure[s] the indigent defendant an adequate opportunity to present his claims fairly in the context of the State's appellate process.'"[123]

Justices Brennan and Marshall dissented. In their view, the position of a criminal defendant for whom counsel is appointed is unique. "'To force a lawyer on a defendant can only lead him to believe that the law contrives against him,'" they noted. "'The defendant, and not his lawyer or the State, will bear the personal consequences of a conviction. It is the defendant, therefore, who must be free personally to decide whether in his particular case counsel is to his advantage.'"[124] They agreed with the majority that clients generally should defer to their lawyers' judgments about which issues should be raised on appeal. But, they continued,

> [t]he Constitution . . . does not require clients to be wise. . . . It is no secret that indigent clients often mistrust the lawyers appointed to represent them. . . . A lawyer and his client do not always have the same interests. Even with paying clients, a lawyer may have a strong interest in having judges and prosecutors think well of him, and, if he is working for a flat fee — a common arrangement for criminal defense attorneys — or if his fees for court appointments are lower than he would receive for other

---

119. [Authors' footnote.] John W. Davis is famous for, among other things, having argued South Carolina's case (against desegregation) in *Brown v. Board of Education.* See Anthony G. Amsterdam, Telling Stories and Stories About Them, 1 Clin. L. Rev. 9 (1994). Davis was the Democratic Party's nominee for president in 1924.

120. *Barnes,* 463 U.S. at 751-753.

121. Id. at 754.

122. Id. at 755 (quoting McMann v. Richardson, 397 U.S. 759, 771 (1970)).

123. Id. (quoting Ross v. Moffitt, 417 U.S. 600, 616 (1974)).

124. Id. at 758 (quoting Faretta v. Cal., 422 U.S. 806, 834 (1975)).

work, he has an obvious financial incentive to conclude cases on his criminal docket swiftly. . . . A constitutional rule that encourages lawyers to disregard their clients' wishes without compelling need can only exacerbate the clients' suspicion of their lawyers. . . . I am not willing to risk deepening the mistrust between clients and lawyers in all cases to ensure optimal presentation for that fraction of a handful in which presentation might really affect the result reached by the court of appeals.

Finally, today's ruling denigrates the values of individual autonomy and dignity central to many constitutional rights, especially those Fifth and Sixth Amendment rights that come into play in the criminal process. . . . The role of the defense lawyer should be above all to function as the instrument and defender of the client's autonomy and dignity in all phases of the criminal process. . . . The Court subtly but unmistakably adopts a different conception of the defense lawyer's role — he need do nothing beyond what the State, not his client, considers most important. In many ways, having a lawyer becomes one of the many indignities visited upon someone who has the ill fortune to run afoul of the criminal justice system. I cannot accept the notion that lawyers are one of the punishments a person receives merely for being accused of a crime. . . .[125]

Notes and Questions about *Jones v. Barnes*

1. **What got settled?** Did *Jones v. Barnes* settle the question of whether lawyers should let their clients decide which issues to raise?

2. **What would you do?** What do you think of Justice Brennan's view that since clients bear the consequences of lawyers' decisions, lawyers should defer to their clients' judgments? If you are appointed to represent a criminal defendant, should you follow your client's guidance in raising issues (at trial or on appeal), against your better judgment and your advice to your client?

3. **A wealthy client.** Suppose you are representing a really wealthy criminal defendant — someone like Martha Stewart, perhaps. Might you be more deferential to the wishes of such a well-heeled client? If so, why?

4. **Paid representation.** In principle, if the defendant can pay, he could fire you and get a new attorney. In practice, that option may not really be available. If the client has already given you a retainer of some thousands of dollars, the client may not have enough money to start over again with a new lawyer. Even if the client has the money, it is often impractical to change lawyers in the middle of a case because of the time required for another lawyer to become familiar

---

125. Id. at 761-762, 763-764.

with the matter. The court may not be willing to delay the case if the defendant changes lawyers. Does this suggest that a criminal defense lawyer should be very deferential to a client regardless of his financial resources?

5. **Civil cases.** The consequence of losing a civil case does not include loss of liberty, but a plaintiff might face loss of compensation for a serious injury. A defendant might face extensive monetary liability or other consequences. Given this, perhaps a lawyer should be just as deferential to a client in a civil case as in a criminal case. Alternatively, perhaps the degree of deference should depend more on the context of a particular case than on whether it is civil or criminal.

6. **The client's brief.** Justice Jackson (quoted in the majority opinion) wrote that "[o]ne of the first tests of a discriminating advocate is to select the question, or questions, that he will present orally." If you think that as a lawyer you should sort through the arguments and present the best case to the court, should you, like Melinger, *also* file the brief that your client wrote, which presents the arguments that you did not want to present?

7. **Ends and means.** Rule 1.2(a) appears to distinguish between the "objectives" of the representation (which the client decides) and the "means by which [the objectives] are to be pursued" (which the lawyer decides after consulting with the client). Is this distinction clear? For example, was Barnes's desire to present his issues to the appellate court one of his "objectives," or was it only a "means" to the end of having his conviction reversed?

8. **Collaboration.** In an article published shortly after the decision in *Jones v. Barnes*, Professor Judith Maute contended that the Model Rules embody a "collaborative joint venture model" of lawyer-client decision making. She sees the vagueness of the rules as a virtue: "By providing only general guidance, the Rules promote genuine dialogue between interdependent persons."[126] The interdependence results from the fact that the client will suffer if she discharges a lawyer who has already put substantial work into a matter, and the lawyer will suffer the economic losses after such a discharge.

Professor Maute's optimism about lawyer-client dialogue may not be justified. When she addresses decisions by lawyers that the rules do not clearly allocate to either the lawyer or the client, she finds that case law supports a fairly traditional lawyer-centered approach. With respect to civil litigation, she reports that

---

126. Judith L. Maute, Allocation of Decisionmaking Authority Under the Model Rules of Professional Conduct, 17 U. Cal. Davis L. Rev. 1049, 1059, 1066 (1984).

> [u]pon hiring a lawyer for litigation representation the client relinquishes control over procedural and tactical issues. The cases are replete with references to the lawyer's plenary powers in litigation. . . . The lawyer's broad authority is justified. . . . A retainer to litigate a matter may impliedly authorize a lawyer to accept service of process, to waive jurisdictional defects, to waive technical filing errors . . . or to consent to a preliminary injunction. . . . Stipulations and concessions by counsel present dilemmas and often fall within the overlap zone of authority. . . . The [few decisions in civil] cases confer principal authority over the litigation process to the lawyer [but] also reflect an ambivalence toward procedural decisions [by lawyers] that threaten clients' substantive interests.[127]

9. **A client's objections to assigned counsel.** Major David Frakt (USAF) was assigned as defense counsel to represent Ali Al-Bahlul, an alleged terrorist, in a trial before a military commission at Guantanamo Bay, Cuba. Al-Bahlul faced a possible sentence of life in prison, but he did not recognize the legitimacy of the tribunal and did not want to participate in its proceedings. He told Frakt that he did not want Frakt or anyone else to represent him. Al-Bahlul told the judge that he did not want Frakt to serve as his lawyer, and Frakt stated in court that he wished to respect Al-Bahlul's wishes. Even so, the judge ordered Frakt to represent Al-Bahlul. Frakt went to court and sat at the table for defense counsel. As the trial began, the government began to introduce evidence that was arguably inadmissible.

Suppose you were in Frakt's shoes. What would you do if you were ordered to represent a client who did not want you to represent him? Would you appear at the court proceedings? Sit at the counsel table? Object to the admission of arguably tainted evidence? Cross-examine the prosecution's witnesses? To hear Major Frakt discuss what he actually did, and why, in an eight-minute recording, go to http://aspenlawschool.com/books/lerman_concise/.

2. Clients with diminished capacity

Lawyers are often called on to represent children or persons with mental disabilities. A client with diminished capacity may be unable to make wise

---

127. Id. at 1089-1093, 1107.

judgments about legal matters. The ethics rules address this issue in Rule 1.14.

> **Rule 1.14 Client with Diminished Capacity**
>
> **(a) When a client's capacity to make adequately considered decisions in connection with a representation is diminished, whether because of minority, mental impairment or for some other reason, the lawyer shall, as far as reasonably possible, maintain a normal client-lawyer relationship with the client.**
>
> **(b) When the lawyer reasonably believes that the client has diminished capacity, is at risk of substantial physical, financial or other harm unless action is taken and cannot adequately act in the client's own interest, the lawyer may take reasonably necessary protective action, including consulting with individuals or entities that have the ability to take action to protect the client and, in appropriate cases, seeking the appointment of a guardian ad litem, conservator or guardian.**
>
> **(c) Information relating to the representation of a client with diminished capacity is protected by Rule 1.6. When taking protective action pursuant to paragraph (b), the lawyer is impliedly authorized under Rule 1.6(a) to reveal information about the client, but only to the extent reasonably necessary to protect the client's interests.**

Subsection (a) of the rule encourages lawyers to maintain "normal" lawyer-client relations with clients who may have some degree of diminished capacity. Subsection (b) acknowledges that in some situations, a lawyer needs the flexibility to assume a more paternalistic role to protect the client from some harm. In such cases, a lawyer may ask a court to appoint a third party who would make some legal decisions on behalf of the client. This raises several issues. Is a lawyer supposed to assess whether and to what extent a client suffers from diminished mental capacity? Most lawyers are not expert in psychological evaluation. How can a lawyer make such an assessment? Is a lawyer who has doubts about a client's mental capacity supposed to send the client for a psychological evaluation? Comment 6 to Rule 1.14 suggests that a lawyer can and should make some assessment of a client's mental capacity. It urges lawyers to consider and balance such factors as the client's ability to articulate reasoning leading to a decision; variability of state of mind; and ability to appreciate the consequences of a decision, the substantive fairness of a decision, and the consistency of a decision with the known long-term commitments and values of the client. In appropriate circumstances, the lawyer may seek guidance from an appropriate diagnostician.

a. Clients who may have mental impairments

The rule assumes that, in at least some cases, a lawyer would know that a client's mental capacity is diminished. In such a case, what should the lawyer do? The rule contemplates that the lawyer may consult about the matter on which the lawyer is representing the client with "individuals or entities" other than the client, such as members of the client's family or public agencies. But it does not explain how the lawyer should know whether to do so. This judgment is important because such contact will involve divulging some client confidences and it will reduce client autonomy.

Sometimes, a client who might have limited competency insists that he or she is fully competent, or directs a lawyer not to raise competency issues. Such a client might be articulate and fully competent to hire a lawyer and to stand trial, but the lawyer may think the client is not making good decisions about the client's own future. What should the lawyer do then?

Can a lawyer avoid making decisions for a possibly impaired client by getting someone else to make those decisions?

A lawyer who represents a client who has an intellectual impairment or a diagnosis of mental illness has several options.

- She might simply follow the client's instructions, to the extent possible.
- She might impose her own ideas of what is best, either because the client is unable to provide instructions or gives instructions that the lawyer believes goes against the client's self-interest.
- She might invite others (the client's friends or family members, social welfare agencies, or courts) to provide substitute guidance.

Also, the lawyer might limit her focus to the matter for which she has been retained, or she might try to help the client with problems other than the particular matter for which the lawyer has been retained. For example, the lawyer (or a third person consulted by the lawyer) might investigate whether the client is able to take care of himself, whether anyone else can care for him, and whether someone else should be given legal authority to do so. If it seems necessary to give someone else legal authority over the client, the lawyer might petition the court to appoint a guardian ad litem, a conservator, or a guardian for the client.

- A guardian ad litem is charged with the duty to determine and advocate for the best interests of the ward; the best interests may not correspond with the expressed wishes of the ward.[128]

---

128. Representation of Incompetent by Guardian Ad Litem or Next Friend, 53 Am. Jur. 2d Mentally Impaired Persons § 165 (2011).

- A conservator is given power to manage the financial affairs of the client, who thereby loses the power to buy, sell, and hold property.[129]
- A guardian has even more authority. A guardian manages the client's financial affairs and may make medical and other personal decisions for the client, who is thereafter the guardian's "ward."[130]

Professor Paul R. Tremblay

Professor Paul Tremblay argues that lawyers should not treat evidently confused or delusional clients as competent but that lawyers should also guard against becoming paternalistic. He suggests that when a lawyer correctly perceives incompetence of her client, some intervention is appropriate, but that the appointment of a guardian is a drastic and virtually complete deprivation of civil rights [depriving the ward of the] right to make legally binding decisions, to vote, to own property, to choose his place and manner of living, to make medical decisions, and so on. . . . A lawyer who is the petitioner is "suing" her own client, who must have other counsel to oppose the petition. . . . Viewed from its harshest perspective, the process looks like this: the client hires the lawyer to serve as his loyal agent and confidante; the lawyer promises him that those expectations are warranted and will be fulfilled; the lawyer then uses her client's confidences to bring a court proceeding that will deprive him of all his rights, and will require him to obtain another lawyer to defend against it; and all the while the lawyer plans to resume representing him once this distraction is over. This representation is obviously full of direct ethical violations.

The serious professional responsibility concerns that inevitably arise in this scenario, however, do not necessarily mandate banning this approach. The consequences of not intervening, and the harm to the client, may well warrant overriding the usual ethical considerations. . . . [But labeling one's client as mentally ill] can hardly be beneficial or even neutral . . . [and] guardianship petitions tend to be granted [because judges do not want to be responsible for harm befalling a potential ward]. . . . Thus, referral actually creates the guardianship. . . . [Also the lawyer usually doesn't tell the client that she played a role in obtaining the guardianship, and this secrecy is itself disloyal.][131]

When a lawyer has an incompetent client, Tremblay would prefer that a lawyer rely on family members to make judgments for the client than that

---

129. Unif. Guardianship & Protective Proc. Act (1997).

130. Id.

131. Paul Tremblay, On Persuasion and Paternalism: Lawyer Decisionmaking and the Questionably Competent Client, 1987 Utah L. Rev. 515.

the lawyer seek appointment of a guardian, which he sees as "unilateral lawyer usurpation of authority." But he concedes that in many jurisdictions family members have no authority to consent on behalf of incompetent family members, and that the law "offers no guidance" on how lawyers should resolve conflicts among family members, each of whom claims to have the client's best interests at heart.

In the end, Tremblay says, there is no perfect solution. He states that "guardianship is legitimate in extreme cases, that reliance on family members may be appropriate, that noncoercive persuasion [of clients] is justified in less extreme cases, and that unilateral usurpation of client autonomy is never appropriate except in emergencies."

PROBLEM 4-2 VINYL WINDOWS

The facts of this problem are drawn from a real case in which the client was represented by students in a law school clinic. The case was supervised by the authors.

You are a staff attorney at the civil legal assistance office. A few days ago, your office was called by Mary McCabe, who had just been sued. McCabe said that she needed legal help, but she was too old to come to your office. You went to see her at her home.

McCabe turned out to be a small, frail woman. During your first conversation, she volunteered that she was 83 years old. Her house was a large, Tudor-style home, which she and her husband had bought nearly 50 years ago. She had been a widow for 8 years. The house appeared to be in good condition, although the living room was very cluttered.

McCabe told you that two salesmen for a company called Stormguard had come to her door about a year ago and talked with her about getting new vinyl windows for her house. She didn't think that she needed new windows, but after conversing with them over a cup of tea, she agreed to let them put some windows in. She signed some papers, and the salesmen asked for some money. She didn't have a checking account or any credit cards, so she went with them to the bank, withdrew money from her account, and gave them a bank check. At the time, she had most of her life savings, $14,000, in that account. She also owns the house. Two weeks later, work on the windows started. Each time the men came to work on the windows, they asked her to go to the bank with them and have the teller give them another bank check for a portion of the amount due.

Eventually the windows were completed, but when the men asked her to pay the last $900, McCabe complained that one of the window frames leaked, and they had damaged one wall while installing one of the windows. She refused to make the last payment. Now the company has sued her for $900. She showed you the complaint from the small claims court, in which Stormguard says that she agreed to pay $8,900 but never paid the final $900 installment.

McCabe was quite confused about how much money she already paid, or when. When you asked to see any contracts, receipts, or other documents the company's men or the bank might have given her, she got distracted and started talking about "those crazy boys" who were putting in the windows. She told you that the red-headed one made a lot of jokes and that the tall one never seemed quite well. She smiled as she remembered how much they liked the brownies that she made for them. You started wondering whether your client bought the windows because she enjoyed her visits with "those crazy boys." However, McCabe thinks that one of the installers stole $400 in cash from underneath her mattress.

You laid out the options for McCabe. You told her that you know from prior experience with Stormguard's lawyer (whose name was on the summons) that when he gets to court, he offers to settle for about 50 percent of the amount stated in the complaint. If he takes this course, she could probably terminate the lawsuit by paying $450. You told her that she could

- pay the full amount now;
- wait until trial and be prepared to accept an offer to pay about $450;
- defend against the lawsuit (you immediately saw possible defenses based on duress, unconscionability, and misrepresentation);
- try to get some or all of her money back by filing a counterclaim for damages (based on the windows leaking, on the damage to the wall, and on the fact that Stormguard is apparently unlicensed, and on a local case holding that unlicensed contractors may not collect any money before completing their work); or
- try to make the company repair the window frame that leaks and repair the wall that was damaged (this might be accomplished as part of a settlement or through a counterclaim for specific performance).

McCabe understood that she was required to respond to the lawsuit, but she had a hard time figuring out what she wanted to do.

Whenever you tried to get her to make a decision, she went on about "those crazy boys." During your first meeting with her, McCabe signed your organization's standard form retainer in which you agreed to represent her in her dispute with Stormguard without charging her a fee.

You asked McCabe if she had any living relatives. She does not; her only brother died a year ago. You asked if there were any friends or neighbors whom she knew well. All of her old friends had passed away, but she said she was friendly with her next-door neighbor, Mrs. Houston, whom she sees every week or two.

The court does not require a written answer if McCabe plans to appear and offer defenses against the claim. You tend to favor fairly aggressive strategies, so you think that she should not pay any more money and should counterclaim. If she wants to file a counterclaim, however, you must file it within a few days. The trial date is in one week, though you probably could obtain a short continuance. You will be seeing McCabe again this afternoon. If she still can't decide how she wants to respond to the lawsuit, what should you do?

---

b. Juveniles

Rule 1.14 applies the same standards to minors that it applies to adults with mental impairments. This means that lawyers should maintain normal lawyer-client relationships with minors to the extent possible. Comment 1 notes that "children as young as five or six years of age, and certainly those of ten or twelve, are regarded as having opinions that are entitled to weight in legal proceedings concerning their custody." The rule makes no distinctions among the various types of proceedings in which minors may be involved. These include delinquency cases (in which the minor has been charged with an offense), custody or adoption proceedings, abuse and neglect proceedings (in which the state is attempting to terminate a parent's custody of a child and remove the child to institutional care or a foster home), and other civil cases (such as personal injury suits by or against minors). Although the ethics rules posit a single rule to cover all these situations, lawyers who represent minors tend to observe norms that are specific to the proceedings involved.

Delinquency cases When they represent children who are charged with juvenile offenses, lawyers typically represent older children, and the cases resemble criminal cases. Therefore most lawyers follow norms of representation similar to the norms they follow when representing adults in court.

"He's talking now, but only through his attorney."

Custody, abuse, and neglect proceedings   Although lawyers are supposed to play essentially the same role as representatives of juveniles in delinquency proceedings that they do for adults who are charged with crimes, their role in other proceedings involving children may be less shaped by the traditional model of the lawyer-client relationship. One difference is that most juveniles who are charged with criminal offenses are teenagers, whereas children in other types of proceedings may be much younger. A second difference is that although the substantive law may permit or require children to have their own lawyers in delinquency cases, it may afford them fewer rights in certain other types of proceedings.

Should a lawyer representing a young child in a child custody matter advocate for the child's stated wishes or the child's "best interests"? Does a lawyer who represents the parents in a matter in which the child has no separate lawyer have duties to the child also? It is problematic for any lawyer in a custody matter to advocate only the child's wishes, on the one hand, or what the lawyer thinks are the child's best interests, on the other. A child might be too young to state goals or too emotionally immature to have the knowledge and judgment needed to evaluate what he or she would prefer to do. On the other hand, if lawyers are free to make their own judgments of what is in their juvenile clients' best interests, the outcome may depend more on who is the lawyer (and what are his presuppositions, biases, and so on) than on the wishes of the child. Also, many lawyers who represent children have large caseloads and do not have time to investigate fully the child's family situation. So the lawyer's judgment might not be fully informed.

While Rule 1.14 lumps representation of children with representation of other persons who have limited mental capacity, other advisory standards, particularly the ABA's Standards of Practice for Lawyers Representing a Child in Abuse and Neglect Cases (1996),[132] which some states have adopted, provide more precise guidance on the role of lawyers in representing children. The ABA standards state that a lawyer for a child "owes the same duties of undivided loyalty, confidentiality and competent representation to the child as is due to an adult client" and that the child's attorney "must advocate the child's articulated position" rather than what the attorney believes would be in the child's best interest. The lawyer should "elicit the child's preferences in a developmentally appropriate manner" and should "follow the child's direction throughout the course of litigation."

E. Terminating a lawyer-client relationship

1. Duties to the client at the conclusion of the relationship

Most lawyer-client relationships end when all the work on the relevant matter has been completed.[133] When the work is finished, the lawyer must return to the client "any papers and property to which the client is entitled" and must return any unearned payment that the client may have made.[134] The relationship is not entirely over at this point because the lawyer has a duty to protect client confidences, a duty that continues indefinitely.[135]

The ethics rules do not specify what types of papers must be returned to a client or whether they must be delivered to the client even if the client does not request them. The Restatement is more specific about a lawyer's

---

132. The ABA Standards are available at http://apps.americanbar.org/child/rclji/repstandwhole. pdf (accessed Nov. 2, 2012). The standards are intended to provide guidance for lawyers, but unlike the Model Rules, they are not intended to be promulgated by state courts as formal disciplinary rules. The ABA regards the standards as current guidance, but they predate the 2002 revision to Model Rule 1.14, which instituted the idea that clients may be of "diminished capacity" and do not simply have or lack a disability.

133. A lawyer does not have a continuing duty to inform former clients about changes in the law pertinent to the former representation. If the lawyer continues to represent the client on the matter or on other matters, a court might eventually infer such a duty, but there are as yet no holdings on point. Restatement § 33, comment h, and reporter's note.

134. Rule 1.16(d).

135. Rule 1.6, Comment 18.

duties to a client, both during and after the representation. Section 46 explains:

> **(2) On request, a lawyer must allow a client or former client to inspect and copy any document[136] possessed by the lawyer relating to the representation, unless substantial grounds exist to refuse.**
>
> **(3) Unless a client or former client consents to non-delivery or substantial grounds exist for refusing to make delivery, a lawyer must deliver to the client or former client, at an appropriate time and *in any event promptly after the representation ends*, such originals and copies of other documents possessed by the lawyer relating to the representation as the client or former client reasonably needs [emphasis added].**

A comment identifies certain types of documents that may be withheld from a client or former client.

> A lawyer may refuse to disclose to the client certain law-firm documents reasonably intended only for internal review, such as a memorandum discussing which lawyers in the firm should be assigned to a case, whether a lawyer must withdraw because of the client's misconduct, or the firm's possible malpractice liability to the client. The need for lawyers to be able to set down their thoughts privately in order to assure effective and appropriate representation warrants keeping such documents secret from the client involved. . . . The lawyer's duty to inform the client can require the lawyer to disclose matters discussed in a document even when the document itself need not be disclosed.[137]

If a client has not paid the bill at the end of the representation, may the lawyer keep the client's documents until the client pays?

If the client has not yet fully paid the lawyer's fee, or the fee is disputed, the lawyer may retain the documents that the lawyer created for the client for which compensation has not been received, unless retention would "un-

---

136. [Authors' footnote.] Restatement § 46, comment a, explains that "a document includes a writing, drawing, graph, chart, photograph, phono-record, tape, disc, or other form of data compilation." Comment d explains that "[t]he client should have an original of documents such as contracts, while a copy will suffice for such documents as legal memoranda and court opinions."

137. Restatement § 46, comment c. In 2009, the Tennessee Bar proposed to the state's supreme court that it adopt a rule requiring lawyers to return to the client, on request, all "client filed materials," which were defined to include "attorney notes, research materials, and other work product prepared by the lawyer for the client, if the lawyer has received payment for creating those materials." Proposed Overhaul of Tennessee Rules Embraces ABA Updates, with Key Changes, 77 U.S.L.W. 2743 (June 9, 2009). The court did not adopt the rule. Joan C. Rogers, Latest Updates to Tennessee Ethics Rules Add Some Unique Standards to ABA Models, ABA/BNA Laws.' Man. on Prof. Conduct 26:617 (Oct. 13, 2010) (available at http://arwebserver.arlaw.com/pdf/tennrevised rules10132010LMPC.pdf).

reasonably harm the client."[138] In all but a few states, statutes and court rules permit a lawyer to obtain a broad retaining lien under which, if the client fails to pay the lawyer's fee or if the amount owed is disputed, the lawyer may decline to return original documents (such as birth certificates and passports) that belong to the client that the client provided to the lawyer to obtain legal assistance. The authors of the Restatement strongly criticize the law that permits such broad retaining liens, urging that it may "impose pressure on a client [to pay a disputed bill or a bill that a client cannot afford to pay] disproportionate to the size or validity of the lawyer's fee claim."[139] Therefore the Restatement authors take the position that "unless otherwise provided by statute or rule," a lawyer may contract with a client only for a narrower retaining lien under which the lawyer might secure payment of his fee by retaining "the proceeds of the representation" up to "the amount of fees and disbursements claimed reasonably and in good faith for the lawyer's services."[140]

What if a lawyer has drafted an affidavit — not yet filed with a court — for a client and comes to believe that it contains false information? If the lawyer is terminating her relationship to the client, and the lawyer thinks the client would simply pass on the draft to his successor lawyer, must the lawyer turn over the draft affidavit to the client?

The Restatement says that absent client consent or unless "substantial grounds exist for refusing to make delivery," a lawyer must deliver to a client "such documents . . . relating to the representation of the client as the client or former client reasonably needs."[141] The comment explains that the lawyer may retain documents based on a valid lien or if turning over the documents "would violate the lawyer's duty to another." As examples, the Restatement mentions if the provision of documents would violate a protective order or "if the lawyer reasonably believed that the client would use the document to commit a crime."[142] If the client provided the affidavit to another lawyer, this could lead to the new lawyer presenting perjured testimony by the client, which would be a criminal offense. In a similar vein, a District of Columbia ethics opinion states that the lawyer may withhold documents of this character if the lawyer believes that the client intends to file them in court or provide them to another lawyer.[143]

---

138. Restatement § 43, comment c.
139. Restatement § 43, comment b.
140. Restatement § 43(2).
141. Restatement § 46(3).
142. Restatement § 46(3), comment c.
143. D.C. B. Leg. Ethics Comm., Op. 350 (2009) (available at http://www.dcbar.org/for_lawyers/ethics/legal_ethics/opinions/opinion350.cfm).

PROBLEM 4-3 THE CANDID NOTES

This problem is based on a situation that arose in a law school clinic. We have changed the setting to a law firm and changed the text of the "candid notes."

You are a partner in a small law firm that has three partners, four associates, and three paralegals. The lawyers have instructed the paralegals to make thorough notes of their work, and especially to record their candid impressions of clients whom they interview, so that the lawyers know what to expect when they encounter these clients.

A few months ago, you represented Winnie Bryzanski in an unsuccessful administrative proceeding to require the local school board to admit her daughter Leona to a special education program. Bryzanski decided not to take the matter to court because she did not have enough money to retain you. At that point, she paid for the work that your firm had performed, and your representation ended. You returned to Bryzanski all of her original documents such as Leona's birth certificate.

Yesterday, you received a letter from Bryzanski asking for a copy of her "entire file" because she is about to retain another less costly lawyer to take the case to court. Before sending it, you reviewed the file. In it, you found several memoranda from one of your paralegals to one of your associates reporting on the paralegal's initial interviews with Bryzanski and Leona. Most of the information was of a factual nature, but the memoranda were sprinkled with the paralegal's impressions and observations, some of which were derogatory. In particular, the memoranda included these passages:

> This interview took much longer than expected because Ms. Bryzanski is very long-winded and pushy. She insists on having her own way 100 percent. I don't think that she will make a good witness and might even argue with or antagonize the judge. . . .
>
> Leona certainly should win this case and be placed in the special education program. Her social worker says that she is severely emotionally disturbed, and I can confirm that from what I saw of her. She can't seem to sit still and she constantly interrupted both me and her mother. . . .
>
> Although I have related the story of Ms. Bryzanski's encounter with the school principal just as she told it, I should add that I don't think that it is entirely accurate. Sometimes I have the feeling that Ms. Bryzanski exaggerates her accounts because she feels so strongly that the school system has wronged her daughter.

Assume that since there is no ethics rule to the contrary, your jurisdiction would follow the Restatement standard. Must you send copies of the memoranda to Bryzanski? If you must send her the documents, should you redact (that is, delete) your paralegal's impressions?

---

2. Grounds for termination before the work is completed

Sometimes, lawyers are required or permitted to end the representation of a client before the work is completed. Rule 1.16 distinguishes between situations where early termination is mandatory and those where it is permissive.

a. When the client fires the lawyer

A lawyer must withdraw if the client fires the lawyer.[144] A client always has the right to change lawyers and need not give a reason, although a client for whom a lawyer has been appointed may not change lawyers without the court's permission. Also, a court may refuse to permit a substitution that would unduly delay a case. A lawyer also must withdraw if the lawyer's illness or loss of capacity would materially impair the representation.[145]

b. When continued representation would involve unethical conduct

A lawyer also must withdraw if representation will require the lawyer to violate the law, including the state's rules of professional conduct.[146] A sudden withdrawal because the representation entailed a possible violation of law may call adverse attention to the client. During litigation, a lawyer's withdrawal may cause the court to become suspicious about the client. Even so, a lawyer is required to withdraw rather than violate the law.

If the client has already used the lawyer's services to commit a crime or fraud but continued representation will not result in a new or continuing crime or fraud, the lawyer may withdraw but is not required to do so.[147]

---

144. Rule 1.16(a)(3). While some large institutional clients can afford to fire a lawyer and hire a new one, most individual clients and small businesses are unable to afford to fire their lawyer and start anew with someone else.

145. Rule 1.16(a)(2).

146. We have already considered one application of this requirement in the problem on Reese's Leases in Chapter 3.

147. Rule 1.16(b)(3).

Similarly, if the client persists in a course of action that the lawyer reasonably believes is a crime or fraud, and the lawyer's services are being used to assist this action, the lawyer may withdraw, even if the actions have not yet been adjudicated to be criminal or fraudulent. Finally, if the client insists on action the lawyer finds "repugnant," the lawyer may withdraw.[148]

c. When the lawyer wants to terminate the relationship

A lawyer may withdraw from representing a client in other circumstances also. Rule 1.16(b)(1) offers the broadest opportunity for exit. The lawyer may withdraw if it is possible to do so "without material adverse effect on the interests of the client." On the eve of trial or just before closing a complex business deal, material adverse effect is likely. If the matter is complex and the lawyer has done extensive work, the client might not be able to change lawyers without substantial additional cost. However, when time is not of the essence and in a matter that is not too complex, it may be possible for a client to hire new counsel who will obtain the prior lawyer's records and become familiar with the matter. If the client is indigent and the lawyer is working without a fee, the option to withdraw depends on the availability of another lawyer to take over.

d. Matters in litigation

If a lawyer has filed suit on behalf of a client or entered an appearance in a matter in litigation, the lawyer generally cannot withdraw from representation of the client without permission from the court that is to hear the case. Rule 1.16(c) acknowledges this by requiring that "[a] lawyer must comply with applicable law requiring notice to or permission of a tribunal when terminating a representation."

A court may be reluctant to permit withdrawal if the case will be delayed or if a substituted lawyer for the client has not been arranged. Although forcing the lawyer to remain in the case may be economically ruinous, a lawyer may not be able to count on a court's granting permission to withdraw.[149]

---

148. Rules 1.16(b)(2), (b)(4). For an example of "repugnant" conduct, see Plunkett v. State, 883 S.W.2d 349 (Tex. App. 1994), in which the court allowed an attorney to withdraw during a jury trial because the client had (without using the services of the lawyer) bribed several jurors.

149. See, e.g., In re Withdrawal of Attorney, 594 N.W.2d 514 (Mich. App. 1999), in which a court repeatedly refused to allow a firm to withdraw from representing prisoners in a class action against the Department of Corrections, even though one of the firm's lawyers had spent ten months doing nothing but observing other lawyers take testimony on behalf of other parties in the case and had been given no date by which she could expect to begin presenting her witnesses, the firm had not been appointed to represent any party, and the firm was not collecting any fees from the prisoners whom it had agreed to represent.

What if an ethical rule requires the lawyer to withdraw, but the judge refuses to grant the lawyer's motion to do so?

The answer may depend on whether the matter is criminal or civil. In a criminal case in California, a defense lawyer discovered a conflict of interest in the middle of his client's trial, when the prosecution called a witness who was also represented by the lawyer and from whom the lawyer had received confidential information.[150] The lawyer understood that her cross-examination of her other client would be improper disloyalty to that client and moved to withdraw, but the judge denied the motion. The California Supreme Court ruled that the judge should have granted the motion.[151] That ruling was based on the defendant's Sixth Amendment right to counsel, not on the ethics rule.

In a civil case, the lawyer must apparently obey the court's ruling even if she is thereby forced to violate an ethics rule, at least in states that have adopted the ABA's Model Rules. Rule 1.16(a) provides that a lawyer shall withdraw to avoid violation of the rules "except as stated in paragraph (c)," which provides that a lawyer "must comply with applicable law requiring . . . permission of a tribunal when terminating a representation." The rules apparently allow a judge's order to trump the mandatory withdrawal provisions, although a lawyer who is ordered to represent her client under these circumstances may find herself in a sticky situation. Suppose the lawyer seeks to withdraw because she knows that her client intends to commit perjury. She can't reveal this reason to the judge without violating a client confidence, so the judge might deny her motion. In that case, maybe she could honor both the rules and the court's requirement that she remain in the case by warning her client that she will have to reveal such perjury to the tribunal.[152] But an even more difficult problem arises if she discovers a conflict of interest, as in the California case, that would require her to cross-examine another of her clients, and the judge refuses to let her withdraw.

e. When the client stops paying the fee

A lawyer may withdraw if the client doesn't pay the lawyer's fee, but the lawyer must first warn the client that nonpayment will lead to withdrawal (or to a motion to withdraw from a matter that is in litigation).[153] This can be very complicated. Sometimes when a client doesn't pay a lawyer's fee, the client is satisfied with the service but doesn't have the money or doesn't want to spend the money. In many cases, however, clients fail to pay

---

150. See the discussion of cross-examining a current client in Chapter 5.
151. Leversen v. Super. Ct., 668 P.2d 755 (Cal. 1983).
152. See Rule 3.3(b), discussed in Chapter 10.
153. Rule 1.16(b)(5).

lawyers' bills because they are dissatisfied with the service or because they believe that the fees are too high. (This is a common problem if a client has agreed to an hourly fee and has not been given an accurate estimate of the total cost of the work.) If the client doesn't have the money to cover the fee, a lawyer should consider reducing the fee to make the representation affordable for a client with limited means.[154] If a client has a complaint about the service or the fee, usually it is best to sit down with the client and work out a resolution of the dispute rather than simply withdrawing from representation.

f. When the case imposes an unreasonable financial burden on the lawyer

If a case turns out to impose an unreasonable financial burden on the lawyer, the lawyer may withdraw. This might arise in any matter that turned out to be more complex than the lawyer originally anticipated.[155]

g. When the client will not cooperate

A lawyer may withdraw if the client makes continued representation by the lawyer "unreasonably difficult." For example, if the client repeatedly fails to show up for scheduled meetings or hearings or if the client refuses to divulge to the lawyer the identities of witnesses who could help the case, the lawyer may withdraw.[156] Finally, Rule 1.16 permits withdrawal for "other good cause."[157]

---

154. See Rule 6.1, which articulates lawyers' professional obligation to spend part of their time providing services to clients who cannot afford to pay their fees.

155. For an extreme example of such problems, consider the plight of the lawyer in Harr, supra n. 109, in which the lawyer did not withdraw, even when on the verge of bankruptcy.

156. Rule 1.16(b)(6); see Bailey v. Va., 568 S.E.2d 440 (Va. App. 2002) (permitting appointed counsel to withdraw from representing a defendant who insisted that his lawyer communicate with him only in writing).

157. Rule 1.16(b)(7); see, e.g., Greig v. Macy's Northeast, 1996 U.S. Dist. LEXIS 22142 (D.N.J. Nov. 21, 1996) ("other good cause" existed for allowing withdrawal, where the lawyer doubted the validity of the client's federal civil rights claim against Macy's for "being wrongfully targeted as a shoplifter" and the mutual failure of lawyer and client to "sustain adequate communication" had caused a "deterioration of the attorney-client relationship").

5 | CONFLICTS OF INTEREST: CURRENT CLIENTS

A. An introduction to conflicts of interest

A basic principle of ethical practice is that lawyers are supposed to avoid conflicts of interest. When a lawyer undertakes representation of a client, the lawyer owes that client a duty of loyalty and a duty to protect confidential information. In some situations, it would be disloyal for the lawyer to agree to represent another client whose interests are adverse to an existing client, or even a former client. Also, in the course of representing one client, the lawyer might (intentionally or accidentally) use or reveal confidential information learned from the other client. This might result in tangible harm to one of the clients.

What defines "conflicts of interest" may have changed over time. A lawyer in Chicago notes that lawyers often used to handle potential conflicts between two clients much more informally than they do now.

> When I was young, ... if a law firm — or in those days, really, a lawyer — had two important clients that got into a dispute, the most natural thing for them to do would be both of them would go in, see their lawyer and hash it out with them. ... And they'd reach an agreement. Maybe it would be worked out in writing, maybe it was a handshake. We can sit back and say, "How unethical that guy was! Here he is collecting a fee from two people who had adverse interests. It's cutting across the lines of loyalty and duty and everything else." But that's not how it was viewed in the '40s and '50s and maybe even into the early '60s. It was: they went to their lawyer; their lawyer is a professional; he's an ethical man; he understands his obligations to both sides, and he can be trusted in that situation. And I think the change that you see is today, what we are saying is, "no, nobody can be trusted in that situation! ... People have a right to independent counsel. People have a right to have a lawyer that's just thinking about their best interests. You know, the adversary system, hooray, hooray!"[1]

The lawyer quoted above was expressing nostalgia for a time when things were more informal and when a lawyer was freer to use his own judgment about whether he could manage — and perhaps intermediate between — two clients whose interests were at least partly at odds. These days, things are not so simple. Law firms are larger and have more complex networks of relationships with client organizations. Some institutional clients are part of networks of interconnected organizations. The size of both lawyer and client organizations multiplies the number of potential conflicts that need to be evaluated. Also, these changes in the profession make it more difficult to identify and evaluate conflicts.

Conflicts of interest often come to the attention of courts through motions to disqualify a party's lawyer. Sometimes a party to a litigation

---

1. Susan Shapiro, Tangled Loyalties: Conflict of Interest in Legal Practice 58 (U. Mich. Press 2002), quoting an interview with a Chicago lawyer in a firm with more than 100 lawyers.

moves to disqualify counsel for another party because of genuine concern that the lawyer's presence as counsel for the other party presents a risk of harm to the moving party. The party seeking disqualification might worry that opposing counsel would misuse confidences that the lawyer previously received from the moving party.

In other situations, a party may move to disqualify counsel for the other party because the facts present an arguable basis for doing so and because litigating the disqualification motion may increase the time and expense to the other party of conducting the litigation. These motions might be described as "pretextual" because their real purpose is not to prevent harm resulting from the conflict but to gain advantage in litigation. This problem has been evident for at least 20 years. In 1988, in *Federal Deposit Insurance Corp. v. Amundson,* Judge James M. Rosenbaum lamented:

> We have reached a difficult and unpleasant stage in our legal-ethical development. We are now in a time when ethics has ceased to be a common guide to virtuous behavior. It is now a sword in hand, to be used to slay a colleague. This kind of ethics does not reflect a heightened awareness of moral responsibility or a means to temper one's zeal for his or her client. It is instead a means to hobble the opposition by driving a spurious wedge between a client and chosen counsel.[2]

The conflicts rules aspire to assist lawyers to avoid or remedy situations in which the representation of one client could be compromised in some way by another obligation of the lawyer. Even so, the conflicts rules are often invoked not based on good faith ethical concerns, but as "a sword in hand, to be used to slay a colleague." As you explore the problems presented in these chapters, ask about each example: "What is the potential harm to a client presented by this situation, and how might the harm best be prevented?"[3]

The conflicts rules guide lawyers on how to distinguish among three categories of conflicts:

1. Conflicts that on close examination do not present a real risk of harm to one or more clients, so the lawyer may proceed without advising the client or asking for consent

---

2. FDIC v. Amundson, 682 F. Supp. 981 (D. Minn. 1988) (denying a motion to disqualify counsel for a bank). The court asked,

> What is the public interest being preserved by this motion? This was a tiny bank with but a few in executive and management positions. The bank, as an entity apart from this managing group, scarcely existed. The FDIC's motion suggests absolutely nothing that was known by or given to challenged counsel. The motion is premised on a stated concern to prevent the appearance of a conflict. The motion devolves into an effort to avoid the created-appearance of an appearance of a conflict. This Court suggests that not only is the FDIC's emperor without clothes; there may well be no emperor.

Id. at 989.

3. This passage was prompted by an insightful e-mail from Professor Tom Andrews to Lisa Lerman (Oct. 23, 2008).

2. Conflicts that may be adequately addressed if the affected clients are willing to provide consent after the lawyer explains all the potential problems

3. Conflicts that are so serious that even consent would not solve the problem, and the lawyer should turn down the second client (or withdraw, if the lawyer already has begun representation)

One of the most important skills that you will need as a lawyer is to identify and analyze conflicts. Some large firms have one or more expert lawyers whose main role is to evaluate potential or actual conflicts.[4] But most lawyers screen their own cases for conflicts, and they vary in how well they understand this complex issue. Real trouble may follow if you don't notice and address conflicts. A lawyer who proceeds in the face of a conflict might be disqualified by a judge, enjoined from further representation,[5] sued for malpractice, or charged with violation of disciplinary rules. The lawyer might forfeit a fee for the conflicted work. The lawyer might even be indicted for ignoring a conflict of interest. The most common type of litigation over conflicts involves one firm moving to disqualify another that has an apparent conflict of interest. Any of these consequences are possible.

Even leaving these various disaster scenarios aside, you need to be able to evaluate potential conflicts to know whether you can take on a particular matter. If you take on a matter that raises a conflict without remedying it, a client may feel betrayed. This could be problematic even if the client doesn't fire or sue you. Your role as a lawyer puts you in a position of trust with each client. Your professional reputation will depend on whether you maintain that trust and inspire confidence in your loyalty and judgment.

Competency in conflict evaluation also is important to your financial interests. If you doze through these difficult chapters on conflicts of interest, you might take on a matter that you shouldn't and wind up losing more than one client as a result. Or, in an abundance of caution, you might turn down a matter that you would be permitted to take on if you obtained

---

4. Many large firms have concluded that having an ethics advisor in the firm to screen conflicts and to help build "ethical infrastructure" helps to avoid professional liability and other problems. Elizabeth Chambliss & David B. Wilkins, The Emerging Role of Ethics Advisors, General Counsel, and Other Compliance Specialists in Large Law Firms, 44 Ariz. L. Rev. 559 (2002); Elizabeth Chambliss & David B. Wilkins, Promoting Ethical Infrastructure in Large Law Firms: A Call for Research and Reporting, 30 Hofstra L. Rev. 691 (2002); Susan Saab Fortney, Are Law Firm Partners Islands unto Themselves? An Empirical Study of Law Firm Peer Review and Culture, 10 Geo. J. Leg. Ethics 271 (1996).

5. If the matter is in litigation, a lawyer might be disqualified. If the representation is transactional, a client aggrieved by conflicting work for another client might seek an injunction prohibiting the lawyer from continuing the work in question. See Maritrans GP, Inc. v. Pepper, Hamilton & Scheetz, 602 A.2d 1277 (Pa. 1992).

client consent. Sometimes the rules do not offer clear guidance, but you will be better off understanding the range of permissible action under the rules.

Some possible consequences of representing a client in the face of a conflict:

Legal sanctions:
- Disqualification
- Discipline
- Malpractice liability
- Injunction against representation (transactional case)
- Fee forfeiture

Business repercussions:
- Client may retain a different lawyer
- Client may mistrust you
- Your professional reputation may suffer

---

1. How the conflicts chapters are organized

The material on conflicts of interest is more complex than the other topics in this book.[6] We divide this material into five chapters. This chapter introduces conflicts of interest. We begin by presenting some basic principles about how to analyze conflicts involving two or more current clients, often called concurrent conflicts. We then examine conflicts that arise in civil litigation. In Chapter 6, we look at some particular types of concurrent conflicts, those that often arise when a lawyer represents an organization and when a lawyer simultaneously represents two or more clients in criminal, domestic relations, estate planning, insurance, immigration, and class action cases.

In Chapter 7, we explore successive conflicts, which occur between the interests of current and former clients. Chapter 7 also discusses imputed conflicts. A conflict is "imputed" if one lawyer in a firm who has a conflict "infects" the other lawyers in the firm with this conflict. Because Chapter 5 involves conflicts among current clients, it explains the imputation of conflicts involving two present clients of a law firm. Chapter 7 explains the

---

6. The volume of this material reflects its bulk in the Model Rules; nearly a third of the pages of the Model Rules and their comments are devoted to the subjects covered in Chapters 5 through 9 of this book. Likewise, many practicing lawyers who are the resident legal ethics experts in their firms would tell you that the majority of their time is devoted to evaluating possible conflicts of interest.

imputation of conflicts that involve one present client and one former client.

Chapter 8 considers conflicts between the interests of a client and a lawyer's own interests. That chapter covers ethical issues relating to legal fees,[7] lawyers' obligations in managing their clients' property, and conflicts that relate to lawyers' personal or business interests.

Chapter 9 discusses conflicts of interest issues for present and former government lawyers and judges. The ethics codes include special successive conflicts rules for present and former government lawyers because so many lawyers move from government service into private law practice or vice versa. Likewise, judicial ethics is addressed in a separate code from the ethics rules that govern lawyers. Lawyers who appear in court should have some background in judicial ethics, for example, so that they can deal with a situation in which the lawyer believes that a judge has a conflict of interest.

2. How the conflicts rules are organized

As you begin your review of the ethics rules on conflicts of interest, a first step is to get a fix on the main categories of conflicts and on which rules address each category. Here is a thumbnail.

- **Conflicting obligations to more than one current client: Rules 1.7, 1.8, and 1.18.** Rule 1.7 offers a template for examining the impact of potentially conflicting obligations on a lawyer's loyalty to current clients. In some cases, a lawyer may seek informed consent from the affected clients to waive a conflict. In other cases, a conflict is nonconsentable — it is so serious that even the client's consent does not remedy it. Rule 1.8 includes some additional, very specific prohibitions affecting lawyers' relationships with their clients. Rule 1.18 addresses the problem of loyalty to existing clients when a lawyer contemplates accepting new clients with potentially conflicting interests.
- **Successive conflicts: Rules 1.7 and 1.9.** The impact of a successive conflict on a former client is analyzed using Rule 1.9. The impact on a present client is analyzed using Rule 1.7.

---

7. Most books on professional responsibility do not include issues about legal fees in the materials on conflicts of interest. We cover them for two reasons. When a lawyer charges a fee to a client, there is usually a conflict of interest, in the ordinary if not the technical sense of the term. The lawyer would like the fee to be higher. The client would like it to be lower. Also, most of the issues that are conventionally thought of as involving lawyer-client conflicts are about money, so we placed all the lawyer-client money issues in one chapter.

- **Imputed conflicts: Rule 1.10.** Rule 1.10 explains how to analyze imputed conflicts. Sometimes imputation can be avoided by screening off the lawyer who is directly conflicted and notifying the former client of the screen. An imputed conflict often may be waived by the informed consent of a potentially disadvantaged client.
- **Conflicts for present and former government lawyers: Rule 1.11.** Rule 1.11 addresses both successive and imputed conflicts of interest for lawyers who move between jobs in government and jobs in the private sector.

The conflicts rules impose more stringent restrictions on conflicts that may cause serious consequences for clients and fewer restrictions on conflicts that may cause less harm. The rules impose a high bar with respect to

- conflicts that may adversely affect current clients rather than former clients;
- conflicts that involve two or more lawyers in the same firm serving two conflicting interests; and
- conflicts involving work handled by a lawyer for her current employer rather than conflicts resulting from work by the lawyer in her previous job.

The following chart summarizes the types of conflicts.

Conflicts spectrum: Time, lawyers, and firms				
Type of conflict	Simultaneous or sequential representation	Is one lawyer or more than one lawyer involved?[8]	Lawyer(s) work for the same firm	Relevant rules
Concurrent	Simultaneous	One lawyer	Yes	1.7, 1.8, 1.13
Successive	Sequential	One lawyer	Yes	1.9, 1.11(a), (c), (d), 1.12(a) & (b)
Imputed	Simultaneous or sequential	Two or more lawyers	Currently in same firm but may previously have been in a different firm	1.10, 1.11(b), 1.12(c)

---

8. A conflict presented between two clients of one lawyer is described here as a one-lawyer conflict. An imputed conflict occurs because of one lawyer's association with another lawyer, not because one lawyer is representing conflicting interests.

B. General principles in evaluating concurrent conflicts

1. Rule 1.7

Rule 1.7 first explains what is considered to be a problematic conflict between two present clients (or one present and one prospective client). It then explains that for some, but not all, of these conflicts, a lawyer may seek informed consent from the affected clients and may proceed if consent is obtained.

Rule 1.7 Conflicts of Interest: Current Clients

Rule language[*]	Authors' explanation[**]
(a) Except as provided in paragraph (b), a lawyer **shall not** represent a client if the representation involves a **concurrent** conflict of interest. A concurrent conflict of interest exists if:	A concurrent conflict is one between two current obligations of the lawyer — two clients, a client and another person, or a client and the lawyer's own interests.
(1) the representation of one client will be **directly adverse** to another client; or	"Directly adverse" means that a lawyer is acting directly against the interests of one of his own clients. (See box below.)
(2) there is a **significant risk** that the **representation** of one or more clients will be **materially limited** by the lawyer's **responsibilities to another** client, a former client or a third person or by a **personal interest** of the lawyer.	Even if there is no direct adversity, there is a conflict if there is a significant "likelihood that a difference in interests will eventuate and, if it does, [that] it will materially interfere with the lawyer's independent professional judgment." Comment 8.
(b) **Notwithstanding** the existence of a concurrent conflict of interest under paragraph (a), a lawyer **may represent** a client if:	Even if a conflict is found under Rule 1.7(a), in most cases a lawyer may represent the conflicting interests if he obtains the clients' informed consent. But if one of the conditions listed in (b)(1), (2), or (3) is not satisfied, the lawyer may not ask for client consent.
(1) the lawyer **reasonably believes** that the lawyer will be able to provide **competent and diligent representation** to each affected client;	A lawyer may not ask for consent "if in the circumstances the lawyer cannot reasonably conclude that the lawyer will be able to provide competent and diligent representation." Comment 15.
(2) the representation is **not prohibited by law**;	"For example, in some states substantive law provides that [even if the clients consent,] the same lawyer may not represent more than one defendant in a capital case." Comment 16.

Rule language[*]	Authors' explanation[**]
(3) the representation does **not** involve the assertion of a **claim by one** client **against another client** represented by the lawyer in the **same litigation or other proceeding before a tribunal**; and	A lawyer may not represent adverse parties in litigation even with their consent. For example, a lawyer cannot represent both plaintiff and defendant in a lawsuit requesting an amicable divorce.
(4) **each affected client gives informed consent**, confirmed in writing.	To get informed consent, a lawyer must explain to each affected client the "ways that the conflict could have adverse effects on the interests of that client." Comment 18. Sometimes this requires disclosure of another client's confidences, which requires that client's consent. Comment 19.

[*]All emphasis added.

[**]This and other authors' explanations draw from the comments to the rules and from other sources. They are not comprehensive but highlight some important interpretive points.

Rule 1.7 addresses how a lawyer should analyze conflicts between two present clients or between two current obligations of the lawyer — the conflicting obligation might run to a third person or to the lawyer's own interests. Under Rule 1.7, a lawyer is prohibited from representing a client if one of the conflicts described in 1.7(a) exists, unless under 1.7(b) the conflict is waivable by the client and the client gives informed consent to allow the lawyer to continue with the representation. Rule 1.7(a) identifies two types of conflicts that might preclude representation of a client:

- One client's interests might be "directly adverse" to those of another client.
- There might be a "significant risk" that a representation will be "materially limited" by another obligation of the lawyer — to another client, to a former client, or to a third person. A representation also could be materially limited by a conflict between the lawyer's interests and the client's interests.[9]

If a conflict is present, a lawyer should evaluate under 1.7(b) whether she may continue to represent the affected clients if they give informed

---

9. "Direct adversity" conflicts are in fact a subset of a larger group of conflicts in which the lawyer's representation could be materially limited by another obligation. The conflicts that involve direct adversity often are the most serious ones. Restatement § 121 subsumes the "direct adversity" and "material limitation" conflicts into one category and asserts that

[a] conflict of interest is involved if there is a substantial risk that the lawyer's representation of the client would be materially and adversely affected by the client's own interests or by the lawyer's duties to another current client, a former client, or a third person.

consent after learning about the conflicts. A lawyer may seek consent to resolve many, but not all, conflicts.

a. Direct adversity

A conflict is said to involve "direct adversity" to the interests of a client if the lawyer's conduct on behalf of one client requires the lawyer to act against the interests of another current client. The most obvious example is a lawyer who files suit on behalf of one client against another of his own clients. If, in the course of representing one client, the lawyer takes action that could directly harm another client, there is direct adversity. Both litigation and nonlitigation situations can involve direct adversity.

Direct adversity: common situations
- A lawyer who represents client A in one matter sues client A in a second matter on behalf of client B. (Another lawyer might be representing client A in the second lawsuit.)
- The lawyer acts adversely to a client in litigation (e.g., by cross-examining him).
- Outside of litigation, a lawyer undertakes adversarial negotiation against another client. (Rule 1.7, Comments 6 and 7.)

---

b. Material limitation

Even if there is no direct adversity, a conflict exists if representation of one client would be "materially limited" by another responsibility of the lawyer. The "other responsibilities" that might materially limit a lawyer's representation of a client include obligations to

- another present client;
- a former client;
- someone else to whom a lawyer owes a duty (e.g., if the lawyer has fiduciary obligations because the lawyer is a trustee, an executor, or a member of a corporate board of directors);
- someone other than the client who is paying the lawyer's fee;
- the lawyer's own financial, employment, personal, or other interests.

FOR EXAMPLE: "A lawyer asked to represent several individuals seeking to form a joint venture is likely to be materially limited in [his] ability to recommend or advocate all possible positions that each might take because of the lawyer's duty of loyalty to the others."[10]

---

10. Rule 1.7, Comment 8.

If a client would receive less vigorous representation from a lawyer because of the lawyer's other responsibilities, there might be a "material limitation" conflict. A "mere possibility" of harm is insufficient to present a conflict. To evaluate whether a conflict is present, a lawyer must ask two questions.

- How likely is it "that a difference in interests will eventuate"?
- If there likely is such a divergence, would it "materially interfere" with the lawyer's advice to or representation of a client?[11]

If there is a conflict that presents either direct adversity or material limitation, the conflict must be evaluated under Rule 1.7(b) to see whether the lawyer may seek informed consent from the affected clients or whether the conflict is nonconsentable.

2. How to evaluate conflicts

To resolve a concurrent conflict under Rule 1.7, a lawyer must

- clearly identify the client or clients and determine whether each is a present client or a former client;
- determine whether a conflict of interest exists;
- decide whether the lawyer is permitted to represent the client despite the existence of a conflict (i.e., whether the conflict is consentable); and
- if so, consult with the clients affected under paragraph (a), obtain their informed consent, and send written confirmation to the client of the informed consent.[12]

Some conflicts are apparent at the time a lawyer undertakes to represent a client; others emerge later because of changes in circumstances or information learned in the course of representation. The rules encourage lawyers to "adopt reasonable procedures, appropriate for the size and type of firm and practice, to determine in both litigation and non-litigation matters the persons and issues involved" for the purpose of identifying conflicts.[13]

If a consentable conflict is identified before a client is accepted, and the affected client gives informed consent after the lawyer explains the possible problems that the conflict might generate, the lawyer may go forward despite the conflict. If the conflict is not consentable, the lawyer must

---

11. Id.
12. Id. at Comment 2.
13. Id. at Comment 3.

decline to accept representation of one or more clients. If a nonconsentable conflict emerges after a lawyer-client relationship has begun, the lawyer might be able to remedy the conflict by withdrawing from representation of one of the affected clients.[14] Sometimes, however, the lawyer will have to give up both clients.

3. Nonconsentable conflicts

Most conflicts are consentable — it is the unusual case in which a court might say that even with the consent of all parties, the lawyer may not continue the representation. But some conflicts are considered so problematic that a lawyer may not continue to represent a client even if the client wishes the lawyer to do so. To determine whether a conflict is consentable, Rule 1.7(b) directs a lawyer to ask

- whether she "reasonably believes that [she] will be able to provide competent and diligent representation" to the relevant clients;
- whether "the representation is . . . prohibited by law"; and
- whether the representation involves litigation in which the lawyer is representing one client against another client whom the lawyer is representing in that matter.

a. The lawyer's reasonable belief

In evaluating a conflict, a lawyer must consider "whether the interests of the clients will be adequately protected if the clients are permitted to give their informed consent to representation burdened by a conflict of interest."[15] The question is whether the lawyer can "reasonably conclude that [he] will be able to provide competent and diligent representation."[16] The inquiry is not whether the lawyer has the subjective impression that the conflict is consentable. The question is what a reasonable lawyer would think.[17]

In considering whether a conflict may be waived by consent, the lawyer should ask: Would there be an adverse effect on the *relationship* with either client? Also, would there be an adverse effect on the *representation* of either

---

14. Id. at Comment 5.

15. Id. at Comment 15.

16. Id. The Restatement formulates this question a little differently, explaining that "if a reasonable and disinterested lawyer would conclude that one or more of the affected clients could not consent . . . because the representation would fall short in either respect, the conflict is nonconsentable." Restatement § 122, comment g(iv).

17. Rule 1.7, Comment 15. The Restatement uses similar language, stating "a lawyer may not represent a client if . . . it is not reasonably likely that the lawyer will be able to provide adequate representation to one or more of the clients." Restatement § 122(2)(c).

client? In addressing these questions, a lawyer should consider the following questions.

- Are the conflicting representations related or unrelated? If the matters involved are not factually interrelated, the conflict may be waivable.[18]
- Does the problem involve joint representation of two parties with very divergent interests? If so, it may not be possible to pursue the interests of one without harming the other.[19]
- Is the conflict between two present clients or between one present and one former client? If the conflict could adversely impact only a former client, the conflict is consentable.[20]
- Does the lawyer have a friendship or a bond of professional loyalty toward one of the two clients? If so, the lawyer might be unable to provide competent and diligent representation to the other, especially if the interests of the two are divergent.[21]
- How sophisticated is the client? If the client is a sophisticated user of legal services, the client's consent is likely to solve the problem. For example, in a practice in which the clients are large institutional clients with general counsels advising them, nearly all conflicts may be waived by consent.[22]

b. Representation prohibited by law

Some conflicts are not consentable because the representation of a client in the face of some conflicts is prohibited by statute or by case law.

> **FOR EXAMPLE:** A federal statute prohibits a federal government lawyer from representing a client against the United States regardless of whether the government consents.[23]

c. Suing one client on behalf of another client

A final category of nonconsentable conflicts consists of cases in which a lawyer is asked to represent two parties who are "aligned directly against

---

18. Restatement § 122, comment g(iv).

19. Id.

20. See Rule 1.9; Restatement § 122, comment g(iv); id. § 132. Note, however, that if the conflict between a present client and a former client might adversely impact the current client, the conflict may not be consentable. See Rule 1.7.

21. Restatement § 122, comment g(iv).

22. Id.

23. 18 U.S.C. § 205 (2007).

each other in the same litigation."[24] A lawyer may not represent "opposing parties in the same litigation, regardless of the clients' consent."[25]

> **FOR EXAMPLE:** Can a lawyer represent both husband and wife in a divorce? Some jurisdictions allow two spouses to hire one lawyer to help them work out the property settlement and other issues. Under this rule, however, the lawyer could not file a divorce action in which the lawyer represented both plaintiff and defendant. The parties might agree, however, that after the lawyer assisted both of them in negotiating terms, the lawyer could represent one of them in the litigation.[26]

4. Informed consent

If the conflict is consentable, a lawyer may ask the affected clients whether they would like to waive the conflict by giving informed consent. If the client declines to give consent, the lawyer cannot take on or continue the conflicting work. A lawyer seeking such consent must communicate to a client all the information needed to understand the possible adverse effects that might befall the client if she waives the conflict. Rule 1.0 defines "informed consent" to refer to an agreement "to a proposed course of conduct after the lawyer has communicated adequate information and explanation about the material risks of and reasonably available alternatives to the proposed course of conduct."[27]

How much information does a lawyer have to give a client to obtain informed consent?

The lawyer must orally explain to the client the risks, advantages, and possible alternatives to the lawyer going forward with the representation. A client's oral consent must be "confirmed in writing" by the lawyer. This means that either the client must sign a waiver of the conflict of interest, or the lawyer must obtain the client's oral waiver of the conflict and, within a reasonable time, send the client a text memorializing the oral communication.[28] Although the client is not required to sign the text, a client must

---

24. Restatement § 122, comment g(iii).

25. Rule 1.7, Comment 23.

26. This example is based on Restatement § 122, comment g(iii), illus. 8. The Restatement notes that some jurisdictions restrict joint representation in situations involving the interests of children. See the discussion of conflicts in domestic relations matters in Chapter 6.

27. Rule 1.0(e). The Restatement uses similar language, stating that to give informed consent, a present or former client must "have reasonably adequate information about the material risks of such representation to that client or former client." Restatement § 122(1).

28. See Rule 1.7, Comment 20.

expressly indicate consent to the conflict. A lawyer may not merely explain the conflict in a letter and state that she will assume consent if the client does not respond.

Empirical research on lawyers' behavior in handling conflicts of interest
Much of our knowledge about how lawyers actually handle conflicts of interest comes from a sociological study undertaken by Dr. Susan Shapiro, a Senior Research Fellow at the American Bar Foundation. She interviewed 128 lawyers in Illinois to examine how the lawyers think about and evaluate conflicts. She reports the results in Tangled Loyalties: Conflict of Interest in Legal Practice (U. Mich. Press 2002). This study is the most comprehensive empirical study to date on how American lawyers think about conflicts of interest.

Dr. Susan Shapiro

Shapiro talked to lawyers from large and small law firms, and to lawyers who worked in large cities and small towns.[29] She talked with lawyers who specialize in many different areas of practice. Ninety-four percent of the lawyers interviewed were men. They ranged in age from late 20s to late 70s.[30] She chose to interview only Illinois lawyers to ensure that all the lawyers in her sample were bound by a common set of conflicts rules. Some aspects of the lawyers' thinking may reflect Illinois legal culture, but her sample covers the gamut of types of private law practice. Ninety-two percent of the firms randomly selected consented to allow Shapiro to conduct interviews. This makes it unlikely that her data is atypical because of a nonresponse bias.[31] We appreciate Dr. Shapiro's willingness to allow us to illustrate conflicts of interest by quoting her research.

When clients are asked to consent to conflicts, do they usually agree?

Many clients consent to waive conflicts, especially if they perceive the conflicts to be technical and believe that it will not harm their interests for the lawyers to pursue the conflicting work. But some clients decline to waive even technical conflicts. Susan Shapiro talked to one lawyer who told the following story:

---

29. Shapiro, supra n. 1, at 29.
30. Id. at 51-53.
31. Id. at 28.

Did some work for a bank in a smaller town in Illinois — for their trust department. We had a client in the firm that wanted to sue the bank with regard to mishandling of a commercial loan. It had nothing to do with their trust department. This bank is represented by every lawyer in . . . their town. So that, from the point of view of finding someone to defend them, they had no legitimate gripe. From the point of view of my knowing anything that would have any bearing upon this suit, they had no legitimate gripe. We thought it would be nice to ask them anyway. And they said no, that they absolutely did not want us representing anybody who was suing them. . . . That was a very surprising reaction.[32]

How often are clients asked to give informed consent? How often do they say yes? Although not much empirical literature is available on informed consent, we can make a couple of guesses. Sophisticated clients such as banks probably rarely consent (except in "advance waivers," which are discussed below), while less wealthy clients, who depend on low-cost or pro bono lawyers, probably often cannot give genuine consent to conflicts because if they refuse consent, they might be abandoned by their lawyers and have no other options.

How can a lawyer make adequate disclosure without revealing confidences of one client to another?

Often the lawyer will need to disclose some confidential information about client A's case to client B so that client B has enough information to know whether he wants to consent. This disclosure may be necessary to help the client to understand the nature of the conflict.

> FOR EXAMPLE: Suppose client A proposes to purchase a video rental business from client B, and both want a single lawyer to handle the transaction. The lawyer knows that client B is leaving the video business to become an evangelical minister. Client A has told the lawyer that he intends to expand the store to include X-rated films. The lawyer might need to disclose this to client B because if client B knew this information, he might not want to sell to client A, much less share a lawyer with client A.

To obtain informed consent from the seller in this example, the lawyer must share confidential information from the buyer. Before doing this, the lawyer must ask the buyer's permission to disclose the buyer's confidences to the seller. If the buyer declines to allow the lawyer to disclose the relevant confidences, the lawyer may not proceed with the representation because the lawyer will not be able to obtain informed consent from the seller.

---

32. Id. at 61.

If the client already knows the information needed to give consent, does the lawyer have to explain it anyway?

No. The lawyer must assure that the client receives the relevant information, either from the lawyer or from another source. For example, if the client has a separate lawyer to advise her about the risks involved in waiving a particular conflict, the client might need less information from the original lawyer than one who is not independently advised.[33]

If a client gives informed consent to a conflict and things turn out worse than expected, can the client change her mind and withdraw consent?

Yes, the client may withdraw consent. Suppose two clients give informed consent to a lawyer's continued representation of both of them in making a business deal. They begin negotiations, and things go badly. It appears that one of them may file suit against the other. Are they stuck with a common lawyer? Clearly not. A client always has the right to fire a lawyer. A client who has waived a conflict may revoke the waiver.[34]

If a client revokes consent to a conflict, may the lawyer continue to represent the other client(s)?

It depends. If a client justifiably revokes consent, her lawyer might need to withdraw from representing both clients, or the lawyer might be able to continue to represent one of them. This depends on the nature of the conflict that has arisen, what if any circumstances have changed, and what harm might result from continuing to represent one of the clients. If a client revoked consent arbitrarily, a lawyer might be permitted to continue to represent another client who had relied on the earlier consent in hiring this lawyer.[35]

During the informed consent process, a lawyer may ask the client whether, if a conflict arises, the lawyer could continue to work with one of the clients, and if so, which one. If there is disclosure and consent to a contingency plan, it is more likely that the lawyer may continue to represent one of them if a conflict arises.

May a law firm ask a client to sign a contract waiving certain conflicts at the outset of the representation?

It is standard practice, especially in large law firms, to seek waiver of certain types of conflicts of interest at the outset of a firm's work on behalf of a

---

33. Restatement § 122, comment c(i).
34. Id. at comment f.
35. Id.

client. These waivers vary in scope and specificity, but all ask the client to agree in writing that a conflict is not presented by the firm's representation of certain clients or its work on certain subject matters. The Arizona bar offers its lawyers the following model language for an advance waiver on work in certain subject areas.

> Therefore, as a condition to our undertaking this matter, Clients must agree that the Firm may continue to represent or may undertake in the future to represent existing or new clients in any matter that is not substantially related to our work for Clients, even if the interests of such entities in those other matters are directly adverse to Clients. We agree, however, that Clients' prospective consent to conflicting representation contained in this paragraph shall not apply in any instances where, as a result of our representation of Clients, we have obtained privileged, proprietary, or other confidential information of a nonpublic nature that, if known to such other entity, could be used in any such other matter by such entity to Clients' material disadvantage.[36]

Are "advance waivers" allowed? In other words, can a client give consent early in the representation to possible conflicts that might arise in the future?

Like so many conflicts questions, the answer is, "It depends." A lawyer may seek advance waivers from clients and may do so when the client first engages the services of the lawyer, but the validity of those waivers depends on

- how well the client understands the risks of the possible future conflicts;
- how thorough and specific is the lawyer's initial disclosure of possible future conflicts;
- how much experience the client has had with the type of legal services being provided and the nature of the conflicts that could arise;
- whether the client has received independent legal advice before giving the advance waiver; and
- whether the conflict that arises is one that can be solved by consent (if it is nonconsentable, the waiver will not be valid as to that particular conflict).[37]

---

36. Michael J. DiLernia, Advance Waivers of Conflicts of Interest in Large Law Firm Practice, 22 Geo. J. Leg. Ethics 97, 100 (2009), quoting Samuel A. Thumma & Lynda C. Shely, Fee Agreements: A to Z, Ariz. Atty. 36 (Jan. 2002).

37. Rule 1.7, Comment 22; see ABA Standing Comm. on Ethics & Prof. Resp., Formal Op. 05-436 (opining that "General and open-ended consent is more likely to be effective when given by a client that is an experienced user of legal services, particularly if . . . the client is independently

FOR EXAMPLE: A law firm has an office in New York and one in Chicago. The firm does commercial collection work for a sophisticated institutional client in New York and gives tax advice to a Chicago client. The law firm might obtain valid advance consent from the New York client to conflicts that would arise if the firm were to file a collection matter against the Chicago client. (The Chicago client would be represented by a different lawyer for the collection matter; otherwise, it would not be a consentable conflict.) In the event of such a suit, the firm would need consent from the tax client as well.[38]

One recent article suggests that courts, bar associations, and academics tend to focus (as does the passage above) on when advance waivers are valid and enforceable, and that attention to this issue has too often focused on the small number of litigated cases that have challenged the use of a waiver.[39] The author interviewed eight lawyers in large law firms and found that they actually ask a more practical set of questions about waivers. For example, "How can I get the waiver I need and still keep my client happy? What sort of disclosures should I make in my engagement letter? Will I scare a client away if I make the waiver into a big deal — or try to enforce it over a client's objection?"[40] The author urges that the current conflicts rules have not kept pace with developments in practice and that the rules should be modified to offer more useful guidance.[41]

In the example of the New York and the Chicago clients, the hypothetical lawyer knew, when asking for the waiver, what type of conflict might arise (a collection matter). In practice, it may be impossible to anticipate most types of future conflicts. If a client signs a blanket advance waiver without any idea of the types of conflicts that may arise in the future, the consent to the waiver might later be found invalid because it was not well informed. The waiver also could be found not to cover a conflict of a type that was not identified and discussed.

---

represented by other counsel in giving consent and the consent is limited to future conflicts unrelated to the subject of the representation."). One scholar recommends amending Rule 1.7 to reduce uncertainties about the effectiveness of advance waivers by encouraging and permitting lawyers and clients to sign agreements defining direct adversity and substantial relatedness for the lawyer's work involving that client. Richard Painter, Advance Waiver of Conflicts, 13 Geo. J. Leg. Ethics 289 (2000).

38. This example is based on Restatement § 122, comment d, illus. 2.

39. DiLernia, supra n. 36, at 97-98.

40. Id.

41. Id.

5. Withdrawal and disqualification

Suppose a lawyer discovers a nonconsentable conflict or the relevant client declines to consent to the lawyer's continued work on the matter. In this case, the lawyer must withdraw from representation. (See Rule 1.16.) The lawyer might take this action (to seek consent and withdraw if consent is not forthcoming) on his own initiative, or he might be prompted to act by his opposing counsel. If a lawyer is representing a client in the face of a conflict without obtaining consent, the lawyer's opposing counsel may file a motion to disqualify the lawyer from continuing the work.

Why do lawyers sometimes move to disqualify opposing counsel on the ground of an asserted conflict of interest?

Some lawyers file motions to disqualify opposing counsel because of a good faith belief that the conflicted representation will adversely affect a client of the lawyer who files the motion. However, some lawyers use disqualification motions to obstruct litigation or to obtain a strategic advantage by requiring an adversary to spend time and money to change lawyers or to defend the disqualification motion. Courts review motions to disqualify filed by adversaries with care to ensure that they are not being enlisted to assist in such tactics.[42]

Sometimes law firms simply turn away clients because the firms have been interviewed by the adverse party. Susan Shapiro notes that "[m]ajor corporations [and individual clients] needlessly [engage] law firms in order to strategically conflict out a firm possessed of rare expertise that might be used against them."[43] One of the Chicago lawyers whom Shapiro interviewed explained that

> in the divorce area ... there are people who deliberately shop around for lawyers, in order to create conflicts so that their spouses can't hire those lawyers.... Obviously, I think it's unethical.... And there are also ... people [who] have been through a divorce ... who ... will encourage friends ... going through a divorce ... to "go see five, six lawyers before you ... sign with the one you intend to sign with, so that your [spouse] can't ... see those lawyers."[44]

---

42. ABA, Annotated Model Rules of Professional Conduct 116-117 (5th ed., ABA 2004); see also the Preamble to the Model Rules, ¶ 20.

43. Shapiro, supra n. 1, at 74.

44. Id. at 74-75. Note, however, that the conduct described may not actually be "unethical," as the rules of professional conduct do not explicitly prohibit this tactic.

Do the rules of professional conduct apply in determining disqualification motions?

Although the ethics rules were written primarily to be a basis for discipline of lawyers who violated them, some courts have come to rely on, or at least give substantial weight to, the rules in various other types of proceedings, including motions to disqualify lawyers because of conflicts of interest or other unethical behavior.[45] Some courts evaluating disqualification motions refer to the ABA Model Rules (rather than the applicable state ethics code) or to the Restatement as evidence of "national standards" for evaluation of conflicts of interest.[46]

6. Imputation of concurrent conflicts

A lawyer can have a conflict of interest because his firm represents two clients whose interests conflict or because his firm represents one client whose interests conflict with those of a client represented by his partner. Here we introduce the rules on imputation of conflicts between current clients of a firm. We discuss imputed conflicts in connection with former clients in Chapter 7.

> **Rule 1.10 Imputation of Conflicts of Interest: General Rule**
> (a) **While lawyers are associated in a firm, none of them shall knowingly represent a client when any one of them practicing alone would be prohibited from doing so by Rules 1.7 or 1.9, unless**
>> (1) **the prohibition is based on a personal interest of the disqualified lawyer and does not present a significant risk of materially limiting the representation of the client by the remaining lawyers in the firm; . . .**
> (c) **A disqualification prescribed by this rule may be waived by the affected client under the conditions stated in Rule 1.7. . . .**

Rule 1.10(a) takes the position that "a firm of lawyers is essentially one lawyer for purposes of the rules governing loyalty to the client. . . ."[47] In general, if one lawyer's client has a conflict with a client of another lawyer represented by the firm, then so do all the other lawyers in the firm. Both partners and associates are "lawyers" in the firm. If such a conflict is presented, the firm may not continue to represent the affected clients unless the clients consent after being fully advised.

---

45. ABA, Annotated Model Rules of Professional Conduct 5 (6th ed., ABA 2007).
46. Id. at 9-10, citing several cases that have relied on the Model Rules or the Restatement.
47. Rule 1.10(a), Comment 2.

If a client's interests conflict, not with the interests of another client, but with the personal interests (e.g., financial interests) of a lawyer in the firm, under Rule 1.10(a), those interests are not imputed to other lawyers in the firm.[48] The firm may proceed with representation in such cases without the informed consent of the affected client.

While the range of conflicts imputed to all lawyers within a firm is very broad, Rule 1.10 provides that such conflicts may be waived by a client affected by the conflict, unless the conflict is not consentable under Rule 1.7(b).

Are conflicts imputed to temporary lawyers and nonlawyer employees?

The imputation rules apply to conflicts presented by all lawyers in a firm (including associates) but do not preclude representation based on conflicts presented by law clerks, paralegals, secretaries, or other nonlawyer employees. Rule 1.10(a) also does not preclude a firm from accepting representation of a client based on conflicts relating to work that a lawyer in the firm did before she became a lawyer.[49] This means that the work you do as a law clerk or as an extern during law school will not be imputed to your future employers. If a conflict is presented by work done by someone who is not a lawyer or was not a lawyer at the time the work was done, a comment to Rule 1.10 explains that the conflicted person "ordinarily must be screened from any personal participation in the matter. . . . "[50] A firm must maintain a conflicts-checking system that lists the clients and former clients of lawyers and nonlawyer employees to identify cases in which screening is necessary.

PROBLEM 5-1   **THE INJURED PASSENGERS, SCENE 1**

Jill and Reema are passengers in a taxicab taking them from the airport to each of their homes. They don't know each other. The taxi driver is a fast driver. He changes lanes and ignores speed limits. He crashes into another car. Both Jill and Reema sustain injuries.

---

48. The exemption of some personal interest conflicts is discussed in Chapter 8.
49. Rule 1.10, Comment 4.
50. Id.

You are a personal injury lawyer in the town where the accident occurred. Jill and Reema come to see you together. They want you to represent both of them in a lawsuit against the cab driver and the cab company. Jill suffered whiplash, which is not too serious but will require physical therapy. Reema suffered several fractures and had some abdominal injuries. She was hospitalized for five weeks. If you were to represent them, you would charge contingent fees. The fee for each one would be calculated as one-third of the amount received by that passenger in a settlement or a judgment.

Questions

1. Can you represent both Jill and Reema? What other information do you need to know to be able to answer this question?
2. Might there be a nonconsentable conflict in this case?
3. Do you need to get informed consent before undertaking the joint representation?
4. Assuming that you need to obtain informed consent, what would you need to disclose to the clients to obtain their consent?

C. Conflicts between current clients in litigation

Having provided a general overview of the process for analyzing concurrent conflicts, we next explore the standards by which a lawyer should judge whether a conflict exists between the interests of two clients, beginning with some conflicts that arise in litigation. We start with the most extreme, dramatic conflicts and then look at some less serious conflicts.

1. Suing a current client

Can a lawyer ever be involved in litigation in which the lawyer represents one client in a lawsuit against another?

Imagine being sued by your own lawyer! Many clients would view this as a betrayal. Let's consider an example. Suppose you are representing a husband, Fred, in a divorce. While that work is progressing, a new client, Mona, asks you to sue a driver who rammed into her car at a stop sign. The ramming driver turns out to be your client Fred. If you sue Fred on behalf of Mona while you represent Fred in another matter, you would be "directly adverse" to Fred. This is true even though the cases are unrelated,[51] and even if a different lawyer represents Fred in the accident case.[52]

Case 1: Divorce

Fred	v.	Wife
(your client)		(another lawyer)

Case 2: Car accident

Mona	v.	Fred
(your client)		(a third lawyer)

How often does a situation like this come up?

One of the large firm lawyers interviewed by sociologist Susan Shapiro said, "That comes up all the time. . . . I'll bet that probably once a week, we're invited to get into a situation where we'd be adverse to a current client."[53]

Are lawyers allowed to sue current clients?

In nearly every state, the ethics rules provide that a lawyer cannot file suit against another present client unless the lawyer reasonably believes that she can represent both without adverse impact on either and unless both clients give informed consent.[54] Many court decisions reach the same conclusion.[55]

---

51. "Unrelated" in this context means that "no work done for, or information learned in, one representation would be relevant to the other." Thomas D. Morgan, Suing a Current Client, 9 Geo. J. Leg. Ethics 1157, 1157 n. 1 (1996).

52. See Rule 1.7, Comment 6.

53. Shapiro, supra n. 1, at 59.

54. Conflicts of Interest, Representation Adverse to Existing Client, ABA/BNA Laws.' Man. on Prof. Conduct 51:101 (2010) (stating that suing a current client or defending against a suit by a current client is "universally condemned" unless both conditions described in the text are met). Comment 6 to Rule 1.7(a) explains that "[a]bsent consent, a lawyer may not act as an advocate in one matter against a person the lawyer represents in some other matter, even when the matters are wholly unrelated." But this prohibition doesn't apply if the relevant clients consent. Restatement § 128, comment e.

55. See, e.g., In re Dresser Indus., 972 F.2d 540, 545 (5th Cir. 1992) (stating that "the national standards of attorney conduct forbid a lawyer from bringing a suit against a current client without the consent of both clients"); IBM v. Levin, 579 F.2d 271 (3d Cir. 1978) (a lawyer cannot sue a present client on behalf of another client even if the lawyer is not working on a matter for the defendant client at the time of the lawsuit unless the client consents to be sued).

Do practicing lawyers think the rule is too restrictive?

Many lawyers would decline to accept a matter that involved suing a current client, regardless of what the rules say. One lawyer at a large firm who talked to Susan Shapiro said:

> If two clients are fighting, we try to stay out.... We're just going to lose.... If we represent somebody who's really adverse to another client, we're guaranteed to lose that other client. I mean, it's like no question! Because if you do as good a job as you can possibly do for the client you're staying with, you're just going to tick the other side off. So, that's a no-brainer; no-win situation.[56]

Questions about suing a current client

1. The rule makes sense in the context of an individual client and an individual lawyer because the client would perceive the lawsuit as a breach of trust, a betrayal. What if a law firm that represents a large corporation in a tax matter wants to represent a plaintiff in a lawsuit against the tax client on a products liability matter? Should it be relevant that the law firm has hundreds of lawyers and several offices in different cities?[57]

2. Likewise, should a longtime client who has an ongoing relationship with a lawyer be required to hire new counsel simply because she wants to sue someone for whom the firm is providing modest service?[58] What if the potential defendant is a large corporation that has hired each of the major firms in town precisely to preclude their being sued by any of those firms?[59] The potential defendant could simply decline to waive the conflict, thereby insulating itself from suit by particular firms.

PROBLEM 5-2 I THOUGHT YOU WERE *MY* LAWYER!

This problem is based on a case that arose in the western United States in the 1970s.

___

You are the ethics counsel for Shelton & Cadenas. It is your job to advise the firm on any ethics problems that it has, particularly conflicts problems.

___

56. Shapiro, supra n. 1, at 60.
57. This question is raised by Professor Thomas Morgan, supra n. 51, at 1157.
58. Id. at 1161-1162.
59. Id. at 1162.

One of the firm's clients, Dori Hathaway, was hit by a bus while she was crossing the street. On her behalf, Shelton & Cadenas is suing the bus company. The firm has already put a lot of work into the case.

While that case was pending, Shelton & Cadenas agreed to represent another client, Kevin Bielaski, who is suing his wife for divorce. His wife is Dori Hathaway. Because Dori Hathaway has a different last name, the firm didn't realize that she is Bielaski's wife.

Kevin was not involved in the bus accident. Both Dori and Kevin have made clear that they want to go ahead with the divorce. They have no children, but they do have some property, and there may be a dispute about the property division.

The lawyer handling the divorce for Bielaski has just discovered that Dori Hathaway is a client of the law firm.

Questions

1. Your firm has signed contracts agreeing to represent Dori in the accident case and Kevin in the divorce case. What, if anything, should you advise the firm to do? Evaluate this conflict under Rule 1.7.
2. What if the law firm has two offices in different cities? If one office is handling Dori's case and the other office is handling Kevin's case, does the analysis change?
3. Assume you decide that the firm cannot represent both Kevin and Dori. Can the firm represent one of them? If so, can the firm choose which client to drop?

---

2. Cross-examining a current client

A lawyer can have an adverse relationship to a current client in litigation even if the client is not a party in the case in which the conflict arises. One such situation occurs when a lawyer is called on to cross-examine one of her clients in a trial involving charges against another of her clients.

FOR EXAMPLE: Suppose you represent Henry, a criminal defendant who is accused of robbing a convenience store. You also represent Roger, who is facing an unrelated arson charge. Roger is a prosecution witness in the robbery case against Henry because he was involved in the convenience store robbery. Therefore, you need to cross-examine Roger to show that

Roger drove Henry to the store and insisted that Henry hold up the store to get cash to pay Roger for drugs that Roger supplied to Henry. The cross-examination of Roger could show that Henry was coerced. It also could lead the prosecutor to file new charges against Roger, so your cross-examination of Roger would be directly adverse to Roger, who also is your client. This cross-examination might not affect the arson matter, but still it could increase the risk that Roger would go to prison.[60]

This kind of conflict can arise before a criminal case is tried. It is very common for criminal defendants to try to get lighter penalties or early release from prison by offering statements that assist the prosecution in obtaining conviction of other defendants. Especially in small communities, it often turns out that a lawyer who represents one defendant also is defending or has previously defended others who might incriminate him. One small-town criminal defense lawyer shared the following story with Susan Shapiro:

> I was trying a murder case here. And, on the eve of trial, two of my clients that I had represented previously . . . made statements against a third client of mine in the murder case. . . . I really found myself in quite a dilemma. . . . [O]n the one hand, I'm still in active representation of a client who's charged with murder. . . . [O]n the other hand, these guys are making statements . . . that, if they make 'em, the likelihood of them coming out of [prison] alive is not great. [The implication is that the statements were more incriminating of the speakers than they realized, and that they might exculpate the murder defendant.] And, obviously, law enforcement's not telling them that. But I was almost in a catch-22 situation. I couldn't get to them to say, "Guys, it's probably not in your interest to say this." And then I almost have a conflict by saying that, because I'm really trying to help my other client.[61]

3. Representation of co-plaintiffs or co-defendants in civil litigation

For a lawyer to sue one client on behalf of another presents perhaps the most serious type of conflict of interest. If a lawyer jointly[62] represents two clients who are both either plaintiffs or defendants in a lawsuit, their re-

---

60. See Rule 1.7, Comment 6 (discussing the potential adverse impact on a current client if the lawyer is required to cross-examine that client).

61. Shapiro, supra n. 1, at 72.

62. The discussion of these issues often refers to the representation of two plaintiffs or two defendants as "joint representation" or "multiple representation." These terms are interchangeable.

lationship is not one of direct adversity, but their interests might conflict anyway. Possible problems include the following.

- One client might have a potential claim against the other.
- If the clients are co-plaintiffs, they might be suing a defendant whose limited assets would make it impossible to satisfy both their claims.
- If a settlement is proposed, the two plaintiffs might have different views on whether to settle. The defendant might try to trade one client's claim off against the other.
- If a lawyer represents two defendants who each have some responsibility for the harm that is the subject of the suit, then each might seek to avoid liability by asserting that the other is responsible.
- If the clients are plaintiffs in a lawsuit seeking injunctive relief as well as damages, they might disagree as to what the remedy should be.[63]

Joint representation often occurs in accident cases in which two passengers or a passenger and driver in one car sue the driver of the other car that was involved in the accident. Several cases have held that a driver and passenger have sufficiently divergent interests that they may not be represented by a single lawyer.[64] The Restatement, however, takes the position that this type of conflict may be waivable by the client after full disclosure.[65]

Another common situation is one in which an employer and an employee are sued for damages. If the employer agrees to cover any damages awarded against it or the employee, the possible conflicts are limited enough that the courts generally allow both defendants to be represented by one lawyer.[66]

How can a lawyer decide whether she may represent co-plaintiffs or co-defendants?

In applying Rule 1.7(b) to evaluate whether a lawyer may represent two plaintiffs or two defendants in a single litigation, the lawyer must ascertain whether the conflict is consentable. The lawyer must ask whether "the

---

63. Restatement § 128, comment d.

64. In re Thornton, 421 A.2d 1 (D.C. 1980). Thornton represented the driver and the passengers in an accident case despite the fact that the judge expressed concern about the conflict. The judge referred the matter to the bar counsel. In response to an inquiry from bar counsel, Thornton submitted a document that purported to reflect the informed consent of the driver and the passengers. This document was found to be "patently unbelievable." Thornton was suspended from practice for one year. See also Restatement § 128, comment d.

65. Restatement § 128, comment d.

66. Smith v. N.Y.C., 611 F. Supp. 1080 (S.D.N.Y. 1985) (corporation counsel properly undertook to represent both the city and police officers in an action alleging misconduct by the officers).

lawyer reasonably believes that the lawyer will be able to provide competent and diligent representation to each affected client."[67]

If the lawyer determines that the conflict is consentable, what must the lawyer disclose to or discuss with each client to obtain truly informed consent?

The lawyer must disclose all the facts and circumstances that might adversely affect the client's interests. The content of the disclosure will depend on the circumstances of the particular case. Comment 18 following Rule 1.7 explains that

> [w]hen representation of multiple clients in a single matter is undertaken, the information must include the implications of the common representation, including the possible effects on loyalty, confidentiality, and the attorney-client privilege and the advantages and risks involved.

The ethics committee of the Arizona State Bar explained further[68] that this disclosure should address

1. the conflicting or potentially conflicting interests of the other clients;
2. the potential courses of action that may be foreclosed or limited by the joint representation;
3. the effect of the representation upon the client's confidential information and on the attorney-client privilege;
4. any reservations the lawyer would have about the representation if the lawyer were representing only the client being advised; and
5. the consequences on the representation if one client later withdraws their consent to the joint representation.[69]

The Arizona committee also offered general guidance on some of the topics that the lawyer should discuss with the client and then in a follow-up confirmatory writing, which Rule 1.7 requires the lawyer to send to the client. The topics flagged by the committee for written and oral disclosure (as summarized in *U.S. Law Week*) include the following.

- ▪ *Conflicting testimony.* The lawyer should identify any potential testimonial conflicts and explain how they would impair the claims of each individual client. In some cases, known testimonial conflicts

---

67. Rule 1.7(b)(1). See section B3 of this chapter for discussion of assessment of consentability.

68. Ariz. State B. Comm. on the R. of Prof. Conduct, Op. 07-04 (available at http://www.azbar.org/Ethics/Ethics.Opinions/ViewEthicsOpinion?id = 696).

69. [Arizona State Bar's citation.] Restatement § 122 cmt c(i) (2000); ABA/BNA Laws.' Man. on Prof. Conduct §51:309-311 (2005).

may make it impossible to accept the representation even with client consent.

■ *Conflicting settlement positions.* The lawyer should disclose that there may be conflicts among clients with respect to settlement, and discuss the advantages and disadvantages of individual settlement offers as opposed to aggregate offers. . . . [T]he lawyer should make clear to each client that information about each individual offer and the response to such an offer cannot be kept secret from the other jointly represented clients.

■ *Attorney-client privilege.* [It will not apply if the clients later become adverse to one another, unless they have a prior agreement preserving the privilege under those circumstances].[70]

■ *Withdrawal in event of conflict.* Counsel must also disclose that the law firm may be forced to withdraw if an untenable conflict arises during the representation, and that expense and delays could result if withdrawal becomes necessary.

■ *Confidentiality.* The . . . attorney's normal confidentiality obligation does not apply as between jointly represented clients, and that information imparted to the lawyer by one co-client will be shared with the other co-clients if it is necessary for their representation. . . . If one joint client instructs the lawyer not to share material information with other joint clients, a conflict is created that may require the lawyer's withdrawal from the joint representation. . . .[71] If a settlement offer is received, the lawyer should reevaluate whether additional disclosure and consent is required under Rule 1.8's provision on aggregate settlements.

■ "Finally . . . ," the opinion states, "lawyers must evaluate on an ongoing basis whether future developments in the case create issues that require additional disclosures and consent to the multiple representation or possible withdrawal."[72]

---

70. This is a clarification of the Arizona opinion, which says that "there is no attorney-client privilege between jointly represented clients during the pendency of the matter." The operative word is "between."

71. As noted in Chapter 3, in most jurisdictions, co-parties may agree that the lawyer either may or may not share their confidences with each other, and the authorities do not agree about the obligations of counsel when no such agreement has been made. In Arizona, apparently, the default position is that there is no confidentiality between co-clients.

72. For Multiple Representation, Disclosures Must Be Molded to Particular Circumstances, 76 U.S.L.W. 2390 (Jan. 8, 2008).

PROBLEM 5-3 **THE INJURED PASSENGERS, SCENE 2**

Let's return to the accident in which both Jill and Reema were injured in an accident while they were passengers in a taxicab. Recall that Reema's injuries are much more serious than Jill's. Assume that you concluded that you could represent them both, and that you have obtained their informed consent. You have filed suit on behalf of each of your clients and done some discovery. The attorney for the taxicab company contacts you to discuss settlement. During settlement negotiations, the attorney for the cab company hints that he may soon offer $350,000 to settle Reema's claim if you'll accept only $50,000 for Jill's claim.

Questions

1. How should you respond?
2. Suppose that you are able to continue representing both clients, and they both reject the settlement offer. During your deposition of the driver, he states that Jill was very drunk when she got into the car and that the accident occurred while Jill was swearing at him for going too fast. You ask Reema about Jill's behavior in the cab, and she confirms what the driver told you. How does this information affect your work on behalf of Jill and Reema?

---

4. Positional conflicts: taking inconsistent legal positions in litigation

If a lawyer makes a legal argument on behalf of one client in one case that is contrary to the interests of another client who is not involved in the case, does that situation present a conflict?

Although a lawyer would confront a conflict of interest if she were to advocate on behalf of one client against another client, normally a lawyer may make inconsistent arguments on a legal issue in different courts at different times without running afoul of the conflicts rules.[73] This situation is called a "positional" conflict. It is usually less problematic than other types of conflicts. Whether a positional conflict presents a serious problem, however, depends on the likelihood that one client would be materially

---

73. See Rule 1.7, Comment 24, quoted below.

harmed if a lawyer made an argument in another case that was contrary to the client's interest. Comment 24 following Rule 1.7 states, in part:

The mere fact that advocating a legal position on behalf of one client might create precedent adverse to the interests of a client represented by the lawyer in an unrelated matter does not create a conflict of interest. A conflict of interest exists, however, if there is a significant risk that a lawyer's action on behalf of one client will materially limit the lawyer's effectiveness in representing another client in a different case; for example, when a decision favoring one client will create a precedent likely to seriously weaken the position taken on behalf of the other client. . . . If there is significant risk of material limitation, then absent informed consent of the affected clients, the lawyer must refuse one of the representations or withdraw from one or both matters.

The comment following Rule 1.7 and the Restatement identify factors to be considered in making this assessment:

- Whether the issue is before a trial or appellate court
- Whether the issue is substantive or procedural
- The temporal relationship between the matters
- The practical significance of the issue to the immediate and long-run interests of the clients involved
- The clients' reasonable expectations in retaining the lawyer[74]

An ABA ethics opinion on this issue concluded that it was not very significant whether the relevant matters were at the trial or appellate level. The committee urged that a lawyer evaluating a positional conflict should consider whether the decision in one case is likely to affect the decision in the other and whether the lawyer might be inclined to "soft-pedal" or otherwise alter one or another argument to avoid affecting the other case.[75]

FOR EXAMPLE: A lawyer is handling damage actions on behalf of two different clients in two different federal district courts. In one case, representing the plaintiff, the lawyer will offer evidence of injury to the client based on a controversial medical test. In the other case, in which the lawyer represents the defendant, the plaintiff will offer similar evidence, and the lawyer will object to its admission. The lawyer may go forward with both these representations without obtaining the informed consent of the clients, even though it is possible that one of

---

74. Restatement § 128, comment f.
75. ABA Standing Comm. on Ethics & Prof. Resp., Formal Op. 93-377.

these courts might publish a ruling that might become a basis for argument in the other matter.[76]

Professor Helen Anderson has critiqued the ABA stance on positional conflicts, arguing that they are not true conflicts and that urging lawyers to avoid positional conflicts "creates incentives for lawyers to avoid the positional conflict by bowing to business conflicts and suppressing arguments for or dropping the less favored client."[77] She states further that "a rule against positional conflicts gives greater control to wealthy clients over the availability of legal services without significantly protecting the rights of poor or middle income clients."[78]

D. Conflicts involving prospective clients

A last topic for this chapter is conflicts that involve prospective clients who consult lawyers while seeking representation but who do not engage those lawyers. During a preliminary discussion with a potential client, a lawyer may learn various confidences for the purpose of assessing whether the lawyer will represent the client. Even if this lawyer ultimately does not represent the client, the lawyer may possess confidential information that could be used adversely to that former prospective client on behalf of another client. Therefore, Rule 1.18 mandates protection of confidences received from prospective clients and lays out a set of standards by which to evaluate conflicts with prospective clients.[79] Rule 1.18 gives prospective clients some protection from conflicts with the lawyer's other clients, but not as much protection as actual clients. Rule 1.18(a) defines a prospective client. Rule 1.18(b) bars a lawyer from using or revealing information learned from a prospective client except to the extent permitted by Rule 1.9. Rule 1.18(c) bars a lawyer from continuing to represent a current client if she receives information from a prospective client that could be "significantly harmful" to her if it were revealed to the other client. Even if one lawyer in a firm is disqualified by this rule because the lawyer received confidential information from a prospective client, under 1.18(d), other lawyers in the firm may continue to

---

76. This example is adapted from Restatement § 128, comment f, illus. 5.

77. Helen A. Anderson, Legal Doubletalk and the Concern with Positional Conflicts: A "Foolish Consistency," 111 Penn St. L. Rev. 1, 4 (2006).

78. Id.

79. This rule makes explicit the duty to protect confidences received from, and to avoid representation that conflicts with the interests of, a prospective client (depending on how much adverse confidential information the lawyer received). Lawyers have other duties to prospective clients also, such as the duty of competence and duties with respect to papers or other property that a prospective client leaves in the lawyer's care. See Rule 1.18, Comment 9.

represent the current client (1) if both the current and prospective clients give informed consent; or (2) if (a) the lawyer who received the potentially damaging information took steps to prevent being exposed to more than the necessary amount of information to determine whether the firm could represent the client, (b) the disqualified lawyer is screened from contact with the matter, and (c) written notice of the conflict is given to the prospective client.

A lawyer dealing with a prospective client must also keep in mind that a court ultimately might find that the "prospective" client had become an actual client through her dealings with the lawyer.[80] The Internet has increased the risk that a lawyer will inadvertently take on the representation of a client because law firms have created interactive websites, some of which allow clients to pose questions to lawyers. As of 2010, 84 percent of law firms had websites, and 81 percent of Americans researched products and services online.[81] The ABA has warned that law firm websites "serve as an effective marketing tool" but that warnings and disclaimers may be necessary "to avoid a misunderstanding by the website visitor that ... a lawyer-client relationship has been created."[82] Comment 2 to Rule 1.18 (as amended by the ABA House of Delegates in August 2012) provides that an electronic consultation with a lawyer can render the client a "prospective client." It further provides that such a consultation

> is likely to have occurred if a lawyer, either in person or through the lawyer's advertising in any medium, specifically requests or invites the submission of information about a potential representation without clear and reasonably understandable warnings and cautionary statements that limit the lawyer's obligations, and a person provides information in response.

The comment also states that a person is not a "prospective client" if the person contacted the lawyer for the purpose of disqualifying the lawyer from representing a potential adversary. This comment responds to a concern that the Internet makes it very easy for individuals to try to disqualify a large number of lawyers from representing an opposing party by sending them confidential information through e-mails or other electronic communications.

80. See the *Togstad* case in Chapter 4.

81. Eileen Libby, Websites May Trigger Unforeseen Ethics Obligations to Prospective Clients, ABA J. 22 (Jan. 1, 2011) (available at http://www.abajournal.com/magazine/article/websites_may_trigger_unforseen_ethics_obligations_to_clients/).

82. ABA Standing Comm. on Ethics & Prof. Resp., Formal Op. 10-457 (available at http://www.lawmarketingmonitor.com/10_457.pdf).

PROBLEM 5-4 **THE SECRET AFFAIR**

This problem is based on events that took place in a western state.

You started a small law firm and, so far, are the firm's only lawyer. To attract potential clients, you put on your firm's website a link asking:

"What are my rights? We may be able to help you."

A visitor who clicks on this line sees an electronic form. The first line in the form asks the visitor:

"Wondering about a legal problem you have?"

The form asks for the visitor's name and contact information and for a statement of facts about the person's legal problem. Then it invites the visitor to pose a question for someone at the firm to answer. Right under that box is this statement:

I acknowledge that I will not be charged for the response that I receive from the firm.

I agree that I am not forming an attorney-client relationship by submitting this question. I also understand that I am not forming a confidential relationship.

I further agree that I may retain the firm only by entering into a written fee agreement.

Below these statements are two buttons:

SUBMIT By submitting this inquiry, I signify my agreement to the foregoing terms.

CANCEL my inquiry.

You are the lawyer at the firm who reads and responds to the inquiries that arrive. You just received one from Maria Decorsi. She writes:

My husband, Nicholas Decorsi, is living with another woman. We have been separated for three months. I am looking for a lawyer to handle my divorce. I want a good property settlement, and I would like to obtain sole custody of my 13-year-old son, who lives with me. I had an extramarital affair several years ago. Nicholas doesn't know about it. I wouldn't want him to find out because he'd probably try to use it to prevent me from getting sole custody. I like your website and would like you to represent me. I have enough money to pay you from my savings.

You type out a quick e-mail to Maria, stating, "Maria: it sounds like you have a genuine need for legal representation. If you like, you can call me at my office tomorrow and we can talk about whether we should represent you." Then you do a quick check for conflicts of interest and discover that your firm has already agreed to represent Nicholas, who wants to divorce Maria.

Questions

1. Is Maria a prospective client?
2. If she is a prospective client, may you decline to represent her and continue to represent Nicholas? If so, may you tell Nicholas about Maria's affair?

---

6 Current Client Conflicts in Particular Practice Settings

We have explored the general principles raised by conflicts between the interests of two clients. Conflicts are especially common in certain practice settings, and each of these situations raises particular issues. In this chapter, we examine conflicts that arise in various types of representation. These include a lawyer's representation of (a) multiple parties to a transaction, (b) organizations, (c) criminal co-defendants, (d) spouses in domestic relations matters and in estate planning, (e) insured persons and their insurance companies, and (f) employers and prospective employees in immigration applications. Nearly all these situations have in common the problem of a lawyer attempting to represent two clients who have some common interests, but who may have some divergent interests.[1] In an ideal world, perhaps each person confronting a legal problem would have his or her own lawyer.[2] This would avoid the possible compromise of the interests of one client on behalf of another.[3] In the real world, however, legal representation is expensive, so many clients prefer to share counsel with someone else who has common interests. This is not always a bad thing. Sometimes joint representation is beneficial because of common interests, pooled information, and cost efficiency. In some cases, however, representation of multiple parties involved in one matter poses problems relating to confidentiality or to loyalty.[4]

A. Representing both parties to a transaction

Suppose you are approached by the buyer and seller of a business. They want you to represent both of them in drawing up the documents of sale.

---

1. A lawyer representing an organization would fit this description if she also was representing an employee of the organization, but if she is representing only the organization, conflicts might arise between her duties to the client organization and her perceived duties to officers of the organization. See, for example, the Worldwide Bribery problem in Chapter 3.

2. See Debra Lyn Bassett, Three's a Crowd: A Proposal to Abolish Joint Representation, 32 Rutgers L.J. 387, 426 (2001) (arguing that joint representation is more problematic than has been generally recognized).

3. This assumes that the ideal representation is one in which a lawyer would pursue the interests of a single client with undivided loyalty. If one assumes that pursuit of self-interest is the name of the game, this looks like a good model. However, sometimes this model foments controversy where compromise would have been possible. If the goal is to resolve conflicts in a way that attends to the interests of all parties instead of helping one party to win every possible advantage, then perhaps one lawyer representing two parties with overlapping interests can be more beneficial than detrimental. See generally Carrie Menkel-Meadow, The Silences of the Restatement of the Law Governing Lawyers: Lawyering as Only Adversary Practice, 10 Geo. J. Leg. Ethics 631 (1997).

4. See generally John S. Dzienkowski, Lawyers as Intermediaries: The Representation of Multiple Clients in the Modern Legal Profession, 1992 U. Ill. L. Rev. 741; William E. Wright Jr., Ethical Considerations in Representing Multiple Parties in Litigation, 79 Tul. L. Rev. 1523 (2005).

Are you allowed to do this? Such conflicts are evaluated using the standards articulated in Rule 1.7, so whether the representation is permitted and whether client consent is required depends on whether there is a "direct adversity" conflict or a "material limitation" conflict under 1.7(a). If so, the lawyer must evaluate whether she reasonably believes that she "will be able to provide competent and diligent representation to each affected client." If that question is answered affirmatively, the lawyer may seek the consent of the affected clients.

In most cases, a lawyer may represent two clients seeking legal assistance with a common goal. But if it appears that the clients' interests could conflict, the lawyer must provide the clients with information about the possible downsides of the joint representation and obtain their consent.[5] The clients might be forming a corporation, settling a dispute without litigation, doing estate planning, or buying a house. Not every such case presents a possible conflict; if no conflict is apparent, informed consent is not required.[6]

On the other hand, there are all sorts of ways that the interests of two parties to a transaction might conflict. One lawyer whom Susan Shapiro interviewed said that representing two parties to a transaction was like "handling a porcupine."[7] Another of her lawyer informants gave this example involving representation of both a buyer and a seller:

> [Consider] two parties who come in and just want to use one lawyer for a property transaction. . . . I think that's almost impossible to do without conflicts. Although people ask you to do it all the time. . . . But it's to the seller's benefit to pro-rate taxes at the current levels. Or to the buyer's benefit to pro-rate taxes at an estimated 110 percent level of previous taxes. Inspection clauses, who's going to pay for repairs if they're required? . . . [T]here's just absolutely no way you can — aggressively, anyway — represent both sides. You always have to kind of compromise in the middle. And I think that's a real, real conflict.[8]

How does a lawyer know whether she needs to obtain informed consent?

The relevant question is whether there is an actual or potential conflict that is "reasonably apparent" to the lawyer. If the clients' interests appear entirely harmonious, there may be no need to obtain consent. If, on the other hand, the clients have some divergent interests or goals, or some tension is

---

5. William Freivogel, Freivogel on Conflicts, Joint/Multiple Representation, http://www. freivogel.com/jointmultiplerepresentation.html (accessed Nov. 13, 2012).
6. Restatement § 130, comment b.
7. Susan Shapiro, Tangled Loyalties: Conflict of Interest in Legal Practice 66 (U. Mich. Press 2002).
8. Id. at 65.

apparent in the communication between them, the lawyer should obtain their consent to be sure they understand the possible disadvantages of being represented by a single lawyer.[9]

Can a lawyer solve the possible conflict by undertaking just to draft documents without giving advice?

No. If a lawyer undertakes joint representation of parties to a transaction, the lawyer should not regard himself as a "mere scrivener" who is simply recording their preferences. He instead should endeavor to provide the same range of services to each of the two clients as he would if he were representing only one of them.[10]

Can a lawyer keep confidences learned from one client from the other client?

A lawyer owes both clients a duty of loyalty, which might be compromised if the lawyer keeps secrets from either one of them.

> **FOR EXAMPLE:** Suppose one member of a domestic partnership pays three-quarters of the price of the house that they purchase jointly but receives only half the ownership interest. The other partner confides to the lawyer that he is unsure how long the partners' relationship will last. Especially if the transaction is not yet completed, the lawyer may have an obligation to reveal this confidence to the partner who is paying more. (The lawyer has an obligation to keep each client informed and to render candid advice under Rule 1.4.) Alternatively, the lawyer may be obliged to withdraw because she cannot continue the representation without violating a rule.

No attorney-client privilege shields information from either of the clients when they are jointly represented (unless the clients have agreed otherwise),[11] but the ethical duty to protect confidences is less clear-cut. Comment 31 to Rule 1.7 suggests that a lawyer usually should not keep confidences received from one joint client from the other:

> The lawyer should, at the outset of the common representation and as part of the process of obtaining each client's informed consent, advise each client that information will be shared and that the lawyer will have to withdraw if one client decides that some matter material to the representation should be kept from the other. In limited circumstances, it may be appropriate for the lawyer to proceed with the representation when the clients have agreed, after being properly informed, that the lawyer will keep certain information confidential.

---

9. Restatement § 130, comment c.
10. Restatement § 130, comment b.
11. Restatement § 75.

The comment goes on to suggest that, in the circumstances of a particular case, the lawyer might reasonably conclude that she could keep one client's trade secrets confidential from another client without adverse impact on her representation of the clients in a joint venture. In that case, she could continue the representation with the informed consent of both clients.

If the two clients wind up in litigation against one another, does the lawyer have to withdraw altogether, or can the lawyer represent one against the other?

If a conflict develops that will lead to litigation, a lawyer may not continue to represent both (or all) of the clients because that would involve the lawyer in suing one client on behalf of another in an adversarial situation. If the lawyer withdraws from representing one client, the other becomes a former client. In this case, the lawyer usually cannot represent one client in a lawsuit against a former client because the suit would be (per Rule 1.9) "the same or a substantially related matter" and its initiation would be materially adverse to the interests of the former client.[12] In such a situation, representation is allowed only with the consent of the former client.[13] The consent of the continuing client might also be required under Rule 1.7 if the lawyer's obligations to the former client (such as protecting confidences) might materially limit the lawyer's continuing representation of the continuing client. A lawyer might be able to continue to represent one (or fewer than all) of the clients if the lawyer obtained a valid advance waiver of this conflict from the clients at the outset of the representation. As part of the informed consent process, the lawyer should work out with the clients what would happen if litigation develops and whether they would consent to the lawyer representing one (or fewer than all) of them against the other.[14]

B. Representing organizations

Lawyers used to spend most of their professional lives representing individual persons. This is no longer the case. These days, the majority of legal services are delivered to organizations rather than persons. Most of these organizations are for-profit corporations, which since the late nineteenth century have been accorded the status of legal personhood.

This section of the chapter explores some of the questions that arise when a lawyer is representing an organization. For example:

---

12. Restatement § 132.
13. See Chapter 7 for discussion of former client conflicts.
14. Restatement § 130, comment c.

■ Who is "the client" of a lawyer who represents an organization?

■ What if one member of an organization seeks to act in a manner contrary to the interests of the organization?

■ May a lawyer represent an organization and its employees, members, and affiliates?

■ If a lawyer is representing an organization, may the lawyer take on representation that might be adverse to an employee, member, or affiliate of the organization? If the conflict may be waived by the clients, who can give consent to waive a conflict on behalf of an organization?

These issues are addressed in Rule 1.13.

Rule 1.13 Organization as Client

Rule language[*]	Authors' explanation[**]
(a) **A lawyer employed** or retained **by an organization represents the organization** acting through its duly authorized constituents.	This section addresses "who is the client" of a lawyer representing an organization. The "client" does not include the "officers, directors, employees, shareholders and other constituents," but is the entity itself. Comments 1 and 2.
(b) If a lawyer for an organization **knows** that an officer, employee or other person associated with the organization is **engaged** in action, **intends to act or refuses to act** in a matter related to the representation that is a **violation of a legal obligation to the organization, or a violation of law that reasonably might be imputed to the organization, and that is likely to result in substantial injury to the organization,** then the lawyer **shall proceed as is reasonably necessary in the best interest of the organization. Unless** the lawyer reasonably believes that it is **not necessary** in the best interest of the organization to do so, the lawyer **shall refer the matter to** higher authority in the organization, including, if warranted by the circumstances to the **highest authority that can act** on behalf of the organization as determined by applicable law.	This section explains the duties of a lawyer if someone associated with the organization is involved in unlawful or other action that could harm the organization. It describes the circumstances under which the lawyer must "report up" to the top of the corporate ladder. A lawyer ordinarily should defer to the decisions of corporate officers on "policy and operations," but if an officer's action is likely to "substantially injure" the organization or if the action is unlawful, the lawyer has duties under this section. See Comment 3. What action is required of the lawyer depends on "the seriousness of the violation and its consequences, the responsibility in the organization and the apparent motivation of the person involved," and other factors. Sometimes the lawyer can fulfill this duty by requesting reconsideration of the matter or by having the matter reviewed by a higher authority in the organization. See Comment 4. Sometimes the lawyer must report the information to someone outside the organization. See Rule 1.13(c).

Rule language[*]	Authors' explanation[**]
(c) Except as provided in paragraph (d), **if** (1) despite the lawyer's efforts in accordance with paragraph (b) the **highest authority** that can act on behalf of the organization **insists upon or fails to address** in a timely and appropriate manner an action, or a refusal to act, that is clearly a violation of law, and	
(2) the lawyer reasonably believes that **the violation is reasonably certain to result in substantial injury to the organization,** then the lawyer **may reveal information relating to the representation whether or not Rule 1.6 permits such disclosure**, but only if and to the extent the lawyer reasonably believes necessary to prevent substantial injury to the organization.	This section of the rule lays out the circumstances under which a lawyer is permitted to disclose confidential information outside the corporation to prevent or remedy conduct by an employee that is reasonably certain to cause significant harm to the organization. Rule 1.13(c) creates another exception (besides those in 1.6(b)) to the rule requiring protection of confidences. See Comment 6.
(d) Paragraph (c) **shall not apply** with respect to information relating to a lawyer's representation of an organization to investigate an alleged violation of law, or to defend the organization or an officer, employee or other constituent associated with the organization against a claim arising out of an alleged violation of law.	This section explains that paragraph (c) does not allow revelation of confidences as to a matter on which the lawyer has been engaged to investigate possible illegal conduct or to defend the organization or an employee against an allegation of illegal action.
(e) A lawyer who **reasonably believes that he or she has been discharged because of the lawyer's actions taken pursuant to paragraphs (b) or (c), or who withdraws under circumstances that require or permit** the lawyer to take action under either of those paragraphs, **shall proceed as the lawyer reasonably believes necessary to assure that the organization's highest authority is informed** of the lawyer's discharge or withdrawal.	This section describes the duties of a lawyer who is fired or who withdraws because of action that the lawyer takes to prevent or remedy unlawful conduct. The lawyer should take steps to inform the board of directors of the lawyer's firing or withdrawal.
(f) **In dealing with an organization's directors, officers, employees, members, shareholders** or other constituents, a lawyer **shall explain** the identity of the client **when the lawyer knows or reasonably should know that the organization's interests are**	This section requires a lawyer who represents an organization to explain her role whenever she is dealing with constituents whose interests may conflict with those of the organization.

Continued

Rule language[*]	Authors' explanation[**]
adverse to those of the constituents with whom the lawyer is dealing.	
(g) **A lawyer representing an organization may also represent any of its directors, officers, employees, members, shareholders or other constituents, subject to the provisions of Rule 1.7.** If the organization's consent to the dual representation is required by Rule 1.7, the consent shall be given by an appropriate official of the organization other than the individual who is to be represented, or by the shareholders.	This section explains that a lawyer who represents an organization may also represent individuals associated with the organization so long as the representation complies with Rule 1.7. It also explains how to obtain the consent of the organization.

[*]This is the text of Kentucky Rule SCR 3.130 (1.13), which is the same as the text of Model Rule 1.13. See the note in the Introduction for a more detailed explanation.

[**]All emphasis added.

[***]This and other authors' explanations draw from the comments to the rules and from other sources. They are not comprehensive but highlight some important interpretive points.

1. Who is the client?

Does the lawyer represent only the corporation, or are the officers, subsidiaries, and other affiliates of the corporation also clients?

If a lawyer is engaged to represent a corporation, usually the lawyer's client is the corporation itself, not the officers or shareholders of the corporation, and not other corporations owned (in part or whole) by the corporation. Rule 1.13(a) provides that "[a] lawyer employed or retained by an organization represents the organization. . . . " Sometimes, however, the lawyer has obligations toward other individuals or organizations affiliated with a client organization, especially if the organization's action will have financial consequences for the other person or organization.[15]

Many lawyers who represent corporations develop close and cooperative working relationships with the corporate representatives — often lawyers in the corporate general counsels' offices — with whom they deal. The general counsel may give instructions to the lawyer, pay the bills, or be responsible for

---

15. See Rule 1.7, Comment 34; Restatement § 121, comment d; ABA Standing Comm. on Ethics & Prof. Resp., Formal Op. 95-390 (concluding that a lawyer for a corporation does not represent affiliates unless the client has a reasonable expectation of representation); Charles W. Wolfram, Corporate Family Conflicts, 2 J. Inst. Study Leg. Ethics 295 (1999).

selection of outside counsel on various matters. The general counsel may decide whether the lawyer will continue to receive work from the corporation. As a practical matter, the general counsel may seem to be "the client." But in fact, the lawyer's obligations run to the organization itself.[16]

The question of who is the lawyer's client comes up in various contexts. Here are a few examples.

- A person or entity related to the primary client organization (such as the chief executive officer) might seek legal advice or services or might seek to blame the organization's lawyer for that person's own misdeeds.
- The corporate representative might ask the lawyer to do something that is in that person's individual interest (for example, shred documents that are embarrassing or incriminating) but that is not in the interest of the organization as a whole.
- Another client of the lawyer might ask the lawyer to file suit against a subsidiary or other entity related to a corporate client of the lawyer. The question is whether the lawyer is precluded from undertaking this work. To figure out whether the subsidiary might be viewed as her client, the lawyer might consider the following criteria.

Factors affecting whether a related entity is a client[17]

Related entity more likely to be a client if:	Related entity less likely to be a client if:
The lawyer received confidential information from or provided advice to the subsidiary.	The lawyer no longer represents the initial corporate client.
The entity was controlled and supervised by the parent organization.	The two entities became linked (e.g., by a merger) after the lawyer began representation of the corporation.
The original client could be materially harmed by the suit against the subsidiary.	

The case law is not consistent with respect to the issues arising from the representation of related entities. Some courts examine the particular circumstances, using the criteria listed in the table. If you represent an entity,

---

16. See Restatement § 131, comment e. Regarding the attorney-client privilege for such communications, see Chapter 3 and Restatement § 73, comment j.

17. Restatement § 121, comment d, reporter's note; see ABA Standing Comm. on Ethics & Prof. Resp., Formal Op. 95-390; John Steele, Corporate-Affiliate Conflicts: A Reasonable Expectations Test, 29 W. St. U. L. Rev. 283, 311-313 (2002).

you need to obtain information about other organizations and individuals that are related to the entity (owners of, owned by, officers and directors of, and so forth) so that if you are asked to take on a matter adverse to one of the related persons or entities, you can evaluate whether there is a conflict.

2. Representing the entity and employees

Can a lawyer who represents a corporation provide legal services to individual employees of the organization?

A lawyer in private practice who represents an organization may represent a member or an employee of the organization unless the interests of the organization and the individual conflict, in which case the lawyer may proceed only with the consent of the affected parties.

Restatement § 131 articulates a standard by which to evaluate whether consent is required in this context:

> A lawyer may not represent both an organization and a director, officer, employee, shareholder, owner, partner, member or other individual or organization associated with the organization if there is a substantial risk that the lawyer's representation of either would be materially and adversely affected by the lawyer's duties to the other.

If consent for such a conflict is required, a designated corporate official can give consent, so long as that person is not the one to be represented by the lawyer.[18] Suppose an organization is accused of misconduct — for example, of grossly overstating its earnings for a few years running. An individual who participated in the decisions to take the questionable actions might also be accused of wrongdoing. A lawyer may not be able to represent both the organization and the individual because each would have an interest in pointing the finger at the other to avoid responsibility.[19] On the other hand, if the individual and the organization would assert the same defense to the accusation, there might be no serious conflict in the lawyer representing them both, but the possibility of divergence down the road requires that the lawyer obtain informed consent from both the organization and the individual.[20]

In general, a lawyer who is an employee of the corporation who represents the corporation may not undertake representation of share-

---

18. Rule 1.13(e).

19. Restatement § 131, comment e.

20. Id. at illus. 3; see Coleman v. Smith, 814 F.2d 1142 (7th Cir. 1987); Dunton v. Suffolk Co., 729 F.2d 903 (2d Cir. 1984) (discussing under what circumstances a lawyer for the police department may also represent individual police officers).

holders of the corporation.[21] Authority is divided about whether a lawyer who works for an insurance company may represent insured persons.[22]

3. Duty to protect confidences of employees

If an employee of a corporation discloses information to the corporation's lawyer in confidence, does the lawyer have an obligation to the employee to protect the confidence?

As usual, it depends.[23] If the lawyer represents only the organization and not any employee, the lawyer generally has no duty to protect confidences of employees. The lawyer's duty is to protect the information belonging to the organization from others outside the organization. If an employee approaches the lawyer for advice, and the lawyer perceives a potential conflict of interest, the lawyer must advise the employee that a potential conflict exists and that the lawyer may have a duty to reveal the content of discussions with the employee to the managers of the organization. The lawyer should decline to represent the employee and should suggest that the employee obtain independent representation.[24] If the lawyer fails to give such a warning and behaves in a manner that would justify the employee in her expectation of confidentiality, then the lawyer might inadvertently create a lawyer-client relationship with the employee, with an attendant duty to protect the employee's communication as confidential. If the employee's interests conflict with those of the organization, the lawyer may need to discontinue representation of both the organization and the employee.[25]

A related issue — the scope of the attorney-client privilege accorded to corporations — is addressed in Chapter 3.

---

21. Sometimes shareholders of an organization file "derivative suits" alleging that officers or directors of the organization have breached a duty to the organization. Usually the organization is an involuntary plaintiff and the officers or directors are defendants. The suit is brought for the benefit of the organization. Some courts have held that the lawyer for the corporation should represent the officers or directors and that the corporation should hire a separate lawyer. See Cannon v. U.S. Acoustics Corp., 398 F. Supp. 209 (N.D. Ill. 1975), *aff'd in relevant part*, 532 F.2d 1118 (7th Cir. 1976); Forrest v. Baeza, 67 Cal. Rptr. 2d 857 (Ct. App. 1997); Restatement § 131, comment g; and Rule 1.13, Comments 13 and 14.

22. Restatement § 4, comment e and reporter's note to comment e.

23. See generally Sarah Helene Duggin, Internal Corporate Investigations: Legal Ethics, Professionalism, and the Employee Interview, 2003 Colum. Bus. L. Rev. 859.

24. Rule 1.13, Comment 10.

25. Restatement § 131, comment e; see also Restatement § 15, comment c; § 103, comment e.

4. Responding to unlawful conduct by corporate officers and other employees

What should a lawyer do if an officer or employee of an organization threatens to do something illegal or something that would harm the organization?

In the course of representing an organization, a lawyer might learn that an officer or employee has done something or is planning to do something that is illegal or that would cause harm to the organization.

> **FOR EXAMPLE:** Suppose that the chief executive officer is planning to use funds belonging to the organization to purchase a luxury car for his mistress.[26] Or suppose that the chief financial officer is planning to include material misinformation in a report that is to be filed with a state regulatory agency.

The lawyer's duty is to the organization, not to the senior executives. Rule 1.13 requires the lawyer to serve the interests of the organization. This usually means that the lawyer should report the misconduct to a higher authority within the organization and, if need be, to the highest authority that can act on behalf of a corporation (the board of directors or its audit committee).[27] If the highest authority refuses to act properly and the lawyer believes that the misconduct will result in substantial injury to the organization, the Model Rules now permit the lawyer to reveal the misconduct to public officials.[28] The Model Rules do not permit revelation to outside entities if the organization retained the lawyer to investigate the misconduct or to defend the organization or its employees against a claim arising out of an alleged violation of law.[29] In these cases, the importance of serving the corporation apparently outweighs the importance of disclosure.[30]

It is risky for a lawyer to report proposed or past misconduct by senior officers to the president or board of directors. For one thing, senior officials whose conduct is reported might fire the lawyer. If the lawyer is fired for reporting to higher authorities within or outside the organization, or if the

---

26. This example is adapted from Restatement § 96, illus. 1.

27. Rule 1.13(b).

28. Rule 1.13(c).

29. Rule 1.13(d).

30. Rule 1.13(c). Not all states permit "reporting out" to officials. The Delaware Rules, for example, do not condone reporting to officials. They merely permit (but do not require) the lawyer to resign. Del. Rule 1.13(c). If the client's activities are regulated by federal agencies such as the Securities and Exchange Commission, federal law may impose additional obligations on the lawyer. See, e.g., the discussion in Chapter 3 of the regulations and proposed regulations under the Sarbanes-Oxley Act.

lawyer withdraws because the lawyer has become aware of the misconduct of an officer, the Model Rules direct the lawyer to inform the organization's highest authority of the discharge or withdrawal.[31] Even if the most senior officers address the misconduct, they might not rehire the lawyer who reported it.

5. Entity lawyers on boards of directors

Is there a conflict of interest if a lawyer sits on the board of directors of a corporation that the lawyer represents?

Lawyers are not forbidden to sit on the boards of directors of organizations that they represent, and some lawyers do so. In many instances, there is no conflict between the two roles, but if there is a potential or an actual conflict, the lawyer must take remedial action.[32] A conflict might be presented, for example, if the directors asked the lawyer to give an opinion on payment of bonuses to a group of corporate officers. If the lawyer would be a recipient of the bonus, his judgment might be affected by his personal interests.[33] Another example: If a lawyer-director is accused of wrongdoing in a derivative suit, the lawyer may not represent the organization in the suit.[34]

If a conflict arises that presents "a substantial risk that the lawyer's representation of the client would be materially and adversely affected" by the lawyer's obligations as a director, the lawyer should cease to represent the corporation on that matter unless the organization waives the conflict.[35] Alternatively, the lawyer could resign from the board of directors to resolve the conflict.[36] If such conflicts are likely to be frequent and serious, a lawyer should not take on the dual roles.[37] If a lawyer is also a director of an organization, communications with him may not be protected by attorney-client privilege.[38]

---

31. Rule 1.13(e).

32. See generally Sarah Helene Duggin, The Pivotal Role of the General Counsel in Promoting Corporate Integrity and Professional Responsibility, 51 St. Louis U. L.J. 989 (2007); Susanna M. Kim, Dual Identities and Dueling Obligations: Preserving Independence in Corporate Representation, 68 Tenn. L. Rev. 179 (2001).

33. Restatement § 135, comment d, illus. 3.

34. See, e.g., Harrison v. Keystone Coca-Cola Bottling Co., 428 F. Supp. 149 (M.D. Pa. 1977).

35. Restatement § 135.

36. Rule 1.7, Comment 35.

37. Id.

38. Restatement § 135, comment d, reporter's note; Rule 1.7, Comment 35.

Do the principles that apply to representation of for-profit corporations also apply to representation of nonprofit corporations and other organizations?

Yes. Rule 1.13 applies the same principles whether the lawyer is representing a business or another type of organization.

PROBLEM 6-1 **MY CLIENT'S SUBSIDIARY**

Let's return to consider the representation of Dori Hathaway, who, as you learned in Problem 5-2, was hit by a bus while crossing the street. You may recall that your firm, Shelton & Cadenas, took on representation of her soon-to-be ex-husband in a divorce action while it was representing Hathaway in a personal injury suit against Pearl Bus Co. and the driver who hit Hathaway. Hathaway was seriously injured in the accident. She had several fractures in her legs and pelvis, spent some weeks in the hospital, and had to have four different surgeries to repair the damage. She still suffers from chronic pain as a result of her injuries, and one of her legs is about an inch shorter than the other.

Assume that the firm continues to represent Dori while her husband found a different law firm to represent him in the divorce. You are still the ethics advisor to Shelton & Cadenas.

A couple of months after the personal injury suit is filed, you discover that Pearl is owned by Transport, Inc., which is an active client of Shelton & Cadenas. The firm's conflicts-checking system doesn't always capture information about companies that own or are owned by client companies. You were not aware of this connection, and you have never had any contact with any Pearl officials. You send an e-mail to the other lawyers at Shelton & Cadenas, and it seems no one at the firm has ever done any work for Pearl.

You call Jason Kerr, the president of Transport, to get more information. He says the corporation purchased the Pearl Bus Co. many years ago. In recent years, Transport has had to take over many management functions at Pearl because the bus company managers kept making costly errors. A couple of times, Transport has had to shell out tens of thousands of dollars to cover damage awards that exceeded Pearl's insurance coverage. After the last one, Kerr says he insisted that Pearl massively increase its insurance coverage. Pearl agreed to do this after Kerr agreed to help cover the increased cost of the insurance. Kerr hopes to prevent another cash drain from Transport. "Anything else you can tell me about this?" you ask.

Kerr pauses. "Well, I guess it might be relevant that my son is the president of Pearl. He just took over a couple of years ago, after we discovered that the former president was embezzling funds from the company. Why do you want to know all this, anyway?"

You say: "I'll explain in a moment. I'm sorry but I've got to put you on hold for a minute — my secretary says I must take another call." You press the hold button to catch your breath and think about what to tell Kerr.

Questions

1. What can you tell Kerr about the reason for your call to him?
2. Must the firm withdraw from representing Hathaway, or Transport, or both?
3. If the firm may continue to represent one or both clients, must it obtain the informed consent of one or both of them?

C. Representing criminal co-defendants

1. Costs and benefits of joint representation of co-defendants

As we have seen, representation of co-plaintiffs or co-defendants in a civil matter can be complicated. While at first glance they may appear to have more common interests than conflicting ones, there may be sufficient divergence in their interests that a lawyer should not even ask the clients to consent to allow her to represent them both. Or the conflict could be such that the lawyer may proceed, but only with informed consent.

Why would criminal co-defendants want to be represented by a single lawyer?

In criminal cases, the stakes are higher than in civil cases since the defendants may face imprisonment if they are convicted. As in civil cases, many co-defendants wish to be represented by a single lawyer because neither one can afford to hire separate counsel. Also, criminal co-defendants' best chance of avoiding conviction may lie in mutual cooperation. If neither one confesses or provides information to the prosecutor, the prosecutor may be unable to convict either

Professor Kenneth Mann

of them. As Professor Peter Tague explains, "any group of clients might benefit from united opposition to the government. If none cooperates . . . the government may be unable to indict any client because no other credible sources possess enough admissible information."[39] Kenneth Mann, a lawyer and a sociologist,[40] surveyed more than 1,000 defense attorneys in New York and interviewed and observed 29 of them who defended white-collar criminals. The remarkable book that resulted from his studies was published more than 25 years ago, but it remains a classic exposition of the realities of criminal law practice. Mann reports:

> When the defense attorney uses his position to facilitate noncooperation on the part of more than one person in an investigation . . . it was not uncommon for an attorney to say, "I am stonewalling," meaning that he was conducting a defense in which he was attempting to keep all persons holding inculpatory information from talking to government investigators and thereby defeat the criminal investigation. There are many benefits . . . including close coordination of statements given to investigators, early warning of investigatorial contacts with third parties, and the making of uniform legal arguments.[41]

Mann notes that sometimes defense lawyers can manage the conflicts through informed consent, to the advantage of some, and occasionally all, co-defendants:

> [If] the government has just enough evidence to consider asking for an indictment against each, but not enough to dismiss the option of granting immunity to one client in order to get determinative evidence against the other . . . it is difficult for an attorney to act without compromising one of the clients' interests. If he advises neither to make a deal because he believes that he may be able to win the case for both, he is sacrificing a certain success for one of them. And he clearly cannot advise one to make a deal against the other's interest. Some attorneys are able to obtain informed consent in this situation, after explaining the implications of the multiple representation. They then continue to represent all clients in a strategy based on total noncooperation [in which all defendants invoke their privilege against self-incrimination]. It is often the case that no client is willing to voluntarily become an informer against other clients. The stonewall defense continues until the government decides to force immunity on one of the clients, at which time the attorney will then have to divide representation. . . . [If the prosecution has less information to

---

39. Peter W. Tague, Multiple Representation of Targets and Witnesses During a Grand Jury Investigation, 17 Am. Crim. L. Rev. 301 (1980).

40. Mann did his research on defense counsel for his Ph.D. dissertation in sociology at Yale. Later he became a law professor and the chief public defender of Israel.

41. Kenneth Mann, Defending White Collar Crime: A Portrait of Attorneys at Work 166 (Yale U. Press 1985).

begin with,] both clients may be able to hold out and save each other the humiliation and embarrassment of becoming either an informant or the subject of a criminal prosecution.[42]

What are the risks for criminal co-defendants represented by a single lawyer?

Although it may be more efficient or strategically appealing for one lawyer to represent multiple plaintiffs or defendants, joint representation could ultimately involve a significant sacrifice of the interests of one client on behalf of another. When multiple people are charged in connection with one crime, the stone wall (referred to by Mann, above) they initially erected may crumble, and one or more of them may seek to reduce any potential penalty by offering to give the prosecutor inculpatory information about another defendant.

2. Ethics rules and the Sixth Amendment

Are lawyers permitted to represent criminal co-defendants?

The Sixth Amendment to the U.S. Constitution provides: "In all criminal prosecutions, the accused shall enjoy the right . . . to have the Assistance of Counsel for his defense." Criminal defendants who can afford to pay lawyers may select their own counsel. Courts appoint lawyers for defendants who cannot afford counsel. An indigent defendant for whom counsel is appointed is not entitled to select his own lawyers, but he does have a right to have a court-appointed lawyer who is free of conflicts.[43] Most criminal co-defendants are entitled to have separate lawyers, but, as Mann explains, some prefer to work with a single lawyer. A criminal defendant can waive her right to have a lawyer who owes no loyalty to a co-defendant,[44] but if the judge perceives that a conflict will emerge, the judge may refuse to allow a single lawyer to represent multiple co-defendants.

Because of the potential for conflicts, case law, ethics rules, and scholarly commentary[45] all discourage joint representation of criminal co-defendants by a single lawyer. The ABA guidelines for criminal defense lawyers strongly discourage lawyers from representing criminal co-defendants, stating:

---

42. Id. at 170.

43. Glasser v. U.S., 315 U.S. 60 (1942).

44. See, e.g., U.S. v. Mers, 701 F.2d 1321, 1324-1325 (11th Cir. 1983).

45. See, e.g., Peter W. Tague, Multiple Representation and Conflicts of Interest in Criminal Cases, 67 Geo. L.J. 1075 (1979).

(c) Except for preliminary matters such as initial hearings or applications for bail, defense counsel who are associated in practice should not undertake to defend more than one defendant in the same criminal case if the duty to one of the defendants may conflict with the duty to another. The potential for conflict of interest in representing multiple defendants is so grave that ordinarily defense counsel should decline to act for more than one of several codefendants except in unusual situations when, after careful investigation, it is clear either that no conflict is likely to develop at trial, sentencing, or at any other time in the proceeding or that common representation will be advantageous to each of the codefendants represented, and in either case, that:

(i) the several defendants give an informed consent to such multiple representation; and

(ii) the consent of the defendants is made a matter of judicial record.[46]

Some scholars urge that this standard should be better implemented to reduce the number of instances in which criminal defendants waive conflicts without fully understanding the implications of their actions.[47] Professor Debra Lyn Bassett proposes the outright prohibition of criminal defense lawyers representing co-defendants.[48]

The Restatement says that a lawyer may not represent criminal co-defendants unless the clients give informed consent and it is "reasonably likely that the lawyer will be able to provide adequate representation to . . . the clients."[49] The Restatement provides the following illustration:

A and B are co-defendants charged with a felony offense of armed robbery. They are both represented by Lawyer. The prosecutor believes that A planned the crime and was the only one carrying a weapon. The prosecutor offers to accept B's plea of guilty to a misdemeanor if B will testify against A. Lawyer's loyalty to A causes Lawyer to persuade B that the prosecutor's proposal should be rejected. Following a trial, both A and B are convicted of the felony. When plea negotiations involving B's separate interests began, B should have received independent counsel. In the

---

46. Standards for Criminal Justice: Prosecution Function and Defense Function, Standard 4-3.5(c), Conflicts of Interest (3d ed., ABA 1993). The Model Rules reach a similar but less nuanced conclusion. Comment 23 to Rule 1.7 states: "The potential for conflict of interest in representing multiple defendants in a criminal case is so grave that ordinarily a lawyer should decline to represent more than one codefendant."

47. See Ross Barr & Brian Friedman, Joint Representation of Criminal Codefendants: A Proposal to Breathe Life into Section 4-3.5(c) of the ABA Standards Relating to the Administration of Criminal Justice, 15 Geo. J. Leg. Ethics 635 (2002).

48. Debra Lyn Bassett, Three's a Crowd: A Proposal to Abolish Joint Representation, 32 Rutgers L.J. 387 (2001).

49. Restatement §§ 122, 129.

circumstances, Lawyer could not properly represent A and B even with the informed consent of both clients.[50]

If a lawyer proposes to represent two criminal defendants in a federal court case, the judge must hold a hearing and advise both defendants of their right to separate counsel.[51] In other courts, judges may not be required to inquire about possible conflicts in joint representation of criminal defendants unless a conflict is apparent to the judge.[52] Even if an inquiry into a possible conflict is not required, it may be advisable.[53]

Do criminal defense lawyers often represent multiple co-defendants?

In some communities, representation of criminal co-defendants is fairly common. However, some lawyers who represent multiple defendants are disqualified or disciplined for proceeding in the face of a conflict.[54] If a defense lawyer is representing multiple co-defendants and the prosecutor perceives a possible conflict of interest, the prosecutor may move to disqualify the defense lawyer from representing one or more of the co-defendants.[55] Joint representation of criminal defendants also can lead to a conviction being reversed.[56]

Public defender offices have to be particularly alert for conflicts of interest because they have so many lawyers and represent so many clients. Most public defenders avoid multiple representation of defendants. A survey published in 1978 indicated that 70 percent of public defender offices had strong preferences against multiple representation in criminal cases, and that 49 percent of the offices surveyed never represent more than one defendant in a multiple defendant case.[57] These offices hire criminal defense lawyers in private practice to represent one defendant in a matter in which the office is representing another.

---

50. Restatement § 129, comment c and illus. 1, based on Alvarez v. Wainwright, 522 F.2d 100 (5th Cir. 1975).

51. Fed. R. Crim. P. 44c.

52. Geoffrey C. Hazard Jr., Susan P. Koniak & Roger C. Cramton, The Law and Ethics of Lawyering 618 (3d ed., Found. Press 1999).

53. Restatement § 129, comment c, reporter's note.

54. Id.

55. See Bruce A. Green, Her Brother's Keeper: The Prosecutor's Responsibility When Defense Counsel Has a Potential Conflict of Interest, 16 Am. J. Crim. L. 323, 328-329 (Spring 1989).

56. Holloway v. Arkansas, 435 U.S. 475 (1978); Kentucky v. Holder, 705 S.W.2d 907 (Ky. 1986).

57. Gary T. Lowenthal, Joint Representation in Criminal Cases: A Critical Appraisal, 64 Va. L. Rev. 939, 950 n. 40 (1978), cited in Cuyler v. Sullivan, 446 U.S. 335, 346 n. 11 (1980).

Do criminal defense lawyers encounter conflicts other than in the representation of co-defendants?

Yes. A criminal defense lawyer may encounter concurrent client conflicts through representation of co-defendants or in certain other circumstances (for example, where a lawyer is called upon to cross-examine his own client, albeit in a different case). The general rule is that a lawyer may not represent a criminal defendant and simultaneously represent either a prosecution witness or the prosecutor.[58]

Does joint representation of criminal co-defendants violate their Sixth Amendment right to counsel?

Joint representation of criminal defendants may violate the conflict of interest rules and also may violate the Sixth Amendment right to counsel of a defendant. A defendant whose lawyer had a conflict of interest may challenge his conviction on the basis that he was denied the effective assistance of counsel. However, a defendant may knowingly waive an objection based on a conflict, unless the judge refuses to accept the waiver. Furthermore, not all conflicts that violate Rule 1.7 are so serious that they would prompt a court to reverse a conviction.[59]

What if a lawyer objects to representing co-defendants because of a conflict in their interests, and the judge requires the lawyer to continue the representation?

If a lawyer objects to jointly representing defendants with conflicting interests and a court nevertheless requires the lawyer to continue to represent them, any resulting conviction may be overturned. In *Holloway v. Arkansas*, a criminal defense lawyer made a timely objection that he could not adequately represent three co-defendants. The judge declined to appoint separate counsel and refused to allow the lawyer to cross-examine any of the three co-defendants on behalf of the other two. In 1978, the U.S. Supreme Court overturned the resulting conviction, stating that "whenever a trial court improperly requires joint representation over timely objection reversal is automatic."[60] No showing of prejudice was required.

---

58. See, e.g., Castillo v. Estelle, 504 F.2d 1243 (5th Cir. 1974).

59. See the discussion of *Strickland v. Washington* in Chapter 4.

60. *Holloway*, 435 U.S. at 488. The Restatement asserts that the holding of *Holloway* is "well-settled" and cites numerous subsequent cases that followed the rule laid down in *Holloway*. Restatement § 129, comment c.

If a lawyer proceeds with representation of co-defendants in the face of a conflict and no one objects, will a resulting conviction be overturned?

If no one objects to joint representation of defendants, a resulting conviction may nevertheless be overturned if the conflict significantly affected the representation. In *Cuyler v. Sullivan*, three co-defendants in a murder case were tried separately but were represented by a single lawyer. No one objected to the multiple representations. The Supreme Court decided that if a defendant who was jointly represented is convicted and no one objected to the joint representation at the time, to overturn the conviction on Sixth Amendment grounds, the defendant must show that there was "a conflict of interest [that] actually affected the adequacy of his representation."[61] The Court held that the defendant need not demonstrate prejudice but only an adverse impact in the representation.[62]

If the court-appointed lawyer who represented a homicide victim on unrelated charges represents a capital defendant, will a conviction be overturned for ineffective assistance?

Such a conviction might be overturned, but only if it is proven that the conflict "significantly affected" the performance of counsel. In *Mickens v. Taylor*,[63] a capital conviction was challenged because the court-appointed counsel for a defendant in a murder case had represented the murder victim on unrelated criminal charges. The lawyer, Bryan Saunders, did not object when he was appointed to represent the defendant in the murder case.

Saunders represented Mickens at the murder trial, apparently believing that he had no further obligation to the victim (his former client) because the victim was dead.[64] Saunders claimed that he had not learned any confidences from the victim that would be relevant to the defense of the murder suspect.[65]

---

61. Cuyler v. Sullivan, 466 U.S. 335, 348-349 (1980).

62. The Court contrasted two situations. In one, a defendant's lawyer failed to cross-examine a prosecution witness because he wanted to persuade the jury that a co-defendant was innocent. This was an actual conflict that impaired the defendant's case. In a contrasting example, a lawyer for a man named Dukes persuaded Dukes to plead guilty and then sought leniency for co-defendants by arguing that their cooperation had induced Dukes's guilty plea. This was not a situation of adverse impact, the Court reasoned, because Dukes retained the right to plead guilty or not guilty. Id.

63. 535 U.S. 162 (2002).

64. Once murdered, the victim became a former client. When he was appointed to represent Mickens, the lawyer should have evaluated the conflict under Virginia's standards for handling successive conflicts.

65. *Mickens*, 535 U.S. at 177-179 (Kennedy, J., concurring).

The post-conviction defense lawyer discovered evidence that Hall, the murder victim, was a male prostitute, and that he and Mickens might have engaged in consensual sex before the homicide. The death penalty could not be imposed without a finding of forcible sodomy, so if the sexual contact was consensual, this penalty would not have been available.[66] It is not clear why Saunders did not offer this evidence. Perhaps he did not know of it, or perhaps he felt an obligation to protect the reputation of his former client.

The Supreme Court, in a 5-4 decision, held that if "the trial judge is not aware of a conflict (and thus not obligated to inquire) . . . prejudice will be presumed only if the conflict has *significantly affected* counsel's performance — thereby rendering the verdict unreliable."[67] Habeas corpus was denied because Mickens and his lawyers had not proved significant impact.[68] The majority opinion stated that the duty to prove adverse impact from the representation is greater if no objection to the conflict was proffered at the trial.

In dissent, Justice Souter questioned why the making of an objection was important, given that the judge should have known that Saunders had been representing the victim until the day before she appointed him to represent the defendant. The judge had signed a docket sheet on the victim's case after he died that listed "BRYAN SAUNDERS" in large, handwritten letters, as counsel for the decedent on assault and battery charges and a concealed weapon charge.[69]

This decision makes it less likely that a criminal conviction will be overturned on the basis that the defense attorney had a conflict of interest.[70]

If a criminal defendant wants to waive a conflict, can the judge disqualify the lawyer anyway?

The constitutional guarantee of right to counsel might be diminished if the conflicts rules intrude too far into a criminal defendant's right to be represented by counsel of her own choosing. In general, a criminal defendant is entitled to give a knowing waiver of a conflict created by her lawyer's representation of another co-defendant in the same case.[71] A

---

66. Id. at 181 (Stevens, J., dissenting).

67. Id. (emphasis added).

68. Id.

69. Id. at 190 n. 1 (Souter, J., dissenting).

70. Justice Breyer, dissenting, questioned whether in this or other similar cases, at the post-trial stage, it would be possible to prove whether the trial lawyer's conflict of interest actually affected the lawyer's judgment about what strategy to pursue, what witnesses to call, what arguments to make, and so on. Id. at 210 (Breyer, J., dissenting).

71. U.S. v. Curcio, 680 F.2d 881 (2d Cir. 1982).

defendant who waives a conflict is foreclosed from challenging a subsequent conviction on the basis of the conflict.[72] But where there is a great risk of prejudice resulting from a conflict, a judge may disqualify counsel from representing co-defendants even if the co-defendants want to waive the conflict.[73]

> **FOR EXAMPLE:**   In *Wheat v. United States*,[74] the defendant wanted to have the same lawyer as two other defendants whose charges arose out of a common situation but who were to be tried separately. The district court denied this request because of the possibility that the various defendants would be witnesses at each other's trials. Wheat appealed to the Supreme Court, which held that a court may disqualify a lawyer on the basis of an actual or a potential conflict even if the defendant prefers to waive the conflict. The Court held that such disqualification would not violate a defendant's Sixth Amendment right to be represented by the counsel of his choice. The Court pointed out that conflicts are hard to anticipate and that judges need broad discretion in such judgments, in part because less ethical attorneys are more willing to seek waivers.[75]

PROBLEM 6-2 POLICE BRUTALITY, SCENE 1

This problem is based on a real case that took place in New York in the 1990s.

Several police officers were indicted in connection with a brutal assault against a man named Louis Alston. Alston was taken into a bathroom after he was arrested and sexually assaulted with a broken broomstick. Officer Tom Babbage pleaded guilty to charges arising out of this incident, but the victim says that at least one other officer participated in the assault. Two other officers, Chip Stone and Bob Morton, are facing charges that they participated in the assault. The Policeman's Benevolent Association (PBA), which provides lawyers for officers who face charges in connection with their work, has asked you and your law partner to represent these two co-defendants.

If you agree to represent Stone and Morton, the PBA would pay your fees. Rule 1.8(f) states that a lawyer may not accept com-

---

72. Id.

73. See, e.g., U.S. v. Flanagan, 679 F.2d 1072 (3d Cir. 1982).

74. 486 U.S. 153 (1988).

75. Id. In California, the defendant has the ultimate call on choice of lawyer. Alcocer v. Super. Ct., 254 Cal. Rptr. 72, 75 (Ct. App. 1988).

pensation from a third person unless the represented client gives informed consent, "there is no interference with the lawyer's independence of professional judgment or with the lawyer-client relationship," and confidences are protected.

Questions

1. What potential conflicts should you consider in deciding whether you can represent Stone while your partner represents Morton?
2. Are these potential conflicts so serious that you must not represent both defendants even if you obtain their consent?

PROBLEM 6-3 POLICE BRUTALITY, SCENE 2

Assume that your firm has agreed to represent both clients. Meanwhile, Alston has filed a civil suit against the PBA, alleging a conspiracy among several officers to injure him and a failure of the association leadership to provide adequate supervision of the officers.

A few months later, the PBA offers your firm a two-year contract for $10 million to handle representation of all PBA members. The PBA would pay an agreed portion of the money at the outset and the remainder in regular installments. The PBA could cancel the contract at any time if it was dissatisfied with the work of your firm.

Meanwhile, another co-defendant, Officer Tony Gutman, has been indicted in the Alston case. Like Stone and Morton, Gutman denies having been present during the assault. The whereabouts of all of the other officers in the station at the time can be accounted for. If Alston is telling the truth, one of those three men participated with Babbage. Gutman is being represented by a lawyer from another firm. However, Gutman is a member of the PBA and an elected member of the PBA board.

Questions

1. If Stone, Morton, and the PBA all consent, can your firm accept the attractive PBA contract?
2. Assume that you conclude that you may seek waivers from your clients. How might your disclosure of the potential conflicts to the two criminal defendants be affected by your desire to obtain the PBA contract?

3. If you ask your clients to waive the potential conflicts and they refuse, what are your options? Can you take on the PBA contract and ask the PBA to get new counsel for Stone and Morton?

PROBLEM 6-4 POLICE BRUTALITY, SCENE 3

Assume that the firm has signed the PBA contract. You are representing Stone, who is charged with having participated in the assault. One of your partners is representing Morton. Stone consents in writing to waive any conflicts caused by your partner's representation of Morton and any conflicts caused by your contract with the PBA. In court, the judge goes over the potential conflicts again, and Stone again states that he wants to waive them. As the case proceeds, statements from other officers to police investigators suggest that Gutman (the PBA board member), not Stone or Morton, was the second police officer in the bathroom. Alston cannot personally identify the second officer, but some of the other officers have stated in interviews that they saw Gutman pushing Alston into the bathroom. If you introduce testimony from these officers as part of your defense of Stone, Stone might be acquitted, but the testimony could be used against Gutman. Also, this testimony could make it more likely that the PBA would be found liable for damages to Alston in the civil suit against the PBA. The PBA might retaliate against you by canceling your contract.

Questions

1. Should you present the testimony of the officers who say that they saw Gutman going toward the bathroom with Alston?
2. Suppose you don't introduce the testimony of the other officers. Instead you decide to rely on the theory that Officer Babbage acted alone. Babbage has already pleaded guilty. Stone is then convicted. He appeals, claiming that your representation of him was "ineffective" because of your conflicting obligations to the PBA and its board member Gutman, and that despite his consent to your representation, the judge should have disqualified you to prevent the violation of his Sixth Amendment right to effective counsel. Is he likely to prevail?

D. Representing family members

1. Representing both spouses in a divorce

Domestic relations lawyers often are asked to represent both spouses in a divorce. Technically this would involve the lawyer in filing a lawsuit on behalf of one client against another client. However, if both parties want to get divorced and have no disagreement about child custody or property division, then perhaps there is no actual adversity, only technical adversity.[76]

If two spouses ask a lawyer to help draft a separation agreement, may the lawyer agree to do it?[77]

Some states allow a lawyer to represent both parties in an uncontested divorce. Others forbid a lawyer from representing both husband and wife in the suit for divorce, but permit a lawyer to assist both parties in preparing a settlement agreement, so long as the clients agree and the resulting settlement seems fair.[78] But some jurisdictions do not allow a lawyer to represent both husband and wife in any divorce action, even with the consent of both spouses.[79] This prohibition is motivated in part by a concern that even if there is no apparent disagreement between the parties, they may in fact have conflicting financial or other interests that would emerge if they were separately advised. A lawyer who improperly represents both spouses in a divorce may be subject to malpractice liability or discipline.

> **FOR EXAMPLE:** A lawyer who had represented both husband and wife in a divorce failed to learn about some of the husband's assets. As a result, the lawyer produced a settlement that gave the wife far less than her share of the property. A court found that these allegations stated a claim for malpractice.[80]

> **FOR EXAMPLE:** A lawyer was suspended from practice after representing both husband and wife in a divorce while simultaneously

---

76. For thoughtful discussions of conflicts of interest faced by lawyers in representing multiple members of families, see Steven H. Hobbs, Family Matters: Nonwaivable Conflicts of Interest in Family Law, 22 Seattle U. L. Rev. 57, 68 (1998); and Russell G. Pearce, Family Values and Legal Ethics: Competing Approaches to Conflicts in Representing Spouses, 62 Fordham L. Rev. 1253, 1274 (1994).

77. For a synthesis of the various rules on joint representation of divorcing spouses, see Restatement § 128, reporter's note to comment c.

78. See, e.g., Klemm v. Super. Ct., 142 Cal. Rptr. 509 (Ct. App. 1977).

79. Restatement § 128, reporter's note to comment c.

80. Ishmael v. Millington, 50 Cal. Rptr. 592 (Ct. App. 1966).

representing the husband on charges of domestic violence and sexual abuse of a child.[81]

2. Representing family members in estate planning

It is quite common for lawyers to draft wills for husbands and wives, and for the beneficiaries of the wills to be other family members. This can be a harmonious process, but a number of problems can arise.[82] What if one spouse has a secret from the other? What if a parent wants to secretly change her will to disinherit a child? Does the lawyer have a duty to disclose this information to the other family member? Does it matter if the other person is formally a client? Some authorities urge that joint representation of two clients should include an agreement that information shared by one is not to be held in confidence from the other.

PROBLEM 6-5 REPRESENTING THE McCARTHYS

The facts of this problem are very similar to those of a case that was litigated in a northeastern state.

You are a partner in the law firm of Kenney & Drogula. Your specialty is estate planning. About 18 months ago, you were approached by Hugh and Joline McCarthy, who wanted you to assist them in planning their estates. You undertook to represent them jointly, drafting a will for each that left his or her property to the other.

At the outset of the representation, you asked Hugh and Joline to sign a letter that explains the possible conflicts of interest inherent in this type of joint representation. The letter explained that one effect of a will leaving property to the other spouse is that he or she could then dispose of the property as she pleased. Also, the letter explained that information disclosed to the firm by one spouse

---

81. In re Houston, 985 P.2d 752 (N.M. 1999).

82. The conflicts that arise in estate planning matters are thoroughly explored in Teresa S. Collett, And the Two Shall Become as One ... Until the Lawyers Are Done, 7 Notre Dame J.L. Ethics & Pub. Policy 101 (1993); Teresa S. Collett, Disclosure, Discretion or Deception: The Estate Planner's Ethical Dilemma from a Unilateral Confidence, 28 Real Prop., Prob. & Tr. J. 683, 743 (1994); Geoffrey Hazard, Conflict of Interest in Estate Planning for Husband and Wife, 20 Prob. L. 1 (1994).

could become available to the other. Both McCarthys signed this disclosure statement.[83]

The wills were written and finalized over the next few weeks. The wills provided that each spouse left part of his or her estate to the other spouse, and part of it in trust for their children. After the wills were finalized, the McCarthys signed a continuing retainer agreement providing that for a small annual fee, the firm would continue to provide periodic advice to them on changes in tax law that might affect the disposition of the property.

The firm maintained a database to check for possible conflicts of interest. The clerk who opened the initial file on the case and entered the data in the firm's conflicts database unfortunately misspelled the McCarthys' last name, writing it as "MacCarthy."

Six months later, a woman named Maureen Carr retained Kenney & Drogula to file a paternity suit on her behalf against Hugh McCarthy. She claims that Hugh is the father of her newborn baby daughter, and she wants to sue him for child support. Gus Kenney, a partner in the family law department, accepted the matter. He did not know that Hugh was a client of the firm. The conflicts check did not identify him as a client because of the misspelling in the database.[84]

Before long, Kenney sent a letter to Hugh McCarthy about Carr's paternity claim. It didn't occur to Hugh to object to the fact that the firm that had written his will was representing Carr. He is not a lawyer and has no training in conflicts of interest. He did not tell you about the matter, probably because he is not eager to talk about it with anyone. Instead, he hired another lawyer, Charlie Bucci, to represent him in connection with the paternity claim. Hugh denied that he was the father of the child, but he agreed to voluntary DNA testing, which would have been ordered by the court if he had not agreed. The DNA test indicated that he *was* in fact the father of Carr's child. At this point, Kenney filed suit against Hugh McCarthy on behalf of Maureen Carr.

The conflict came to light when Maureen Carr's lawyer, Kenney, asked Bucci for information about Hugh's assets. Bucci politely informed Kenney that his firm already had the relevant financial information. (Hugh had told him that a lawyer at Kenney & Drogula had written his will.) He suggested that Kenney check Hugh's

---

83. For sample letters to clients disclosing various types of conflicts of interest and requesting consent, see Freivogel, supra n. 5.

84. This really happened, although the misspelling was, obviously, of a different name.

file in the firm's estate department and then call him back if he needed anything else.

Questions

1. You (the McCarthys' estate planning lawyer) just got off the phone with your partner, Gus Kenney, who told you he is representing Maureen Carr in a paternity suit against Hugh McCarthy. Now what? Does the firm have a conflict of interest under Rule 1.7? If so, is it consentable? If so, from whom would the firm need consent?
2. Assume that the conflict is not consentable. May Kenney & Drogula continue to represent one or two of these clients, or must it withdraw from representation of all three?
3. You are pretty sure that Joline McCarthy has no idea that her husband is allegedly the father of Maureen Carr's child. Assume that even if you have made a decision to withdraw, you have not done so yet, so Joline is still your client. Do you have an obligation to disclose this information to her?

E. Representing insurance companies and insured persons

Insurance policies usually provide that when the insured person is sued over an event covered in the policy, such as a car accident, the insurance company will provide the insured person with a lawyer to defend him or her. If damages are awarded, the insurance company will cover the damages up to the amount of the insurance policy. The lawyer who defends the insured person may work at a private law firm paid by the insurance company to handle claims against its insured. The lawyer's contact at the insurance company usually is an insurance adjuster, who evaluates each claim and determines what, if anything, the insurance company should agree to pay.

The insurance defense lawyer's dilemma[85] is fundamentally about money. The lawyer is being paid by one client (the insurer) to represent both itself and another client (the insured). While this relationship is

---

85. See generally Charles Silver & Kent D. Syverud, The Professional Responsibilities of Insurance Defense Lawyers, 45 Duke L.J. 255 (1995).

governed in part by contract law and by insurance law,[86] the ethical rules provide useful guidance as well.

Who is the client of the insurance defense lawyer?

If a lawyer is working for an insurance company but handling a matter for an insured person, the question is "who is the client?"[87] The Restatement says "that a lawyer designated to defend the insured has a client-lawyer relationship with the insured. The insurer is not, simply by the fact that it designates the lawyer, a client of the lawyer."[88] The insurance company may be a client as well, depending on the contract and on state law. But the insured is always a client. Even if the insurer is not a client of the lawyer, the Restatement continues, communications between the insurer and counsel for the insured "should be regarded as privileged and otherwise immune from discovery by the claimant or another party to the proceeding."[89] Likewise, because of the insurer's financial stake in the matter, "the insurer should be accorded standing to assert a claim for appropriate relief from the lawyer for financial loss proximately caused by professional negligence or other wrongful act of the lawyer."[90]

Much case law takes the position that a lawyer may represent both the insurer and the insured so long as there is no conflict between their interests. For example, if a claim will be covered entirely by the insurance policy, then usually the insurer and insured's interests are largely aligned.

Can the lawyer reveal confidential information from the insured person to the insurer?

Suppose a lawyer is assigned by an insurer to represent an insured on a fire insurance claim. Suppose the insured person reveals to the lawyer that he caused the fire by smoking in bed. This information probably would lead the insurer to decide to contest coverage of the claim. Can the lawyer tell the insurer what the insured has told him? The answer is no, even if the insurer also is a client of the lawyer and even if "the insurer has asserted a 'reservation of rights'" in this matter and informed the insured that it may refuse to pay the claim.[91] In one case, a lawyer learned that an assault on a child had been intentional and therefore would not be covered by the

---

86. The Restatement addresses the law that governs a lawyer representing an insured person and takes the position that "the law governing the relationship between the insured and the insurer is . . . beyond the scope of the Restatement." See Restatement § 134, comment f.

87. For thoughtful exploration of the conflicts faced by insurance defense lawyers, see Geoffrey Hazard, Triangular Lawyer Relationships: An Exploratory Analysis, 1 Geo. J. Leg. Ethics 15 (1987); and John Leubsdorf, Pluralizing the Lawyer-Client Relationship, 77 Cornell L. Rev. 825 (1992).

88. Restatement § 134, comment f.

89. Id.

90. Id.

91. Restatement § 60, comment l.

insurance policy.[92] The court held that the lawyer was obliged to keep the information confidential and to withdraw from representing the parties.[93] In this circumstance, the lawyer used the information to benefit the insurer, so the company was estopped from denying coverage.[94]

When is there a conflict between the interests of the insurer and the insured?

> **Rule 1.8(f) provides:**
> **A lawyer shall not accept compensation for representing a client from one other than the client unless:**
> > **(1) the client gives informed consent;**
> > **(2) there is no interference with the lawyer's independence of professional judgment or with the client-lawyer relationship; and**
> > **(3) information relating to representation of a client is protected as required by Rule 1.6.[95]**

Comments 11 and 12 after Rule 1.8 explain how to evaluate whether there is a conflict between insurer and insured and how a lawyer should respond when there is a conflict:

> Because third-party payers frequently have interests that differ from those of the client, including interests in minimizing the amount spent on the representation and in learning how the representation is progressing, lawyers are prohibited from accepting or continuing such representations unless the lawyer determines that there will be no interference with the lawyer's independent professional judgment and there is informed consent from the client. . . .

Sometimes, it will be sufficient for the lawyer to obtain the client's informed consent regarding the fact of the payment and the identity of the third party payer. If, however, the fee arrangement creates a conflict of interest for the lawyer, then the lawyer must comply with Rule. 1.7. The lawyer must also conform to the requirements of Rule 1.6 concerning confidentiality. Under Rule 1.7(a), a conflict of interest exists if there is significant risk that the lawyer's representation of the client will be materially limited by the lawyer's own interest in the fee arrangement or by the lawyer's responsibilities to the third party payer (for example, when the

---

92. Parsons v. Continental Natl. Am. Group, 550 P.2d 94 (Ariz. 1976).

93. Id. at 98.

94. Id. at 99.

95. See also Rule 5.4(c), which states: "A lawyer shall not permit a person who recommends, employs, or pays the lawyer to render legal services for another to direct or regulate the lawyer's professional judgment in rendering such legal services."

third party payer is a co-client). Under Rule 1.7(b), the lawyer may accept or continue the representation with the informed consent of each affected client, unless the conflict is nonconsentable under that paragraph. Under Rule 1.7(b), the informed consent must be confirmed in writing.

If it appears that a damage award may exceed the amount covered by an insurance policy, a conflict may exist. The more likely a conflict, the more careful a lawyer should be about consulting with the insurer and the insured to obtain informed consent before proceeding.[96]

If a conflict of interest arises between the insured and the insurer, what is the lawyer supposed to do?

If there is a conflict, the lawyer should act in the best interests of the insured, except that the lawyer may not assist client fraud. If the insurer is also the lawyer's client, the lawyer should try to act in the best interests of both clients. If that is not possible, the lawyer must withdraw from representation of both clients.[97] Many insurance policies provide that when a claim is made, the insured person and the insurer will be represented by a single lawyer, but if there is a conflict between the interests of the insured and the insurer (for example, if the insurer asserts that the claim is not covered), the insurer will pay the cost of hiring a separate lawyer for the insured.[98] Most jurisdictions have held (as an insurance law matter) that if an insurer contests coverage, the insurer has to pay for a lawyer selected by the insured unless the insured has agreed or agrees to be represented by a lawyer selected by the insurer.[99]

Can a lawyer accept direction from an insurer as to how much to spend on discovery and other aspects of litigation?

If a lawyer represents an insured but his fee is paid by the insurer, the lawyer owes the client a duty of competent representation. However, as to duties that go beyond a duty of competency, the contract between the insurer and the insured may delegate to the insurer the authority to make decisions about discretionary efforts or expenses in litigation.[100] Nevertheless, if the insured might incur liability exceeding the policy limits, the lawyer may not follow a direction by the insurer that would substantially increase the risk of such liability.[101]

---

96. Restatement § 134, comment f.

97. Id.

98. Id.; see, e.g., Nandorf, Inc. v. CNA Ins. Cos., 479 N.E.2d 988 (Ill. App. 1985). If the insurer selects the alternate lawyer, the insured must give informed consent. See, e.g., N.Y. St. Urb. Dev. Corp. v. VSL Corp., 738 F.2d 61 (2d Cir. 1984).

99. Restatement § 134, comment f, reporter's note.

100. Id. at illus. 5.

101. Id. at comment f.

What if the insurer and the insured disagree about whether to settle?

What if the insurer wants to settle and the insured does not? Although an insured person can agree by contract to allow the insurer to control some aspects of her defense, the lawyer's professional obligations to the insured should govern the lawyer's conduct in the event of a dispute about settlement.[102] ABA Opinion 96-403 concludes that if the insurer and the insured disagree about whether to settle, the lawyer must withdraw from representing both of them in that matter. Once the insured is a former client, the lawyer still cannot assist the insurer in settling the matter against the interests of his former client.[103] Of course, if the lawyer seeks to withdraw after the lawsuit has been partly litigated, the insured will have to hire a new lawyer. If the insurance company asserts that the policy does not cover the claim, she will have to do so at her own expense.

On the other hand, what if the plaintiff offers to settle the claim within the policy limits, the insured wants to do so, and the insurer insists on turning down the settlement? If the insurer turns down a settlement and then damages are awarded in excess of the policy limits, the insurer often is required to cover those costs.[104]

F. Representing employers and immigrant employees

Many U.S. companies need employees with special skills, such as the ability to use certain types of advanced software as well as to speak and write Chinese.[105] Often, employers want to hire foreign nationals who have these specialized skills and who already live in the United States under temporary work visas or student visas, which allow students to stay for one year after completing their education. An employer who wants to hire such an employee for an indefinite period must sponsor him for an immigrant visa. The outcome of the sponsorship application matters to both the employer and the employee, so each may want to be represented by a lawyer. But it is costly and inefficient for each of them to hire a lawyer. Typically, the employer selects a lawyer to represent both parties. Both the employer and the employee may be clients of the lawyer

---

102. Id.

103. Id.

104. Parsons v. Continental Natl. Am. Group, 550 P.2d 94 (Ariz. 1976).

105. The discussion is this section draws on Austin T. Fragomen Jr. & Nadia H. Yakoob, No Easy Way Out: The Ethical Dilemmas of Dual Representation, 21 Geo. Immig. L.J. 621 (2007).

regardless of whether joint representation is formally acknowledged, since the lawyer provides advice and services to both.

Conflicts can arise, just as they can when a single lawyer represents an insurer and an insured. For example, the immigrant may give the lawyer information (for example, by revealing a prior criminal conviction) that would lead the employer to revoke the job offer. The employee might expect protection of such a confidence, while the employer may expect to be advised of any adverse information. Likewise, the lawyer may know that the employer's financial position is shaky and that the job is therefore not secure, but the employer may not want the employee to know this.

Some immigration lawyers try to solve the potential conflict by telling the immigrant at the outset, in writing, that the lawyer represents only the employer and that the employee may retain her own lawyer. This disclosure often is not very effective. The employee may have limited command of English, may not appreciate the types of conflicts that could arise, or may not be able to afford separate counsel. Furthermore, a lawyer's statement may not be an effective disclaimer of a lawyer-client relationship because the lawyer usually has already prepared the documents and advised the employee.

Other lawyers ask each party to sign written conflict waivers and create separate groups within the law firm to represent the employers and immigrants; they may wall each group off from the other ("screening"). These techniques may also be ineffective. Advance waivers written in very general terms, with no disclosure of the specific types of conflicts and risks that could arise, may not be upheld or may not be found to cover particular conflicts that arise. The immigrant's signature may not be viewed as a genuine consent because the potentially adverse employer is paying the lawyer and could terminate the immigration petition, dashing any possibility of success. Also, screening is permitted as a solution to conflicts problems only in limited circumstances. And while both sides sign waivers, the agreement might be ruled invalid because typically such agreements call for the immigrant, but not the employer, to waive confidentiality.

Two experienced immigration practitioners write that dual representation "pervades immigration law," but that current ethics rules offer "no easy way out." They suggest that the ABA should modify the confidentiality and conflicts rules for immigration lawyers, although they do not specify what changes would be in order. Meanwhile, they suggest that while "a uniform approach to dual representation that fits all clients is untenable," in many cases "obtaining consent in advance from the foreign national after full disclosure may be the answer."[106] However, as the authors themselves note, it may be impossible to imagine in advance all of the conflicts that could arise or to obtain advance disclosure that is fair and effective.

---

106. Id. at 636-640.

7 CONFLICTS INVOLVING FORMER CLIENTS

This chapter examines conflicts that involve the interests of former clients. It looks at what duties lawyers owe to former clients and what lawyers should do if those duties conflict with the duties they owe to current or new clients.

A. Nature of conflicts between present and former clients

Sometimes a lawyer wants to take on work that poses a conflict with the interests of a person or an organization that the lawyer represented in the past. A conflict with a former client's interests may develop or become apparent after a lawyer is well into some work on behalf of a current client. In the event of a conflict between a former client and a present client, a lawyer might

- betray confidences of a former client to a present client,
- make *adverse use* of confidences that the lawyer learned during the representation of the former client,
- attack or challenge work that the lawyer did on behalf of the former client, or
- engage in work that is in some other way disloyal to the former client or at least causes the former client to feel betrayed.

If the interests of a former client and a present client present a conflict, a lawyer who has a strong sense of loyalty to the former client might be less zealous on behalf of the present client. For example, suppose the lawyer knows information from the former representation that could help the present client, but does not use or reveal that information because of his duty to protect the former client's confidences. His advocacy on behalf of the new client is somewhat compromised by his duties to the former client.

We might recast this abstract issue in more concrete terms. A lawyer might compromise the interests of a prior client in favor of a current client because the latter is currently paying fees. On the other hand, previous financial relationships, the expectation of future work, or continuing emotional ties might cause a lawyer to favor her former client and to be a less vigorous advocate for her present one.

If a conflict involves a present client and a former client, which ethical rule applies?

Protections for former clients are provided by Rule 1.9, so a lawyer should evaluate the impact of such a conflict on a former client using the standards articulated in Rule 1.9. Protections for present clients are provided in Rule 1.7, which is discussed in Chapters 5 and 6. If a present and former client's interests conflict, a lawyer should refer to Rule 1.7 for guidance on protecting the interests of the present client and to Rule 1.9 for guidance on protecting the former client's interests.

So is a conflict between a present and a former client both a successive conflict and a current conflict?

Yes. Rule 1.7(a)(2) defines a current conflict to include a situation in which "there is a significant risk that the representation of one or more clients will be materially limited by a lawyer's responsibilities to another client, a former client, a third person or by a personal interest of the lawyer." Comment 9 explains that "a lawyer's duties of loyalty and independence may be materially limited by responsibilities to former clients under Rule 1.9."

The following table illustrates the applicability of both rules.

Which rule to apply to conflicts involving present and former clients

Situation	Possible interest harmed	Can this conflict be waived?	Rule
Lawyer knows (or might have had access to) information from a former client that could be used adversely to the former client.	Breach of commitment to keep confidences of **former client**	Yes, by informed consent of former client	1.9
New client wants lawyer to sue lawyer's former client, whom lawyer represented for years on a variety of matters.	• Possible adverse use of confidences of **former client**, depending on subject matter • Lawyer's advocacy on behalf of **new client** might be compromised by relationship to former client	Yes, by informed consent of present and former clients, unless the conflict is so severe that the lawyer could not reasonably believe that he could provide competent and diligent representation to the new client	1.9 1.7

Are the ethical rules less restrictive as to successive conflicts than they are as to concurrent conflicts?

Yes. The ethics rules reflect an assumption that the problems relating to former clients may not be quite as serious as those with present clients. A lawyer's duties to a former client are limited mainly to protecting confidences, avoiding side-switching, and refraining from attacking the work the lawyer did for the former client. The passage of time often reduces the likelihood that a lawyer will deliberately or inadvertently misuse information she received from one client while representing another client. In addition, the legal profession does not want to hamstring lawyers by imposing lifetime loyalty obligations to former clients that would preclude too broad a range of future work.[1]

Although the rules on former clients are not as restrictive as those on current client conflicts, they do preclude a lawyer from proceeding in many situations without the consent of the former client.

B. Duties to former clients

What duties does a lawyer owe a former client?

The primary duty that lawyers owe to former clients is to protect their confidences.[2] A lawyer must decline any new matter that presents a substantial risk that the lawyer would make material adverse use of the former client's confidences, unless the former client consents. Rule 1.9 articulates the standards against which lawyers should evaluate the risk of harm to former clients.

Rule 1.9   Duties to Former Clients

Rule language*	Authors' explanation**
(a) A lawyer who has **formerly represented a client** in a matter **shall not** thereafter **represent** another person in **the same or a substantially related matter** in which that person's interests are **materially adverse** to the interests of the former client **unless the former client gives informed consent, confirmed in writing.**	This section bars representation of a new client (absent consent) if the new representation would involve a substantially related matter and material adversity. See Comment 3 for explanation of "substantial relationship."
(b) A lawyer **shall not** knowingly represent a person in the **same or a substantially related matter** in which **a firm with which the lawyer formerly was associated had previously represented a client**	This section should be used to evaluate conflicts that arise when a lawyer moves from one firm to another.
(1) whose interests are **materially adverse** to that person; **and**	

---

1. Restatement § 132, comment b. While the profession is reluctant to impose lifetime *loyalty* obligations, Rule 1.6 does impose a lifetime *confidentiality* obligation.

2. See, e.g., Analytica v. NPD Research, 708 F.2d 1263 (7th Cir. 1983).

Rule language[*]	Authors' explanation[**]
(2) about whom the lawyer had **acquired information protected by Rules 1.6 and 1.9(c)** that is **material** to the matter;	
unless the former client gives informed consent, confirmed in writing.	
(c) A lawyer who has **formerly represented** a client in a matter **or whose present or former firm has formerly represented** a client in a matter **shall not** thereafter:	This section bars *use or revelation* of confidences of former clients or clients of a former firm to the same extent as such use or revelation is barred for present clients.
(1) **use information relating to the representation to the disadvantage of the former client except** as these Rules would permit or require with respect to a client, or when the information has become **generally known**; or	
(2) **reveal** information relating to the representation except as these Rules would permit or require with respect to a client.	

*All emphasis added.

**This and other authors' explanations draw from the comments to the rules and from other sources. They are not comprehensive but highlight some important interpretive points.

Under Rule 1.9(a), a lawyer may not do work on behalf of a new client if that work involves "the same or a substantially related matter" as a former representation *and* the new client's interests are "materially adverse to the interests of the former client, *unless* the former client gives informed consent, confirmed in writing" (emphasis added). One difference between the rule on conflicts that impact present clients and those that might *adversely impact former clients* is that, if the only adverse impact would be on a former client, a lawyer is *always* permitted to proceed with the new work if the lawyer can secure informed consent from the former client. However, as discussed in Chapter 5, a conflict that could *adversely impact a present client* might not be waivable.[3]

Here is another distinction to consider. Conflicts that impact present clients may be problematic regardless of the subject matter of the two representations. Conflicts that impact former clients raise a problem only if there is a "substantial relationship" between the work done for the former client and the new matter.

---

3. Rule 1.7(b).

C. Distinguishing present and former clients

How do you know whether a client is a present client or a former client?

William Freivogel

This sounds like a dumb question, but it isn't. A concurrent conflict involves two present clients or one present and one prospective client. A successive conflict involves one present or prospective client and one former client. But it is not so simple. If a lawyer has completed work for a particular client, the lawyer may view that client as a former client. However, if the lawyer has not formally terminated the relationship, that client may consider himself a present client. As conflicts expert William Freivogel notes, things would be simpler if every lawyer, upon completion of a piece of work (such as writing a will), wrote a letter to a client saying: "This matter has concluded. We plan to do no further work for you, and you are no longer our client."[4]

The problem, says Freivogel, is that "[l]awyers hate to write letters like that. A truly effective letter may offend the client. Moreover, the lawyer wants to maintain a bond with the client so that it will send more business. Thus, these letters are rarely written."[5]

One Chicago lawyer who was interviewed by Susan Shapiro, for example, puts it this way:

> Do you think that anyone in their right mind is going to . . . send a letter to that client [for whom a deal had been handled] saying, "It was a pleasure working for you. We don't work for you any more. We consider our relationship terminated. Very truly yours?" No. They might send a letter . . . saying "It's been a pleasure handling this deal. We look forward to working with you again."[6]

Even if there is not a clear statement by the lawyer or the client or in the contract between them confirming that the relationship is over, the Restatement says the lawyer's representational authority can also end "because the lawyer has completed the contemplated services."[7] But whether the

---

4. William Freivogel, Freivogel on Conflicts, Former Client — The Substantial Relationship Test, http://www.freivogel.com/formerclientparti.html (accessed Nov. 14, 2012).

5. Id.

6. Susan Shapiro, Tangled Loyalties: Conflict of Interest in Legal Practice 192 (U. Mich. Press 2002), quoting an interview with a Chicago lawyer in a firm with more than 100 lawyers.

7. Restatement § 31(2)(e). Comment h states that this question depends on examination of the course of dealing between the parties. The comment notes that "[b]ecause contracts with a client are to be construed from the client's viewpoint, the client's reasonable understanding of the scope of representation controls."

relationship is over depends on examination of the course of dealing between the parties. The Restatement explains that "[b]ecause contracts with a client are to be construed from the client's viewpoint, the client's reasonable understanding of the scope of representation controls."[8]

This question of who is a present client and who is a former one is fraught with practical pressures. As firms grow larger and as institutional clients increasingly tend to use multiple firms, the problems multiply. The desire to get repeat business from the client pushes in the direction of treating former clients as current or continuing clients. At the same time, the ethics rules push lawyers to regard such clients as former clients because the conflicts rules are more forgiving with respect to conflicts between current clients and former clients. But even treating a client as a former client doesn't solve all the problems. A lawyer might face ethical or practical risks if she takes on work that conflicts with the interests of an arguably former client without that person's consent. The former client might consider himself a present client and might intend to use the firm in the future. Susan Shapiro elaborates:

> As monogamous general counsel relationships are increasingly being transformed into promiscuous one-night stands with special counsel, law firms can ill afford to shelter their uncommitted paramours from the former-client category. As many respondents observe, they face both potential ethical and financial consequences when they consider one-shot patrons former clients and financial consequences when they do not.[9]

What if a lawyer has a long-term client, but the lawyer has not done anything for that client in a year or more?

If a lawyer has not formally concluded representation of the client, a court might still find that the client is a present one and that a conflict with another client should be evaluated as a concurrent conflict.[10]

One Chicago lawyer raises the following question:

> Ours is primarily a transactional practice. A client may call you up to do one thing. It is completed. The firm continues to send a newsletter to the client. Lawyers occasionally make a sales call to them.[11] How does this fit into the assessment of whether someone is a former client?[12]

---

8. Id. at comment h.

9. Shapiro, supra n. 6, at 195.

10. Restatement § 132, comment c, reporter's note, citing Shearing v. Allergan, Inc., 1994 WL 396139 (D. Nev. May 1994) (lawyer had represented a client for 13 years but had not done any work for that client in more than a year — still found to be a current client).

11. [Authors' footnote.] Under the ethics rules in most jurisdictions, there are some restrictions on in-person or telephonic solicitation of business from new clients, but once a client has engaged the services of a firm, the firm may contact the client to suggest additional services that the firm could provide. See, e.g., Rule 7.3.

12. Shapiro, supra n. 6, at 192, quoting a Chicago lawyer in a firm with between 50 and 99 lawyers.

Can a lawyer drop one client to clear the way to take on representation of a more lucrative matter for a new client?

Suppose a lawyer represents one client in a small transaction, and then a second client seeks to retain the lawyer to work on a major transaction (a different one) that would be adverse to the first client but would be far more profitable for the lawyer? In general, the lawyer may not drop the client. "[T]he attempt to drop one client to accept another — the so-called hot-potato gambit [because it involves dropping the first client like a "hot potato"] — has been roundly condemned."[13] So a lawyer can't fire a client to lower the conflicts bar on a new client. On the other hand, if one of the following conditions is satisfied, the lawyer may use the more lenient successive conflict standards to evaluate the conflict.

- The lawyer withdraws at the natural end point in the representation.
- The client fires the lawyer for reasons other than the impending conflict.
- The client triggers a conflict for the lawyer by some action (e.g., acquiring a company that is a defendant in a matter in which the lawyer represents the plaintiff) that was unforeseeable to the lawyer. This type of conflict is sometimes referred to as one "thrust upon" a lawyer by the client.[14] In this case, the lawyer's withdrawal makes this client a former client.
- The lawyer withdraws for some other good reason (e.g., if the client insists that the lawyer assist in committing a fraud or if the client refuses to pay the fees she owes).[15]

Can a client preclude an adversary from hiring certain firms by engaging those firms for small, continuing matters, thereby creating concurrent conflicts for the firms if an adversary approaches them?

In theory, a client could preclude an adversary from hiring a certain lawyer by hiring that lawyer for some other matter. However, it is unethical for a lawyer to suggest or participate in this practice.[16] Nevertheless, law firms sometimes realize that new clients who want to hire them for small matters

---

13. ABA, Annotated Model Rules of Professional Conduct 161 (6th ed. 2007) citing, among others, Pioneer-Standard Elecs., Inc. v. Cap Gemini Am., Inc., No. 1:01CV2185, 2002 WL 553460 (N.D. Ohio Mar. 11, 2002).

14. Restatement § 132, comment j, reporter's note, citing Gould, Inc. v. Mitsui Mining & Smelting Co., 738 F. Supp. 1121 (N.D. Ohio 1990); see D.C. B., Leg. Ethics Comm., Op. 292 (1999) (available at http://www.dcbar.org/for_lawyers/ethics/legal_ethics/opinions/opinion292.cfm).

15. Restatement § 132, comment c.

16. Ind. State B., Op. 2 (2000) (available at http://www.inbar.org/LinkClick.aspx?fileticket=Ea4m5rvTNVI%3d&tabid=81&mid=886) (improper for divorce lawyer to suggest that client consult a firm so that the firm will be disqualified from representing his spouse).

may be trying to set up conflicts for them. They may refuse the business or attempt to avoid the conflicts by asking the new clients for advance waivers of future conflicts of interest. At least in some jurisdictions, such advance waivers are effective.[17] Comment 22 to Rule 1.7 explicitly condones advance waivers of conflicts under some circumstances, particularly if the client is an "experienced user . . . of legal services" and the client signing the waiver is familiar with the type of conflict it waives.[18]

If a lawyer used to work in the law department of a corporation, is the corporation his former client on all matters that were going on during his employment?

Not necessarily. Former in-house counsels have been disqualified for such conflicts in several cases,[19] but the mere fact of employment does not make a lawyer the corporation's lawyer on every matter. If a lawyer worked on a matter (more than a trivial amount) on behalf of his employer corporation, the corporation will be viewed as a former client as to that matter. However, if the lawyer did not work on a certain matter and received no confidences about it, the corporation will not be viewed as a "former client" even as to matters that took place during the lawyer's work for the corporation.[20]

D. Evaluating successive conflicts

The critical question about conflicts between present and former clients is whether the conflict is serious enough that the lawyer may not go forward with the new work without the former client's informed consent. To answer this question, the lawyer, applying Rule 1.9, must ask two things about the new matter:

- Is it the "same matter" as the previous one?
- If not, is it "substantially related" to the previous one?
- Beware! Both these questions use terms of art that must be understood to answer them correctly.

---

17. Kennecott Copper Corp. v. Curtiss-Wright Corp., 449 F. Supp. 951 (S.D.N.Y.), *aff'd and rev'd*, 584 F.2d 1195 (2d Cir. 1978), discussed in Richard W. Painter, Advance Waiver of Conflicts, 13 Geo. J. Leg. Ethics 289, 297-298 (2000).

18. Rule 1.7, Comment 22. Conversely, as we noted in Chapter 6, if the client being asked to sign an advance waiver is an unsophisticated individual, such as a prospective immigrant employee whose lawyer is also representing and being paid by the prospective lawyer, the waiver may be ineffective.

19. See, e.g., NCK Org., Ltd. v. Bregman, 542 F.2d 128 (2d Cir. 1976).

20. ABA Standing Comm. on Ethics & Prof. Resp., Formal Op. 99-415.

- If one of the two questions above is answered "yes," the lawyer must ask whether the new client's interests are "materially adverse to the interests of the former client."
- If the matter is the same or substantially related and there is material adversity, the lawyer may not go forward with the new representation without the former client's informed consent.
- There must be written confirmation of the consent.

The discussion that follows explores each of these steps. Keep in mind that if the conflict might adversely impact your representation of a current client, you must also do a separate analysis of the conflict under Rule 1.7.

1. The same matter

When is one matter "the same matter" as a previous one?

First of all, what is a "matter"? A matter can be anything that is the subject of representation: litigation, a transaction, a subject on which a client requests advice.[21] A conflict may occur between a former matter that did not involve adversarial advocacy — perhaps the client just sought advice — and a subsequent, more adversarial matter.[22]

The most obvious "same matter" is a single transaction or lawsuit. In addition, it is the "same matter" if the new representation involves a document that the lawyer was involved in producing — the subject matter is the same.[23]

Under Rule 1.9, a lawyer may not switch sides in the midst of a negotiation or litigation (same matter, materially adverse interests) unless the former client gives written consent, which would be unlikely.[24] Likewise, a lawyer may not "switch sides" and attack an instrument that the lawyer drafted.

> **FOR EXAMPLE:** A lawyer drafts a will for a client who wishes to disinherit his eldest son. After the client dies, the eldest son asks the lawyer to represent him to challenge the validity of this will. The lawyer may not take on this work.

2. Substantial relationship

The law governing when two matters are substantially related seems maddeningly complex and indeterminate. William Freivogel places the

---

21. Restatement § 132, comment d(iii).
22. Id. at reporter's note.
23. Id. at comment d(ii).
24. Id. at comment d(i).

following notice near the beginning of his summary of this body of law:

> *Warning*: More cases deal with former client issues than just about any other issue relating to conflicts of interest. The cases also tend to be more fact-specific than those in other areas — particularly as to what is "substantially related." Thus, many of them have relatively little value as precedent.[25]

As you study the application of this slippery standard, then, focus on exploring the facts of a problem and on what a lawyer *might have* learned during the first matter that could be used adversely to the former client in the second. Once you have delved into all the available facts, you will be able to use the doctrinal framework explained below to evaluate the nature of the conflict.

When is there a "substantial relationship" between one matter and another?

A commonsense interpretation of this question would be to ask if there is some connection between the earlier matter and the new matter. There are many possible connections: Two matters might involve the same parties, the same lawsuit, the same legal issues, or the same (or overlapping) facts. The legal definition of "substantial relationship," however, is far narrower and focuses on likely access to relevant confidential information.

The dominant legal definition of "substantial relationship" asks whether the lawyer, in the course of her work in the first matter, would normally have learned information that could be used adversely to the former client in the second. Comment 3 to Rule 1.9 explains:

> Matters are "substantially related" for purposes of this Rule if they involve the same transaction or legal dispute *or* if there otherwise is a substantial risk that confidential factual information as would normally have been obtained in the prior representation would materially advance the client's position in the subsequent matter.[26]

Does the existence of a "substantial relationship" between the present and former matter depend on common *facts* or common *legal issues*?

Most ethics codes and most courts take the position that the relationship between the two matters depends on whether factual information would normally have been learned during the first matter that could be used

---

25. Freivogel, supra n. 4.

26. The Restatement defines "substantial relationship" very similarly. Restatement § 132, comment d(iii).

adversely to the first client during the second representation. The inquiry is not about common legal issues, but about common facts. Under this interpretation, a lawyer who becomes expert in a legal topic (say, the law of escheat) in one matter may use that legal knowledge in any subsequent representation that does not present a conflict based on the facts. A few courts define "substantial relationship" to include matters that involve common legal issues, but the better analysis is the fact-based one. The Restatement suggests that the better analysis is to look at overlapping facts and to ask whether "there is a substantial risk that representation of the present client will involve use of information acquired in the course of representing the former client."[27]

Are two matters substantially related? Questions to ask:
- Do the matters involve the **same transaction or legal dispute?**
- If yes, they are substantially related.
- Is there a substantial risk that a lawyer representing a client in a matter like the one handled for the former client **would normally have learned confidential information in the first matter that could be used to materially advance the new client's position in the second matter?** To answer this question, ask:

  - What types of information a lawyer handling a matter like the first one would normally acquire?
  - Would that information (if revealed or used on behalf of the second client) provide the second client with a material advantage?

- If both these questions are answered yes, the two matters are substantially related.
- If the matters are substantially related, the lawyer may not represent the new client unless the former client gives informed consent.

Does a "substantial relationship" depend on whether a lawyer actually learned information in the first representation that could be used adversely to the former client in the later matter?

No. The existence of a substantial relationship depends not on what the lawyer *actually learned,* but on what kinds of confidences a lawyer *ordinarily would have learned* in the prior matter that could be used in the second matter in a way that would materially advance the new client's position,

---

27. Id.

presumably harming the former client. The reason for the hypothetical format of this inquiry is that the goal of the inquiry is to protect the former client's confidences. If those same confidences had to be disclosed to a judge (in the event of a disqualification motion) to determine whether their protection was threatened by the lawyer's role in the subsequent matter, the goal of preserving confidences would be defeated. The comments to Rule 1.9 offer an example that illustrates this point.

> A lawyer who has represented a businessperson and learned extensive private financial information about that person may not then represent that person's former spouse in seeking an increase in alimony and child support.[28]

During the representation of the businessperson, the lawyer learned specific information about the husband's assets. This information could be used to materially advance the wife's position if the lawyer represented the wife in the divorce proceeding. If the husband tried to conceal assets, his former lawyer would know of the existence of those assets and could disclose their existence to the wife. Even if it would be improper for the husband to conceal assets, it also would be improper for the wife's lawyer to reveal confidences about the husband that the lawyer learned while representing the husband.

The existence of a "substantial relationship" does not depend on whether the lawyer *actually learned* of these assets in the prior representation; one question is whether there is a *substantial risk* that this sort of information *normally would have been obtained* in the prior representation. Also, it doesn't matter whether the lawyer *actually used* such information adversely to his former client. The second question is whether there is a substantial risk that the lawyer obtained information that could be used to the material advantage of the second client.[29]

If a former client moves to disqualify a lawyer from working on a new matter, does she have to reveal the relevant confidences to make the case?

No. That would defeat the purpose of the motion. The former client may give a general description of the lawyer's previous services, and a judge may draw inferences about the type of confidences that ordinarily would be learned in that type of representation.[30] By examining "the general features

---

28. Rule 1.9, Comment 3.

29. If there is a substantial relationship and if the new representation involves "material adversity" toward the former client (obviously true of this divorce), the lawyer may not represent the wife in the divorce without the consent of the husband, his former client. Unless the divorce is an entirely harmonious one, the odds that the husband would consent are low.

30. Rule 1.9, Comment 3.

of the matters involved," the judge can assess "the likelihood that confidences were imparted by the former client that could be used to adverse effect in the subsequent representation."[31]

If the present and former matters appear on their face not to have common facts, can one safely assume that there is no substantial relationship?

No. There are many cases that appear at first not to have factual overlap but that turn out to present a risk of adverse use of prior confidences. It is worthwhile to find out as many facts as possible before evaluating whether there might be a substantial relationship between two matters. Here's another example from the comments to Rule 1.9:

> A lawyer who has previously represented a client in securing environmental permits to build a shopping center would be precluded from representing neighbors seeking to oppose rezoning of the property on the basis of environmental considerations; however, the lawyer would not be precluded, on the grounds of substantial relationship, from defending a tenant of the completed shopping center in resisting eviction for nonpayment of rent.[32]

Because the lawyer got the environmental permits, he probably possesses confidential information on the environmental features of the property that might be at issue in the new matter. For example, he might know how much solid waste the shopping center produces annually. These facts could help the neighbors to oppose rezoning. There is a substantial relationship between these two matters because a lawyer working on environmental permits *would normally have had access* to confidences that could be used adversely to his former client in a dispute about rezoning the property.

The comment assumes that the environmental information is irrelevant to the eviction case, so there would be no opportunity to make adverse use of the confidential information. On this basis, the comment concludes that there is no substantial relationship. But what if the tenant stopped paying rent because there was toxic waste seeping into her ground floor space? If there is a substantial risk that the lawyer would have learned about toxic waste on the property in the first representation, there would in fact be a substantial relationship after all. Since there is material adversity, the lawyer would need to withdraw unless the former client consented to his continued work.

---

31. Restatement § 132, comment d(iii).
32. Rule 1.9, Comment 3.

If, during the first representation, the lawyer learned only general information about a client's business operations, is there a substantial relationship?

If during the first representation, a lawyer normally would have learned only general knowledge that has only slight relevance to the new matter, such knowledge may not create a substantial relationship.[33] Comment 3 to Rule 1.9 explains:

> In the case of an organizational client, general knowledge of the client's policies and practices ordinarily will not preclude a subsequent representation; on the other hand, knowledge of specific facts gained in a prior representation that are relevant to the matter in question ordinarily will preclude such a representation.

> FOR EXAMPLE: A lawyer, once general counsel to a corporation, now works in private practice. Another company asks the lawyer to file an antitrust suit against the lawyer's former employer. The suit is predicated on events that occurred after the lawyer left the corporation. However, the allegations involve a pattern of business practices that extend back through the period when the lawyer was general counsel. Unless the former client (the corporation) consents, the lawyer may not handle the antitrust suit because he knows too much about the operations of the defendant company.[34]

What if the lawyer knows how the former client approaches legal disputes? Does this "playbook" knowledge create a substantial relationship?

Suppose a lawyer has represented a client in several lawsuits or nonlitigation matters unrelated to the new client's matter. As a result of the prior representation, the lawyer knows how the client tends to react to legal problems—disposition toward settlement, attitude about cooperation with discovery requests, and so on.[35] This type of knowledge might give the lawyer and her new client an advantage in subsequent litigation against the former client. Whether such knowledge amounts to a substantial

---

33. Restatement § 132, comment d(iii).

34. This example is based on Restatement § 132, comment d(iii), illus. 3, which is based on Chugach Elec. Assn. v. U.S. Dist. Ct., 370 F.2d 441 (9th Cir. 1966); see also In re Corrugated Container Antitrust Litig., 659 F.2d 1341, 1346 (5th Cir. 1982) (more recent case, similar facts); but see ABA Standing Comm. on Ethics & Prof. Resp., Formal Op. 99-415, criticizing the *Chugach* opinion as overbroad. Restatement § 132, comment d(iii), reporter's note, refers to some cases that say possession of general information is an insufficient basis for disqualification.

35. Professor Charles Wolfram refers to this type of knowledge as a "playbook view" of the former client. Charles W. Wolfram, Former Client Conflicts, 10 Geo. J. Leg. Ethics 677 (1997).

relationship depends on the range of information that a lawyer could be expected to have learned during the former representation. If the lawyer represented the former client for a long period of time, it is more likely that the lawyer's prior representation would be found to be substantially related to the new matter.[36]

What if the information that the lawyer learned in the previous representation has become public or is obsolete?

If the confidential information that a lawyer learned from the former client has become public, the lawyer is not precluded from representing the new client by the possession of that knowledge. Similarly, if the information learned in the previous representation is so out of date that it is not relevant, it is unlikely that the new matter would be found to be substantially related to the old one.[37]

Is the likelihood of disqualification affected by how much responsibility a lawyer had on the prior matter?

It could be. In *Silver Chrysler Plymouth, Inc. v. Chrysler Motors Corp.*,[38] the court declined to disqualify a lawyer based on his work on a matter as an associate at his previous firm. In the previous position, the lawyer had helped to defend Chrysler Motors against an antitrust claim brought by a taxicab company. At his new firm, he represented a Chrysler dealer suing Chrysler Motors in a dispute about the terms of a real estate lease. There was testimony that when the lawyer was an associate, he "did not work directly or indirectly on Chrysler dealer litigation, with the possible exception of researching a few specific points of law that may have been involved in a dealer case."[39] The court declined to presume that this former associate had been exposed to the confidences possessed by other lawyers in the 80-lawyer firm. Therefore, the two matters were found not to be substantially related. The court said that especially in a motion to disqualify a lawyer who had been in a subordinate role on the prior matter, a movant would need to allege "actual activities on specific cases . . . which would make it reasonable to infer that he gained some information about his former client of some value to his present client."[40]

---

36. Freivogel, supra n. 4.
37. Rule 1.9, Comment 3.
38. 370 F. Supp. 581 (E.D.N.Y. 1973), *aff'd*, 518 F.2d 751 (2d Cir. 1975).
39. Id. at 585.
40. Id. at 589.

Do the courts use the "substantial relationship" test to decide a motion to disqualify a lawyer, or is this standard only used in lawyer discipline?

The standard is used in lawyer disciplinary matters and in disqualification matters. The purpose of the "substantial relationship" standard articulated in Rule 1.9 and its state counterparts is to evaluate whether a lawyer should be disciplined for representing a client whose interests are in conflict with a former client, rather than as a yardstick by which to judge whether a lawyer or law firm should be disqualified from handling a particular case. However, much of the case law on successive conflicts of interest involves motions to disqualify lawyers. In fact, a wide variety of litigation occurs in which one party seeks some remedy for an alleged conflict of interest of the lawyer for another party. As lawyer and professor Richard Flamm explains,

> [t]he use of the ABA conflict rules as a cudgel, rather than as a compass, has not been confined to a single type of proceeding. On the contrary, claims that a lawyer has engaged in conflicted representation, or failed to disclose such a conflict, have supplied the basis for breach of contract actions, legal malpractice claims, and lawsuits filed for the express purpose of enjoining the challenged attorney or firm from continuing to engage in conflicted representation, as well as for proceedings seeking to preclude a "conflicted" lawyer or firm from collecting a fee, or to affirmatively "disgorge" fees that have already been paid.[41]

In ruling on motions to disqualify lawyers because of conflicts of interest, the courts are not bound to use the ethics rules as standards.[42] Their analysis focuses on whether there is a substantial relationship, but, as explained above, there is some divergence in the courts' definitions of that standard.[43]

---

41. Richard E. Flamm, Looking Ahead to Ethics 2015: Or Why I Still Do Not Get the ABA Model Conflict of Interest Rules, 19 N. Ill. U. L. Rev. 273 (1999); see Damron v. Herzog, 67 F.3d 211 (9th Cir. 1995) (conflict with former client was the predicate for a malpractice claim); Maritrans GP Inc. v. Pepper, Hamilton & Scheetz, 602 A.2d 1277 (Pa. 1992) (conflict with former client led to claim of breach of fiduciary duty).

42. The divergence between the conflicts standards on discipline and disqualification doesn't make too much difference as a practical matter. If a judge *denies* a motion to disqualify a lawyer because of a conflict, it is unlikely that a bar counsel would impose discipline. If a judge *grants* such a motion, discipline would not necessarily be initiated, and in fact, the matter usually ends there. But it is not out of the question that the disciplinary authorities would go forward with an investigation.

43. See Restatement § 132 and comment d(iii). Because of the variations in state law, it is important to study the law of the jurisdiction in which you intend to practice. However, since the Ethics 2000 Commission definition of "substantial relationship" and the Restatement definition are so similar, perhaps we will see a greater degree of uniformity in future cases.

Do federal courts follow state law in deciding motions to disqualify lawyers based on conflicts with former clients?

Sometimes. One authority has concluded that "federal courts have used a cacophony of legal sources to analyze ethics issues" and that they "articulate a variety of attitudes toward disqualification."[44] Some federal courts have urged that state law governs disqualification motions in diversity cases, but others have urged that federal courts may consider a variety of sources in deciding the legal standards on disqualification; state ethics codes are sometimes held not to be controlling.

May a lawyer sue a former client on behalf of a new client, without the former client's consent, if the new matter is not substantially related to the previous one?

Yes. No consent is required unless the new matter is "the same or substantially related" and the new representation is "materially adverse" to the interests of the former client.

> FOR EXAMPLE: A law firm had represented the publisher of the *Village Voice* in a defamation case. Subsequently, the same firm filed suit against the publisher on behalf of a reporter who had been fired, claiming, among other things, that the editor of the newspaper had made defamatory statements about the reporter. The newspaper moved to disqualify the firm in the second case. The court denied the motion, finding no substantial relationship between the two matters. Newfield, the editor of the *Village Voice*, claimed that in the previous matter, the firm now suing his paper had learned confidential information about "my work habits, my past, my views on journalism generally . . . my methods and the care with which I practice my trade. . . ."[45] The court found that "[w]hile these may have been involved in an action arising out of a [previous] series of published articles [in the *Village Voice*], they are not 'substantially related' to Newfield's opinions of the plaintiff expressed in an interview conducted by a reporter for another newspaper."[46]

Other cases involving unrelated suits against former clients have been resolved similarly.[47]

44. Judith A. McMorrow & Daniel R. Coquillette, Moore's Federal Practice §§ 808.01[7][a], 808.02[2][a][iii] (3d ed., LexisNexis 2001).

45. Nichols v. Village Voice, Inc., 417 N.Y.S.2d 415, 419 (App. Div. 1979).

46. Id.

47. See examples listed in Restatement § 132, comment d(iii), reporter's note.

Is it ever a good idea to sue a former client?

Maybe not. Although a lawyer is permitted to sue a former client on an unrelated matter, as in the previous example, it may be a bad idea.

> **FOR EXAMPLE:** Suppose that Otto, a lawyer in a small community, represented a family-owned business, Mickey's Hardware, for 25 years in various corporate matters. Then Mickey's switched lawyers because the original owner's son, who had inherited the business, wanted to hire a close friend. Two years later, Otto is asked to sue Mickey's in a slip-and-fall case unrelated to any prior representation. Even if Otto *may* accept this matter, he might be better advised to refer the client to a different lawyer. Mickey's might be dismayed to find Otto on the other side of a case. If the owners of Mickey's feel betrayed, they might make negative comments about Otto to other business owners, damaging his reputation in the community. Also, Otto's sense of professional duty might counsel against suing Mickey's even if no harm would result.

An example of substantial relationship analysis: *Westinghouse v. Gulf*

One case that illustrates the application of the substantial relationship test is *Westinghouse Electric Corp. v. Gulf Oil Corp.*[48] This was a price-fixing case

Mount Taylor

in which Gulf moved to disqualify the Bigbee law firm from representing one of the other defendants because the firm had previously represented Gulf on matters that were urged to be substantially related to the price-fixing litigation. Here's what happened.

Gulf had acquired an interest in some uranium reserves in New Mexico located on the Mount Taylor properties. In 1971, Gulf hired the Bigbee firm to provide a variety of services, including

> the patenting of fifty-nine mining claims, drafting leases required for uranium exploration, representing Gulf in litigation involving title disputes, counseling Gulf in relation to the resolution of certain problems relating to mine waters, and lobbying on behalf of Gulf in front of the New Mexico state legislature on tax and environmental matters. One of Bigbee's name partners . . . alone spent over 2,000 hours working on behalf of Gulf.[49]

---

48. 588 F.2d 221 (7th Cir. 1978). The well-articulated definition of the term "substantial relationship" in this opinion (excerpted below) is quoted in Restatement § 132, comment d(iii).

49. *Westinghouse Elec.*, 588 F.2d at 222-223.

Gulf argued that this work was substantially related to the later Westing-house litigation. In the *Westinghouse* case, it was alleged that Gulf had failed to produce uranium from the Mount Taylor properties because of a con-spiracy to fix prices. Gulf urged that it had shared confidences with the Bigbee firm about "the quantity and quality of uranium reserves in the Mt. Taylor properties." In the Westinghouse litigation, the Bigbee firm was representing UNC, a co-defendant of Gulf's. Gulf urged that this was problematic because UNC "was attempting to exculpate itself by incul-pating Gulf."[50]

The Seventh Circuit explained the substantial relationship test this way:

> [T]he determination of whether there is a substantial relationship turns on the possibility, or appearance thereof, that confidential information might have been given to the attorney in relation to the subsequent matter in which disqualification is sought. The rule thus does not necessarily involve any inquiry into the imponderables involved in the degree of relationship between the two matters but instead involves a realistic appraisal of the possibility that confidences had been disclosed in the one matter which will be harmful to the client in the other. . . . [In evaluating a conflict, it is necessary] to restrict the inquiry to the possibility of dis-closure; it is not appropriate for the court to inquire into whether actual confidences were disclosed.[51]

The court explained that the evaluation of an alleged conflict under this rule

> require[s] three levels of inquiry. Initially, the trial judge must make a factual reconstruction of the scope of the prior legal representation. Second, it must be determined whether it is reasonable to infer that the confidential information allegedly given would have been given to a lawyer representing a client in those matters. Finally, it must be deter-mined whether that information is relevant to the issues raised in the litigation pending against the former client.[52]

The district court had found it reasonable to infer that the Bigbee firm did obtain confidential information from Gulf about its uranium reserves, but it declined to disqualify the Bigbee firm because it assumed that this information was not relevant in the Westinghouse litigation. The district court thought that a price-fixing conspiracy would mainly be proven by showing direct evidence of communication among the conspirators.

The Seventh Circuit reversed the district court, noting that circum-stantial evidence could be highly probative in proving a price-fixing

---

50. Id. at 223.
51. Id. at 224.
52. Id.

conspiracy. The court stated that "proof that Gulf was restricting its output of uranium would be highly relevant circumstantial evidence if its competitors were behaving in a parallel fashion."[53] The court also concluded that "evidence of Gulf's quantity and quality of uranium reserves could serve as a central element [to prove the] violation alleged. . . . Therefore the incentives to disclose and abuse the confidential information are present, and disqualification is required."[54]

3. Material adversity

What does it mean for a matter to be "materially adverse" to the interests of a former client?

According to Rule 1.9, if a new representation is substantially related to a previous one *and* presents "material adversity" to the interests of a former client, the lawyer may not pursue the new matter without the consent of the former client. Neither Rule 1.9 nor the comments that follow it define "material adversity." Rule 1.7 uses the term "direct adversity" in defining conflicts that impact present clients. The question is whether "material adversity" is intended to be synonymous with "direct adversity," to be broader in scope, or to be narrower.

Logic suggests that if the drafters of the rule had intended the two terms to mean the same thing, they would have used the same term. Likewise, logic suggests that "material adversity" should be the less restrictive of the two standards because one would assume that the more rigorous standard would be used to protect present clients from conflicts of interest.

The apparent intention of the rule is to require consent if the use of the former client's confidences might harm the former client's interests. If the subsequent use of the confidences would not harm the former client's interests, consent is not required. One court held that "adversity is a product of the likelihood of the risk and the seriousness of its consequences."[55]

> **FOR EXAMPLE:** A lawyer was to depose a former client in a lawsuit related to the prior representation. A federal court found this situation to present material adversity under Rule 1.9 because of a slight risk that the former client would be exposed to liability or would suffer harm to her business reputation if the lawyer were permitted to depose her. The

---

53. Id. at 226.
54. Id. at 227.
55. Natl. Med. Enters., Inc. v. Godbey, 924 S.W.2d 123 (Tex. 1996).

court said that the former client "has a right to expect that her credibility and integrity will not be impugned by her former attorney in a substantially related matter."[56]

Authorities differ as to the meaning of the phrase "material adversity." The ABA ethics committee once urged that "material adversity" in Rule 1.9 should be read to refer only to "direct adversity" as defined in Rule 1.7.[57] The Restatement, on the other hand, concludes that material adversity is limited to potential harm to the type of interests that the lawyer sought to advance on behalf of the former client. If the new matter is adverse to interests of a former client that are unrelated to the lawyer's previous work, this would not constitute material adversity.[58]

> **FOR EXAMPLE:**   Suppose a lawyer negotiates a lease for office space for a company that manufactures shower curtains. In the course of the representation, the lawyer does not learn anything about the manufacturing process but is solely concerned with securing favorable terms in the lease. At a later time, the lawyer is approached by a new client who wants the lawyer to assist with a patent application for a new process to create material that would be used for shower curtains. The new client intends to start a company that would manufacture shower curtains. It would become a competitor with the lawyer's former client.

Under the Restatement definition, the new representation would not present "material adversity" because it does not relate to the interests sought to be advanced in the prior representation. Under the ABA ethics committee definition, this work would not present material adversity because it involves neither a suit against the old client nor participation in some similarly adversarial process. Consent would not be required under either approach. It is not clear whether there are any circumstances under which the two approaches would yield different results.

---

56. Selby v. Revlon Consumer Prods. Corp., 6 F. Supp. 2d 577 (N.D. Tex. 1997) (noting also that there is "a paucity of authority" on the meaning of "material adversity" as it is used in Rule 1.9).

57. ABA Standing Comm. on Ethics & Prof. Resp., Formal Op. 99-415. However, the committee reached this conclusion based on a sentence in Rule 1.9, Comment 1, which read, "The principles in Rule 1.7 determine whether the interests of the present and former client are adverse." This sentence was deleted from the comments by the Ethics 2000 Committee. The opinion dealt with disqualification of former in-house corporate counsel from subsequent adverse work on matters handled by the legal departments of their former employers.

58. Restatement § 132, comment e. This analysis would appear to effectively narrow the substantial relationship test so that a lawyer need not obtain consent unless the lawyer could have learned adverse facts in representing the first client that could be used against that client in the new representation *and* the new representation would attack the interests of the former client that were at stake in the first representation.

PROBLEM 7-1   KEEPING IN TOUCH

You work for a law firm that five years ago did some work for Almond Enterprises, a small business. The firm's prior work for Almond was to provide an opinion on the tax consequences of purchasing certain bonds. This work took one day. Almond paid $2,500. Your firm sends its annual newsletter to all of its previous clients as well as its current clients. The newsletter alerts recipients to changes in tax law and other laws that might affect small businesses. One purpose of sending the newsletter is to encourage small-business clients to contact and retain the law firm for more specific advice about the implications of these changes. The firm also called Almond several times over the years to ask whether it needed additional services. Almond always declined.

Now Star Information Systems, a computer service company, wants to hire the law firm to sue Almond to collect unpaid bills for 40 hours of consulting services it provided when Almond was installing a new e-mail system. The computer consulting services have nothing to do with the bond purchase five years ago. The managing partner has asked you to assess whether any present or prior work of the firm creates a conflict of interest that precludes the firm from accepting the offer of Star Information Systems or that requires the firm to obtain consent before doing so.

Your preliminary review suggests that the only problem relates to the firm's previous work for Almond Enterprises. You need to evaluate whether Almond is a current client, because if so, the more stringent restrictions of Rule 1.7 would apply. Is Almond a current client? If you decide that Almond is a former client, would Rule 1.9 permit you to represent Star?

E. Addressing former client conflicts in practice

If a lawyer discovers a conflict between a former client and a present client, what courses of action are available to the lawyer?

A lawyer who encounters a conflict that impacts a former client might choose one of three courses of action, depending on the lawyer's analysis of the conflict.

■ The lawyer might conclude that the two matters are unrelated and simply proceed with the new matter without seeking consent.

- The lawyer might conclude that there is both a substantial relationship between the matters and material adversity, and therefore tell the new client that the firm cannot accept the matter.
- The lawyer might disclose the problem to the former client and ask for consent.[59]

Even though the critical question is whether consent is required to proceed, lawyers don't often seek consent from former clients. More often, they either decide they don't need consent or they decide not to go forward.

Asking a former client for a conflicts waiver can be problematic. A lawyer is bound to protect the confidences of both the new client and the former client from each other, so disclosure of that information would require client permission. If the lawyer asks for this consent, the new client might decide to hire a different firm rather than to allow disclosure of confidences. If a lawyer seeks consent from a former client to represent a new client whose interests conflict with those of the former client, the former client (a) would have little reason to give consent, (b) might claim that it was a current rather than a former client, or (c) might later claim that the request for a waiver constitutes an admission that a waiver was needed. It may be that lawyers don't seek consent from former clients very often because of these complexities.[60]

Can a lawyer make a reliable assessment of a successive conflict?

Many lawyers have difficulty evaluating whether a new matter is substantially related to an old one. When a new case comes in, a law firm must make this assessment to decide whether the consent of a former client is needed. If a lawyer decides there is no substantial relationship and goes forward without consent, she may face a motion to disqualify. Susan Shapiro notes that a "number of respondents ... shared troubling memories of instances in which they guessed wrong and were disqualified from a matter that a judge considered substantially related to a prior representation."[61] Some of the lawyers Shapiro interviewed expressed frustration that

---

59. See Rule 1.7. As we explained in Chapter 5, if there is a conflict between two *current* clients, both parties must consent (provided that the conflict is consentable). In a *successive* conflict situation, if the only person potentially adversely affected is the former client (a Rule 1.9 issue), then only the former client must consent. But if, in addition, the present client's interests might be compromised by a lawyer's duties to the former client, then the lawyer must obtain the consent of the present client under Rule 1.7 and of the former client under Rule 1.9.

60. See e-mails from William Freivogel to Lisa Lerman, June 17, 2004, and June 21, 2004 (on file with authors). Freivogel reports that he had no data on the frequency of requests for conflicts waivers from former clients, but he wrote: "I cannot recall counseling a firm on it in 16+ years of doing this." Id.

61. Shapiro, supra n. 6, at 195.

there seemed to be no "reliably predictive formula by which to classify matters as related or unrelated."[62]

In some cases, common sense and gut judgment seems useful. One large-firm Chicago lawyer suggested that the length and depth of the firm's relationship with the former client was the key:

> A law firm knows so much about the inner workings of that particular company that judges will say, "Maybe this case has nothing to do with any of the work you did for that former client. But you were so close to that client and you defended so many cases that had issues that were touched on . . . that you just got into their skin and bones. And until more time has passed, you can't be an adversary."[63]

F. Conflicts between the interests of a present client and a client who was represented by a lawyer's former firm

So far we have discussed successive conflicts that involve a single lawyer. But what if the former client was not represented by the lawyer personally but by another lawyer at a law firm where one of the lawyers in the firm used to work?

> **FOR EXAMPLE:** A lawyer named Hank used to work at the firm of Barr & Thornburgh. While Hank worked there, some other lawyers at Barr & Thornburgh represented The Toy Chest, a small chain of toy stores, in employment matters. Hank didn't work on any Toy Chest matters. Now Hank works at Reno & Days. Hank has been asked to represent a new client, Jenny, in a suit against her former employer, The Toy Chest.

T1:
Hank works for B & T.
Other B & T lawyers defend The Toy Chest in employment cases.
T2:
Hank works for R & D.
Jenny wants Hank to sue The Toy Chest for wrongful discharge.

---

62. Id. at 196.
63. Id.

This is just like the successive conflicts cases we have discussed above except that the prior representation was not handled by Hank personally but by other lawyers at his former firm. Rule 1.9(b) addresses this type of situation.

> **Rule 1.9(b)**
> **A lawyer shall not knowingly represent a person in the same or a substantially related matter in which a firm with which the lawyer formerly was associated had previously represented a client**
>
> **(1) whose interests are materially adverse to that person; and**
>
> **(2) about whom the lawyer had acquired information protected by Rules 1.6 and 1.9(c) that is material to the matter; unless the former client gives informed consent, confirmed in writing.**

The analysis is similar to the questions raised by Rule 1.9(a): Is the matter the same or substantially related? Is there material adversity? If so, you need informed consent. But there is a critical difference. Under (b), which applies to lawyers whose former firms represented the prior client, consent is not required unless "the lawyer had acquired information protected by Rules 1.6 and 1.9(c) that is material to the matter." Under 1.9(a), one asks whether the lawyer *could have acquired* confidential information in the first representation that might be used adversely to the former client's interests. Here, by contrast, one asks whether the lawyer *actually acquired* material confidential information.

Like the other conflicts rules, this one attempts to strike a balance among competing values — protection of confidences shared by former clients, provision of relative freedom to clients in their choice of counsel, and assurance of relative freedom to lawyers in moving from one firm to another and in taking on new clients.

Several decades ago, most lawyers stayed in one law firm for their entire careers.[64] In the last few decades, a new pattern has emerged. Many lawyers change law firms several times, both early in their careers and later on. Similarly, many clients used to employ one lawyer or one firm to service all their legal needs. Not so any more. Many institutional clients employ multiple law firms at any given time and switch lawyers often. Rule 1.9(b) attempts to protect client interests from harmful conflicts while avoiding undue interference with the desire of both lawyers and clients to play "musical law firms."[65]

---

64. Marc Galanter & Thomas Palay, Tournament of Lawyers: The Transformation of the Big Law Firm 24 (U. Chi. Press 1991).

65. See Rule 1.9, Comment 4.

1. Analyzing former firm conflicts

If a lawyer switched firms, how would anyone other than the lawyer know what confidences he had acquired at the first firm?

It can be difficult to figure out whether a lawyer who has changed firms acquired material confidences about a particular matter at her old firm. Susan Shapiro comments that possible conflicts with "baggage left behind" (meaning the lawyer's former firm's clients) is "insidious because it is harder to inventory (and remember) everything on which the lateral hire actively worked, in which he or she was only tangentially involved, or that he or she inadvertently overheard."[66]

To know whether a lawyer has acquired material confidences, one must analyze the specific facts relating to the lawyer's access to or information about the relevant matter. Comment 6 after Rule 1.9 directs analysts to use certain assumptions. For example, a lawyer who had management responsibility at a former firm may be presumed to have received confidential information about all firm matters. This is because firm managers often have access to all client files and are involved in discussions about many different matters. On the other hand, one might assume that a junior lawyer with no management duties had access to or information about only the matters that she worked on or perhaps only matters handled by her department. She would not be presumed to have information about other matters.[67]

A party seeking to disqualify opposing counsel based on this type of successive conflict may not have access to information about exactly what the lawyer worked on or learned about at the former firm. Therefore, the comment to Rule 1.9 urges that the firm whose disqualification is sought (in the example above, Hank's current firm) should have the burden to prove that the lawyer who changed firms does not possess confidential information that is material to the new matter.[68] Proving a negative is difficult, but it would be unfair to make the opposing party prove that Hank did possess confidential information.

2. Using or revealing a former client's confidences

The duty to protect client confidences does not end when the representation is concluded but continues indefinitely. Rule 1.9(c) explains the nature of this duty to former clients.

---

66. Shapiro, supra n. 6, at 208.
67. Rule 1.9, Comment 6.
68. Id.

Rule 1.9(c)

A lawyer who has formerly represented a client in a matter or whose present or former firm has formerly represented a client in a matter shall not thereafter:

> **(1) use information relating to the representation to the disadvantage of the former client except as these Rules would permit or require with respect to a client, or when the information has become generally known; or**

> **(2) reveal information relating to the representation except as these Rules would permit or require with respect to a client.**

A lawyer must protect confidences of his own present and former clients, of other present and former clients of law firms where he works or used to work, and of prospective clients. If a lawyer represents an organization and receives information about a member or a subsidiary entity, the lawyer has a duty to the client organization to protect those confidences. In any situation in which there is a substantial risk that the lawyer would normally have obtained confidences in a former matter that could be used adversely to the former client in a subsequent matter, the lawyer may not be able to handle the second matter unless the former client consents. But regardless of whether the possible receipt of confidences in a prior matter precludes representation of a new client, Rule 1.9(c) prohibits the *revelation* of confidences received from former clients and prohibits the *adverse use* of such confidences.

Rule 1.9 exempts from protection any confidences that may or must be revealed pursuant to other rules. So, for example, if a former client sues a lawyer for malpractice, the lawyer is permitted under Rule 1.6(b)(3) to reveal confidential information to the extent necessary to defend herself against the action. Also, as explained in Chapter 3, a lawyer is not barred from all use of client confidences, just from uses that would adversely impact the client on whose behalf the lawyer learned them.

Rule 1.9(c) includes one additional exception to the mandate to protect confidences of former clients. If the information received in confidence has since become generally known, the lawyer must keep the information confidential but is not barred from using the information adversely to the client.

PROBLEM 7-2 A DYSFUNCTIONAL FAMILY BUSINESS

This problem is loosely based on a case that arose in a southern state.

For many years, you represented a family-owned retail clothing business. The business consisted of two corporations created after the family's patriarch Henry Elliston Rice Jr. bequeathed his assets to his sons. One corporation was called "HER, Inc." (This company name is derived from the founder's initials.) The other was called HER Fashions, Inc. HER, Inc. owned a factory and three retail clothing outlets. HER Fashions, Inc. owned a larger factory and one retail clothing outlet.

Until a few years ago, two brothers, Henry Elliston Rice III and Joseph Rice, jointly owned both corporations. At the time, they were on good terms. You were the general counsel for both corporations, and each paid half your salary. Among other things, you handled an application to register a trademark consisting of a drawing of a fashionably dressed teenage girl that was the company emblem. The trademarks were issued in the name of HER, Inc., but the public was unaware that there were two separate companies and thought that there was simply a company called "HER." The drawing became the recognized symbol of both companies.

The original concept for these two companies, which started in the 1960s, was to design and manufacture tasteful and stylish clothing for girls and women aged 15 to 30. Henry III was distressed by the styles (ranging from way-too-short skirts to disheveled rags) prevalent in the '60s. He wanted to provide a positive alternative. More recently, his brother Joseph began authorizing production of clothing designs that featured bare midriffs and outerwear that looked like underwear. Henry was horrified; he felt that Joseph was undermining the entire purpose of the business. After many attempts to work out these problems, the brothers decided they had to split the business.

In the wake of the fraternal dispute, the family business was reorganized. Henry obtained ownership of HER, Inc., which still owned the smaller factory and two of the retail outlets. Joseph obtained sole ownership of HER Fashions, Inc., which now owned the other factory and the other two retail outlets.

When the company split, you realized that with so much enmity and rivalry between the brothers, you could not represent both companies. You resigned as general counsel of HER, Inc. (Henry's company) but continued as general counsel of HER Fashions, Inc. (Joseph's company).

After the split, both corporations continued using the HER trademarks, although at the time of the split, there had been no discussion of whether both companies would continue to use them. Henry just assumed that Joseph would commission a new logo for HER Fashions. But Joseph, being aware of the good reputation and brand-name recognition of HER, continued to use the registered drawing.

Then Henry's company sued Joseph's company for an injunction to prohibit HER Fashions from using the trademark. In this lawsuit, you entered your appearance as the lawyer for HER Fashions, the defendant. Henry's new lawyer telephoned you immediately and asked you to withdraw from representing Joseph's company. He claimed that your participation would violate Rule 1.9. He said that if you refused to withdraw, he would move to disqualify you. But Joseph has told you that using the logo is very important to his business, and he very much wants you to help him fight the suit.

Must you withdraw?

If a lawyer moves from one firm to another, may the lawyer reveal a certain amount of information about her former clients or her former firm's clients to the new firm for the purpose of doing a conflicts check?

Yes, at least in many cases. The new firm hiring a lateral lawyer is obliged to check whether that lawyer's prior work, and sometimes her firm's prior work, conflicts with the obligations owed to clients of the lawyer's new firm. Likewise, the lateral lawyer must ensure that she does not take on representation that conflicts with her obligations to her former clients. Rule 1.9(c) points out that a lawyer is not permitted to make adverse use of or to reveal confidences of former clients except if the revelation is permitted under the rules or if the information has become generally known.

Professor Paul Tremblay identifies five types of information that a lawyer entering a new firm might have and that the new firm might want to obtain:

> (1) the identity of those clients whom the lateral has represented in the past; (2) the nature of the work she did for those clients; (3) the identity of clients of the lateral's prior firm whom she did not represent but about whom she learned information; (4) the information she learned about her firm's clients; and (5) the amount of money the lateral earned from her prior clients, especially those who might follow her to the new firm.[69]

Tremblay concludes that some revelations are necessary to accomplish adequate conflicts checks, that other revelations are impermissible, and that guidance to distinguish among these types of revelations is inadequate. He

---

69. Paul R. Tremblay, Migrating Lawyers and the Ethics of Conflict Checking, 19 Geo. J. Leg. Ethics 489 (2006). In the next section, we explain how problems involving screening and confidentiality arise with respect to work that an employee did before becoming a lawyer.

urges some changes in the rules that would provide better direction for lateral lawyers and their new firms to do conflicts checking when they are hiring new lawyers.[70] In the meantime, lateral lawyers and their hiring firms might look to Professor Tremblay's analysis of these issues for guidance.

G. Imputation of former client conflicts to affiliated lawyers

In Chapter 5, we examined conflicts between current clients and the imputation of such conflicts from one lawyer in a firm to another. Here we address a related question: To what extent are conflicts caused by work done for former clients imputed to other lawyers in a firm?

Rule 1.10 (which we also encountered in Chapter 5 when we considered current conflicts) explains the rules on imputation for private sector lawyers. (Rule 1.11 covers government lawyers, for whom slightly different standards apply.) The general rule stated in Rule 1.10 is that if one lawyer in a firm is disqualified from working on a matter because of a conflict, none of the other lawyers in the firm is permitted to work on the matter either, unless one of the exceptions listed in Rule 1.10 applies. One of those exceptions allows the use of a screening procedure to avoid imputation to a firm of conflicts of a lateral lawyer. Many state ethics codes also permit screening under some conditions to avoid otherwise impermissible conflicts.

What are all the situations in which the Model Rules permit screening?

The Model Rules allow screening in six situations:

1. where a lawyer has moved from one firm to another (Rule 1.10(a)(2));
2. where one lawyer in a firm has a conflict that is based on a personal interest (family, political, financial) that does not present a significant risk of materially impacting the other lawyers' representation of the client (Rule 1.10(a)(1));
3. where a former nonlawyer employee has become a lawyer (Rule 1.10, Comment 4);
4. where a former government lawyer entered a law firm (Rule 1.11, discussed in Chapter 9);

---

70. Id.

5. where a lawyer received confidential information from a prospective client who did not become an actual client (Rule 1.18, discussed in Chapter 5); and

6. where a lawyer is disqualified from working on a matter because the lawyer previously worked on the matter as a judge, a law clerk, an arbitrator, a mediator, or in some similar role (Rule 1.12).

The most important of these screening rules is Rule 1.10(a)(2), which allows a firm to erect a screen around a lateral lawyer — one who has come from another firm — to avoid imputing to the new firm conflicts stemming from the work of the lawyer at the lawyer's former firm.

When did the ABA incorporate language into Rule 1.10 allowing screening in some cases?

The rules have allowed screening to avoid imputation of conflicts of former government lawyers for a long time. Use of screening to avoid imputation in other circumstances has been the subject of bitter controversy in the ABA for many years. The Ethics 2000 Commission proposed language to allow screening for "personal interest" conflicts and for conflicts of lateral lawyers. This was prompted because of the multiplying problems experienced by law firms who hired lateral lawyers, and because by then, many states had modified their rules to allow screening in these instances. However, Lawrence J. Fox, a partner at Drinker, Biddle & Reath, proposed an amendment to delete the language allowing screening of lateral lawyers from Rule 1.10. He argued that if screening is allowed, "the client gets no choice at all when a lawyer goes to a firm on the other side."[71] The ABA House of Delegates approved the Fox amendment and rejected screening of laterals by a vote of 176 to 130,[72] declining to adopt the recommendation of the Ethics 2000 Commission. The ABA did, however, adopt the language permitting screening to avoid personal interest conflicts.[73]

Discussion and debate over whether and when to allow screening continued. Finally, at its 2009 midyear meeting, the House of Delegates adopted the current language of Rule 1.10, which allows screening for lateral lawyers. The central change in 2009 was the addition of 1.10(a)(2), which allows screening to prevent imputation of lateral lawyers' conflicts. This means that the lawyer's new firm need not seek informed consent from the lateral lawyer's former clients, but under the rule, the firm is required to

---

71. Model Rules: ABA Stands Firm on Client Confidentiality, Rejects "Screening" for Conflicts of Interest, ABA/BNA Laws.' Man. on Prof. Conduct 17:492 (Aug. 15, 2001).

72. Id.

73. ABA, A Legislative History: The Development of the ABA Model Rules of Professional Conduct, 1982-2005, at 250-258 (ABA 2006).

provide detailed notice of its screening procedures to the relevant former client.

Are the state rules the same as the new Model Rule 1.10?

As you know, many states use the Model Rules as a basis for their own rules, but many states adopted screening language long before the ABA rule was amended to do so. Other states adopted some version of Rule 1.10 after 2009. At least 25 states have versions of Rule 1.10 to allow law firms to avoid imputation of conflicts presented by the previous work of a lateral lawyer by "screening" the conflicted lawyer from any contact with the matter that presents the problem.[74] In these jurisdictions, if an adequate screening process has been implemented, and the firm has complied with any notice requirements to former clients, the firm may proceed with a matter that would present an imputed conflict.

Do the state rules on imputation of conflicts apply in federal courts?

Not always. Some federal courts have ruled that if the firm can demonstrate that effective screening mechanisms are in place, the firm can avoid being disqualified because of an imputed conflict. A federal court may apply the relevant state ethics rule or it may apply common law standards that are independent of the ethics code. Some federal courts have permitted screening as a remedy for imputed disqualification even if the state ethics code does not allow this.[75] A California appellate court also has recognized screening as a valid basis to avoid imputed disqualification of a firm based on the prior work of a lateral lawyer.[76]

Despite the many variations on the rules on screening lateral lawyers, our primary focus here is on the Model Rules. Therefore, we move on now to a close examination of Rule 1.10 and how it works.

---

74. As of 2011, these states are among those that permit screening to avoid imputation of conflicts in at least some cases: Arizona, Illinois, Maine, Massachusetts, Michigan, Minnesota, Nebraska, New Jersey, North Carolina, Ohio, Oregon, Pennsylvania, South Carolina, Tennessee, Washington, and Wisconsin. No state has yet adopted the precise language of amended Rule 1.10. See Stephen Gillers, Roy D. Simon & Andrew M. Perlman, Regulation of Lawyers: Statutes and Standards 149-152 (Wolters Kluwer 2011); Susan R. Martyn, Lawrence J. Fox & W. Bradley Wendel, State Lawyer Code Screening Rules that Prevent Imputed Disqualification, in The Law Governing Lawyers: National Rules, Standards, Statutes, and State Lawyer Codes 120-123 (Wolters Kluwer 2010-2011 ed.); Wash. R. Prof. Conduct 1.10 (2011) (available at http://www.courts.wa.gov/court_rules/?fa=court_rules.display&group=ga&set=rpc&ruleid=garpc1.10).

75. See Conflicts of Interest: Lawyer's Substantial Work at Former Firm Doesn't Prevent Screening in Federal Case, ABA/BNA Laws.' Man. on Prof. Conduct 26:632 (Oct. 27, 2010), 2010 WL 4214670.

76. See Joan C. Rogers, California Court Recognizes Ethics Screens as a Method of Avoiding Firms' Disqualification, 78 U.S.L.W. 1655 (Apr. 27, 2010).

Rule 1.10 Imputation of Conflicts of Interest: General Rule*

Rule language**	Authors' explanation***
(a) **While lawyers are associated in a firm**, **none** of them **shall** knowingly **represent a client when any one of them practicing alone would be prohibited from doing so by Rules 1.7 or 1.9**, *unless*	This section states the general rule that if one lawyer in a firm is barred by Rule 1.7 or 1.9 from handling a matter, then everyone else in the firm is barred as well, unless one of the exceptions below applies.
(1) the prohibition is based on a **personal interest** of the disqualified lawyer *and* **does not present a significant risk of materially limiting the representation** of the client by the remaining lawyers in the firm; or	This first exemption from the general imputation rule states that a conflict is not imputed if it involves a personal interest of the lawyer and does not threaten client loyalty or protection of confidences. Comment 3. Examples of lawyers' personal interests are strong political beliefs antagonistic to the goals of a client being represented by the firm or a family relationship with a party who is in litigation against a client of the firm.
(2) the prohibition is **based upon Rule 1.9(a) or (b) and arises out of the disqualified lawyer's association with a prior firm**, *and*	The second exemption applies *only* to conflicts that involve the work a lateral lawyer did at a former firm or the work that other lawyers did at the former firm. In these cases, the firm may proceed without seeking the informed consent of the former client if it complies with the screening and notification conditions listed below.[77] *Note:* Screening is not permitted under this rule as a solution to any conflict that involves two present clients of a firm or one present client and one former client of a firm.
(i) the **disqualified lawyer is timely screened from any participation** in the matter	Rule 1.0(k) explains that the word "screened" "denotes the isolation of a lawyer from any participation in a matter through the timely imposition of procedures within a firm that are reasonably adequate under the circumstances to protect information that the isolated lawyer is obligated to protect under these Rules or other law."[78]
and is apportioned no part of the fee therefrom;	Comment 8 explains that this "does not prohibit the screened lawyer from receiving

---

77. Comment 7 after Rule 1.10 refers to this language in 1.0(k) as "a description of effective screening mechanisms."

78. A conflict that would adversely affect a former client might, of course, also involve adverse impact on a present client. The impact on the present client is evaluated under Rule 1.7; on account of that impact, the lawyer might need to seek the current client's consent. See Chapter 5.

Rule language**	Authors' explanation***
	a salary or partnership share established by prior independent agreement," but she may not receive "compensation directly related to the matter."
(ii) **written notice is promptly given to any affected former client** to enable the former client to ascertain compliance with the provisions of this Rule, which **shall include a description of the screening procedures** employed; a **statement of the firm's and of the screened lawyer's compliance** with these Rules; a statement that **review may be available before a tribunal**; and an agreement by the firm to respond promptly to any written inquiries or objections by the former client about the screening procedures; and	Comment 9 explains that this notice "should include a description of the screened lawyer's prior representation and be given as soon as practicable after the need for screening becomes apparent. It also should include a statement by the screened lawyer and the firm that the client's material confidential information has not been disclosed or used in violation of the Rules."
(iii) **certifications of compliance** with these Rules and with the screening procedures are **provided to the former client** by the screened lawyer and by a partner of the firm, **at reasonable intervals upon the former client's written request** and **upon termination of the screening procedures**.	Comment 10 says these certifications will "give the former client assurance that the client's material confidential information has not been disclosed or used inappropriately, either prior to timely implementation of a screen or thereafter. If compliance cannot be certified, the certificate must describe the failure to comply."
(b) **When a lawyer has terminated an association with a firm**, the firm is not prohibited from thereafter representing a person with interests **materially adverse to those of a client represented by the formerly associated lawyer** and not currently represented by the firm, **unless:**	If a lawyer leaves a firm, his former firm should use this rule to evaluate new business that conflicts with the former lawyer's work at the firm. Conflict leaves the firm with the lawyer unless:
(1) the matter is **the same or substantially related** to that in which the formerly associated lawyer represented the client; and	the matter is the same or substantially related and
(2) **any lawyer** remaining in the firm has **information protected by Rules 1.6 and 1.9(c) that is material** to the matter.	a remaining lawyer knows material confidential information.
(c) A disqualification prescribed by this rule **may be waived** by the affected client under the conditions stated in Rule 1.7.	Most imputed conflicts may be waived. See Comment 6.

Continued

Rule language**	Authors' explanation***
(d) The disqualification of lawyers associated in a firm with the former or current government lawyers is governed by Rule 1.11.	

*This will be the text of Connecticut Rule 1.10 if the state's court system accepts the 2011 unanimous recommendation of the House of Delegates of the Connecticut Bar Association. See Wick Chambers, House of Delegates Votes Unanimously in Favor of ABA Model Rule 1.10, http://forctlawyers.com/?p=4102 (June 21, 2011) (Rule 1.10(a) as proposed to be amended) and Conn. Rules of Prof. Conduct, http://www.jud.ct.gov/Publications/PracticeBook/PB_2011.pdf#page=29 (Rule 1.10(b) through (d), to which no amendments are proposed). It is identical to Model Rule 1.10. The Connecticut comments diverge from the comments after the Model Rule, but our authors' explanations refer to the comments after Model Rule 1.10.

**All emphasis added.

***This and other authors' explanations draw from the comments to the rules and from other sources. They are not comprehensive but highlight some important interpretive points.

When a lawyer moves from one firm to another, are all of her former client conflicts imputed to the lawyers in the new firm?

To understand how conflicts may travel with a lawyer who changes firms, consider a variant of the problem we encountered earlier. Hank, the lawyer in the hypothetical situation posed at the very beginning of this section, used to work at the firm of Barr & Thornburgh. Barr & Thornburgh represented The Toy Chest in employment matters, and it still does so. Hank didn't work on any Toy Chest matters. However, Hank often chatted with his colleagues about their cases. Suppose that Hank learned in passing that one of the personnel managers at The Toy Chest, who later left the company, believed that women were good cashiers and wholesale buyers but were poor executives. Now Hank works at Reno & Days. The Reno firm has been asked to represent Jenny in a suit against her former employer, The Toy Chest. The firm would like several of its other lawyers (but not Hank) to work on Jenny's case. Hank has never discussed any Toy Chest matters with the lawyers who would work on the case, and he doesn't plan to do so. May Reno & Days accept Jenny as a client?

> T1:
> Hank works for B & T.
> Other B & T lawyers defend The Toy Chest in employment cases.
> Hank knows about these cases but does not work on them.
> T2:
> Hank works for R & D.
> R & D wants its lawyers — but not Hank — to sue The Toy Chest for the wrongful discharge of prospective client Jenny.
> Hank has not discussed The Toy Chest with these lawyers.

Whether Reno & Days may represent Jenny depends on whether the firm is in a jurisdiction that allows a firm to screen off a lateral lawyer to avoid imputation of a conflict based on the lawyer's work at his former firm or based on the work of others at the former firm. If the Model Rules apply in the jurisdiction where this firm is located, the analysis would go this way:

- Hank probably would be prohibited from representing Jenny because, under Rule 1.9(b), one would conclude that Hank's former firm represented a client (Toy Chest) in a substantially related matter (other employment matters), Toy Chest's interests are materially adverse to Jenny's, and Hank arguably acquired confidential information about Toy Chest matters that might be used adversely to Toy Chest on behalf of Jenny. Therefore, probably Hank could not represent Jenny unless Toy Chest gave informed consent.

- Under Rule 1.10(a), no one at Reno & Days may represent a client when any one of them practicing alone would be prohibited from doing so, unless one of the exceptions in (a) applies.

- The conflict here is not a "personal interest" conflict but a former firm's former client conflict, so Rule 1.10(a)(1) is inapplicable.

- Rule 1.10(a)(2) applies here because the prohibition is based on Rule 1.9(b) and arises out of the disqualified lawyer's association with a prior firm. Therefore, the firm may represent Jenny without seeking the consent of Toy Chest if it complies with the requirements in (2) that Hank be screened from participation, that he be apportioned no part of the fee, and that the firm and Hank complete the written notice and certification of compliance required by the rule.

This analysis addresses whether the firm must obtain informed consent from Hank's former firm's former client, Toy Chest, before accepting representation of Jenny. In addition, one should consider the unlikely possibility that Hank's presence in the firm would adversely affect the representation of Jenny, which then would require her informed consent as well. This question would be evaluated by application of Rule 1.7.[79]

What is a "firm" for the purpose of imputing conflicts?

This rule applies to lawyers in a "firm." A comment explains that this term includes "lawyers in a law partnership, professional corporation, sole proprietorship or other association" as well as "lawyers employed in a legal services organization or the legal department of a corporation or other organization."[80] This rule applies to firms of two lawyers, firms of 1,500 lawyers, and firms with offices in many cities or on different continents.

---

79. See Rule 1.10, Comment 6.
80. Rule 1.10, Comment 1.

The conflicts of a lawyer in Chicago are imputed to another lawyer in the Hong Kong office of the same firm. This remains so even if the Chicago lawyer and the Hong Kong lawyer have never spoken, practice in different fields, represent different clients, and will never come into contact with one another. The imputation of conflicts to all lawyers in the same firm multiplies the number of conflicts that must be evaluated and for which consent must be sought. The larger the firm, the larger the number of conflicts. Most firms use computer software, which may be one component of a practice management system,[81] among other methods, to identify actual or potential conflicts.

Lawyers who have separate practices but who share office space may be considered a law firm for conflicts purposes if their file management and communication might permit one lawyer in a suite to have access to confidential information about a matter being handled by another lawyer.[82] Rule 1.10 governs all practicing lawyers except those who work for governments.[83]

What kinds of steps are needed to effectively screen off one lawyer from a matter that he is disqualified from working on?

What is needed to erect an effective screen varies from one situation to another and from one jurisdiction to another. The question for each case is whether the procedures adopted are "reasonably adequate under the circumstances to protect information that the isolated lawyer is obligated to protect."[84] The Massachusetts Rules of Professional Conduct offer a more detailed set of criteria to use in erecting a screen than do most other rules. They state that

> **a firm will be deemed to have been screened from any participation in a matter if:**
>
> **(1) all material information which the personally disqualified lawyer [PDL] has has been isolated from the firm;**
>
> **(2) the [PDL] has been isolated from all contact with the client relating to the matter, and any witness for or against the client;**
>
> **(3) the [PDL] and the firm have been precluded from discussing the matter with each other;**
>
> **(4) the former client of the [PDL] or [his former firm] . . . receives notice of the conflict and an affidavit of the [PDL] and**

---

81. See ABA, FYI: Conflict Checking, http://www.americanbar.org/groups/departments_offices/legal_technology_resources/resources/charts_fyis/coninterestfyi.html (accessed Nov. 14, 2012).

82. Rule 1.10, Comment 1.

83. The imputation rules for government lawyers are stated in Rule 1.11.

84. Rule 1.0(k).

the firm describing the procedures being used effectively to screen the [PDL], and attesting that (i) the [PDL] will not participate in the matter and will not discuss the matter or the representation with any other lawyer or employee of his or her current firm, (ii) no material information was transmitted by the [PDL] before implementation of the screening procedures and notice to the former client; and (iii) during the period of the lawyer's personal disqualification those lawyers or employees who do participate in the matter will be apprised that the [PDL] is screened from participating in or discussing the matter; and

(5) the [PDL] and the firm with which he is associated reasonably believe that the steps taken to accomplish the screening of material information are likely to be effective in preventing material information from being disclosed to the firm and its client.[85]

A California decision identified six factors that can help to make a screen of a lateral lawyer effective:

1. Isolation of the tainted attorney through physical, geographic, and departmental separation.
2. Prohibitions against discussion of the confidential information.
3. Establishment of rules and procedures to prevent access to confidential information and files.
4. Establishment of rules and procedures to prevent a disqualified attorney from sharing profits in the representation.
5. The absence of any supervisory relationship between the tainted attorney and the lawyers involved in the current matter.
6. Notice to the former client.[86]

The California judge mentioned that a careful analysis of the effectiveness of a screen cannot best be evaluated by a list of criteria, but must focus on "whether the court is satisfied that the tainted attorney has not had and will not have any improper communication with others at the firm concerning the litigation."[87]

---

85. Mass. R. Prof. Conduct 1.10(e), http://www.mass.gov/obcbbo/rpc1.htm# (accessed Nov. 13, 2012).

86. Joan Rogers, Opinion Mulls Elements of Effective Screening to Deal with Lateral Conflicts, ABA/BNA Laws.' Man. on Prof. Conduct 26:241 (Apr. 14, 2010) (describing Kirk v. First Am. Title Ins. Co., Cal. Ct. App. No. B218956 (Apr. 7, 2010)).

87. Id.

Can clients waive imputed conflicts?

Yes. Rule 1.10 explains that a conflict imputed to one lawyer from another may be resolved by obtaining the informed consent of the affected client to the new representation. The analysis for waiver of imputed conflicts is the same as that for concurrent conflicts under Rule 1.7(b). (See discussions of conflict waiver in Chapters 5 and 6.) If an imputed conflict is waivable, the lawyer must make the appropriate disclosures and the necessary consent must be in writing.

If law clerks, paralegals, or law students change jobs, are conflicts presented by their previous employment imputed to their new firms?

This is another situation in which screening is permitted to solve a conflicts problem.[88] Conflicts are not imputed to a firm from nonlawyer employees of the firm so long as employees who have previously done conflicting work are properly screened by the firm. Comment 4 following Rule 1.10 explains:

> The rule in paragraph (a) also does not prohibit representation by others in the law firm where the person prohibited from involvement in a matter is a nonlawyer, such as a paralegal or legal secretary. Nor does paragraph (a) prohibit representation if the lawyer is prohibited from acting because of events before the person became a lawyer, for example, work that the person did as a law student. Such persons, however, ordinarily must be screened from any personal participation in the matter to avoid communication to others in the firm of confidential information that both the nonlawyers and the firm have a legal duty to protect.

In a jurisdiction that follows this guidance, a law firm should request information about a nonlawyer employee's previous work so that it can check whether there are conflicts with current work and have a database through which to identify conflicts with clients who come to the firm after the nonlawyer employee arrives. If such conflicts are identified, the erection of a screen appears to be considered an adequate safeguard to prevent the nonlawyer from revealing confidences learned during previous employment.[89] However, it is not always a simple matter for a law firm to learn even the names of the clients formerly served by a prospective lawyer employee when she worked as a law student (in a clinic or part-time job) or paralegal. The employee may not remember the names of her clinic or law firm's clients. In some cases, revelation of the names may violate Rule 1.6 or create risks for the former clients. For example, the revelation of the name of a former client for whom a law student had obtained political asylum

---

88. Rule 1.10, Comment 4.
89. See Tremblay, supra n. 69.

could jeopardize relatives of that client who were still in the client's country.[90]

Suppose a law firm in a jurisdiction that does not permit screening tries to screen a newly hired, conflicted lawyer to avoid an imputed conflict. Or suppose a firm in a state that does allow screening erects an insufficient screen. What consequences could be expected?

Bar discipline is unlikely unless the new lawyer actually revealed confidential information. Professor Andrew Perlman reports that "[t]here is rarely, if ever, discipline for the mere deployment of a screen in the lateral attorney context, even when such a screen is found not to be authorized by the relevant conflicts rule."[91] But the conflicted lawyer's former client may move to disqualify the new firm from representing that former client. If the motion is successful, the effort could cost the new firm's client a great deal of time and money because the client would have to retain a new firm and bring it up to speed. The disqualified firm could lose a substantial fee. Professor Perlman notes, however, that when courts consider motions to disqualify lawyers for inadequately screening lawyers who have moved laterally, they usually apply their own judge-made standards rather than those of Rule 1.10 to assess the adequacy of the screen.[92]

PROBLEM 7-3 THE FIRM'S NEW PARTNER

This problem is based on events that occurred in an eastern city in 2010.

Leonard Toll was a lawyer at Masters & Schon, LLP, which had 250 lawyers. He was the senior associate representing Galaxy Recordings, Inc., a recording company that was suing Hipster, LLC, an Internet file-sharing company, for damages. Hipster's website allowed customers to download and share their music files, allegedly violating Galaxy's copyrights, cutting its profits, and reducing its artists' royalties. Toll spent hundreds of hours on the case and learned a great deal about Galaxy's business and its litigation strategies. Three and a half years ago, while the suit was pending, Toll left the Masters firm and became a partner at Parks, Foster &

---

90. These issues are explored in Tremblay, supra n. 69.

91. Andrew Perlman, Civil Procedure and the Legal Profession: The Parallel Law of Lawyering in Civil Litigation, 79 Fordham L. Rev. 1965, 1971 n. 59 (2011).

92. According to Perlman, because the screening guidelines in Rule 1.10(a)(2) are not in practice enforced either by disciplinary bodies or by the courts in disqualification disputes, they "ha[ve] become less law-like and no longer suppl[y] lawyers with adequate guidance regarding their conduct." Id. at 1971.

Bane, a firm with more than 500 lawyers. Soon thereafter, Galaxy Recordings decided to switch counsel. It hired O'Malley & Associates.

One year later, Avon Winters, president of Hipster, contacted Morton Bane, a partner at the Parks firm, Toll's new employer. Winters knew nothing of Toll or his new employment. Winters told Bane he was unhappy with Hipster's current representation; he asked Bane to consider accepting his company as a client. Bane agreed to investigate possible conflicts to see whether the Parks firm could take over representing Hipster in this matter. Bane mentioned the possible case to Toll. Toll explained the significant role he had played in representing Galaxy in the Hipster matter, but he did not reveal any client confidences. Toll and Bane agreed that they would not discuss the matter any further. Bane did not follow the firm's usual practice of entering the names of Galaxy or Hipster into its conflicts database. Winters continued to shop around for new counsel and did not then hire the Parks firm to represent Hipster.

A year and a half later, the case was still in litigation. Winters approached Bane again about possibly representing Hipster. The two men agreed that the Parks firm would take over the defense of the case. Bane did not mention that Toll was now a partner in the Parks firm, but he remembered his prior conversation with Toll, so he notified Toll that the firm was going to represent Hipster.

Six weeks later, Bane circulated a memo to the lawyers who would be working on the Hipster matter. Bane wrote that Toll had been "walled off from the *Galaxy v. Hipster* matter" and said that no communications concerning Hipster should occur when Toll was present. Bane filled out the firm's "new case" form. The form asked, "Are there any conflicts concerns?" Bane checked the "no" box.

Three weeks later, the document manager of Parks, Foster & Bane sent Bane an e-mail: "Just a reminder: I'm expecting a memo from you to wall off Leonard Toll from a current matter, but I haven't yet received it." Bane instructed the manager to exclude Toll from all e-mails or other correspondence relating to Hipster. The next day, the firm's records department created an electronic and paper "wall" so that Toll would not see any documents relating to Hipster. Even so, on one occasion, an electronic folder of documents labeled "Hipster" appeared on Toll's computer screen, but he did not open it to see the documents it contained.

Bane chatted again with Toll about his work for Galaxy in his former job. Toll said it was so long ago now that he could not remember anything of substance about the case. At this point, Bane circulated a memo to all the lawyers explaining that the firm was representing Hipster in the Galaxy litigation and that there were no conflict concerns. He also sent a memo to the five lawyers working on the Galaxy case, reminding them not to discuss the case with Toll. Still, no entry was made in the conflicts database.

You are the newly hired ethics counsel at Parks, Foster & Bane. You just started work in this newly created position. One of the junior associates working on the Galaxy case has come to see you to discuss the memo she just received from Bane. She said "I'm not sure that the firm is in compliance with the ethics code. I was just wondering if you could review the situation and see if we are okay."

You interviewed the people involved in the Hipster matter, and you interviewed Toll. You have now learned the facts stated above.

1. Why does this matter? Why might Galaxy care that its former lawyer is now working for the law firm representing Hipster?
2. Has Toll or the firm done anything that contradicts the mandates of Rule 1.7, 1.9, or 1.10?
3. Do you have guidance to offer the firm as to additional steps it should take?

If lawyers are sharing office space but are not part of the same law firm, are conflicts imputed among them?

If lawyers are practicing as a law firm, it is obvious that the imputation rules apply among them. It doesn't matter whether the firm is organized as a partnership, a professional corporation, a limited liability corporation, or in some other way. It doesn't matter whether the lawyers involved are partners, associates, or counsel. It doesn't even matter whether one lawyer is the most senior partner in the New York office and the other lawyer is the most junior associate in the Moscow office.[93] If they are practicing in a firm, their conflicts are imputed to one another to the same extent as if they were in the same firm.

But some lawyers share office space without any formal association of their practices. One advisory opinion notes that lawyers who share office space

- should not leave confidential client files in unlocked file cabinets or storage areas;
- must ensure that any common staff members preserve confidences (apparently to prevent sharing each lawyer's confidential information with the other lawyer); and

---

93. Westinghouse Elec. Corp. v. Kerr-McGee Corp., 580 F.2d 1311 (7th Cir. 1978).

■ must protect the confidences of each of their clients from each other, because they are not in fact partners. If they consult about case matters, they must do so without revealing client identity.[94]

When a lawyer has left a firm, are her conflicts still imputed to her former firm?

Suppose that while she was at firm A, a lawyer named Allyson represented a printing company called Ink, Inc. When she moves to firm B, Ink wants her to continue as its lawyer, so it moves its legal business to firm B. After Allyson and Ink are gone, can firm A accept work that would conflict with the interests of Ink?

Rule 1.10(b) addresses this question. The analysis is conceptually similar to analysis prescribed by Rule 1.9(b). Firm A can take on a new client whose interests are materially adverse to those of Ink, unless the matter is substantially related to the work that Allyson did for Ink while at firm A and a lawyer who still works at firm A has material confidential information learned in connection with the work done for Ink. In that case, consent is required. In both cases, lawyers in the firm that seek to take on the new work should determine whether there is (a) material adversity, (b) substantial relationship, and (c) possession of material confidences by a lawyer in the firm. If the answer is yes to all three questions, the firm can't take on the work without the consent of the affected client.

Many lawyers and law students find these two rules maddeningly similar and therefore very confusing. One antidote to this confusion is to reread Rules 1.9(b) and 1.10(b) and then reread the two preceding paragraphs. Focus on *when* each of these rules applies. Both rules deal with conflicts precipitated by a lawyer changing jobs. Rule 1.9(b) examines whether the lawyer brings the old firm's conflicts with her. Rule 1.10(b) looks at whether the old firm retains the conflicts created by the work of the moving lawyer. This point may be diagrammed as follows:

Lawyer moves from firm A to firm B. The lawyer does not bring any clients with him.

To analyze conflicts the lawyer carries with him **into firm B** based on confidences learned at firm A: 1.9(b).

To analyze conflicts that other lawyers at firm B may have because of the lawyer's work at firm A: 1.10(a).

To analyze conflicts **remaining at firm A** as a result of work the lawyer did while there: 1.10(b).

---

94. D.C. B. Op. 303 (2001).

8 CONFLICTS BETWEEN LAWYERS AND CLIENTS

A. **Legal fees**
   1. Lawyer-client fee contracts
   2. Regulation of hourly billing and billing for expenses
   3. Contingent fees
   4. Forbidden and restricted fee and expense arrangements
   5. Fee disputes
   6. Dividing fees with other firms or with nonlawyers
   7. Payment of fees by a third party

B. **Lawyer as custodian of client property and documents**
   1. Client trust accounts
   2. Responsibility for client property
   3. Administering estates and trusts

C. **Conflicts with lawyers' personal or business interests**
   1. In general
   2. Business transactions between lawyer and client
   3. Gifts from clients
   4. Sexual relationships with clients
   5. Intimate or family relationships with adverse lawyers
   6. Imputation of lawyer-client conflicts to other lawyers in a firm

*"My fees are quite high, and yet you say you have little money.
I think I'm seeing a conflict of interest here."*

Lawyers encounter conflicting interests nearly as often as they breathe. Hypothetically, a lawyer who wanted to avoid possible conflicts with other present or former clients might represent only one client for his entire career. In addition, to avoid possible conflicts between the client's interests and the lawyer's *own* interests, the lawyer might

- work for the client without charging a fee, since fee agreements involve some level of conflict between the interests of the lawyer and those of the client (the lawyer wants to be paid more, the client wants to pay less);
- avoid any acquisitions of property from or business arrangements with the client, or with anyone whose property or business interests might have some impact on the client; or
- make no other time commitments to activities such as family vacations or hobbies that might interfere with the lawyer's ability to devote his full attention to the client's interests.

The point is that lawyers encounter conflicts between their interests and the interests of clients all the time. The ethical rules, liability rules, and disqualification rules on conflicts of interest tend to identify certain conflicts that may harm the representation of a client or the client's interests. A lawyer must learn the law on conflicts of interest, but also must develop sensitivity to the whole spectrum of possible conflicts of interest that are not discussed in formal rules. A lawyer is not expected to forgo having a family, taking vacations, or representing other clients to avoid conflicts of interest. However, a lawyer is expected to be aware of and attentive to the constant collision of these various competing interests and to exercise judgment about how she juggles them. It is the essence of professionalism to exercise care, judgment, and restraint that goes far beyond the boundaries set by ethical or legal rules.

In this chapter, we explore some of the possible conflicts between the interests of client and lawyer. Many of these problems involve lawyers' pursuit of financial self-interest by setting fees without adequate consultation with or disclosure to clients. Some situations involve deliberate theft and deception. Some involve standard practices in contracting between lawyers and clients that allow lawyers almost unfettered discretion in setting fees. And some involve business transactions between lawyers and their clients.

The first part of this chapter looks at lawyer-client fee contracts. It explains the types of fee arrangements lawyers use, the rules requiring that fees be reasonable, the principle that lawyers should communicate with clients about fees, and the requirements for modification of fee agreements. We then examine the developing law on regulation of lawyer billing practices and restrictions on use of contingent fees by lawyers. We consider some particular fee and expense arrangements that have been prohibited or restricted, such as providing financial assistance to clients during representation. Then we discuss the law relating to fee disputes between lawyers and clients, collection of fees by lawyers, the rules governing division of fees between lawyers who are not in the same firm, limits on fee-sharing with nonlawyers, and restrictions on payment of legal fees by someone other than the client.

The second part of the chapter looks at rules governing lawyers who have custody of clients' documents or property. We discuss the rules on management of client trust accounts, on duties relating to client property, and on administration of estates and trusts for clients.

The final part of the chapter examines other conflicts between the interests of lawyers and clients. We explain the restrictions on business transactions, gifts, and sexual relationships between lawyers and clients; the handling of situations in which two opposing lawyers are family members; and the imputation of lawyer-client conflicts to other lawyers in a firm.

A. Legal fees

1. Lawyer-client fee contracts

When a client hires a lawyer to represent him, the client and the lawyer enter into a contract. The contract may involve a formal written agreement, or it may involve a conversation followed by a perfunctory letter in which the lawyer confirms how much she will charge for each hour of her time. Regardless of whether the terms are written or even stated, hiring a lawyer creates a contract that is subject to all the usual rules of contract law. If the client fails to pay the fee, the lawyer may sue the client for breach of contract. Likewise, if the lawyer fails to do the work she was hired to do or does it poorly, the client may sue for breach of contract. If, in the course of making a contract, a lawyer deceives a client about the cost or nature of the service to be provided, the contract might be voidable for misrepresentation.[1]

In addition to the rules of contract law, lawyer-client fee contracts are governed by the relevant state ethics code. In bankruptcy, probate, public benefits, and other areas, additional rules are imposed about how billing is to be done and how much a lawyer may charge.[2]

a. Types of fee agreements

About 70 percent of legal services provided by American lawyers are billed on the basis of time spent.[3] Some firms charge only for lawyer time, but other firms also charge for the time of paralegals and secretaries. In personal injury cases, plaintiffs' lawyers often charge contingent fees in which the lawyer gets a percentage of the damages (if any) that are paid to the client. If the client receives no recovery, the lawyer gets nothing. In recent years, some lawyers have begun to experiment with other methods of billing. Some charge flat fees for certain standard services. Some use fee schedules in which specified fees are charged for particular tasks.

In recent years, corporate clients have become much more concerned about controlling expenditures on outside counsel fees. Some have adopted policies restricting what outside counsel may bill for. Some invite

---

1. Restatement (Second) of Contracts §§ 162, 164 (1981).

2. For example, federal law limits the fee that a lawyer may receive for helping a veteran to obtain benefits from the Department of Veterans Affairs. A fee greater than 33 1/3 percent of the past-due benefits awarded is presumed unreasonable and may be disallowed. 38 C.F.R. § 14.636(f) (2010).

3. William Ross, The Honest Hour: The Ethics of Time-Based Billing by Attorneys (Carolina Acad. Press 1996).

competitive bidding by law firms for various projects. Many corporations hire several different law firms to handle different matters. For an amusing parody of a fee negotiation between a corporate counsel and a lawyer, see Riverview Law, Cometh the Hour, http://www.youtube.com/watch?v= BfXhn3tf_vE&feature=plcp.

Individual clients typically have far less bargaining power in negotiating fee arrangements than institutional clients. When clients consult lawyers for the first time, the lawyers may inform new clients of their hourly rates. At that time, lawyers often require initial payments from clients against which the first hours will be charged. Despite the confusion, both the agreements that initiate most lawyer-client relationships and the initial fees that clients pay are usually called "retainers." Clients rarely question retainer fees or bargain about their size. Lawyers are not required to charge retainer fees, but charging for a certain number of hours in advance is common when a lawyer is going to be paid on the basis of time spent and the lawyer and client do not already have an ongoing relationship.

Lawyers often provide little information to individual clients about the projected cost of the service. It is difficult to predict how much time legal work will take, but this approach to fee contracts requires a client essentially to sign a blank check for legal services. A client who is unhappy with his legal bills could fire the lawyer and stop the meter, but hiring a replacement lawyer may increase the overall cost of the services sought. A new lawyer would have to learn the case afresh and might, in the long run, charge just as much as the previous lawyer. Many clients wind up feeling blindsided by the steep legal bills and angry that they were not given more information at the outset of the representation about the likely total cost.

b. Reasonable fees

The ethical rules impose a few "bright line" restrictions on legal fees, and case law imposes some additional boundaries, but lawyers have wide discretion in deciding how much to charge. Rule 1.5(a) requires that fees be reasonable and provides a shopping list of criteria that lawyers should use to evaluate whether they are charging reasonable fees.[4]

> **Rule 1.5(a)**
> **A lawyer shall not make an agreement for, charge, or collect an unreasonable fee or an unreasonable amount for expenses. The factors to be considered in determining the reasonableness of a fee include the following:**

---

4. The *Restatement (Third) of Law Governing Lawyers*, similarly, states that a lawyer may not charge a fee "larger than reasonable under the circumstances." Restatement § 34.

> **(1)** the time and labor required, the novelty and difficulty of the questions involved, and the skill requisite to perform the legal service properly;
>
> **(2)** the likelihood, if apparent to the client, that the acceptance of the particular employment will preclude other employment by the lawyer;
>
> **(3)** the fee customarily charged in the locality for similar legal services;
>
> **(4)** the amount involved and the results obtained;
>
> **(5)** the time limitations imposed by the client or by the circumstances;
>
> **(6)** the nature and length of the professional relationship with the client;
>
> **(7)** the experience, reputation, and ability of the lawyer or lawyers performing the services; and
>
> **(8)** whether the fee is fixed or contingent.

Lawyers have been disciplined for charging unreasonable fees, but the guidance offered by this rule makes it difficult for any lawyer to know whether a particular fee would violate the rule. In evaluating whether a fee is reasonable, the courts rely on various combinations among the eight factors listed.[5] The chart that follows offers some examples of cases in which fees have been found to violate Rule 1.5.

Unreasonable fees: A few examples

Fees have been found unreasonable:	For example:
if the lawyer charges a higher than usual rate because he is unfamiliar with the law and charges for the time of an assistant as if it were his own time.	**North Dakota, 2006:** An elderly client signed a retainer agreeing to pay a lawyer $275 per hour for "all attorney's time and services expended" to administer a simple estate mainly of cash. The lawyer's usual rate was about $200, but he charged more because he did not know the state's law. His assistant did some of the work, but the lawyer billed it as if it were his own time. The client did not object to the fees, but a beneficiary did. The lawyer was reprimanded and forced to disgorge about a third of his fee.[6]

---

5. ABA, Annotated Model Rules of Professional Conduct 68-69 (6th ed., ABA 2007).
6. Disc. Bd. v. Hellurd, 714 N.W.2d 38 (N.D. 2006).

Fees have been found unreasonable:	For example:
if the fee charged is disproportionate to the services provided.	**South Dakota, 2000:** A lawyer charged more than $47,000 for representing a client on a standard child custody and support matter.[7]
if the lawyer requires a client to have sex with him as part of his fee.	**Louisiana, 2004:** A lawyer tried to coerce a client facing a misdemeanor drug charge to have sex with him as a late payment fee. In a recorded conversation, he analogized his demand for sex "as a penalty fee, like, [on a] Discover card." The lawyer was suspended for two years. A dissenting judge noted that the lawyer and his client had previously had consensual sex.[8]
if the lawyer fabricates or inflates records of time or expenses, bills for time not worked, bills lawyer rates for nonlawyer work, or engages in other dishonesty about what the lawyer is billing for.	**Maryland, 1999:** A partner in a large law firm gave one important client a promised 15 percent discount on fees in exchange for a promise to pay fees on time. Even so, the partner directed employees of his firm to set up a computer program that would add the discounted amount back into the bills without disclosing this to the client. The lawyer was suspended for two years.[9] **Wisconsin, 2001:** A lawyer who contracted with the public defender to serve indigent clients billed for 16 to more than 24 hours a day and for fictitious travel from a remote office. He was convicted of theft by fraud and sentenced to five years in jail.[10]
if the lawyer bills a client for providing little or no service, or for providing inadequate service.	**Delaware, 2005:** A lawyer charged more than $25,000 for work on one estate when the lawyer took longer than 15 years to complete the work; the lawyer charged a similar amount on a different estate in which he failed to file an inventory or accounting. The lawyer was suspended from practice for three years.[11]

---

7. See, e.g., In re Dorothy, 605 N.W.2d 493 (S.D. 2000).

8. In re DeFrancesch, 877 So. 2d 71 (La. 2004).

9. Atty. Grievance Commn. of Md. v. Hess, 722 A.2d 905 (Md. 1999).

10. State v. LeRose, 693 N.W.2d 803 (Wis. App. 2001) (criminal conviction); Matter of Disc. Proceedings Against LeRose, 514 N.W.2d 412 (Wis. 1994) (disbarment). For a story about his sentencing, see Mark Hertzberg, Journal Entry, https://groups.google.com/forum/?fromgroups=#!topic/bit.listserv.nppa-l/2KgV7CyvifQ (accessed Nov. 24, 2012). The disciplinary charges against him were based on Rule 8.4, but violations of Rule 5.1 could also have been charged.

11. In re McCann, 894 A.2d 1087 (Del. 2005).

Relatively small fees sometimes have been found unreasonable. In Oklahoma in 2003, a legal fee of $750 was found unreasonable because the lawyer could not prove having done any work to earn it.[12] Very large fees sometimes have been found reasonable. A Nebraska court in 1997 found a fee agreement that might produce a fee of $4 million not to be excessive. The lawyer was providing services relating to a business venture that was unlikely to succeed. He was to receive no fee unless it succeeded. Also, the lawyer had already expended $250,000 worth of time on the project and had lost other business as a consequence.[13]

Much of the calculus of what is reasonable depends on the norms in a local legal community and in a particular area of practice. But there is reason to believe that the price of legal services is not very well controlled through competition. Legal services are intangible, so it is difficult for clients to compare the quality of services offered by different firms or to judge whether one firm will do the work more quickly and efficiently than another.

Many industries have publications that evaluate and compare the services provided by different vendors. A local consumer magazine, for example, might publish a comparative survey of the price and quality of work of the auto mechanics in a particular community. While lawyer-rating websites are being established,[14] as a general rule, consumer information about lawyers is scarce. Many clients have very limited information about the lawyers or firms that they hire. Although clients may learn something from a firm's advertising, website, or brochures, it is difficult for most clients to ascertain which firm will provide better service or to learn anything about the potential cost of services.

From the early 1990s until the U.S. economy began to contract in 2008, the fees that lawyers charged to large corporate clients increased significantly, despite the growing unease of those clients. For example, the hourly rate at which large law firms billed corporate clients for bankruptcy work increased at four times the rate of inflation between 1998 and 2007, with at least one firm charging $18.50 per minute for bankruptcy assistance.[15] Even in the midst of a recession, some of the nation's largest firms were billing

---

12. See, e.g., State ex rel. Okla. B. Assn. v. Sheridan, 84 P.3d 710 (Okla. 2003).

13. See, e.g., Bauermeister v. McReynolds, 571 N.W.2d 79 (Neb. 1997), *modified on denial of reh'g*, 575 N.W.2d 354 (Neb. 1998).

14. One lawyer-rating site that is expanding rapidly is http://www.avvo.com (accessed Nov. 15, 2012), which allows consumers and lawyers to rate the quality of service of lawyers. The site also provides information about which of the lawyers have received disciplinary sanctions. See Adam Liptak, On Second Thought, Let's Just Rate All the Lawyers, N.Y. Times A9 (July 2, 2007) (available at http://www.nytimes.com/2007/07/02/us/02bar.html).

15. Lindsay Fortado & Linda Sandler, Bankruptcy Lawyers Seek $18.50 a Minute from Court, Bloomberg, http://www.bloomberg.com/apps/news?pid=newsarchive&sid=agfjWe9ZN25Y&refer=us (Jan. 28, 2009).

"I'm going to get you acquitted, but I want my fee to be a lesson to you."

their bankruptcy clients at a rate of more than $1,000 an hour.[16] One lawyer who charges $1,100 an hour earns less than 20 percent of his income based on hourly billing because he can earn even more money using other methods to calculate fees.[17] Another lawyer who bills $950 per hour says, "when I go on cruises, I still put in six, eight hours a day."[18]

Matter of Fordham[19]:

When a fee may be considered excessive. In 1989, Timothy Clark, age 21, was stopped by the police for speeding. When the police discovered that the car was unregistered, that Clark was driving with a suspended license, and that he had a partly full bottle of vodka in the car, they gave Clark a field sobriety test, which he failed. He was then arrested and taken to a police facility where he submitted to two breathalyzer tests, which showed his

---

16. Id.

17. Terry Carter, The G-Man: A Week in the Life of a $1,000-per-hour Lawyer (Feb. 1, 2008) (available at http://www.abajournal.com/magazine/article/the_g_man/).

18. Martha Neil, Bankruptcy Lawyer Bills $950/Hour, Finds Out of Office Work Can Be Productive, ABA J. (Aug. 23, 2010) (available at http://www.abajournal.com/news/article/bankruptcy_lawyer_bills_950hour_finds_out-of-office_work_can_be_productive/).

19. Matter of Fordham, 668 N.E.2d 816 (Mass. 1996).

blood alcohol level to be .10 and .12. He was charged with driving under the influence of alcohol.

He and his father consulted three lawyers, who offered to represent him for amounts between $3,000 and $10,000. During this period, Clark's father happened to go to Laurence Fordham's house to service an alarm system. While there, he told Fordham's wife about the arrest. She suggested that he talk to Fordham, who was the managing partner of Foley, Hoag & Eliot, a major Boston law firm. When they met, Fordham told father and son that he had never represented anyone in a DUI case or, for that matter, in any criminal matter, but that he was hard-working and believed that he could competently represent Timothy. He also said that he worked at an hourly rate and billed monthly, and that others in his firm would also work on the case. The Clarks agreed to hire Fordham.

After much work on the case, Fordham filed a pretrial motion requesting suppression of the breathalyzer tests on the ground that state law rendered them valid only if they were "within" .02 of each other. He argued that results of .10 and .12 were not "within" .02. The judge acquitted Clark. Fordham had come up with a defense that no criminal defense lawyer in Massachusetts had ever hit upon.

Meanwhile, Fordham had been sending monthly bills to Clark's father. The bills totaled $50,022, representing 227 hours of work, two-thirds of which were performed by Fordham himself. Clark paid $10,000 in late June; Fordham told Clark at that time that most of the work on the matter was done, except for the trial. When Clark failed to make additional payments, Fordham asked him to sign a promissory note, which he did. Six days before the scheduled trial date in October, Fordham sent a bill for a $5,000 "retroactive increase." In early November, Fordham sent a bill for an additional $15,000.

After Clark complained to the bar that the fee was unreasonable, the bar counsel charged Fordham with violating the rules on fees. The bar counsel stipulated, along with Fordham, that "that all the work billed by Fordham was actually done, . . . that Fordham and his associates spent the time they claim to have spent, [and] that Fordham acted conscientiously, diligently, and in good faith in representing Timothy and in his billing." Expert witnesses testified before a review board and disagreed about whether the charge was unreasonable, though even those who thought it was reasonable conceded that the usual charge for a similar case was $10,000 or less. The hearing committee and the review board dismissed the charge against Fordham, finding that his fee was reasonable.

On appeal, Massachusetts' highest court acknowledged that Fordham's work was novel and successful, and that both the fee arrangement and Fordham's lack of criminal law experience had been disclosed at the outset of the representation. Nevertheless, the court reversed the finding that the fee was reasonable. Although Clark knew that Fordham's fee was $200 an hour, Fordham had never estimated how many hours the case would require. The court found that Fordham had spent many hours preparing himself to work in an area of law that was new for him, and the fee was objectively out of line with other lawyers' fees for comparable work. The court imposed a public censure.[20]

Questions about *Fordham*

1. No one would quibble with a lawyer who spent extra time on a case to increase the odds of getting a desired result for a client. The issue in this case is whether a lawyer may bill for the extra time. There is no indication that Fordham was lying about the amount of time he actually worked. The parties stipulated that he and his associates really spent 227 hours on the case. Do you think that Fordham billed Clark for too many hours on Timothy Clark's matter?

2. Review the standard for a reasonable fee under Rule 1.5(a). This was the standard that was applied in the *Fordham* case. Is the guidance provided by the rule clear enough to be a basis for discipline? Draft some changes to clarify this rule.

3. Should the court have concluded that the fee was reasonable because the client signed a promissory note and apparently acquiesced after he objected?

4. The court noted that one of the bills included an additional amount for a retroactive rate increase. Assuming this was the first that Clark knew about the rate increase, was this proper?

5. The general concept behind hourly billing is that if a lawyer contracts to bill by the hour, and honestly and diligently works the actual number of hours billed to the client, the resulting fee should be regarded as reasonable. Should the courts follow this principle as to lawyers who bill for "initial study time"? Should a lawyer be allowed to bill for study time if she discloses to her client that she is inexperienced in the area of law in question and intends to charge the client for learning a new field?

6. Several years after the *Fordham* case was decided, the attorney general of Massachusetts hired several law firms, on a contingent fee basis, to assist it in novel and highly uncertain litigation against several tobacco companies, in which it claimed damages for its expenses in providing medical treatment for cancer victims over many decades. At the time, the tobacco industry had won 800 court cases and had never lost a case. The law firms declined to work on the case unless the state was willing to pay 25 percent of any damages

---

20. A "censure" was at that time Massachusetts' term for what is now called a public reprimand. See Roger Geller & Susan Strauss Weisberg, Dues and Dont's [sic], http://www.mass.gov/obcbbo/dues.htm (Jan. 2002).

that the state was awarded. They urged that this fee was appropriate because they would have to devote the time of more than 100 lawyers to this work with no certainty that they would ever be paid. The state agreed to these terms, in writing. Eventually, the state won an $8.3 billion dollar settlement from the tobacco companies, but the public (and the state government) balked at paying approximately $2 billion to the lawyers. If the firms had charged by the hour, at their normal rates, the bill would have been about $20 million. The state agreed to pay only $775 million, and two law firms sued the state for $1.2 billion, their share of the balance owed under the contingent fee agreement.[21] Should the lawyers have won their suit against the state?

c. Communication about fee arrangements

As we explained above, many conflicts between lawyers and clients over fees are caused by inadequate disclosure about fees at the outset of the representation or inadequate consultation with the client about fees as the representation progresses. Rule 1.5(b) requires lawyers to make some disclosures to clients about the fees they intend to charge.

> **Rule 1.5(b)**
> **The scope of the representation and the basis or rate of the fee and expenses for which the client will be responsible shall be communicated to the client, preferably in writing, before or within a reasonable time after commencing the representation, except when the lawyer will charge a regularly represented client on the same basis or rate. Any changes in the basis or rate of the fee or expenses shall also be communicated to the client.**

Let's examine what this rule requires.

What must be disclosed?

A lawyer must disclose information about the scope of the representation. What does this mean? A comment says that the lawyer must disclose "the general nature of the legal services to be provided." Perhaps this comment isn't very helpful to lawyers who are trying to draft letters to their clients. The term "general nature" doesn't add very much to the term "scope."

A lawyer must disclose the "basis or rate of the fee and expenses." The comments suggest that a lawyer must disclose information about "the

---

21. Thanassis Cambanis, Law Firms Accuse State of Breaching Tobacco Deal, Boston Globe (Nov. 5, 2003) (available at http://www.boston.com/news/local/articles/2003/11/05/law_firms_accuse_state_of_breaching_tobacco_deal/).

lawyer's customary fee arrangements" and "the basis, rate, or total amount of the fee and . . . any costs or expenses or disbursements" that will be charged to the client. If the lawyer is billing by the hour, then the lawyer should reveal his hourly rate. If the client will be billed 25 cents a page for photocopying or charged for the cost of hiring a court reporter for a deposition, the client should be so informed.[22]

Must the disclosure be in writing?

No, unless the lawyer intends to charge a contingent fee (see below). The rule recommends but does not require that the disclosure be in writing. The Ethics 2000 Commission recommended that the word "preferably" be eliminated from the rule; this change would have required a written disclosure. The ABA House of Delegates, however, rejected this suggestion, preferring to give lawyers the discretion to decide whether to disclose information about fees and expenses in writing. One group of lawyers that specializes in reviewing legal bills by other firms has published a model "Client-Friendly Retention Agreement" to create a "more level relationship" between lawyers and clients.[23]

Does the lawyer have to disclose fee and expense information before starting work on the matter?

No. The rule says the disclosure must occur "before or within a reasonable time after commencing the representation." If client needs services urgently, such as a client who is in jail and needs legal assistance to be released, it might be appropriate to postpone discussion of fee information until after the work has begun. Absent such circumstances, principles of contract law require articulation of terms before an enforceable fee agreement comes into existence.[24]

Must the lawyer estimate the amount of time she will spend or the total fee?

No. Auto repair people (who also bill by the hour) must give written estimates before providing services,[25] but lawyers are not required to do so.

---

22. See ABA Standing Comm. on Ethics & Prof. Resp., Formal Op. 94-389 (before entering into a contingent fee arrangement with a client, a lawyer should discuss possible choices of fee arrangements).

23. John Toothman, The Devil's Advocate, Our Client-Friendly Retention Agreement, http://www.devilsadvocate.com/Articles/retagr.html (accessed Nov. 16, 2012).

24. Restatement § 38, comment b, notes, for example, that if a lawyer says "I will charge what I think fair, in light of the hours expended and the results obtained," this might be part of a valid contract, but it "does not bind the client or tribunal to accept whatever fee the lawyer thinks fair."

25. See, e.g., Colo. Rev. Stat. Ann. § 42-9-104 (2003) (requiring auto repair shops to give customers specific written price estimates before performing repair work).

Some lawyers urge that it is impossible to estimate the cost of legal services because it is so hard to predict how much time a matter will require.

Even though such disclosure is not required and can be difficult to calculate, it is good business practice to provide clients with a realistic assessment of the possible cost of the representation. One reason why people don't trust lawyers is that so many clients have been blindsided by legal fees far higher than they had been led to expect.[26] A client who commits time and money to a relationship with a lawyer but who gets no price information until a bill arrives may feel that he was manipulated into an agreement. Even if the client doesn't object to the first bills from the lawyer, she may become increasingly concerned as months pass and the total fee climbs beyond her cost expectations.

If a lawyer is uncertain about the amount of time a matter will consume, he could provide an estimate that includes a high and low prediction. A lawyer who wants good relations with clients whose resources are limited would be well advised to disclose more information in advance and perhaps to commit to a ceiling on what he will charge for a specified service.

PROBLEM 8-1 AN UNREASONABLE FEE?

A lawyer called one of the authors for advice about a situation similar to the one described in this problem.

Ingrid Sanders hired a lawyer, Colin Horlock, to settle a dispute with her landlord about who was responsible for the cost of clean-up and renovation following a flood in her luxury apartment. The landlord had refused to cover the repairs. The work cost Ingrid $70,000. Colin told Ingrid that his rate was $250 per hour, and she agreed that he should pursue the matter. He did so vigorously, devoting so much time to the matter that his bills to Ingrid totaled $60,000. Initially, Colin spent many hours on legal research into a landlord's responsibility for repairs caused by flooding. He spent even more time on fact investigation. He interviewed many other tenants in Ingrid's building to determine what, if any, problems they had had with the landlord, what costs they had incurred as a result of the flood, and whether the landlord had reimbursed them

---

26. ABA Formal Op. 93-379 explains that "[o]ne major contributing factor to the discouraging public opinion of the legal profession appears to be the billing practices of some of its members." ABA Standing Comm. on Ethics & Prof. Resp., Formal Op. 93-379. See generally Marc Galanter, The Faces of Mistrust: The Image of Lawyers in Public Opinion, Jokes, and Political Discourse, 66 U. Cin. L. Rev. 805 (1998); Leonard E. Gross, The Public Hates Lawyers: Why Should We Care? 29 Seton Hall L. Rev. 1405 (1999).

for those costs. Then he persuaded the landlord's lawyer to participate in a mediation process, which took many hours of time but which ultimately produced no settlement. Eventually, Colin filed a lawsuit and deposed the landlord and the landlord's accountant. During the course of the work, Colin and Ingrid never talked about whether she wanted him to expend this much time on the matter.

When Ingrid got the bill from Colin, she was aghast. She came to consult you about whether Colin's bill was excessive. Ingrid pointed out to you that even if she ultimately collected the full $70,000 from the landlord for the repair work, she would have spent nearly the same amount on the legal fees to obtain this recovery.

Questions

1. How would you evaluate whether Colin actually has charged an excessive fee? What other information do you need?
2. Apart from Rule 1.5, has Colin violated any other duties to Ingrid under the rules of professional conduct or other law?

---

d. Modification of fee agreements

If a lawyer represents a client over a long period of time, the lawyer's regular hourly rate might increase during that period. In contractual terms, the lawyer is seeking a modification of an ongoing contract. An agreement modifying an initial contract is enforceable if it is "fair and equitable in view of circumstances not anticipated by the parties when the contract was made."[27]

The courts vary in the standards imposed for enforcement of fee modification contracts. Some cases hold that a lawyer may not simply notify a client of an increase in the hourly rates charged.[28] Others require client consent before a lawyer increases the percentage of a settlement

---

27. Restatement (Second) of Contracts § 89(a)(1981). The *Restatement (Third) of the Law Governing Lawyers* asserts that "the client may avoid [such an agreement] unless the lawyer shows that the contract and the circumstances of its formation were fair and reasonable to the client." Restatement § 18(1)(a). Some courts have held that modifications of legal fee agreements are "presumptively fraudulent" unless the lawyer "demonstrates full disclosure of all the relevant information, client consent based on adequate consideration, and client opportunity to seek independent legal advice before agreeing to the modification." Durr v. Beatty, 491 N.E.2d 902 (Ill. App. 1986); see also Corti v. Fleisher, 417 N.E.2d 764 (Ill. App. 1981); Christian v. Gordon, 2001 WL 883551 (Terr. V.I. June 20, 2001).

28. See, e.g., Severson, Werson, Berke & Melchior v. Bolinger, 1 Cal. Rptr. 2d 531 (Ct. App. 1991) (where a fee agreement provided that law firm would charge client its "regular hourly rates," the law firm was not permitted to raise its rates without the client's consent).

retained as a contingent fee.[29] If a lawyer holds up distribution of a settlement until the client consents, the consent may be invalid.[30]

2. Regulation of hourly billing and billing for expenses

Until about 1990, many lawyers sent their clients bills that read only "for professional services rendered" along with the amount owed. Few clients inquired as to how the total was arrived at. Since then, however, many clients have become less trusting of their lawyers and have begun to demand more information about the basis of their legal bills. The numerous public examples of lawyers guilty of billing and expense fraud have contributed greatly to clients' mistrust. Some of these cases involved lawyers who inflated the number of billable hours they recorded, who worked more hours than necessary to complete a task, or who billed clients at professional rates for time they spent doing ministerial tasks. Some cases have involved lawyers who billed clients for personal expenses or who marked up the actual cost of legitimate expenses. Although very many lawyers are scrupulously honest about how they calculate fees, some lawyers engage in various forms of chicanery to generate higher bills.[31]

How many lawyers engage in unethical billing practices?

No one really knows how many lawyers have engaged in occasional "padding" or in even more serious misrepresentation of their time or expenses, but recent scholarship provides tentative answers to these questions. A majority of the lawyers surveyed by Professor William Ross in 1991 admitted that they at least occasionally inflate the hours billed to clients. A smaller percentage of them admitted to larger-scale inflation of hours or fabrication of time records.[32] Most lawyers reported to Ross that other lawyers engage in billing fraud more often than they themselves do.[33]

---

29. See, e.g., In re Thayer, 745 N.E.2d 207 (Ind. 2001) (lawyer violated Rules 1.5(a) and 1.8(a) by presenting client with a fee modification agreement on the day of settlement that increased his fee from 40 percent to 50 percent).

30. Id.

31. One authority has called bill padding "the perfect crime . . . [because] much padding of hours is simply impossible to detect." Ross, supra n. 3, at 23.

32. Professor William Ross of Cumberland School of Law surveyed 500 lawyers and received responses from 272. Of that group, 49 percent of the respondents said that they either "rarely" or "occasionally" billed two clients for the same period of time (engaged in double-billing), while 1.2 percent admitted to "frequent" double-billing. William G. Ross, The Ethics of Hourly Billing by Attorneys, 44 Rutgers L. Rev. 1, 78-83 (1991).

33. Ross asked how often the respondents thought that other lawyers "padded" their hours (recording more time than actually worked) and found that 12.3 percent said other lawyers pad their hours "frequently"; 80.4 percent said "rarely" or "occasionally"; 7.3 percent said "never." Id. at 16.

In 1994-1995, Professor Ross conducted a second survey about lawyer billing practices that drew responses from 106 lawyers in private practice and 91 lawyers who work for corporations.[34] In this survey, Ross asked what percentage of the time billed by American lawyers "consists of 'padding' for work not actually performed?" Sixteen percent of the lawyers in private practice who responded estimated that 25 percent or more of the total hours billed by lawyers were phony.[35] The second survey asked whether the lawyers had ever engaged in "double-billing" (billing two clients for the same period of time) or billed for "recycled" work (billing one client for work that was originally done for another). Seventy-seven percent of the lawyers said they had "never" engaged in double-billing, but 23 percent admitted that they had done so. Sixty-five percent said they had never billed a client for recycled work, but 35 percent reported that they had done so.[36]

In 1999-2000, Professor Susan Saab Fortney sent a survey on billing practices and other questions to a group of randomly selected law firm associates in Texas. She received responses from 487 lawyers. Eighty-six

percent of her respondents reported that they had not engaged in double-billing, and 83 percent reported that they had not billed clients for recycled work,[37] meaning that about one in six lawyers in this group indirectly admitted to double-billing or billing for recycled work.

Professor Susan Saab Fortney

These surveys suggest that a very high percentage of lawyers are careful about keeping accurate time records when billing clients, but that between 15 and 50 percent of American lawyers at least occasionally engage in dishonest billing practices.

---

34. Ross, supra n. 3, at 6.

35. Id. at 265-266. Of the corporate counsel who responded, 17.4 percent estimated that 25 percent or more of the hours billed reflected padding. Id. at 269.

36. Id. at 267. On the double-billing question, 15 percent checked "rarely," 7 percent checked "a moderate number of times," and 1 percent checked "often." On the recycled work question, 18.8 percent checked "rarely," 11.3 percent checked "a moderate number of times," and 4.8 percent checked "often." Id.

37. Susan Saab Fortney, Soul for Sale: An Empirical Study of Associate Satisfaction, Law Firm Culture, and the Effects of Billable Hour Requirements, 69 UMKC L. Rev. 239, 258 (2000).

Shouldn't it be obvious that if a lawyer is billing based on time worked, the lawyer is obliged to keep accurate time records and not to "fudge," "pad," or even estimate?

Perhaps it should be, but apparently some lawyers do not perceive that writing down phony hours is dishonest. Law firms make more money if they bill more hours, so there are financial reasons not to be too specific in guiding junior lawyers as to what is or is not proper in billing clients. Also,

Patrick J. Schiltz

many firms put considerable pressure on their lawyers to bill a certain number of hours. The firms set annual targets, often between 1,800 and 2,400 hours per year, and they give bonuses to lawyers who bill various astronomical numbers of hours.[38] This system creates incentives for lawyers to find ways to record extra hours — their incomes depend on it, and at some firms, the odds of retention and promotion are greatly improved by billing more hours than one's peers.[39]

Patrick J. Schiltz, On Being a Happy, Healthy, and Ethical Member of an Unhappy, Unhealthy, and Unethical Profession

52 Vand. L. Rev. 871, 916-918 (1999)

[Patrick J. Schiltz, a former law clerk to Justice Antonin Scalia, worked as an associate and then as a partner in a large law firm before resigning to begin teaching at Notre Dame Law School. Later, he became associate dean at the University of St. Thomas School of Law. In 2006, President George W. Bush appointed him to be a federal district judge in Minnesota.]

Unethical lawyers do not start out being unethical; they start out just like you — as perfectly decent young men or women who have every intention of practicing law ethically. They do not become unethical overnight; they become unethical just as you will (if you become unethical) — a little bit at

---

38. For example, in 2002, a group of associates at the law firm of Clifford Chance sent a memorandum to the partners in the law firm to protest the firm's requirement that, to qualify for a bonus, an associate had to bill 2,420 hours per year. Adam Liptak, Stop the Clock: Critics Call the Billable Hour a Legal Fiction, N.Y. Times G7 (Oct. 29, 2002) (available at http://www.nytimes.com/2002/10/29/jobs/on-the-job-stop-the-clock-critics-call-the-billable-hour-a-legal-fiction.html?pagewanted=all&src=pm).

39. See Deborah L. Rhode, In the Interests of Justice: Reforming the Legal Profession 171 (Oxford U. Press 2000); Dennis Curtis & Judith Resnik, Teaching Billing: Metrics of Value in Law Firms and Law Schools, 54 Stan. L. Rev. 1409 (2002); Gerald Phillips, It's Not Hourly Billing But How It's Abused That Causes the Poor Image of Attorneys, 2007 Prof. Law. 21.

a time. And they do not become unethical by shredding incriminating documents or bribing jurors; they become unethical just as you are likely to — by cutting a corner here, by stretching the truth a bit there.

Let me tell you how you will start acting unethically: It will start with your time sheets. One day, not too long after you start practicing law, you will sit down at the end of a long, tiring day, and you just won't have much to show for your efforts in terms of billable hours. It will be near the end of the month. You will know that all of the partners will be looking at your monthly time report in a few days, so what you'll do is pad your time sheet just a bit.

Maybe you will bill a client for ninety minutes for a task that really took you only sixty minutes to perform. However, you will promise yourself that you will repay the client at the first opportunity by doing thirty minutes of work for the client for "free." In this way, you will be "borrowing," not "stealing."

And then what will happen is that it will become easier and easier to take these little loans against future work. And then, after a while, you will stop paying back these little loans. You will convince yourself that, although you billed for ninety minutes and spent only sixty minutes on the project, you did such good work that your client should pay a bit more for it. After all, your billing rate is awfully low, and your client is awfully rich.

And then you will pad more and more — every two minute telephone conversation will go down on the sheet as ten minutes, every three hour research project will go down with an extra quarter hour or so. You will continue to rationalize your dishonesty to yourself in various ways until one day you stop doing even that.

And, before long — it won't take you much more than three or four years — you will be stealing from your clients almost every day, and you won't even notice it.

You know what? You will also likely become a liar. A deadline will come up one day, and, for reasons that are entirely your fault, you will not be able to meet it. So you will call your senior partner or your client and make up a white lie for why you missed the deadline. And then you will get busy and a partner will ask whether you proofread a lengthy prospectus and you will say yes, even though you didn't. And then you will be drafting a brief and you will quote language from a Supreme Court opinion even though you will know that, when read in context, the language does not remotely suggest what you are implying it suggests. And then, in preparing a client for a deposition, you will help the client to formulate an answer to a difficult question that will likely be asked — an answer that will be "legally accurate" but that will mislead your opponent. And then you will be reading through a big box of your client's documents — a box that has not been opened in twenty years — and you will find a document that would hurt your client's case, but that no one except you knows exists, and you

"'Is it right? ... Is it fair?' Get a grip Carlton—we're a law firm!"

will simply "forget" to produce it in response to your opponent's discovery requests.

Do you see what will happen? After a couple years of this, you won't even notice that you are lying and cheating and stealing every day that you practice law. None of these things will seem like a big deal in itself—an extra fifteen minutes added to a time sheet here, a little white lie to cover a missed deadline there. But, after a while, your entire frame of reference will change. You will still be making dozens of quick, instinctive decisions every day, but those decisions, instead of reflecting the notions of right and wrong by which you conduct your personal life, will instead reflect the set of values by which you will conduct your professional life—a set of values that embodies not what is right or wrong, but what is profitable, and what you can get away with. The system will have succeeded in replacing your values with the system's values, and the system will be profiting as a result.

Does this happen to every big firm lawyer? Of course not. It's all a matter of degree. The culture in some big firms is better than in others. . . . The big firm at which I practiced was as decent and humane as a big firm can be. Similarly, some big firm lawyers have better values than others. I owe a lot to a partner who sacrificed hundreds of hours of his time and tens of thousands of dollars of income to act as a mentor to me and to many other young lawyers like me. At the same time, you should not under-estimate the likelihood that you will practice law unethically. It is true, for example, that not every lawyer knowingly and blatantly lies on his time sheets. But there is a reason why padding time sheets has been called "a silent epidemic."[40]

Do some firms train lawyers to be honest and ethical in billing hours?

Yes, there are firms that care more about ethical practices than about "the bottom line." Some firms develop clear written policies to guide their lawyers and their other employees as to what is proper or improper. Some firms offer periodic training to implement those policies. Some firms hire ethics specialists who advise firm employees on ethical questions about billing and other matters that come up in the course of their work.[41]

But many lawyers still make decisions about what is proper without the benefit of firm policy or training. In Fortney's 1999-2000 survey, she asked whether the respondents worked at law firms that "had written billing guidelines other than those imposed by clients." Forty percent said that their firms did have such guidelines. Thirty-six percent said their firms did not have billing guidelines. Twenty-four percent of the lawyers checked the box that said "I don't know."[42]

After it became evident that some lawyers were taking liberties with their time sheets and expense records, judges and ethics committees began to produce opinions spelling out some boundaries on permissible and impermissible billing practices. Some of these boundaries are summarized below.

No padding or time inflation: A lawyer billing by the hour may not bill for more hours than she actually worked

A lawyer who has agreed to bill based on time worked may not increase the amount of time recorded above the actual time recorded for any reason.[43] Sometimes lawyers pad their hours because they think their work is "worth" more than the amount that would be billed based on time. Sometimes they do this to meet firm demands that they bill a certain

---

40. The ethics counsel at a large Minneapolis law firm asserts that Professor Schiltz's "characterizations of large law firms [particularly Schiltz's claims about the unethical conduct they tolerate] miss or distort several fundamental points." William J. Wernz, The Ethics of Large Law Firms — Responses and Reflections, 16 Geo. J. Leg. Ethics 175, 176 (2002).

41. Elizabeth Chambliss & David B. Wilkins, The Emerging Role of Ethics Advisors, General Counsel and Other Compliance Specialists in Large Law Firms, 44 Ariz. L. Rev. 559, 560-561 (2002).

42. Fortney, supra n. 37, at 253.

43. ABA Standing Comm. on Ethics & Prof. Resp., Formal Op. 93-379.

number of hours. The ABA ethics committee has made clear, however, that this is impermissible: "It goes without saying that a lawyer who has undertaken to bill on an hourly basis is never justified in charging a client for hours not actually expended."[44]

May a lawyer increase the amount of time recorded by rounding up to a "billing increment"?

The ABA ethics committee clearly stated that when a client has agreed to an hourly fee, a lawyer may not bill more hours than she actually works, except for rounding up to a minimum billing increment (such as one-quarter or one-tenth of an hour).[45] Conventional notions on rounding would allow a lawyer to round up only if he or she has worked more than half of the minimum billing increment for a client. If the lawyer works less than half the minimum billing increment, the lawyer should round down.[46] The ABA opinion refers only to "rounding up," so some lawyers might interpret the opinion to allow lawyers to behave like owners of parking lots, charging their customers for an additional increment of time if they provide even one additional minute of service beyond the previous unit of time changed.

> **FOR EXAMPLE:** A senior partner in a California firm billed $175 per hour and used 18-minute increments as his routine billing period. He "recorded a one-minute telephone call as eighteen minutes, [and] billed

---

44. Id.

45. Id.

46. One typical description of rounding is supplied by Jeff Kenney, professor of astronomy at Yale University:

Rules for rounding off numbers:

   1. If the digit to be dropped is greater than 5, the last retained digit is increased by one. For example, 12.6 is rounded to 13.

   2. If the digit to be dropped is less than 5, the last remaining digit is left as is. For example, 12.4 is rounded to 12.

   3. If the digit to be dropped is 5, and if any digit following it is not zero, the last remaining digit is increased by one. For example, 12.51 is rounded to 13.

   4. If the digit to be dropped is 5 and is followed only by zeros, the last remaining digit is increased by one if it is odd, but left as is if even. For example, 11.5 is rounded to 12, 12.5 is [also] rounded to 12. This rule means that if the digit to be dropped is 5 followed only by zeros, the result is always rounded to the even digit. The rationale is to avoid bias in rounding; half the time we round up, half the time we round down.

Jeff Kenney, A Short Guide to Significant Figures, http://www.astro.yale.edu/astro120/SigFig.pdf (accessed Nov. 16, 2012); see also Russell Hurlburt, Comprehending Behavioral Statistics 12 (Wadsworth 1994).

"Remember to round each billable hour off to the nearest week."

the client $52.50 for work that should have cost only $3 if billed for the time actually spent."[47]

Gerald Phillips, the lawyer who reported this example, believes that undisclosed rounding combined with large billing increments imposes on clients millions of dollars of unearned legal fees every year.[48]

No inventing hours that weren't really worked

The ABA opinion made clear that padding hours is unethical. But some lawyers simply fabricate time records out of thin air and then bill for them as if the hours were real.

---

47. Gerald F. Phillips, Time Bandits: Attempts by Lawyers to Pad Hours Can Often Be Uncovered by a Careful Examination of Billing Statements, 29 W. St. U. L. Rev. 265, 273 (2002). Phillips is in a position to speak with authority on where the bar should draw the line between acceptable and fraudulent billing methods. He practiced for 38 years in the firm of Phillips, Nizer, Benjamin, Krim & Ballon.

48. Id. at 273 n. 38.

FOR EXAMPLE: Bill Duker got a Ph.D. from the University of Cambridge, England, and then a law degree from Yale. After a clerkship, he spent several years as an associate at Cravath, Swain & Moore. After a few years as a law professor, he started his own firm in New York and became an expert in litigation involving professional misconduct.

Between 1990 and 1995, he earned between $1 million and $5 million per year. As managing partner of his firm, Duker reviewed the time records of all the other lawyers in his firm. As he reviewed them, he wrote instructions to his bookkeeper as to how many hours should be added to those recorded by the lawyers, systematically increasing the number of hours billed out to the federal banking agency that was his biggest client. He overbilled a major client by at least $1.4 million. Duker was convicted of mail fraud and other crimes, sentenced to 33 months in prison and disbarred.[49]

In recent years, a surprising number of highly educated, intelligent, and successful lawyers have been prosecuted for federal mail fraud or other crimes because of dishonest billing practices.[50] Others have been disciplined for fabricating hours. Jeffery Luckett billed Cook County, Illinois, for more than 20 hours of work daily (sometimes more than 24 hours in a day) while representing juveniles at county expense.[51] In 2011, he was suspended for at least 21 months.[52]

Some lawyers who bill for fictitious hours are not detected or punished. One large-firm associate related these examples:

> I used to prepare the bills for a client. . . . I was working on a bill . . . and . . . one of the managing partners of the firm was written down [as having spent] ten or twenty hours [working for that client that] month. I went in to my boss . . . and said, "Did [Steve Whitman] work on this case?" . . . And he said, "No, no. He didn't." . . . He . . . [explained] that [Steve] spends so much time managing the firm and not doing client business, that in order to justify his existence and salary every month, he

---

49. This story through 1999 is recounted in Lisa G. Lerman, Blue-Chip Bilking: Regulation of Billing and Expense Fraud by Lawyers, 12 Geo. J. Leg. Ethics 205 (1999). After release from prison, Duker founded a company called Amici and sold it in 2006 for $174 million. For the Amici part of the story, see Nic Rossmuller, Xerox Acquires Document Manager Amici LLC, LetsGoDigital, http://www.letsgodigital.org/en/8605/xerox_documents_manager_amici/ (June 17, 2006); Peter Lattman, Xerox Acquires Amici: A Banner Day for the Boies Brood?, Wall St. J. Law Blog, http://blogs.wsj.com/law/2006/06/15/ (June 15, 2006).

50. Lerman, supra n. 49, at 263.

51. Debra Cassens Weiss, Lawyer Accused of Billing County for More than 24 Hours of Work in a Day, ABA J. (June 6, 2008) (available at http://www.abajournal.com/news/article/lawyer_accused_of_billing_county_for_more_than_24_hours_of_work_in_a_day/).

52. Ill. Atty. Registration & Disc. Commn., Jeffery Luckett, http://www.iardc.org/ldetail.asp?id=457310975 (accessed Nov. 24, 2012).

just sort of [picks] some clients that are decent-sized clients and throws a few hours onto their bills. This was known in the firm as the [Whitman] Tax. Someone later [asked], "Oh, you didn't know about the Whitman Tax" — "Oh, that was the first time you got socked with the Whitman Tax?" And you had to hide it in the bill. You couldn't put this guy's name [down] at a billing rate of $285 an hour — and you just sort of had to swallow it. There were lots of things like that where you were really in a tough spot. You were told to do it. . . . [Y]ou couldn't run and tell the management of the firm . . . because they were the ones doing it. And if you tattled to the client . . . [you would get] fired. So you really were [stuck]. [Lisa G. Lerman, Gross Profits? Questions about Lawyer Billing Practices, 22 Hofstra L. Rev. 645, 646 (1994).]

No profits on costs: A lawyer may not bill for "overhead" or markup costs

A lawyer may bill a client for costs incurred in the course of representation, such as postage or messenger service. However, a lawyer may not bill the client more than the actual cost of the service to the lawyer. The ABA ethics committee said very clearly that turning your copy room into a profit center is prohibited. "The lawyer's stock in trade is the sale of legal services, not photocopy paper, tuna fish sandwiches, computer time or messenger services."[53] It also concluded that while a lawyer may bill a client at cost for disbursements and for services provided in-house, it is improper to bill clients for general overhead costs, which should be covered by lawyers' ample hourly fees.[54] What counts as nonbillable overhead? The committee offered as examples the cost of running a library, purchasing malpractice insurance, or paying for office space, heating, or air conditioning.

The ABA opinion was triggered in part by a 1991 article in *American Lawyer* reporting a fee dispute involving Skadden, Arps, Meagher & Flom in which the client had discovered that the law firm had added surcharges onto many costs billed to clients. For example, the firm billed the client $33.60 for coffee and pastries for four people, which in 1991 seemed like an outrageous sum. But the firm also billed for faxes (both incoming and outgoing) by the page, as well as $35 to $45 per hour for the staff person who watched over the fax machine.[55]

Once the ABA made clear that lawyers might earn profits from legal services but not by marking up other costs, one would have assumed that

---

53. See also In re Zaleon, 504 S.E.2d 702 (Ga. 1998) (lawyer disciplined for charging the client above cost for disbursements without disclosing to the client that the lawyer was doing so).

54. ABA Standing Comm. on Ethics & Prof. Resp., Formal Op. 93-379; see also Restatement § 38(3)(a).

55. Skaddenomics, Am. Law. 3 (Sept. 1991).

law firms, especially large prominent law firms, would have changed policy to comply with this interpretation of the ethics rules. Apparently this isn't what happened. In 1995, one large firm surveyed 30 others and found that markups on costs were still commonplace. The results of the survey were leaked to *American Lawyer*, which reported:

> Eleven of the 30 firms charged at least $2 per page for an outgoing domestic fax. Twenty-one of the firms marked up telephone charges. Eighteen firms charged 20 cents or more a page for photocopying. And 13 of the 30 firms admitted to marking up LEXIS charges, five by as much as 50 percent.[56]

No double-billing: A lawyer may not bill two clients for one period of time

If a lawyer does work that benefits two clients, and the lawyer is billing both clients based on time, the lawyer may bill each client for half the time expended or, with their consent, may allocate the time in some other way. But the lawyer may not bill the block of time twice. This may seem obvious and logical, but double-billing has been common practice in some firms.[57] A former paralegal at a large firm remembered this story:

> In preparation for litigation and anticipated discovery on behalf of Client A, I was sent on a trip . . . to the client's HQ to review document files. . . . Meanwhile, a matter involving Client B was heating up. . . . The partner handling the Client B matter was also handling Client A. He asked that I take some of the [Client B] depositions with me and digest them while on the road. He also said something to the effect, "Besides, it will give you something to do on the plane." Apprising the partner of the firm policy to bill transportation time to the client (in this case Client A), I asked how I should bill the time I spent digesting the depositions for Client B. He responded that I should bill the total transportation time to Client A and the time spent digesting depositions to Client B. In other words, double bill. . . . [L]ater, in similar situations, the senior paralegal in charge of assignments let it be known that this is how billing was to be handled.[58]

This incident took place before the ABA ethics opinion made clear that double-billing was unethical. This practice is less common than it used to be, but it still occurs.

---

56. Karen Dillon, Dumb and Dumber, Am. Law. 5 (Oct. 1995).

57. See, e.g., Kevin Hopkins, Law Firms, Technology, and the Double-Billing Dilemma, 12 Geo. J. Leg. Ethics 93 (1998).

58. This story is recounted in Lisa G. Lerman, Lying to Clients, 138 U. Pa. L. Rev. 659, 710 (1990).

No billing a second client for recycled work

ABA Opinion 93-379 asks, what if a lawyer does "research on a particular topic for one client that later turns out to be relevant to an inquiry from a second client. May the firm bill the second client, who agreed to be charged on the basis of time spent on his case, the same amount for the recycled work product that it charged the first client?" The ABA says that it may not:

> A lawyer who is able to reuse old work product has not re-earned the hours previously billed and compensated when the work product was first generated. Rather than looking to profit from . . . the luck of being asked the identical question twice, the lawyer who has agreed to bill solely on the basis of time spent is obliged to pass the benefits of these economies on to the client. The practice of billing several clients for the same time or work product, since it results in the earning of an unreasonable fee, therefore is contrary to the mandate of Model Rule 1.5.

No churning or running the meter: A lawyer may not do unnecessary extra work to justify billing more hours

One of the biggest problems with hourly billing is that it provides lawyers with an enormous incentive to be inefficient. The more time the work takes, the more they get paid. Often the judgment of what "needs" to be done is extremely subjective, so a lawyer can err on the side of thoroughness, spend lots of extra time, and be well within the range of normal professional conduct. One lawyer whom we call "Winston Hall" described this problem:

> The most common [type of deception], by far, is make-work that the client pays for but that didn't lead very directly to the result. That describes an enormous percentage of the activity that I think goes on in law firms.[59]

One partner in Hall's firm had explained to him that

> law practice is somewhat supply-side driven. You can decide how heavily you are going to bill on a matter. There is a wide range of acceptability. If you've got the people, you do more work; if you don't have the people, then you don't.

Hall described a major lobbying matter that his firm handled for a big industry. "We spent half a million dollars tracking this legislation — eight people working on it essentially full-time." The firm billed this time

---

59. Id. at 706-708, quoting an associate at a large firm. The subsequent quotes from the Hall interview are excerpted from this article.

primarily to two clients. The firm hoped to attract additional clients in this area, so part of the work product (reports analyzing the legislation) was sent to 300 people. The reports covered many issues that would have no impact on the clients who were paying for the work. Hall thinks that "it was all done without the client knowing that it was being billed to them."

Comment 5 to Rule 1.5 says: "A lawyer should not exploit a fee arrangement based primarily on hourly charges by using wasteful procedures." ABA Opinion 93-379 also addressed this question with an unequivocal "don't do it."

> Continuous toil on or overstaffing a project for the purpose of churning out hours is also not properly considered "earning" one's fees. . . . Just as a lawyer is expected to discharge a matter on summary judgment if possible rather than proceed to trial, so too is the lawyer expected to complete other projects for a client efficiently. A lawyer should take as much time as is reasonably required to complete a project, and should certainly never be motivated by anything other than the best interests of the client when determining how to staff or how much time to spend on any particular project.

No billing clients or the firm for personal expenses or marking up expense receipts

Lots of lawyers have gotten in bad trouble (discipline, prosecution, civil liability, and loss of employment, to name a few) for charging their clients or their firms for personal expenses or for inflating their claimed business expenses.

Some cases involve small amounts. A first-year associate named Thomas Schneider simply added a "1" in front of eight receipts for under $100. He claimed he did that to get reimbursed for some expenses for which he didn't have receipts. He was suspended from practice for 30 days.[60]

Other cases involve much larger amounts of money. Webster Hubbell, while managing partner of his firm, paid personal credit card bills on ten different cards out of firm accounts. These were among over 400 instances of financial fraud, which also included inflation of hours billed, that amounted to $480,000 in billing and expense fraud. The discovery of this misconduct required his resignation from his position as associate attorney general in the Clinton administration. Hubbell was also disbarred and pleaded guilty to criminal charges of mail fraud. He was sentenced to 21 months in prison.[61]

Charging clients at lawyers' rates for work that could be done by support staff

Clients may assume that lawyers delegate to paralegals and secretaries the work that could be done by nonlawyers and that senior lawyers delegate simpler work to less experienced (and cheaper) lawyers. But most lawyers spend some time doing administrative work that does not involve a high level of professional skill. It may be perfectly legitimate for lawyers to charge clients at lawyer rates for certain types of administrative work that can be done only by the lawyers themselves. (For example, at the end of work on a matter, a lawyer might know best which documents could be discarded and how to assemble those that should be retained.) But may lawyers bill at their usual rates for administrative tasks that they actually perform but that could have been delegated to a staff person? In 2000, the Colorado Supreme Court held that lawyers should not bill at their hourly rates for clerical

---

60. In re Schneider, 553 A.2d 206 (D.C. 1989). Curiously, like Bill Duker, Mr. Schneider had earned a Ph.D. in addition to his law degree; Duker's was from Cambridge, Schneider's was from Oxford.

61. Lerman, supra n. 49, at 213.

services. In the case before the court, there were "multiple entries reflecting the faxing of documents to the client and opposing counsel, entries for calls made to the court of appeals clerk's office, and the delivery of documents to opposing counsel." Applying Colorado's Rule 1.5, the court concluded that "charging an attorney's hourly rate for clerical services that are generally performed by a non-lawyer, and thus for which an attorney's professional skill and knowledge add no value to the service, is unreasonable as a matter of law."[62]

Billing for billing

If a lawyer bills by the hour, may the lawyer bill the client for time she spends explaining her billing practices to the client? What about the time she spends preparing the bills? Or time spent writing or calling clients to urge them to pay their bills? At least one court held that "the practice of charging clients for 'accounting services' — that is, billing clients for time spent completing time sheets and calculating bills therefrom — [without express agreement from the client in advance] was unreasonable and a violation" of Rule 1.5.[63]

3. Contingent fees

a. In general

Though the ethical rules impose relatively few constraints on lawyers regarding legal fees, they impose more restrictions if the fee is contingent on the result achieved for the client. A common type of contingent fee is calculated as a percentage of the client's recovery. In another type, the client pays an hourly or a flat fee, but pays the lawyer an additional amount if a specified result is achieved.[64]

Historically, the bar has concerned itself more with lawyers who charge contingent fees than hourly ones (although we have seen that dishonest lawyers who charge hourly fees manipulate the system just as easily). The reasoning is that lawyers who hold financial stakes in their clients' recoveries may engage in improper tactics to make sure their clients get good

---

62. In re Green, 11 P.3d 1078, 1088-1089 (Colo. 2000). The court cited other decisions that reached similar conclusions.

63. Atty. Grievance Commn. of Md. v. Kreamer, 946 A.2d 500 (Md. 2008). The attorney in question had previously been suspended for other violations, and the violation in this case involved several complaints in addition to billing for billing. Ms. Kreamer was disbarred.

64. Restatement § 35, comment a.

"First, we discuss my percentage of any water you find, real or imagined."

recoveries (in which they will share) or, conversely, may settle cases too cheaply and quickly in order to move on to the next client.[65]

Until the latter part of the twentieth century, the bar frowned on contingent fees and viewed them with suspicion. Over time, the use of contingent fees has become more accepted. One reason is that many clients who do not have the funds to hire lawyers cannot obtain representation unless the fee is paid out of the client's recovery. Contingent fees allow access to justice for people who are not wealthy. Also, while the use of an hourly fee sets up a conflict between the lawyer's interests and the client's, the use of a contingent fee usually aligns the interests of lawyer and client. If the lawyer is to be paid a percentage of the client's recovery, the better the client does, the better the lawyer does. While some ethical concerns about contingent fees persist, the rules allow lawyers to charge contingent fees except if the fee is contingent on achieving a particular outcome in a

---

65. Rule 1.8(i), restricting lawyers from acquiring a proprietary interest in litigation, is discussed later in this chapter.

criminal case or a domestic relations case.[66] Still, the rules impose more specific disclosure requirements for contingent fees than for other legal fees.

Rule 1.5(c)

Rule language*	Authors' explanation**
A fee may be contingent on the outcome of the matter for which the service is rendered, except in a matter in which a contingent fee is **prohibited by paragraph (d) or other law.**	Rule 1.5(d) bars contingent fees in many criminal and domestic relations cases. See Section b below. Other law sometimes bars such fees. Rule 1.5(a) requires that contingent fees be reasonable. Comment 3.
A contingent fee agreement shall be in a writing signed **by the client** and shall **state the method by which the fee is to be determined,** including the **percentage** or percentages that shall accrue to the lawyer in the event of settlement, trial or appeal; litigation and other expenses to be deducted from the recovery; and whether such expenses are to be deducted before or after the contingent fee is calculated.	The agreement must specify the percentage of the recovery to be earned by the lawyer and indicate whether the percentage to be charged depends on how the case proceeds. The agreement must explain whether expenses are to be deducted from the total settlement or judgment before or after the lawyer's fee is calculated.
The agreement must clearly **notify** the client of any **expenses for which the client will be liable** whether or not the client is the prevailing party.	The agreement needs to explain which expenses the client must pay even if she gets no recovery.
Upon conclusion of a contingent fee matter, the lawyer shall provide the client with a written statement stating the outcome of the matter and, if there is a recovery, showing the remittance to the client and the method of its determination.	When the matter is concluded, the lawyer must provide this client with another writing explaining what fee and expenses were charged and how they were calculated.

*All emphasis added.

**This and other authors' explanations draw from the comments to the rules and from other sources. They are not comprehensive but highlight some important interpretive points.

What difference does it make whether expenses are deducted from the client's recovery before or after the lawyer's fee is calculated?

This is best explained by example. Suppose a client is injured in a car accident. The lawyer sues the other driver, who was at fault, and obtains a verdict for the client of $100,000. Litigation expenses were $10,000. The lawyer is to receive a contingent fee of 40 percent of the recovery. If the

---

66. See Restatement § 35(1).

lawyer's fee is calculated before expenses are taken out, here's what happens:

Fee calculated before expenses subtracted	
Total recovery:	$100,000
Lawyer's fee:	40,000
Expenses:	10,000
Client's recovery:	50,000

Suppose instead that the expenses are deducted from the total amount before the lawyer's fee is calculated. Here's what happens:

Fee calculated after expenses subtracted	
Total recovery:	$100,000
Expenses:	10,000
Lawyer's fee:	36,000
Client's recovery:	54,000

If the litigation expenses are higher, the client's recovery would be affected even more than in this example by whether the fee is calculated before or after expenses are taken out. The rule requires a lawyer to disclose to a client how the lawyer intends to calculate the fee. Note that the rule does not require lawyers to deduct expenses before calculating their fees or to offer clients an option to do so.

Is there any limit on what percentage of the recovery a lawyer may charge as a contingent fee?

The rule does not specify a maximum percentage that may be charged, but contingent fees, like other fees, are subject to the requirement of Rule 1.5 that they be "reasonable." In some jurisdictions, however, other law imposes a ceiling on the percentage that may be charged or imposes other restrictions.

Is it fair for a lawyer to take 30 or 40 percent of a client's recovery as a contingent fee?

That depends. One justification for the use of contingent fees is that, in some cases, it is very uncertain whether the client will obtain any recovery.

The lawyer takes a risk in such cases that he will invest substantial time and obtain no fee for the work. If the contingent fee in successful cases is generous to the lawyer, it compensates for the risk of obtaining no fee in unsuccessful cases.

In some cases, it is fair for the lawyer to get 30 or 40 percent of the client's damages because the lawyer has invested substantial time to obtain that recovery. In other cases, however, the risk of nonrecovery is minimal or nonexistent, and the work required to obtain the recovery is modest. In such cases, some scholars argue, it is not fair for a lawyer to take such a hefty percentage of the recovery. They assert that the norm of a one-third contingent fee in the legal profession allows lawyers to take more than their fair share of the recovery in some percentage of these cases.[67] Other scholars suggest that contingent fee lawyers do not earn higher fees than those of other lawyers.[68] If, however, legal fees are unreasonably high, it's not much comfort if contingent fees are comparable to others.[69]

Another justification often offered for large contingent fees is that many lawyers who handle contingent fee matters earn fees in some matters but not others. The relatively high fee in some cases cross-subsidizes lawyers to handle matters that generate no fees at all.[70] The notion is that it is valuable for plaintiffs to have access to contingent fee lawyers since so many people could not afford to hire lawyers otherwise. If these lawyers were limited to lower percentage contingent fees across the board, they might decline to accept cases that posed a risk of nonrecovery. Some of these cases are meritorious but risky. Or these lawyers might cease handling contingent fee matters altogether. The 30 to 40 percent contingent fee is urged to be fair because lawyers need the cross-subsidy to maintain viable practices.

Professor Nora Freeman Engstrom

A fascinating recent study by Professor Nora Freeman Engstrom suggests that, at least in California, many firms that do personal injury work on a contingency fee basis have become "settlement mills" that advertise on late-night television, handle tens of thousands of claims a year, and avoid litigation. They work cooperatively with insurance companies to settle the vast majority of cases, not on the basis of what courts

---

67. See Lester Brickman, Contingent Fees without Contingencies: Hamlet without the Prince of Denmark? 37 UCLA L. Rev. 29, 105-111 (1989).

68. See Herbert M. Kritzer, The Wages of Risk: The Returns of Contingency Fee Legal Practice, 47 DePaul L. Rev. 267, 290-299, 302 (1998).

69. See Ted Schneyer, Empirical Research with a Policy Payoff: Market Dynamics for Lawyers Who Represent Plaintiffs for a Contingent Fee, 80 Tex. L. Rev. 1829, 1831 n. 15 (2002) (making this point at n. 15 but also providing a lucid review of the empirical analysis of contingent fees).

70. See Restatement § 35, comment b.

have done with comparable cases, but on the basis of past settlements. Engstrom tentatively concludes that victims with modest injuries do relatively well when represented by these mills, but that those with significant injuries would get better settlements or judgments if they were represented by attorneys who took fewer cases and were prepared to litigate if necessary. Insurance companies are willing to offer favorable settlements to the clients of the mills precisely because the mills are willing to recommend modest settlements even for their clients who are severely injured.[71]

Some lawyers who represent defendants in personal injury cases charge their clients (as part of their fee) a percentage of the difference between what a plaintiff sought and what the defendant ultimately had to pay. Is this practice ethically permissible?

The ABA ethics committee concluded that the Model Rules do not prohibit "reverse contingent fees," but it noted that plaintiffs often sue for unrealistically high damage amounts. This makes it difficult to assess the actual benefit to a defendant from the lawyer's work. Therefore, the committee said, a lawyer proposing to charge such a fee should take pains to obtain genuinely informed consent from the client.[72]

b. Criminal and domestic relations cases

Rule 1.5 prohibits lawyers from charging contingent fees in criminal and in most domestic relations cases.[73]

> **Rule 1.5(d)**
> **A lawyer shall not enter into an arrangement for, charge, or collect:**
> **(1) any fee in a domestic relations matter, the payment or amount of which is contingent upon the securing of a divorce or upon the amount of alimony or support, or property settlement in lieu thereof; or**
> **(2) a contingent fee for representing a defendant in a criminal case.**

One concern underlying the bar on contingent fees in domestic relations cases is that lawyers should not have a financial stake in their clients' ultimate divorce. Traditionally, lawyers were obliged to make efforts to

---

71. Nora Freeman Engstrom, Run of the Mill Justice, 22 Geo. J. Leg. Ethics 1485 (2009).

72. ABA Standing Comm. on Ethics & Prof. Resp., Formal Op. 93-373.

73. New Jersey authorities have concluded that the ban on contingent fees in criminal cases also applies to representation of clients defending against charges of traffic violations. N.J. Sup. Ct. Advisory Comm. on Prof. Ethics, Op. 717 (2010) (available at http://www.judiciary.state.nj.us/notices/2010/n100308d.pdf).

encourage a divorcing couple to reconcile. If the lawyer's fee depended on the parties actually divorcing, lawyers might foment further discord between the parties to ensure that they would get paid. However, after a divorce has been granted, a lawyer may charge a contingent fee to collect past due alimony or child support.[74]

There are several potential problems with the use of fees that are contingent on successful outcomes in criminal cases. The concerns are primarily with possible conflicts between the interests of lawyer and client, and with the possibility that the lawyer will charge an excessive fee.

> **FOR EXAMPLE:** Suppose that a criminal defense lawyer agrees that her client will pay her a substantial fee if the client is acquitted. Suppose then that the client wants to go to trial and give false testimony as to her alibi. The lawyer's financial stake in the acquittal might tempt the lawyer to allow the client to give false testimony. What if, instead, the client wanted to accept a favorable plea agreement in which the client would plead guilty to a criminal charge in exchange for the dismissal of other charges and a light penalty? The lawyer might be tempted to discourage the client from pleading guilty because her doing so would result in the lawyer not getting paid.

Another possible problem with the use of contingent fees in criminal cases is that clients facing criminal charges may be vulnerable and may accept fee agreements that overcompensate the lawyer. Because a contingent fee is uncertain, a client might agree to a high contingent fee, doubting that it would ever come due.[75]

Note that Rule 1.5(d) applies only to defense attorneys and not to prosecutors. In 2010, the district attorney in Denver gave bonuses averaging $1,100 to prosecutors who tried at least five cases and won convictions in at least 70 percent of them. Defense attorneys challenged the convictions that these prosecutors had obtained on the ground that the prosecutors had a financial stake in the outcomes. The prosecutor argued that this created only a "perceived conflict" and that the defendants could not get new prosecutors unless they proved "actual" conflicts.[76]

---

74. Rule 1.5, Comment 6.

75. Criminal defendants are often vulnerable regardless of the nature of the fee arrangement. It is not uncommon, for example, for a criminal defense lawyer to insist that a client pay, for example, $10,000 before the lawyer will agree to accept the case. For a low-income client, the amount may be enormous, but the stakes are so high that the client may feel tremendous pressure to produce the cash.

76. Jessica Fender, Defense Attorney Cites DA Bonuses in Bid for New Prosecutor, Denver Post (Mar. 29, 2011) (available at http://www.denverpost.com/news/ci_17722035).

"My client got twenty years, yet he paid me in full. It just shows the system works."

4. Forbidden and restricted fee and expense arrangements

a. Buying legal claims

Can a collection lawyer purchase claims from a client and then pursue collection on his own behalf?

Some lawyers do collection work for retailers and lenders, suing purchasers and borrowers who have not paid their bills. Rule 1.8(i) states that a lawyer may not "acquire a proprietary interest in the . . . subject matter of litigation the lawyer is conducting for a client," except for permitted liens and contingent fees.[77] Under this rule, a lawyer may not obtain an interest in a claim on which the lawyer is representing the client. However, if a lawyer purchases a claim from a client and ceases to represent the client in the collection of that claim, the transaction would no longer violate Rule 1.8(i).

---

77. See In re Rivera-Arvelo, 830 F. Supp. 665 (D.P.R. 1993) (in which a lawyer was disbarred because he had acquired an interest in property that was the subject of a lawsuit in which he was representing a client).

b. Financial assistance to a client

The same concerns that led lawyers to look askance at contingent fees have led to restrictions on lawyers providing financial assistance to clients during the course of litigation. These are stated in Rule 1.8(e).

> **Rule 1.8(e)**
> **A lawyer shall not provide financial assistance to a client in connection with pending or contemplated litigation, except that:**
> **(1) a lawyer may advance court costs and expenses of litigation, the repayment of which may be contingent on the outcome of the matter; and**
> **(2) a lawyer representing an indigent client may pay court costs and expenses of litigation on behalf of the client.**

One goal of this rule is to prevent lawyers from having too big a stake in the outcome of litigation, for fear that this will produce an improper level of zeal. Likewise, if a lawyer offers to pay a client's living expenses while the lawsuit is going on, a client might pursue a frivolous suit to obtain the offered financial support.[78]

Despite these concerns, the rule allows lawyers to pay court costs and litigation expenses, including the cost of needed medical examinations or other costs to obtain evidence.[79] If the client is not indigent, the client is ultimately responsible for paying these costs, but they may be taken out of the client's recovery. If the client is indigent, the lawyer need not attempt to collect these sums from the client.

PROBLEM 8-2 AN IMPOVERISHED CLIENT

This problem is based on a real case handled by students who were supervised by one of the authors.

You have your own private practice. One of your clients is Gerald Mahoney, a 62-year-old man who recently lost his job as a night security guard at a local mall. According to Mr. Mahoney, the manager who fired him said that Mahoney seemed to be "slowing down" and that "it was time to get some younger blood around here." He was given two weeks' notice. He came to see you because he has no pension plan and almost no savings.

---

78. Rule 1.8, Comment 10.
79. Id.

You brought suit against Mahoney's employer under the Age Discrimination in Employment Act. In its answer to your complaint, the employer admitted that it fired Mahoney, but said that the firing was justified because he was sitting around too much and not making rounds often enough. Nevertheless, your preliminary investigation suggests that other employees have been fired because of their age. You think there is a decent chance that Mahoney will win his case. The case probably will come to trial in about three months. If he prevails, Mahoney could be awarded $50,000 in damages, of which you would collect one-third under your contingency fee agreement.

Yesterday, Mahoney showed up in your office. He said that he had used up his savings and was no longer able to pay his $400 per month rent. He had been served with an eviction notice. His telephone had been disconnected because he had no money to pay the phone bill. Mahoney said that because he has no living relatives, if he is evicted next month, he will have to live on the streets.

If Mahoney is evicted, it will be difficult for you to continue to represent him because it will be hard to stay in contact. Even if he stays in his apartment, the fact that he no longer has a phone will make it difficult for you to prepare him for trial. More important, probably, is that unless he gets some emergency funds while the case is pending, he may not have enough to eat.

You would like to give Mahoney some money to help him to get by while the case is pending and avoid his having to drop the case for lack of funds. Specifically, you would like to buy him a prepaid cell phone so that you can call him when you need to talk to him about the case, and you would like to pay his rent for the next three months so that he is not put on the street before his case gets to trial. Also, you'd like to give him some cash for groceries.

May you pay these expenses?

---

c. Publication rights

Suppose a famous pop star asks you to represent him in a criminal case. His fortune is spent, his financial situation disastrous. Can you agree to take on the matter in exchange for a promise that when it is all over, you will have exclusive rights to publish a book about the case? Rule 1.8(d) says that you may not.

Rule 1.8(d)
Prior to the conclusion of representation of a client, a lawyer shall not make or negotiate an agreement giving the lawyer literary or

media rights to a portrayal or account based in substantial part on information relating to the representation.

Why not? Isn't this just another version of a contingent fee? The drafters of the rules think not. The problem is that if the case is quickly settled in a quiet plea bargain, no one will want to read the book. On the other hand, if there is a lengthy trial that makes lots of headlines in the newspaper, the book might be a bestseller. A lawyer in such a situation might be tempted to do things that would be bad for the client and good for the book.

The prohibition is on the making of such an arrangement before the case is over. If after the case has concluded the pop star owes you a hefty fee, you and the client could agree to forgive part or all of the debt in exchange for transfer of literary or media rights.

This rule applies to transfer of literary or media rights to the story of the representation. It does not restrict lawyers representing clients in book or movie contracts where the book or movie is not about a case handled by the lawyer.

> **FOR EXAMPLE:** If a cartoonist makes a contract with an independent film company to write a screenplay based on one of her graphic novels, the lawyer who negotiates the contract on her behalf may make an agreement that her fee will be a percentage of the royalties paid to the cartoonist for the movie. However, such an agreement would be subject to Rule 1.8(a), so the lawyer would have to comply with its disclosure requirements.[80]

d. Advance payment of fees and nonrefundable retainer fees

As we have noted, lawyers often ask clients to pay retainer fees for a specified service before the service is performed. When a client pays a retainer fee at the outset, the lawyer has some protection against a client who becomes unwilling or unable to pay for services that the lawyer has already rendered. The lawyer will charge fees against the advance payment as she earns them. The advance is deposited in the lawyer's client trust account (discussed below), and the lawyer withdraws portions of the advance as they are earned. If the lawyer does not earn the whole amount advanced, the unearned portion of the advance must be returned to the client.[81] After the advance payment has been exhausted, if the lawyer

---

80. Rule 1.8, Comment 9.
81. Rule 1.16(d). Apparently no rule requires lawyers to tell clients, upon receiving a retainer fee, that any unearned portion will be refunded or that the client may discharge the lawyer and receive a refund of any unearned portion. We wonder how many clients become dissatisfied with their lawyers soon after representation begins but decline to discharge their lawyers because they

continues to do work for the client, the lawyer usually bills the client periodically.

Another type of fee paid in advance is a lump-sum payment to secure the lawyer's availability for a period of time or for a particular task. For example, a company might pay a lawyer some thousands of dollars each month to advise the company on tax matters if and when the company needs tax advice. This type of retainer, sometimes called a classic retainer or a general retainer, may be treated by the lawyer as having been earned when it is received, because the payment secures the lawyer's availability but does not depend on the performance of any particular task.[82] The lawyer may have to forgo other obligations to maintain his availability.[83] Similarly, a lawyer who conducts interviews with a prospective divorce client often learns confidential information that would preclude her from representing the spouse. That lawyer may charge a reasonable fee for the interview and for having to forgo an opportunity to represent an adverse party.

Some types of representation do not present a genuine risk that the lawyer will have to turn away other business to avoid a conflict. For example, a lawyer who is considering representation of a criminal defendant with no accomplices has little prospect of giving up another client if that client terminates the representation at an early stage. Some states recognize this distinction and prohibit a lawyer from treating a fee paid in advance as earned before the lawyer performs any services, unless proposed representation would create a conflict with other prospective clients.[84]

May a lawyer require a nonrefundable advance payment from an individual client with whom the lawyer has no prior relationship?

This practice is controversial. Such a payment, it is argued, locks the client into the relationship with the lawyer and tends to constrain the client from firing the lawyer if, for example, the lawyer fails to perform adequately. Courts consider it very important to protect the right of clients to fire their lawyers. Public policy disfavors nonrefundable retainers as inconsistent with a lawyer's fiduciary obligations to his client.[85]

---

erroneously believe that the lawyer would then keep their money, just as the seller of a house would keep the buyer's deposit if the buyer changes her mind and decides not to close on the sale.

82. If a lawyer accepts such a payment and then fails to perform his duties under the agreement, he would be subject to suit for breach of contract and might be obliged to return the payment.

83. See In re Lochow, 469 N.W.2d 91, 98 (Minn. 1991) (explaining that most advance payments of fees should be placed in the client trust account, but if a lawyer must forgo other opportunities to be available to serve a client, a retainer may be considered to be earned when paid. The purpose of this type of retainer must be recorded in writing and approved by the client.).

84. In re Mance, 980 A.2d 1196 (D.C. 2009); Advisory Comm. of the Sup. Ct. of Mo., Formal Op. 128 (2010) (available at http://www.mobar.org/ethics/formalopinions/frontpage.htm?terms=Formal%20Op.%20128%20).

85. See Wong v. Michael Kennedy, P.C., 853 F. Supp. 73 (E.D.N.Y. 1994).

A New York lawyer was suspended for two years because he charged nonrefundable retainers to his divorce clients.[86] One of the respondent's written fee agreements with his clients read as follows:

> My minimum fee for appearing for you in this matter is fifteen thousand ($15,000) dollars. This fee is not refundable for any reason whatsoever once I file a notice of appearance on your behalf.[87]

5. Fee disputes

a. Prospective limitations of lawyers' liability and settlement of claims against lawyers

These days, legal malpractice suits are common. Suppose a lawyer decides it is not worth practicing law with a risk of liability hanging over his head. He wants to ask each client to agree in advance not to sue the lawyer for malpractice, no matter what. May the lawyer do that? Rule 1.8(h)(1) says that she may, but only if each client has independent legal representation in making that agreement.

> **Rule 1.8(h)**
> **A lawyer shall not**
> > **(1) make an agreement prospectively limiting the lawyer's liability to a client for malpractice unless the client is independently represented in making the agreement. . . .**

Therefore, usually it is impractical to include a waiver of malpractice liability in a contract for legal services.

---

86. In re Cooperman, 591 N.Y.S.2d 855 (App. Div. 1993), *aff'd*, 633 N.E.2d 1069 (N.Y. 1994). While the law is not entirely settled about which, if any, nonrefundable retainers are enforceable, most judges and ethics committees scrutinize such fee arrangements with a skeptical eye. For discussion of nonrefundable retainers, see Lester Brickman & Lawrence A. Cunningham, Nonrefundable Retainers Revisited, 72 N.C. L. Rev. 1 (1993); Steven Lubet, The Rush to Remedies: Some Conceptual Questions About Nonrefundable Retainers, 73 N.C. L. Rev. 271 (1994).

87. Another one used this language:

> This is the minimum fee no matter how much or how little work I do in this investigatory stage . . . and will remain the minimum fee and not refundable even if you decide prior to my completion of the investigation that you wish to discontinue the use of my services for any reason whatsoever.

Cooperman, 591 N.Y.S.2d at 856.

If a lawyer and a client settle a malpractice claim against the lawyer, does the client have to be separately represented?

If a lawyer makes a mistake for which the lawyer might be liable, the lawyer might contact her malpractice insurance company and/or notify the client. The lawyer and client might well work out a settlement of the potential claim short of litigation. A lawyer may settle with a client who does not have independent legal advice, but the lawyer must advise the client in writing that it is a good idea to get advice from another lawyer before making such a settlement. The lawyer also must give the client a chance to consult another lawyer. Rule 1.8(h)(2) explains.

> **Rule 1.8(h)**
> **A lawyer shall not: ...**
>> **(2) settle a claim or potential claim for such liability with an unrepresented client or former client unless that person is advised in writing of the desirability of seeking and is given a reasonable opportunity to seek the advice of independent legal counsel in connection therewith.**

Also, the settlement of a malpractice claim may not bar the client from filing a disciplinary complaint or require the client to withdraw a complaint that was already filed.[88]

Are lawyers allowed to organize law firms in ways that limit their liability for acts or omissions of their partners?

To answer this question, we need to ask a prior question: To what extent are law partners liable for the acts of others? A partnership involves "[a] voluntary contract between two or more competent persons to place their money, effects, labor and skill ... in lawful commerce or business, with the understanding that there shall be a proportional sharing of profits and losses between them."[89] Until the 1960s, most lawyers who practiced with other lawyers formed general partnerships.[90] In a general partnership, "each partner in the firm [is] vicariously liable, jointly and severally, for the malpractice of each other partner or lawyer-employee. 'Vicarious' liability ... means that the plaintiff [is] not required to demonstrate any personal

---

88. Ohio Sup. Ct. Bd. of Commrs. on Grievances & Disc., Op. 2010-3 (available at http://www.supremecourt.ohio.gov/Boards/BOC/Advisory_Opinions/2010/Op_10-003.doc).

89. Black's Law Dictionary 1120 (6th ed., West 1990), cited in Susan Saab Fortney, Professional Liability Issues Related to Limited Liability Partnerships, 39 S. Tex. L. Rev. 399, 400 n. 4 (1998).

90. Thomas D. Morgan, Conflicts of Interest and the New Forms of Professional Associations, 39 S. Tex. L. Rev. 215, 216 (1998).

wrongdoing of a particular firm lawyer in order to hold the firm lawyer [liable]."[91]

Other organizational structures allow lawyers to invest resources together and share profits but limit their liability for the acts or omissions of their partners.[92] One common structure is a "limited liability partnership" or "LLP."[93] This form of organization offers lawyers a degree of protection from malpractice liability for their partners' actions. The point is to "make their pockets shallower."[94] If a firm is organized as an LLP, one partner is liable for his own conduct and that of others he supervises, but is otherwise not vicariously liable for the conduct of his partners.[95] The District of Columbia and every state have passed legislation allowing lawyers to organize firms as LLPs.[96]

So are lawyers prohibited from these organizational limitations of liability? Though the LLP might protect lawyers to some extent from liability for the malpractice of their partners, Rule 1.18 does not prohibit this arrangement, "provided that each lawyer remains personally liable to the client for his or her own conduct" and provided that the firm complies with other restrictions imposed by law.[97]

Why aren't all law firms LLPs?

Perhaps some clients aren't enthusiastic about retaining firms that limit their liability for malpractice this way. In addition, some analysts have suggested that the LLP formula may harm a firm in the long run. It "means that [the partners] are less careful in making decisions about what risks and

---

91. Charles W. Wolfram, Inherent Powers in the Crucible of Lawyer Self-Protection: Reflections on the LLP Campaign, 39 S. Tex. L. Rev. 359, 365 (1998).

92. Morgan, supra n. 90, at 216-217.

93. The LLP structure was authorized by state statutes in the early 1990s in the wake of the savings and loan scandals, which had resulted in many cases in which law partners at elite firms such as Kaye, Scholer and Jones Day found themselves personally liable for millions of dollars because of the misfeasance of certain of their partners in representing the savings and loans. See John S. Dzienkowski, Legal Malpractice and the Multistate Law Firm: Supervision of Multistate Offices; Firms as Limited Liability Partnerships; and Predispute Agreements to Arbitrate Client Malpractice Claims, 36 S. Tex L. Rev. 967, 981-982 (1995) (recounting how the savings and loan mess led to the creation of LLPs).

94. Dennis E. Curtis, Old Knights and New Champions: Kaye, Scholer, the Office of Thrift Supervision, and the Pursuit of the Dollar, 66 S. Cal. L. Rev. 985, 1014 (1993).

95. Fortney, supra n. 89, at 402.

96. Id. at 403-404. A related development is the creation of limited liability companies, which offer similar benefits for corporate entities. LLCs differ from LLPs in that the LLCs are subject to more regulatory formalities than LLPs. Id. at 402 n. 18.

97. Rule 1.8, Comment 14. Similarly, Restatement § 58 acknowledges that lawyers who are partners in LLPs may be protected from the vicarious liability imposed on general partners. Some drafters of the Restatement preferred to articulate a general rule of vicarious liability for law partners. See Wolfram, supra n. 91, at 370 n. 32.

expenses to take on [and] have less incentive to commit themselves to a long and difficult turnaround when the firm gets into trouble."[98]

b. Fee arbitration

Many bar associations have established committees to intermediate between lawyers and clients who have disputes over fees. The lawyer might initiate this process in connection with a client who refuses to pay. A client might initiate this process because the client believes that the lawyer is charging too much. A comment to Rule 1.5 notes that if a jurisdiction has set a mandatory mediation or arbitration process for resolution of fee disputes, a lawyer must comply with it. If the available process is voluntary, the comment urges that a lawyer "should conscientiously consider submitting to it."[99]

May a lawyer ask clients to agree in advance to arbitrate any disputes about the lawyer's services?

Many lawyers include clauses in their retainer agreements in which both parties agree to go to binding arbitration in the event of a fee dispute. Some of these also require clients to agree to binding arbitration of any malpractice claims. Some have questioned the use of such clauses because clients are asked to waive their right to sue before the service is provided. However, the ABA ethics committee concluded that such an agreement is proper when the client is carefully advised of the advantages and disadvantages of arbitration, the client gives informed consent, and the provision does not insulate the lawyer from liability that might otherwise be imposed by law.[100] For example, the lawyer should explain that in agreeing to arbitration, the client would waive her right to a jury trial, some of her discovery rights, and her right to appeal. Some other ethics committees, however, have declared that it is unethical for a lawyer to require a client to sign an agreement to arbitrate any dispute before a dispute has arisen, unless the client has the advice of independent counsel before signing the agreement.[101]

---

98. Columnist Steven Pearlstein, quoted in Debra Cassens Weiss, Three Letters — LLP — Helped Spur Howrey's Downfall, Columnist Says, ABA J. (Mar. 21, 2011) (available at http://www.abajournal.com/news/article/three_lettersllphelped_spur_howreys_downfall_columnist_says).

99. Rule 1.5, Comment 14 [Delaware]. In the ABA's Model Rules, it is Comment 9.

100. ABA Standing Comm. on Ethics & Prof. Resp., Formal Op. 02-425.

101. Jean Fleming Powers, Ethical Implications of Attorneys Requiring Clients to Submit Malpractice Claims to ADR, 38 S. Tex. L. Rev. 625, 633 (1997) (citing ethics opinions in Washington, D.C., Maryland, and Michigan).

c. Collection of fees

What if your client doesn't pay?

If a client doesn't pay a fee that is due, a lawyer may contact the client to request payment. The lawyer may sue the client to collect the fee (though it is a good idea to think carefully before doing so because some clients counterclaim for malpractice). A lawyer may use a collection agency or hire another lawyer to collect a fee owed by a client, but it is important to be sure that the agency or lawyer will not use improper methods of fee collection (see below). As discussed in Chapter 4, many jurisdictions allow lawyers to withhold documents prepared by the lawyer for which payment has not been received, but only if doing so will not unreasonably harm the client.[102]

Does state or federal law restrict lawyers' methods of fee collection?

Lawyers are subject to the Fair Debt Collection Practices Act[103] if they regularly engage in consumer debt collection activities.[104] This means they may not make "false or misleading representations" or engage in various abusive and unfair practices.[105] Violators are subject to civil liability in claims by harassed debtors and subject to enforcement actions by the Federal Trade Commission.[106]

Several state consumer statutes (including those in Connecticut, Louisiana, Massachusetts, and Texas) apply to lawyers and forbid various unfair and deceptive practices.[107] Some of the consumer statutes impose quite specific prohibitions, and violation may result in the award of double,

---

102. In Chapter 4, see the section on "Terminating a Lawyer-Client Relationship"; see also Restatement § 43, comment c.

103. 15 U.S.C. § 1692 et seq. (2006).

104. Heintz v. Jenkins, 514 U.S. 291 (1995). The act, one version of which was enacted in 1977, exempted lawyers from coverage, but in 1986, Congress repealed this exemption. Id. at 294-295.

105. Id. at 292.

106. Id. at 293.

107. Susan P. Koniak & George M. Cohen, Under Cloak of Settlement, 82 Va. L. Rev. 1051, 1079 n. 88 (1996). These authors also state that

> [c]ourts in four other states — Montana, Oregon, South Carolina and Washington — have suggested such claims would be upheld in appropriate circumstances. . . . Three states — Maryland, North Carolina and Ohio — have statutes that exclude lawyers from coverage. . . . Cases in three more states — Illinois, New Hampshire and New Jersey — have rejected the application of consumer protection statutes to lawyers. . . . Cases in Arkansas, Idaho and Pennsylvania suggest that lawyers may be exempt from liability under consumer protection statutes in those states.

Id.

treble, or punitive damages. In addition, some allow the award of attorneys' fees against the violator.[108]

While the application of the state consumer statutes to lawyers is variable, lawyers are well advised to avoid some of the debt collection practices prohibited by those statutes. For example, a lawyer should not

- commit any acts of harassment against a debtor or make a frivolous claim,
- retain documents or unearned fees that should be turned over to a client as leverage to secure payment of fees,
- make any false or misleading statements about the fee claim,
- reveal information to a third party (or threaten to do so) to get a client to pay a fee.[109]

May lawyers obtain liens on client property?[110]

As we explained earlier, historically the rules have prohibited a lawyer from acquiring a "proprietary interest" in a client's case. However, Rule 1.8(i) allows a lawyer to charge an otherwise permitted contingent fee or to "acquire a lien authorized by law to secure the lawyer's fee or expenses."

How would a lawyer acquire a lien on a client's property?

Each state has law that authorizes liens — some by statute, some by common law, and some by contract. A lawyer who agrees to represent a client in a matter might contract with the client to secure the payment of the legal fee by a lien on the client's summer home. If the client did not pay the fee, the lawyer might assert a claim against the property.

The comments following Rule 1.8 explain that such a lien, acquired by contract, constitutes a business transaction with a client and is covered by Rule 1.8(a).[111] This means that the client is entitled to fair terms, a clear explanation of the terms in writing, and written encouragement and opportunity to seek the advice of an independent lawyer before the client agrees to give the lawyer a lien on the property.

---

108. See, e.g., N.C. Gen. Stat. § 75-16.1 (2010).

109. Restatement § 41, comment c, reporter's note (listing cases in which lawyers were alleged to have engaged in the listed behavior as methods of fee collection).

110. This section refers to client property other than documents that the client provided to the lawyer or that the lawyer created during the course of the representation. The lawyer's obligation to return documents is discussed in Chapter 4, in the section on termination of representation.

111. The Restatement also provides that "acquisition of . . . a security interest [in property not connected to the representation] is a business or financial transaction with a client within the meaning of § 126." Restatement § 43(4).

d. Fees owed to a lawyer who withdraws or is fired before the matter is completed

If a lawyer withdraws from representing a client before the representation is completed, whether the lawyer is entitled to payment for the work done depends on the reason she withdrew. This most often comes up in contingent fee cases, where the lawyer generally receives no payment until after the case is settled or tried. If the client has breached the contract with the lawyer — by failing to cooperate in the representation, for example — the lawyer may be considered justified in withdrawing. (See Rule 1.16(b) for a list of reasons a lawyer would be justified in withdrawing.) In such a case, the lawyer would be entitled to compensation on a quantum meruit basis (an equitable assessment of the value of the work done). On the other hand, if the lawyer withdraws from representing the client without good cause, then the lawyer is breaching the contract and may forfeit her right to recover any fees for the work done.[112]

If a client fires his lawyer in a contingent fee case, the lawyer may charge a quantum meruit fee for services already performed, assuming that those services had some value. A retainer agreement that provides for payment of more fees than would be recovered on a quantum meruit basis would violate the prohibition on charging excessive fees.[113]

6. Dividing fees with other firms or with nonlawyers

a. Division of fees between lawyers not in the same firm

If two lawyers in different firms work on a case, may they split the fee? Two lawyers in different firms may work on a single matter for various reasons. An inexperienced lawyer might enlist an expert in a certain field to assist her on a matter. A lawyer might ask another lawyer to assist because a matter must be litigated in a jurisdiction in which she is not licensed to practice. One lawyer might collaborate with another because of the amount of work that needs to be done or to ensure that counsel would be available during the vacation or sick leave of one of the lawyers.

---

112. See, e.g., Augustson v. Linea Aera Nacional-Chile, S.A., 76 F.3d 658 (5th Cir. 1996) (whether a lawyer is entitled to quantum meruit compensation upon withdrawal depends on whether the lawyer can prove that there was just cause for withdrawal).

113. See, e.g., Fla. B. v. Hollander, 607 So. 2d 412 (Fla. 1992) (fee agreement that provided for substantial fees upon discharge of lawyer was found improper because it provided for excessive fees; lawyer suspended for six months); see generally Lester Brickman, Setting the Fee When the Client Discharges a Contingent Fee Attorney, 41 Emory L.J. 367 (1992).

If two lawyers in different law firms work on a case, both should be paid for their services. If the fee agreement provides for hourly fees, it is easy to calculate which lawyer is entitled to be paid what amount. However, if the agreement provides for a contingent fee, the allocation of the fee is less obvious, especially because some contingent fee lawyers do not keep time records, so it is not easy to measure the relative contributions of the two lawyers. Rule 1.5(e) allows the lawyers to share a fee, but the rule imposes conditions to protect clients.

> **Rule 1.5(e)**
> **A division of a fee between lawyers who are not in the same firm may be made only if:**
>> **(1) the division is in proportion to the services performed by each lawyer or each lawyer assumes joint responsibility for the representation;**
>> **(2) the client agrees to the arrangement, including the share each lawyer will receive, and the agreement is confirmed in writing; and**
>> **(3) the total fee is reasonable.**[114]

If one lawyer refers a case to another lawyer, may the first lawyer be paid a referral fee?

Suppose a client seeking a divorce approaches a lawyer who handles only medical malpractice cases. This lawyer refers the client to another lawyer who does domestic relations work. Under the rule quoted above, the referring lawyer may indeed collect a referral fee, and it could be a large part of the total fee, provided that she meets various conditions. First, she must take on "financial and ethical responsibility for the representation as if the lawyers were associated in a partnership."[115] In addition, the proposed share that each lawyer receives must be disclosed to and approved by the client, the fee-sharing arrangement must be confirmed in writing, and the total fee must be reasonable.

If the referring lawyer is planning to do some work on the case, the lawyers and the client may agree in writing that the lawyers will divide the fee based on the proportion of time spent or work done. In that case, each

---

114. This is North Carolina's version of Rule 1.5(e). This rule varies considerably across states, reflecting policy differences. Although this book usually quotes the Delaware Rules of Professional Conduct because Delaware adopted most of the Model Rules after those rules were revised in 2002, Delaware did not adopt the revised version of Rule 1.5(e). North Carolina did adopt the ABA's revised wording for Rule 1.5(e).

115. Rule 1.5, Comment 8 [North Carolina]. The corresponding comment in the Model Rules is Comment 7.

one will have to take financial and ethical responsibility for that lawyer's work, but not for the case as a whole.

What does it mean for a lawyer to take "financial and ethical responsibility for the representation"?

This phrase means that in the event of disciplinary action or a malpractice suit, the lawyers agree to share responsibility as if they were law partners. It follows from their equal responsibility that each lawyer has a duty of supervision under Rule 5.1. That rule makes lawyers in supervisory positions responsible to ensure compliance with the rules and makes them responsible for some violations of the ethics rules by others working on a matter.[116]

A lawyer who collects a fee for referring a case and who does not plan to collaborate on the case is well advised to follow the referred case closely because if the lawyer to whom the case is referred commits an ethical breach or is negligent, the referring lawyer could be disciplined or sued. The Utah State Bar Ethics Advisory Opinion Committee explained:

> Lawyers contemplating a joint-responsibility arrangement must realize that each lawyer's responsibility is significant. The lawyer receiving a referral fee under a joint-responsibility arrangement cannot simply "hand off" the client to the receiving lawyer.... [A] referring and receiving lawyer must work out arrangements that give reasonable assurance that neither will violate the Rules of Professional Conduct in the matter in question. Partners are responsible for each others' violations of the rules if they order the violations, knowingly ratify them, or knowingly fail to take reasonable, potentially effective remedial action. Under these circumstances, therefore, both referring and receiving lawyers would be responsible for each others' ethical violations.[117]

Lawyers often make fee-splitting agreements that do not comply with Rule 1.5(e). Some courts refuse to enforce such agreements because they violate

---

116. While lawyers in different firms are not partners, the "joint responsibility" fee-sharing arrangement gives them responsibility for the work of the other as if they were partners. See ABA Standing Comm. on Ethics & Prof. Resp., Informal Ethics Op. 85-1514 (joint responsibility means that each lawyer assumes responsibility to client "comparable to that of a partner in a law firm under similar circumstances, including financial responsibility [and] ethical responsibility to the extent a partner would have ethical responsibility for actions of other partners in a law firm in accordance with Rule 5.1"). When Rule 1.5 was amended in 2002, Comment 7 was amended to delete a reference to the obligations stated in 5.1, but this was replaced by a reference to "financial and ethical responsibility for the representation as if the lawyers were associated in a partnership." This language was based on Informal Opinion 85-1514. ABA Center for Professional Responsibility, Model Rule 1.5, Reporter's Explanation of Changes, Comment 7, http://www.americanbar.org/groups/professional_responsibility/policy/ethics_2000_commission/e2k_rule15rem.html (accessed Nov. 16, 2012).

117. Utah St. B., Ethics Advisory Op. Comm., Op. No. 93-121.

the public policy stated in the rule.[118] But some have held that a lawyer may recover a share of the fees on a quantum meruit basis even if the fee-splitting agreement is unenforceable.[119]

b. Sharing fees with nonlawyers

While lawyers are allowed to share legal fees with other lawyers, they are not allowed to share legal fees with nonlawyers, except in certain narrow circumstances. As to splitting fees with nonlawyers in general, Rule 5.4(a) provides that "[a] lawyer or law firm shall not share legal fees with a nonlawyer, except that: . . . (3) a lawyer or law firm may include nonlawyer employees in a compensation or retirement plan, even though the plan is based in whole or in part on a profit-sharing arrangement." The purpose of the rule is to protect the lawyer's independent judgment from being affected by influence or pressure from nonlawyers. Rule 5.4 is being subjected to increasing criticism because other countries are allowing their lawyers to form multidisciplinary service firms with nonlawyers.

Law firms may pay salaries and bonuses to nonlawyer employees but may not routinely divide profits among lawyers and nonlawyers. So, for example, if a firm employed a paralegal with skills like those of Erin Brockovich (the paralegal made famous by the movie about her) and made millions as a result of her work, it could give her a big bonus but not a share of the annual profits.[120]

Can lawyers pay "runners" who find them clients who are accident victims?

In most states, lawyers may not pay referral fees to nonlawyers who send them clients,[121] except that they may pay lawyer referral services for making information available about their practices.[122] Some personal injury lawyers nevertheless employ "runners" to go to the scene of accidents or to hospital emergency rooms to distribute business cards or brochures; some of them have been disbarred.[123] Likewise, a lawyer may not pay an

---

118. See, e.g., Post v. Bregman, 707 A.2d 806 (Md. 1998).

119. Daynard v. Ness, Motley, Loadholt, Richardson & Poole, P.A., 178 F. Supp. 2d 9 (D. Mass. 2001).

120. For a brief biography of Erin Brockovich Ellis, see http://exsmo.com/museum/famous/brockovich/brockovich.pdf (accessed Nov. 16, 2012).

121. Restatement § 10, comment d.

122. See ABA Standing Comm. on Ethics & Prof. Resp., Informal Op. 85-1510.

123. In one notable case, a lawyer had used a runner to solicit cases from accident victims while they were hospitalized, paid the runner so much that it amounted to fee-splitting with a nonlawyer, provided financial assistance to clients, and committed other ethical violations. The court noted that some amount of solicitation is constitutionally protected but concluded that the manner in which the solicitations were conducted in this case was unreasonable and that the runner was not merely a

accountant, a real estate broker, or anyone else who comes into contact with a potential client group for sending potential clients her way.

7. Payment of fees by a third party

The principle of maintaining a lawyer's independent judgment has produced restrictions on allowing one person to pay a lawyer to represent another person. As a practical matter, it is necessary to allow parents to pay for the representation of minor children who need lawyers. Automobile insurance policies typically provide that the insurance company will provide and pay for a lawyer to represent the insured person if a suit is filed based on a claim covered by the policy. Likewise, some employers pay for the legal representation of employees in matters that arise out of workplace activities. Consequently, the rules allow a third party to pay a lawyer's fee, but only if the client consents after being advised, the third person does not direct the lawyer's decisions or otherwise interfere in the representation, and the lawyer avoids sharing with the third person any confidences learned in the course of the representation.[124]

B. Lawyer as custodian of client property and documents

Lawyers very often have responsibility for money, documents, and other valuables that belong to clients. They have a fiduciary duty to protect their clients' possessions and to turn money and property over to clients upon request or, in some cases, promptly after receiving it. Some of a lawyer's responsibilities with respect to client property are addressed in Rule 1.15, which you should read with care.

---

paid employee but a person with whom the lawyer was unlawfully sharing a fee. The lawyer was disbarred. In re Pajerowski, 721 A.2d 992 (N.J. 1998).

124. Rule 1.8(f). The Restatement articulates similar restrictions but provides that a third person may direct the lawyer's judgment if the client consents and the direction is reasonable. Restatement § 134. See generally Nancy Moore, Ethical Issues in Third-Party Payment: Beyond the Insurance Defense Paradigm, 16 Rev. Litig. 585 (1997) (exploring the relationship of lawyers to third parties who pay their fees such as parents of children represented by the lawyers, employers who pay legal fees of employees, and other examples).

1. Client trust accounts

One important aspect of the lawyer-client relationship involves a lawyer's management of the client trust account, the bank account in which the lawyer keeps funds that belong to various clients. If a lawyer takes possession of money from a client or third party in connection with a representation, she must keep it "separate from the lawyer's own property. Funds shall be kept in a separate account maintained in the state where the lawyer's office is situated, or elsewhere with the consent of the client or third person."[125]

Property other than money must be "appropriately safeguarded," and the lawyer must keep "complete records" of the funds or other property for a period specified in state rules (the ABA recommends five years) after the events that they record.[126]

This rule permits a lawyer to keep funds that belong to multiple clients in a single account, but the funds that belong to clients must be kept in a separate account from any funds that belong to the lawyer.[127] This rule seeks to ensure that the lawyer does not spend client funds improperly and that the lawyer's creditors are not able to seize funds held by the lawyer that belong to clients.

If a client pays a lawyer in advance a sum against which the lawyer may charge fees, this sum should be deposited into the client trust account. The lawyer may withdraw funds against this payment only as fees are earned or expenses incurred.[128] If the lawyer charges a flat fee and collects it in advance, the funds must be kept in trust until the services have been performed.[129]

Rule 1.15 bars lawyers from depositing their own funds into the client trust account, to ensure that lawyers do not attempt to hide their own monies from creditors in their client accounts.

> **FOR EXAMPLE:** J. Kevin Lund, a Kansas lawyer, was divorced from his wife and ordered to pay child support. When he fell behind in his payments, his wife obtained a judgment for some past-due amounts. Lund deposited some of his personal funds into his client trust account, thus protecting them from attachment by his wife. He was suspended from practice for a year.[130]

---

125. Rule 1.15(a).
126. Id.
127. Rule 1.15, Comment 1.
128. Rule 1.15, Comment 7(b) [Delaware]; Rule 1.15(c) [ABA Model Rules].
129. In re Mance, 980 A.2d 1196 (D.C. 2009).
130. In re Lund, 19 P.3d 110 (Kan. 2001).

The rule also requires lawyers to keep detailed records of deposits into and withdrawals from the client trust account. Many state bars have initiated programs to conduct random audits of client trust accounts to ensure that lawyers comply with these rules.

Once you have a license to practice law, one of the quickest and surest ways to lose it is to put funds that belong to a client into your own account (rather than your client trust account) or to "borrow" funds from the client trust account that you have not yet earned. In many jurisdictions, these offenses are considered most grave and are grounds for disbarment. A lawyer may be disciplined for commingling or misappropriation even if the violation was unintentional, even if no client funds were lost, and even if the lawyer's mental capacity is compromised by illness.[131]

2. Responsibility for client property

a. Prompt delivery of funds or property

When a lawyer receives a settlement check or other funds that should be paid (at least in part) to a client, the lawyer is obliged to notify the client and to make prompt payment of all funds due to the client. If the client asks, the lawyer must provide a record of the amount received and of how much was paid to whom.[132] The same obligation applies if the person who has an interest in the funds is someone other than a client. This sounds fairly routine, but some lawyers contrive to obtain funds that belong to others as a result of settlement negotiations; they then conceal their misconduct by giving clients inadequate or inaccurate information.

> **FOR EXAMPLE:** James O'Hagan was a partner at Dorsey & Whitney, one of the largest firms in Minneapolis. One of his clients was the famous Mayo Clinic, which he represented in medical malpractice cases. O'Hagan settled some cases but was not always honest with his client about the amounts of the settlements. O'Hagan reportedly settled

---

131. ABA, Annotated Model Rules of Professional Conduct 230-231 (6th ed., ABA 2007); see generally Irene Ricci, Client Trust Funds: How to Avoid Ethical Problems, 11 Geo. J. Leg. Ethics 245 (1998).

132. Rule 1.15(d) provides:

Upon receiving funds or other property in which a client or third person has an interest, a lawyer shall promptly notify the client or third person. Except as stated in this Rule or otherwise permitted by law or by agreement with the client, a lawyer shall promptly deliver to the client or third person any funds or other property that the client or third person is entitled to receive and, upon request by the client or third person, shall promptly render a full accounting regarding such property.

one case for $270,000, but then told the Mayo Clinic that it had settled for $595,000. The Mayo Clinic gave O'Hagan a check for $595,000. He paid $270,000 to the plaintiff's attorney and used the remainder to pay off personal loan obligations. For this and other similar offenses that added up to alleged theft of $3 million, O'Hagan was fined and sentenced to 30 months in prison.[133]

b. Disputes about money or property in lawyer's possession

Suppose a lawyer and her plaintiff client make a contingent fee agreement under which the lawyer will receive one-third of the amount of any settlement. The case then settles for $25,000. The defendant writes a check and sends it to the lawyer, who deposits it in the trust account. The client, upon learning of the settlement, points out to the lawyer that the settlement took place after the lawyer had done only a few hours' work on the matter. The client claims that the original agreement would overcompensate the lawyer. Can the lawyer withdraw her one-third from the trust account?

Model Rule 1.15(e)[134] provides that if there is a dispute about the amount of the fee, the lawyer is to distribute undisputed portions of the settlement and keep the disputed portion in the client trust account. So the lawyer should pay out to the client two-thirds of the settlement amount and should not transfer the remaining third to herself until the dispute is resolved. Even if the lawyer thinks that the client is wrong and that the lawyer is entitled to one-third, the client's inquiry places that amount in dispute.[135]

3. Administering estates and trusts

May a lawyer act as executor of a client's estate?

A lawyer may recommend and may accept appointment as executor of a client's estate. Executors often are paid substantial sums for their services in

---

133. State v. O'Hagan, 474 N.W.2d 613 (Minn. App. 1991). O'Hagan's conduct also would violate Rule 1.15 because he arranged to be in possession of funds that belonged to his client and neither notified the client nor distributed the funds to the client. This conduct also would violate the prohibition against dishonesty in Rule 8.4. O'Hagan was disbarred in the wake of these allegations, but no findings were made as to which Minnesota rules were violated. Instead, O'Hagan was disbarred because he failed to respond to the disciplinary action filed against him. In re O'Hagan, 450 N.W.2d 571 (Minn. 1990). In 1994, O'Hagan was also convicted on federal mail fraud, securities fraud, and money laundering charges and sentenced to 41 months in prison. U.S. v. O'Hagan, 521 U.S. 642 (1997).

134. Rule 1.15(c) in Delaware.

135. See In re Haar, 698 A.2d 412 (D.C. App. 1997) (lawyer who withdrew a legal fee that was disputed by the client because he believed he was entitled to the payment was found to have engaged in negligent misappropriation).

settling estates, but the solicitation of such appointment is not prohibited by Rule 1.8(c) because the payment would be for services rendered. However, a lawyer giving advice about whom to appoint as executor or carrying out the functions of executor for a client might be improperly biased by self-interest in doing so. A lawyer must comply with Rule 1.7 in giving such advice or in acting as executor for a client's estate.[136] This means, for example, that the lawyer must consider whether there is a significant risk that her representation of the estate would be materially limited by the lawyer's responsibilities to another present or former client, to a third person, or by a personal interest of the lawyer. If such a risk is present, the lawyer must assess whether she would be able to provide competent and diligent representation to each affected client. If so, the lawyer may accept appointment as executor, but only if each affected client provides informed consent, confirmed in writing.

C. Conflicts with lawyers' personal or business interests

1. In general

Rule 1.7(a)(2) states that a lawyer has a conflict of interest if "there is a significant risk that the representation of one or more clients will be materially limited . . . by a personal interest of a lawyer." If the lawyer's personal or business interest in a matter is at odds with the interests of her client, she might be unable to provide disinterested advice or advocacy.[137] If such a conflict exists, a lawyer must not represent the client unless all of the conditions in Rule 1.7(b) are met.[138] Here are some hypothetical examples of such conflicts:

■ A lawyer is engaged in settlement negotiations with a lawyer from another firm. The other lawyer happens to be the hiring partner of a firm to which the first lawyer has applied for a job. The lawyer's advocacy on behalf of his client might be compromised by his efforts to appear cooperative to the adverse lawyer.[139]

---

136. Rule 1.8, Comment 8.

137. Rule 1.7, Comment 10.

138. The lawyer must reasonably believe that she will be able to provide competent and diligent representation despite the conflict; the representation must not be prohibited by law; the matter must not involve a lawyer in representing two clients on opposite sides in litigation; and each of the clients must give written informed consent. See Rule 1.7(b).

139. This example is adapted from Rule 1.7, Comment 10.

■ A lawyer who handles Social Security disability cases often refers his clients to a physical therapy clinic. He is part owner of the clinic but does not mention this. The lawyer's obligation to look out for his client's best interests might be compromised by his interest in the profitability of the clinic.[140]

■ A state attorney general is in charge of an investigation of a large corporation whose main offices are located in the state capital. The investigation could lead to criminal fraud charges against the corporation and its officers. This particular corporation was the largest contributor to a campaign fund that assisted the attorney general in his last campaign for election and is likely to do so again — depending on the outcome of the investigation. The attorney general's obligation to the citizens of his state may be compromised by his concerns about the impact of the investigation on his campaign funds.[141]

2. Business transactions between lawyer and client

Sometimes lawyers and clients have strong incentives to do nonlegal business with each other. A client may benefit from doing business with his lawyer because his lawyer may give him loans or equity investments, reduced fees for legal services, and sophisticated business and legal advice. A lawyer may benefit from a business deal with a client by getting in on the ground floor of a new and promising company or by obtaining compensation in the form of an equity investment in a client who is too short of cash to pay legal fees. For decades, real estate lawyers have bought interests in their clients' ventures. More recently, many lawyers who helped in the formation of new dot-com companies were paid with company stock rather than with cash. The attitude of the bar toward deals like these has gradually become more permissive.

The traditional view is that lawyers should avoid doing business with clients. Lawyers have fiduciary obligations to clients. If a lawyer does business with or invests financially in a client, the lawyer's interest in making money or gaining other advantages is likely to conflict with his ability to look out for his client's interests. Because clients trust their lawyers' judgment, it is easy for lawyers to take advantage of that trust in a business deal. It is better to maintain clear boundaries as to the lawyer's role and not to muddy the provision of legal services with other transactions.

---

140. Id.

141. This example was drawn from a story about fund-raising by Alabama Attorney General William Pryor Jr. when he was being considered for a federal judicial appointment. R. Jeffrey Smith & Tania Branigan, GOP Attorneys General Asked for Corporate Contributions, Wash. Post A1 (July 17, 2003).

Rule 1.8(a) does not flatly prohibit lawyers from doing business with clients but strongly discourages them from doing so.

Rule 1.8(a)

A lawyer shall not enter into a business transaction with a client or knowingly acquire an ownership, possessory, security or other pecuniary interest adverse to a client unless:

(1) the transaction and terms on which the lawyer acquires the interest are fair and reasonable to the client and are fully disclosed and transmitted in writing in a manner that can be reasonably understood by the client;

(2) the client is advised in writing of the desirability of seeking and is given a reasonable opportunity to seek the advice of independent legal counsel on the transaction; and

(3) the client gives informed consent, in a writing signed by the client, to the essential terms of the transaction and the lawyer's role in the transaction, including whether the lawyer is representing the client in the transaction.[142]

If you want to buy a client's house or undertake any such transaction, you need to satisfy the conditions articulated in Rule 1.8(a).

Before you make a deal with a client, ask these questions:
- Are the terms fair to the client?
- Have you explained the terms to the client clearly and in writing?
- Have you advised the client in writing that she should get legal advice about the deal from a lawyer not associated with you?
- Has the client had a chance to get advice from another lawyer?
- Has the client given informed consent in writing to the terms of the deal and to your role in the deal?

Do the restrictions on lawyer-client business deals apply to every lawyer-client contract?

No. The rule applies to contracts for goods and services regardless of whether the lawyer is the buyer or the seller. There are a couple of exceptions. The restrictions do not apply

---

142. This is the version of the rule that has been adopted in Pennsylvania; it is identical to Model Rule 1.8(a).

- to a contract for legal services, unless part or all of the fee is to be paid by the transfer of property to the lawyer; so a standard contract for legal services in which the client pays a fee is not covered;
- to a contract in which the client sells the lawyer some product or service that the client normally sells to others. For example, a lawyer may go to a doctor who is his client and pay for the doctor's services without worrying about Rule 1.8(a).[143]

The rule covers business deals between lawyers and clients whether the contracts are related or unrelated to the matter on which the lawyer represents the client.[144] For example, a real estate lawyer who sells title insurance must comply with this provision for the sale of the title insurance.[145] Likewise, if the same lawyer sold his golf clubs to the client, he must comply with the rule.

The rule does not apply to all contracts made by lawyers, only to those in which another party to the contract is a client. As we have observed in earlier chapters, it may be unclear whether a particular individual is a client of a lawyer. The relationship may be tenuous, the legal services may have been completed, or the relationship may involve a mix of business and legal advice.

The cases in which lawyers have been disciplined for violating Rule 1.8 are a gallery of stupid mistakes by lawyers who took advantage of their access to clients' funds or took advantage of their clients' trust. Here are some rules of thumb that can save you from an untimely professional demise.

Several simple steps to avoid inadvertent professional suicide

Don't borrow money from your clients or lend money to your clients unless you take great care to comply with Rule 1.8 (except for litigation expenses, discussed above). Some lawyers have been disbarred for making loans to or borrowing money from clients without making adequate disclosures.[146] Especially in dealing with non-institutional clients, a good

---

143. Rule 1.8, Comment 1.

144. Id.

145. Id.

146. See In re Cordova-Gonzalez, 996 F.2d 1334 (1st Cir. 1993) (Cordova was disbarred because, among other things, he "violated ABA Model Rule 1.8(a) when he borrowed $100,000 from his client Jose Lopez-Nieves. . . . Cordova borrowed money from Lopez-Nieves without disclosing to his client (a) that he did not own the property pledged as collateral, (b) that his wife—who did own the collateral—and he were involved in bankruptcy proceedings, and (c) that the collateral was subject to the jurisdiction of the bankruptcy court, which had not approved the pledge."); People v. Johnson, 35 P.3d 168 (Colo. O.P.D.J. 1999) (court syllabus explained that "disbarment was appropriate sanction for attorney who, along with misconduct involving two other clients, obtained two loans totaling $50,000 from client during pendency of an estate proceeding, having been aware

rule of thumb is: If you or your client needs to borrow money, get it from a bank.

Don't ever borrow a penny from client funds that are entrusted to you. Not even just for a day. Many lawyers with cash-flow problems have junked their careers by temporary appropriation of client funds. Most disciplinary agencies regard this as an extremely serious offense — a sure path to disbarment.

Don't sell your house, your wife's old car, or anything else to a client. Find another buyer. While you can make such a sale to a client if you jump through the hoops listed above, it is risky.[147] What if you sell the car to a client, the car dies a week later, and the client accuses you of having made inadequate disclosures?

Don't ask your client to invest in your business. Suppose your client just got a hefty personal injury settlement. She's got cash on hand. How about suggesting that you and she buy some real estate together? Or maybe you and she could buy old Coca-Cola paraphernalia and then sell it for a profit? Forget it! One lawyer in Indiana got an 18-month suspension for various instances of unethical behavior, including trying out this idea.[148]

Can a lawyer accept stock or stock options as payment for legal services instead of cash?

A lawyer may be paid in the form of stock or stock options, but this type of transaction requires compliance with Rule 1.8.[149] This means that the terms of the transfer must be fair to the client. The lawyer must make a full written disclosure of the terms to the client and must explain that the lawyer's ownership of stock in a client corporation could cause a conflict of interest between the lawyer and the client that would require the lawyer to withdraw from representing the client. The problem is that if the lawyer becomes a shareholder, the lawyer has a personal financial stake in the entity that might be at odds with the interests of the entity as a whole. The

---

that the client had received a bequest from the estate, and failed to advise client to seek independent advice concerning the loan, or obtain her written consent to the loan, and after having made some initial repayment, he thereafter knowingly misled client into believing that he would repay the loan.").

147. See In re Hartke, 529 N.W.2d 678 (Minn. 1995) (lawyer suspended indefinitely for selling his wife's car to a client without making adequate disclosures, and other offenses).

148. In re Davis, 740 N.E.2d 855 (Ind. 2001).

149. The transaction also requires compliance with Rule 1.7, and it may be subject to regulations of the Securities and Exchange Commission. See John S. Dzienkowski & Robert J. Peroni, The Decline in Lawyer Independence: Lawyer Equity Investments in Clients, 81 Tex. L. Rev. 405, 477 (2002).

lawyer-shareholder, for example, might want short-term financial benefits that could be had only if needed research was forgone. The client must be given a chance to get independent legal advice before the stock transfer. The client's consent must be in writing.[150]

PROBLEM 8-3 STARTING A BUSINESS

Events similar to these occurred in Rhode Island.

Ten years ago, you successfully defended Jose Lopez against a misdemeanor charge. As a result, the two of you became friends. You have never represented him on a legal matter since then, and he has never paid you any money since that time, although from time to time, you have given him advice about buying and selling property.

A few months ago, Lopez, who is expert in appliance repair, decided to set up his own appliance repair company, and he asked you to help him in various ways. Together, you found a suitable building, which is the only asset owned by the 1404 Forest Street Corporation (Forest). That corporation is owned by Pasha Harari (she owns all 100 shares).

You are planning to make the following arrangements:

- You will provide $25,000 in start-up money to buy all of the stock in the corporation from Harari. Lopez will put up only a small amount of money, but he will work full-time running the company. You expect to own 20 percent of the company, and Lopez will own 80 percent.
- When you pay the money to Harari, you will have her transfer 80 shares of Forest to Lopez and 20 shares to you.
- You and Lopez have agreed orally that Lopez will get another lawyer to represent him in connection with the purchase of the stock from Harari, but you will prepare the relevant documents.
- Lopez will serve as the president and sole director of Forest. You will serve as its general counsel and will handle its legal matters. You will be paid a salary.

---

150. See ABA Standing Comm. on Ethics & Prof. Resp., Formal Op. 00-418 (available at http://www.americanbar.org/content/dam/aba/publications/YourABA/00_418.authcheckdam.pdf); D.C.B., Ethics Op. 300 (2000) (available at http://www.dcbar.org/for_lawyers/ethics/legal_ethics/opinions/opinion300.cfm); N.Y.C. B. Assn., Ethics Op. 2000-3 (available at http://www2.nycbar.org/Ethics/eth2000-3.htm).

You would prefer to enter into these arrangements without having to make a lot of disclosures to Lopez. He gets nervous about complicated legal information, so if you go overboard on disclosure, he might back out of this deal with you.

What, if any, warnings or disclosures do you have to give to Lopez?

---

3. Gifts from clients

Gifts from clients to lawyers can be problematic.[151] A gift from a client to a lawyer could represent a disguised fee in excess of the "reasonable" limit imposed by Rule 1.5. Or a client could make a gift in response to unfair pressure by the lawyer. For example, a lawyer might suggest to a client that in lieu of paying overdue bills for legal services, the client should change his will to leave his house to the lawyer. Rule 1.8(c) prohibits a lawyer from soliciting substantial gifts or bequests from a client. It also prohibits a lawyer from preparing for a client any instrument (such as a will) giving a gift to the lawyer or his relatives.[152] The rule allows a lawyer to prepare such an instrument on behalf of a close relative, however.

> **Rule 1.8(c)**
> **A lawyer shall not solicit any substantial gift from a client, including a testamentary gift, or prepare on behalf of a client an instrument giving the lawyer or a person related to the lawyer any substantial gift unless the lawyer or other recipient of the gift is related to the client. For purposes of this paragraph, related persons include a spouse, child, grandchild, parent, grandparent or other relative or individual with whom the lawyer or the client maintains a close, familial relationship.**

The rule does not bar lawyers from receiving unsolicited gifts from clients. However, if the gift is too large, the client could later sue for its return.[153]

Therefore, if your client offers you a holiday gift or some other modest thank-you gift, you may accept it. But you may not ask a client for a substantial gift or prepare a document transferring client property to you or

---

151. Also, Rule 1.8(e), discussed earlier in this chapter, bars certain types of financial assistance to clients by lawyers.

152. The practice of writing a client's will in the lawyer's favor is prohibited unless the lawyer is a close relative. For example, in Clements v. Ky. B. Assn., 983 S.W.2d 512 (Ky. 1999), a lawyer was suspended from practice for preparing a will under which she would inherit $50,000.

153. Rule 1.8, Comment 6.

one of your relatives, unless the client is a close relative or the functional equivalent of a close relative. This rule reflects a concern that some lawyers might take advantage of their clients' trust and appreciation by persuading clients to give them property.

4. Sexual relationships with clients

"Can we talk about our attorney-client relationship?"

Lawyers and clients sometimes develop sexual relationships. It is obvious that if a lawyer coerces a client into a sexual relationship (for example, in lieu of paying a fee), the relationship is improper because it is exploitative.[154] However, it is not as clear that there is anything wrong with a truly consensual sexual relationship between a lawyer and a client, especially if there is no harm to the quality of the legal representation. Perhaps there is always a possibility of adverse impact, if only because the romance might

---

154. Many of the reported cases involve clients who retained lawyers for divorce proceedings, at a time when they may have been particularly vulnerable. See, e.g., In re Halverson, 998 P.2d 833 (Wash. 2000) (abrogated in part, not pertinent to the merits, by In re Disciplinary Proceeding Against Anschell, 69 P.3d 844 (Wash. 2003)) (former president of the state bar was a divorce specialist who had edited a book discussing the adverse consequences of lawyer-client sexual relationships but was suspended for one year for having sex with six female divorce clients).

end and then the professional relationship would become strained. In 1996, the ABA Committee on Ethics and Professional Responsibility declined to conclude that sexual relationships with clients were inherently unprofessional, but it advised lawyers to avoid them "because of the danger of impairment to the lawyer's representation." The Committee wrote that "the lawyer would be well advised to refrain from such a relationship. If such a sexual relationship occurs and the impairment is not avoided, the lawyer will have violated ethical obligations to the client."[155]

Some states have suspended lawyers from practice because of consensual lawyer-client sexual relations, even though no disciplinary rule explicitly prohibited the relationship and even though there was no evidence of harm to the client.

> **FOR EXAMPLE:** While Dale Feneli was representing a female client in her claim for damages following an automobile accident, he had oral sex with her. Later, he suggested that she pay her legal fees by engaging in certain sexual acts, specifying a price for each one. He told her that she had other methods of payment that he would enjoy more than money. She sued him, and he paid $25,000 to settle the civil case. In addition, his license was suspended for 18 months.[156]

In one case, a male lawyer was disciplined because he had a sexual relationship with a female client while handling a matter for her. Then, after the work and the romance ended, she hired him to handle another matter for her. In imposing a one-month suspension, the court reasoned:

> First, because of the dependence that so often characterizes the attorney-client relationship, there is a significant possibility that the sexual relationship will have resulted from the exploitation of the lawyer's dominant position and influence and, thus, breached the lawyer's fiduciary obligations to the client. Second, a sexual relationship with a client may affect the independence of the lawyer's judgment. Third, the lawyer's engaging in a sexual relationship with a client may create a prohibited conflict between the interests of the lawyer and those of the client. Fourth, a non-professional, yet emotionally charged, relationship between attorney and client may result in confidences being imparted in circumstances where the attorney-client privilege is not available, yet would have been, absent the personal relationship.[157]

---

155. ABA Standing Comm. on Ethics & Prof. Resp., Formal Op. 92-364.

156. Cleveland B. Assn. v. Feneli, 712 N.E.2d 119 (Ohio 1999).

157. Matter of Tsoutsouris, 748 N.E.2d 856 (Ind. 2004); see also Fla. B. v. Bryant, 813 So. 2d 38 (Fla. 2002) (lawyer suspended for one year for sex with a client, even though the referee had found that the relationship was not exploitative because the client was a prostitute).

In 2002, at the recommendation of the Ethics 2000 Commission, the ABA amended the Model Rules to prohibit sexual relationships with clients, even if the client is not prejudiced, except for sexual relationships that existed before the lawyer-client relationship began. If a lawyer represents a corporation, Rule 1.8(j) bars the lawyer from a sexual relationship with any person in the corporation "who supervises, directs, or regularly consults with that lawyer concerning the organization's legal matters."[158]

Note that the rule does not prohibit lawyers from having romances with former clients. Therefore, a lawyer who wishes to initiate a romantic relationship with a client might first assist the client in finding new counsel.

5. Intimate or family relationships with adverse lawyers

**"God help me, Henry, but I think I've fallen
in love with my wife's divorce attorney."**

One common "personal interest" conflict occurs when two lawyers who are members of the same family represent clients with adverse interests in a matter. If the relationship between the two lawyers is that of "parent, child, sibling or spouse," they normally may not represent clients who are

---

158. Rule 1.8, Comment 17.

adversaries unless the clients have been informed of the relationship, advised of the possible problems, and given informed consent.[159]

> **FOR EXAMPLE:** Sandra is a district attorney prosecuting a murder case. Her husband, Abdul, is a public defender who has been assigned to represent the defendant. Both lawyers must inform their clients (or, in Sandra's case, the representative of an institutional client) of their relationship and the possible ways that it could compromise their work on behalf of their clients (for example, through sharing of confidences) and seek consent.

As with other personal interest conflicts, this type of conflict is not imputed to other lawyers in the firm, so if one of the clients is not willing to consent, another lawyer in the firm may take over the representation.

6. Imputation of lawyer-client conflicts to other lawyers in a firm

a. Financial interest conflicts

Rule 1.8 lays out rules on many particular situations in which lawyers' financial interests may conflict with those of clients. Rule 1.8(k) provides that financial interest conflicts of one lawyer in a firm are imputed to all other lawyers in the firm. This means, for example, that "one lawyer in a firm may not enter into a business transaction with a client of another member of the firm without complying with paragraph (a), even if the first lawyer is not personally involved in the representation of the client."[160]

b. General rule on imputation of conflicts with a lawyer's interests

While Rule 1.8 governs imputation of financial conflicts between the interests of client and lawyer, Rule 1.10(a) addresses imputation to other lawyers in a firm of other conflicts between a client's interests and a lawyer's personal interests.

As we discussed in Chapter 5, Rule 1.10(a) imputes to all lawyers in a firm any conflicts of one client with the interests of another present or former client of another lawyer in the firm. The rule also imputes some conflicts created by the personal interests of a lawyer in the firm. However,

---

159. Rule 1.7, Comment 11. This type of conflict is not imputed to members of the lawyers' firms. Id. If two adverse lawyers have an intimate relationship that is not one of those listed in Comment 11, it may be advisable nevertheless to seek consent before going forward.

160. Rule 1.8, Comment 20.

if a "personal interest" conflict "does not present a significant risk of materially limiting the representation of the client by the remaining lawyers in the firm," the conflict is not imputed to other lawyers in the firm.[161] A comment explains that whether a personal interest conflict is imputed depends on whether it presents "questions of client loyalty [or] protection of confidential information."[162]

> **FOR EXAMPLE:** One lawyer in a firm wants to represent an organization that advocates for the rights of Palestinians in Israel. Another lawyer in the firm neither wants nor is able to handle this work because he has family in Israel and is unsympathetic to this organization. This lawyer's views create a personal conflict for him because if he were to handle this matter, his representation of the organization might be less vigorous because of his political beliefs. This conflict would not be imputed to the other lawyers in the firm so long as the conflicted lawyer does not do any work on the matter.

> **FOR EXAMPLE:** One lawyer in a firm wishes to represent a worker at a thermos factory who was injured on the job while operating a machine. One of the partners in the firm owns the thermos factory and therefore is not able to handle the suit. This conflict would be imputed to the other lawyers in the firm because the other lawyers in the firm "would be materially limited in pursuing the matter because of loyalty to that lawyer."[163]

From these examples, it is apparent that one must evaluate each such conflict on its facts rather than attempting to make categorical distinctions. Suppose that the first example involved a small firm of five lawyers and that the lawyer with the conflict had lost a family member to a Palestinian suicide bomber. In that case, the loyalty of the other lawyers to the first lawyer might require imputation of this conflict for the same reasons as in the second example.

---

161. Rule 1.10(a).

162. Rule 1.10, Comment 3. If the personal interest of the affected lawyer involves a prohibition to undertake certain transactions under Rule 1.8, one should refer to Rule 1.8(k) rather than Rule 1.10 to determine whether that conflict is imputed to other lawyers in the firm. Rule 1.10, Comment 8.

163. Rule 1.10, Comment 3. Both of these examples are elaborations on the examples offered in Comment 3.

9 Conflicts Issues for Government Lawyers and Judges

A. Successive conflicts of former and present government lawyers
   1. Conflicts of former government lawyers in private practice
   2. Conflicts of government lawyers who formerly worked in private practice

B. Conflicts involving judges, arbitrators, and mediators
   1. Overview of the Model Code of Judicial Conduct
   2. Impartiality and fairness; avoidance of bias, prejudice, and harassment
   3. Ex parte communications
   4. Disqualification of judges
   5. Conflicts rules for former judges, law clerks, arbitrators, and mediators

A. Successive conflicts of former and present government lawyers

If a lawyer works for a government agency for a period of years and then joins a private law firm, some of the lawyer's previous work may conflict with her new practice. Logically, all successive conflicts would be governed by the standard articulated in Rule 1.9. Government lawyers are expected to comply with the applicable rules of professional conduct just as are lawyers in private practice.[1] However, Rule 1.11 imposes less stringent standards regarding successive conflicts that arise from a lawyer's present or past government service, and allows organizations to resolve former client conflicts of former government lawyers by screening the conflicted lawyer from the matter. The main reason for the less demanding rule is that too-stringent conflict standards would make it more difficult for government lawyers to obtain positions in law firms because their government work might preclude the firms from representing many clients. This bar, in turn, might unduly discourage lawyers from serving in the government. Likewise, if conflicts barriers were higher, government agencies might be precluded from hiring lawyers from private practice because of prior conflicting work.

From about 1970 through about 2008, the gap between government lawyers' salaries and those of lawyers in large law firms widened, making it more difficult for government agencies to compete with part of the private sector in hiring lawyers. But many lawyers wanted to work in government early in their careers, in part to gain expertise to use later in private practice. Also, as a result of the recession that began in 2008, many new law school graduates could not obtain the jobs they desired in law firms and sought government employment as a temporary measure. These salary gaps make it even more important not to impose successive conflicts rules that discourage movement between the private and public sectors. However, current and former government officials, including lawyers, are subject to some statutory and regulatory conflicts rules in addition to those imposed by the state ethics codes. Civil service rules or other federal, state, or local laws (usually applicable to officials whether or not they are lawyers) may impose significant restrictions.

> **FOR EXAMPLE:** 18 U.S.C. § 205 (2004), originally enacted in the mid-nineteenth century, prohibits current officers and employees of the United States from bringing claims against the United States or representing any party before any agency or court in connection with a matter in which the United States has a direct and substantial interest.[2]

> **FOR EXAMPLE:** 18 U.S.C. § 207(a)(1)(B) (2007) prohibits, for two years, former officers and employees of the United States from bringing

---

1. See Rule 1.11, Comment 1. There has been some dispute about whether prosecutors are subject to Rules 4.1 and 4.2, which restrict lawyers and their agents from falsifying their identities and communicating directly with persons known to be represented by counsel. This issue is discussed in Chapter 11.

2. For a discussion of the history and impact of this statute, especially as it restricts pro bono work by federal government lawyers, see Lisa G. Lerman, Public Service by Public Servants, 19 Hofstra L. Rev. 1141 (1991).

claims against the United States or helping others to bring claims in which the United States is a party or has a direct and substantial interest and in which the former officer or employee participated personally and substantially while a federal employee.

FOR EXAMPLE: 18 U.S.C. §207(c) (2007) bars former government employees from trying to influence employees of their former agency for a period of one year after leaving office on behalf of any other person. In his first term, President Barack Obama issued an executive order on his second day in office that expanded this prohibition; the order bars all appointees to federal office from participating, for two years, in any particular matter involving specific parties that is directly or substantially related to their former employer or clients and imposes limitations on communications with employees of their agencies for two years after they leave the government.[3]

1. Conflicts of former government lawyers in private practice

Rule 1.11(a) articulates the standard by which former government lawyers are to evaluate potential conflicts between prior government work and subsequent work.

> **Rule 1.11(a)**
> **Except as law may otherwise expressly permit, a lawyer who has formerly served as a public officer or employee of the government:**
> **(1) is subject to Rule 1.9(c); and**
> **(2) shall not otherwise represent a client in connection with a matter in which the lawyer participated personally and substantially as a public officer or employee, unless the appropriate government agency gives its informed consent, confirmed in writing, to the representation.[4]**

Rule 1.9, the general successive conflicts standard, precludes representation (absent informed consent) if a new client's interests are "materially adverse" to those of the former client and the matter is "the same or . . . substantially related." Rule 1.11(a), in contrast, precludes a former government lawyer from representing a client in "a matter in which the

---

3. Executive Order — Ethics Commitments by Executive Branch Personnel (Jan. 21, 2009) (available at http://www.whitehouse.gov/the_press_office/ExecutiveOrder-EthicsCommitments).

4. An additional conflict standard is stated in Rule 1.11(c); this is discussed below.

lawyer participated personally and substantially" while in government service. Former government lawyers are guided by Rule 1.11(a) instead of by 1.9(a) with respect to conflicts between prior government work and present work in private practice.[5] The rule requires no inquiry about the degree of adversity between the new client's interests and the government's interests. If the lawyer participated personally and substantially in the matter, the lawyer may not take on the subsequent work unless the government agency gives informed consent. If the matter is one that the lawyer worked on while in the government and the lawyer's participation was personal and substantial, then the relevant agency must give its informed consent before the lawyer can take on the matter.

The following table illustrates the similarities and differences in the two successive conflicts rules.

Rule and conflicts subject to rule	Lawyer may not represent a new client without the consent of the former client in:
Rule 1.9(a): Applies to all successive conflicts except those related to former government work	**"the same or a substantially related matter"** if the new client's interests are **"materially adverse"** to those of the former client
Rule 1.11(a): Applies to conflicts related to former government work	"a matter in which the lawyer participated personally and substantially"

a. What is a "matter"?

Whether a representation involves the same "matter" as a previous one sounds like a commonsense assessment, but it's not always so simple. Here is the definition in the rule.

> **Rule 1.11(e)**
>
> **As used in this Rule, the term "matter" includes:**
>
> > **(1) any judicial or other proceeding, application, request for a ruling or other determination, contract, claim, controversy, investigation, charge, accusation, arrest or other particular matter involving a specific party or parties, and**

---

5. The Ethics 2000 Commission had proposed that former government lawyers should be bound by Rules 1.9(a) and (b) in addition to Rule 1.11, except for a narrower definition of "matter." This proposal was rejected by the ABA House of Delegates. The result is that former government lawyers are guided by Rule 1.11 instead of Rules 1.9(a) and (b). Stephen Gillers, Roy D. Simon & Andrew M. Perlman, Regulation of Lawyers: Statutes and Standards 157-158 (Wolters Kluwer 2011).

(2) any other matter covered by the conflict of interest rules of the appropriate government agency.

The comments offer two further explanations:

> [Paragraph (a)(2) of Rule 1.11 disqualifies lawyers only from work on] matters involving a specific party or parties, rather than extending disqualification to all substantive issues on which the lawyer worked.[6]

> For purposes of paragraph (e) of this Rule, a "matter" may continue in another form. In determining whether two particular matters are the same, the lawyer should consider the extent to which the matters involve the same basic facts, the same or related parties, and the time elapsed.[7]

FOR EXAMPLE: Suppose a lawyer at the U.S. Department of Justice helped to defend the government against a lawsuit by a group of citizens challenging the validity of a rule on toxic waste cleanup. After leaving the Department, the lawyer went to work at a private firm. Consider which of the following work by the firm would constitute the "same matter":

- Representation of the citizen group on an appeal of the lawsuit
- Representation of the citizen group in a petition to modify the rule that was challenged in the lawsuit
- Representation of a different organization in a petition to modify the rule
- Representation of the citizen group or the other organization in lobbying Congress for legislation to overturn the rule

Suppose instead that the lawyer was not involved in any prior litigation over the rule but assisted in drafting the rule. Can he or the firm later participate in litigation over the validity of the rule?

All of these questions turn on whether the new work is part of the same matter that the lawyer worked on while in the government. If the work does involve the same matter, Rule 1.11 might bar the former government lawyer from participation absent agency consent and might bar the firm from participation absent screening and notice to the agency pursuant to Rule 1.11(b).

On one hand, what is the same matter is not necessarily defined by the boundaries of one litigation or other proceeding. If the citizen group lost the case and six months later started a petition to achieve the same result through regulatory or congressional action, perhaps the second round would be regarded as the same matter. On the other hand, if five years

---

6. Rule 1.11, Comment 4.
7. Id. at Comment 10.

elapse, the players change, and another initiative is undertaken to change the rule, then the new initiative probably is not the same matter.

b. Personal and substantial participation

The comments to Rule 1.11 do not define "personal and substantial participation." However, the drafters of the ethics code borrowed this standard from a federal conflict of interest statute that imposes a two-year bar on former federal employees from bringing certain claims against the United States and from helping others to bring such claims.[8] The bar applies if the matter is one in which the former federal employee participated personally and substantially while working for the government.[9] The regulations implementing the federal statute offer useful guidance on the meaning of "personal and substantial participation":

> The restrictions of section 207(a) apply only to those matters in which a former Government employee had "personal and substantial participation," exercised "through decision, approval, disapproval, recommendation, the rendering of advice, investigation or otherwise." To participate "personally" means directly, and includes the participation of a subordinate when actually directed by the former Government employee in the matter. "Substantially," means that the employee's involvement must be of significance to the matter, or form a basis for a reasonable appearance of such significance. It requires more than official responsibility, knowledge, perfunctory involvement, or involvement on an administrative or peripheral issue. . . . [T]he single act of approving or participation in a critical step may be substantial. It is essential that the participation be related to a "particular matter involving a specific party."[10]

c. Screening of former government lawyers

As we discussed in Chapter 5, Rule 1.10 provides that if one lawyer in a firm has a conflict of interest based on previous legal work (not a conflict with

---

8. While federal regulations implementing a criminal statute cannot usually be considered a dictionary for the ethical rules, in this case the standard "personal and substantial participation" "comes from the Ethics in Government Act, 18 U.S.C. § 207." ABA, Annotated Model Rules of Professional Conduct 186 (6th ed., ABA 2007). Some cases interpreting this language in Rule 1.11 have used the analysis of "personal and substantial participation" that is directed by the federal statute and its regulations. See, e.g., U.S. v. Philip Morris, 312 F. Supp. 2d 27 (D.D.C. 2004) (ordering the disqualification of a former Department of Justice lawyer from representing a tobacco company seeking to intervene in the government's suit against a related tobacco company because the former DOJ lawyer had been "personally and substantially involved" in preparing for and responding to tobacco company suits challenging FDA regulations on tobacco during his time at DOJ).

9. 18 U.S.C. § 207(a)(1)(B) (2007).

10. 5 C.F.R. § 2637.201(d) (2007).

the lawyer's personal interests), the ethical rules impute that conflict to all other lawyers in the law firm. Other lawyers in the firm are prohibited from handling the conflicting work unless the affected client gives informed consent.[11] The Model Rules and the rules of most states do not allow the conflicted lawyer to be screened from involvement in or communication about the conflicting work to prevent imputation of the conflict. However, if the conflict is with work that a lawyer did while employed by a government agency, the ethics codes allow screening to avoid imputation. Rule 1.11(b) explains this exception to the general rule.

> **Rule 1.11(b)**
>
> **When a lawyer is disqualified from representation under paragraph (a), no lawyer in a firm with which that lawyer is associated may knowingly undertake or continue representation in such a matter unless:**
>
> > **(1) the disqualified lawyer is timely screened from any participation in the matter and is apportioned no part of the fee therefrom; and**
> >
> > **(2) written notice is promptly given to the appropriate government agency to enable it to ascertain compliance with the provisions of this rule.**

Under this rule, the former government lawyer's firm must screen the former government lawyer from any contact with the work and see that he earns no part of the fee unless it is part of a regular salary or partnership share.[12] The firm need not seek consent from the government agency as a prerequisite to taking on the conflicting work; it must screen the conflicted lawyer and notify the government agency about its work on the matter.[13]

d. Confidential government information

Even if a former government lawyer is not precluded from representing a client on the basis of "personal and substantial participation" in a "matter," the lawyer might be precluded because, while in the government, she learned "confidential government information" about a person and the new matter could involve material adverse use of that information. Rule 1.11(c) imposes this restriction, defines "confidential government information," and permits screening to avoid imputation of conflicts resulting from possession of such information.

---

11. See Rules 1.10(a) and (c).

12. See Rule 1.11, Comment 6.

13. The notice should include "a description of the screened lawyer's prior representation and of the screening procedures employed." Rule 1.11, Comment 7.

Rule 1.11(c)

Rule language[*]	Authors' explanation[**]
Except as law may otherwise expressly permit,	
a lawyer having information that the lawyer knows is **confidential government information** about a **person** acquired when the lawyer was a public officer or employee,	This prohibition applies only if the lawyer has actual knowledge of the information. See Comment 8. The rule is triggered only by possession of confidential government information about a person.
may not represent a private client **whose interests are adverse** to that person in a **matter** in which the **information could be used to the material disadvantage** of that person.	This type of conflict occurs only with respect to a matter in which the lawyer could use the information in a way that would harm the person.
As used in this Rule, the term "confidential government information" means **information that has been obtained under governmental authority** and which, at the time this Rule is applied, the **government is prohibited by law from disclosing to the public** or has a **legal privilege** not to disclose **and** which is **not otherwise available** to the public.	— The information whose possession triggers the rule must have been obtained through governmental power (such as through threat of subpoena); — the government must be barred from disclosing it or entitled to assert a privilege against disclosure; and — the information must not be in the public domain.
A firm with which that lawyer is associated **may undertake or continue** representation in the matter only if the **disqualified lawyer is timely screened** from any participation in the matter and is apportioned **no part of the fee** therefrom.	If the former government lawyer has such information, the firm may go ahead with the representation if the conflicted lawyer is screened and does not earn specific fees from the work.

*All emphasis added.

**This and other authors' explanations draw from the comments to the rules and from other sources. They are not comprehensive but highlight some important interpretive points.

Government law enforcement and other agencies have the power to collect information not normally available to members of the public. This rule seeks to prevent the use of governmental power in aid of private interests and to avoid giving an unfair advantage to a party whose lawyer has confidential government information about individuals.[14] If a former government lawyer has actually learned information[15] about a person that

---

14. Id. at Comment 4.

15. Rule 1.11, Comment 8, explains that a former government lawyer is precluded by this section only by having "actual knowledge" about a person, and that knowledge cannot be imputed to her.

was obtained under governmental authority and that could be used to the material disadvantage of that person in a new representation, the former government lawyer cannot take on that work. This type of conflict cannot be cured by obtaining consent.

In a case in which a former government lawyer has confidential government information, the lawyer's firm may handle the matter that presents a conflict for the former government lawyer if the conflicted lawyer is screened. For this type of conflict, the firm need not notify the government agency about its work on the matter.

Bases for disqualification of former government lawyers:

- Subsequent work involves a "matter" in which the government lawyer was "personally and substantially involved" while in the government. (This can be cured by agency consent.) Rule 1.11(a) (type 1).
- Subsequent work could involve use of "confidential government information" about a person known to the lawyer in a way that would materially disadvantage that person. (This cannot be cured by consent.) Rule 1.11(c) (type 2).

---

2. Conflicts of government lawyers who formerly worked in private practice

We have explored the successive conflicts rules that apply to lawyers who worked for government agencies and then switched jobs. Now we take up the opposite question, about how a government lawyer should evaluate conflicts that arise because of work that the lawyer did in a previous private law job. Former client conflicts are addressed by Rule 1.11(d).[16]

> **Rule 1.11(d)**
>
> **Except as law may otherwise expressly permit, a lawyer currently serving as a public officer or employee:**
>
> **(1) is subject to Rules 1.7 and 1.9; and**
>
> **(2) shall not: . . . participate in a matter in which the lawyer participated personally and substantially while in private practice or nongovernmental employment, unless the**

---

16. Rule 1.11(d)(2)(ii) deals with a different question, one about restrictions on government lawyers who wish to apply for jobs with persons who are involved in matters on which the government lawyers are working. This question is discussed below in connection with a similar provision for former judges in Rule 1.12.

appropriate government agency gives its informed consent, confirmed in writing. . . .

Former government lawyers are to evaluate the potential impact of conflicts on former government clients under Rule 1.11(a) through (c) *instead of* Rule 1.9(a). (Rule 1.9(c) still applies to them.) Present government lawyers, on the other hand, are subject to the restrictions of Rule 1.9(a) *in addition to* those stated in Rule 1.11. Both groups are subject to the restrictions imposed by Rule 1.7 (concurrent conflicts). Rule 1.9(a) prohibits a lawyer from working on "the same or a substantially related matter in which that person's interests are materially adverse to the interests of a *former* client unless that client gives informed consent, confirmed in writing."[17]

Both present and former government lawyers are subject to Rule 1.9(c) on protecting confidences of former clients. The differences in the rules governing these two groups are in the standards used to evaluate other successive conflicts and in who must consent.

If the work would be adverse to a former client, the government lawyer must ask whether it is both substantially related and involves material adversity. If so, the lawyer can't do the work without the consent of the former client. Even if the new work is not adverse to the interests of a former client but involves a matter on which the lawyer did a lot of work in private practice, the government lawyer is precluded from working on it unless the current employing agency gives its consent.

PROBLEM 9-1 THE DISTRICT ATTORNEY

This is a problem that arose for a prosecutor in a city in New England.

You are the district attorney of your city. Twelve years ago, when you were in private practice, you represented Zeke Brick, then 5 years old, who was injured in an automobile accident. Brick suffered a concussion and three fractures in the accident. You negotiated a good settlement for him. You don't remember anything about the case, and you haven't looked at the file since the case was settled.

Last month, Brick (now 17) was arrested and charged with murder. His lawyer, the public defender, has served notice that he

---

17. Rule 1.9(a).

plans to rely on a defense of "mental disease or defect." In the letter, the lawyer demanded that you disqualify yourself from prosecuting him because you previously represented him in the automobile accident case.

Your old firm has already turned over Brick's case file to the public defender, and you haven't asked for or received a copy.

Under Rule 1.11(d), should you withdraw from representing the state in the prosecution of Brick, or may you proceed?

B. Conflicts involving judges, arbitrators, and mediators

Chapters 5 through 8 and the first part of this chapter have addressed concurrent, successive, and imputed conflicts of interest of lawyers. Here we shift gears and offer a brief introduction to some of the conflicts issues that arise for present and former adjudicators and for their law clerks. While there is not time in a survey course on the law that governs lawyers to treat judicial ethics issues in any depth, we offer an overview and discuss some key topics.

Why does a law student need to learn about judicial ethics?

Some law student readers of this book will become judges, but few will do so in the next decade. However, many law students work for judges as externs or become judicial law clerks after graduation. Many provisions of the judicial ethics code apply indirectly to those who work for judges, so some degree of familiarity with the code is useful.

Suppose you are a judicial extern in a state appellate court. You are drafting an opinion in a contract dispute and wishing you had studied harder when your contracts class addressed "the battle of the forms." You are too embarrassed to tell your judge how confused you are. May you make an appointment with your former contracts teacher to discuss "a hypothetical"? May you consult with your roommate about the matter?

Also, some law students enroll in clinical courses in which they are admitted under student practice rules. These students may represent clients in court. Even novice practitioners sometimes encounter problematic judicial behavior and sometimes work on matters in which judicial bias could be a real problem. Finally, the Multistate Professional Responsibility Examination always includes some questions involving judicial ethics. So law students need to be familiar with judicial ethics rules.

1. Overview of the Model Code of Judicial Conduct

What are the central principles articulated in the ABA Code of Judicial Conduct?

The ABA Model Code of Judicial Conduct is organized into four canons, which espouse some of the qualities most valued in judicial conduct. Here they are:

Canon 1: A judge shall uphold and promote the independence, integrity, and impartiality of the judiciary, and shall avoid impropriety and the appearance of impropriety.

Canon 2: A judge shall perform the duties of judicial office impartially, competently, and diligently.

Canon 3: A judge shall conduct the judge's personal and extrajudicial activities to minimize the risk of conflict with the obligations of judicial office.

Canon 4: A judge or candidate for judicial office shall not engage in political or campaign activity that is inconsistent with the independence, integrity or impartiality of the judiciary.[18]

It is hard to argue with any of the general principles that are articulated in these canons. Most of the controversy in the drafting of this code focused on the particular rules explicating the behavioral restrictions relevant to each of the canons. Some of these issues are explained below.

Is the ABA Model Code of Judicial Conduct binding on state or federal judges?

No. Like lawyers admitted in a particular state, state court judges must comply with the code of judicial conduct adopted by the highest court of the particular state. The state supreme courts review the ABA Model Codes and then adopt their own codes, which may mirror or diverge from the ABA model. Federal judges, except for justices of the U.S. Supreme Court, must comply with the Code of Conduct for Federal Judges, which was issued by the U.S. Judicial Conference.[19]

---

18. ABA Model Code of Jud. Conduct (ABA 2010).

19. 175 F.R.D. 364 (1998). The Code of Conduct for United States Judges also is available at http://www.uscourts.gov/Viewer.aspx?doc=/uscourts/RulesAndPolicies/conduct/Vol02A-Ch02.pdf (accessed Nov. 19, 2012).

Shouldn't the Supreme Court also have an ethical code?

The U.S. Supreme Court has never adopted a code of ethics like those that govern most other judges. Perhaps it was thought unnecessary in such hallowed halls. In recent years, however, some policy advocates have urged that the justices of the U.S. Supreme Court should be bound to comply with the judicial ethics code. In 2007 and 2008, Justices Scalia and Thomas attended "private political meetings sponsored by David and Charles Koch, conservative billionaires" who own large oil and gas investments and are major backers of the tea party movement.[20] They were reimbursed for their travel by the Federalist Society, which had received at least $11.4 million from the Kochs' foundations over the years. Koch-owned companies were involved in hundreds of cases in federal court. In response, in 2011, more than a hundred law professors wrote to Congress asking it to extend the Code of Conduct for Federal Judges to the Supreme Court.[21]

If a judge violates a provision of the applicable judicial code of ethics, what consequences might follow?

The state courts have set up judicial disciplinary commissions that can review allegations of unethical behavior by judges and can impose sanctions ranging from a reprimand to removal from the bench.[22] Federal judges may also face disciplinary sanctions, but removal of a federal judge requires impeachment by Congress.[23]

---

20. For more information on the Koch brothers and their impact on public policy, see Jane Mayer, Covert Operations: The Billionaire Brothers Who Are Waging a War Against Obama (Aug. 3, 2010) (available at http://www.newyorker.com/reporting/2010/08/30/100830fa_fact_mayer).

21. R. Jeffrey Smith, Professors Ask Congress for an Ethics Code for Supreme Court, Wash. Post (Feb. 24, 2011) (available at http://www.washingtonpost.com/national/law-group-seeks-ethics-code-for-supreme-court/2011/02/23/AB8rKgI_story.html). Justice Stephen G. Breyer testified to Congress in April 2011 that Supreme Court justices do follow the Judicial Code of Conduct but that it would be "unprecedented" for the Judicial Conference of the United States, composed of district court and appellate judges, to bind the members of the Supreme Court. Justice Anthony M. Kennedy said that such action would create a "constitutional problem." Supreme Court Justices Already Comply with Ethics Rules, Kennedy, Breyer Say, 79 U.S.L.W. 2389 (Apr. 19, 2011). The number of signatories later rose to 135. Alliance for Justice, Judicial Ethics Sign-On Letter, http://www.afj.org/judicial-ethics-sign-on-letter.html (accessed Nov. 19, 2012). Professor Lerman, one of the authors of this book, signed this letter.

22. For a list of these organizations, see Am. Judicature Socy., State Judicial Conduct Organizations, http://www.ajs.org/ethics/eth_conduct-orgs.asp (accessed Nov. 19, 2012).

23. See Am. Judicature Socy., Federal Judicial Conduct, http://www.ajs.org/ethics/eth_fed-jud-conduct.asp (accessed Nov. 19, 2012).

2. Impartiality and fairness; avoidance of bias, prejudice, and harassment

One of the most important provisions of the Model Code of Judicial Ethics is the requirement that judges perform their duties "fairly and impartially."[24] Most obviously, judges must not have personal interests in the cases that they adjudicate. They may be disciplined for violating their public trust by enriching themselves through their decisions. Many cases present troubling stories, but the following one makes many readers' hair stand on end.

FOR EXAMPLE: Judges Mark Ciavarella and Michael Conahan ran the juvenile court in Luzerne County, Pennsylvania, for twelve years. They worked out a secret plan with Robert J. Powell, one of Judge Conahan's wealthy friends, through which Powell and Robert Mericle would build a private juvenile detention center. The court would pay the rent and the state would pay millions of dollars to Powell and Mericle to house children who were determined by the judges to be juvenile offenders. Judge Conahan managed to terminate public financing for the competing county-run detention center. For the next several years, the two judges sentenced juveniles to detention in the new private juvenile center at a rate that was twice the state average. The judges typically spent two minutes on each case. The judges did not allow lawyers for the children to present defenses. Thousands of children, some as young as ten, were sent to detention in the institution. The grateful developers gave the judges $2.6 million in kickbacks. With this money, the judges secretly bought a condominium in Florida and a 56-foot yacht, putting the property in their wives' names to conceal it. The "kids for cash" kickback scheme was finally uncovered because a "reputed mob boss-turned-informant" revealed it, apparently in exchange for a sentence reduction. The judges eventually were convicted of racketeering. Ciavarella, who maintained his innocence throughout his trial, was sentenced to 28 years. Conahan received 17 years; his lesser sentence was based on his cooperation with prosecutors, his guilty plea, and his statement of responsibility and apology.[25] Four thousand juvenile convictions were dismissed. This was little comfort to the thousands of

---

24. ABA Model Code of Jud. Conduct Rule 2.2.

25. Dave Janoski, At Sentencing, Defense Cites Conahan's Upbringing for Ex-judge's Role in Scandal, Scranton Times-Trib. (Sept. 24, 2011) (available at http://thetimes-tribune.com/news/at-sentencing-defense-cites-conahan-s-upbringing-for-ex-judge-s-role-in-scandal-1.1208423#axzz1bdIeeh2A); Ex-Luzerne County Judge Michael Conahan Sentenced to 17 1/2 Years in Kids-for-Cash Case, Associated Press (Sept. 23, 2011) (available at http://www.pennlive.com/midstate/index.ssf/2011/09/ex-luzerne_county_judge_michae.html).

children who had spent time in the institution because of the judges' corrupt decision making. One child had committed suicide.[26]

Are judges barred from discriminatory behavior?

Yes. Judges must avoid conduct that manifests bias. As the code has evolved, the list of groups against whom biased behavior is prohibited has grown, as has the list of examples of conduct that might violate the rule. The following chart offers details.

Judges must avoid biased or prejudiced behavior or harassment based upon:	Examples of conduct that could manifest bias or prejudice:
• Race • Sex • Gender • Religion • National origin • Ethnicity • Disability • Age • Sexual orientation • Marital status • Socioeconomic status • Political affiliation[27]	• Epithets • Slurs • Demeaning nicknames • Negative stereotyping • Attempted humor based on stereotypes • Threatening, intimidating, or hostile acts • Suggestions of connections between race, ethnicity, or nationality and crime • Irrelevant references to personal characteristics • These could be communicated by facial expressions or body language.[28]

A new ABA rule also prohibits judges from participating in organizations that discriminate.

---

26. Ian Urbina, Despite Red Flags About Judges, a Kickback Scheme Flourished, N.Y. Times (Mar. 28, 2009) (available at http://www.nytimes.com/2009/03/28/us/28judges.html); Dave Janoski, Judges' "Finder's Fee" in Focus as Mericle, Powell Testify, Scranton Times-Trib. (Feb. 11, 2011) (available at http://thetimes-tribune.com/news/judges-finder-s-fee-in-focus-as-mericle-powell-testify-1.1102832#axzz1HpxIeXXE); Michael Rubinkam, Pa. Judge Guilty of Racketeering in Kickback Case, Associated Press (Feb. 18, 2011) (available at http://www.aolnews.com/2011/02/18/former-pa-judge-mark-ciavarella-guilty-of-racketeering-in-kick/); Dave Janoski & Michael R. Sisak, Prosecutor Heralds "Full Justice" in Ciavarella's 28-Year Sentence, Scranton Times-Trib. (Aug. 12, 2011) (available at http://thetimes-tribune.com/prosecutor-heralds-full-justice-in-ciavarella-s-28-year-sentence-1.1187808# axzz1UpMwO3v0); Philip Caulfield, "Rot in Hell!" Heartbroken Mom Whose Son Committed Suicide Confronts Crooked Judge, N.Y. Daily News (Feb. 21, 2011) (available at http://articles.nydailynews.com/2011-02-21/news/28639615_1_mark-ciavarella-sentencing-hundreds-michael-conahan). Ciavarella is appealing his conviction and sentence. Terrie Morgan-Besecker, Ciavarella Appeals Sentence, Conviction, Scranton Times Leader) Aug. 18, 2011 (available at http://www.timesleader.com/news/Ciavarella__appeals__sentence___conviction_08-17-2011.html).

27. ABA Model Code of Jud. Conduct Rule 2.3.

28. Id. at Comment 2.

Rule 3.6 Affiliation with Discriminatory Organizations

(A) A judge shall not hold membership in any organization that practices invidious discrimination on the basis of race, sex, gender, religion, national origin, ethnicity, or sexual orientation.

(B) A judge shall not use the benefits or facilities of an organization if the judge knows or should know that the organization practices invidious discrimination on one or more of the bases identified in paragraph (A). A judge's attendance at an event in a facility of an organization that the judge is not permitted to join is not a violation of this Rule when the judge's attendance is an isolated event that could not reasonably be perceived as an endorsement of the organization's practices.

If a newly appointed judge is a member of an organization that discriminates on the basis of sexual orientation, must the judge resign from membership?

Probably so. If a newly appointed judge is an Eagle Scout and a longtime gay Boy Scout troop leader, and the Boy Scouts of America persist in barring gay men from being scout troop leaders,[29] the judge would have to resign from the organization.

> **FOR EXAMPLE:** Justice Sonia Sotomayor resigned from the all-women's "Belizean Grove" when she was nominated for her Supreme Court post and Republicans questioned her membership. The club, composed largely of high-powered female corporate executives, met annually in Central America or New York for "fun, substantive programs, and bonding." She stated that the Grove did not practice "invidious discrimination" but did not want questions about her participation to distract from senators' consideration of her qualifications.[30]

On the other hand, in 2011, George C. Pain II, the chief bankruptcy judge in Nashville, refused to resign from the Belle Meade Country Club, whose 600 voting members were all white men. In a "confidential" 10-8 decision, the Judicial Council of the Sixth Circuit declined to take any action. A retired federal judge who was a member of the club and did not

---

29. CNN.com, Supreme Court Says Boy Scouts Can Bar Gay Troop Leaders (June 28, 2000), http://archives.cnn.com/2000/LAW/06/28/scotus.gay.boyscouts.

30. Charlie Savage & David D. Kirkpatrick, Sotomayor Defends Ties to Association, N.Y. Times (June 16, 2009) (available at http://www.nytimes.com/2009/06/16/us/politics/16judge.html?ref= politics); Sotomayor Resigns from All-Women's Club, N.Y. Times (June 19, 2009) (available at http://www.nytimes.com/2009/06/20/us/politics/20grove.html).

participate in the Judicial Council's decision commented that the club did not discriminate, but said that African Americans did not apply for membership because "maybe they would not feel comfortable."[31]

3. Ex parte communications

Another judicial rule that frequently impacts practicing lawyers is the rule requiring judges to avoid most ex parte communications. In general, a judge is prohibited from initiating, permitting, or considering communications about a pending (or about to be filed) matter by the parties or their lawyers, unless all relevant parties or their lawyers are present.[32] The rule lays out a list of circumstances in which ex parte contact is permissible:

- For "scheduling, administrative or emergency purposes" so long as the substance of the matter is not addressed, the judge reasonably believes that the communicating party won't be advantaged, and the other parties are promptly notified and given a chance to respond.
- "A judge may obtain the written advice of a disinterested expert on the law applicable to a proceeding" so long as the judge gives advance notice of the advice sought and gives them a chance to object to the request and to respond to it.
- "A judge may consult with court staff and court officials . . . or with other judges, provided the judge makes reasonable efforts to avoid receiving factual information that is not part of the record. . . ."
- If a judge is overseeing an effort to settle a pending matter, then with the parties' consent, the judge can meet separately with the parties or their lawyers.
- Other ex parte communication permitted by other law is allowed,[33] "such as when [a judge is] serving on therapeutic or problem-solving courts, mental health courts, or drug courts . . . [where a judge] may assume a more interactive role. . . ."[34]

One component of a judge's duty to avoid ex parte communication is the duty to "consider only the evidence presented and any facts that may properly be judicially noticed."[35] This means that a judge may not conduct

---

31. Adam Liptak, Weighing the Place of a Judge in a Club of 600 White Men, N.Y. Times (May 17, 2011) (available at http://www.nytimes.com/2011/05/17/us/17bar.html).

32. ABA Model Code of Jud. Conduct Rule 2.9.

33. Id.

34. Id. at Comment 4.

35. Id. at Rule 2.9(C).

any independent fact investigation, including conducting Internet searches to learn information that may not be in the record presented to the judge.[36]

4. Disqualification of judges

The judicial ethics code provides that a judge may not hear a matter because of a conflicting interest or a possible bias, if "the judge's impartiality might reasonably be questioned." This is an objective standard—the question is whether a reasonable person might think that the judge is not impartial. The reason for the use of this standard is that it is important for the public to have confidence in the impartiality of the judicial system, so both actual bias and the appearance of bias are problems.

May judges be Facebook "friends" with lawyers who appear before them regularly?

This issue is a new one, but the Ohio Board of Commissioners on Grievances and Discipline concluded that social networking by judges is permissible, just as other social relationships with members of the bar are acceptable, provided that judges do not suggest that some people have more influence over them than others and do not investigate facts of pending cases on the social networking site.[37]

If a judge believes that he should not hear a case because of a conflict of interest or a bias, should the judge disqualify himself?

Yes. Model Code of Judicial Conduct Rule 2.11 states that "[a] judge shall disqualify himself or herself in any proceeding in which the judge's impartiality might reasonably be questioned." The Model Code then provides an illustrative list of such situations. Rather than providing the entire list, we offer some illustrative examples.

- Suppose that the judge's former wife files for divorce against her second husband. The judge might have "a personal bias or prejudice concerning a party . . . or personal knowledge of facts that are in dispute in the proceeding."[38]

---

36. Id. and Comment 6. Much ink has been spilled on the question of whether our system of adjudication is equipped to do a competent job of fact-finding. See, e.g., Richard Danzig & Geoffrey Watson, The Capability Problem in Contract Law (2d ed. Found. Press 2004). In the era of the Internet, one might wonder whether our justice system would be better served by allowing judges to seek information about the facts as well as about the law.

37. Ohio Sup. Ct. Bd. of Commrs. on Grievances & Disc., Op. 2010-7 (available at http://www.supremecourt.ohio.gov/Boards/BOC/Advisory_Opinions/2010/Op_10-007.doc).

38. ABA Model Code of Jud. Conduct Rule 2.11(A); hypothetical facts supplied.

- Suppose that the judge's spouse or domestic partner[39] is on the board of directors of a corporation that is a party in a matter that is presented to a judge. What if the judge's partner is the lawyer for one of the parties or owns substantial stock in one corporate party?[40]

- Suppose that the judge's nephew, who has been living in her house for the last year, is a 25 percent owner of a corporation that is a party to a dispute presented to the judge.[41]

- Suppose that a judge is secretly sleeping with the prosecutor who is seeking the death penalty against a defendant in a case before the judge.[42]

- Suppose that the judge, during the last election campaign to retain his seat, said, "If elected, I *will* impose the death penalty on any defendant convicted of first degree murder." Then the judge is elected, and a defendant in his courtroom is convicted of first degree murder. May the judge hear the matter?[43]

In all these cases, the judge's impartiality might reasonably be questioned. In such situations, a judge is supposed to disqualify herself, even if no party files a recusal motion. It does not always happen this way.

> **FOR EXAMPLE:** Two nonprofit organizations, Sierra Club and Judicial Watch, sued Vice President Dick Cheney to obtain records of a task force chaired by Cheney that had made energy policy recommendations

---

39. A "domestic partner" is "a person with whom another person maintains a household and an intimate relationship, other than a person to whom he or she is legally married." ABA Model Code of Jud. Conduct, Terminology.

40. ABA Model Code of Jud. Conduct Rule 2.11(A)(2); hypothetical facts supplied.

41. Id. at Rule 2.11(A)(3); hypothetical facts supplied. Each judge is obliged to "keep informed" about his or her own economic interests and about the "personal economic interests of the judge's spouse or domestic partner and minor children residing in the judge's household." Id. at Rule 2.11(B). This might mean that the judge in the hypothetical example could claim "excused ignorance" of the nephew's economic interests.

42. This is not a hypothetical case. For six years, Judge Verla Sue Holland was having a secret affair with Tom O'Connell, the district attorney of Collin County, Texas. In a case that he prosecuted, she sentenced Charles Hood to death for murder. It took 20 years for Hood's lawyer to be able to prove the affair; he finally did so after a former assistant district attorney revealed the liaison. An appellate court held that Hood's lawyer waited too long before raising the issue, over a dissent that argued that the deadline was missed because of the judge's "deliberate measures to ensure that the affair would remain secret." Ex parte Hood (Ct. Crim. App. Tex. Sept. 16, 2009) (dissenting opinion) (available at http://www.cca.courts.state.tx.us/OPINIONS/PDFOPINIONINFO2.ASP?OPINIONID= 18735&FILENAME=WR-41,168-11.PDF). There was much criticism of the decision by ethics experts; the U.S. Supreme Court denied a writ of certiorari. Adam Liptak, Questions of an Affair Tainting a Trial, N.Y. Times (Feb. 22, 2010) (available at http://www.nytimes.com/2010/02/23/us/23bar.html); Bill Mears, High Court Rejects Death Row Appeals from Texas, CNN.com (Apr. 19, 2010), http://www.cnn.com/2010/CRIME/04/19/scotus.texas.death.row/. Two years later, the Texas courts ordered a new sentencing hearing for Hood. Ex parte Hood, 304 S.W.3d 397 (Ct. Crim. App. Tex. 2010).

43. ABA Model Code of Jud. Conduct Rule 2.11(5); hypothetical facts supplied.

favored by oil companies. They wanted access to the records to ascertain the degree of industry influence over the policy recommendations. The case raised a novel legal issue: whether the kind of task force that Cheney chaired was subject to laws requiring public disclosure of task force proceedings. While the suit was being appealed to the Supreme Court, Justice Antonin Scalia went on a duck-hunting trip with Cheney, flying to a private hunting camp on *Air Force Two*. Scalia later denied a motion by the Sierra Club asking the justice to recuse himself. Justice Scalia stated that he might have granted the motion if he had been an ordinary federal appellate judge, who could be replaced by any other judge, but that a recusal by a Supreme Court justice would leave the Court with an even number of judges, which would risk a tie vote.[44] He later voted with a 7-2 majority in favor of Cheney.[45]

Judges are elected in 38 states. May a lawyer who contributes to a judge's campaign be appointed by the judge to a compensated position as a special master or receiver?

Model Rule 7.6 imposes a limited restriction on lawyers and firms that contribute to judicial election campaigns, barring a lawyer from accepting an appointment (such as a job as a special master) from a judge if the lawyer makes or solicits political contributions *for the purpose of obtaining* that appointment.

The comments following the rule reaffirm the right of lawyers and law firms to contribute to judicial election campaigns just as they may participate in other parts of the political process. But they explain that if lawyers were to contribute to judicial or other campaigns for the purpose of obtaining compensated appointments, the public would lose confidence that such appointments were merit-based, and the integrity of the profession would be undermined.[46] This rule, adopted by the ABA in 2000, attempts to deter "pay to play" political contributions by subjecting lawyers who engage in this practice to disciplinary action.[47]

---

44. Cheney v. U.S. Dist. Ct., 541 U.S. 913, 915 (2004). The *New York Times* editorialized that "[f]ederal judges at all levels are legally mandated to disqualify themselves from cases in which their 'impartiality might reasonably be questioned.' This case plainly meets that standard." Editorial, Beyond the Duck Blind, N.Y. Times (Mar. 15, 2004).

45. Cheney v. U.S. Dist. Ct., 542 U.S. 367 (2004).

46. Model Rule 7.6, Comments 1 and 3.

47. ABA, A Legislative History: The Development of the ABA Model Rules of Professional Conduct, 1982-2005, at 785 (ABA 2006).

In the states in which judges are elected, may a judge decide a case in which one of the parties gave the judge a large campaign contribution?

The controversial practice of electing state court judges has long created concerns that some people would use campaign contributions to "buy justice." The amount of money raised in judicial election campaigns is large and growing. In the 2006 judicial election cycle, candidates seeking seats on state supreme courts raised more than $34 million. This figure is 20 percent higher than the amounts for the previous four election cycles combined. Businesses contribute 44 percent of the money, but 72 percent of business leaders are very concerned that the contributions undermine the independence of the judiciary.[48]

Parties to pending cases and lawyers sometimes give campaign contributions to the judges who hear their cases. Also, some organized commercial interests and ideologically driven groups aim to vote out incumbent judges because they disagree with particular "hot button" decisions. Sometimes these interests try to inject controversy into judicial elections to increase turnout favoring their sides in nonjudicial elections being conducted at the same time.[49]

Despite longstanding concerns about the propriety of lawyers' lining judges' pockets, lawyers may contribute to judicial election campaigns even if they may appear before the judges to whom they give money, at least in states that follow the ABA Model Rules of Professional Conduct or ABA Model Code of Judicial Conduct.

The ABA judicial code allows the campaign committee for a judgeship candidate to solicit contributions that are "reasonable" in amount.[50] The code does not require a judge to recuse himself from a case in which one party made a substantial contribution to the judge's campaign. But it does require a judge to recuse himself if his "impartiality might reasonably be questioned." One of the circumstances listed as a possible basis for recusal is if one of the parties, or a lawyer or law firm for one of the parties, has made a contribution exceeding an amount to be

---

48. Jonathan Berman, You May Know the Law, But I Own the Judge: Why Congress Can and Should Get Involved in State Judicial Election Reform, 34 J. Leg. Prof. 145, 147-148 (2009). In 2011-2012, $28 million was spent just on television advertising for state supreme court candidates. Brennan Center for Justice, Judicial Election TV Spending Sets New Record, Yet Voters Reject Campaigns to Politicize the Judiciary (Nov. 7, 2012).

49. Roy A. Schotland, Iowa's 2010 Judicial Election: Appropriate Accountability or Rampant Passion?, 46 Ct. Rev. 118 (2009-2010) (available at aja.ncsc.dni.us/publications/courtrv/cr46-4/CR46-4Final.pdf).

50. ABA Model Code of Jud. Conduct Rule 4.4(B)(1).

specified by the state adopting the rule, if the state chooses to specify a limit.[51]

Many judges decide cases in which past contributors are parties, though scholars have criticized the practice. A 2008 study of the Louisiana Supreme Court by Professor Vernon Valentine Palmer found that "justices voted in favor of their contributors 65 percent of the time, and two of the justices did so 80 percent of the time."[52] One of them, Justice John L. Weimer, voted for plaintiffs

- 47 percent of the time in cases in which neither side had contributed to his campaigns,
- 90 percent of the time when the plaintiffs gave him larger contributions than the defendants did, and
- only 25 percent of the time when the defendants had given him larger contributions.[53]

If you believe that a judge assigned to your case is biased, your only options are to go forward with the case or to file a motion for recusal with the very judge whose recusal you desire. Awkward, don't you think? Suppose the judge disagrees with you that recusal is required, turns down your motion, and insists on hearing the case. Will your client be disadvantaged by your having more or less accused the judge of unethical behavior? Despite the awkwardness of the procedure for challenging the impartiality of a judge, it is the usual path by which lawyers seek recusal of judges who appear to have a conflict of interest in a particular matter.

PROBLEM 9-2   THE JUDGE'S FORMER PROFESSOR

This problem is based on a news report about a judge who was presiding over a case involving a prominent public figure.

You are a lawyer for Carl Ahr, a government official who is a defendant in a suit for sexual harassment. The suit was filed in federal court and was assigned to Mindy Lynch, a respected judge.

---

51. Id. at Rule 2.11(A)(4). In a very extreme case, for a judge to preside in a case in which a party made huge contributions to that judge's election may violate an opposing party's right to due process. See Caperton v. A. T. Massey Coal Co., 556 U.S. 868 (2009).

52. Adam Liptak, Looking Anew at Campaign Cash and Elected Judges, N.Y. Times (Jan. 29, 2008) (available at http://www.nytimes.com/2008/01/29/us/29bar.html); see also Adam Liptak, Campaign Cash Mirrors a High Court's Rulings, N.Y. Times (Oct. 1, 2006) (available at http://www. nytimes.com/2006/10/01/us/01judges.html?pagewanted=all) (Wisconsin Supreme Court justices voted in favor of campaign contributors 70 percent of the time, and one voted for his contributors 91 percent of the time).

53. Liptak, Looking Anew, supra n. 52.

Your client did a brief stint as a law professor many years ago, before becoming a public official. The judge was actually a student in one of his classes. He says the judge was a very good student and he enjoyed having her in class, so maybe the former relationship will have a positive impact on the outcome of the case.

There's a possible hitch, however. Just after the end of the semester in which Mindy Lynch took his class, Ahr went away on vacation. He says he still doesn't know what happened, but he mislaid a pile of bluebooks from the course in which Lynch was enrolled.

After Ahr established that the exams were gone, never to be seen again, he consulted with the dean and offered the students whose bluebooks he had lost grades of B+ in the class. Every student accepted the offer except for Lynch. She urged that her grade point average was higher than B+, and she felt she deserved a higher grade. After some negotiation, Ahr gave her an A.

There's another funny coincidence as well. Judge Lynch's husband is now a law professor at the same law school where Ahr once was a professor. Mr. Lynch joined the faculty after Ahr left, but because Ahr returns to the law school for various events, Ahr knows the Lynches personally. Even weirder, when the lawyers went to meet with the judge for a status conference a couple of weeks ago, Mr. Lynch was present during the meeting and participated in the discussion of the issues in the case. There are rumors that Mr. Lynch helps his wife to evaluate and decide the cases before her.

Questions about the Judge's Former Professor

1. What impact does the prior relationship between Lynch and Ahr have on the case? If the plaintiff's lawyer learns about the prior relationship between Ahr and Lynch, is he likely to file a motion requesting that the judge recuse herself? Why or why not? If the plaintiff's lawyer does not file such a motion, should you do so?

2. Assuming that the ABA Model Code of Judicial Conduct applies, if a motion requesting recusal is filed, will the judge have to disqualify herself? (Review Rule 2.11 to answer this question.)[54]

3. Model Code of Judicial Conduct Rule 2.4 prohibits a judge from allowing "family, social, political, financial, or other interests relationships to influence the judge's judicial conduct or judgment."

---

54. If you have a statutory supplement, the code may appear there. Otherwise, you can find it at http://www.americanbar.org/content/dam/aba/migrated/judicialethics/ABA_MCJC_approved. authcheckdam.pdf (accessed Nov. 19, 2012).

Rule 2.9 allows a judge to obtain the advice of "a disinterested expert" on the law that applies to a particular matter if the judge notifies the parties as to who is consulted and of the substance of the communication and allows the parties to respond. Has Judge Lynch violated either of these rules? If so, should you object on behalf of your client to Mr. Lynch's involvement? (Review the relevant rules before you answer this question.)

---

5. Conflicts rules for former judges, law clerks, arbitrators, and mediators

Some judges remain on the bench for the duration of their professional lives. Others return to practice after a period of judicial service. Many other lawyers do part-time or occasional adjudicative work as special masters, arbitrators, or mediators.[55] An even larger group of lawyers have worked as law clerks for judges or as staff attorneys (professional law clerks) for courts. Consequently, a considerable number of lawyers have had adjudicative responsibility on various matters. Rule 1.12 lays out conflicts rules for those lawyer-adjudicators.[56]

> **Rule 1.12(a)**
>
> ... **[A] lawyer shall not represent anyone in connection with a matter in which the lawyer participated personally and substantially as a judge or other adjudicative officer or law clerk to such a person or as an arbitrator, mediator or other third-party neutral, unless all parties to the proceeding give informed consent, confirmed in writing.**[57]

a. Personal and substantial participation

The "personal and substantial participation" standard is the same as that used for conflicts of government lawyers in Rule 1.11.

---

55. Rule 1.12, Comment 1, explains, "The term 'adjudicative officer' includes such officials as judges pro tempore, referees, special masters, hearing officers, and other parajudicial officers, and also lawyers who serve as part-time judges."

56. We use this term to refer to people who have occupied any of the judicial or quasi-judicial roles covered by this rule.

57. The rule makes an exception from this prohibition for "an arbitrator selected as a partisan of a party in a multi-member arbitration panel." Rule 1.12(d).

FOR EXAMPLE: Suppose a lawyer had been a law clerk for a judge on a state court of appeals that has nine sitting judges and hears cases in panels of three. The former clerk would be considered to have participated personally and substantially in a case in which he drafted the opinion or for which his judge sat on the three-judge panel, but not one that was handled by another panel.[58] He could not thereafter "represent anyone in connection with" a matter in which he was involved "unless all parties to the proceeding give informed consent, confirmed in writing."[59]

b. Imputation

What if a former judge leaves the bench and, a year later, joins a firm that represents one of the parties in a complex matter on which he handled the early motions? The former judge would be disqualified under Rule 1.12(a). Would his conflict be imputed to the firm? Rule 1.12(c) says no, so long as the judge "is timely screened from any participation in the matter and is apportioned no part of the fee there from; and . . . written notice is promptly given to the parties and any appropriate tribunal" so that they can check whether the rule is observed. The prohibition on receiving profits from conflicted work "does not prohibit the screened lawyer from receiving a salary or partnership share established by prior independent agreement."[60]

c. Employment negotiation

Like Rule 1.11(d)(2)(ii), applicable to government lawyers, Rule 1.12(b) prohibits lawyer-adjudicators from negotiating for employment with any party or lawyer for a party to a matter in which the adjudicator is "participating personally and substantially":[61]

---

58. This example is adapted from the explanation in Rule 1.12, Comment 1. The comment also makes clear that the exercise of "remote or incidental administrative responsibility that did not affect the merits" would not constitute personal and substantial participation. Id.

59. Rule 1.12(a).

60. Rule 1.12, Comment 4.

61. A similar prohibition is imposed on government lawyers by Rule 1.11:

(d) Except as law may otherwise expressly permit, a lawyer currently serving as a public officer or employee: . . . shall not . . . negotiate for private employment with any person who is involved as a party or as lawyer for a party in a matter in which the lawyer is participating personally and substantially, except that a lawyer serving as a law clerk to a judge, other adjudicative officer or arbitrator may negotiate for private employment as permitted by Rule 1.12(b) and subject to the conditions stated in Rule 1.12(b).

Rule 1.12(b)

A lawyer shall not negotiate for employment with any person who is involved as a party or as lawyer for a party in a matter in which the lawyer is participating personally and substantially as a judge or other adjudicative officer or as an arbitrator, mediator or other third-party neutral. A lawyer serving as a law clerk to a judge or other adjudicative officer may negotiate for employment with a party or lawyer involved in a matter in which the clerk is participating personally and substantially, but only after the lawyer has notified the judge or other adjudicative officer.

This language uses the present tense; it appears not to prohibit the lawyer-adjudicator from employment negotiation after the adjudication has concluded.

Law clerks, fortunately, are permitted to apply for jobs, even with parties or lawyers involved in matters that are pending before their judges, but "only after the lawyer has notified the judge or other adjudicative officer."[62] This may be especially important in smaller communities, in which every firm in town may have matters before each judge in town.[63] Since most clerkships are one or two years in duration, law clerks need more latitude in applying for new jobs.

Several states have also adopted specific ethics codes for judicial law clerks.[64] Law students who accept judicial clerkships should take care to read their state's code before commencing such employment. If you encounter an ethical issue while you are in such a position, you may be able to obtain advice from an official body.

---

62. Rule 1.12(b).

63. When the authors taught in Morgantown, West Virginia, for example, two judges and four magistrates served the community of 40,000.

64. See, e.g., Code of Conduct for Law Clerks & Staff Attys. of the Sup. Ct. of Tex. (2002) (available at http://www.supreme.courts.state.tx.us/rules/pdf/clk-conduct-atty.pdf); Rules of the Sup. Ct. of N.H., Law Clerk Code of Conduct Rule 46, http://www.courts.state.nh.us/rules/scr/scr-46.htm (accessed Nov. 19, 2012).

10 | LAWYERS' DUTIES TO COURTS

So far we have examined the obligations that lawyers owe to their clients — the duties of confidentiality, competence, diligence, communication, deference, loyalty, and fair dealing. Our system of justice also requires lawyers to behave in certain ways toward people who are not their clients. Those other people include judges and other government officials, adversary parties and their lawyers, potential witnesses, and other members of society with whom lawyers have contact. In Chapters 10 and 11, we explore lawyers' obligations to nonclients and how they may conflict with the duties that lawyers owe to clients. Conflicting duties are inherent in an adversary system of justice. In the interest of justice, lawyers are directed to be fiercely loyal to their clients. But if there were no bounds on such loyalty, lawyers could subvert justice, for example, by helping clients to commit crimes or by supplying courts with false evidence.

This chapter focuses primarily on lawyers' duties to judges and adversaries in proceedings to resolve disputes. In Chapter 11 we will consider lawyers' duties to witnesses and others and the special duties of prosecutors to criminal defendants and potential defendants.

This chapter investigates the tension between "zealous advocacy" for one's client and obligations to the system of justice. We ask when our profession's ethical rules encourage, or at least tolerate, making a client's interests primary, particularly in situations of conflict such as litigation, and to what extent rules of law (including the rules of professional conduct) constrain such advocacy in the interest of fair adjudication and decent treatment of adversaries and others.

A. Being a good person in an adversary system

Many articles and books ask whether conscientious lawyers should seek every advantage for their clients, short of violating any laws or clearly defined ethical prohibitions. Should lawyers look out for the interests of people other than their clients even when no law or rule compels it? The laws and rules occasionally require or forbid particular conduct, but very often they allow lawyers the discretion to act as they think best. And even the most ethically responsible lawyers differ in their views of what is proper. Most would agree, for example, that a lawyer representing a defendant in a civil case may (but need not) assert a technical defense to defeat a plaintiff's claim, even if that tactic would defeat an otherwise legitimate lawsuit.[1]

---

1. An example of such a technical defense would be that the process server was not a resident of the forum state as required by that state's law. Some lawyers might say that if a client wants the lawyer to use such a defense, the lawyer is bound to follow the client's wishes. However, most would

Imagine a spectrum of lawyers' attitudes about the relative importance of their duties to clients versus their duties to others. At one end are "hired guns" who typically pursue every possible tactic on behalf of their clients. A single-minded client-centered approach is perhaps most appropriate for criminal defense attorneys, who must counter the immense resources that the state brings to bear against defendants.

At the other end are lawyers who believe that their duties of fairness to all parties and as "officers of the court" are as important as their duties to clients.[2] Such lawyers might decline to make technical arguments that would create unfair outcomes for other parties. They might disclose information to prevent harm to others if permitted by the ethics rules. In the middle of this hypothetical spectrum are lawyers who balance devotion to client interests with a concern to be responsible officers of the court and to be fair to and considerate toward adversaries and others involved in the justice system. Lawyers who have ongoing interaction with judges and opposing counsel seek to avoid tactics that might damage those relationships.

The debate about how client-centered lawyers should be is sometimes couched in terms of whether a good lawyer can also be a good person or, conversely, whether to be a decent human being, a lawyer must sometimes eschew lawful tactics that would help his clients. Charles Fried, a Harvard law professor who served as the U.S. solicitor general during the Reagan administration, argued for a model of intense loyalty to a client, even if doing so would bring about an unjust result. He asked his readers to consider "asserting the statute of limitations or the lack of a written memorandum [that would satisfy the statute of frauds] to defeat what you know to be a just claim against your client." He concluded that this is not the defending lawyer's problem: "[I]f an injustice is worked, it is because the legal system . . . which authorizes both the injustice . . . and the formal gesture for working it insulates [the lawyer] from personal moral responsibility."

But in the final analysis, Fried tempered his conclusion slightly:

> [The lawyer] may exploit the system for his client even if the system consequently works injustice. He may, but must he? . . . [I]f you are the last lawyer in town, is there a moral obligation to help the finance

---

say either that this question is one of means rather than objectives, requiring the lawyer only to consult the client under Rule 1.2, or that the issue is so technical that not even client consultation is needed before the lawyer decides either to assert or not to assert the defense.

2. Perhaps the familiar term "officer of the court" should be taken with a grain of salt. Lawyers are allowed to exercise some traditionally public powers. For example, in most or perhaps all jurisdictions, they may sign subpoenas as if they were court officials. But lawyers who represent clients are not court or government employees, and their primary loyalties are to those whom they represent.

company foreclose on the widow's refrigerator? If the client pursues the foreclosure in order to establish a legal right of some significance, I do not flinch from the conclusion that the lawyer is bound to use this right. So also if the finance company cannot foreclose because of an ideological boycott by the local bar. But if all the other lawyers happen to be on vacation and the case means no more to the finance company than the resale value of one more used refrigerator, common sense says the lawyer can say no. One should be able to distinguish between establishing a legal right and being a cog in a routine, repetitive business operation, part of which just happens to play itself out in court.[3]

Professor Stephen Gillers explores the same issue. He constructs a pair of interesting hypotheticals and suggests that a lawyer who uses permitted (but not required) tactics to produce unjust results can properly be criticized, along with her client, for immoral conduct.

Stephen Gillers, Can a Good Lawyer Be a Bad Person?

84 Mich. L. Rev. 1011, 1011-1022 (1986)[4]

Professor Stephen Gillers

[Professor Gillers is the Crystal Eastman Professor of Law at New York University School of Law.]

If the lawyer uses only legal means, can a coherent theory of moral philosophy nevertheless label the lawyer's conduct immoral? Can a good lawyer be a bad person?

[Consider these hypotheticals. First,] a man whose lifelong dream has been to open a restaurant persuades a wealthy cousin to lend him $50,000. The man is unsophisticated in business matters, while the cousin is not. The man signs a demand note for the loan and opens the restaurant. Food critics give it excellent reviews; great success is predicted. Seeing this, the cousin calls the note, then brings an action on it, intending to acquire the restaurant in a foreclosure sale. The man goes to a lawyer who sees improbable defenses on the merits and who proceeds to make a series of nonfrivolous procedural motions calculated to gain time for her client until either the restaurant's cash flow is great enough to pay the note or a bank loan can be obtained. The motions are either weak, with the lawyer expecting them to fail, or they are highly technical. [For example, one motion points out that the law

3. Charles Fried, The Lawyer as Friend: The Moral Foundation of the Lawyer-Client Relation, 85 Yale L.J. 1060, 1086-1087 (1976).

4. A revised version of this article appears at 2 J. Inst. Study Leg. Ethics 131 (1999).

requires process servers to be 18, but the process server in this case was one month under that age.]

[Second,] while on her way home from a job as a housekeeper, a single mother of three children is hurt by falling debris at a construction site. She suffers permanent injuries that prevent her from resuming gainful employment. She sues the construction company. Its lawyer, recognizing only weak defenses on the merits, makes [the same procedural motion with] the effect of increasing pressure on the financially desperate plaintiff to settle for a tenth of what she could reasonably expect to recover at trial. . . .

Even if law and the governing ethical document permit the motions, does the lawyer who makes them act immorally by "frustrating an opposing party's attempt to obtain rightful redress or repose?" I believe she does. On these facts, a good lawyer may be a bad person. . . .

A lawyer may refrain from making the motions, even if requested to do so by her client, without violating [ethical norms]. Because the tactic is discretionary, the lawyer who invokes it by making the motions is as morally accountable as the client on whose behalf she acts. . . . Whether the conduct of a lawyer and client may be morally criticized hinges on the entire factual context, including the particular circumstances of the case and the behavior of the opposition. It may be that the conduct in [the first hypothetical] can be defended, while the conduct in [the second] cannot.

Question about Being a Good Person

Fried and Gillers use examples of lawyers interposing valid but technical defenses, such as a defense based on the age of the process server, to defeat otherwise valid legal claims. Do you expect to use such tactics? If your answer is yes, do you expect to have any moral qualms about doing so? What would you actually do in the two cases that Gillers describes? If both clients want you to do whatever you can to win the case and yet you would inject the service of process defense in the first case but not the second, what gives you the right to make those decisions?

B. Investigation before filing a complaint

Fried and Gillers ask whether a good lawyer can be a good person if the lawyer uses all of the permitted tools of the legal system on behalf of a client. Often the legal rules do not draw clear lines between what is permitted and what is forbidden. Lawyers often must interpret imprecise regulatory language or apply that language to unique facts to know whether they may take particular actions on behalf of clients. If they make judgments with which others disagree, they may find themselves subject to bar discipline, civil suits, or even (like Belge in Chapter 3) criminal indictments.

How much fact investigation must a lawyer do before filing a lawsuit?

One ethical problem lurks at the threshold of every lawsuit: Does the lawyer for the party initiating the proceedings have enough of a factual and legal basis to justify starting a case that will impose burdens of time and expense on others? Lawyers are not expected to limit themselves to filing "sure winners," but they are not allowed to file "frivolous" lawsuits — those that have virtually no chance of succeeding.

This is the rule.

Rule 3.1 Meritorious Claims and Contentions

A lawyer shall not bring or defend a proceeding, or assert or controvert an issue therein, unless there is a basis in law and fact for doing so that is not frivolous, which includes a good faith argument for an extension, modification or reversal of existing law. A lawyer for the defendant in a criminal proceeding, or the respondent in a proceeding that could result in incarceration, may nevertheless so defend the proceeding as to require that every element of the case be established.

Rule 3.1 prohibits the filing of "frivolous" claims, but it does not define that term. A lawyer may not file a suit on the basis of mere speculation that a prospective defendant has done something wrong. But how much more is required? Comment 2 states that the facts need not be "fully substantiated" before suit is filed. It recognizes that a lawyer may need to use discovery to "develop vital evidence." On the other hand, lawyers must "inform themselves about the facts of their clients' cases and the applicable law and determine that they can make good faith arguments in support of their clients' positions."

Some court rules further elaborate a lawyer's duty before filing a case. In federal civil cases, Federal Rule of Civil Procedure 11(b) is similar to Rule 3.1, but it is more detailed.[5] Under Rule 11, a party's legal theory must be "warranted by existing law or by a nonfrivolous argument for the extension, modification, or reversal of existing law or the establishment of new law."[6]

---

5. All states have similar rules, and most are modeled on Fed. R. Civ. P. 11.

6. Fed. R. Civ. P. 11(b)(2). The importance of permitting good faith arguments for outcomes that are inconsistent with existing law cannot be understated. If lawyers were not permitted to make such arguments, they could not urge changes in the common law and could not ask courts to correct erroneous or outdated precedents. The law would become frozen. Because ethical standards encourage American lawyers to challenge even recent precedents if they seem wrongly decided, courts, including the Supreme Court, can correct their own mistakes relatively quickly. See, e.g., Lawrence v.

Factual assertions must "have evidentiary support or, if specifically so identified, [be] likely to have evidentiary support after a reasonable opportunity for further investigation or discovery."[7]

This standard is subject to widely ranging interpretation. Evidence can consist of documents or testimony. Even unpersuasive statements of a witness who is willing to testify may constitute "evidentiary support." Juries are allowed to draw inferences, so evidence can be circumstantial. And for some factual assertions, the pleader need not have evidentiary support if the lawyer justifiably believes (and asserts) that discovery will "likely" produce such support.[8] On the other hand, FRCP 11 also may be interpreted to require a party to have some evidence in hand with respect to every element of the case for which the party has the burden of pleading. This interpretation would require considerable prefiling investigation in some cases.

We do not have definitive answers to these questions about how to interpret Rule 3.1 or FRCP 11. Most of the cases decided since Rule 11 was amended in 1993 are very fact-specific trial court decisions.[9] This makes it difficult to generalize about what lawyers need to do in other cases.

What are the differences between Rule 3.1 and FRCP 11?

Rule 3.1 and FRCP 11 articulate similar standards, but there are important distinctions between them.

- **Sanctions.** Violation of Rule 3.1 can result in bar disciplinary action against an attorney. A violation of FRCP 11 is punished not by the state bar but by the judge in the civil action, and it can result in nonmonetary directives or monetary sanctions against a lawyer or a party.
- **Safe harbor.** FRCP 11 has a "safe harbor" provision not found in Rule 3.1. If an opposing party makes a motion complaining that a lawyer has violated FRCP 11, the lawyer may withdraw the allegedly frivolous pleading within 21 days after opposing counsel's motion and suffer no sanction other than having to pay the attorneys' fees that the opposing party incurred for making the motion. Although

---

Texas, 539 U.S. 558 (2003) (statutes making it a crime for persons of the same sex to engage in private sexual activity violated the Due Process Clause), *overruling* Bowers v. Hardwick, 478 U.S. 186 (1986) (because it was incorrectly decided).

7. Fed. R. Civ. P. 11(b)(3).

8. Lawyers are not fond of conceding that they don't currently have critically needed support for their claims and need discovery to obtain it. That admission could invite the opposing party to resist discovery more strongly.

9. Among other changes, the 1993 amendment added the section allowing lawyers to file cases that include identified allegations for which they do not yet have evidentiary support.

"This firm has a long history of bringing gravitas to frivolous lawsuits."

Rule 3.1 has no safe harbor provision, a bar counsel would be unlikely to file a charge against a lawyer for filing a frivolous case or defense that the lawyer withdrew pursuant to the safe harbor provision of the FRCP.[10]

What penalties (beyond losing the cases) may apply when lawyers bring unsubstantiated suits?[11]

Rule 11 penalties   A lawyer who initiates a federal court lawsuit in good faith and later finds out (for example, through discovery) that the lawsuit is groundless may be subject to sanctions under FRCP 11.

---

10. In 2005, the House of Representatives approved H.R. 420, which would have eliminated the safe harbor provision from FRCP 11 and would also have imposed new types of sanctions on lawyers who violate that rule. The bill was not approved by the Senate and did not become law, but congressional efforts to make FRCP 11 more strict may continue.

11. If a plaintiff cannot substantiate the basis of a lawsuit, the plaintiff will lose the case for not meeting the burdens of production and persuasion. In a civil suit in federal court, if the facts alleged in the complaint are not sufficient to persuade the judge that the claim is "plausible," the judge might grant a motion to dismiss the suit without allowing discovery, even though Rule 11 suggests that some facts can be alleged subject to discovery that will likely produce evidentiary support. Ashcroft v. Iqbal, 556 U.S. 662 (2009). For an effort to reconcile *Iqbal* and Rule 11, see Adam Steinman, The Pleading Problem, 62 Stan. L. Rev. 1293, 1331 (2010).

Attorneys' fees A federal statute provides that a lawyer who "multiplies the proceedings in any case unreasonably and vexatiously" may be required to pay the other party's attorneys' fees.[12]

> FOR EXAMPLE: In one famous case, two U.S. journalists were seriously injured when a bomb was detonated at a press conference in Nicaragua. Their lawyer relied on unreliable hearsay evidence as the basis for the claim that CIA operatives who were "main figures in the Irangate scandal"[13] (often referred to as the Iran-Contra affair) had set the bomb as part of a conspiracy to assassinate a Nicaraguan opposition leader. The lawyer continued the case even though he could not substantiate the claims through discovery. Relying on Rule 11 and on the federal sanctions statute, the court imposed counsel fees and other sanctions of more than $1 million against the lawyer and the nonprofit organization that employed him.[14] This sanction bankrupted the nonprofit organization.[15]

Liability for malicious prosecution In some states, a defendant who has been sued on the basis of virtually no evidence may sue the plaintiff or the plaintiff's lawyer for the tort of malicious prosecution.[16] Most courts impose higher burdens of proof for winning such cases than for granting sanctions under FRCP 11. A plaintiff usually must prove

- that she won the previous suit in which she was a defendant,
- that the prior suit was brought without probable cause,

---

12. 28 U.S.C. § 1927 (2007).

13. Mark Tan, Appeal Against 1 Million Dollars Costs in Irangate Case, Guardian (London) (Feb. 7, 1989). During the Reagan administration, it was revealed that federal government officials had used profits from secret arms sales to Iran to fund an off-the-books insurgency against the government of Nicaragua.

14. Avirgan v. Hull, 932 F.2d 1572 (11th Cir. 1991). The court probably would have imposed a sanction if this case had arisen under the 1993 version of FRCP 11 because the plaintiffs did not withdraw the case when discovery failed to provide the necessary evidence.

15. Gregg Easterbrook, Blond Ghost: Ted Shackley and the CIA's Crusades, Wash. Monthly (Sept. 1994) (available at http://www.thefreelibrary.com/Blond+Ghost%3A+Ted+Shackley+and+the+C.I.A.+'s+Crusades.-a015856838) (bankruptcy of the Christic Institute); Nick Schou, Who Killed Col. James Sabow? Orange Co. Wkly. (Feb. 18-24, 2000) (available at http://www.ocweekly.com/2000-02-24/news/who-killed-col-james-sabow/) (plaintiff in the suit charged the lawyer with poor work, tried to get him disbarred, and sued him to recover investigative material he collected during the litigation).

16. In some states, the tort is called "wrongful use of civil proceedings." See, e.g., N.W. Natl. Cas. Co. v. Century III Chevrolet, 863 F. Supp. 247 (W.D. Pa. 1994); In re Smith, 989 P.2d 165 (Colo. 1999); Morse Bros. v. Webster, 772 A.2d 842 (Me. 2001).

■ that the prior suit was brought with malice (a motivation other than obtaining a proper adjudication of the case), and

■ that the plaintiff was injured despite having won the prior suit.[17]

Some states, such as Michigan, also require a plaintiff to show "special injury"—that is, that he was injured in his reputation, his person, or his liberty. It is not enough to claim only that the suit was costly or time-consuming.[18]

A lawyer can prove that there was "probable cause" for the previous suit, defeating a claim for malicious prosecution, if the lawyer had a "reasonable belief" that facts could be established and that, under those facts, the client had a valid claim.[19]

PROBLEM 10-1 YOUR VISIT FROM PAULA JONES

The facts of this problem are drawn from the complaint filed in Jones
v. Clinton, *858 F. Supp. 902 (E.D. Ark. 1994).*

Paula Jones

Paula Jones, an employee of a state agency in Arkansas, comes to see you at your law office. She wants you to file a lawsuit against the president of the United States for sexually harassing her while he was the governor of Arkansas. She tells you the following story.

She claims that she was working at the conference registration desk at a hotel where the governor was speaking. The governor's bodyguard appeared at her desk with a piece of paper with a hotel suite number on it and told her that the governor (whom she had never met) wanted to meet her. She thought she might be considered for promotion, so she went to the governor's suite. He closed the door, told her that her superior in the state government was his good friend and appointee, and said "I love your curves." Then he put his hand on her leg and attempted to kiss her. She walked away

---

17. See Wal-Mart Stores Inc. v. Goodman, 789 So. 2d 166, 174 (Ala. 2000).
18. See Friedman v. Dozorc, 312 N.W.2d 585 (Mich. 1981).
19. Restatement § 57, comment d.

from him, but he lowered his trousers and underwear and asked her to kiss his erect penis. She fled but feared that her job would be jeopardized by her having refused his advances. She was so afraid of being fired for reporting the incident that she did not even tell her best friends about it. Some years later, after she had taken maternity leave, she was transferred to a position from which she could not earn a promotion. She was told that her previous position had been abolished, but in fact it had not been abolished.

What, if anything, must you do to corroborate Jones's allegations before you may sue the president?

In answering this question, assume that a jury could infer from these facts, *if proved*, that the president committed the tort of sexual harassment. Also assume, as is the case, that the president is not constitutionally immune from being sued for his unofficial acts.[20] Finally, exclude from your consideration any knowledge of Monica Lewinsky, the White House intern whose sexual liaison with President Clinton became the subject of an impeachment proceeding. At the time Jones visits you (and at the time the actual lawsuit on which this problem is based arose), Lewinsky is not yet on the scene.

C. Truth and falsity in litigation

Once a case has been filed, the lawyers are bound by court rules and ethical rules to be honest with the tribunal. The rules vary from one state to another. The lawyers' duties also vary depending on the stage of the proceeding and whether the lawyer herself or a witness is communicating to the court.

1. The rules on candor to tribunals

Rules 3.3 and 8.4(c) are the starting points for analysis.

---

20. Clinton v. Jones, 520 U.S. 681 (1997).

Rule 3.3 Candor Toward the Tribunal

Rule language[*]	Authors' explanation[**]
(a) **A lawyer shall not knowingly**: (1) **make a false statement of law or fact** to a tribunal or **fail to correct a false statement of material fact or law previously made to the tribunal by the lawyer**;	• Rule 3.3(a)(1) bars false statements to courts by lawyers themselves, as opposed to false testimony by clients or other witnesses. • If a lawyer discovers that she has made a false statement, the lawyer must correct it.[21]
(2) **fail to disclose** to the tribunal **legal authority** in the **controlling jurisdiction** known to the lawyer to be **directly adverse** to the position of the client and not disclosed by opposing counsel;	Rule 3.3(a)(2) requires more than avoiding falsehood. Lawyers must affirmatively disclose directly adverse law in the controlling jurisdiction if the opponent doesn't do so.
(3) **offer evidence that the lawyer knows to be false.** If a lawyer, the lawyer's client, or a witness called by the lawyer, **has offered material evidence and the lawyer comes to know of its falsity, the lawyer shall take reasonable remedial measures, including, if necessary, disclosure to the tribunal.** A lawyer may refuse to offer evidence, other than the testimony of a defendant in a criminal matter, that the lawyer reasonably believes is false.	• A lawyer who knows that his client or other witness is going to lie to the court may not allow the witness to do so. • If the witness does lie, the lawyer must call on the witness to correct the lie, and if he won't, the lawyer must disclose the lie. • This rule applies to trial testimony, depositions, and other testimony related to adjudication. Comment 1. • If a lawyer reasonably believes, but is not certain, that evidence is false, the lawyer "may" (or may not) refuse to offer the evidence. • In a criminal case, a lawyer must allow the defendant to testify if the lawyer reasonably believes but is not certain that the evidence is false.
(b) A lawyer who **represents a client** in an **adjudicative proceeding** and who knows that a person intends to engage, is engaging or has engaged in **criminal or fraudulent conduct related to the proceeding shall take reasonable remedial measures**, including, if necessary, disclosure to the tribunal.	This rule imposes on lawyers a duty to prevent not only false testimony but also "criminal or fraudulent conduct" in connection with a case before a tribunal.

---

21. A lawyer's intentional misrepresentations meant to deceive the court or an opposing party may have ramifications beyond discipline for violating the rules. Some state statutes expressly permit civil actions against lawyers for such conduct. See, e.g., N.Y. Jud. Law § 487 (McKinney 2006).

Rule language*	Authors' explanation**
(c) The duties stated in paragraphs (a) and (b) continue **to the conclusion of the proceeding**, and apply **even if compliance requires disclosure of information otherwise protected by Rule 1.6.**	• If a lawyer learns that a witness gave false testimony, the lawyer must take steps to correct the record unless the case, including any appeals, has been completed. • The duty to correct the record overrides the duty of confidentiality.
(d) In an ex parte proceeding, a lawyer shall inform the tribunal of all material facts known to the lawyer that will enable the tribunal to make an informed decision, whether or not the facts are adverse.	In a proceeding in which only one side makes a presentation to the court, the lawyer has a duty to tell the court about adverse facts as well as adverse law.

*All emphasis added.
**This and other authors' explanations draw from the comments to the rules and from other sources. They are not comprehensive but highlight some important interpretive points.

Rule 8.4(c) Misconduct

Rule language*	Authors' explanation**
It is professional misconduct for a lawyer to . . . engage in conduct involving **dishonesty, fraud, deceit or misrepresentation**.	This rule applies to *all* conduct by lawyers, including conduct before tribunals. The bans on "deceit" and "misrepresentation" may be broader than the Rule 3.3(a)(1) ban on false statements.

*All emphasis added.
**This and other authors' explanations draw from the comments to the rules and from other sources. They are not comprehensive but highlight some important interpretive points.

2. Which rule applies when? A taxonomy of truth-telling problems in litigation[22]

Rules 3.3, 4.1, and 8.4 apply to many different situations. One way to understand these rules is to inventory some of the situations in which these obligations arise and to explain which rule applies in each circumstance.

---

22. As noted in Chapter 3, Rules 1.2(d), 1.6(b), and 4.1 impose additional obligations in settings unrelated to litigation.

Which truth-telling rule applies

Who might lie or deceive	Situation (Court, administrative hearing, or discovery)	Lawyer's obligation
Lawyer	Lawyer *is considering* making a false statement of fact or law to a judge.	Lawyer must not do it. Rules 3.3(a)(1), 8.4.
Client	Lawyer *knows*[23] that her client is considering testifying falsely in court or in a deposition.	Lawyer must counsel client and refrain from asking client questions that would elicit the false testimony. Rule 3.3(a)(3).
Civil client or witness in any proceeding	Lawyer *suspects* but does not know that planned testimony may be false; witness is not criminal defendant.	If lawyer "reasonably believes" it is false, lawyer may refuse to offer the testimony — or may allow it. Rule 3.3(a)(3).
Criminal defendant	Lawyer *suspects* but does not know that planned testimony may be false; witness is a criminal defendant.	If defendant insists on testifying, lawyer must allow it even if lawyer "reasonably believes it is false." Rule 3.3(a)(3).
Client or witness	Lawyer *knows* that her client or other witness has testified falsely during direct or cross-examination.	Lawyers must counsel client to correct the record; consider withdrawing; correct record if necessary to undo the effect of the false evidence. Rules 3.3(b) and (c), and Comment 10.
Client or witness	Witness has *misled* the court by making statements that are literally true but deceptive.	Lawyer may have duty to counsel client and correct the record. Rules 3.3(b), 8.4(c).
Lawyer	Lawyer *knows* of directly adverse controlling *legal authority* that has not been disclosed by opposing counsel.	Lawyer must bring it to court's attention (and distinguish it or explain why it is not authoritative). Rule 3.3(a)(2).

---

23. How does a lawyer "know" that testimony will be false? See discussion of intended false testimony below. For a discussion of when a lawyer should seek to learn all of the facts of a client's case and when a lawyer might properly warn a client not to reveal adverse information that the lawyer would be obliged or would have discretion to reveal, see Stephen Ellmann, Truth and Consequences, 69 Fordham L. Rev. 895 (2000).

Who might lie or deceive	Situation (Court, administrative hearing, or discovery)	Lawyer's obligation
Lawyer	Lawyer *knows* of *facts adverse* to client's interest, not requested in discovery or required to be disclosed by a court rule.	No need to disclose unless the proceeding is ex parte. Rule 3.3(d).

3. A lawyer's duties if a client or witness intends to give false testimony

a. When the lawyer believes that a criminal defendant intends to lie on the stand

Rule 3.3 states that a lawyer may not present testimony that the lawyer knows to be false. On the other hand, a client expects a lawyer's assistance in presenting his version of the facts to a court, and nowhere is the lawyer's assistance more important than in criminal cases. What should a lawyer do when a criminal defendant wants the lawyer to help him present a patently false case?

Nix v. Whiteside: No Sixth Amendment right to testify falsely

The leading case on this subject is the Supreme Court's decision in *Nix v. Whiteside*,[24] although it arose under the Sixth Amendment, not the ethics rules. In 1977, three men, including Whiteside, went to the apartment of a man named Love, seeking marijuana. Love was in bed when they arrived. An argument ensued. During the argument, Love told his girlfriend to get his "piece." Later, he got up and returned to his bed. Shortly thereafter, according to Whiteside, Love started to reach under his pillow and to move toward Whiteside. Whiteside then stabbed Love in the chest, killing him. An attorney named Robinson was appointed to defend Whiteside in his murder trial. Whiteside told Robinson that Love "was pulling a pistol from underneath the pillow on the bed." Robinson asked whether Whiteside had actually seen a gun. Whiteside conceded that he had not, but he said that he was convinced that Love had a gun. None of the men who went to the apartment with Whiteside saw a gun, and no pistol was found there.

Robinson told Whiteside that for a self-defense argument, he did not need to assert that he'd seen a gun; he needed only to have had a reasonable belief that Love had a gun nearby. But a week before trial, Whiteside told Robinson (for the first time) that he had seen "something metallic" in Love's hand. When Robinson asked why Whiteside was telling him this for

---

24. 475 U.S. 157 (1986).

the first time, White said, "[In] Howard Cook's case there was a gun. If I don't say I saw a gun, I'm dead."

Robinson was convinced that Whiteside was planning to lie and told him that lying was perjury. Robinson threatened to advise the court about the perjury and to withdraw from the case if Whiteside insisted on saying that he had seen something metallic. Whiteside agreed that in his testimony, he would not say that he'd seen something metallic. Whiteside testified in his own defense and said he knew that Love had a gun, and that he acted in self defense because he believed Love was reaching for a gun. Robinson produced testimony that Love had been seen with a sawed-off shotgun on other occasions and that the victim's family had removed everything from the apartment shortly after the crime, but a jury convicted Whiteside.

In a post-conviction habeas corpus challenge, Whiteside claimed that his Sixth Amendment right to counsel implied a duty for Robinson to allow Whiteside to testify as he desired, even if it was untruthful.

Reversing the Eighth Circuit, the Supreme Court held that a lawyer's duty to advocate for his client "is limited to legitimate, lawful conduct compatible with the very nature of a trial as a search for truth." It noted that the Model Rules require disclosure of client perjury, and that although the Model Rules are not the same as the Sixth Amendment, they "confirm that the legal profession has accepted" the principles that a lawyer may not help a client to present false evidence and that a lawyer must disclose perjury to the court. Robinson's threat to disclose perjured testimony or to withdraw therefore fell "within accepted standards of professional conduct" and involved no Sixth Amendment violation.

A concurring opinion by four justices noted that "[t]he only federal issue in this case is whether Robinson's behavior deprived Whiteside of the effective assistance of counsel; it is not whether Robinson's behavior conformed to any particular code of legal ethics."[25] That opinion also noted that some states had adopted variants of the Model Rules' requirement that perjury be disclosed to the court and objected to "the Court's implicit adoption of a set of standards of professional responsibility for attorneys in state criminal proceedings," preferring to "allow the States to maintain their 'differing approaches' to a complex ethical question."[26]

b. A lawyer's "knowledge" of a client's intent to give false testimony

In most cases, lawyers are presented with more ambiguous facts than those presented in *Nix*. It is very common for witnesses in a case to disagree with each other about what happened. Often, a lawyer cannot tell which of them

---

25. Id. at 188 (Blackmun, Brennan, Marshall, and Stevens, JJ., concurring).
26. Id. at 189-190.

"O.K.—let's review what you didn't know and when you didn't know it."

is telling the truth. The rules of professional responsibility do not require lawyers to present only truthful evidence, so a lawyer may present evidence about which he is unsure. But if the lawyer "knows" that the evidence is false, he may not present it.

Under the rules, a lawyer's obligation depends on her belief as to the truth or falsity of a witness's statement. It depends also on whether the witness is a criminal defendant. If the lawyer thinks (or reasonably believes) that the intended testimony of a witness is true, the lawyer may offer it to the court. In a civil case, if the lawyer reasonably believes that the testimony is false, the lawyer may refuse to offer it. Alternatively, the lawyer who reasonably believes that the testimony is false may give the client or other witness the benefit of the doubt and agree to present the testimony. Only if the lawyer *actually knows* that the witness is going to testify falsely must the lawyer refrain from offering the testimony. On the other hand, if the person testifying is a criminal defendant, the lawyer must not present false testimony if the lawyer *knows* that it is false, but (in contrast to the lawyer's option in civil cases) *must allow* the testimony if he does not *know* but *only reasonably believes* it to be false.

How can a lawyer ever *know* that planned testimony is false? The most obvious case is one, like Whiteside, in which the client essentially admits to the lawyer that his planned testimony is a lie. But suppose that the facts were slightly different. Imagine, for example, that in his first statement to Robinson, Whiteside had said only that he knew that Love owned a gun and that he saw Love reach under his pillow. Whiteside did not mention seeing an object there, and Robinson didn't ask whether Whiteside saw one. Suppose that in his second statement to Robinson, two weeks later, Whiteside said that he saw something metallic under Love's pillow.

In these circumstances, could Robinson allow Whiteside to testify about seeing "something metallic" because Robinson cannot be certain that Whiteside simply omitted that detail in his first statement? Or would anyone in Whiteside's shoes have reported seeing something metallic in his very first statement if indeed he had really seen such an object?

This question about a variation on the Whiteside theme is merely hypothetical. But consider this problem from an actual case.

PROBLEM 10-2 FLIGHT FROM SUDAN, SCENE 1

This problem is based on a case handled by two students in a law school clinic who were supervised by Professor Schrag. As usual, we have changed the names of the individuals, but in this case we have also changed the country, the name of the newspaper, and a few other details to protect the identity of the client.

You are a staff lawyer for the Immigrants' Rights Center. You represent Joseph Barragabi, an applicant for political asylum. You met him two months ago when he was referred to your office by a human rights organization. You interviewed him and accepted his case. He seemed terrified that he might lose his case and be forcibly returned to Sudan, which he had fled. In fact, he seems to be one of the most frightened clients you had ever met. You have interviewed him at five different meetings. He has always seemed very anxious about his case. You suspect that if he loses and all his appeals fail, he might commit suicide rather than return home.

Sudan is ruled by a brutal dictator. Political opponents of the regime are tortured and killed. Barragabi says that for a year, six or seven years ago, he was a staff member for the underground opposition newspaper, *Democracy*. He did not write any articles under his own name, however. He worked on several articles with other staff members, but they were published under a fictitious name so that the authors would be less at risk of government reprisal.

Six years ago, in April, the government raided and closed the newspaper and arrested several of the editors. Barragabi says he escaped, left his family, and went into hiding with a friend in a small village. Some of the editors who were arrested have been in jail ever since.

Eventually, Barragabi made it out of the country into Ethiopia, where he worked under a false name and earned enough money to buy a counterfeit passport and an airline ticket to New York City. When he got to the airport in the United States, he admitted having a false passport and he requested asylum. As a result, he was automatically placed in deportation proceedings.

If a person in such proceedings persuades a judge that he qualifies for asylum, the person can remain in the United States. To qualify, the person must show a "well-founded fear" of political or religious persecution in his home country. If the person fails to persuade the judge (either because his story doesn't seem true or because his fear of returning is based on a nonpolitical reason, such as fear of reprisals from a creditor), then he will be deported.

Only about one-third of asylum applicants are successful. A major barrier to victory is a federal statute requiring corroborating evidence (documents or the testimony of other witnesses) unless it cannot reasonably be obtained.[27] In your first interview with Barragabi, you told him about the corroboration requirement and asked him whether it was all right with him if you searched for corroboration. He said that it was.

It is easy to corroborate some of the facts of Barragabi's case through newspaper accounts and respected human rights reports. You find published accounts of the crackdown on the opposition press in Sudan, the closing of *Democracy*, and the incarceration of some of the editors. You have documents showing Barragabi's travel through Ethiopia to the United States. However, Barragabi has been unable to document that he ever worked for *Democracy*. He has no employment card, payroll stub, or other such documents. This is not surprising, however. Refugees often leave most of their documents behind when they are fleeing their home countries.

During the last month, you have done two things. First, you have prepared a detailed affidavit (sworn statement) that your client will sign and file in court, telling his whole story. Under court rules, the affidavit must be filed the day after tomorrow. In a hearing in two weeks, he will be expected to testify consistently with the affidavit. Second, you have been searching for some corroboration of his employment with the newspaper. The other editors seemed to be either in jail or in hiding.

This morning, you had a major breakthrough. You discovered that the editor in chief of *Democracy*, Hamid Al-Parah, escaped from jail and from Sudan, and he is now living in Canada. You

----

27. 8 U.S.C. § 1158(b)(1)(B)(ii) (2007).

called him right away and told him that you were representing Barragabi, who was seeking asylum. You asked him to supply an affidavit and perhaps to come to the United States to testify regarding Barragabi's former employment. Much to your surprise, Al-Parah told you that he had never heard of Barragabi. You described your client's appearance. Al-Parah insists that he knew all of his employees and that Barragabi never worked for him, either under the name Barragabi or any other name.

Questions about Flight from Sudan, Scene 1

1. Should you tell Barragabi about your conversation with Al-Parah?
2. Should you file the affidavit?
3. Should you ask the court for permission to withdraw from representing Barragabi?
4. Did you violate Rule 1.6 by contacting Al-Parah and discussing Barragabi's case with him without first obtaining Barragabi's consent, or was his agreement to let you seek corroboration sufficient?
5. Did you make a mistake by doing your job too well? After learning that Al-Parah was in Canada, should you have said to Barragabi, "I've found a number for Al-Parah in Canada. Of course, I want to call him only if he will corroborate your story. Should I call Al-Parah?" Before you respond to this part of the problem, consider the following question.

Can lawyers protect themselves and their clients by deliberately not knowing all the facts?

Up to a point, they can. Several important obligations, such as the duty not to collaborate in a client's crime (Rule 1.2(d)), the duty to report the misconduct of corporate officials to a client corporation (Rule 1.13), and the duty to correct a client's testimony that the lawyer knows to have been false (Rule 3.3(b)), depend on how much the lawyer knows. Lawyers usually think that they cannot responsibly represent clients without learning as much as possible about their cases. But sometimes, particularly in criminal defense work, lawyers avoid learning all of the facts. Many criminal defense lawyers, for example, do not ask their clients if they committed the crime of which they are accused. They reason that after a client admits that he committed a robbery, they could not allow that client to testify that he was elsewhere at the time. Of course, one can legitimately ask whether the rules of legal ethics *should* give lawyers an incentive not to dig too deeply.[28] Is it even possible to write ethical rules that would encourage lawyers and clients to share all of the facts while still prohibiting lawyers from using perjured testimony?

In recent years, deliberate ignorance has become so pervasive in corporate and professional culture that it is now a field of study. Professor Robert N. Proctor of Stanford University coined the term "agnotology" to describe a new academic enterprise: the study of ignorance. He believes that in recent years, corporations and other institutions have increasingly resisted investigating potential wrongdoing, both because investigations are expensive and because they don't want to know that their employees have acted illegally or immorally. For example, when the chief executive of the Enron Corp. was warned of financial irregularities several months before the company collapsed and a scandal erupted, he could have hired outside investigators to find out what was going on. "But instead of hiring people with no relation to the company and a reputation for tough investigations, he employed the company's longtime law firm and requested a narrow inquiry."[29]

c. A lawyer's duties if a client intends to mislead the court without lying

Many issues involving possible deception of tribunals involve partial truths rather than bald-faced lies. The ethics rules prohibit false statements but permit some less direct forms of deception. A partial truth is a statement that may literally be true but that deceives another person by omitting relevant information or twisting information in a way that distorts it. Many people believe that partial truths and deception by omission are morally more defensible than false affirmative assertions.[30] As we are about to see, the criminal law of perjury makes a sharp distinction between the two types of deception.

Perjury — lying under oath — is a crime. If a lawyer knowingly puts on perjured testimony, the lawyer might be disbarred[31] or even convicted of

---

28. For a particularly thoughtful discussion of the willful ignorance problem, see David Luban, Contrived Ignorance, 87 Geo. L.J. 957 (1999).

29. Karen W. Arenson, What Organizations Don't Want to Know Can Hurt, N.Y. Times (Aug. 22, 2006) (available at http://www.nytimes.com/2006/08/22/business/22mistakes.html?page wanted=print).

30. One scholar attempts to explain this difference by arguing that "a victim who is deceived by a [deliberate] non-lie feels foolish and embarrassed, presumably because he believes he has contributed to his own harm by drawing unwarranted inferences from misleading premises. By contrast, a victim of lies is much more likely to feel 'brutalized' . . . by some external force." Stuart P. Green, Lying, Misleading, and Falsely Denying: How Moral Concepts Inform the Law of Perjury, Fraud, and False Statements, 53 Hastings L.J. 157, 167-168 (2001).

31. Matter of Mitchell, 262 S.E.2d 89 (Ga. 1979).

the crime of subornation of perjury.[32] The crime of perjury is a very extreme form of dishonesty, and precisely because it is a crime, the definition of what constitutes perjury is quite narrow. The leading case is *Bronston v. United States*.[33] Bronston had a personal bank account in Switzerland for five years, which he closed just before filing for bankruptcy. In the bankruptcy proceeding, he was being questioned about his assets, and he testified as follows:

> Q: Do you have any bank accounts in Swiss banks, Mr. Bronston?
> A: No sir.
> Q: Have you ever?
> A: The company had an account there for about six months in Zurich.

Bronston was charged with perjury under a federal statute that made it a crime when a witness under oath "states or subscribes any material matter which he does not believe to be true." Prosecutors argued that Bronston's evasive answer tended to mislead his creditors into thinking that he had never had a personal Swiss bank account. He was convicted. The Supreme Court unanimously reversed the conviction. The Court noted that Bronston may well have intended to mislead his questioner by giving a "nonresponsive" answer. But his answer was not literally a false statement, and the Court declined to interpret the federal perjury law to prohibit intentionally misleading nonresponsive statements:

> Under the pressures and tensions of interrogation, it is not uncommon for the most earnest witnesses to give answers that are not entirely responsive. Sometimes the witness does not understand the question, or may in an excess of caution or apprehension read too much or too little into it. It should come as no surprise that a participant in a bankruptcy proceeding may have something to conceal and consciously tries to do so, or that a debtor may be embarrassed at his plight and yield information reluctantly. It is the responsibility of the [examining] lawyer to probe; testimonial interrogation, and cross-examination in particular, is a probing, prying, pressing form of inquiry. If a witness evades, it is the lawyer's responsibility to recognize the evasion and to bring the witness back to the mark, to flush out the whole truth with the tools of adversary examination.[34]

Under the *Bronston* standard, deliberately false statements by lawyers or witnesses may be prosecuted as perjury under federal and state perjury statutes, and lawyers who commit perjury can be disciplined for making

---

32. Sheriff v. Hecht, 710 P.2d 728 (Nev. 1985) (subornation of perjury where a lawyer advised a witness to testify falsely that he did not remember a fact); Butler v. Texas, 429 S.W.2d 497 (Tex. Crim. App. 1968).

33. 409 U.S. 352 (1973).

34. Id. at 358-359.

false statements to courts.[35] But under *Bronston*, many of the corners that lawyers and witnesses cut do not involve actual perjury. The disciplinary standards, however, require a more exacting degree of truthfulness from lawyers than does the criminal law of perjury.

The most relevant ethics rules are the state rules corresponding to Rule 3.3(b) (requiring lawyers to correct "fraudulent" conduct by their witnesses) and Rule 8.4(c) (barring "deceit"). But neither these nor other rules deal expressly with the problem of half-truths. Rule 7.1, which mainly regulates lawyer advertising but which uses very general language about lawyers' communications, bars lawyers from making false or misleading statements about themselves or their services. It provides that when a lawyer communicates about himself or about his services, the statement "is false or misleading if it contains a material misrepresentation of fact or law, or omits a fact necessary to make the statement considered as a whole not materially misleading." That explanation does not appear in Rule 3.3 or Rule 8.4.

Curiously, very little case law speaks to whether lawyers can be disciplined because they or their witnesses mislead courts with partially true but deceptive testimony. We did a LEXIS search of 201 bar disciplinary cases that mentioned "deceit" and "omission," together with either "3.3" or "8.4." Nearly all these cases involved deceptive conduct by lawyers outside of the context of litigation before tribunals — for example, tax fraud, embezzlement of client funds, false statements on bar applications, or misrepresentation of the lawyer's own qualifications. Not one of the cases resulted in discipline of a lawyer because the lawyer or a witness called by the lawyer misled a tribunal or an opposing lawyer without actually making a false statement of fact.[36]

Even if lawyers are never or rarely disciplined or sanctioned for the half-truths of their testifying clients or witnesses, what should lawyers do when their clients engage in nonperjurious deceptive behavior?

---

35. See, e.g., People v. Cardwell, 2001 WL 1174299 (Colo. July 11, 2001) (lawyer suspended for three years for falsely telling the court that his client had no prior convictions for driving under the influence of alcohol).

36. Although not a lawyer discipline case, *Technomed v. Santiago* imposed a monetary sanction of $1,000 against attorney Emilio Santiago for misleading a New York trial court by a half-true statement. On behalf of a client, Santiago moved for (and received) a default judgment, representing to the court that the defendant had neither filed an answer to his complaint nor moved for an extension of time. Those statements were true, but Santiago failed to mention that the defendant had moved to dismiss. Anthony Lin, Lawyer Liable for Malicious Prosecution in Bronx Case, N.Y.L.J. (July 1, 2003).

PROBLEM 10-3   FLIGHT FROM SUDAN, SCENE 2

This problem is also based on a case handled by two law students in an immigration clinic.[37]

Al-Parah, the former editor in chief of *Democracy*, told you that Barragabi, your asylum client, never worked for him. After some reflection, you decide that you have no basis to believe him over your client. You decide to continue to represent Barragabi in his deportation proceeding.

Barragabi said that during the months while his asylum application was pending, he participated in three demonstrations against the government of Sudan outside of the embassy of Sudan. This tends to support his claim that he is an opponent of the government. You have evidence that embassy officials photograph demonstrators so that the government can punish them if they ever return to Sudan. Therefore, if you can prove that he participated in the demonstrations, this would help to demonstrate that he would be at risk if he were deported.

The only person who can corroborate Barragabi's participation in the demonstration is his roommate, Farik Massariah, another Sudanese refugee whom Barragabi met after he came to the United States. You interviewed Massariah and learned that he, too, had applied for asylum. He had been a dissident leader in Sudan. The government's interviewer provisionally recommended that he be granted asylum, subject to the results of an FBI fingerprint check. The FBI report stated that there was an outstanding arrest warrant from Pennsylvania for Massariah. The government directed Massariah to supply a certificate from the Pennsylvania state police showing that he had not been convicted of any crimes in that state. He did so, but the government nevertheless withdrew the provisional recommendation and initiated deportation proceedings against Massariah. His hearing is scheduled in six months.

At Barragabi's asylum hearing, you put Massariah on the stand. He testifies that Barragabi and he participated in three demonstrations outside the Sudanese embassy. The government lawyer cross-examined Massariah as follows:

Q: What is your own immigration status, Mr. Massariah?
A: I was provisionally recommended for asylum. But there was something wrong with my fingerprints, and I had to get some records from the

---

37. Actually, it involved a client other than the one on whose case Scene 1 is based, but we have adapted it so that after working on the problem in Scene 1, you don't have to learn a new set of facts.

police in Pennsylvania showing that I had not been convicted of any crimes there. I got those records and I supplied them to the immigration officials.

Q: How many people attended the first demonstration in which you and Mr. Barragabi participated?

The government lawyer asked more questions about the demonstrations but never returned to the subject of Massariah's immigration status. Massariah never stated that he himself was still a respondent in deportation proceedings.

Should you take steps (including your own disclosure, if necessary) to inform the government or the court that immigration officials withdrew the provisional recommendation that Massariah be given asylum and instead put Massariah into deportation proceedings?

---

d. Variations in state rules on candor to tribunals

Most states have adopted language similar to Rule 3.3. Under some conditions, a lawyer may not allow his client or any other witness to testify falsely and must disclose confidential information to correct false testimony if the client will not do so. Several jurisdictions have adopted different rules for some or all types of cases. For example, in the District of Columbia, a lawyer who is not able to dissuade a criminal defendant client from giving testimony that the lawyer believes to be false may allow the client to give the testimony in a "narrative" fashion. The client may tell his story without the lawyer asking questions that would elicit the false testimony.[38] During closing argument, the lawyer must not refer to the facts stated by the defendant as if they were true. The D.C. approach protects a defendant whose lawyer may have misjudged him and protects his right to a day in court. At the same time, a lawyer who uses this approach signals the trial judge that the client is lying. However, if the case is tried to a jury, the judge's perception may be irrelevant because many jurors would not realize that the different style of providing testimony has a hidden meaning.[39]

---

38. D.C. R. Prof. Conduct 3.3(b) (lawyer must first try to dissuade the client from lying and, if that fails, must move to withdraw, but if the motion is denied, the lawyer may allow the client to testify "in a narrative fashion"); see Mass. R. Prof. Conduct 3.3(e), Comment 10 (lawyer who cannot dissuade defendant from lying should make a motion to withdraw to a judge other than the trial judge, but if a trial has already started, the lawyer need not make the motion if that would prejudice the defendant. If the motion is denied, the lawyer may allow the defendant to relate his testimony without the usual question-and-answer participation of his lawyer.). Although the client initially tells his story in this unusual manner, he is still subject to ordinary cross-examination.

39. Note that *Nix* decided only that a lawyer's refusal to permit perjured testimony doesn't violate the defendant's constitutional rights. *Nix* therefore left states free to adopt ethics rules, such as this one, that direct other solutions to the problem of expected false testimony by clients.

As for lawyers who did not expect their clients to lie but discover that clients are giving or already have given false testimony, at least two jurisdictions prohibit them from "ratting" on their clients rather than requiring them to do so.[40] These jurisdictions appear to put a higher value on preserving the lawyer-client relationship than on making the lawyer a warrantor that a client is not lying.

Finally, in some states, the duty to inform the court if the client has lied and refuses to correct the false testimony may be negated by the attorney-client privilege, particularly if (as in New York) the privilege is embodied in a statute rather than in the common law. The New York State Bar Association has concluded that while the obligation in Rule 3.3 to take remedial measures to correct false testimony overrides the confidentiality requirements of Rule 1.6, Rule 3.3 cannot trump the statutory privilege.[41]

4. False impressions created by lawyers during litigation

Up to this point, we have considered the duties of a lawyer whose witness may lie or mislead a tribunal or has already done so. Most lawyers take their obligations of candor to tribunals very seriously and would not themselves mislead an adjudicator. However, because many lawyers also take their obligations to their clients very seriously, it sometimes does happen that a lawyer gives a false impression to a court. Furthermore, the problems that arise for lawyers, like those that arise for witnesses, are rarely as simple as making clearly false statements to courts. Lawyers often must decide whether their efforts to shade or embellish the truth in favor of their clients represent good advocacy or punishable deception. The editorial that follows provides an example for your consideration.

How Simpson Lawyers Bamboozled a Jury

Omaha World Herald (Oct. 10, 1996)

[O.J. Simpson is a famous African American football player and actor who was charged with murdering his ex-wife, Nicole Brown Simpson, and her friend, Ronald Goldman. During the trial, the court allowed the jury

---

40. D.C. R. Prof. Conduct 3.3(d) (lawyer should call upon the client to rectify a fraud on the tribunal, but if the lawyer is unsuccessful, the lawyer should abide by the ban imposed by Rule 1.6 on disclosing confidential information); Mass. R. Prof. Conduct 3.3(e) (in a criminal case, if client will not rectify false testimony, the lawyer shall not reveal the falsity to the tribunal).

41. N.Y. State B. Assn., Op. 837 (2010) (available at http://www.nysba.org/AM/Template.cfm?Section=Home&TEMPLATE=/CM/ContentDisplay.cfm&CONTENTID=36773). The committee noted that in some, but not all, circumstances, depending on the precise nature of the falsehood, the attorney-client privilege would be inapplicable because of the crime-fraud exception. Id. at n. 3.

to visit Brown Simpson's house, the scene of her murder. Over the objection of the prosecutor, the court also allowed the jury to tour Mr. Simpson's nearby house, where some of the evidence had been found.]

Another sordid revelation for the O.J. Simpson file: A soon-to-be-published book about Simpson's criminal trial says that defense lawyers did some redecorating at Simpson's home before the jury toured the home during the trial.

The book says a nude photo of Simpson's white girlfriend, Paula Barbieri, was removed from his bedroom and a framed picture of Simpson's mother was placed by his bed. Pictures of other white friends were taken down and replaced by pictures of black friends.

Defense attorney Johnnie Cochran took from his own office a Norman Rockwell print of a black girl being escorted to school by federal marshals and hung it in Simpson's home in a place where the jury would be sure to see it.

Any sensible defense attorney wants his client to make a favorable impression on the jury. Granted, having an unkempt lout shave, get a haircut and put on a new suit is a little disingenuous if the defendant has seldom done so. But a fellow ought to be allowed to put himself in the best possible light. And the argument can be made that everyone ought to clean up out of respect for the court.

If the pictures of Ms. Barbieri and others had been replaced with pictures of football highlights or scenic landscapes, that might have been branded sneaky but similar to cleaning up oneself for a court appearance.

The replacement of white people's pictures with pictures of black people takes on a more sinister quality because race was a major issue in the Simpson trial. Some African Americans had questioned Simpson's commitment to fellow blacks. Nine of the 12 jurors were black. Cochran would later call the case against Simpson a [conspiracy] of lies and doctored evidence produced by a racist police force that was jealous of Simpson's wealth and fame.

In that context, the attempt to give the jury a different picture of Simpson through the swapping of pictures and the display of a civil-rights poster becomes a contemptible, despicable fraud that tarnishes the reputations of all involved.

Question about *Omaha World Herald* Editorial

Do you agree that Cochran's substitution of the pictures was a "contemptible, despicable fraud" in the murder trial of O.J. Simpson? Did it violate any rule of professional conduct? Or was it a good and ethically responsible piece of lawyering, similar to providing the defendant with a nice suit? Would you have done the same thing?

PROBLEM 10-4 THE DRUG TEST

This problem is based closely on a case that was decided in a midwestern state early in the twenty-first century.

You work in a small law firm and represent Frederic Krause in a divorce action against his wife, Maria. Maria's lawyer has made a motion to suspend Frederic's right to visit the couple's three-year-old daughter, Darlene. Maria claims that Frederic uses methamphetamines. Under the law, a judge may suspend the visitation rights of any parent who currently uses illegal drugs.

The judge scheduled a hearing on Maria's motion in five days. In preparing for the hearing, you asked Frederic whether he was using methamphetamines. He said that he did so at one time while living with Maria, but that he had not used this drug in more than four years. You advised him to get a drug test to prove that he was not using methamphetamines. Frederic then went to your town's hospital and asked to have his urine tested for methamphetamines. He instructed the hospital to send the report on the drug test to you.

The hospital's laboratory technician telephoned you and reported that Frederic tested negative for methamphetamines. However, the test screened for eight substances, and Frederic had tested positive for marijuana. She faxed you a copy of the printout.

There were no allegations of marijuana use in Frederic's legal case, so you told the technician that you needed a report showing only the methamphetamine results. You asked for a new test, for methamphetamines only. She said that she could do only a multi-substance screen, but she could provide you with a second report, omitting the marijuana results.

You asked her to do that. She mailed you part of the original printout. In comparing the report she mailed you with the technician's earlier fax, you saw that she had simply used a scissors to cut off the bottom portion of the original report and sent you only the top portion showing that your client tested negative for methamphetamines.

Questions about the Drug Test

1. When you received the telephoned report from the laboratory, would it have been proper for you to thank the hospital, dispense with a written report, and advise Frederic to get a new test at another hospital, making sure to find a laboratory that uses a test for methamphetamines only and not for other substances?
2. Now that you have received the partial report in the mail, would it be ethically proper for you to send a copy of it to Mrs. Krause's

lawyer and then offer it as an exhibit that will be part of the evidence?

3. Assume that you do introduce it as evidence. The judge then asks you (as the judge in the real case did), "Is this the entire report?" Which of the following possible responses is best? (If you don't approve of any of these responses, devise a better one.)

   a. "Yes, your honor."

   b. "That's what I have, judge. That's what I asked them to screen for."

   c. "No, your honor. Mr. Krause tested positive for marijuana, but I asked the lab technician to exclude that result from the report since Mrs. Krause accused Mr. Krause only of using methamphetamines."

   d. "Actually, your honor, I have just decided to withdraw the exhibit."

---

5. Lawyers' duties of truthfulness in preparing witnesses to testify

A lawyer is not permitted to offer evidence known to be false, so it follows that a lawyer may not advise a client or other witness to give false evidence. But what about more subtle advice? For example, may a lawyer who is preparing a witness for trial urge the witness to use particular truthful words or phrases that the witness normally would not use? Alternatively, may a lawyer coach a witness on nonverbal behavior such as facial expressions and tone of voice?[42] What about rehearsing testimony so that the witness hesitates less and is less likely to contradict herself? All of these methods of preparation may enhance the credibility of the witness or the clarity of the testimony, but they also may give a misleading impression of the witness or of the events at issue.

Even if lawyers do not try to distort the testimony of a witness, preparation for a trial may inevitably change how a witness recalls events and

---

42. This discussion focuses on the ethical propriety of coaching while preparing a witness who is going to testify in a trial or a deposition. Coaching a witness who has already taken the stand or begun to give testimony during a deposition, particularly while a question is pending, may violate the rules of a tribunal. See, e.g., Hall v. Clifton Precision, 150 F.R.D. 525 (E.D. Pa. 1993) (analogizing depositions to trials and prohibiting coaching during either type of proceeding); S.C. R. Civ. P. 30(j)(5) and (6) (prohibiting coaching during depositions). Only a few courts have taken this position, however. The American Bar Association has taken the position that lawyer-client conversations during recesses should be permitted and that the attorney-client privilege should apply to any such discussions. ABA Section of Litigation, Civil Discovery Standard 18(b)(i) (2004).

therefore change the substance of the testimony. Professor Richard C. Wydick of the University of California illustrates the problem with this pretrial dialogue:

> Q: When Bloggs came into the pub, did he have a knife in his hand?
> A: I don't remember.
> Q: Did you see him clearly?
> A: Yes.
> Q: Do people in that neighborhood often walk into pubs with knives in their hands?
> A: No, certainly not.
> Q: If you had seen Bloggs with a knife in his hand, would you remember that?
> A: Yes, of course.
> Q: And you don't remember any knife?
> A: No, I don't remember any knife.

During the days or months between the interview and the trial, the story can harden, and what started as "I don't remember" may come out like this at trial:

> Q: When Bloggs came into the pub, did he have a knife in his hand?
> A: No, he did not.[43]

Wydick points out, however, that American law tolerates a considerable amount of coaching because uncoached witnesses often ramble and contradict themselves. Lawyers help courts to process cases efficiently by preparing witnesses to give clearer and more cogent, coherent, and pertinent testimony than the witnesses would give without preparation.[44]

Anecdotal evidence also suggests that pretrial coaching is routine. A former federal prosecutor who later moved to a prominent law firm explained to a reporter that when preparing a witness for testimony, it is "okay to point out additional facts or show them documents that would refresh their recollection. It's entirely proper for someone to come in and do a mock cross-examination to draw out what might be vulnerabilities in the witness's testimony." Professor Yale Kamisar, criticizing a government lawyer who had given a witness transcripts of other witnesses' testimony so that the stories would be consistent, said that such behavior is "not the way you coach. In the real world, it's more of just, 'Let's go over your testimony.' Here, there was not even a pretense, not even a cover."[45]

---

43. Richard C. Wydick, The Ethics of Witness Coaching, 17 Cardozo L. Rev. 1, 11-12 (1995).

44. Id. at 12-13.

45. Adam Liptak, Crossing a Fine Line on Witness Coaching, N.Y. Times (Mar. 16, 2006) (available at http://www.nytimes.com/2006/03/16/national/16assess.html?pagewanted=print).

What do the ethics rules say about coaching?

There is very little "law" on the subject of coaching.[46] The ethical rules address this subject only in the most general terms.

> **Rule 3.4 Fairness to Opposing Party and Counsel**
> **A lawyer shall not . . .**
>
> > **(b) falsify evidence, counsel or assist a witness to testify falsely, or offer an inducement to a witness that is prohibited by law.[47] . . .**

The focus on false testimony may imply that if lawyers avoid conduct that leads witnesses to testify falsely, coaching is ethically unobjectionable. Alternatively, perhaps the drafters were simply in such disagreement about the propriety of coaching that they decided not to address the issue.

"I love my testimony. You've really captured my voice."

---

46. There may be relatively little law because information about coaching takes place in private, and no one who might complain about it really knows what coaching took place. If someone did complain, communications between lawyers and their clients are effectively shielded by the attorney-client privilege, and even communications with nonclient witnesses are usually protected by the more limited work product doctrine. As a result, courts and disciplinary authorities are not likely to learn the nature of any pretrial coaching, and it is difficult to find reported cases with information about such coaching.

47. In the ABA Model Rules, this section ends with a semicolon rather than a period.

The Restatement more explicitly allows coaching that does not induce false evidence:

> In preparing a witness to testify, a lawyer may invite the witness to provide truthful testimony favorable to the lawyer's client. Preparation . . . may include discussing the role of the witness and effective courtroom demeanor; discussing the witness's recollection and probable testimony; revealing to the witness other testimony or evidence that will be presented and asking the witness to reconsider the witness's recollection or recounting of events in that light. . . . Witness preparation may include rehearsal of testimony. A lawyer may suggest choice of words that might be employed to make the witness's meaning clear. However, a lawyer may not assist the witness to testify falsely as to a material fact.[48]

The D.C. Bar Legal Ethics Committee took the view, consistent with the Restatement, that lawyers may suggest answers to witnesses even when the basis for the answers did not derive from the witnesses themselves, provided that the substance of the testimony given "is not, so far as the lawyer knows or ought to know, false or misleading."[49] Some experts criticize this approach. Professors Fred Zacharias and Shaun Martin argue that "attorneys who 'coach' their clients or witnesses to fashion a story that is consistent with the written record can simultaneously foster the introduction of false testimony while remaining ignorant of the true set of facts." "Under the D.C. Bar Opinion's approach," they write, "lawyers are justified in introducing the altered testimony on the grounds that the lawyers do not 'know' that it is false."[50] Wydick states that if "the lawyer uses [a] role-playing session as an occasion for scripting the witness's answers, then it is unethical."[51]

PROBLEM 10-5 REFRESHING RECOLLECTION

You represent Nancy Magill, who is being sued by the Superior Mortgage Co. The company is attempting to take Magill's house from her because she became unable to keep up her mortgage payments. She said she never realized that the interest rate for the mortgage would be so high, so she didn't anticipate how hard it would be to make the payments.

When you interviewed Magill initially, you asked her whether the loan agent, Spencer Martinelli, made any statements to her about

---

48. Restatement § 116, comment b. The Restatement adds that this comment "is supported by relatively sparse authority but, it is believed, by the uniform practice of lawyers in all jurisdictions." Id. at comment b, reporter's note.

49. D.C. B. Leg. Ethics Comm., Formal Op. 79 (1979).

50. Fred C. Zacharias & Shaun Martin, Coaching Witnesses, 87 Ky. L.J. 1001, 1015 n. 59 (1998).

51. Wydick, supra n. 43, at 16.

what interest rate Superior would charge for the loan. She said that he did not. In fact, although the loan documents show that Martinelli was her loan agent, she does not remember him very well and is not able to describe him.

After you began to work on the Magill case, you agreed to represent several other homeowners in the neighborhood who also had obtained mortgages from Superior. Nearly all of your other clients said that Martinelli had falsely asserted that "Superior's interest rates were the lowest in the region." Actually, they were a quarter of a percentage point higher than the rates offered by City Mortgage Co.

When you took Martinelli's deposition in the Magill case, he denied having made such statements. You have settled two cases on favorable terms after Superior's lawyer deposed your clients and heard their credible testimony about Martinelli's lies. You are about to meet with Magill to prepare her for her own deposition.

If you remind Magill to testify truthfully, during this meeting may you do any of the following?

1. Ask Magill whether Martinelli made any statements to her to the effect that Superior's rates were lower than those of other companies?
2. Tell her that Superior settled other cases favorably because the borrowers remembered that Martinelli said that "Superior's interest rates were the lowest in the region"? (Assume that you could share this information without disclosing any confidences of other clients.)
3. Remind her what Martinelli looks like?
4. Suppose you tell her that other customers of Martinelli have testified that he told them that Superior's rates were lower than those of other companies, and she then recalls that he told her the same thing. May you advise her to sound forceful and confident about this fact when she testifies?

May a lawyer coach a client or other witness, or discuss that person's prior testimony, during breaks in the person's deposition?

The authorities are deeply divided on whether this type of coaching is permitted. In some jurisdictions it is permitted; in some it is forbidden; in some it is permitted if initiated by the client or witness rather than the lawyer; and in some its propriety depends on the duration of the recess.[52]

---

52. The different rules and their rationales are discussed in Joseph R. Wilbert, Muzzling Rambo Attorneys: Preventing Abusive Witness Coaching by Banning Attorney-Initiated Consultations with

D. Concealment of physical evidence and documents

Of course, a lawyer should not conceal evidence. Do we need to discuss this topic? Consider the duty of confidentiality, which requires lawyers to conceal quite a lot of information. In the "Missing Persons" case considered in Chapter 3, a lawyer felt pinned between his duty of confidentiality to his clients and his duty (reinforced by a criminal statute) to reveal to authorities the location of undiscovered cadavers. In that case, the client told the lawyer where the bodies of two murder victims were located. The lawyer saw the physical evidence but did not come into the possession or control of it.[53] Sometimes lawyers are given or independently discover physical evidence or documents related to an impending or ongoing case. This section explores how lawyers should balance their duty to protect client confidences against their responsibilities to the system of justice.

As we shall see, the relevant ethics rules are painted with a broad brush. They do not distinguish between civil and criminal cases, or between physical evidence and documentary evidence, or between material generated for the purpose of obtaining legal assistance and material that would have been created even if no lawyer were involved. In practice, these distinctions are important.

1. Duties of criminal defense lawyers with respect to evidence of crimes

What should a lawyer do when a criminal defendant hands the lawyer a weapon or other tangible evidence of a crime?

In criminal cases, prosecutors may not use discovery to obtain information from defendants. If a prosecutor requires a suspect to answer questions before a grand jury, the suspect may refuse to testify to avoid self-

---

Deponents, 21 Geo. J. Leg. Ethics 1129 (2008). The last variation is found in Del. R. Civ. P. for the Super. Ct. 30(d)(1) (such conversations are permitted if the recess lasts longer than five days).

53. Actually, Mr. Belge, one of the two lawyers for defendant Robert Garrow, had not only seen and photographed the evidence, but touched part of it when he moved some bones that had been carried away by animals. Did he thereby conceal evidence, make it easier to discover, or neither? This aspect of his actions apparently was not discussed in the judicial opinions on the case. Was it ethically significant? Perhaps so: An opinion of the New York State Bar, released four years after the case was over, stated that "there could be an appearance of impropriety . . . in moving a part of one of the bodies" even if the only purpose in doing so was to bring the body part within camera range and not to conceal any evidence. N.Y. State B. Assn., Formal Op. 479 (prepared in 1974 but publication withheld until Feb. 28, 1978) (available at http://www.nysba.org/AM/Template.cfm?Section=Ethics_Opinions&ContentID=49076&template=/CM/ContentDisplay.cfm).

incrimination. But law enforcement officials may obtain search warrants to look for physical evidence (which law enforcement officials and judges sometimes refer to as "real evidence"). If a lawyer for a suspect in a criminal case were to take possession of physical evidence, the lawyer could help the client to avoid prosecution by hiding it. On rare occasions, judges grant warrants to search lawyers' offices, but because such searches could breach attorney-client privilege in all of the lawyer's cases, prosecutors are reluctant to ask for such searches and judges hesitate to authorize them.[54] The rules of professional responsibility therefore restrict lawyers from hiding evidence of criminal misconduct.

> **Rule 3.4(a) Fairness to Opposing Party and Counsel**
> **A lawyer shall not: . . . unlawfully obstruct another party's access to evidence or unlawfully alter, destroy or conceal a document or other material having potential evidentiary value. A lawyer shall not counsel or assist another person to do any such act.**

This rule does not prohibit all concealment or destruction of evidence but only "unlawful" concealment or destruction. Nor does the rule prohibit concealment or destruction of every object or document in the possession of a suspect or other witness, but only material having "potential evidentiary value." In a state that adopts this rule, the ban applies only if some other law makes the concealment or destruction unlawful. The word "unlawful" is not defined in the rules, but the ABA Annotated Model Rules of Professional Conduct explain that concealment of evidence is a violation of the ethical rule only if the lawyer already has some obligation to disclose it, such as if the evidence is the subject of a discovery request to which no objection has been made, or is the fruit or instrumentality of a crime and the lawyer is required by law to turn it over to law enforcement officials.[55]

If the conduct at issue would violate a criminal obstruction of justice statute, the destruction or concealment is unlawful. If the conduct violates a court order, it is unlawful because it is a contempt of court. Similarly, a

---

54. The U.S. Department of Justice has issued rules that prosecutors must follow before lawyers' offices are searched. 28 C.F.R. § 59.4 (2007). In addition, Rule 3.8(e) bars a prosecutor from issuing subpoenas to lawyers to try to force them to present evidence against their clients unless the prosecutor reasonably believes that the information is not protected by privilege, is essential to an investigation or a prosecution, and is not obtainable by other means.

55. ABA, Annotated Model Rules of Professional Conduct 325 (6th ed., ABA 2007). This passage refers only to concealment, not destruction, and there is an important difference. A lawyer who withholds evidence while making an objection remains able to produce it if a tribunal determines that the objection is not valid.

lawyer may violate Rule 3.4(a) by failing to comply with a discovery request or with discovery rules imposing an ongoing duty of disclosure.[56]

Concealment or destruction of evidence also may be unlawful under Rule 3.4 if it would constitute a tort, but this is less clear than the above cases in which the lawyer has a legal duty to protect or to disclose certain evidence. For example, in some jurisdictions, destroying or concealing documents for the purpose of preventing an adversary from using them constitutes the tort of spoliation.[57] If certain conduct is tortious, then one who engages in that conduct may be obliged to pay damages. But that doesn't necessarily mean that the act in question is illegal or unlawful.

So one problem with Rule 3.4 is the lack of clarity about the meaning of "unlawful." Another problem is that some state obstruction of justice and evidence tampering statutes are very ambiguous, which makes it hard for lawyers to know what is prohibited.[58]

Two other problems make enforcement of this rule quite difficult. To begin with, violations are often difficult to detect. If a lawyer is destroying or concealing evidence, who will find out? In addition, even if a prosecutor accuses a lawyer of concealing evidence for a defendant, the lawyer inevitably cites the attorney-client and work product privileges to avoid revealing information. The prosecutor must find some way to prove the misconduct without any admission by the lawyer.

The conflict between loyalty to clients and loyalty to the justice system with respect to real evidence relevant to criminal investigations has arisen and been adjudicated in a variety of procedural contexts.

---

56. See, e.g., Briggs v. McWeeny, 796 A.2d 516 (Conn. 2002) (affirming a trial court finding that "the plaintiff had violated Rule 3.4 by suppressing relevant, discoverable evidence to which the opposing parties and their counsel were entitled in accordance with the plaintiff's continuing duty to disclose under [Connecticut's] Practice Book § 3-15").

57. The development of this tort appears to have begun with a case decided by an intermediate appellate court in California, Smith v. Super. Ct., 151 Cal. App. 3d 491 (1984), but 14 years later, the Supreme Court of California held that the tort does not exist in that state except, perhaps, in favor of a party who could not have known about the spoliation during the underlying lawsuit (the suit for which the evidence was concealed) and who therefore could not have moved for sanctions or other remedies in that case. Cedars-Sinai Med. Ctr. v. Super. Ct., 954 P.2d 511 (Cal. 1998). Meanwhile, other states recognized the tort. See, e.g., Hazen v. Anchorage, 718 P.2d 456 (Alaska 1996); Oliver v. Stimson Lumber Co., 993 P.2d 11 (Mont. 1999).

58. For example, the D.C. Code makes it a crime to destroy or conceal a record, document, or other object "with intent to impair its integrity or its availability" for use in an "official proceeding" if the defendant knew or had reason to believe that the proceeding had begun or was "likely to be instituted." D.C. Code Ann. § 22-723 (2007). A defendant accused of violating this law, or a lawyer accused of violating a state rule based on Rule 3.4(a), could dispute her intent, the likelihood that a proceeding would be instituted, her knowledge or reason to believe that it would be instituted, and whether whatever process was foreseeable was an "official proceeding." Obviously a criminal prosecution is such a proceeding, but what if all that was in the offing was a legislative investigation, the inquiry of a commission, or the institution of a civil lawsuit?

State v. Olwell, **1964**[59]   Warren was stabbed to death, and Gray was arrested for murder. Gray admitted killing Warren but said he didn't know what happened to the knife. Two days later, he retained Olwell to represent him. The coroner subpoenaed Olwell to attend an inquest and asked whether Olwell had a knife belonging to Gray. Olwell refused to answer, claiming attorney-client privilege. He was held in contempt. The appellate court reversed the contempt order because the subpoena had not been drafted properly, but it offered guidance for lawyers who are given evidence by their clients. The court said that Olwell, who had come into possession of a knife that he believed belonged to Gray, could have kept it for a reasonable period of time for purposes of examining it and conducting tests on it. After that, he should have turned it over to the prosecution at his own initiative, "as an officer of the court," without being asked or issued a subpoena. "The attorney should not be a depository for criminal evidence (such as a knife, other weapons, stolen property, etc.), which in itself has little, if any, material value for the purposes of aiding counsel in the preparation of the defense of his client's case." To encourage lawyer-client confidentiality, however, the prosecutor "when attempting to introduce such evidence at the trial, should take extreme precautions to make certain that the source of the evidence is not disclosed in the presence of the jury...." If Olwell had given Gray's knife to the prosecutor, law enforcement officials would have been more certain that Gray was the murderer. This could have made it more likely that they would charge Gray with the crime or that they would demand more in a plea bargain. However, if the prosecutor refrained from informing the jury that the knife came from Olwell, the jury would not be able to use the lawyer's cooperation to convict his client. (It turned out that the knife in Olwell's possession did belong to Gray, but it was not the murder weapon! Gray was convicted anyway.)

In re Ryder, **1967**[60]   A man robbed a bank, using a sawed-off shotgun, and stole $7,500, including a number of marked $10 bills. Two days later, a man named Cook rented a safe deposit box. Later that day, FBI agents visited Cook at his home. At their request, Cook gave the agents some money in his possession, probably not realizing that it was marked. Also he called his lawyer, whose name was Ryder. (Ryder was admitted to the bar in 1953 and served for five years as an assistant U.S. attorney before he embarked on the private practice of law.) After the agents left (without arresting Cook), Cook persuaded Ryder that he had won the money gambling. Despite this conversation, Ryder asked the FBI whether Cook's

---

59. 394 P.2d 681 (Wash. 1964).
60. 263 F. Supp. 360, 361 (E.D. Va), *aff'd*, 381 F.2d 713 (4th Cir. 1967).

money had been stolen. The FBI told Ryder that Cook's money included some of the marked bills. Now disbelieving Cook, Ryder asked Cook to authorize Ryder to have access to Cook's safe deposit box. Ryder went to the bank and transferred the money and the gun from Cook's safe deposit box to his own. He apparently intended to prevent Cook from disposing of the evidence. Soon after that, Cook was arrested. The FBI obtained a warrant and searched Ryder's box (this was one of those rare searches of a lawyer's property), and it found the evidence.

Ryder was barred from practicing before the federal court because he had engaged in unethical conduct.[61] His motivation for moving the money was deemed to be irrelevant because he had helped to conceal the evidence. "Ryder knew that the law against concealing stolen property and the law forbidding receipt and possession of a sawed-off shotgun contain no exemptions for a lawyer who takes possession with the intent of protecting a criminal from the consequences of his crime." The appellate court, affirming his suspension, said that Ryder made himself an "accessory after the fact" to the robbery.[62]

***People v. Meredith*, 1981**[63]   Scott helped to rob and kill Wade. After Scott took the money out of Wade's wallet, he tried to burn the wallet. Unable to do that, he threw the partially burned wallet, with Wade's credit cards, into a trash can behind his house. He told Schenk, his lawyer, where it was. Schenk sent his investigator to retrieve the wallet, turned it over to the police, and withdrew as counsel. The prosecutor called the (former) defense lawyer's investigator to testify as to where he had found the wallet. Scott was convicted. In appealing his conviction, Scott argued that the investigator's testimony violated the attorney-client privilege. The court held that the testimony was proper. Schenk could have left the wallet in place. Then the communication about its location would have been fully privileged. But when Schenk's investigator removed the wallet, the privilege was partly abrogated. When he removed the wallet, the investigator prevented the police from finding it in the trash and testifying about the find. The only way the prosecution could prove the location of the evidence was to call the defense investigator as a witness. Furthermore, the prosecutor properly protected what was left of the privilege by not asking the investigator, in the presence of the jury, to reveal that he was employed by Scott's lawyer.

---

61. Ryder was charged with violation of Canons 15 and 32 of the Canons of Professional Ethics of the Virginia State Bar. (Most states at this time had adopted a set of canons of ethics, which were later replaced by the Code of Professional Responsibility and later by Rules of Professional Conduct.)

62. 381 F.2d at 714.

63. 631 P.2d 46 (Cal. 1981).

Are documents treated differently from other physical evidence?

No. Rule 3.4(a) applies both to physical evidence and to documents. Different rules apply to documents created by or for lawyers, but documents such as maps or plans used in the perpetration of crimes are considered to be physical evidence. Just as a lawyer may not conceal incriminating other types of physical evidence, the lawyer may not destroy such documents or counsel the client to do so. Destruction would be even more problematic than concealment because there would be no possibility of recovering the evidence.

Morrell v. State, **1978**[64]   A document was at the center of *Morrell v. State.* Morrell was charged with kidnapping and rape, and Cline, a public defender, was appointed to represent him. A friend of Morrell cleaned out Morrell's car and found a written kidnap plan. He gave it to Cline, who consulted the Ethics Committee of the Alaska Bar Association about what to do with it. On the committee's advice, he returned the plan to the friend and resigned from the case. With some assistance from Cline (who telephoned the police), the friend gave the plan to the police, and it was used as evidence against Morrell, who was convicted. On appeal, Morrell claimed that Cline's actions violated his constitutional right to counsel. The Alaska Supreme Court applied the rule from *Olwell* and held that Cline had a duty to turn over the plan to the prosecutor, even without having been asked for it. If Morrell's friend had not been willing to turn it over, Cline would have had to do so himself. This duty derived from Alaska's statute prohibiting concealment of evidence.[65]

It is difficult to say whether the *Morrell* case applies to documents used in white collar crimes, such as an exchange of letters between a client and a competitor in which they conspired to fix prices in violation of the antitrust laws. Morrell's kidnap plan was not the kind of document that a lawyer might receive from a business client. We are not aware of any reported cases requiring lawyers to give prosecutors paper or electronic documents in their possession that were used in the course of committing white collar crimes. The Restatement, however, includes the white-collar crime of mail fraud in its explanation of the duty of lawyers to provide physical evidence to prosecutors.[66] One arguable distinction between the kidnap plan and routine business correspondence is that the kidnap plan is presumably a

---

64. 575 P.2d 1200 (Alaska 1978).

65. Since the plan was not part of a privileged communication from Morrell to Cline, the caution in *Olwell* that the prosecutor should avoid telling the jury that the lawyer was ultimately the source of the information was inapplicable.

66. The duty to turn physical evidence over to prosecutors "includes such material as documents and material in electronically retrievable form used by the client to plan the offense,

unique, original document. If it is in the lawyer's possession, it is rendered unavailable to criminal investigators. If a lawyer has photocopies or electronic copies of correspondence, however, usually there are other copies of the documents that remain in their usual location and could be found by investigators. It remains to be seen whether the courts will oblige lawyers to turn over business documents as they do physical evidence.

Do lawyers who have possession of documentary evidence have to be concerned about criminal statutes as well as ethical rules?

Yes. The federal obstruction of justice statute[67] prohibits the concealment, alternation, and destruction of documents by any person who knows that the documents are covered by a grand jury subpoena, whether or not the subpoena has been served.[68] An additional criminal statute was enacted in 2002 as part of the Sarbanes-Oxley law. It provides that

> whoever knowingly alters, destroys, mutilates, conceals, covers up, falsifies, or makes a false entry in any record, document, or tangible object with the intent to impede, obstruct, or influence the investigation or proper administration of any matter within the jurisdiction of any department or agency of the United States may be punished by up to 20 years in jail.[69]

In some of the recent corporate scandals, lawyers were thought to have destroyed files and deleted e-mail messages before criminal charges could be brought. The statute was intended to deter lawyers from helping to destroy evidence of their corporate clients' misdeeds.

A number of court decisions and statutes offer the following guidance for lawyers:[70]

- ■ If a client tells a lawyer about the location of evidence, the lawyer may inspect the evidence but should not disturb it or move it unless doing so is necessary to examine or test the evidence.[71]
- ■ If the lawyer merely inspects the evidence without disturbing it, the lawyer's knowledge of its location remains privileged.[72]

---

documents used in the course of a mail-fraud violation, or transaction documents evidencing a crime." Restatement § 119, comment a.

67. 18 U.S.C. § 1503 (2006); United States v. Rasheed, 663 F.2d 843 (9th Cir. 1981).

68. Arianna Berg & Jeffrey Levinson, Obstruction of Justice, 37 Am. Crim. L. Rev. 757, 767 (2000).

69. 18 U.S.C. § 1519 (2006).

70. Note, however, that none of these opinions directly construe Rule 3.4. All of them predate the ABA's initial adoption of Rule 3.4 in 1983. Also, these decisions arise from only a few jurisdictions. Most jurisdictions do not have reported decisions on these issues. Nevertheless, these three cases have been important in establishing the principles articulated here.

71. People v. Meredith, 631 P.2d 46, 53 (Cal. 1981).

72. Id. at 54.

- In many states, a lawyer may "take temporary possession of physical evidence of client crimes for the purpose of conducting a limited examination that will not alter or destroy material characteristics of the evidence. . . . Applicable law may require the lawyer to turn the evidence over to the police or other prosecuting authority. . . ."[73]
- If a client delivers physical evidence of a crime to a lawyer, the lawyer must turn the evidence over to the law enforcement authorities within a reasonable period of time — at least in some jurisdictions.[74] This rule applies to documents as it does to other physical evidence.[75]
- A prosecutor who receives evidence of a crime from the lawyer for a suspect should take steps to avoid revealing to a jury the fact that the incriminating evidence came from the defendant's lawyer.[76]

Do all jurisdictions require lawyers to contact prosecutors about physical evidence in their possession?

No. In the District of Columbia, a lawyer may turn evidence over to the D.C. bar counsel, which then gives it to the prosecutor. Under this system, the prosecutor would not learn the identity of the lawyer from whom the real evidence came, much less the identity of the client. A D.C. lawyer who receives incriminating physical evidence from a client may return it to its rightful owner (the client or a third party) if it is not yet under subpoena and if it can be done without revealing client confidences or violating other law. If returning the evidence would give away confidences, the lawyer may ask the D.C. bar counsel to turn it over to the owner.[77]

How cases involving a lawyer's concealment of physical evidence may arise

These cases reveal the many fora and procedural postures in which issues about lawyers and physical evidence can arise.

- *Olwell*: A lawyer was resisting a coroner's subpoena.
- *Ryder*: The FBI obtained a warrant to search a lawyer's safe deposit box.
- *Meredith*: A defendant appealed his conviction based on an alleged violation of the rules of evidence (specifically, attorney-client privilege).
- *Morrell*: A defendant appealed his conviction alleging that his lawyer's revelations deprived him of the effective assistance of counsel.

---

73. Rule 3.4, Comment 2.
74. State v. Olwell, 394 P.2d 681, 684 (Wash. 1964).
75. Morrell v. State, 575 P.2d 1200 (Alaska 1978).
76. *Olwell*, 394 P.2d at 685.
77. D.C. R. Prof. Conduct 3.4(a) and Comments 5, 6, and 7.

> The issue could also arise in other contexts, such as state bar disciplinary proceedings against a lawyer who either did or did not reveal evidence to a prosecutor.

PROBLEM 10-6   CHILD PORNOGRAPHY

This problem is based on a situation faced by a New England lawyer a few years ago.

You are a prominent criminal defense attorney and a past president of your city's bar association. For years, you have represented one of the most respected churches in your town, a church at which the family of an American president once worshipped. Howard Gardiner, the church's choir director, worked for the church for 30 years. Two days ago, Gardiner loaned his laptop computer for a few hours to Art Hefferline, another church employee. While he was using Gardiner's computer, Hefferline discovered that it contained hundreds of images of naked boys. Possession of images of child pornography is a federal crime.

Hefferline informed the rector. The rector called you. Together, you and the rector confronted Gardiner, who promptly admitted that he owned the computer and resigned. The rector handed you the laptop computer. There has been no publicity about the incident, and the church wants to keep it that way. No charges have been filed against Gardiner. You realize that if the pictures on this computer become public (which would probably happen in court if Gardiner is prosecuted), the reputation of the church may be destroyed.

What will you do? Some options include the following:

- Try to erase the files (this might be impossible because you don't have the technical skill to erase all of the images; you suspect that some or all of them would survive in hidden files on the computer's hard disk)
- Keep the computer in your office
- Return the computer to Gardiner
- Deliver the computer to the FBI
- Destroy the computer

You may think of other options. Consider the pros and cons of the various options, and then decide what you will do.

2. Concealment of documents and other evidence in civil and criminal cases

a. A more limited obligation to reveal

May a lawyer hide or destroy, or counsel a client to hide or destroy, potential evidence when only a civil lawsuit is likely?

Rule 3.4(a) applies both to civil and criminal cases, but as noted above, it bans only "unlawful" concealment. Some state laws allow lawyers to keep possession of tangible evidence, including documents that are not pertinent to criminal investigations. The standard for civil cases is different (in some states) because the possession of such documents may not cover up a crime. Also, in a civil case, discovery can be used to obtain the evidence, even if it is in the physical custody of an opposing party's lawyer.

At what point in a criminal or civil matter does the lawyer's obligation not to conceal or destroy objects or documents begin?

It is not possible to state these rules succinctly or with accuracy on a national basis, both because state laws vary considerably and because there is very little case law on this subject. In general, however, the rules on concealment and destruction of documents break down as follows:

Criminal matters

- If a lawyer has no knowledge that a violation of law has been committed and no criminal investigation is foreseeable, a lawyer has no duty to turn evidence over to a prosecutor.[78]
- In some states, the lawyer's duty not to conceal tangible evidence takes effect as soon as the lawyer believes that an official investigation is about to be instituted. In other states, it does not begin until an investigation has actually started.[79]

Civil matters

- Obligations in civil cases are governed by civil discovery rules[80] as well as by professional responsibility rules.[81] Soon after a civil case is commenced, a lawyer may have a duty under the pertinent rules of

---

78. Cf. Restatement § 119 (affirming the lawyer's duty to turn over physical evidence of "a client crime" to authorities).

79. Deborah L. Rhode & David Luban, Legal Ethics 341-342 (5th ed., Found. Press 2009).

80. E.g., Fed. R. Civ. P. 26 et seq., and particularly R. 26 and R. 34.

81. Rule 3.4(a), discussed in the text, prohibits destruction of documents, and Rule 3.4(c) bars a lawyer from knowingly disobeying an obligation under the rules of a tribunal (including discovery rules), except for an open refusal based on an assertion that no valid obligation exists.

procedure to turn over some information to the opposing party, even in the absence of a discovery request.[82]

■ Some state laws require the preservation of business records for specified periods of time even if no dispute is on the horizon. In general, when a lawsuit is pending or foreseeable, individuals and businesses have more stringent duties to protect and eventually to disclose relevant material.[83]

■ As in the case of tangible evidence, where no specific record preservation statute applies but a lawyer has some reason to believe that wrongdoing has occurred, state law varies as to when the duty to preserve evidence arises (that is, whether a lawsuit or government investigation must have begun, be imminent, or merely be foreseeable).[84]

■ In any event, once a duty to preserve documents applies, relevant records and objects should be retained even if they could otherwise routinely be destroyed.

Even within a particular jurisdiction, a lawyer may need to do serious research to understand when documents or objects may be destroyed. The Restatement warns:

> It may be difficult under applicable criminal law to define the point at which legitimate destruction becomes unlawful obstruction of justice. Under criminal law, a lawyer generally is subject to constraints no different from those imposed on others. Obstruction of justice and similar statutes generally apply only when an official proceeding is ongoing or imminent. For example, the American Law Institute Model Penal Code Sec. 241.7 (1985) provides that the offense of tampering with or fabricating physical evidence occurs only if "an official proceeding or investigation is pending or about to be instituted...."
>
> Difficult questions of interpretation can arise with respect to destruction of documents in anticipation of a subpoena or similar process that has not yet issued at the time of destruction.... No general statement can accurately describe the legality of record destruction; statutes and decisions in the particular jurisdiction must be consulted. In many jurisdic-

---

82. See, e.g., Fed. R. Civ. P. 26(a)(1), requiring disclosure without a prior request of a copy of, or a description by category and location of, all documents, data compilations, and tangible things in the possession and control of the party and that the disclosing party may use to support its claims and defenses, unless solely for impeachment, and any liability insurance agreement that may make an insurance company liable to satisfy a judgment. Note that the party is *not* obligated to disclose the existence of documents that would *contradict* its claims and defenses (that is, the damaging documents that the other side's lawyers would most like to inspect).

83. See generally Restatement § 118, comment c.

84. Id.

tions, there is no applicable precedent. Legality may turn on such factual questions as the state of mind of the client or a lawyer.[85]

The bottom line is that a lawyer should never assume that documents that are or could be pertinent to a civil lawsuit may be concealed or destroyed, even if a suit has not yet been filed. Obstruction of justice or evidence tampering statutes may still apply. These laws may trigger obligations under Rule 3.4(a).

b. A lawyer's duties in responding to discovery requests

Once documents or tangible evidence have been requested through discovery procedures, lawyers involved in civil litigation are subject to court rules that require litigants to comply with discovery requests or else to object to make formal objections to the requests.[86] The courts may enforce their rules by sanctioning the parties or their lawyers.[87] Discovery abuse is also punishable by bar discipline under Rule 3.4.

> **Rule 3.4(d) Fairness to Opposing Party and Counsel**
> **A lawyer shall not . . . in pretrial procedure, make a frivolous discovery request or fail to make reasonably diligent efforts[88] to comply with a legally proper discovery request by an opposing counsel.**

Despite the discovery rules and the rules of professional conduct, lawyers in practice often seek discovery of many more documents than they really need. This increases the cost of litigation. Also, many lawyers work hard to avoid disclosing embarrassing or damning information or documents that an opponent dearly wants to discover.[89]

E. The duty to disclose adverse legal authority

Unless a disclosure rule or a discovery rule applies,[90] or unless a lawyer is required to remedy false testimony or some other ethical

---

85. Id.

86. See, e.g., Fed. R. Civ. P. 26.

87. See, e.g., Fed. R. Civ. P. 26(g), 30(d)(2), and 37.

88. In the ABA Model Rule, this word is "effort" rather than "efforts."

89. See Symposium, Ethics: Beyond the Rules, 67 Fordham L. Rev. 697 (1998); Wayne D. Brazil, Views from the Front Lines: Observations by Chicago Lawyers About the System of Civil Discovery, 1980 ABA Found. Research J. 219.

90. "Disclosure" refers to lawyers' revelations of fact that are required by court rules even when no discovery has been requested, such as disclosure under Fed. R. Civ. P. 26(a)(1) of documents on which a party will later rely. As a matter of professional responsibility, prosecutors also must disclose

breach,[91] a lawyer representing a client in litigation need not inform an adversary of adverse facts. However, Rule 3.3(a)(2) prohibits a lawyer from knowingly failing to disclose legal authority in the controlling jurisdiction that the lawyer knows is directly adverse to her client's position, if an opponent has not already informed the judge of the adverse authority.

Isn't this backwards? Shouldn't a lawyer have a stronger duty to disclose adverse facts than adverse law?

At first it may seem strange that a lawyer has a duty to reveal adverse law but not adverse facts. After all, if a lawyer hides the law, the court and the opposing party can find it by doing research. If the lawyer hides the facts, the court might never find out about them.

There is a certain logic to the idea that the lawyer's first duty should be to ensure that the facts are on the table. However, the idea of a lawyer volunteering facts that are adverse to a client is contrary to the principles of confidentiality and client loyalty. Disclosure and discovery rules also require lawyers to give away inculpatory information about their clients, but those rules are subject to the attorney-client privilege and the work product doctrine.

But why does the rule require lawyers to disclose adverse legal authority? The premise of this rule is that cases should be decided within the framework of the law — the whole body of law, not only the favorable parts of it that parties told the judge about or about which the judge learned through independent research.[92] Neither judges nor opposing counsel always find relevant adverse authority: hence, this duty of disclosure.

How often do lawyers actually have to disclose adverse legal authority?

This provision of the rules doesn't create very many problems for lawyers. Most of the time, an opponent will tell the judge of any authority adverse to your position. If the opponent has not yet done so but has the right to file another brief, such as a reply brief, the lawyer may not (yet) have a duty to disclose.[93] Even if the opponent has filed her last permitted brief without disclosing some legal authority adverse to a lawyer's client, the lawyer still may have no duty of disclosure.

■ If the adverse law is from another jurisdiction, it need not be disclosed because only law from the controlling jurisdiction matters.

---

any exculpatory evidence to criminal defendants. Rule 3.8(d). The term "discovery" refers to providing information, as required by court rules, in response to requests.

91. See Rules 3.3(a)(1), (a)(3), and (b).
92. Restatement § 111, comment c.
93. Id.

- Only authority that is "directly adverse" need be disclosed. Dicta and holdings that are applicable only by analogy do not have to be disclosed.
- Persuasive authority, such as statements in treatises and law review articles, need not be disclosed.

Can a lawyer be disciplined for overlooking a directly adverse case?

No, because the prohibition is for "knowingly" failing to reveal the adverse authority. On the other hand, knowledge under the ethics rules can be inferred from circumstances.[94]

F. Disclosures in ex parte proceedings

Rule 3.3(d) requires that in ex parte (one-sided) proceedings, a lawyer must inform the tribunal of "all material facts known to the lawyer that will enable the tribunal to make an informed decision, whether or not the facts are adverse."

Doesn't this exception violate the client's expectation of confidentiality?

Yes, the duty overrides the obligation to protect confidences under Rule 1.6.[95] However, lawyers are not required to reveal information protected by the attorney-client privilege and the work product doctrine.[96]

Why are lawyers required to disclose known adverse facts in ex parte proceedings?

The ethics rules illustrate the need for disclosure of facts in an ex parte proceeding through the example of a request for a temporary restraining order, in which one party rushes into court to try to stop an irreparable injury that may occur before the opposing party can even be notified that the matter will be contested in court.[97]

---

94. Rule 1.0(f).

95. Technically, a state court that has promulgated Rule 3.3(d) and created the legal obligation to disclose under these circumstances has excused lawyers from the obligation of confidentiality because Rule 1.6(b)(6) allows disclosures that are required "to comply with other law."

96. Restatement § 112, comment b. The Restatement doesn't cite authority, but presumably the theory is that the privileges are ordinarily understood to trump other law (as in the *Belge* case, discussed in Chapter 3), unless the state legislature explicitly narrows their scope.

97. See, e.g., Fed. R. Civ. P. 65(b).

> **FOR EXAMPLE:** If a mother has reason to believe that her former husband, with whom she has had a great deal of conflict, is about to take their 12-year-old daughter to another country, the mother might seek a court order prohibiting the father from leaving the country with the child. The mother might seek a temporary restraining order ex parte, without first alerting the father, because advance disclosure might trigger immediate departure.

Under circumstances like these, it is plain why the petitioner's lawyer arguably should disclose all known adverse facts. Suppose that the father and mother in the previous example are living separately and are bitterly angry at each other. Suppose the father has been threatening to take the daughter abroad for a long period of time. Suppose further that the mother's lawyer knows, however, that the father is not planning to leave the country permanently but is going to give a lecture in Paris and has invited his daughter to accompany him. Since the father's lawyer will not be in court, his side of the story would not come out unless the mother's lawyer is required to reveal it.

Does a lawyer have to disclose adverse facts in nonemergency ex parte hearings?

There are other types of ex parte proceedings. Some of them, such as patent applications and Social Security disability hearings, are hearings on the merits of the cases, as opposed to preliminary matters. The application of this rule to those proceedings might be unfair.

In a state that has adopted Rule 3.3, an advocate who represents claimants in Social Security disability hearings may be in a serious bind. The lawyers' clients are going to hearings because government officials claim that they are not truly disabled. In a hearing before a federal administrative law judge (ALJ), the lawyer must prove that the client is disabled. The hearing consists of an examination of documentary evidence and searching questioning by the ALJ. It is formally ex parte; that is, the government does not send a lawyer to argue that the claimant is able to work. In preparing for such a hearing, the claimant's lawyer collects all of her client's medical records, which often include conflicting reports about the degree of disease or injury.[98] The ALJ can order his own "consultative examination," but most do not do so.

---

98. The documentation may be equivocal; for example, if the client's doctor was trying to minimize his description of an illness to encourage his patient to get back on her feet, or if the client was injured on the job and was examined by a doctor hired by the employer who was trying to show that the injury was minor.

Must the lawyer provide the ALJ with all the medical reports, including those that would justify denying disability benefits? If so, might the client have a valid complaint that the lawyer failed to act as her advocate? Comment 14 after Rule 3.3 explains that the purpose of Rule 3.3(d) is to allow the judge to "accord the absent party just consideration." This suggests that if the matter is not truly adversarial, perhaps 3.3(d) does not apply. The bar authorities that have considered these questions in the context of Rule 3.3(d) are divided. Some read the rule literally as requiring disclosure. Others conclude that "a lawyer has no duty to defeat his own case."[99] At least one jurisdiction, the District of Columbia, did not adopt Rule 3.3(d).

G. Improper influences on judges and juries

The goal of lawyers who litigate is to persuade judges and juries. But some methods of persuasion are improper. All states make it a crime to bribe a judge, for example. Likewise Rule 3.5(a) states that a lawyer may not "seek to influence a judge, prospective juror or other official by means prohibited by law."

1. Improper influences on judges

a. Ex parte communication with judges

A lawyer must not communicate with a judge about a pending case, orally or in writing, unless the lawyers for all parties to the case are privy to the communication. Rule 3.5(b) states that a lawyer shall not "communicate . . .

---

99. The quotation is from an unpublished opinion of the chairman of the Missouri Bar Administration Advisory Committee, while the general counsel of the Alabama State Bar Disciplinary Commission held that the rule compels disclosure. Robert E. Rains, The Advocate's Conflicting Obligations Vis-a-Vis Adverse Medical Evidence in Social Security Proceedings, 1995 B.Y.U. L. Rev. 99, 113-114. Rains concludes that the law is "totally unsettled." Id. at 135. He recommends that a lawyer should produce the adverse evidence because that plan "is not only prudent in terms of the attorney's good standing with the bar, but also as a litigation strategy." Id. at 134. He suggests, however, that the lawyer should seek to subpoena any doctor who wrote the adverse report and then move to exclude the adverse report if (as will often be the case) the doctor does not honor the subpoena. Id. at 134-135. After Rains published his article, North Carolina issued Formal Ethics Op. 98-1, concluding that Rule 3.3(d) does not apply to Social Security hearings. Vermont concluded that a lawyer need not disclose medical opinions harmful to a Social Security client if there is "reasonable justification for rejecting the opinion and accepting another" and the judge has not asked for such materials. Vt. B. Assn., Op. 95-8. Vermont apparently distinguishes between medical "fact," which should be disclosed, and medical "opinion," which need not be disclosed. Rains points out in an update to his article that "anyone who has ever dealt with forensic medicine will readily understand that the distinction between a medical fact and a medical opinion is an elusive one at best." E-mail from Professor Rains to the authors (Aug. 2, 2003).

ex parte with [a judge, juror, prospective juror, or other official] during the proceeding unless authorized to do so by law or court order. . . ."[100]

Should lawyers avoid becoming friends with judges?

The lawyers and judges in any community often have attended the same law schools and belong to the same professional associations, so friendships are commonplace. Rule 3.5 prohibits only communications related to particular proceedings, not personal communications. However, a lawyer who has a case pending before a judge who is a friend, or who even works with a lawyer who has a case pending, should be careful to avoid communications that could touch on the subject of the case.

> **FOR EXAMPLE:** John Gerstle, a lawyer who was a friend of Judge Russell, stopped by Russell's chambers and suggested that they have a beer. Judge Russell was putting the finishing touches on an opinion. Gerstle asked her about it. Judge Russell said the case involved Subway Restaurants and a party named Kessler, and that she was imposing sanctions on a lawyer named Duree. Gerstle told Judge Russell that Duree was a "great guy" who had paid Gerstle's fees to represent Kessler in a different case. Judge Russell had to recuse herself from the case, and, citing Rule 3.5, the Supreme Court of Kansas said that Gerstle's questioning had been inappropriate.[101]

May a lawyer contact a judge's chambers to ask a procedural question, such as whether a motion is likely to be decided soon?

Yes. As explained in Chapter 9, lawyers are allowed to call judges' secretaries or clerks to make minor, routine procedural inquiries about pending cases without having to notify the other parties.[102] But they may not discuss the substance of cases with judges or their secretaries or clerks unless all parties' representatives have been notified and given an opportunity to participate.

Are these limits scrupulously observed?

Every community has its own norms, and in some communities, some ex parte communication is accepted. The chief justice of Indiana reports that

> during the course of a busy day in a courthouse, all sorts of administrivia [sic] passes between various actors that no objective observer would deem to violate [the goals of even-handedness and fair process]. "Judge, my

---

100. A similar provision in the judges' code of professional responsibility imposes on them the obligation to avoid ex parte communications. Model Code Jud. Conduct Rule 2.9 (2007).

101. Subway Restaurants Inc. v. Kessler, 970 P.2d 526 (Kan. 1998).

102. A judge who responds to such an inquiry has a duty to inform all other parties of the substance of the communication. Model Code Jud. Conduct Rule 2.9(A)(1)(b).

client says he'll plead if the prosecutor recommends probation. Is that a deal you might approve?" "Yes, probably, but I'd like to hear what the prosecutor says about it. Subject to reading the presentence report it sounds all right." While we tend to label such communications as improper, they advance the practice of litigation. Our profession not only condones these conversations, it relies on them. We usually sanction the participants when some unexpected force arises, like a runaway client who complains loudly.[103]

b. Campaign contributions

In many states, state court judges have to run for election.[104] Lawyers are often the main contributors to judicial election campaigns. It is not improper for a lawyer to make a contribution to a judge's campaign. However, the ABA recommends that states set limits on the amount of money that a judge may receive from a lawyer without having to disqualify herself from all proceedings in which that lawyer is involved.[105] The state judges' response to this suggestion has been muted. Many states have not adopted a rule restricting lawyers' contributions to judges' campaigns. Some states have contribution limits applicable to all contributors.[106]

2. Improper influences on juries

a. Lawyers' comments to the press

Pick up almost any newspaper or watch TV news for a few days, and you will see lawyers commenting to the press about pending cases. Although the practice is common, the ethics rules impose some limits, particularly when a case is going to be tried by a jury. Courts must balance the free speech rights of lawyers and their clients against the possibility that jurors would

---

103. Randall T. Shepard, Judicial Professionalism and the Relations Between Judges and Lawyers, 14 Notre Dame J.L. Ethics & Pub. Poly. 223, 228 (2000).

104. For an analysis of the merits of various state judge selection systems, see Judith L. Maute, Selecting Justice in State Courts, 41 S. Tex. L. Rev. 1197 (2000).

105. See Model Code Jud. Conduct Rule 2.11(A)(4).

106. A Wisconsin statute limits individual contributions to campaigns for trial judges in large cities to $3,000. Wis. Stat. § 11.26 (2002). In contrast, Texas allows a political action committee to contribute up to $52,000 to a trial judge's campaign, with the limit depending on the population of the judicial district. Am. Judicature Socy., Judicial Campaigns and Elections, http://www.judicialselection.us/judicial_selection/campaigns_and_elections/campaign_financing.cfm?state= (accessed Nov. 20, 2012). Critics charge that large campaign contributions by lawyers influence the outcomes of litigation there. See Texans for Public Justice, Pay to Play: How Big Money Buys Access to the Texas Supreme Court (2001) (available at http://info.tpj.org/docs/2001/04/reports/paytoplay/) (Texas Supreme Court justices receive 52 percent of their campaign contributions from litigants and lawyers, and contributors account for 70 percent of the petitions that the court accepts for review).

base decisions on what they learned about the case from the media rather than on the evidence they heard in court. The ethical rules reflect concerns about comments that might prejudice a finder of fact and they reflect constitutional concerns.

The *Gentile* case

Dominic Gentile

In 1987, the Las Vegas police discovered large amounts of money and cocaine missing from their safe deposit box at Western Vault Corp. (The funds and drugs had been used as part of an undercover operation.) Other people also reported that property was missing from their safe deposit boxes. The thief could have been a police detective with access to the vault or the owner of the vault company, Grady Sanders. The sheriff spoke to the press, announcing his faith in the police officers. The deputy police chief eventually announced that two detectives who had access to the vault had been cleared. Seventeen major newspaper stories and several television reports cast suspicion on Sanders. The police leaked that Sanders was about to be indicted. With the indictment imminent but a trial at least six months away, Sanders's lawyer, Dominic Gentile, held a press conference. He hoped to counter the publicity directed against Sanders. He said that when the case was tried, the evidence would show that Sanders was innocent and that one of the detectives was most likely to have taken the property. He asserted that his client was being made into a scapegoat and that four of the other victims of the alleged theft were known drug dealers who might be currying favor with the police.

Six months later, Gentile represented Sanders in the jury trial. Sanders was acquitted. The jury foreman called Gentile to say that if the detective had been charged, the jury would have found him guilty.

The state bar then accused Gentile of violating Nevada's rule against pretrial publicity, prohibiting public comments that "will have a substantial likelihood of materially prejudicing an adjudicative proceeding," but nevertheless allowing a lawyer to "state without elaboration . . . the general nature of the . . . defense." Gentile was reprimanded, but he appealed to the U.S. Supreme Court.

By a 5-4 vote, the Supreme Court held the disciplinary rule void because the "elaboration" and "general nature" clauses were too vague to convey clear information about what was prohibited, so the state bar might enforce the rule in a discriminatory manner.[107] Four of the five justices who sided with Gentile said that an attorney may "take reasonable steps to defend a

---

107. Gentile v. St. B. Nev., 501 U.S. 1030 (1991).

client's reputation and reduce the adverse consequences of indictment . . . [and] attempt to demonstrate in the court of public opinion that the client does not deserve to be tried."[108] The ABA amended its Model Rule to delete the clause that the Supreme Court had criticized.

Rule 3.6 governs pretrial publicity for lawyers. Rule 3.8(f) imposes some additional restrictions on prosecutors, which we will consider in the next chapter.

Rules 3.6(a) and (b) Trial Publicity

Rule language[*]	Authors' explanation[**]
(a) A **lawyer** who is participating or has participated in the investigation or litigation of a matter **shall not make** an **extrajudicial statement** that the lawyer knows or reasonably should know will be disseminated by means of public communication and will have a **substantial likelihood of materially prejudicing** an adjudicative proceeding in the matter.	
(b) Notwithstanding paragraph (a), a **lawyer may state**: (1) the **claim, offense or defense involved** and, except when prohibited by law, the identity of the persons involved; (2) information contained in a **public record**; (3) that an investigation of a matter is in progress; (4) the scheduling or **result of any step in litigation**; (5) a **request for assistance in obtaining evidence** and information necessary thereto; (6) a **warning of danger** concerning the behavior of a person involved, when there is reason to believe that there exists the	"Paragraph (b) is not intended to be an exhaustive listing of the subjects upon which a lawyer may make a statement, but statements on other matters may be subject to paragraph (a)." Comment 4. Comment 5 lists some "subjects that are more likely than not to have a material prejudicial effect on a proceeding" including, for example, the credibility or reputation of a party, the expected testimony of a witness, the possibility of a guilty plea or the contents of a confession or admission, the nature of evidence to be presented, an opinion as to guilt or innocence, or any information that is likely to be inadmissible as evidence.[109]

Continued

---

108. Id. at 1043.

109. The Nevada rule that was declared void for vagueness by the Supreme Court (and which was almost identical to the ABA Model Rule at that time) included this list of potentially prejudicial types of statements in the black-letter rule rather than in the comment, but also stated that information on the list "ordinarily is likely to" result in material prejudice. 501 U.S. at 1060-1061.

Rule language[*]	Authors' explanation[**]
likelihood of substantial harm to an individual or to the public interest; and (7) in a **criminal case**, in addition to subparagraphs (1) through (6): (i) the identity, residence, occupation and family status of the accused; (ii) if the accused has not been apprehended, information necessary to aid in apprehension of that person; (iii) the fact, time and place of arrest; and (iv) the identity of investigating and arresting officers or agencies and the length of the investigation.	

[*]All emphasis added.

[**]This and other authors' explanations draw from the comments to the rules and from other sources. They are not comprehensive but highlight some important interpretive points.

Rule 3.6(c) allows a lawyer to make a statement that a "reasonable lawyer would believe is required to protect a client from the substantial undue prejudicial effect of recent publicity" initiated by others. Subsection (d) makes clear that if one lawyer in a firm or organization cannot make a statement, the others in the organization may not do so either.

May a lawyer repeat to the press anything that is contained in a document that the lawyer filed in court?

It is generally thought "safe" to give the press a copy of documents that have been filed in court. Lawyers sometimes send copies of pleadings to the press in cases in which publicity might advance a client's cause. This strategy is probably more risky if the case is to be tried by a jury in the near future, but pleadings and pretrial motions usually are filed long before trials take place. If a complaint is defamatory, its filing in court is absolutely protected from a libel claim by a doctrine called judicial privilege. But in some states, even if the complaint has been filed and is a public document, a lawyer may have only a "qualified" privilege (justifying an inquiry into the lawyer's good faith) if he sends a copy to the press.[110]

---

110. *Bochetto v. Gibson*, 860 A.2d 67 (Pa. 2004). This appears to be a minority view and was adopted over a dissent that pointed out that reporters could as easily obtain litigation documents from court clerks.

Do lawyers often talk about their cases with journalists?

Professor Michele DeStefano Beardslee

Increasingly so, and particularly in big cases involving large, publicly traded corporations. Professor Michele DeStefano Beardslee sent questionnaires about press relations to the general counsels of the S&P 500 and interviewed 57 general counsels, law firm partners, and public relations consultants. She found that corporate lawyers often work hand in hand with public relations teams to coordinate daily messages to influence public opinion about ongoing litigation involving the corporations for whom they work. Noting that most litigation eventually settles, one general counsel observed that "the negotiation is in the newspaper." Others pointed out that spinning the press coverage was equally important in cases that did go to trial because "judges read newspapers."[111]

b. Impeachment of truthful witnesses

If a lawyer believes that an opposition witness is truthful, may the lawyer cross-examine the witness in a way that suggests that the witness is lying?

The rules of professional conduct do not explicitly address a problem sometimes faced by criminal defense lawyers and sometimes by others. A lawyer defending a client whom the lawyer knows to be guilty may assist the client in pleading not guilty and may force the state to present its evidence. The lawyer may object to proffered evidence that may be inadmissible (e.g., unlawfully seized evidence). May the lawyer cross-examine the victim (or some other witness) in a way that implies that the victim may be lying if the lawyer in fact believes that the victim is telling the truth? The ethics rules do not address this question directly. Rule 4.4(a) states that a lawyer may not use means that "have no substantial purpose other than to embarrass, delay, or burden a third person. . . ." Of course, the tactic of discrediting an honest witness is not undertaken merely to embarrass or burden the witness but to make the testimony of the witness seem false.

Although this question comes up frequently, there are no reported disciplinary or other cases that address it.[112] The Restatement terms this problem "particularly difficult," but it takes the position that a lawyer may

---

111. Michele DeStefano Beardslee, Advocacy in the Court of Public Opinion, Part I: Broadening the Role of Corporate Attorneys, 22 Geo. J. Leg. Ethics 1259 (2009).

112. Restatement § 106, comment c, reporter's note.

"cross-examine a witness with respect to testimony that the lawyer knows to be truthful, including harsh implied criticism of the witness's testimony, character or capacity for truth-telling."[113] But the Restatement notes that "even if legally permissible, a lawyer would presumably do so only where that would not cause the lawyer to lose credibility with the tribunal or alienate the factfinder."[114]

Harry I. Subin, The Criminal Defense Lawyer's "Different Mission": Reflections on the "Right" to Present a False Case

1 Geo. J. Leg. Ethics 125, 129-135 (1987)[115]

Professor Harry I. Subin

[Professor Subin is professor of law emeritus at New York University Law School.]

About fifteen years ago I represented a man charged with rape and robbery. The victim's account was as follows: Returning from work in the early morning hours, she was accosted by a man who pointed a gun at her and took a watch from her wrist. He told her to go with him to a nearby lot, where he ordered her to lie down on the ground and disrobe. When she complained that the ground was hurting her, he took her to his apartment, located across the street. During the next hour there, he had intercourse with her. Ultimately, he said that they had to leave to avoid being discovered by the woman with whom he lived. The complainant responded that since he had gotten what he wanted, he should give her back her watch. He said that he would.

As the two left the apartment, he said he was going to get a car. Before leaving the building, however, he went to the apartment next door, leaving her to wait in the hallway. When asked why she waited, she said that she was still hoping for the return of her watch, which was a valued gift, apparently from her boyfriend.

She never did get the watch. When they left the building, the man told her to wait on the street while he got the car. At that point she went to a nearby police precinct and reported the incident. She gave a full description of the assailant that matched my client. She also accurately described the

---

113. Id. at comment c.

114. Id.

115. The reference in the title is a quotation from Justice Byron White: "[D]efense counsel has no . . . obligation to . . . present the truth. Our system assigns him a different mission. . . . If he can confuse a witness, even a truthful one . . . that will be his normal course. . . . [A]s part of the duty imposed on the most honorable defense counsel, we countenance or require conduct which in many instances has little, if any, relation to the search for truth." U.S. v. Wade, 388 U.S. 218, 256-258 (1967) (White, J., concurring).

inside of his apartment. [The man was arrested, and a gun was found, but the woman was unable to identify the gun as the weapon he had used.] No watch was recovered. . . .

[The client had an alibi, which I investigated and was unable to corroborate. Then he came up with an entirely different alibi, which was obviously false. Finally he confessed to me that he had committed the crime. Meanwhile, at a preliminary hearing, the complainant testified and told her story under oath] in an objective manner that, far from seeming contrived, convinced me that she was telling the truth. She seemed a person who, if not at home with the meanness of the streets, was resigned to it. To me that explained why she was able to react in what I perceived to be a non-stereotypical manner to the ugly events in which she had been involved. . . .

[Since consent is a defense to a rape charge, and the robbery charge would fail if the woman seemed to be a liar, the best defense would be] to raise a reasonable doubt as to whether he had compelled the woman to have sex with him. The doubt would be based on the scenario that the woman and the defendant met, and she voluntarily returned to his apartment. Her watch, the object of the alleged robbery, was either left there by mistake or, perhaps better, never there at all.

The consent defense could be made out entirely through cross-examination of the complainant, coupled with argument to the jury about her lack of credibility on the issue of force. I could emphasize the parts of her story that sounded the most curious, such as the defendant's solicitude in taking his victim back to his apartment, and her waiting for her watch when she could have gone immediately to the nearby precinct that she went to later. I could point to her inability to identify the gun she claimed was used (although it was the one actually used), that the allegedly stolen watch was never found, that there was no sign of physical violence, and that no one heard screaming or other signs of a struggle. . . . The defendant would not have to prove whether the complainant made the false charge to account for her whereabouts that evening, or to explain what happened to her missing watch. If the jury had reason to doubt the complainant's charges it would be bound to acquit the defendant.

Question about the Subin Article

> In Subin's account of this case, he reports that he considered cross-examining this complaining witness to make the points listed above. Would it be proper for him to cross-examine the complainant in a manner that implies that she consented to go to the defendant's apartment and have sex with him, even though the defendant has privately confessed that he raped her?

c. Statements by lawyers during jury trials

The advocate-witness rule   In general, lawyers may not testify as witnesses in cases that they are handling. Rule 3.7 explains this rule and states some important exceptions.

Rule 3.7   Lawyer as Witness

Rule language[*]	Authors' explanation[**]
(a) **A lawyer shall not act as advocate** at a trial in which the lawyer is likely to be a necessary witness unless:	The rule purports to apply only to trials, but the advocate-witness rule has been held to apply to all contested proceedings, including hearings on motions at which evidence is taken and evidentiary administrative proceedings.[116] This rule is often enforced through motions by opposing parties either to disqualify a lawyer or to prevent her from testifying for her client.
(1) the testimony relates to an **uncontested issue**;	Example: If the issue is not contested, a lawyer attempting to introduce a letter into evidence may testify that she received the letter from her client's brother.
(2) the testimony relates to the **nature and value of legal services** rendered in the case; or	Example: If a lawyer wins a case and is filing a petition for attorneys' fees to be paid by the losing party, the lawyer may testify about how much time he spent on the case.
(3) disqualification of the lawyer would work **substantial hardship on the client**.	Example: A lawyer who has handled the financial affairs of a client with a mental disability might seek to testify for the client in a small tax claim where the lawyer had personal knowledge of the issues and was representing the client pro bono, and no other lawyer would accept a case involving such a small amount.

---

116. Restatement § 108, comment c. The version of the rule in § 108 is slightly different from the version in the Model Rules. For example, the Restatement version would apply to any case in which the lawyer "is expected to testify for the lawyer's client" or the lawyer does not intend to testify but (i) the lawyer's testimony would be material to establishing a claim or defense of the client, and (ii) the client has not consented . . . to the lawyer's intention not to testify." Rule 3.7 applies where the lawyer "is likely to be a necessary witness."

Rule language[*]	Authors' explanation[**]
(b) A lawyer **may act as advocate in a trial in which another lawyer in the lawyer's firm is likely to be called** as a witness unless precluded from doing so by Rule 1.7 or Rule 1.9.	• If another lawyer in the advocate's firm has the same information as the advocate, the other lawyer usually is not barred from being a witness. • None of the exceptions to the advocate-witness rules excuses a lawyer from the conflict of interest rules, although those rules include their own exceptions (e.g., for consent under some conditions). See Comment 7.

[*]All emphasis added.

[**]This and other authors' explanations draw from the comments to the rules and from other sources. They are not comprehensive but highlight some important interpretive points.

The advocate-witness rule has two purposes. First, it seeks to avoid a situation that could "prejudice the tribunal and the opposing party."[117] This concern apparently relates primarily to jury trials, for it is said that "it may not be clear whether a statement by an advocate-witness should be taken as proof or as an analysis of the proof."[118] Second, it seeks to avoid "a conflict of interest between the lawyer and client"[119] because a lawyer who has unprivileged, personal knowledge of a case might give testimony that was adverse to the client. This could arise even if the lawyer is called as a witness on behalf of the client. If there is a conflict, the lawyer must assess whether it is consentable, and if so, "the lawyer must secure the client's informed consent, confirmed in writing."[120]

Comments by lawyers appealing to racial or other prejudice of jurors Lawyers should avoid attempting to appeal to jurors' racial or other prejudices. The rules of professional conduct address this issue in one of the comments that follows Rule 8.4, explaining that manifestation of prejudice could be a basis for discipline.

A lawyer who, in the course of representing a client, knowingly manifests by words or conduct, bias or prejudice based upon race, sex, religion, national origin, disability, age, sexual orientation or socioeconomic status, violates paragraph (d) when such actions are prejudicial to the adminis-

---

117. Rule 3.7, Comment 1.
118. Id. at Comment 2.
119. Id. at Comment 1.
120. Id. at Comment 6.

tration of justice. Legitimate advocacy respecting the foregoing factors does not violate paragraph (d). . . .[121]

Some judges will declare a mistrial or order a new trial if a lawyer makes a discriminatory appeal to a jury, but other courts may be willing to allow trial lawyers a certain degree of latitude.

> **FOR EXAMPLE:** Smokers and their survivors sued tobacco companies in a Florida state court class action, claiming that the nation's tobacco companies had tortiously caused widespread disease, including cancer. The court certified the class, estimated to consist of 700,000 Floridians, and the case proceeded to trial by a six-person jury that included four African Americans.[122] During the closing argument, the plaintiffs' lawyer, Stanley Rosenblatt, told the jury that the tobacco companies "study races" and divide consumers into "white" and "black." He told the jury that it could fight "unjust laws" as Martin Luther King had done, implying that they could ignore the judge's instructions about the legality of cigarette sales. Also, he informed the jury that in the 1960s, "in this building, a temple to the law, there were drinking fountains which said Whites Only."

The jury ruled in favor of the plaintiffs and granted damages to the class in the amount of *$145 billion*. This verdict, one of the largest in American history, was reversed on appeal. The principal ground for reversal was that the court had improperly certified a class. The intermediate appellate court also noted that the case had to be reversed because "plaintiffs' counsel's improper race-based appeals for nullification caused irreparable prejudice."[123] The Supreme Court of Florida largely sustained the denial of class action certification but stated with respect to Mr. Rosenblatt's remarks that related to race:

> We condemn these tactics of Mr. Rosenblatt. His attempt to incite racial passions was conduct unbecoming an attorney practicing in our state courts. Nevertheless, we note that the trial court sustained objections to several of these remarks and no motion for mistrial was made or curative instruction requested. In addition, there was no further race-based argument during the remainder of the closing.[124]

---

121. Rule 8.4, Comment 3.
122. Robert A. Levy, Tobacco Class Decertified in Florida, Sanity Restored, The Hill (June 11, 2003).
123. Liggett Group Inc. v. Engle, 853 So. 2d 434 (Fla. Dist. App. 2003).
124. Engle v. Liggett Group, Inc., 945 So. 2d 1246, 1273 (Fla. 2006).

Other restrictions   Rule 3.4(e) imposes further limits on what lawyers may say in court — particularly restricting comments that might prejudice the judgment of juries.

Rule 3.4(e) Fairness to Opposing Party and Counsel

Rule language[*]	Authors' explanation[**]
A lawyer shall not: . . . in trial, **allude to any matter that the lawyer does not reasonably believe is relevant**	Example: Even if a witness blurted out that he was the father of twins, and even though that fact might endear the witness to the jury, the lawyer who put the witness on the stand should not mention the fact unless it is relevant to the case.
or that will not be supported by admissible evidence,	Example: Police officer Justin Volpe was tried for raping Abner Louima with a broom handle and causing severe internal injuries. Volpe's lawyer, Marvyn Kornberg, said in his opening statement that the DNA of another man was found in the feces of Louima, implying that the injuries were the result of consensual gay sex. Volpe pled guilty during the trial after four eyewitnesses testified against him, so no evidence on this subject was introduced on this point. (Kornberg later justified his opening statement by saying that he never directly said that Louima was gay.)[125] If Kornberg's opening statement "had only fumes of evidence to back it up,"[126] his statement would violate this rule.
assert personal knowledge of facts in issue except when testifying as a witness,	A lawyer should not evade the advocate-witness rule by providing factual information to the jury. If the lawyer must state facts within her unique personal knowledge, she should attempt to take the stand under one of the exceptions to the advocate-witness rule.

Continued

---

125. Laura Mansnerus, When the Job Requires a Walk on the Ethical Line, N.Y. Times (May 30, 1999) (available at http://www.nytimes.com/1999/05/30/weekinreview/the-nation-when-the-job-requires-a-walk-on-the-ethical-line.html); David Barstow, Officer, Seeking Some Mercy, Admits to Louima's Torture, N.Y. Times (May 26, 1999) (available at http://www.nytimes.com/1999/05/26/nyregion/louima-case-overview-officer-seeking-some-mercy-admits-louima-s-torture.html?pagewanted=all&src=pm).

126. David Barstow, Brash Defense Lawyer Shrugs Off Attacks on Tactics in Louima Case, N.Y. Times (June 13, 1999) (available at http://www.nytimes.com/1999/06/13/nyregion/brash-defense-lawyer-shrugs-off-attacks-on-tactics-in-louima-case.html?ref=marvynmkornberg&pagewanted=1).

Rule language*	Authors' explanation**
or state a personal opinion as to the justness of a cause, the credibility of a witness, the culpability of a civil litigant or the guilt or innocence of an accused accused; . . .	• Example: In a closing statement, a lawyer should not say that she believes that her client is telling the truth. • The reason for this rule is probably the concern that juries may trust lawyers more than they should, given the lawyer's partisan role; also, the views of nontestifying lawyers are not subject to cross-examination.

*All emphasis added.

**This and other authors' explanations draw from the comments to the rules and from other sources. They are not comprehensive but highlight some important interpretive points.

Can a lawyer communicate his own knowledge or opinions if he includes them in questions posed to witnesses?

No. A jury can obtain information by hearing a question as well as by listening to its answer, so a lawyer should not ask an improper or objectionable question to plant an idea in the minds of the jurors. When two defendants are being tried separately for a crime they allegedly committed together, a prosecutor may not call one of them to the stand in the trial of the other and ask whether he participated in the crime, knowing that the witness will invoke his right not to incriminate himself. That tactic could suggest to the jury that the witness was guilty even though a jury is not entitled to draw that inference from invocation of the right.[127]

> **FOR EXAMPLE:** In *Douglas v. Alabama,* the prosecutor called co-conspirator Loyd to the stand and had him sworn in. After Loyd invoked his right not to incriminate himself, the prosecutor had him declared a hostile witness. Then the prosecutor read the alleged confession of Loyd, under the guise of asking Loyd questions about it, even though he knew that Loyd would refuse to answer. Douglas, of course, was unable to cross-examine either the prosecutor or Loyd because the prosecutor was not a witness and Loyd refused to answer any questions. The court held that Douglas's Sixth Amendment rights had been violated.[128]

---

127. See Restatement § 107, comment c. Many judges will sanction prosecutors for deliberately engaging in this conduct. E-mail from Ellen Yaroshefsky, Clinical Prof. of Law & Director, Jacob Burns Center for Ethics in the Practice of Law, to the authors (Apr. 24, 2007).

128. Douglas v. Alabama, 380 U.S. 415 (1965).

What consequences might a lawyer face for violating the rules against making personal comments on the evidence or asking improper questions to prejudice a jury?

Improper conduct in violation of these rules is usually punished by the trial judge. The judge may sustain objections to the lawyer's improper statements, order them stricken from the record, and give corrective instructions to the jury (e.g., to disregard the statements). That remedy may not be sufficient if jurors have already heard the lawyer's improper statements or questions. In that event, the court may declare a mistrial, or an appellate court might order a new trial. If the conduct is repeated, the trial court may order sanctions against the lawyer or hold the lawyer in contempt of court. The state bar might bring disciplinary proceedings against the lawyer.

Are there still other limitations on what lawyers may say in court?

Rule 3.5(d) commands that lawyers should not "engage in conduct intended to disrupt a tribunal." Comment 4 elaborates that lawyers should refrain from "abusive or obstreperous" conduct. Even if a judge screams at a lawyer or otherwise acts in inappropriate ways, a "judge's default is no justification for similar dereliction by an advocate." This rule applies during depositions as well as in hearings.[129]

In addition to the ethical rules, rules of evidence, procedural rules of particular courts, and the substantive law of a jurisdiction may impose further limitations on what lawyers may say in court.[130] For example, lawyers are generally permitted to discuss the law in closing statements but not in opening statements. In practice, however, most judges do not strictly enforce this rule but allow lawyers to "steer a middle course" and permit them to "frame the legal issues" for the jury.[131]

Are lawyers permitted to interview jurors after trials to find out why they were successful or unsuccessful?

Rule 3.5 regulates contacts between lawyers and jurors outside the courtroom. Lawyers may not influence jurors (or judges) illegally (for example, by bribing them), and they may not communicate with jurors during a proceeding unless permitted by law or by the judge. After a case is over and the jury has been discharged, a lawyer may talk to any juror who is willing to talk to the lawyer. However, such communication is prohibited if barred by law or a court order, or if the juror has stated that she does not want to communicate. Finally, a lawyer may not mislead, coerce, pressure, or harass

---

129. Rule 3.5, Comment 5.
130. Restatement § 107, comment a.
131. Steven Lubet, Modern Trial Advocacy 315 (student ed., Natl. Inst. Tr. Advoc. 2000).

jurors. For example, a lawyer may not pretend to be a member of the press in order to find out what happened during jury deliberations.

H. Lawyers' duties in nonadjudicative proceedings

Up to this point, we have considered only the rules governing lawyers who appear in courts or other adjudicative[132] proceedings. However, under Rule 3.9, some of these rules also apply when lawyers represent clients in legislative hearings, in rulemaking, or in other nonadjudicative proceedings before government agencies "in which the lawyer or the lawyer's client is presenting evidence or argument."[133] The idea is that if a lawyer is involved in presenting factual or legal material to a decision maker, the lawyer has a responsibility to the decision maker to assure the accuracy of the information presented and to conduct himself in a manner that assists the administration of justice.[134]

> **Rule 3.9 Advocate in Nonadjudicative Proceedings**
> **A lawyer representing a client before a legislative body or administrative agency in a nonadjudicative proceeding shall disclose that the appearance is in a representative capacity and shall conform to the provisions of Rules 3.3(a) through (c), 3.4(a) through (c) and 3.5.[135]**

Rule 3.9 does not apply all of these rules to negotiations with or inquiries to government agencies that are unconnected to an "official hearing or meeting." Comment 3 explains:

> It does not apply to representation of a client in a negotiation or other bilateral transaction with a governmental agency or in connection with an application for a license or other privilege or the client's compliance with generally applicable reporting requirements, such as the filing of income-tax returns. Nor does it apply to the representation of a client in connection with an investigation or examination of the client's affairs

---

132. Adjudication refers to a proceeding whose purpose is to decide a case involving a specific set of persons or facts. Rule 3.3 specifically refers to proceedings before "tribunals." Rule 1.0(m) defines "tribunal" to refer to a court, an arbitrator in a binding arbitration proceeding or a legislative body, administrative agency or other body acting in an adjudicative capacity. A legislative body, administrative agency or other body acts in an adjudicative capacity when a neutral official, after the presentation of evidence or legal argument by a party or parties, will render a binding legal judgment directly affecting a party's interests in a particular matter.

133. Rule 3.9, Comment 3.

134. Id. at Comment 1.

135. This is Pennsylvania's version of Rule 3.9, which is identical to Model Rule 3.9.

conducted by government investigators or examiners. Representation in such matters is governed by Rules 4.1 through 4.4.

The Restatement simply provides that in administrative proceedings that are adjudicative in nature or that involve a government agency as a participant, lawyers have the same responsibilities that they do in courts. In other types of government proceedings, the Restatement concludes that lawyers have the same duties that they have when they deal with private persons.[136] The Restatement candidly notes that "few decided cases have considered a lawyer's obligations in dealing with legislative bodies and administrative agencies" and that "the proper classification of a particular proceeding may be unclear."[137]

---

136. Agency adjudications (such as proceedings before a zoning board to determine the proper zoning for a client's property) are of the first type, while consideration of legislation is of the second variety. Restatement § 104.

137. Id. at comments b and d.

11 LAWYERS' DUTIES TO ADVERSARIES AND THIRD PERSONS

Chapters 3 through 9 discussed lawyers' duties to clients. Chapter 10 explained their duties to courts and to other tribunals in which they appear. This chapter explores lawyers' duties to third persons such as adversaries, witnesses, and the justice system. These duties are sometimes the same as the duties that lawyers owe to courts. For example, a lawyer may not lie in court because she would mislead both the judge and her adversary. But sometimes the duties to third persons differ from those owed to courts.

A. Communications with lawyers and third persons

When lawyers communicate with others on behalf of clients outside of "proceedings," Rules 4.1 through 4.4 apply. Some of the obligations are very similar to those that apply in proceedings, but others are quite different.

1. Deception of third persons

a. The duty to avoid material false statements

> **Rule 4.1(a) Truthfulness in Statements to Others**
> **In the course of representing a client a lawyer shall not knowingly ... make a false statement of material fact or law to a third person. ...**

Rule 4.1(a) is similar to the first part of Rule 3.3(a)(1) — both rules instruct lawyers not to lie. While Rule 3.3 applies only to proceedings before tribunals, Rule 4.1(a) applies whenever a lawyer is representing a client, such as when the lawyer is talking to a potential witness or to an opposing lawyer.

> **FOR EXAMPLE:** Criminal defense lawyer Thomas Broderick's son was charged with battery in Florida. The prosecutor agreed to defer prosecution. Two years later, the son was arrested in Indiana for driving while intoxicated. Broderick asked the Indiana prosecutor to defer prosecution so that the matter could be resolved without a conviction. The prosecutor did not ask about prior arrests, and Broderick did not mention the Florida charge. The administrator of Indiana's deferred prosecution program drafted and gave Broderick and his son a three-page "deferral agreement" to sign. Broderick did not read it before he and his son signed it, but the agreement included the incorrect statement that his son had no prior arrests. Although Rule 4.1 prohibits only false statements that are made "knowingly," Broderick was publicly reprimanded for violating the rule. The court said that under the circumstances (where Broderick had criminal defense experience), willful ignorance of the content of the statement he signed was no defense to the charge of violating the rule.[1]

---

1. Matter of Broderick, 929 N.E.2d 199 (Ind. 2010).

Rule 4.1 also differs from Rule 3.3 in that Rule 3.3 bars a lawyer from making any false statements to tribunals, while Rule 4.1 prohibits only "material" false statements of fact or law to third persons. Rule 8.4(c), which prohibits lawyers from engaging in conduct involving "deceit or misrepresentation," has no qualifier excusing false statements that are not "material."

PROBLEM 11-1 EMERGENCY FOOD STAMPS

William Simon, a former legal services advocate, is Arthur Levitt Professor of Law at Columbia University. This problem is his account of one of his cases, excerpted from a law review article.[2]

One Friday in 1980, a man named Jessie Rogers walked into our legal aid office in Boston to complain that he had just been denied "emergency" food stamps by the neighborhood welfare office. He had been released from prison the prior day. The prison authorities had arranged temporary lodging for him in a small room with primitive cooking facilities, given him a little cash, and told him he could receive food stamps on application at the welfare office. A social service agency would assess him for employment the following week.

The prison authorities' expectation that he would receive food stamps was not unreasonable. Statutes and regulations entitled financially eligible people in Rogers' residential circumstances to an "over-the-counter" issue of stamps on application if they were in "immediate need." The application process called for various documents, such as proof of residence and a Social Security card, which Rogers had satisfied. He was, however, unable to satisfy one of the demands: He did not have a "picture ID," and neither he nor the welfare worker to whom he applied knew how he could get one in less than five days. Although the regulations stated that documentation requirements should be waived in cases of "immediate need" where there was a reasonable explanation of inability to comply, the worker told Rogers that he could not receive any benefits until he could produce the "picture ID."

---

2. William H. Simon, Virtuous Lying: A Critique of Quasi-Categorical Moralism, 12 Geo. J. Leg. Ethics 433, 433-439 (1999).

On hearing Rogers' story, our paralegal telephoned the welfare worker to argue that Rogers was entitled to a waiver of the ID requirement. While the paralegal waited, the welfare worker went to consult the office director and returned to confirm the office's refusal to provide benefits. When Rogers and the paralegal told me their stories, I called the office. The welfare worker told me that the director had instructed her not to grant benefits without a "picture ID." I asked to speak to the director. The worker, after hesitating suspiciously, said that the director had "left for the day." The paralegal did not believe this: "They're stonewalling. They hate to waive documentation. On Monday, when we finally get to see the director, he'll claim that the worker never told him Mr. Rogers was in immediate need. In the meantime, they'll have had the satisfaction of jerking Mr. Rogers and us around."

I proposed that the paralegal call the office back and, in a secretarial tone, tell the receptionist that Theresa Taylor wished to speak to the director. Theresa Taylor was the welfare department district manager to whom the office director reported. It worked. Within seconds, the office director came on the line. His initially obsequious tone became first irritated and then sheepish as I explained who I was and why his office was clearly obliged to issue stamps immediately to Rogers. Vindicating our paralegal, the director said with ineptly feigned surprise, "Oh, he's in immediate need! He should have told us that." He finally agreed to yield up the stamps that afternoon.

Questions about Emergency Food Stamps

1. A Massachusetts rule in effect at the time these events took place imposed the same obligation that Rules 4.1 and 8.4(c) impose now. Did Professor Simon violate those rules?
2. If so, did he do the right thing?

What about false statements by clients? If a lawyer knows that her client is lying in her presence to someone other than a court, must the lawyer ask the client to tell the truth or tell the third party herself?

As we have seen, if a lawyer knows that her client or any witness she presents is lying to a tribunal or in a pretrial deposition, Rule 3.3(b) requires the lawyer to take remedial measures, which could include informing the tribunal if the client refuses to correct the record herself. Also, even if the client is not testifying before a tribunal, the lawyer must withdraw from representing a client who is using the lawyer's services (such as documents prepared by the lawyer) to perpetrate a fraud.[3] But suppose that no proceeding has commenced, and the client is not using the lawyer's services to perpetrate a fraud, but the lawyer nevertheless knows that the client is providing false information to a third party. For example, suppose that in the course of a criminal investigation, the police question a suspect in his lawyer's presence, and the lawyer knows that her client is providing incorrect information.

The lawyer probably would be foolish to allow her client to lie under these circumstances because the client could be charged with a crime such as obstructing justice. To serve her client well, the lawyer should interrupt the questioning, take her client aside, and advise her to tell the truth. However, if the lawyer does not do so, or if the client refuses to accept her advice, no rule appears to require the lawyer to correct the record.

It could be argued that the lawyer's presence during an event at which the client provides false information is a "use" of the lawyer's services to commit a fraud, permitting disclosure under Rule 1.6(b) and therefore perhaps requiring the disclosure under Rule 4.1(b). However, we are unaware of any holding to that effect.

Nevertheless, a lawyer might be disciplined for sitting by silently while a client perpetrates a fraud, particularly if any action by the lawyer could be construed as participation in the fraud.

> **FOR EXAMPLE:**   David Austern, a lawyer, represented the seller at a real estate closing. The buyers feared that once they closed the sale, the seller would not complete work on the apartment units it was selling. They insisted that the seller give Austern a check for $10,000 to be held in escrow to guarantee completion. Austern accepted the check, but his client told him privately that there was no money in the account and that the check was therefore worthless. Nevertheless, Austern went ahead with the closing, without informing the buyers that the check had no backing. Austern delayed opening the escrow account until two months later, when he received a good check. He was publicly censured for assisting his client in a fraud; the District of Columbia Court of Appeals said that he should have withdrawn, but instead he "used his status as an attorney to lend legitimacy to a transaction which had none."[4]

---

3. See the discussion in Chapter 3.

4. In re Austern, 524 A.2d 680, 687 (D.C. 1987). This case is somewhat different from the hypothetical question posed in the text in which the lawyer is entirely passive because Austern did more than sit silently while his client committed a fraud. The court found that he signed the escrow agreement after knowing of the fraud. Nevertheless, the case is a warning that even more subtle activity by a lawyer in connection with a client's false representations to third parties could subject the lawyer to discipline. The sanction imposed on Austern was light because of his excellent professional reputation and achievements.

b. Lawyers' duties of truthfulness in fact investigation

A lawyer is obliged to undertake a "reasonable" inquiry before filing a suit. Even if this were not required, simple economics would compel most lawyers to investigate potential suits before filing them to avoid investing time and money in lawsuits that have little chance of success. Discovery under court rules is unavailable before a case begins, so lawyers must investigate cases privately. Sometimes the needed investigation can be accomplished through interviews with witnesses and collection of available documents. But in some cases, lawyers or their investigators believe that they can obtain the required information only by misrepresenting their identity or the purpose of their inquiry.

> **FOR EXAMPLE:** An aspiring tenant believes that the landlord of a desirable building rejected his application to rent an apartment because the tenant is African American. If questioned, the landlord would almost surely deny that his motivation was unlawful racial discrimination. A lawyer might want to *test* the landlord's willingness to rent to African Americans by sending, for example, four investigators — two of them white and two of them black — to pose as possible tenants and fill out rental applications, giving similar family information and credit histories. If the landlord agreed to sign leases with the white applicants but not the black applicants, this would substantiate the claim of discrimination.

The testing process requires that the lawyer direct his investigators to lie about their interest in renting apartments in the building, and probably also about their identities, families, and credit histories. Rule 8.4(a) states that it is professional misconduct for a lawyer to violate one of the rules or to "knowingly assist or induce another lawyer to do so" or to "do so through the acts of another." So if the lawyer could not ethically do this work himself, he cannot enlist another person to do it either. Do Rules 4.1 and 8.4(c) preclude the use of testers?[5]

The *Beatles* case

Similar issues arise in other types of litigation. For example, a person contemplating litigation might use deception to seek proof that another person is violating her trademark, breaching a contract, or engaging in unfair competitive tactics. A lawyer for Yoko Ono Lennon posed as a

---

5. For discussion of the ethical issues relating to use of testers, see David B. Isbell & Lucantonio N. Salvi, Ethical Responsibility of Lawyers for Deception by Undercover Investigators and Discrimination Testers: An Analysis of the Provisions Prohibiting Misrepresentation Under the Model Rules of Professional Conduct, 8 Geo. J. Leg. Ethics 791 (1995).

consumer to investigate a possible trademark violation. The International Collectors Society (ICS) sold foreign postage stamps bearing pictures of celebrities, including the Beatles. Lennon sued ICS to enjoin the sales, claiming that the stamps included copyrighted photographs. In court, ICS agreed to a judgment ordering it to terminate the sales. Under this consent decree, however, ICS could sell off a few thousand stamps to persons who had already become members of the "Beatles/Lennon Club" by having purchased Beatles stamps in the past. Two months later, Dorothy Weber, one of Lennon's lawyers, called ICS, posing as a consumer by using her married name, Dorothy Meltzer. She said that her husband was a John Lennon fan. She bought stamps over the phone. At Weber's direction, her secretary and several investigators also posed as consumers who were not Beatles/Lennon Club members, and they too were able to buy stamps over the phone. Lennon then sought to hold ICS in contempt for violating the consent decree. ICS defended, partly relying on the theory that Lennon should not be able to enforce the court's order because Weber had violated Rule 8.4(c). Professor Bruce Green, who teaches professional responsibility at Fordham Law School, filed a statement with the court on behalf of Lennon, arguing (as an ethics expert) that Weber had not violated the rule.[6] Relying heavily on Green's statement, the court refused to find Weber in contempt. It concluded that Rule 8.4(c) "does not apply to misrepresentation solely as to identity or purpose and solely for evidence-gathering purposes." It noted that courts had not condemned lawyers who directed undercover agents in criminal cases or anti-discrimination testers, and it recognized that private lawyers had to use undercover investigators when it would be difficult to discover the violations by other means.[7]

The *Gatti* case

Across the country on the West Coast, however, lawyer Daniel Gatti got in trouble for misrepresenting his identity while investigating whether to file a civil lawsuit. Gatti represented chiropractors. One chiropractor told him that he suspected that a company called California Medical Review (CMR), which reviewed medical claims submitted to insurance companies, was using people who lacked medical training to evaluate insurance claims. When one of Gatti's chiropractor clients had a claim rejected based on a recommendation from a "Dr. Becker" who worked for CMR, Gatti began to investigate a possible fraud case against CMR. He called Becker, pretended

---

6. [Authors' footnote.] Professor Green's declaration, on file with the authors, cited one authority that did not involve civil rights testing or criminal law enforcement—Ala. Ethics Op. RO-89-31 (1989)—suggesting (in Green's words) that "a lawyer may direct an investigator to pose as a buyer for the plaintiff's machine in order to determine whether the plaintiff can lift the machine and must therefore have lied about the extent of his injuries."

7. Apple Corps, Ltd. v. Intl. Collectors Socy., 15 F. Supp. 2d 456 (D.N.J. 1998).

Daniel Gatti

to be a chiropractor, and asked Becker to describe his qualifications. He also called a Mr. Adams at CMR, stated (falsely) that he was a doctor,[8] that he'd been referred to CMR by Becker and an insurance company, that he was interested in working as a claims reviewer, and that he wanted to learn about CMR's educational programs for insurance adjusters.

Adams complained to the Oregon Bar, which initiated disciplinary proceedings against Gatti for misrepresenting his identity in violation of its version of Rule 8.4(c). Gatti defended in part by quoting from a letter he had once received from the Oregon Bar, stating that government prosecutors could use deception in undercover investigations. The case ended up in the Oregon Supreme Court, where Gatti cited the *Beatles* case in his defense. The U.S. attorney for Oregon and the Oregon attorney general urged the court at least to uphold the use of undercover tactics by public law enforcement officials. But the court said that the state's ethics rules applied to all lawyers in all circumstances. It held that Gatti had violated the rule by misrepresenting his identity and purpose to deceive Adams and Becker, and it publicly reprimanded him.[9] In the course of its opinion, it suggested that even prosecutors could not make false statements or direct others to do so, a holding that shocked the state's law enforcement establishment and jeopardized all prosecutor-directed undercover investigations of criminal activity in the state.

Notes About *Gatti*

1. A year after the case was decided, law enforcement officials persuaded the legislature to pass an emergency law allowing any lawyer working for any federal, state, or local government agency to "provide legal advice and direction to" and to "participate in" covert law enforcement activities, "even though the activities may require the use of deceit or mis-representation."[10] The statute made no such exception for private lawyers. Subsequently, the Oregon Supreme

---

8. Gatti claimed that this particular assertion was not actually false since he held the degree of Juris Doctor.

9. In re Gatti, 8 P.3d 966 (Or. 2000).

10. Or. Rev. Stat. Ann. § 9.528 (West 2003). The Utah State Bar ethics committee evaluated the question and reached a conclusion similar to the Oregon legislature, carving an exception for governmental lawyers but reserving for another day the question of whether the exception would also apply to private lawyers who were attempting to investigate fraud or other wrongdoing. Utah St. B., Ethics Advisory Op. Comm., Op. 02-05.

Court drew the line between permitted and prohibited conduct in a quite different place. It amended its rules of professional responsibility to allow both government lawyers and private lawyers to supervise undercover investigations involving deception, but the amendment did not authorize lawyers of either type to participate personally in the deceptions. The new rule permits lawyers to "advise clients or others about, or to supervise lawful covert activity, in the investigation of violations of civil or criminal law or constitutional rights, provided the lawyer's conduct is otherwise in compliance with these disciplinary rules." "Covert activity" is defined as an "effort to obtain information on unlawful activity through the use of misrepresentations or other subterfuge." The rule added that covert activity could be commenced or supervised by a lawyer "only when the lawyer in good faith believes there is a reasonable possibility that unlawful activity has taken place, is taking place or will take place in the foreseeable future."[11]

2. Daniel Gatti's reprimand stood. He published a novel, *White Knuckle*, and said that he wished that a reformed disciplinary rule "could have come about another way."[12]

Despite the ICS and Gatti cases, the issue of undercover investigations by nongovernment lawyers remains unsettled. Some courts have refused to exclude evidence obtained by testers, noting that testing is a legitimate method to identify violations of the civil rights laws.[13] Others have excluded evidence obtained by investigators who posed as customers.[14] In a case that captured national media attention, Hewlett-Packard attorney Kevin Hunsaker was indicted for helping company investigators to misrepresent their identities to obtain private telephone records of members of the company's board of directors. These directors were suspected of leaking company information to the media. Ultimately, Hunsaker was fired; the criminal charges were dropped in exchange for 96 hours of community service.[15]

---

11. Or. Code Prof. Resp. DR 1-102(D) (2004), subsequently enacted as Or. R. Prof. Conduct 8.4(b) (2005).

12. Ashbel S. Green, Lawyers' No-Lying Dispute Comes to a Close, Oregonian (Jan. 30, 2002).

13. Havens Realty Corp. v. Coleman, 455 U.S. 363 (1982).

14. Midwest Motor Sports v. Arctic Cat Sales, 347 F.3d 693 (8th Cir. 2003) (lawyer in franchise dispute hired former FBI agent to visit a snowmobile showroom with his wife, posing as a consumer, and secretly record statements by the sales personnel; court excluded the recording because the behavior was dishonest and violated Rule 8.4(c), and noted that the lawyer also violated Rule 4.2, discussed below).

15. Matt Richtel & Damon Darlin, Ex-Leader of HP Is Charged in California, N.Y. Times (Oct. 4, 2006) (available at http://www.nytimes.com/2006/10/04/business/04hewlettcnd.html); Jessica

No disciplinary case seems to have addressed the issue, but at least one bar association has issued an opinion endorsing "dissemblance" by investigators if

> (i) either (a) the investigation is of a violation of civil rights or intellectual property rights and the lawyer believes in good faith that such violation is taking place or will take place imminently or (b) the dissemblance is expressly authorized by law; and (ii) the evidence sought is not reasonably available through other means; and (iii) the lawyer's conduct and the investigators' conduct that the lawyer is supervising do not otherwise violate [Rule 4.2 or any other ethics rule]; and (iv) the dissemblance does not unlawfully or unethically violate the rights of third parties.[16]

May a lawyer investigating a matter "friend" a witness or prospective defendant on Facebook or another social networking site to search for information that might be helpful to the lawyer's clients?

The answer depends in part on whether the Facebook page in question is that of a witness or a party. The ethics committee of the Association of the Bar of the City of New York found that lawyers have "increasingly turned to social networking sites such as Facebook, Twitter and YouTube, as potential sources of evidence [such as evidence of infidelity in divorce cases] for use in litigation." The committee concluded that a lawyer may send "a friend request" to a potential witness if she uses her real name and profile, and that the lawyer or investigator need not reveal her true reason for the request. The lawyer may not use deception, for example, by creating a false name or profile. The committee pointed out that a lawyer also can subpoena "nonparties in possession" of information contained on Facebook, although federal law imposes some restrictions on obtaining certain information from Facebook and other providers.[17]

The ethics committee of the Philadelphia Bar addressed whether a lawyer may ask a third person (such as a friend of the lawyer) to "friend" the witness, using the third person's own name and profile. That committee concluded that this conduct would be unethical because hiding behind the identity of another person would omit a highly material fact — that that third person was acting at the behest of the lawyer.[18] Presumably, then, the lawyer also may not ask her investigator to "friend" the witness.

Guynn, Final Charges Dropped in HP "Pretexting" Case, San Fran. Chron. (June 29, 2007) (available at http://articles.sfgate.com/2007-06-29/business/17248690_1_pretexting-phone-records-hewlett-packard-chairwoman-patricia-dunn).

16. N.Y. Co. B. Assn., Formal Op. 737 (2007) (available at http://www.nycla.org/siteFiles/Publications/Publications519_0.pdf).

17. Assn. of the B. of the City of N.Y., Formal Op. 2010-2 (available at http://www.nycbar.org/pdf/report/uploads/20071997-FormalOpinion2010-2.pdf).

18. Prof. Guidance Comm., Phila. B. Assn., Op. 2009-02 (available at http://uponfurtherreview.philadelphiabar.org/page/Article?articleID=3e3477ea-c75b-4a34-abb5-885c98faa3c3).

Is a lawyer more restricted from "friending" an adverse party on Facebook than from "friending" a witness?

Probably so. Rule 4.2 states that "a lawyer shall not communicate about the subject of the representation with a person the lawyer knows to be represented by another lawyer in the matter" without permission of opposing counsel. If the lawyer knows that the adverse party is represented by counsel, the lawyer should not contact the adverse party in person, by telephone, through e-mail, or otherwise without permission of opposing counsel if the communication relates to the subject of the representation. If the lawyer does not know that the adverse party is represented, the lawyer should ask this question before other communication occurs. If the adverse party is not represented, the lawyer must comply with the guidance provided by Rule 4.3.[19]

Rule 4.2 bars the lawyer only from communicating with the represented party about the subject of the representation. One question is whether "friending" without identifying one's reason for contact would "count" as a contact prohibited by Rule 4.2. The likely answer is yes if the lawyer has no other good faith reason to contact the opposing party.

Even if "friending" is very restricted, what about surfing Facebook or other Internet sites to obtain information about an opposing party or a witness without making any direct contact?

Suppose you represent a woman in a divorce whose husband has an informative Facebook page with very limited privacy settings. Let's say the soon-to-be-ex-husband also has an open page on "OK Cupid" or another Internet dating site. Assume that without making any direct contact, you see the ex-husband's "relationship status"; whether he is interested in women, men, or both; his recent vacation photos; and more. May a lawyer or the lawyer's investigator view and collect this information?

The likely answer is yes. Lawyers usually are allowed to search public sources in the course of their work. This should be a cautionary note for anyone interested in protecting personal privacy, but some people have little to hide or little interest in being less visible. While we don't know of any authority on this yet, we think that using Google as an investigative tool is permissible. However, cyberlaw may develop rapidly to allow individuals to request exclusion of their names from search engines.[20]

---

19. N.Y. St. B. Assn., Op. 843, n. 1 (2010) (available at http://www.nysba.org/AM/Template. cfm?Section=Home&ContentID=49630&Template=/CM/ContentDisplay.cfm).

20. See Suzanne Daley, On Its Own, Europe Backs Web Privacy Rights, N.Y. Times 1 (Aug. 9, 2011) (available at http://www.nytimes.com/2011/08/10/world/europe/10spain.html?pagewanted= all).

c. Lawyers' duties of truthfulness in negotiation

The text of Rule 4.1 does not allow lawyers to lie for the purpose of bargaining. More precisely, it does not allow a lawyer knowingly to "make a false statement of material fact or law." So is it professional misconduct if a lawyer tells opposing counsel that she believes that her client would not accept a settlement of less than $80,000, knowing that her client would be quite happy to walk away with $75,000? Comment 2 qualifies the rule:

> This Rule refers to statements of fact. Whether a particular statement should be regarded as one of fact can depend on the circumstances. Under generally accepted conventions in negotiation, certain types of statements ordinarily are not taken as statements of material fact. Estimates of price or value placed on the subject of a transaction and a party's intentions as to an acceptable settlement of a claim are ordinarily in this category, and so is the existence of an undisclosed principal except where nondisclosure of the principal would constitute fraud.[21]

The contrary messages in the rule and the comment may reflect a profession that is deeply divided about the acceptability of certain lies during negotiations (e.g., about acceptable levels of settlement or about a lawyer's authority to settle for a certain amount). One author surveyed 15 leading academics, practitioners, and judges about whether, under the ethical rules, they could falsely state that they were not authorized by their defendant client to settle for the amount that the plaintiff wanted to receive. Six said that the rules would not allow such a statement, and 7 said that such a statement was permissible. All but one said that for tactical reasons or because of their personal ethics, they would evade the question rather than lie.[22]

Some authorities justify a "negotiation" exception to the requirement of honesty. Professor James J. White argued in an article published in 1980 that because most negotiation takes place in private, a duty of honesty in negotiation would be virtually impossible to enforce. He also argued that, on the one hand, a "negotiator must be fair and truthful; on the other, he must mislead his opponent. Like the poker player, a negotiator hopes that his opponent will overestimate the value of [the negotiator's] hand [and] must facilitate his opponent's inaccurate assessment. . . . Even the most

---

21. The last part of this comment refers to a situation in which the person on the other side of the negotiation from the lawyer thinks that the lawyer is representing a particular person or institution, but the lawyer is really representing other interests, perhaps entities that could afford to pay much more to the unwitting person.

22. Larry Lempert, In Settlement Talks, Does Telling the Truth Have Its Limits? 2 Inside Litig. 1 (1988).

*Professor Carrie
Menkel-Meadow*

forthright, honest, and trustworthy negotiators [are] actively engaged in misleading their opponents about their true positions."[23]

Some academic authorities have criticized Comment 2 to Rule 4.1, arguing that it enshrines, without justification, an overly adversarial model of negotiation. Professor Carrie Menkel-Meadow has noted that in 1980, the commission that drafted what became the 1983 Model Rules suggested that lawyers should have to be "fair" when dealing with third parties in negotiation, but that the bar rejected this suggestion to "preserve the caveat emptor culture of both the litigator and the transactional dealmaker." She reports that published guides to negotiation often advise negotiators to "deflect" questions or "answer different questions" or "change the subject" as a way of avoiding giving incomplete or untruthful answers to specific requests for information, but she suggests that these tactics sometimes lead to subsequent claims of misrepresentation. She observes that the legal profession generally justifies Comment 2 to Rule 4.1 by reference to "expectations about how the legal-negotiation game is played." Menkel-Meadow asks why "accepted conventions" of advocacy should prevail in an ethics code. She notes that some lawyers might object to a proposal that lawyers be as truthful in negotiation as in their other dealings. Such lawyers might urge that it is impossible to monitor whether a lawyer was telling the truth about his client's intentions. To this she replies, "It would be difficult, but who knows? We have never tried it."[24]

Question About Lying in Negotiation

Professor White (quoted above) asks what a lawyer should do in this situation:[25] Your defendant client has told you that he would like to have to pay the plaintiff as little money as possible but, if necessary, would be willing to pay $100,000. The plaintiff's lawyer says, "I think that my client would accept $90,000. Will your client pay that much?" If you say "yes," you will tell the truth, but your client will have to pay $90,000 when you might have been able to negotiate for a lower payment. If you say something like, "No, $50,000 is the limit," or even,

---

23. James J. White, Machiavelli and the Bar: Ethical Limitations on Lying in Negotiation, 1980 Am. B. Found. Res. J. 926, 927.

24. Carrie Menkel-Meadow, Ethics, Morality and Professional Responsibility in Negotiation Dispute Resolution Ethics: A Comprehensive Guide 119, 127-128, 134-135, 144-145, 154 (Phyllis Bernard & Bryant Garth eds., ABA 2002).

25. White, supra n. 23, at 932-933.

"I don't think he will," you will keep the negotiation open and may end up settling for an amount between $50,000 and $90,000, but you will have lied. What will you say?

d. Receipt of inadvertently transmitted information, including metadata

The nature of the adversary system might lead you to think that if the lawyer opposing you in litigation or negotiating with you in a transaction accidentally sends you a document (e.g., faxes you an internal memorandum with information about the weaknesses of her own case), you might use it as you wish and need not reveal that you had received it. This is only partly right; you are allowed to use the information, but you have to let the other side know that you have it. Rule 4.4(b) provides:

> **A lawyer who receives a document or electronically stored information relating to the representation of the lawyer's client and knows or reasonably should know that the document or electronically stored information was inadvertently sent shall promptly notify the sender.**

> **Comment** [2] Paragraph (b) recognizes that lawyers sometimes receive documents or electronically stored information that was mistakenly sent or produced by opposing parties or their lawyers. . . . If a lawyer knows or reasonably should know that such a document or electronically stored information was sent inadvertently, then this Rule requires the lawyer to promptly notify the sender in order to permit that person to take protective measures. . . .

Word processing programs produce documents that contain "metadata" that does not appear in print but that is embedded in electronic copies of the documents. Metadata can reveal who worked on the document, what changes were made, and the content of supposedly deleted suggestions from one lawyer to another regarding litigation or negotiation strategy. Lawyers who send documents to other lawyers electronically can avoid the risk of sending metadata by sending paper copies or by using commercial software to "scrub" documents before sending them, unless the documents, including their metadata, are being produced as discovery materials.[26] Even though transmission of metadata may be avoidable, many

---

26. ABA Standing Comm. on Ethics & Prof. Resp., Formal Op. 06-442; see ABA, Lawyers Receiving Electronic Documents Are Free to Examine "Hidden" Metadata: ABA Ethics Opinion (Nov. 9, 2006), http://jenner.com/system/assets/assets/3895/original/ABA_Formal_Opinion_06_442_Press_Release.pdf?1319665504.

lawyers are not yet aware of the risks of electronic transmission of documents, so documents that contain metadata remain commonplace. At the other extreme, some lawyers reportedly insert false information into metadata in documents that they send to their adversaries, hoping that the recipients will peek into the metadata and thereby be misled.[27]

If a lawyer e-mails a document containing metadata to another lawyer, may the receiving lawyer "mine" it for the metadata?

States differ on this issue. The ABA and more than a dozen state bar ethics committees have addressed the issue in recent years, and their opinions are sharply divided. The ethics committees of the ABA and the Colorado, District of Columbia, Maryland, Pennsylvania, and Vermont bars concluded that receiving lawyers have no ethical duty either to refrain from viewing the metadata or to notify the sender. The Pennsylvania bar suggested that if the lawyer concluded that the inclusion of metadata was inadvertent, the lawyer should notify the sender, but the mere fact that metadata was embedded in the document did not warrant a presumption that its inclusion was inadvertent. The opinion went on to advise that if the metadata was beneficial to the receiving lawyer's client, that lawyer was not only permitted but required to use it. On the other hand, the ethics committees of the Alabama, Arizona, Florida, Maine, New Hampshire, New York, and North Carolina bars interpret the ethics rules to prohibit the receiving lawyer from even attempting to view the metadata.[28]

Although the Model Rule as amended by the American Bar Association in 2012 requires notification to the sender, it takes no position on whether the lawyer may use inadvertently sent information. So the ABA did not resolve the question of when, if ever, consideration for an adversary should override loyalty to one's own client in these circumstances. Comment 3 states that "where a lawyer is not required by applicable law to do so, the decision to voluntarily return such a document or delete electronically stored information is a matter of professional judgment ordinarily reserved to the lawyer."

---

27. David Hricik, I Can Tell When You're Telling Lies, 30 J. Leg. Prof. 79, 101 (2005).

28. E.g., ABA Standing Comm. on Ethics & Prof. Resp., Formal Op. 06-442); Ala. St. B. Disc. Commn., Op. 2007-02 (available at http://www.alabar.org/ogc/fopDisplay.cfm?oneId=412); Md. St. B. Assn. Comm. on Ethics, Op. 2007-09 (2006) (available at http://icw.lexisnexis.com/applieddiscovery/LawLibrary/CourtRulesArticles/MarylandEOonMetadata.pdf); N.Y. St. Ethics Op. 782 (2004) (available at http://www.nysba.org/AM/Template.cfm?Section=Ethics_Opinions& CONTENTID=13630&TEMPLATE=/CM/ContentDisplay.cfm). For analyses that agree with the Alabama and New York view, see Hricik, supra n. 27; David Hricik, Mining for Embedded Data: Is It Ethical to Take Intentional Advantage of Other People's Failures?, 8 N.C. J. L. & Tech. 231 (2007).

Suppose an employee sues her employer, and the employer then reads all the confidential e-mail that the employee exchanged with her lawyer through the employer's computer system. Does Rule 4.4(b) require the employer's lawyer to disclose this interception to the employee's lawyer?

Perhaps surprisingly, there is no such obligation, according to an ABA ethics opinion. The reasoning is that these communications between lawyer and client were not "inadvertently" sent. The opinion cautioned, however, that other law or court rules might require the disclosure.[29]

e. Obligation of disclosure to third persons

Rule 4.1(b) imposes on lawyers a limited duty to make affirmative disclosures to others when necessary to avoid assisting a criminal or fraudulent act by a client. However, the duty to disclose is subordinate to the duty under Rule 1.6 to protect confidential information. The issues raised by the obligation and by that limitation are explored in Chapter 3 as part of the discussion of when a lawyer may reveal a crime or fraud.

2. Restrictions on contact with represented persons

We move on from a series of questions about deception to some about the proper relationship of a lawyer who is representing a client to a nonlawyer who is involved in the matter but is not the lawyer's client. The ethical rules impose some restrictions on communication between lawyers and adverse persons out of concerns about possible overreaching. The rules first address restrictions on contact with a person (not just an adverse party) who is represented by a lawyer.

> **Rule 4.2 Communication with Person Represented by Counsel**
> **In representing a client, a lawyer shall not communicate about the subject of the representation with a person the lawyer knows to be represented by another lawyer in the matter, unless the lawyer has the consent of the other lawyer or is authorized to do so by law or a court order.**

A major purpose of this rule is to prevent lawyers from making "end runs" around other lawyers to get information from the other lawyers'

---

29. ABA Standing Comm. on Ethics & Prof. Resp., Formal Op. 11-460 (available at http://www.americanbar.org/content/dam/aba/administrative/professional_responsibility/11_460_nm_formal_opinion.authcheckdam.pdf).

clients.[30] If a lawyer contacts a represented person without his lawyer's consent, the represented person might make disclosures or concessions that his lawyer would have counseled him to avoid. The rule applies to all contacts with represented persons, not only to parties in litigation.[31]

> **FOR EXAMPLE:** An employee sued her employer, who was a lawyer, on an employment claim. About 45 minutes after receiving the summons and complaint, the lawyer walked into the employee's office, showed her papers, and asked her what they were and whose idea the suit had been. The employee said that they should not be discussing the suit. The lawyer left her office, saying they would talk about it the following week. The conversation lasted less than one minute. The Supreme Court of Oregon found that the conversation violated Oregon's version of Rule 4.2 because the conversation risked interfering with the employee's relationship to her lawyer and soliciting confidential information.[32]

Comments to Rule 4.2 and an ABA opinion elaborate and qualify these restrictions:

- Rule 4.2 applies to communications initiated by the lawyer and to those initiated by the represented person.[33]
- If a represented client contacts a second lawyer to obtain a second opinion or to explore changing lawyers, the second lawyer may talk to the represented client.[34]
- If a lawyer starts a conversation with another person erroneously believing that the person is unrepresented, the lawyer must end the conversation upon learning that the person has a lawyer.[35]
- The rule applies only to communications with persons known to be represented by a lawyer in "the matter" that is the subject of the communication. The lawyer may communicate with the person

---

30. Another purpose is to prevent lawyers from interfering with the lawyer-client relationships of their adversaries. Rule 4.2, Comment 1. Note that it is possible for a lawyer simultaneously to violate both Rule 4.1 and Rule 4.2 by misrepresenting his relationship to the case (e.g., by misrepresenting his identity) while contacting an adverse party improperly.

31. The ABA revised Rule 4.2 and its comments in 2002. Professor Carl A. Pierce has written three articles exhaustively exploring the effect of the changes. Variations on a Basic Theme: Revisiting the ABA's Revision or Model Rule 4.2, 70 Tenn. L. Rev. 121 (2002) (Part I); 70 Tenn. L. Rev. 321 (2003) (Part II); 70 Tenn. L. Rev. 643 (2003) (Part III).

32. In re Conduct of Knappenberger, 108 P.3d 1161 (Or. 2005).

33. Rule 4.2, Comment 3. Another way to state this proposition is that the consent of the client of another lawyer is not sufficient to overcome the "anti-contact" rule; the consent of the client's lawyer is necessary to permit the contact. Restatement § 99, comment b.

34. Restatement § 99, comment c.

35. Rule 4.2, Comment 3.

about other subjects, even closely related subjects, if they involve a different "matter," as in the following situation.

FOR EXAMPLE: A lawyer for the Jonquil Corp. knows that the Romero Corp. uses the law firm of Hampton & Kim for all of its legal matters. The lawyer may nevertheless call the president of the Romero Corp. directly to ask whether the Romero Corp. would sell one of its subsidiaries to the Jonquil Corp. Even though the lawyer knows that Hampton & Kim always represents Romero on its legal matters, it does not know that Hampton & Kim represents Romero on the new matter of the possible transfer of its subsidiary.[36]

May a lawyer get around this rule by having a paralegal or investigator call the opposing party?

No. A lawyer may not circumvent any of the rules by directing anyone else to do so. Rule 8.4(a) states that a lawyer may not attempt to violate any rule "through the acts of another."

May the lawyer suggest that her client call the represented person directly, even if that person is represented?

Two people who are represented by lawyers may talk with one another without their lawyers' permission. Rule 4.2 applies to lawyers, not to clients, so if a client calls an opposing party on his own initiative, no rule is violated. State bar ethics committees are divided, however, as to whether a lawyer may suggest that a client call a represented adversary in connection with a case. Some state bar opinions permit the practice, some allow it only if the lawyer doesn't "script" the conversation, and others forbid it.[37] In 2011, the ABA's ethics committee weighed in, concluding that Rule 4.2 allows a lawyer to recommend that a client contact a represented opposing party, may suggest what the client should say and what strategies the client should follow during the contact, and may accede to a client's request to draft a proposed settlement agreement that the client would present. However, the lawyer

> must, at a minimum, advise her client to encourage the other party to consult with counsel before entering into obligations, making admissions

---

36. ABA Standing Comm. on Ethics & Prof. Resp., Formal Op. 95-396. This conclusion seems philosophically, although not technically, at odds with the ABA's view that if a lawyer has reason to believe, but does not know for certain, that a lawyer is representing a person in a particular matter, the lawyers may not evade the rule "by closing eyes to the obvious." Rule 4.2, Comment 8.

37. See state bar decisions reviewed in ABA Standing Comm. on Ethics & Prof. Resp., Formal Op. 11-461 (available at http://www.americanbar.org/content/dam/aba/administrative/professional_ responsibility/formal_opinion_11_461_nm.authcheckdam.pdf).

or disclosing confidential information. If counsel has drafted a proposed agreement for the client to deliver to her represented adversary for execution, counsel should include in such agreement conspicuous language on the signature page that warns the other party to consult with his lawyer before signing the agreement.[38]

Does Rule 4.2 mean that lawyers representing clients who have disputes with government agencies must contact the general counsel's office of the agency and may not make direct contact with government officials?

No. The First Amendment's guarantee of the right to petition government overrides any state ethical rule. However, in that situation, an ABA ethics opinion urges that the lawyer must first notify the government's lawyer of her intent to talk directly with the policy official or officials, to give the lawyer a chance to advise them not to talk to the lawyer, or to advise them what to say.[39]

What if a lawyer wants to contact an employee of a corporation that is represented by another lawyer?

Here we explore some issues related to those addressed in our discussion of the *Upjohn* case in Chapter 3. That case dealt with the extent to which a corporation is entitled to the protection of attorney-client evidentiary privilege. There a plaintiff suing a corporation sought access through discovery to the paper records of an internal investigation of the corporation that had been conducted by the corporation's lawyers. The question was whether the corporation was entitled not to disclose the documents based on a claim that they were privileged communications.

Rule 4.2 imposes certain constraints on lawyers who want to interview employees of an adverse corporation without permission of counsel for the corporation. In deciding the scope of the attorney-client privilege for corporations and in interpreting Rule 4.2 as it applies to corporations, judges and rule writers must strike a balance between the desire not to intrude on the attorney-client relationship and the desire to provide litigants, the public, and the courts with access needed to investigate disputed facts. Here is a diagram of the relationship between these two sets of issues, and a summary of the relevant rules.

---

38. Id.; accord Restatement § 99, comment k.

39. ABA Standing Comm. on Ethics & Prof. Resp., Formal Op. 97-408. Some jurisdictions allow lawyers to contact policy officials of government agencies to discuss the substance of pending litigation against the agency without first obtaining the consent of the government's lawyer if they disclose their identities to the officials and state that they represent parties who are adverse to the employee's employer. See D.C. B. Op. 340 (2007) (available at http://www.dcbar.org/for_lawyers/ethics/legal_ethics/opinions/opinion340.cfm).

Comparison of corporate attorney-client privilege and Rule 4.2

Applicable law	If a party that is in litigation with a corporation wants to:	Restrictions imposed
Attorney-client privilege, after *Upjohn v. U.S.*, 449 U.S. 383 (1981)	Compel the corporation to produce documents prepared by the corporation's lawyer as part of an internal investigation.	The corporation may deny access to documents reflecting communications between the corporation's lawyers and employees if the communications are within the scope of the attorney-client privilege. See Chapter 3.
Rule 4.2, Comment 7 (Comment 4 in previous editions of the rules)	Interview employees of the corporation to learn facts relevant to the litigation without permission from the corporation's lawyer.	The adverse lawyer may not interview an employee who: • "supervises, directs or regularly consults with the organization's lawyer concerning the matter," • "has authority to obligate the organization with respect to the matter," or • is one "whose act or omission in connection with the matter may be imputed to the organization for purposes of civil or criminal liability."

Comment 7 to Rule 4.2 attempts to balance two competing policies. One objective is to enable lawyers to conduct inexpensive fact-gathering before and after initiating lawsuits. The other is to protect clients from overreaching by opposing lawyers. Because states have different views of which policy is more important, the proper test for barring lawyers from speaking with organizational employees has been "extensively debated."[40] Some states have adopted various formal standards on when lawyers may contact corporate employees.[41] Other states have evolved their own interpretations of Comment 7 or similar language, through bar ethics opinions or case law. The *Messing* case is an example.

The *Messing* case

Kathleen Stanford, a sergeant with the Harvard University Police Department, retained the law firm of Messing, Rudavsky & Weliky to file a complaint against Harvard for gender discrimination. In the course of its investigation, the firm interviewed five employees of the Harvard police

---

40. Restatement § 100, comment b, reporter's note.
41. See, e.g., Va. R. Prof. Conduct 4.2, Comment 7 (2009-2010); Tex. Disc. R. Prof. Conduct 4.02 (1989).

department, without first notifying Harvard's counsel. None of those employees had management responsibilities, but two of them had some supervisory authority over Stanford.

At the time, Massachusetts had adopted what was then the ABA's Comment to Rule 4.2, which provided that a lawyer in litigation against an organization could not communicate (without prior permission from opposing counsel) with any employee of the organization "whose statement may constitute an admission on the part of the organization." Harvard sought sanctions against the Messing law firm, alleging that it had violated Rule 4.2. The trial court agreed, and ordered the firm to pay $94,418.14 for violating the rule. It interpreted the word "admission" in this comment to mean the same thing that it meant in evidence law. That is, if the employee's statement would be admissible under the evidence rules, a lawyer was barred from talking to that employee. The trial judge conceded that this interpretation was "strikingly protective of corporations regarding employee interviews."[42]

The Messing firm appealed to the state's highest court, which reversed. The court adopted the Restatement position on which employees may be interviewed without permission of opposing counsel. The court banned contact only with those employees "who 'have managing authority sufficient to give them the right to speak for, and bind, the corporation.' Employees who can commit the organization are those with authority to make decisions about the course of the litigation, such as when to initiate suit, and when to settle a pending case."[43] This view, the court said

> would prohibit ex parte contact only with those employees who exercise managerial responsibility in the matter, who are alleged to have committed the wrongful acts at issue in the litigation, or who have authority on behalf of the corporation to make decisions about the course of the litigation. . . . Fairness to the organization does not require the presence of an attorney every time an employee may make a statement admissible in evidence against his or her employer. The public policy of promoting efficient discovery is better advanced by adopting a rule which favors the revelation of the truth by making it more difficult for an organization to prevent the disclosure of relevant evidence.[44]

Even the interviews that the law firm conducted of the two employees with some supervisory authority over Stanford were not barred because the workers did not make managerial decisions regarding the evaluation of Stanford's work.

---

42. Messing, Rudavsky & Weliky, PC v. President & Fellows of Harvard Coll., 764 N.E.2d 825, 831 (Mass. 2002).

43. Id. at 833 (quoting Wright v. Group Health Hosp., 103 Wash. 2d 192, 200 (1984)).

44. Id. at 832.

Note About *Messing*

Amendment to Rule 4.2. The ABA revised Model Rule 4.2 in 2002. It changed the comment to eliminate the restriction on contacting those whose statements could be "admissions on the part of the organization." In explaining this deletion, the Ethics 2000 Reporter's memo stated that "[t]his reference has been read by some as prohibiting communication with any person whose testimony would be admissible against the organization as an exception to the hearsay rule." The ABA also amended the comment to narrow the language restricting access to "persons having a managerial responsibility on behalf of the organization" to restrict access only to those who had managerial authority over the matter at issue.[45]

3. Restrictions on contact with unrepresented persons

On behalf of clients, lawyers routinely contact people who do not have lawyers of their own. When a lawyer or the lawyer's agent contacts an unrepresented person to obtain information or to negotiate, there is a risk that the lawyer will take advantage of his greater knowledge and sophistication. Also there is a risk that the unrepresented person will not understand if the lawyer is representing a client whose interests are adverse to his. The unrepresented person may provide information or agree to settlement terms that he would have rejected if he had obtained the advice of a lawyer. These risks are particularly worrisome when lawyers deal with unrepresented people who are indigent or who have limited education.[46] Rule 4.3 imposes some limits on lawyers' contacts with such persons. The unrepresented persons protected by this rule include, among others, those with whom a client has a dispute, potential witnesses, and experts.

---

45. ABA Ethics 2000 Commn., Reporter's Explanation of Changes to Rule 4.2, http://www.americanbar.org/groups/professional_responsibility/policy/ethics_2000_commission/e2k_rule42rem.html (last visited Nov. 23, 2012). The ABA also amended the comment to narrow the language restricting access to "persons having a managerial responsibility on behalf of the organization" to restrict access only to those who had managerial authority over the matter at issue. The Ethics 2000 Reporter's memo explaining the changes noted that the previous language had been criticized as "vague and overly broad." Id.

46. See Russell Engler, Out of Sight and Out of Line: The Need for Regulation of Lawyers' Negotiations with Unrepresented Poor Persons, 85 Cal. L. Rev. 79, 81-82 (1997).

Rule 4.3 Dealing with Unrepresented Person

Rule language*	Authors' explanation**
In dealing on behalf of a client with a person who is not represented by counsel, **a lawyer shall not state or imply that the lawyer is disinterested**.	• This part of the rule tells a lawyer what *not* to do. The lawyer should not mislead the person into thinking that the lawyer doesn't represent a client. • The lawyer should not state or imply that the lawyer is looking out for the interests of both the client and the unrepresented person.
When the lawyer knows or reasonably should know that the **unrepresented person misunderstands** the lawyer's role in the matter, the **lawyer shall** make reasonable efforts to **correct the misunderstanding**.	• This part of the rule imposes an affirmative duty on lawyers. • If the lawyer should know that the person doesn't understand the lawyer's role, the lawyer should correct any misimpression.
The lawyer shall not give legal advice to an unrepresented person, other than the advice to secure counsel, **if** the lawyer knows or reasonably should know that the interests of such a person are or have a **reasonable possibility of being in conflict with the interests of the client**.	• If there may be a conflict of interest between the client and the person with whom the lawyer is communicating, the lawyer must refrain from giving any legal advice except the advice to obtain independent counsel. • In some jurisdictions, such as the District of Columbia and Pennsylvania, Rule 4.3 bars the lawyer from giving any advice, not just legal advice, to such an unrepresented party.

*All emphasis added.

**This and other authors' explanations draw from the comments to the rules and from other sources. They are not comprehensive but highlight some important interpretive points.

How would a lawyer know that an unrepresented person misunderstands the lawyer's role?

The lawyer has to be alert to the circumstances. For example, suppose a lawyer meets with an unrepresented person on behalf of a client to negotiate a contract. If the unrepresented person says, "I have a few legal questions about this transaction that you are handling for me," it would be obvious that the unrepresented person thinks the lawyer is *his* lawyer.[47] The statement, "I have a few legal questions about this transaction," while not as clear a warning sign, at least raises the possibility that the person thinks that the lawyer's role was to serve the speaker's interests.

---

47. See Restatement § 103, comment d, illus. 2.

Must a lawyer representing a client refrain from negotiating a deal or settling a lawsuit with an unrepresented person?

No. The lawyer may even prepare the relevant documents for both parties to sign. The rule requires only that the lawyer not mislead the unrepresented party about the fact that the lawyer is representing a client.[48] The lawyer has no affirmative duty to clarify her role unless she knows or should know that the other person is confused. And if the other person's interests are at odds with those of the lawyer's client, she should not give advice to the unrepresented person except for advising the person to get a lawyer.

May a prosecutor negotiate a plea bargain with an unrepresented defendant?

The answer to this question may depend on the version of Model Rule 3.8(c) that the state has adopted. The Model Rule, which used to be the rule in Wisconsin, provides that a prosecutor should not "seek to obtain from an unrepresented accused a waiver of important pretrial rights." Many prosecutors, including those in Wisconsin, interpreted this to preclude prosecutors from bargaining for guilty pleas with unrepresented defendants, thereby waiving the defendants' right to trial.[49] But Wisconsin amended its version of Rule 3.8 to provide that a prosecutor may communicate with an unrepresented person and "negotiate a resolution which may include a waiver of constitutional and statutory rights." A subsequent Wisconsin bar opinion clarified that this language allowed plea bargaining, but that other provisions of the Wisconsin ethics code prohibited prosecutors from giving advice to unrepresented persons. Therefore, the bar concluded, the prosecutor can "discuss" negotiated resolutions of a charge but could not advise the defendant to accept a proffered bargain. The bar acknowledged that "the line between discussion and advice may not always be bright."

Does Rule 4.3 apply to a lawyer for a corporation who is dealing with employees of the corporation?

Yes. Employees of the corporation may not understand that the lawyer's duties are to the corporation, not to its officers or employees.

> FOR EXAMPLE: Suppose a corporation lawyer is investigating possible wrongdoing by an employee, and she plans to interview the employee. Because the lawyer represents the company that employs the person

---

48. See Restatement § 103, comment d.

49. Wis. St. B. Comm. on Prof. Ethics, Op. E-09-02 (2009) (available at http://www.wisbar.org/AM/Template.cfm?Section=Wisconsin_ethics_opinions&TEMPLATE=/CM/ContentDisplay.cfm&CONTENTID=79725).

being interviewed, the employee may think that he and the lawyer are "on the same side."

What disclosures should a lawyer make to an employee of an organization to clarify her role?

Rule 4.3 doesn't specify what disclosures a lawyer should make to an employee of her client organization. Professor Sarah Duggin studied internal corporate investigations and offered these and other suggestions.

- The lawyer should advise the employee at the beginning of the interview that the lawyer represents the organization rather than the individual.
- The lawyer should explain that she may share any information that the employee reveals with officers of the corporation or with law enforcement personnel or other third persons, if such disclosure is in the interest of the organization.
- The lawyer should periodically assess whether there is a risk of criminal liability for the employee being interviewed or for others and, if so, whether she should advise the employee of the option of hiring his own lawyer and of having his lawyer present during the interview.[50]

May a lawyer advise an unrepresented witness that he has a right not to talk to her opposing counsel?

Suppose a criminal defense lawyer interviews a witness about the event that led to charges against her client. Assume the witness understands the lawyer's role and that there is no conflict or potential conflict between the client's interests and those of the witness. May the lawyer tell the witness that someone from the prosecutor's office might seek to interview him, but that he doesn't have to talk to that person?

Yes. Rule 4.3 prohibits a lawyer who is communicating with an unrepresented third person on behalf of a client from giving advice to the third person if that person's interests may conflict with those of the client. If there is no such conflict, the lawyer may give this advice. In this example, the lawyer is merely advising the witness that he is not obliged to talk with the prosecutor's office.

---

50. Sarah Helene Duggin, Internal Corporate Investigations: Legal Ethics, Professionalism and the Employee Interview, 2003 Colum. Bus. L. Rev. 859, 958 (recommending several proposed ground rules for "investigative employee interviews").

May the lawyer request the unrepresented witness not to talk to the opposing counsel?

No, but there is an exception. Rule 4.3 does not address the issue of asking witnesses to refrain from talking to an adversary lawyer, but Rule 3.4(f) precludes a lawyer from asking a person other than the lawyer's own client "to refrain from voluntarily giving relevant information to another party" unless the unrepresented "person is a relative, employee, or other agent of the lawyer's client" and the lawyer believes that the witness's interests won't be harmed by his clamming up. So if the witness is a *friend* of the client, such advice is not permitted. Even if the witness were a relative, employee, or agent of the client, a lawyer should not advise him not to talk to the prosecutor unless the lawyer is sure that there would be no harm to the witness from his following the advice.[51]

If a lawyer conducts a witness interview on the telephone, may the lawyer secretly tape-record the conversation?

In some states, it is a crime to record a conversation without the consent of *all* parties. In most states, however, the consent of *one* party (e.g., the lawyer) is sufficient.[52] In 1974, the ABA issued an ethics opinion stating that secretly recording conversations was professionally improper regardless of state law.[53] Few jurisdictions agreed with the ABA opinion, however, and in 2001, the Committee on Ethics and Professionalism withdrew the old opinion and issued a new one that concluded only that lawyers should not make secret recordings in violation of state law and that secretly recording one's own client is "at the least, inadvisable."[54] The more recent opinion explained that "it is questionable whether anyone today justifiably relies on an expectation that a conversation is not being recorded by the other party, absent a special relationship with or conduct by that party inducing a belief that the conversation will not be recorded."

---

51. Comment 4 to Rule 3.4 notes that the rule "permits a lawyer to advise employees of a client to refrain from giving information to another party," but it does not advert to the Rule 3.4(f)'s second clause, allowing such advice only if the person's interests apparently would not be adversely affected.

52. Stacy L. Mills, Note, He Wouldn't Listen to Me Before, But Now . . . : Interspousal Wiretapping and an Analysis of State Wiretapping Statutes, 37 Brandeis L.J. 415, 429 (1998). For discussion of restrictions on surreptitious recording, see Clifford S. Fishman & Anne T. McKenna, Wiretapping and Eavesdropping (3d ed., Thomson Reuters/West 2007).

53. ABA Standing Comm. on Ethics & Prof. Resp., Formal Op. 74-337.

54. ABA Standing Comm. on Ethics & Prof. Resp., Formal Op. 01-422. The ABA did not conclude that surreptitiously recording a conversation with one's own client was unethical but strongly advised against it.

PROBLEM 11-2   THE COMPLAINING WITNESS

This problem is based on a hypothetical that was considered by a bar ethics committee in response to an inquiry involving facts like these.

___

You are a criminal defense lawyer. The court has appointed you to represent Nick Krutko, who has been charged with contempt of court by violating a civil protection order.

Krutko's ex-girlfriend, Lucille DiBello, claimed that Krutko had repeatedly beaten her. She went to court without a lawyer and obtained a civil protection order (a domestic violence restraining order) prohibiting Krutko from visiting or communicating with her in any way. Three weeks later, she went back to court, still with no lawyer. She claimed that Krutko had violated the order by calling her several times, pleading with her to resume their relationship, and threatening that if she did not take him back, he would beat or kill her. The judge signed the forms that initiated the pending contempt case. If DiBello can prove that Krutko threatened her after she obtained the protection order, Krutko could go to jail.

Krutko denies that he ever beat DiBello. He also denies that he called or threatened DiBello after she obtained the order. He says that she often lies. You aren't sure whether you believe him. You are aware that men who are violent toward their partners often deny that there has been any violence. Nevertheless, it is your job to represent Krutko, and DiBello has the burden of proof. Your office employs Sally Fox as a part-time investigator to interview witnesses in upcoming cases. Sally is a 19-year-old college student. She is five feet tall and very friendly; nobody ever feels threatened by her. She is congenial and charming in dealing with witnesses. Usually the people she interviews give her the information she seeks.

You are planning to send Fox to interview DiBello. She will tell DiBello that she works for Krutko's court-appointed counsel. She will ask DiBello for a detailed, signed written statement of what Krutko said and did to her. When DiBello testifies at Krutko's contempt trial, you will use any inconsistencies between her testimony and her written statement to impeach her testimony. This is standard procedure for criminal defense lawyers.

You also would like Fox to get DiBello's signature on a medical release form so that you can obtain copies of her recent medical records, especially those for treatment after the civil protection order was issued. This will allow you to identify any inconsistencies between the injuries she claims occurred and those, if any, that appear in the medical records.

You ask Krutko whether DiBello is likely to slam the door in Fox's face. He says that DiBello is likely to talk to Fox. DiBello once refused to talk to a guardian ad litem that the court had appointed for her son. When she went to a hearing on the matter, the judge chastised her for not cooperating. This really shook her up.

Questions

1. May Fox visit DiBello at all? (As your investigator, Fox must live by any ethical rules that apply to you.)[55]
2. If Fox may visit DiBello, must she advise DiBello that DiBello has no obligation to speak to her, that anything that DiBello says may be used against her in court, or that DiBello should obtain a lawyer?
3. May Fox say that she works for a lawyer who is Krutko's "court-appointed" counsel?
4. May Fox ask DiBello to sign a written statement?
5. May Fox say that DiBello "needs" to sign the release form so that you can obtain her medical records?

Up to this point, we have considered lawyers' duties to persons other than their clients, adversaries, or witnesses primarily in the context of their efforts to investigate facts. But lawyers also have duties to avoid infringing on the rights of other people, particularly their right to privacy.

If a lawyer acquires evidence of wrongdoing by someone who is not a client, should the lawyer always reveal it to public authorities?

If a lawyer learns that a person who is not a client may be engaged in wrongdoing, one might assume that the lawyer owes no duty to that person and might have a duty as a citizen to report the matter to the police or other authorities. However, Rule 4.4(a) articulates additional duties that lawyers owe to third persons. Also, a lawyer could be civilly or criminally liable for failure to respect the rights of a third party. For example, if a lawyer violates

---

55. The ethical rules bind only lawyers. But lawyers are required under Rule 5.3 to "make reasonable efforts to ensure" that their employees comply with the rules. A lawyer could be disciplined for not giving an employee proper guidance. Lawyers are responsible for rules violations by their employees if they order the misconduct or ratify it. Also, Rule 8.4(a) prohibits a lawyer from violating an ethical rule through the acts of another.

the privacy of the third party or takes possession of property stolen from the third party, the lawyer could be liable for such conduct.

Rule 4.4(a) Respect for Rights of Third Persons
In representing a client, a lawyer shall not use means that have no substantial purpose other than to embarrass, delay, or burden a third person, or use methods of obtaining evidence that violate the legal rights of such a person.

Comment

[1] Responsibility to a client requires a lawyer to subordinate the interests of others to those of the client, but that responsibility does not imply that a lawyer may disregard the rights of third persons. It is impractical to catalogue all such rights, but they include legal restrictions on methods of obtaining evidence from third persons. . . .

[2]. . . . [T]his Rule does not address the legal duties of a lawyer who receives a document that the lawyer knows or reasonably should know may have been wrongfully obtained by the sending person. . . .

PROBLEM 11-3 THE BREAK-IN

This problem is based on a case that Professor Lerman handled many years ago.

You represent Cheryl Gardner in a suit against her ex-husband Ron to obtain sole custody of her two daughters, Evie and Rachel, who are five and seven. Cheryl believes that Ron has been molesting the girls during visitation and that he is about to kidnap them and take them to Kuwait, where he is going to work for a petroleum company. You are worried about the children's safety, but it is not clear whether or to what extent Cheryl's fears are well grounded. You have ascertained that Ron has obtained passports for the children. Neither girl says that her father has molested her, and the county's sex abuse program has examined the girls and found no evidence of abuse. Ron's lawyer has been arguing vigorously that Ron should have at least joint custody.

One day Cheryl bursts into your office looking furious but excited. For months she's been saying that her ex-husband was molesting the girls, but Department of Social Services officials have not believed her, and she hasn't had a shred of tangible evidence.

She opens her tote bag and produces a stack of documents. She reports that she broke into Ron's house, climbing in through an unlocked window, and "borrowed" the originals of these documents, which she photocopied and then returned to the house. Cheryl leaves the documents with you to review.

You have examined the product of Cheryl's expedition. One set of documents consists of photocopies of photos of the two girls, both nude and posed in positions that might be considered titillating. Another is a photocopy of Ron's girlfriend's diary, including an entry observing that Ron often crawls into bed with his daughters to sleep. A third is a draft of a novel by Ron in which the population of the planet has been annihilated by a nuclear war, except for two people, a father and his young teenage daughter. During the course of the novel, the daughter persuades the father that they must procreate for the preservation of the human race. Then she seduces him.

What should you do with these documents? Your client is willing to allow you to make whatever use of them you think best. But these are private documents containing information that Cheryl stole from Ron's house, in violation of state law. Consider Rules 1.2(d), 3.4(a), 4.4, and 8.4. (Assume that the state's child abuse reporting statute does not apply to lawyers.)

Evaluate the following options:

- Return? Does any disciplinary rule require you to return the copies to Ron or to notify him that you have received them?
- Negotiate? Would it violate any rules to use these documents in negotiating with Ron's lawyer about custody or to push for a better financial settlement for Cheryl?

Note: Stolen documents as evidence

Some courts have excluded evidence that was improperly or illegally obtained from the opposing party.[56] When such evidence is excluded, the court may also disqualify the lawyer who received the evidence from representing her own client. But some courts have excluded the

---

56. In re Shell Oil Refinery, 143 F.R.D. 105 (E.D. La. 1992) (ordering the suppression of documents obtained by the plaintiff outside the discovery process from an anonymous employee of the defendant); see also Lipin v. Bender, 644 N.E.2d 1300 (N.Y. 1994) (plaintiff's action dismissed because during a deposition, while lawyers were arguing outside the room, plaintiff took and copied documents left sitting on deposition table).

57. Restatement § 60, comment m, reporter's note.

improperly obtained evidence without disqualifying the lawyer.[57] Uncertainty about whether the evidence would be excluded at trial may be a factor in each side's judgment about terms on which to settle a case.

B. Duties of prosecutors

In general, the rules of conduct apply uniformly to all lawyers. Large- and small-firm lawyers, legal aid lawyers, and solo practitioners all have the same obligations. But prosecutors have some extra duties because they have extra powers. Prosecutors can influence decisions that may ultimately lead to the deprivation of a person's liberty or even life. As a comment to the rules puts it, a prosecutor is a "minister of justice."[58] In addition, even if the target of a prosecutor's investigation is not convicted, an indictment or even an investigation of the person may destroy his reputation and require him to spend thousands of dollars on legal fees. Therefore the ethics rules impose a few particular additional responsibilities on prosecutors.[59]

Do we need special ethical rules for prosecutors? Prosecutors are government officials and law enforcement officers. Don't they take care to protect the rights of both victims and defendants?[60]

Many prosecutors have an acute sense of responsibility to the justice system. But a number of them have political ambitions, and many others have made their reputations by aggressively prosecuting high-profile cases. In certain offices, those who obtain "the highest conviction rates (and, thus, reputations as the best performers) stand the greatest chance for advancement internally,"[61] so some prosecutors are tempted to win their cases at any cost. In 1999, two *Chicago Tribune* reporters wrote a five-part series

---

58. Rule 3.8, Comment 1.

59. In addition to the obligations discussed here, Rule 3.8 requires prosecutors to make reasonable efforts to assure that an accused has been advised of the right to counsel and has had reasonable opportunity to obtain counsel; bars prosecutors from seeking waivers of important rights from unrepresented persons; directs prosecutors to refrain from issuing subpoenas to lawyers about their clients "unless the prosecutor reasonably believes" that a lawyer's evidence is not privileged and is "essential"; and bars extrajudicial statements about pending cases "that have a substantial likelihood of heightening public condemnation of the accused" except for those that "serve a legitimate law enforcement purpose."

60. See Berger v. U.S., 295 U.S. 78, 88 (1935) (prosecutor's duty is not to "win a case, but that justice shall be done").

61. Daniel S. Medwed, The Zeal Deal: Prosecutorial Resistance to Post-Conviction Claims of Innocence, 84 B.U. L. Rev. 125, 134-135 (2004).

of articles describing extensive prosecutorial misconduct.[62] The entire series is worth reading. We offer an excerpt from the first article.

Ken Armstrong & Maurice Possley, Trial and Error, Part 1: Verdict: Dishonor

Chicago Tribune (Jan. 10, 1999)

With impunity, prosecutors across the country have violated their oaths and the law, committing the worst kinds of deception in the most serious of cases. They have prosecuted black men, hiding evidence the real killers were white. They have prosecuted a wife, hiding evidence her husband committed suicide. They have prosecuted parents, hiding evidence their daughter was killed by wild dogs.

They do it to win.

They do it because they won't get punished.

They have done it to defendants who came within hours of being executed, only to be exonerated.

In the first study of its kind, a *Chicago Tribune* analysis of thousands of court records, appellate rulings and lawyer disciplinary records from across the United States has found:

■ Since a 1963 U.S. Supreme Court ruling designed to curb misconduct by prosecutors, at least 381 defendants nationally have had a homicide conviction thrown out because prosecutors concealed evidence suggesting innocence or presented evidence they knew to be false. Of all the ways that prosecutors can cheat, those two are considered the worst by the courts. And that number represents only a fraction of how often such cheating occurs.

■ The U.S. Supreme Court has declared such misconduct by prosecutors to be so reprehensible that it warrants criminal charges and disbarment. But not one of those prosecutors was convicted of a crime. Not one was barred from practicing law. Instead, many saw their careers advance, becoming judges or district attorneys. One became a congressman.

■ Of the 381 defendants, 67 had been sentenced to death. They include Verneal Jimerson of Illinois and Kirk Bloodsworth of Maryland, both later exonerated by DNA tests; Randall Dale Adams of Texas, whose wrongful conviction was revealed by the documentary *The Thin Blue*

---

62. Ken Armstrong & Maurice Possley, Trial and Error: How Prosecutors Sacrifice Justice to Win, Chi. Trib. (Jan. 10-14, 1999) (series is available at http://www.chicagotribune.com/news/nationworld/chi-dptrialerror-special,1,1581428.special).

Line; and Sonia Jacobs of Florida, who was eventually freed but whose boyfriend, convicted on virtually identical evidence, had already been executed by the time her appeal prevailed.

■ Nearly 30 of those 67 Death Row inmates — or about half of those whose cases have been resolved — were subsequently freed. But almost all first spent at least five years in prison. One served 26 years before his conviction was reversed and the charges dropped. . . .

■ The failure of prosecutors to obey the demands of justice — and the legal system's failure to hold them accountable for it — leads to wrongful convictions, and retrials and appeals that cost taxpayers millions of dollars. It also fosters a corrosive distrust in a branch of government that America holds up as a standard to the world.

Other studies have come to similar conclusions. A study of 707 California cases in which judges found prosecutorial misconduct — such as improperly withholding exculpatory evidence from the defense — during the period 1997 to 2009 revealed that convictions were nevertheless upheld in 548 of them, on the ground that the defendants received fair trials anyway. Despite 600 judicial findings of prosecutorial misconduct in which the court had named the offending prosecutor, in only 10 cases during this period was a prosecutor subjected to discipline by the bar.[63]

1. Undercover investigations

Do prosecutors' undercover investigations (e.g., those that infiltrate police officers into criminal conspiracies) violate Rules 4.1 and 4.2?

In some undercover investigations, prosecutors direct police officers to conceal their identities while infiltrating criminal groups. (Some such investigations are not directed by lawyers.) If a prosecutor is directing an investigation, she arguably violates the rule prohibiting materially false statements and the rule against contact with represented persons. There is little case law interpreting Rule 4.1 in application to criminal investigations,[64] but numerous cases have involved alleged violations of Rule 4.2 by prosecutors or their delegates. A 2007 decision from the Supreme Court of

---

63. Kathleen M. Ridolfi & Maurice Possley, Preventable Error: A Report on Prosecutorial Misconduct in California, 1997-2009 (Oct. 2010) (available at http://law.scu.edu/ncip/file/ProsecutorialMisconduct_BookEntire_online%20version.pdf).

64. One exception is U.S. v. Whittaker, 201 F.R.D. 363 (2001), where a district court found that an assistant U.S. attorney violated Rule 4.1 by sending a letter to the target of a fraud investigation (who was later indicted) falsely notifying him that the government believed he was a victim of fraud. The court disqualified the U.S. Attorney's Office from prosecuting the target. The court of appeals

Minnesota summarized the application of Minnesota Rule 4.2 in this context as follows:

> When a government attorney is involved in a criminal matter such that [Rule 4.2] applies, the state may not have *any* communication with a represented criminal defendant about the subject of the representation unless (1) the state first obtains the lawyer's consent; (2) the communication is "authorized by law" . . . ; or (3) the state obtains a court order authorizing the communication.[65]

The court referenced Comment 5 following Rule 4.2 to explain that the "authorized by law" exception may cover communications that occur prior to the filing of charges. Comment 5 provides:

> Communications authorized by law may . . . include investigative activities of lawyers representing governmental entities, directly or through investigative agents, prior to the commencement of criminal or civil enforcement proceedings.[66]

The Minnesota court found that Rule 4.2 had been violated by two law enforcement officers conducting post-arraignment interviews with a defendant without the consent of his lawyer, but that suppression of the resulting evidence was not warranted in that case.

Some courts have found that pre-indictment contact by prosecutors with represented persons does not violate Rule 4.2. One decision by then-Judge Samuel Alito concluded that prohibiting such contacts "would significantly hamper legitimate law enforcement operations by making it very difficult to investigate certain individuals."[67]

In Virginia, as in other states, practicing law without a license is a crime.[68] But some unscrupulous people commit the crime, preying on clients (including many new immigrants) who would not think to verify that a "lawyer" offering to represent them was in fact a lawyer. In the years after the *Gatti* decision, the Virginia bar's committee on unauthorized practice was fearful that undercover "sting" operations to ferret out unlicensed practitioners would violate Rules 4.1 and 4.2. It simply stopped

---

reversed the disqualification because the U.S. Attorney's Office had sent the letter containing the false statement by mistake. U.S. v. Whittaker, 268 F.3d 185 (3d Cir. 2001).

65. State v. Clark, 2007 WL 2671264 (Minn. 2007); see also In re Howes, 940 P.2d 159, 167 (N.M. 1997) (federal prosecutor disciplined for post-arrest interview; "even where an attorney's actions do not violate constitutional standards, they may still be in violation" of the rule).

66. Comment 5 continues: "When communicating with the accused in a criminal matter, a government lawyer must comply with this Rule in addition to honoring the constitutional rights of the accused. The fact that a communication does not violate a state or federal constitutional right is insufficient to establish that the communication is permissible under this Rule."

67. U.S. v. Balter, 91 F.3d 427, 436 (3d Cir. 1996).

68. This crime is discussed in the next chapter.

conducting undercover investigations. But in June 2009, the Virginia bar issued an opinion authorizing such operations, provided that there was no reasonable alternative method for collecting the evidence.[69]

Federal prosecutors have faced similar issues. For years they fought for a blanket exemption from state ethics' rules limitations on their investigative contacts and deceptive tactics in undercover investigations. In 1994, the Department of Justice adopted a policy allowing its prosecutors to communicate directly with suspects who were known to have lawyers without first informing the lawyers or getting permission from a court.[70] This practice was successfully challenged by Representative Joseph McDade (R-Pa.), who "had been out to harness federal prosecutors since he was acquitted of bribery and racketeering charges."[71]

In 1998, Congress passed the McDade Amendment, which provides that "an attorney for the Government shall be subject to State laws and rules, and local Federal court rules, governing attorneys in each State where such attorney engages in that attorney's duties, to the same extent and in the same manner as other attorneys in that State."[72] This amendment evidently subjects lawyers working for the federal government to all applicable state ethics rules, not merely Rule 4.2. For several years the executive branch of the federal government tried to persuade Congress to repeal the McDade Amendment, arguing that "abiding by state ethics rules . . . would hamper use of undercover agents and informants."[73] Congress did not repeal the amendment, and in 1999, the Department of Justice established its Professional Responsibility Advisory Office.[74] That office helps the Department's lawyers comply with the obligations that the amendment imposes.[75] The enactment of the McDade Amendment seems to have had little effect on the ability of federal prosecutors to direct pre-indictment communications with a represented suspect. This is because "[t]he McDade Amendment's lone function was to make state rules of professional responsibility applicable to the conduct of Government attorneys . . . [and the authorized by law exception for prosecutors] is part and parcel of Rule 4.2."[76] The Justice Department states that "generally, the case law recognizes

---

69. Karen Sloan, Virginia Bar Investigators Dust Off Their Cloaks and Daggers, Law.com (July 17, 2009), http://www.law.com/jsp/law/LawArticleFriendly.jsp?id=1202432340841.

70. Stephanie B. Goldberg, Questioning New DOJ Rule: Direct-Contact Policy Disregards ABA Rule 4.2, 80 ABA J. 101 (1994).

71. Walter Pincus, Revisiting Rules for Federal Prosecutors; Senate Bill Aims to Resolve Long-Running Dispute Between Justice Dept., State Bars, Wash. Post A6 (Feb. 10, 1999).

72. 28 U.S.C. § 530B (2006).

73. Pincus, supra n. 71.

74. U.S. Dept. of Justice, Professional Responsibility Advisory Office, http://www.usdoj.gov/prao/ (accessed Nov. 23, 2012).

75. Dept. of Justice, Prof. Resp. Advisory Off., 70 Fed. Reg. 76163-64 (2005).

76. U.S. v. Grass, 239 F. Supp. 2d 535, 545 (M.D. Pa. 2003).

covert contacts in non-custodial and pre-indictment situations as 'authorized by law' [and] a few courts have recognized such an exception [to Rule 4.2] in connection with overt, pre-indictment contacts during a criminal investigation."[77] While the case law on this issue remains sparse, the same distinction may evolve in applying Rule 4.2 to state prosecutors. That is, 4.2 may be interpreted in favor of allowing prosecutors to have contact with suspects before they are charged (or allowing them to direct investigations involving contact with such suspects), but it may be held to prohibit such contact, without the consent of the defendant's lawyer, once a charge is filed.

PROBLEM 11-4 THE PROSECUTOR'S MASQUERADE

This problem is closely based on actual events in a western city.

You are the district attorney in a small city. The police have called you to a crime scene in an apartment. Three women lie brutally murdered. Their heads have been split open with an axe. Stacey Blankenwell, an eyewitness to the murders, is in the apartment.

Stacey recounts the following story. A man abducted her and the other women and took them, one by one, to the apartment. He identified himself as Ward Flood. Then he tied Blankenwell to a bed, raped her, and forced her to watch as he killed the others. He also dictated details of his crimes into a tape recorder. Finally, he left the apartment, instructing Blankenwell to call the police and to page him by calling a specified telephone number when they arrived. She followed his instructions. Flood then telephoned the apartment from a cell phone.

When Flood called, a police officer who was in the apartment answered the phone and talked with him for three and a half hours. Flood told the officer all the details of his crimes. The police recorded the call but were unable to trace Flood's location.

Flood told the police that he could still kill more people and that he would not surrender until he had legal representation. He demanded guarantees that if he turned himself in, he would be isolated from other prisoners and would be allowed cigarettes. He wanted assistant public defender Harrison Biaggi to be his lawyer. Biaggi had represented him on a previous criminal charge.

77. U.S. Dept. of Justice, Communications with Represented Persons — Issues for Consideration, 9 U.S. Atty.'s Man. § 296(G), http://www.usdoj.gov/usao/eousa/foia_reading_room/usam/title9/crm00296.htm (accessed Nov. 23, 2012).

The police told Flood that they would try to locate a public defender for him. Then they consulted you about whether they should call any lawyer for Flood while he was still at large and capable of killing more people. You were ambivalent about doing so because you knew that any lawyer would tell Flood not to continue talking with the police. You found Biaggi's number in a telephone book that was in the apartment. He was now apparently in private practice. You called the number and felt relieved when a recording stated that the number was no longer in service.

Suddenly, a plan occurred to you. You could get on the telephone and tell Flood that you were an assistant public defender. You could then "negotiate" with the police and arrange for his peaceful surrender in exchange for the promises he sought of isolation and cigarettes. You will see to it that he in fact receives those minor benefits after he surrenders.

Should you do it? If so, should you simply negotiate the terms of the surrender, or should you try to get information during your conversation with Flood that would assist in obtaining his conviction?

---

2. Required investigation by prosecutors before charges are filed

> **Rule 3.8(a) Special Responsibilities of a Prosecutor**
> **The prosecutor in a criminal case shall ... refrain from prosecuting a charge that the prosecutor knows is not supported by probable cause.**

Rule 3.8(a) is the prosecutor's analogue to Rule 3.1. The Restatement elaborates the special responsibility of prosecutors articulated in Rule 3.8, explaining that a prosecutor may not file a criminal case without a "belief, formed after due investigation, that there are good factual and legal grounds" for it.[78] This rule imposes a standard for filing criminal charges similar to the standard imposed by Rule 11 for civil plaintiffs' lawyers.

---

78. Restatement § 97(3). The ABA's Standards Relating to the Administration of Criminal Justice, The Prosecution Function (ABA 1993), are not binding on officials, but they would impose a higher standard. They provide that a prosecutor should not institute a criminal charge in the absence of "sufficient admissible evidence to support a conviction." Standard 3-3.9(a). At least some commentators argue, however, that a prosecutor may appropriately bring a charge even though on the basis of the evidence the prosecutor herself, applying the "beyond a reasonable doubt" standard, would not, in the role of a juror, vote to convict. Thus, where a prosecutor knows from years of experience that identification of a black defendant by an elderly white robbery victim who glimpsed

Professor
Bruce A. Green

As to criminal cases, Professor Bruce Green notes that Rule 3.8(a) "adds nothing to the standard already established by law" because the law already requires criminal charges to be supported by probable cause. Rather than imposing extra duties on prosecutors, then, this rule simply imports the existing legal standard into the ethics code.

The probable cause standard, Green points out, is pretty low. "Under the probable cause standard," Green writes, "it does not have to be 'more likely than not' that the accused is guilty. All that is needed is a fair possibility of guilt, something more than a 'reasonable suspicion.'"[79] He notes that the ethics rule does not require a prosecutor to seek readily available exculpatory evidence, so a decision to prosecute can be based on one-sided information.[80] By contrast, the District of Columbia's ethics rules direct that a prosecutor may not "intentionally avoid pursuit of evidence or information because it may damage the prosecution's case or aid the defense."[81]

Professor Fred Zacharias explains that prosecutors are rarely disciplined for initiating proceedings based on skimpy evidence because "so long as some evidence supports a criminal charge, observers typically disagree over the propriety of a prosecutor's decision to support a police arrest pending further investigation."[82] Despite the relative infrequency of discipline, it is important for prosecutors to conduct independent investigations into the evidence before initiating criminal charges. If a prosecutor files charges without an adequate basis, then even if the defendant is ultimately acquitted, the charges may damage the reputation of the person charged and disrupt his life.[83]

3. Concealment of exculpatory evidence

In 1963, the U.S. Supreme Court held in *Brady v. Maryland* that "the suppression by the prosecution of evidence favorable to an accused upon request violates due process where the evidence is material either to guilt or to punishment, irrespective of the good faith or bad faith of the

---

him only briefly may be flawed despite the victim's apparent certainty and would vote to acquit on this basis, the prosecutor, it is argued, may nevertheless bring the robbery charge. H. Richard Uviller, The Virtuous Prosecutor in Quest of an Ethical Standard: Guidance from the ABA, 71 Mich. L. Rev. 1145, 1157-1159 (1973).

79. Bruce Green, Prosecutorial Ethics as Usual, 2003 U. Ill. L. Rev. 1573, 1589-1590.
80. Id.
81. D.C. R. Prof. Conduct 3.8.
82. Fred Zacharias, The Professional Discipline of Prosecutors, 79 N.C. L. Rev. 721, 736 (2001).
83. Restatement § 97, comment h.

prosecution."[84] The Supreme Court later decided that prosecutors must disclose exculpatory evidence to the defense even if the defendant has not requested it.[85] This rule is codified in Rule 3.8(d), which states:

The prosecutor in a criminal case shall: ...

(d) make timely disclosure to the defense of all evidence or information known to the prosecutor that tends to negate the guilt of the accused or mitigates the offense, and, in connection with sentencing, disclose to the defense and to the tribunal all unprivileged mitigating information known to the prosecutor, except when the prosecutor is relieved of this responsibility by a protective order of the tribunal.

Notes about prosecutorial misconduct

1. *Nifong.* Even though the law is clear, prosecutors do not always disclose exculpatory evidence. For example, in 2006, Michael B. Nifong, the district attorney of Durham, North Carolina, was facing an election primary. During this period, a young African American woman who had worked as a stripper at a party hosted by some Duke University students claimed that some of the students had sexually assaulted her during the party. Nifong filed charges against three men who were identified by the young woman. The defendants were members of the Duke lacrosse team. The accusation was all over the print and broadcast media throughout the country. A month later, Nifong learned that DNA testing showed that genetic material from several men had been found on the stripper, but none of it matched the DNA of the accused athletes. Nifong withheld this information from defense counsel for six months and lied to the court, saying he had turned over all exculpatory evidence to the defense. Eventually Nifong released the information to defense counsel, but buried it in more than 1800 pages of laboratory data. It took defense lawyers another month to find the exonerating evidence. Nifong was disbarred and convicted of contempt of court. He was sentenced to only a single day in jail.[86]

---

84. 373 U.S. 83, 87 (1963).

85. U.S. v. Agurs, 427 U.S. 97 (1976).

86. Duff Wilson, Hearing Ends in Disbarment for Prosecutor in Duke Case, N.Y. Times (June 16, 2007) (available at http://query.nytimes.com/gst/fullpage.html?res=950 CE3DE123FF934A25755C0A9619C8B63); Duke Lacrosse Prosecutor to be Disbarred, District Attorney's Actions Motivated by Upcoming Election, Disciplinary Committee Chairman Says, Grand Rapid Press (June 17, 2007); WRAL.com, Nifong Guilty of Criminal Contempt; Sentenced to 1 Day in Jail (Sept. 1, 2007) (available at http://www.wral.com/news/local/story/1763323/).

The most unusual aspect of the *Nifong* case is that it occurred at all; a prosecutor not only was charged by a state bar but actually disbarred for misconduct in a criminal prosecution. In fact, "as scholars note, prosecutors rarely receive ethical sanctions for their misconduct, even when it leads to wrongful conviction."[87] The North Carolina bar may have acted so swiftly and decisively in this case because both Nifong's charges against the athletes and their lawyers' complaints about prosecutorial misconduct (including improper statements to the press and withholding of exculpatory evidence) received national media attention for months.

2. **Evidence from DNA exonerations.** Prosecutorial suppression of exculpatory evidence may not be as rare as one would hope. The Innocence Project found that prosecutorial misconduct was a "factor" in 33 of the first 74 exonerations as a result of DNA evidence. More than a third of those 33 instances were cases in which prosecutors had destroyed or suppressed exculpatory evidence.[88] Another study looked at all death penalty verdicts that were imposed and fully reviewed from 1973 to 1995. Sixty-eight of them were reversed by courts due to serious error.[89] In that study, prosecutorial suppression of evidence or other police or prosecutorial misconduct accounted for 18 to 19 percent of the reversals.[90]

3. **The California controversy.** In 2010, the California State Bar's Board of Governors proposed a major revision of the state's ethics code to the California Supreme Court. It included adding Rule 3.8(d) to the state code. But California prosecutors "protested strenuously," insisting that the ethics code should not demand more extensive or more prompt disclosure of exculpatory evidence than the Constitution required. In the next draft of the proposal, Rule 3.8(d) was omitted. The draft proposed only that prosecutors had to comply with all statutory and constitutional requirements for disclosure. The prosecutors objected to that requirement as well, on the ground that case law in California, interpreting state statutes, imputed the misconduct of junior prosecutors to their boss, and prosecutors should not be subject to discipline if a member of a prosecution team withheld information without the knowledge of the chief prosecutor.

---

87. Jane Campbell Moriarty, Misconvictions, Science and the Ministers of Justice, 86 Neb. L. Rev. 1 (2007).

88. Innocence Project, Understand the Causes: Government Misconduct, http://www.innocenceproject.org/understand/Government-Misconduct.php (last visited Nov. 23, 2012).

89. James S. Liebman, Jeffrey Fagan, Andrew Gelman, Valerie West, Garth Davies & Alexander Kiss, A Broken System Part II: Why There Is So Much Error in Capital Cases and What Can Be Done About It (Feb. 11, 2002) (available at http://www2.law.columbia.edu/brokensystem2/index2.html).

90. Id. at § II.C (available at http://www2.law.columbia.edu/brokensystem2/sectionIIc.html).

The proposal was watered down further to require only that prosecutors comply with their constitutional obligations.[91]

4. Unreliable evidence

A study published in 2005 concluded that "erroneous forensic science expert testimony [was] the second most common contributing factor to wrongful convictions."[92] The evidence referred to is erroneous expert testimony identifying a defendant through faulty lab work, such as erroneous microscopic hair comparisons. Usually the errors are simply mistakes by expert witnesses, although deliberate falsification of laboratory results has occurred as well.[93]

Professor Jane Moriarty

Professor Jane Moriarty argues that except for DNA evidence, much of the forensic comparison evidence admitted in criminal cases (including bullet lead, microscopic hair, shoe prints, and even fingerprint comparisons) does not meet scientific reliability standards. She explains that in criminal cases, judges routinely admit forensic evidence that does not comply with acceptable scientific methodology and likely would not satisfy courts in civil cases. To curb excessive reliance on dubious forensic expert testimony, Moriarty advocates amending the ABA Model Rules to require prosecutors to "make reasonable efforts to assure that only reliable expert evidence is admitted into evidence" and to prohibit them from using evidence that they know or reasonably should know is unreliable.[94]

Suppose that a prosecutor obtains a conviction without committing misconduct but later learns information that suggests the defendant may be innocent. Do the ethical rules impose any duty on the prosecutor to try to reopen the case?

Until 2008, prosecutors who learned that a convicted defendant might be innocent had no duty to act. In 2008, however, the ABA's House of

---

91. Joan C. Rogers, Model Rules: In Its Final Look at Full Set of Updates, California Bar Endorses Last Seven Rules, ABA/BNA Laws.' Man. on Prof. Conduct 26:619 (Oct. 13, 2010), 2010 WL 3973601.

92. Michael J. Saks & Jonathan J. Koehler, The Coming Paradigm Shift in Forensic Identification Science, 309 Sci. 892, 893 (2005) (available at http://www.sciencemag.org/content/309/5736/892.abstract).

93. See In the Matter of an Investigation of the W. Va. St. Police Crime Lab., Serology Div., 438 S.E.2d 501, 503 (W. Va. 1993).

94. Moriarty, supra n. 87, at 28.

Delegates amended Rule 3.8 to add new obligations for prosecutors in this situation. In states that adopt the amendment, a prosecutor who obtains "new, credible and material evidence creating a reasonable likelihood that a convicted defendant did not commit an offense of which the defendant was convicted" must disclose the evidence to an "appropriate court or authority." Also, if the defendant had been prosecuted locally, the prosecutor must make a reasonable effort to investigate whether an innocent person was convicted. Prosecutors with clear and convincing evidence of the innocence of a convicted person must seek to remedy the conviction.[95]

It is not always easy for a prosecutor to decide when to seek the exoneration of a person who may have been wrongfully convicted. This problem is even more difficult when a more senior prosecutor disagrees with the person making the judgment.

> **FOR EXAMPLE:** In 2005, Daniel Bibb was an assistant district attorney in New York, reporting to District Attorney Robert M. Morgenthau. Bibb had worked in the district attorney's office for 21 years and was planning to spend his whole career there; it was the only job he had ever wanted.
>
> Fifteen years earlier, Bibb's office had obtained murder convictions of Olmedo Hidalgo and David Lemus for killing a man outside a famous nightclub. The defendants had been in prison ever since. But after press investigations suggested that someone else had committed the murder, Hidalgo and Lemus's lawyers moved to reopen the conviction. Morgenthau told Bibb to investigate. After interviewing some eyewitnesses who were unknown to Hidalgo and Lemus's lawyers, Bibb became fully convinced that the two men had been wrongly convicted. Bibb urged Morgenthau that the district attorney's office should join the effort to exonerate the men. But Morgenthau was facing a contentious reelection contest,[96] and he ordered Bibb to defend the convictions in court. Bibb did so, but he also secretly collaborated with the defense counsel. Bibb told them about the existence of the witnesses he'd uncovered, told witnesses what questions he would ask them, and refrained from cross-examining defense witnesses aggressively. He said he "did the best I could — to lose." "I was angry," he said, "that I was being put in a position to defend convictions that I didn't believe in." Hidalgo and Lemus were exonerated.
>
> In 2008, when Bibb revealed what he'd done, the New York bar authorities opened an investigation of whether he had violated his

---

95. ABA Model R. Prof. Conduct 3.8(g) and (h).

96. Morgenthau was being opposed for reelection by Leslie Crocker Snyder, who accused Morgenthau of prosecuting innocent men.

ethical obligations to his client. Bibb resigned from his job. The bar eventually ended its investigation without recommending discipline. Ethics experts split in their evaluation of what Bibb should have done.[97]

5. Enforcement

How should the ethical rules against prosecutorial misconduct be enforced? Professor Ellen Yaroshefsky suggests that state bar discipline cannot be relied upon to ensure proper conduct by prosecutors.

Ellen Yaroshefsky, Wrongful Convictions: It Is Time to Take Prosecution Discipline Seriously

8 D.C. L. Rev. 275 (2004)

Professor Ellen Yaroshefsky

Few public prosecutors are brought before disciplinary committees. . . . While all courts, prosecutors, and defenders would certainly agree that it is "highly reprehensible" to suppress facts or secrete evidence "capable of establishing the innocence of the accused," when that happens, the disciplinary consequence is often nil. . . . The prosecutorial misconduct in [the cases of defendants who were convicted, sentenced to death, and later exonerated] cannot be readily excused as mistakes or errors of judgment. In the vast majority of cases, the misconduct was deemed to be grossly negligent or intentional. Few of those prosecutors were disciplined, either internally or through the state disciplinary system. And, while there has yet to be a systematic analysis of the

---

97. Professor Steven Lubet has said that what Bibb did was wrong, and Professor Stephen Gillers has said that Bibb's "conscience does not entitle him to subvert his client's case." But Professor David Luban has argued that Bibb "did the right thing" because "the prosecutor's role is to seek justice, not merely to convict." Benjamin Weiser, Lawyer Who Threw a City Case Is Vindicated, N.Y. Times (Mar. 5, 2009) (available at http://www.nytimes.com/2009/03/05/nyregion/05da.html? ref=palladiumnyc); David Luban, When a Good Prosecutor Throws a Case, Legal Profession Blog, http://lawprofessors.typepad.com/legal_profession/2008/06/when-a-good-pro.html (June 24, 2008); David Luban, The Conscience of a Prosecutor, 45 Val. U. L. Rev. 1 (2010) (available at http:// scholarship.law.georgetown.edu/cgi/viewcontent.cgi?article=1366&context=facpub).   New York paid $2.6 million to Hidalgo. Benjamin Weiser, Settlement for Man Wrongly Convicted in Palladium Killing, N.Y. Times (Mar. 30, 2009) (available at http://www.nytimes.com/2009/03/31/ nyregion/31palladium.html). Professor Luban notes that although Rule 3.8(h) had not been adopted at the time of Bibb's actions, the applicable standard in New York as well as the Supreme Court's statement in *Berger*, quoted in n. 60, supra, provided that the duty of a prosecutor was to seek justice, not merely convictions.

now 140 exonerations by category and severity of error, the existent analyses confirm that prosecutors have rarely been held accountable for their behavior. With rare exception, there has been no discipline for egregious instances of misconduct that led to these convictions. . . .

Secrecy is the hallmark of most disciplinary proceedings and significant change in openness of the process is highly unlikely in most jurisdictions. If discipline is to serve as a deterrent to prosecutorial misconduct, the process and its results cannot be secret.[98] It is more likely that the creation of an independent disciplinary body will begin as an open process.

[Also,] without significant additional resources, state bar disciplinary authorities are unlikely to undertake this work. Even, however, in the unlikely event that sufficient funds were made available to consider adequately allegations of prosecutorial misconduct, and even if such disciplinary committees hired criminal justice professionals, both the lack of perceived influence of those committees in most jurisdictions and the orientation of disciplinary committees as reactive to individual complaints are sufficient reasons to establish an independent commission to monitor disciplinary matters for the prosecutors. Obviously, these issues merit serious discussion in each state.

However configured, a system of highly regarded professionals independent of prosecutors' offices is essential to a workable system of accountability. Only such a commission can assume the mantle of authority and engender the respect necessary to undertake such a task. To be a serious effort, it should be one of peer review by experienced criminal justice professionals with the power to sanction prosecutors who engage in misconduct. While such an alternative to existing disciplinary committees might be termed "overenthusiastic," there does not appear to be a realistic alternative. . . .

What happens to prosecutors whose convictions are reversed because prosecutorial misconduct is discovered?

Often, nothing. In fact, judges who overturn convictions because of prosecutorial misconduct usually take care not to mention the name of the

---

98. [Yaroshefsky here cites Bruce Green, Policing Federal Prosecutors: Do Too Many Regulators Produce Too Little Enforcement?, 8 St. Thomas L. Rev. 69 (1995).] Green's article states that "Despite recent calls for increased accountability, most state disciplinary authorities continue to conduct their investigations and hearings in secret, with no public record made of the filing of a complaint and, in many instances, no public disclosure of the committee's ultimate determination. Many disciplinary committees make liberal use of private sanctions when minor wrongdoing is found. Only when the committee imposes either a public reprimand or a more serious sanction, such as suspension or disbarment, will the public learn of its proceedings. As a consequence, it is impossible to know how often federal prosecutors have come under investigation by state disciplinary committees or even how often federal prosecutors have been sanctioned for misconduct." Id. at 88.

offending prosecutors in their opinions. The names are made public only about 25 percent of the time. One authority has called for naming the prosecutor in all cases of serious prosecutorial misconduct, both to deter it and to enable judges to monitor the conduct of those who repeatedly cause problems.[99]

C. Conduct prejudicial to the administration of justice

In this chapter, we have considered many duties that lawyers owe to people whom they encounter, including judges, adversaries, and witnesses. Some of the rules governing lawyers' conduct are quite specific, like the advocate-witness rule; others are very general, like the prohibition of "deceit" in Rule 8.4(c). Lawyers should also be aware of the most general of all of the rules, Rule 8.4(d), which provides that it is professional misconduct for a lawyer to "engage in conduct that is prejudicial to the administration of justice." Under this rule, lawyers have been disciplined for improper actions relating both to clients and to other persons.

This provision is a kind of catchall that exhorts people to act honorably, without defining the behavior that could cause a lawyer to be disciplined or even disbarred. It has been challenged repeatedly on the ground that it is unconstitutionally vague, but all of the challenges have been rejected by the courts.[100]

The comments that follow Rule 8.4 mention that a lawyer who knowingly manifests bias or prejudice on such grounds as race, sex, religion, and sexual orientation "in the course of representing a client" violates the rule if "such actions are prejudicial to the administration of justice."[101] Lawyers have been disciplined under the standard of Rule 8.4(c) for a very wide range of conduct. Here are some examples.[102]

---

99. Adam M. Gershowitz, Prosecutorial Shaming: Name Attorneys to Reduce Prosecutorial Misconduct, 42 U.C. Davis L. Rev. 1059 (2009). For a compelling account of prosecutorial misconduct, see Angela J. Davis, Arbitrary Justice: The Power of the American Prosecutor (Oxford U. Press 2007).

100. See cases cited in Restatement § 5, comment c, reporter's note; ABA, Annotated Model Rules of Professional Conduct 614 (5th ed., ABA 2003).

101. Rule 8.4, Comment 3.

102. The same standard appeared in the Model Code of Professional Responsibility, and some of the following decisions are from states whose rules follow the Model Code. Some bar opinions also address Rule 8.4(d). In New Jersey, the bar's ethics committee determined that lawyers would violate Rule 8.4(d) if they told prospective clients that the job of a prosecutor is to find you guilty, or that the Internal Revenue Service "pulls out all of the stops. They simply seize your assets and sell them at an auction!" N.J. St. B. Advisory Comm. on Prof. Ethics, Op. 698 (2005).

■ A lawyer heard that a police drug raid was likely to be conducted in Wooster, Ohio. She called a former client and advised him to "clean up his act." The client agreed to cooperate with the police and to testify against his lawyer, who was then convicted of attempted obstruction of justice. (One-year suspension, six months stayed.)[103]

■ In an Internet chat room, a male lawyer asked girls between the ages of 13 and 16 to meet him for the purpose of having sex. Some of them met him, but he did not have sex with any of them. (Indefinite suspension.)[104]

■ A paralegal was being prosecuted by the county attorney's office for driving with an expired license plate. The lawyer who employed the paralegal wrote to the deputy county attorney in charge of the prosecution that the county attorney was guilty of the same offense. He enclosed a photo of the county attorney's license plate and said that if the prosecution of his paralegal was dismissed, he would not move for the appointment of a special prosecutor to prosecute the county attorney. (Four-month suspension.)[105]

■ After a client won a judgment against her lawyer requiring him to refund her $5,000 retainer, the lawyer did not pay the money he owed her. There was no finding that the lawyer intended to obstruct the suit against him, merely that he failed to pay the judgment. (Reprimand.)[106]

■ Samir Zia Chowhan advertised on Craigslist for a legal secretary and required applicants to submit their measurements. He told a woman who answered the ad that a requirement of the job would be to have "sexual interaction" with him. To demonstrate her willingness to perform this duty, she would have to have sex with him as part of her job interview. Chowhan then lied to the administrator of the Illinois disciplinary board, claiming that he had not placed the ad. (He was suspended for one year, after a disciplinary hearing committee noted that his conduct was "not as serious" as that of another attorney who was suspended for two years after, on three occasions, he tied female job applicants and employees up with rope.)[107]

---

103. Off. of Disc. Counsel v. Klaas, 742 N.E.2d 612 (Ohio 2001).

104. Atty. Grievance Commn. of Md. v. Childress, 770 A.2d 685 (Md. 2001).

105. Counsel for Disc. of the Neb. Sup. Ct. v. Koenig, 769 N.W.2d 378 (Neb. 2009).

106. Daniels v. Statewide Grievance Comm., 804 A.2d 1027 (Conn. App. 2002).

107. Illinois: Attorney's Employment Ad Leads to Ethics Violation, Legal Ethics Blog, http://legalethicsinfo.blogspot.com/2010/06/illinois-attorneys-employment-ad-leads.html (June 2, 2010); Kashmir Hill, Lawyer of Last Week: Seeking a Sexy Secretary, Above the Law, http://abovethelaw.com/2009/10/lawyer-of-the-day-last-week-seeking-a-sexy-secretary/ (Oct. 25, 2009); Ill. Atty. Regulatory & Disc. Comm. Report (July 15, 2011) (available at https://www.iardc.org/09PR0053HB.html); Ill. S. Ct., In re: Chowhan, M.R. 24851 (Nov. 22, 2011) (suspension order).

■ President Bill Clinton, a member of the Arkansas bar, "knowingly gave evasive and misleading answers" regarding his relationship with Monica Lewinsky while being deposed in the lawsuit brought by Paula Jones. (Five-year suspension.)[108]

D. Are lawyers really too zealous?

In the excerpt below, Professor Ted Schneyer suggests that contrary to the popular impression that lawyers are too doggedly concerned only with the interests of their own clients, most lawyers may actually give *too much* weight to the interests of others.[109]

Ted Schneyer, Moral Philosophy's Standard Misconception of Legal Ethics

1984 Wis. L. Rev. 1529

[Professor Schneyer is Milton O. Riepe Professor of Law at the University of Arizona.]

Professor Ted Schneyer

[The sociological literature does not support the critics' claims that lawyers are too zealous in advocating for their clients.] Take criminal defense work. Sociologist Abraham Blumberg found, in what remains one of the most important empirical studies of the field, that defense lawyers sometimes behave more like professional wrestlers than zealous combatants.[110] Generally, criminal defense lawyers represent their clients on a one-shot basis and are paid by a third party. For these structural reasons, Blumberg found, defense lawyers are understandably tempted to sacrifice individual clients, or even their clients as a class, in order to maintain good personal relations with the prosecutors, police, and court and jail personnel with whom they must deal on a long-term basis.

---

108. ABA/BNA Laws.' Man. on Prof. Conduct 17:73 (2001).

109. Schneyer's counterexamples do not review the empirical literature on civil discovery, an arena in which, according to writings such as those excerpted in this book, the prevailing legal culture may be particularly directed toward adversary behavior. Also, Schneyer's article does not deal with the question of zeal among prosecutors.

110. [Schneyer's footnote 54.] Abraham Blumberg, The Practice of Law as Confidence Game: Organizational Cooptation of a Profession, 1 Law and Socy. Rev. 16 (1967).

Moreover, they sometimes succumb to the temptation, [forgoing] meritorious defenses to avoid antagonizing busy prosecutors and judges, and even acting as "double agents" for the criminal justice bureaucracy by advising clients to cop pleas when it might not be in their interest and by "cooling out" clients who fail at first to see the wisdom of the advice. . . .

The vivid and influential ties Blumberg observed between criminal defense lawyers and third parties can sometimes be found in civil litigation as well. Sociologist Donald Landon recently interviewed 200 trial lawyers who practice in small communities and often know an opposing party or counsel personally.[111] Landon began by supposing that lawyers are strongly influenced by the Code and that the Code tilts sharply toward the client in defining the lawyer's proper role as advocate. He was therefore surprised to find that his lawyers were far from single-minded advocates willing to push to the hilt any and all of a client's legally defensible positions.

Landon's advocates were sometimes reluctant to accept cases, not because of moral qualms, but because it would make them unpopular in their community and be bad for business; one lawyer, for instance, called his decision to handle a malpractice suit against the local doctor a ruinous mistake he would never repeat. . . . Landon's advocates were unwilling to use sharp tactics to gain an advantage over a lawyer they knew and regularly dealt with. As one said: "You don't file a five-day motion on Charley Jones when he's on a two-week vacation, or try to take advantage of him. If he's forgot to file an answer, you don't ask the judge for default. You call him. . . . [F]airness is more important than winning." . . .

Putting criminal and civil litigation aside, consider the way lawyers behave as negotiators, advisers and draftsmen. Regarding negotiations, several years ago my colleague Stewart Macaulay surveyed 100 Wisconsin lawyers practicing in a wide range of settings who had experience representing buyers or sellers in the settlement of minor consumer complaints.[112] His conclusions about the way lawyers behave in the negotiation process were these:

> Rather than playing hired gun for one side, lawyers often mediate between their client and those not represented by lawyers. They seek to educate, persuade and coerce both sides to adopt the best available compromise rather than to engage in legal warfare. Moreover, in playing all of their roles, . . . lawyers are influenced by their own values and self-interest. . . .

---

111. [Schneyer's footnote 64.] Donald Landon, Clients, Colleagues, and Community: The Shaping of Zealous Advocacy in Country Law Practice, [1985 Am. B. Found. Res. J. 81].

112. [Schneyer's footnote 72.] Stewart Macaulay, Lawyers and Consumer Protection Laws, 14 Law and Socy. Rev. 115 (1979).

Notes and Questions About the Schneyer Article

1. What do your own observations of lawyers among your friends, family, and employers suggest about whether lawyers are too zealous or not zealous enough? Do the lawyers you know move heaven and earth for their clients, perhaps even to the point of unfairness to adversaries or third persons, as in some of the problems in this chapter? Or are they sometimes disrespectful or disdainful of their clients' rights, desires, or finances?

2. In your experience, does how lawyers treat their clients and how assiduously they advocate for them depend on whom the clients are or how much money they are paying?

3. To what extent is the ethical behavior of lawyers and their loyalty to clients influenced by the economic and social settings in which the lawyers are employed?

12 | THE PROVISION OF LEGAL SERVICES

A. The unmet need for legal services

B. Sources of free legal services for those who cannot afford legal fees
1. Right to counsel for indigent litigants
2. Civil legal aid
3. Pro bono representation
4. Loan forgiveness and scholarships for public service lawyers

C. Restrictions on legal services
1. Restrictions on lawyers
2. Restrictions on nonlawyers

This chapter examines the extent to which the legal profession is meeting the public's needs for legal services. It also examines the laws and institutions that benefit clients who cannot afford to pay for legal services. We begin with a survey of the empirical literature on the need for legal services in the United States. Then we examine rules and institutions that act to expand the supply of legal services available to those who cannot afford to pay. These include the constitutional guarantee of legal services to indigent criminal defendants (but not to impoverished civil litigants), legal aid organizations, the rule of professional conduct that encourages pro bono service to the poor, and loan repayment assistance to low-salaried individual lawyers who offer legal services to those in need. Finally we turn to important limitations on the provision of legal services or information to people who cannot afford them. These include limitations on lawyers' ability to "solicit" clients who may need their services, the state-by-state licensing system that limits lawyers' abilities to serve clients in states other than their own: and state laws that prohibit persons other than licensed lawyers from providing such assistance.

A. The unmet need for legal services

In the mid-1990s, for the first time in 20 years, the American Bar Association (ABA) conducted a comprehensive empirical assessment of the extent to which Americans' needs for legal services were being met. The study was based on interviews with adults in 3,000 randomly selected American

"You have a pretty good case, Mr. Pitkin. How much justice can you afford?"

households.[1] The ABA study remains the most authoritative national survey of the extent to which the legal profession is meeting Americans' need for legal services. Although this study is somewhat dated, more recent statewide surveys reach essentially the same results.[2]

The research assumed that the wealthiest one-fifth of Americans were able to afford legal services, so the study focused on households with incomes in the lowest 80 percent of the population.[3] Each person interviewed was asked a battery of questions to determine whether that person's family had experienced, during the previous year, problems involving any of 67 specific sets of circumstances that might have required legal assistance. About half of the respondents had faced serious situations involving civil legal problems, but most either tried to solve them by themselves or took no action.

For low-income households, the main reason for inaction was that "it would not help and it would cost too much." For moderate-income households, "the three dominant reasons [for not consulting lawyers] were that the situation was not really a problem, that they could handle it on their own, and that a lawyer's involvement would not help."[4]

Among low-income people who tried to solve their legal problems on their own, only about 27 percent were satisfied with the outcomes. This percentage rose to about 40 percent for moderate-income people who tried to solve their own legal problems. But among people who sought help from the legal system, these figures rose to 48 percent and 64 percent.[5]

The researchers concluded that

> even counting the efforts many people make to handle problems on their own or to get help from outside the legal system, substantial proportions of low- and moderate-income households still may need legal help. Meanwhile, over the last twenty years, legal services to individuals and households have declined as a proportion of all legal services provided by the civil justice system.[6]

The newer studies have echoed the findings of the ABA report. Most recently, a study by the Legal Services Corporation (which summarized

---

1. The results were published in 1994. ABA, Legal Needs and Civil Justice: A Survey of Americans (1994) (available at http://www.abanet.org/legalservices/downloads/sclaid/legalneed study.pdf). The ABA published a follow-up report two years later. ABA, Agenda for Access: The American People and Civil Justice (1996) (available at http://www.americanbar.org/content/dam/aba/migrated/legalservices/downloads/sclaid/agendaforaccess.authcheckdam.pdf).

2. See Legal Servs. Corp., Documenting the Justice Gap in America (Sept. 2009) (available at http://www.lafla.org/pdf/justice_Gap09.pdf) (survey of the unmet legal needs of the poor in seven states).

3. This excluded households with 1992 incomes above $60,000. ABA, Legal Needs, supra n. 1, at 1.

4. Id. at 15.

5. Id. at 17-19.

6. ABA, Agenda for Access, supra n. 1, at vii.

seven state-based surveys) determined that in all of those states, only about one in five legal problems of low-income people are addressed with the help of a lawyer.[7]

We can also look at the distribution of legal services in the United States by estimating the value of legal services for different demographic groups and by calculating the number of clients per lawyer for each of these groups. Professor David Luban has done the arithmetic, focusing particularly on those most in need:

> Law is a $100 billion per year industry. Of that $100 billion, however, less than $1 billion is dedicated to delivering [civil] legal services to low-income Americans. Put in terms of people rather than dollars, there is about one lawyer for every 240 nonpoor Americans, but only one lawyer for every 9000 Americans whose low income would qualify them for legal aid.[8]

What do these studies prove?

Most people think that the studies demonstrate that ordinary Americans have an immense, unmet need for legal services.[9] On the other hand, maybe the researchers took account of trivial problems and inflated the perceived need. Or maybe the research shows that many people really don't need lawyers because they find other ways, such as enlisting the help of neighbors or clergy, to address their legal problems, or that it is reasonable for most people to accept a certain amount of un-redressed injustice as a normal part of life or at least as a reasonable alternative to an abundance of lawyers.[10]

Do low-income people need lawyers more urgently or more often than middle- or high-income people?

Wealth inequalities affect access to all types of goods and services. But at least some types of legal services are not like other consumer needs. In some situations, people desperately need lawyers. If a person is arrested and faces possible imprisonment, she must have access to counsel. Criminal defendants have a right to state-subsidized counsel if they cannot afford to pay attorneys. The payment often is too low or the lawyer's caseload too high to

---

7. Legal Servs. Corp., supra n. 2, at 17. This study also found, consistent with the earlier ABA study, that "most people who appear in state courts without an attorney do so because they cannot afford one." Id. at 27.

8. David Luban, Taking Out the Adversary: The Assault on Progressive Public-Interest Lawyers, 91 Cal. L. Rev. 209, 211 (2003).

9. Roger C. Cramton, Delivery of Services to Ordinary Americans, 44 Case W. Res. L. Rev. 531, 542 (1994) (discussing the "prevailing consensus").

10. Some argue that what the nation needs is fewer lawyers. David Gergen, who served as communications director for President Ronald Reagan and who appears often as a CNN commentator, argues that "we need to de-lawyer our society." David Gergen, America's Legal Mess, U.S. News & World Rep. 72 (Aug. 19, 1991).

provide adequate representation, but at least society accepts the principle of providing help to indigent criminal defendants. Other situations also present "legal emergencies." If someone is about to be evicted or have her heat shut off, the need for legal help is urgent. That is also true where a person faces deportation, domestic violence, or termination of parental rights or child custody. Even if a situation is not a legal emergency, the need for legal services may be much greater than the need for ordinary consumer goods or services. Litigants are much more likely to obtain favorable outcomes if they have legal representation. Lawyers are much more likely to understand the culture of the court, the strategies of successful advocacy, and the rules of procedure and evidence.[11]

What is the bar doing to increase the availability of legal services to people who are not wealthy?

The ethical rules and the organized bar strongly support publicly funded programs of criminal defense and pro bono civil legal aid to people who cannot afford the services of lawyers. They also encourage private lawyers to offer pro bono assistance to those who cannot pay lawyers. On the other hand, the bar associations also support state "unauthorized practice" laws that prevent nonlawyers from helping low-income people to solve relatively simple problems that have legal components. These restrictions arguably preserve an unwarranted "monopoly" for lawyers. We consider unauthorized practice statutes in the final section of the chapter. Restrictions on collaborative practice with members of other (sometimes less expensive) disciplines may also constrain competition within the legal profession, keeping the cost of legal services artificially high, perhaps beyond the reach of some consumers.

B. Sources of free legal services for those who cannot afford legal fees

1. Right to counsel for indigent litigants

a. Criminal defendants

Most criminal defendants are too poor to hire lawyers.[12] In 1938, the Supreme Court held that the Constitution requires the government to provide

---

11. See Frank I. Michelman, The Supreme Court and Litigation Access Fees: The Right to Protect One's Rights — Part I, 1973 Duke L.J. 1153, 1172-1177.

12. In 1996, more than 80 percent of felony defendants charged with a violent crime in the country's largest counties were represented by publicly financed lawyers, and 74 percent of state prison inmates had been represented by appointed counsel. U.S. Dept. of Justice, Defense Counsel in Criminal Cases 1, 7 (Nov. 2000) (available at http://bjs.ojp.usdoj.gov/content/pub/pdf/dccc.pdf).

counsel for indigent defendants in federal criminal cases.[13] In 1963, in the famous case of *Gideon v. Wainwright*,[14] the Court extended that ruling to felony defendants in state prosecutions. Within a decade, the Court held that misdemeanor defendants who could be subjected to imprisonment and juveniles who were accused of offenses[15] also were entitled to have lawyers appointed to represent them if they could not afford to hire private counsel.

How effectively have the states provided court-appointed counsel for indigent criminal defendants?

States and counties spend about $3.5 billion annually for criminal defense services.[16] This amount is about 2 percent of the amount spent for state and local police, judicial services, and corrections.[17] Despite decades of efforts to obtain solid data on the extent to which this money actually provides counsel to all those entitled to it under *Gideon* and its progeny, however, "we have no idea how many defendants are represented by the indigent defense systems in this country, how many misdemeanor defendants have a right to counsel, or what percentage of defendants who are entitled to court-appointed representation go unrepresented. The limited data we do have certainly suggest that many jurisdictions are violating defendants' constitutional right to counsel."[18]

If a judge appoints a lawyer to represent an indigent criminal defendant, must the lawyer accept the appointment?

Some judges appoint lawyers to represent indigent criminal defendants even if there are no funds available to pay them. Rule 6.2 urges lawyers to accept such appointments except for "good cause."

> **Rule 6.2 Accepting Appointments**
> **A lawyer shall not seek to avoid appointment by a tribunal to represent a person except for good cause, such as:**
> > **(a) representing the client is likely to result in violation of the Rules of Professional Conduct or other law;**

---

13. Johnson v. Zerbst, 304 U.S. 458 (1938), *partially overruled on other grounds*, Edwards v. Ariz., 451 U.S. 477 (1981).

14. 372 U.S. 335 (1963).

15. In re Gault, 387 U.S. 1 (1967); Argersinger v. Hamlin, 407 U.S. 25 (1972).

16. ABA Bar Information Program, State and County Expenditures for Indigent Defense Services in Fiscal Year 2005 (2006) (available at http://www.americanbar.org/content/dam/aba/administrative/legal_aid_indigent_defendants/ls_sclaid_def_final_report_fy_2005_expenditure_report.authcheckdam.pdf).

17. See U.S. Dept. of Justice, Bureau of Justice Statistics, Justice Expenditure and Employment in the United States, 2003 (Apr. 2006) (available at http://www.prisonpolicy.org/scans/bjs/jeeus03.pdf).

18. Erica Hashimoto, Assessing the Indigent Defense System, Am. Const. Socy. Issue Br. (Sept. 2010) (available at http://www.acslaw.org/files/Hashimoto%20Indigent%20Defense.pdf).

(b) representing the client is likely to result in an unreasonable financial burden on the lawyer;

(c) the client or the cause is so repugnant to the lawyer as to be likely to impair the client-lawyer relationship or the lawyer's ability to represent the client.

b. Parties in civil and administrative proceedings

People who need to go to court to resolve family, landlord-tenant, consumer, or other "civil" problems do not have a right to receive court-appointed counsel. This is true even when they are defendants or when they face such serious outcomes as eviction, deportation, or loss of child custody.

Is there a right to counsel in some civil cases under the Due Process Clause of the U.S. Constitution?

Some indigent litigants have claimed that not appointing counsel for them denies their due process rights. Since 1923, scholars have written dozens of articles calling for recognition of a right to counsel in at least some types of civil and administrative cases.[19] But the courts have consistently rejected both the claims of indigent litigants and the recommendations of the legal scholars.

FOR EXAMPLE: Robert William Kras had once worked as an insurance agent for Metropolitan Life. The company fired him when about $1,000 in premiums he had collected was stolen from his home and he could not repay his employer. For two years, he was unemployed, living in a two-and-a-half room apartment with his wife, his mother, his mother's six-year-old daughter, and his two small children, one of whom suffered from cystic fibrosis. From welfare funds, he was barely able to pay his rent. He had no car and no other assets except for $50 worth of clothing and a couch that was in storage (for which he had to pay $6 a month). He was $6,000 in debt and was harassed by his creditors. He wanted to file for bankruptcy so that he could start a new life and end the harassment. But he had no money with which to pay the $50 filing fee, even in monthly installments.

The Supreme Court rejected Kras's claim that he was being unconstitutionally denied access to the court system. The Court acknowledged that it had held unconstitutional, as applied to indigents, a

---

19. John MacArthur Maguire, Poverty and Civil Litigation, 36 Harv. L. Rev. 361 (1923); for a bibliography of more recent scholarship, see Paul Marvy, Thinking About a Civil Right to Counsel Since 1923, Clearinghouse Rev. 170 (July-Aug. 2006) (available at http://civilrighttocounsel.org/pdfs/marvy.pdf).

state statute requiring a filing fee for a divorce.[20] But it held that divorce cases were unique because "marriage involves interests of basic importance in our society" and "resort to state courts was the only avenue to dissolution of marriages." In the Court's view, "however unrealistic the remedy may be in a particular situation, a debtor [such as Kras], in theory, and often in actuality, may adjust his debts by negotiated agreement with his creditors. . . . Resort to the court, therefore, is not Kras' sole path to relief."[21] Although *Kras* involved a filing fee, this decision has been interpreted to preclude due process claims to the right to counsel in civil cases.[22]

In 1981, the Supreme Court held (in a case involving a state's termination of an incarcerated mother's right to child custody) that the Constitution requires appointment of counsel for indigent civil litigants only when proceeding without such counsel would be fundamentally unfair. The Court stated that trial judges should make this decision on a case-by-case basis.[23] Professor Deborah Rhode notes that "although that standard is not unreasonable on its face, courts have applied it in such restrictive fashion that counsel is almost never required in civil cases."[24]

In 2011, the Supreme Court reaffirmed that indigent civil litigants rarely, if ever, have a constitutional right to counsel. A judge in South Carolina ordered Michael Turner to pay $51.73 a week in child support to Rebecca Rogers, the mother of his child. He fell behind in his payments and was required to appear in court to face charges of civil contempt of court for willful refusal to comply with the order. He could not afford an attorney, so he defended himself. His excuse for nonpayment was that he had been on drugs but was no longer using them, and that he had had a broken back, rendering him unable rather than unwilling to pay as ordered. The judge did not make any express finding on whether Turner could have made the payments but said that Turner had willfully refused to pay. He sentenced Turner to 12 months in jail unless he made the payments. On appeal, the Supreme Court held that even when a person is faced with incarceration for a substantial period of time, he enjoys no automatic right to counsel. But the Court suggested that if counsel is not provided, certain "substitute procedural

---

20. Boddie v. Conn., 401 U.S. 371 (1971).

21. U.S. v. Kras, 409 U.S. 434, 437-446 (1973); see also Ortwein v. Schwab, 410 U.S. 656 (1973) (a state need not allow an indigent to file an appeal of a civil case without paying the statutory filing fee).

22. See, e.g., Deborah L. Rhode & David Luban, Legal Ethics 873 n. 37 (5th ed., Thomson Reuters/Found. Press 2009).

23. Lassiter v. Dept. of Soc. Servs., 452 U.S. 18 (1981).

24. Deborah Rhode, Access to Justice: Connecting Principles to Practice, 17 Geo. J. Leg. Ethics 369, 375 (2004).

safeguards" would be required to make the proceedings fair. In a case like *Turner*, in which a person's ability to pay would be the key issue in the court hearing, these safeguards would include notice to Turner that the issue would be whether his nonpayment was due to unwillingness or inability, a form that would elicit information about his financial circumstances, and an express finding by the trial court stating whether he was able to make the payments.[25]

Is any state providing substantial funding to assist low-income persons in civil cases?

In 2009, California took "civil Gideon" a step further when its legislature passed a law increasing most court filing fees by $10 and directing that, beginning in 2011, the funds would be used to provide legal aid in such matters as child custody and foreclosure suits.[26] In 2011, California allocated $9.5 million in grants to seven legal service organizations for pilot projects that will provide legal assistance to low-income litigants in cases involving housing, child custody, and probate guardianship. Applicants had requested $25.6 million during this first year of the program.[27]

2. Civil legal aid

a. Legal Services Corporation

Although most court decisions have denied indigents a constitutional right to counsel at government expense, Congress, state and local governments, and private donors have created a network of salaried legal aid lawyers who provide advice and representation to some poor people. The nation's largest program of civil legal aid is operated by the federally funded Legal Services Corporation (LSC).[28] However, the funds appropriated are far less than what is needed, and there are strings attached to the services that law offices funded through the corporation can provide.[29] The budget of the Legal

---

25. Turner v. Rogers, 131 S. Ct. 2507 (2011).

26. Cal. Govt. Code ch. 2.1, §§ 68650 & 68651 (eff. July 1, 2011).

27. Judicial Council of Cal., Report to the Judicial Council (Apr. 7, 2011) (available at http://www.courts.ca.gov/documents/20110429itemp-revt.pdf) (listing all funds requested by project proposers); Judicial Council of Cal., Minutes of April 29, 2011, Meeting, Item P (Apr. 29, 2011) (available at http://www.courts.ca.gov/documents/20110429jcminutes.pdf) (approval).

28. For an excellent history of legal aid, see Alan W. Houseman & Linda E. Perle, Securing Equal Justice for All: A Brief History of Civil Legal Assistance in the United States (Jan. 2007) (available at http://www.clasp.org/admin/site/publications/files/0158.pdf).

29. Since the 1996 law was passed, lawyers in offices that receive LSC funding may not use those funds to attempt to influence legislation (and may not even use other funds to do so unless in response to an unsolicited official request for information); participate in administrative rulemaking; attempt to influence a local, state, or federal adjudicatory proceeding that is even partly aimed at making policy; initiate or participate in a class action; participate in most suits on behalf of persons

Services Corporation was $420 million in FY 2010. But by FY 2012, Congress had reduced the budget below the FY 1992 level of $350 million.[30]

Questions About Publicly Funded Legal Aid

1. What is the rationale for the government to provide free legal services for poor people in civil matters? Is this type of service important to the operation of our legal system, and if so, why?

2. What is the rationale for opposing the provision of free legal services for poor people in civil matters? Likewise, what is the rationale for restricting the available services to exclude law reform work and to exclude representation of certain groups? Why do you think that our policymakers have been deeply divided about whether or how to fund legal services?

3. In 2007, two corporate law firms each received more than $2 billion in legal fees to serve a few wealthy clients.[31] That was nearly twice as much as all the legal aid programs in the United States receive from all sources to benefit 50 to 90 million people.[32] Is this just the free market system at work, or do these figures reflect injustice in our system?

4. Some people have noted that the wealthy can afford legal assistance and the very poor (with family income less than 125 percent of the poverty level) may be eligible for legal aid subsidized by the government or by charity, but that working-class people are neither able to afford legal services themselves nor eligible for subsidized assistance. Should the public subsidize or otherwise provide legal aid for working-class individuals and families?

5. Some legal problems involve amounts of money so small that legal fees to obtain justice would exceed the amount in controversy. For example, no rational person would pay the thousands or tens of thousands of dollars that most lawyers would charge to initiate litigation, simply to recover several hundreds of dollars lost to a dis-

---

incarcerated in any prison (even, for example, a divorce or termination of parental rights matter involving an indigent prisoner); defend a person in a proceeding to evict the person from a federally subsidized public housing project on the ground that the person was charged with the sale or distribution of a controlled substance; participate in litigation, lobbying, or rulemaking involving an effort "to reform a Federal or state welfare system"; represent most undocumented immigrants seeking asylum in the United States; or participate in any litigation involving abortion. See Pub. L. No. 104-134, § 504 (1996), and regulations in 45 C.F.R. §§ 1612, 1617, and 1637.

30. Legal Servs. Corp., LSC Funding, http://www.lsc.gov/congress/lsc-funding (last visited Nov. 24, 2012) ($348 million).

31. Am. Law Media, Two Firms Pass the $2 Billion Mark, Am. Law. 175 (May 1, 2008) (available at http://www.law.com/jsp/tal/PubArticleTAL.jsp?&id=1208947716661).

32. Earl Johnson Jr., Justice for America's Poor in the Year 2020: Some Possibilities Based on Experiences Here and Abroad, 58 DePaul L. Rev 393, 396 (2009).

honest automobile repair shop. Many, but not all, states and counties have small claims courts in which individuals may bring and defend cases without lawyers, but most people do better, even in these forums, if they have experienced counsel. Should our society have a concept of "practical indigency" justifying government-subsidized legal services when the amount in controversy is so small that profit-making lawyers would not accept the case?

b. Other civil legal services

The federal LSC is the largest single source of funding for civil legal aid for the poor, but it pays for only about one-third of the $1.3 billion spent annually on civil legal services in the United States. LSC funds 137 "full-service" programs (offering a range of legal services to the poor, other than those prohibited by congressional restrictions). There are also more than 1,500 full-service and specialized programs (e.g., handling only one type of case) funded by foundations, charitable donations, and other sources.[33] Also, students in law school clinics contribute about 3 million hours a year (worth perhaps $150 million)[34] in uncompensated service to poor people.[35] However, in some states, clinics avoid participating in litigation against corporations (such as companies that pollute areas in which poor people live) because of threatened or actual adverse university or governmental reactions.[36]

3. Pro bono representation

Private lawyers' voluntary assistance to low-income clients also helps to meet the legal needs of the poor. One hundred fifty-five law firms and 600 bar or other associations have formal programs through which lawyers offer assistance to indigent clients.[37] If all American lawyers offered pro bono help to those who could not afford to pay, our profession would take a huge step toward meeting the unmet need for legal services. Suppose, for example, that each of the million lawyers in the United States contributed 50 hours of their time each year to helping indigent clients. If those services

---

33. Alan W. Houseman, Civil Legal Aid in the United States: An Update for 2009 (July 2009) (available at http://clasp.org/admin/site/publications/files/0527.pdf).

34. Of course, help from law students is priceless, but we are assuming a nominal billing rate of $50 per hour.

35. Luban, supra n. 8, at 236 n. 108.

36. Robert R. Kuehn & Bridget M. McCormack, Lessons from Forty Years of Interference in Law School Clinics, 24 Geo. J. Leg. Ethics 59, 77 et seq. (2010) (summarizing political interference with representation by clinics and noting that one-third of clinic faculty fear adverse reactions).

37. Houseman, supra n. 33.

were valued at $200 per hour, the value of the total contribution would be $10 billion, or about 25 times as much as the entire annual budget of the LSC.[38]

The organized bar recognizes the importance of pro bono contributions. The ABA's Model Rule 6.1 encourages — but does not require — each lawyer to spend at least 50 hours per year providing pro bono assistance to those in need.

Rule 6.1 Voluntary Pro Bono Publico Service[39]

Rule language*	Authors' explanation**
Every lawyer has a professional responsibility to provide legal services to those unable to pay. **A lawyer should aspire to render at least 50 hours of pro bono publico legal services per year.** In fulfilling this responsibility, the lawyer should:	Despite the words "professional responsibility" in the first sentence, the words "should aspire" in the second sentence and "should" in the third sentence have been universally interpreted to mean that the "responsibility" is only a moral one, not a legal or ethical requirement.
(a) provide a **substantial majority of the 50 hours** of legal services without fee or expectation of fee **to** (1) **persons of limited means** or (2) charitable, religious, civic, community, governmental and educational organizations in matters that are designed primarily to address the needs of persons of limited means; and	The comments to the Model Rules explain that the need for assistance to persons of limited means is so great that lawyers should aspire to provide at least 25 hours per year of such assistance (and at least 25 additional hours in pro bono work that could be of other types).
(b) **provide additional services through:** (1) delivery of legal services at no fee or substantially reduced fee to individuals, **groups or organizations seeking to secure or protect civil rights, civil liberties or public rights**, or charitable, religious, civic, community, governmental and educational organizations in matters in furtherance of their organizational purposes, where the payment of standard legal fees would significantly deplete the organization's economic resources or would be otherwise inappropriate;	Comment 6 after ABA Rule 6.1 says that a lawyer who provides at least 25 pro bono hours a year to poor clients may satisfy the rest of her professional obligation by serving a wide variety of individuals and groups. The services might include help to religious institutions, vindication of First Amendment claims, and protection of the environment. The lawyer may charge a substantially reduced fee for these services rather than waiving compensation altogether.

---

38. This comparison may be a bit unfair because legal services lawyers who specialize in areas of law such as welfare and low-income housing may provide services more efficiently than pro bono lawyers who have to train themselves.

39. This is the text of Minnesota's Rule 6.1, which is identical to the ABA's Model Rule 6.1 except that in the Model Rule, the number "50" is in parentheses.

Rule language*	Authors' explanation**
(2) **delivery of legal services at a substantially reduced fee to persons of limited means; or**	Acceptance of court-appointed criminal defense work at a low rate of compensation qualifies as pro bono assistance for purposes of Rule 6.1(b). ABA Model Rule, Comment 7.
(3) **participation in activities for improving the law**, the legal system, or the legal profession.	Serving on bar association committees also qualifies under Rule 6.1(b). ABA Model Rule, Comment 8.
In addition, a lawyer should voluntarily contribute financial support to organizations that provide legal services to persons of limited means.	Lawyers' financial contributions should be made in addition to, not instead of, pro bono service. ABA Model Rule, Comment 10.

*All emphasis added.

**This and other authors' explanations draw from the comments to the rules and from other sources. They are not comprehensive but highlight some important interpretive points.

"Remember, we can only afford to do all this pro bono because of how much anti bono pays."

It is difficult to ascertain how many lawyers meet or exceed the ABA's aspirational 50-hour standard for pro bono work. In 2005, a survey of ABA members concluded that they average 39 hours per year of free service to people of limited means and another 38 hours of service to community groups.[40] Other evidence suggests that this survey overstates lawyers' pro bono commitments (perhaps because those who perform such services are the ones who responded to the survey). For example, one empirical study found that the median annual pro bono contribution of New York lawyers was 20 hours per year, but the corresponding figure for Texas lawyers was only 5 hours per year.[41] A Wisconsin state bar survey reported that lawyers in private practice provided a median of 25 hours of free service to individuals. A survey by *American Lawyer* magazine found that only 37 percent of lawyers in the 200 largest firms performed at least 20 hours of pro bono work.[42]

Do large firms treat pro bono clients the same way they treat their corporate clients?

Large firms attempt to treat pro bono cases similarly to billable cases and often do so. Once a large law firm accepts a pro bono case, it typically pours substantial resources into the representation, devoting to the case the time of associates, sometimes partners, paralegals, and secretaries, and often the other costs of representation. However, there are distinctive pressures that sometimes militate against equal treatment. At some firms pro bono work must give way to work that can be billed, with the pro bono work done after hours, on the associates' "own time." In some firms, partner supervision is less rigorous on pro bono cases, in part because partners are not well versed in the relevant law.[43]

Do corporate law firms avoid accepting certain kinds of pro bono matters?

Professor Scott Cummings notes that firms that encourage their lawyers to do pro bono work are likely to shy away from taking cases that their paying business clients would disfavor, even when there is no conflict that would require rejecting a pro bono matter. According to Cummings,

---

40. ABA Standing Comm. on Pro Bono & Pub. Serv., Supporting Justice: A Report on the Work of America's Pro Bono Lawyers (Aug. 2005) (available at http://www.americanbar.org/content/dam/aba/migrated/2011_build/probono_public_service/report_2011.authcheckdam.pdf).

41. Deborah L. Rhode, Pro Bono in Principle and in Practice, 53 J. Leg. Educ. 413, 429 (2003). "Only two-fifths of surveyed in-house legal departments participate in pro bono work, and the average yearly commitment is less than 8 hours per legal department employee." Id.

42. Michael Aneiro, The Pro Bono Report, Am. Law. (July 2006).

43. Scott L. Cummings & Deborah L. Rhode, Managing Pro Bono: Doing Well by Doing Better, 78 Fordham L. Rev. 2357, 2394-2399 (2010).

[t]he most noticeable effect is to exclude pro bono cases that strike at the heart of corporate client interests, particularly employment, environmental, and consumer cases in which plaintiffs seek pro bono counsel to sue major companies. Thus, pro bono employment discrimination suits, particularly impact cases against major corporate employers, are regularly rejected by big firms. For instance, the pro bono coordinator at Skadden, Arps, Slate, Meagher & Flom indicated that it was difficult to get the firm to take on employment-related civil rights cases because of conflicts with labor clients—in contrast to cases in the voting rights or housing areas that were much easier to place. Similarly, the pro bono coordinator at Kilpatrick Stockton in Atlanta stated that the firm did not sue employers. In a similar vein, environmental lawyers complain that big firms will not touch many environmental issues, forcing their organizations to rely on smaller boutique environmental firms for support. Again, the key is that big firms avoid environmental issues that directly impact corporate client interests. They do not, therefore, accept pro bono environmental justice cases, in which community groups challenge the location of environmental hazards in low-income neighborhoods. Nor do they take on cases seeking to enforce emissions standards against corporate actors. . . . Even when positional conflicts are not technically at issue, firms can take a dim view of "pro bono activities that might merely offend the firm's regular clients or its prospective clients." Some firms therefore decline to take pro bono cases on either side of the abortion debate, while others shy away from cases involving hate speech, gun control, or religion. One lawyer recounted how she was forced to stop representing the Queer Nation when her pro bono work drew rousing criticism from other lawyers in her firm, one of whom went so far as to try to amend the firm's pro bono policy to bar the Queer Nation as a client.[44]

Do lawyers at small firms do pro bono work?

Compared with lawyers in large firms, fewer lawyers in small firms do free work for people who are not their regular clients. They don't have as many wealthy corporate clients whose fees can in effect subsidize a substantial number of clients who can't pay for legal assistance. In addition, "pro bono is rarely important for small firm recruiting and may actually be discouraged by firm partners due to economic concerns."[45] But many small firm

---

44. Scott Cummings, The Politics of Pro Bono, 52 UCLA L. Rev. 1, 118-119, 122-123 (2004). More generally, Professor Russell Pearce has suggested that "as for pro bono, like other forms of charity, it is a good deed. But unless you place it within the context of broad moral obligation, it serves to relegate the public good to the margins of legal practice." Russell Pearce, How Law Firms Can Do Good While Doing Well (and the Answer Is Not Pro Bono), 33 Fordham Urb. L.J. 211 (2005).

45. Leslie C. Levin, Pro Bono Publico in a Parallel Universe: The Meaning of Pro Bono in Solo and Small Law Firms, 27 Hofstra L. Rev. 699, 701-702 (2009). "Pro bono" has a different meaning to many medium- and small-firm lawyers than it does to big-firm lawyers, so when small-firm lawyers

lawyers cut their rates or provide some free service for regular clients who cannot afford to pay their bills. One reason they do this is to keep those clients, who may be better able to afford to pay regular rates in later years.

Should lawyers be required rather than merely encouraged to perform pro bono work?

Professor Deborah L. Rhode

In 2000, the Ethics 2000 Commission debated whether the 50 hours per year goal should be converted, in the Model Rules, to a mandatory requirement (which a lawyer or firm could satisfy by contributing $25 per hour for each hour not worked to an organization that offered such services). The Commission voted, 6-5, to make the pro bono service mandatory. Then it voted to reconsider and ultimately voted 7-6 not to require lawyers to perform pro bono service.

Professor Deborah L. Rhode of Stanford Law School has summarized some of the strongest arguments for and against a mandatory pro bono requirement. She lists several arguments in favor of a mandatory pro bono requirement. (These are paraphrased unless otherwise noted.)

- Lawyers have special privileges; only they are allowed to provide legal services.
- Lawyers have a special responsibility to improve society.
- Pro bono service exposes new lawyers to the ways the legal system fails those who have little wealth or power.
- Pro bono service benefits lawyers by providing valuable training.

Professor Rhode also notes these arguments against required pro bono service:

- "Compulsory charity is a contradiction in terms."
- Other occupations don't have such requirements; for example, grocers are not required to feed poor people.
- Forced labor is "involuntary servitude."

---

report that they do pro bono work, they may be reporting on cut-rate services to regular clients or court-appointed criminal defense work for which they are paid. On the other hand, small firms are not monolithic, and some do provide free services to indigent clients or to support specific causes. Id. at 716-719. Levin recommends rewriting Rule 6.1 to recognize the types of service that small firms provide at less than their highest rates, and to reward such service with the same kind of public approval that large-firm lawyers receive for their pro bono contributions.

- Most lawyers would evade a pro bono requirement by providing free service to middle class individuals (including friends) and to institutions such as museums and churches.
- Forcing corporate lawyers who have not been trained in poverty law or in how to relate to low-income individuals will result in incompetent service.[46]
- "Requiring all attorneys to contribute minimal services of largely unverifiable quality cannot begin to satisfy this nation's unmet legal needs [but] may deflect public attention from . . . more productive ways of addressing them [including] simplification of legal procedures, expanded subsidies for poverty law programs, and elimination of the legal monopoly over routine legal services."

Professor Rhode concludes that the arguments against mandatory pro bono requirements

> have considerable force, but they are not as conclusive as critics often assume. . . . One option is to allow lawyers to buy out of their required service by making a specified financial contribution to a legal-aid program. Another possibility is to give credit for time spent in training. . . . A final objection to pro bono requirements involves the cost of enforcing them. Opponents often worry about the "Burgeoning Bureaucratic Boondoggle" that they assume would be necessary to monitor compliance. . . . There is, however, a strong argument for attempting to impose pro bono requirements even if they cannot be fully enforced. At the very least, such requirements would support lawyers who want to participate in public-interest projects but work in organizations that have failed to provide adequate resources or credit for these efforts.[47]

In recent years, seven states have rejected proposed rules that would make pro bono service mandatory, but these seven have required lawyers to report annually on how much pro bono work they have done.[48] For example, Illinois lawyers must report annually the number of pro bono hours they provided to the poor and the amount of their monetary contributions,

---

46. The response of the private bar in New Orleans after Hurricane Katrina struck the city in 2005 suggests the power of this critique. Few civil practitioners volunteered to help the public defenders. "Most believed they . . . [did] not have a clue how the criminal justice system worked and thought they lacked the skill set to do criminal defense work." Douglas L. Colbert, 51 How. L.J. 677, 729 (2008). Colbert concludes, however, that mandatory pro bono "may be the only means to ensure that the legal profession is present in sufficient numbers to serve the public interest." Id.

47. Deborah L. Rhode, Cultures of Commitment: Pro Bono for Lawyers and Law Students, 67 Fordham L. Rev. 2415 (1999)

48. ABA Standing Comm. on Pro Bono & Public Service, Overview of State Pro Bono Reporting Policies, http://apps.americanbar.org/legalservices/probono/reporting.html (accessed Nov. 24, 2012).

though this information is not made public except on an aggregate basis.[49] No state has yet required lawyers to contribute pro bono services. In 2010 the Supreme Court of Mississippi proposed such a rule. It would require lawyers to contribute 20 hours a year to representation of poor clients or to pay $500 to the bar for legal services programs. The reaction to the proposal from members of the bar was overwhelmingly negative,[50] and a year later, the proposal seemed to be "on the back burner."[51]

PROBLEM 12-1 MANDATORY PRO BONO SERVICE

Each year, three law students are elected to serve as members of the House of Delegates of the American Bar Association, the ABA's highest governing body.[52] You have been elected to one of these positions.

Because the ABA Ethics 2000 Commission was almost evenly divided in 2000 on making pro bono service mandatory, that proposal has been brought up once again. An ABA committee has recommended that Rule 6.1 be amended to make service mandatory (with a $25/hour buyout), and the House of Delegates is scheduled to vote on the matter this afternoon.

How will you vote? Why?

4. Loan forgiveness and scholarships for public service lawyers

Another strategy to expand resources for clients who cannot afford high legal fees is to remove the barriers to public service caused by the very high

---

49. Ill. S. Ct. R. 756(f) (as amended June 14, 2006).

50. Debra Cassens Weiss, Mississippi Weighs Mandatory Pro Bono, to Lawyers' Dismay, ABA J. (Sept. 20, 2010) (available at http://www.abajournal.com/mobile/article/mississippi_weighs_ mandatory_pro_bono_to_lawyers_dismay/). Mississippi is 50th in the nation for expenditure on provision of counsel to indigent criminal defendants. Monica Davey, Budget Woes Hit Defense Lawyers for the Indigent, N.Y. Times (Sept. 9, 2010) (available at http://www.nytimes.com/2010/09/ 10/us/10defenders.html). Perhaps the proposal aims to compensate for taxpayer resistance to state-financed public defender services by requiring lawyers to contribute time to the defense of the poor. If so, this attempt to draft lawyers to represent people accused of crimes may not work because pro bono obligations need not be satisfied by serving criminal defendants.

51. Lisa Borden, Mandatory Pro Bono Programs May Do More Harm Than Good (Sept. 16, 2011), http://www.bakerdonelson.com/one_good_turn/?entry=111.

52. See ABA Law Student Div., Delegate to House of Delegates Position Description, http:// www.americanbar.org/groups/law_students/about_us/leadership/leadership_opportunities/dels.html (accessed Nov. 24, 2012).

cost of attending law school.[53] Many people want to become lawyers in order to assist people in need. However, as law students approach their graduation dates, many no longer believe they can afford to follow their chosen path. By the time most graduate, they owe $100,000 or more in educational loans (requiring annual repayment of about $10,000); public service lawyers' annual starting salaries are approximately $43,000.[54]

More than 20 law schools have created public interest law scholarship programs. These programs provide special educational enrichment for selected students who are planning careers as public interest lawyers; many also reduce the cost of attendance (and consequently the debt burden) by offering partial or full tuition rebates.[55] However, a study published by the National Association for Public Interest Law showed that in 1999, just 3 law schools (New York University, Georgetown, and the University of

---

53. The public service scholarship and loan repayment programs discussed here help both the individual lawyers who receive the benefits and the clients served by the programs in which they become employed. The scholarships and loan forgiveness payments enable public service employers to hire more lawyers to carry out their missions because the benefits to the law students partially subsidize the salaries that the employers provide to their legal staffs. The benefits also enable employers to retain experienced lawyers who would otherwise have to resign after a year or two because of their debt repayment burdens.

54. See NALP, Starting Salaries — What New Law Graduates Earn — Class of 2010, NALP Bull. (Nov. 2011). For a thorough discussion of this issue, replete with useful statistical information, see ABA Commn. on Loan Repayment & Forgiveness, Lifting the Burden: Law Student Debt as a Barrier to Public Service (ABA 2003) (available at http://www.americanbar.org/content/dam/aba/migrated/legalservices/downloads/lrap/lrapfinalreport.authcheckdam.pdf). As of 2003, the average three-year cost of attendance at the nation's private law schools was $108,113. Id. at 19. It has subsequently increased, reaching $165,000 by 2009. Philip G. Schrag & Charles W. Pruett, Coordinating Law School Loan Repayment Assistance Programs with New Federal Loan Repayment and Forgiveness Legislation, 60 J. Leg. Educ. 583 (2011) (available at http://www.swlaw.edu/pdfs/jle/jle604Schrag.pdf). Even in 2003, the average law student at these schools borrowed $86,378 for education (an amount that exceeded $100,000 on average by 2009), but 25 percent of the students borrowed more than $100,000. ABA Commn. on Loan Repayment & Forgiveness, supra, at 20-24. At an interest rate of 8.25 percent, repaying an $86,378 loan over 10 years would require paying $12,780 per year; repaying over 20 years would cost only $9,000 per year but would cost a total of $210,000 as opposed to $106,000 in current dollars over that period of time. Id. at 21-22. The ABA report noted that for the class of 2002, the median starting salary in public interest law was $36,000. Even if a 2002 graduate had found a public service job paying $40,000 per year and repaid on a 20-year schedule, the first year's loan repayment would be more than 30 percent of her after-tax income. (On a 10-year repayment plan, it would be 43 percent of after-tax income.) Id.

55. Heather Wells Jarvis, Financing the Future: Responses to the Rising Debt of Law Students (2d ed., Equal Justice Works 2006) (available at http://www.equaljusticeworks.org/sites/default/files/financing-the-future2006.pdf). A 2007 study of lawyers who graduated in 2000 found that those with the lowest remaining debt "were the public interest lawyers, a finding that probably reflects that they had taken advantage of the debt relief offered by Loan Repayment Assistance programs." Am. B. Found., Seven Years into a Lawyer's Career, 20 Researching L. No. 2 (Spring 2009) (available at http://www.americanbarfoundation.org/uploads/cms/documents/abf_rl_spring09_final.pdf).

Denver) provided 76 percent of all of the funds for these scholarships.[56] Nearly half of the accredited American law schools offer loan repayment assistance, usually including partial or complete loan forgiveness, to their graduates who take low-paying public service jobs.[57] However, in 2008, as in earlier years, just 6 schools (Yale, New York University, Harvard, Columbia, Stanford, and Georgetown) provided 70 percent of all of the funds for loan forgiveness,[58] and although the number of schools with such programs continues to grow, more than half of American law schools have no loan forgiveness program at all. In addition, 24 states have loan forgiveness programs for graduates of their state's schools, their state's public service lawyers, or both.[59] However, funding under these programs has been very limited.[60]

But there is good news for students seeking careers in public service. Under the federal government's Pay As You Earn (PAYE) and Public Service Loan Forgiveness (PSLF) Programs, law graduates (as well as others who borrowed for higher education) who spend 10 years of full-time employment in public service may repay their government-guaranteed and government-extended educational loans (including Grad PLUS loans) at a very affordable rate and obtain substantial forgiveness of the debt. Public service employment is defined to include all employment by federal, state, local and tribal agencies, as well as all non-profit organizations that are tax-exempt under Section 501(c)(3) of the Internal Revenue Code. Under PAYE, a borrower need repay annually only 10 percent of discretionary income, defined as the borrower's adjusted gross income minus 150 percent of the federal poverty level.[61] This works out to about 7% of actual income.[62] Interest that is unpaid because of this income-based cap is added

56. Natl. Assn. for Public Interest Law (NAPIL), Financing the Future: NAPIL's 2000 Report on Law School Loan Repayment Assistance and Public Interest Scholarship Programs 301-358 (NAPIL 2000). NAPIL is now called Equal Justice Works.

57. Id.

58. Schrag & Pruett, supra n. 54, at 588.

59. Id.

60. See ABA Standing Comm. on Legal Aid & Indigent Defendants, Annual Amount of Assistance Funded (Aug. 2012) (available at http://www.americanbar.org/content/dam/aba/administrative/legal_aid_indigent_defendants/ls_slcaid_lrap_state_chart_funding_amounts_sources.authcheckdam.pdf) (total 2012 annual funding for Iowa was $20,000, and for Indiana, $4,625; funding was suspended altogether for 2012 in South Carolina).

61. U.S. Dept. of Education, Final Regulations, Federal Perkins Loan Program, Federal Family Education Loan Program, and William D. Ford Federal Direct Loan Program, 77 Fed. Reg. 66088 (Nov. 1, 2012). For married borrowers who file joint tax returns, adjusted gross income includes that of the borrower's spouse, but married borrowers (except those in community property states) may avoid that inclusion by filing separate returns. Pub. L. No. 110-153 (2007) (codified at 20 U.S.C. § 1098(e)).

62. Graduates who had government or government-guaranteed loans before October 2007, or who graduated before 2012, are not eligible for PAYE, but they can repay for ten years through the income-based repayment (IBR) plan. This will require them to pay 15% of discretionary income, or

to principal, but through PSLF, any principal or interest remaining after the borrower makes 120 payments while employed in full-time public service work is forgiven,[63] and the forgiveness is tax-exempt.[64]

Under PAYE, forgiveness can be substantial, particularly for those who perform 10 years of full-time public service, and even for those with relatively low incomes who do not perform public service.[65] For example, consider a borrower with $100,000 of educational debt payable at a weighted average of 7.22 percent, who works in a legal aid office for 10 years, starting at $40,000 a year and receiving 4 percent increases annually. In the first month, the borrower would repay $198, compared with $1,173 under a standard (10-year) repayment plan. After 10 years of repayment, during which monthly payments will increase gradually to $298, the borrower will have repaid nearly $30,000 and will still owe more than $142,000 in unpaid principal and interest. The government will forgive that remaining balance.[66]

---

about 10% of actual income. A more complete description of IBR is provided in Philip G. Schrag, Federal Student Loan Repayment Assistance for Public Interest Lawyers and Other Employees of Governments and Nonprofit Organizations, 36 Hofstra L. Rev. 27 (2007) (available at http://www.law.georgetown.edu/news/documents/Forgiveness.pdf). FinAid.org provides a web-based calculator that students can use to quickly determine how PAYE and IBR repayment and loan forgiveness would affect repayment of debts. The calculators for both repayment plans are at http://www.finaid.org/calculators/ibr.phtml (accessed Nov. 24, 2012). Law schools can now create significant loan repayment assistance programs at much less cost than before the CCRAA was enacted because they can lower their public service graduates' loan repayment expenses to zero (and thereby enable those graduates to go to law school for free) by reimbursing the graduates, for ten years, the approximately 7 percent (or 10 percent) of their incomes that the graduates would have to repay under IBR. See Schrag & Pruett, supra n. 54.

63. Pub. L. No. 110-84, § § 203, 401 (2007) (codified at 20 U.S.C. §§ 1078-3, 1087e, 1087e(m)(1), and 1098e). See http://studentaid.ed.gov/repay-loans/forgiveness-cancellation/charts/public-service. Borrowers who received government-guaranteed loans rather than direct loans from the U.S. Department of Education must consolidate into federal direct consolidation loans before their monthly payments will qualify under the federal program for forgiveness after 10 years. The law guarantees them the right to do so. Id. Loans that qualify for forgiveness include Stafford loans, Grad PLUS loans, and, under some conditions, Perkins loans. See FinAid.org, Public Service Loan Forgiveness, http://www.finaid.org/loans/publicservice.phtml (accessed Nov. 24, 2012); Equal Justice Works, The Federal Student Loan Forgiveness Law: College Cost Reduction and Access Act of 2007, http://www.equaljusticeworks.org/resource/ccraa (accessed Nov. 24, 2012).

64. Letter to Rep. Sander Levin from Eric Soloman, Assistant Sec'y of the Treasury, Sept. 19, 2008, available at http://www.ibrinfo.org/files/Treasury_response_levin.pdf. If the borrower's income rises so much that the PAYE formula would require repayment at a rate higher than so-called "standard" (10-year) repayment, the borrower must change to standard repayment terms.

65. Graduates who do not do 10 years of public service, but whose incomes are low compared to their educational debts, may benefit from PAYE but not from PSLF. For these graduates, forgiveness takes place only after 20 years of repayment under the PAYE formula, and forgiveness is not tax-exempt.

66. If the borrower is eligible only for IBR rather than PAYE, the amount of monthly payments will be somewhat greater, and the amount that is forgiven correspondingly lower.

C. Restrictions on legal services

1. Restrictions on lawyers

a. Advertising and solicitation

Until the 1970s, states restricted the availability of legal services to the public by severely limiting advertising by lawyers. Advertising was seen as unseemly and unethical. But prohibitions on advertising made it difficult for people, other than those in the business world, to find lawyers who had experience with the problems they faced. Also, bans on advertising limited competition and therefore kept fees high. But a group of lawyers who wanted to advertise low-cost legal services litigated the constitutionality of Arizona's ban. In a landmark decision, the Supreme Court held that most advertising by lawyers is protected by the First Amendment.[67] Today, many small law firms advertise on billboards, on local television stations, on the Internet, and in the yellow pages of the phone book (where yellow pages still exist).

Questions About Lawyer Advertising

1. Look at some display advertisements for lawyers in the yellow pages of the phone book, in newspapers and magazines, on billboards, and online, and consider these examples. In recent years, the authors' local yellow pages have included the following ads.

   - "You are David. They are Goliath. We are your slingshot. We sue employers that discriminate and wrongfully fire employees. We know how to prove your employer's true motivation or intentional disregard for your rights. If they won't provide fair severance pay, we will sue for all legal damages."
   - A picture of two lawyers who are "attorneys experienced in representing the seriously injured and their families. NEGLIGENT FAILURE TO DIAGNOSE CERVICAL, BREAST, COLON, LUNG, SKIN AND PROSTATE CANCER."
   - A two-page, four-color ad with a large photo of a child in a wheelchair and another of an overturned car. The text includes a list of "SERIOUS ACCIDENTS" such as "AUTO ACCIDENTS," "SPINAL INJURIES," "BURNS," "AMPUTATIONS" and "PARALYSIS" and a notice on what appears to be a $1,000 bill. The notice says, "In many cases we can assist you in arranging for LOANS to cover housing, medical bills, food, etc. while you are

---

67. Bates v. St. B. of Ariz., 433 U.S. 350 (1977).

injured. HOW? Through lending institutions that respect our judgement [sic] and ability. Are we the ONLY LAW FIRM that offers this service? Look for Yourself!!!"

Also consider the ads that lawyers may run on late-night television in your area. When the Staten Island ferry crashed into a pier in New York in 2003, injuring many passengers, lawyers published television and newspaper advertisements to recruit clients. One TV commercial showed a "ghostly image of a ferry washed over by a tidal wave of green dollar signs" and proclaimed, "If you were injured, you may be entitled to money damages." The *New York Times* quoted legal experts and personal injury lawyers as saying that some of these ads "dangle at the edge of what is morally and ethically appropriate after a fatal accident."

The examples don't stop there. What is titled the "Tackiest Lawyer Commercial . . . Ever" appears on YouTube, and a billboard put up by a Chicago firm that specializes in family law was described by ABC News as including a photo of "the six-pack abs of a headless male torso and tanned female cleavage heaving forth from a black lace bra" along with the message "Life's Short. Get a divorce." The Illinois bar authorities declined to take action against the firm, but a local alderman had city workers take it down on the ground that the firm did not have the proper billboard permit.

Should any of these ads or other examples you identify be prohibited by law or by ethics rules, either because they are misleading or for any other reason?

2. Should lawyers be allowed to tout their past success records in their ads, even though past success is no assurance of future success for any particular client?

Some lawyers seek to attract clients through advertising. Others do so by contacting prospective clients to offer their services. Before ethics rules curbed the practice, lawyers sometimes contacted accident victims in person to solicit cases, and they sometimes hired "runners" who would approach prospective clients at the scene of an accident or elsewhere and give out the lawyer's business cards. Although it has protected advertising by lawyers by extending First Amendment protection, the U.S. Supreme Court has shown greater willingness to allow regulation of solicitation by lawyers. The analysis has focused on the means by which the lawyer contacts prospective clients.

FOR EXAMPLE: Florida Rule 4-7.4(b) provides that "(1) A lawyer shall not send . . . an unsolicited written communication directly or indirectly to a prospective client for the purpose of obtaining professional employment if . . . the written communication concerns an action for personal injury or wrongful death or otherwise relates to an accident or disaster involving the person to whom the communication is addressed or a relative of that person, unless the accident or disaster occurred more than 30 days prior to the mailing of the communication. . . . The first page of such written communications shall be plainly marked 'advertisement' in red ink, and the lower left corner of the face of the envelope containing a written communication likewise shall carry a prominent, red 'advertisement' mark." Two lawyers challenged the 30-day rule on First Amendment grounds, noting that insurance adjusters rush in to settle claims well before 30 days after an accident occurs, and the settlements extinguish any further rights that might be asserted by accident victims. The state bar's rule against contact applied only to lawyers, not insurance agents, and the state bar had no authority to regulate insurance agents. Nevertheless, the Supreme Court upheld the Florida rule.[68]

May lawyers solicit clients over the Internet?

The development of the Internet has led to new means by which lawyers may reach potential clients. Lawyers are able to advertise on their own webpages, provide further information to people who click on links on those pages, and purchase pop-up ads on other people's webpages. Lawyers also may pay third parties, such as Groupon, a fixed amount of money for each new client attracted by the third party's website. One law firm gave out free t-shirts with its name on them and offered a chance to win a prize to all who posted photos of themselves wearing the t-shirt on their Facebook pages. Do any of these devices amount to improper solicitation or to sharing fees with nonlawyers in violation of Rule 5.4? For example, does the use of Groupon, or the creation of the t-shirt lottery, turn the Groupon company, or the t-shirt wearers, into the twenty-first-century equivalent of runners? In 2012, the ABA amended Comment 5 to Model Rule 7.2 to clarify that pay-per-lead services are permissible and that lawyers may pay an Internet "lead generator" such as Groupon, provided that the compensated entity does not recommend the lawyer, that it does not advertise in a manner forbidden to lawyers themselves, and that Rule 1.5(e)'s limitations on divisions of fees are not violated. The amended comment provides that lawyers may not pay lead generators if the lead generator

---

68. Fla. B. v. Went For It, Inc., 515 U.S. 618 (1995).

implies that the lawyer has not paid for the lead or that it has analyzed a client's problem when determining which lawyer receives the referral.[69]

b. Multi-jurisdictional practice

As you know from Chapter 1, lawyers are licensed by states, not by the federal government. As a result, interstate competition among lawyers is limited, a fact that may keep fees higher than they would be in a national market for legal services.

Suppose a man who lives in New Jersey and works in New York asks his regular lawyer, who is licensed to practice only in New York, for advice about whether New Jersey would impose a tax on the sale of his New Jersey home. If the New York lawyer knows or can obtain the answer, may she give this advice about New Jersey law? If so, does it matter where the lawyer or her client is when he gives the advice? May the New York lawyer give the advice while having dinner at his friend's New Jersey home? May the lawyer give the advice on the telephone from his Manhattan office if the client is at his own home in New Jersey?

Or suppose a lawyer who is admitted to practice in New York wants to advertise for clients in New Jersey newspapers. May New Jersey prohibit this out-of-state lawyer from advertising, even though it could not ban ads by New Jersey lawyers?

In the name of consumer protection, state bars have tended to protect their lawyers from "outside" competition. They have regarded poaching by out-of-state lawyers as unauthorized practice, just as if an out-of-state lawyer were not a lawyer at all.

Europe imposes fewer geographic restrictions on law practice. European lawyers may practice throughout their own countries and in other countries that are part of the European Union (EU). One expert explains: "Lawyers and law firms from any EU state are able to represent clients on a continuous basis throughout the European Union, practice in almost all commercial law fields in any EU country, and form multinational law firms with offices as desired in any EU commercial center."

Contrast this European flexibility with a decision by the California Supreme Court in a case often referred to as *Birbrower*. A California company retained New York lawyers to help it make claims against another California company. The lawyers went to California, met with their client's accountants, and advised them about how to settle the dispute. Over a period of two days, they also met with representatives of the other Cali-

---

69. The ABA did not address whether lotteries are permitted. Even before the 2012 amendment, some state bars ethics committees had already approved lawyers' use of "daily deal" websites. See, e.g., S.C. B., Ethics Advisory Op. 11-05 (available at http://www.scbar.org/MemberResources/Ethics AdvisoryOpinions/OpinionView/ArticleId/1012/Ethics-Advisory-Opinion-11-05.aspx).

fornia company. On a second trip, they discussed settlement with both parties. Arbitration was contemplated, but the case was eventually settled without arbitration. The New York lawyers sued their client for their fee, and the client defended against payment by claiming that the New York lawyers' work in California was unauthorized practice of law. The California Supreme Court held that the fee agreement was unenforceable because the New York lawyers had not been admitted to practice in California. The court stated that a lawyer could engage in unauthorized practice not only by appearing in court but also by giving advice or providing other legal services. The court noted that an out-of-state lawyer could commit unauthorized practice in California without even setting foot in the state by advising a California client by telephone or e-mail about California law. The court also observed that California law prohibited out-of-state lawyers from giving advice or performing other legal services in California, even if they affiliated with local California law firms.

The *Birbrower* decision was overturned in part by a California state statute. It also shocked the organized bar into initiating a modest effort, on a national scale, to allow attorneys from one state to perform some services in another state. That effort produced an amendment to Model Rule 5.5, which now permits a lawyer otherwise in good standing to perform legal services in another host state on a temporary basis if any one of four factors applies:

> The lawyer is affiliated with another lawyer licensed in the host state who actively participates in the matter.
>
> The lawyer is preparing for pending or potential litigation and is admitted to appear in the proceedings or reasonably expects to be admitted.
>
> The lawyer's work in the host state is incident to a pending or potential alternative-dispute-resolution proceeding and is reasonably related to the lawyer's practice in a state in which he or she is admitted.
>
> The lawyer's work arises out of practice in a jurisdiction in which the lawyer is licensed. (In other words, the lawyer can practice temporarily in another state if she is working for a client in her own state or on a matter connected with her home state.)

The amendment to Rule 5.5 has been adopted in at least 44 states, sometimes with local variations. But it is very narrow. It might not even have protected the New York lawyers in *Birbrower* from committing unauthorized practice. They were not affiliated with a California firm. They did not contemplate litigation for which they expected to be admitted by a court. The case did involve a potential alternative dispute resolution. But the proceeding was not directly related to the firm's New York practice, although possibly it was "reasonably related" to that practice. In any event, amended Rule 5.5 does not go nearly as far in permitting cross-border practice in the United States as Europe has gone in permitting cross-border international practice.

2. Restrictions on nonlawyers

Since many Americans need legal help but cannot afford it and the legal profession is unable to meet the need, perhaps trained paralegals or other nonlawyers should be allowed to provide some basic legal services. Persons with a few weeks or months of training, for example, might staff storefront offices and review lease forms for prospective tenants, help people draft documents to obtain uncontested divorces, or assist with claims for public benefits. The courts could create an examination that would test these basic skills and certify those who passed to provide some services for limited fees or on a pro bono basis. These providers would not be allowed to engage in the full range of activities that are now reserved to lawyers. On the other hand, some people think that legal services should be provided only by those who have had three years of legal education, have passed a bar examination and a character review, and are subject to the lawyer disciplinary system. That is the essential issue in the debate over the proper role for nonlawyers in the solution of routine legal problems.

From 1914 to 1940, professional bar associations, including the ABA, organized successful campaigns that often resorted to litigation to bar nonlawyers from competing with lawyers.[70] Today nearly every state has a statute barring nonlawyers from practicing law or a court doctrine permitting the state bar association or state officials to bring suits to enjoin unauthorized practice.[71]

A central question in the prohibition of unauthorized practice of law (UPL) is the definition of "practice of law." The ABA tried to craft a uniform national definition of what activities constitute the "practice of law," but it eventually abandoned this project.[72] The wording of the UPL statute varies from state to state, but Connecticut's somewhat circular law is representative.

> **Conn. Gen. Stat. § 51-88 (2006)**
> A person who has not been admitted as an attorney ... shall not: (1) Practice law or appear as an attorney-at-law for another, in any

---

70. Derek A. Denckla, Nonlawyers and the Unauthorized Practice of Law: An Overview of the Legal and Ethical Parameters, 67 Fordham L. Rev. 2581, 2583-2584 (1999).

71. Id. at 2585-2586.

72. Utah and Arizona Define Practice of Law; ABA Group Opts Not to Set Model Definition, 71 U.S.L.W. 2642 (Apr. 15, 2003). The ABA abandoned its effort after the U.S. Department of Justice and the Federal Trade Commission warned that its draft rule would reduce consumer choice.

court of record in this state, [or] (2) make it a business to practice law, or appear as an attorney-at-law for another in any such court. . . . Any person who violates any provision of this section shall be fined not more than two hundred and fifty dollars or imprisoned not more than two months or both.

Responding to criticism of the rules on UPL in the 1990s, the ABA's Commission on Non-lawyer Practice recommended reforming the rules. For example, it recommended that states should consider allowing non-lawyer representation of individuals in state administrative agency proceedings and that the ABA should examine its own ethical rules regarding unauthorized practice. It also recommended that the ABA assess, for each type of prohibition of nonlawyer activity, whether the benefits of regulation were outweighed by the negative consequences.[73] "The report was sent to a committee of the Board of Governors but was never presented to the House of Delegates. Its recommendations were never implemented."[74]

Are nonlawyers ever allowed to help people with their legal problems?

Yes. Lawyers are allowed to hire and train nonlawyers as paraprofessionals (sometimes called "paralegals" but called "nonlawyer assistants" by Rule 5.3). These employees may help clients with routine legal problems, such as filling out forms, and they may offer routine advice. However, the employing lawyer must supervise the paraprofessionals and take responsibility for their advice and other work. If a paraprofessional violates a rule of professional responsibility, the supervising lawyer may be disciplined for the violation.[75] Paraprofessionals' work is often billed to clients at an hourly rate.

Some statutes, court rules, and administrative agencies explicitly permit lay advocacy. For example, the Social Security Administration allows unsuccessful claimants to obtain hearings to challenge denials of benefits (such as disability benefits). In those hearings, the claimants may be represented by persons of their choice.[76] Similarly, the Department of Homeland Security has a process of certifying nonlawyer staff members of "religious, charitable, social service, or similar" organizations to represent immigrants claiming certain immigration benefits.[77] Also, many courts and agencies allow law students to provide free representation to indigent cli-

---

73. ABA, Non-lawyer Activity in Law-Related Situations: A Report with Recommendations 8-10 (ABA 1995) (copy on file with the authors).
74. Debra Baker, Is This Woman a Threat to Lawyers? ABA J. 54 (June 1999).
75. Rule 5.3. The standards for disciplining the supervising lawyer are very similar to the standards for disciplining supervisors of associates under Rule 5.1, which is discussed in Chapter 2.
76. 20 C.F.R. § 404.1705 (2006).
77. 8 C.F.R. §§ 292.1-292.2 (2006).

ents. The students must be supervised by clinical teachers or (in some cases) legal aid lawyers.

California licenses "legal document assistants" who may help consumers who are representing themselves in official proceedings. If a consumer with a legal problem knows enough to find and select the proper form, a document assistant may help her fill it out but may not "provide any kind of advice, explanation, opinion, or recommendation to a consumer about possible legal rights, remedies, defenses, options, selection of forms, or strategies."[78] Washington State has taken the licensing of what it calls "limited legal license technicians" a step further, requiring such persons to have more education and experience than those in California, and to pass a licensing examination, but allowing them to undertake more actions than in California without attorney supervision.[79]

The prohibition against UPL is more blurry in some commercial contexts than in noncommercial contexts. For example, accountants routinely prepare tax returns for their clients, even though the tax code is very complex and almost any judgment about how income or expenditures should be treated for tax purposes involves interpretation of law. Similarly, in many states, realtors prepare deeds to property and manage the execution of the closing documents. In some states, real estate salespersons are allowed to attend the actual closings.[80]

Is it a violation of the unauthorized practice laws to publish a manual on how to write a will or a lease?

Maybe. A federal district court in Texas enjoined the publication of the software Quicken Family Lawyer, which included forms for wills, leases, premarital agreements, and 100 other situations. The software itself (but not the packaging) cautioned that the program did not provide individualized information and that purchasers should use their own judgment about whether to consult lawyers. The court found that publication of the software constituted UPL and that the Texas UPL rule did not violate the First or Fourteenth Amendment.[81] The Texas legislature overturned the court decision by passing a statute that stated that the publication of

---

78. Cal. Bus. & Prof. Code § 6400(d) (2011); see also id. § 6401. Suppose a form asks, "Do you claim that the merchant committed fraud?" and the consumer asks the document assistant to explain what the question means. May the assistant answer, or would any answer constitute an unlawful offer of an "explanation" regarding the consumer's "rights"?

79. Sup. Ct. of Wash., Admission to Practice Rule 28 (adopted June 15, 2012) (available at http://www.courts.wa.gov/content/publicUpload/Press%20Releases/25700-A-1005.pdf).

80. See ABA, Standing Comm. on Client Protection, 2009 Survey of Unlicensed Practice of Law Committees, Chart II and notes thereto (May 2009) (available at http://www.americanbar.org/content/dam/aba/migrated/cpr/clientpro/09_upl_survey.authcheckdam.pdf).

81. Unauth. Prac. L. Comm. v. Parsons Tech., 1999 WL 47235 (N.D. Tex. Jan. 22, 1999).

"computer software or similar products" does not constitute UPL if the products state conspicuously that they are not a substitute for the advice of a lawyer.[82] After the legislature enacted this new law, the U.S. court of appeals dissolved the injunction.[83]

More recently, a company called LegalZoom created software through which, for a small fee, customers enter information in windows on their computer screens to generate documents such as bills of sale, leases, wills, promissory notes, trademark applications, or releases. A LegalZoom employee who is not a lawyer reviews the information for completeness and advises the customer about inconsistencies and spelling or grammatical errors. Then the employee electronically pastes the individual's information into a legal forms template to create the document and mails it to the customer. Two consumers who used the website admitted that they had no complaint about the services rendered to them, but they brought a class action seeking refunds on the ground that the website constituted UPL and that therefore LegalZoom could not keep their fees. Denying LegalZoom's motion for summary judgment, a federal district court concluded that a jury could find that this system constitutes UPL. A company may print blank legal forms, but this service is different because an employee translates the raw information into a legal form. Furthermore, the court reasoned, even the creation of a computer program that uses principles of state law to determine which form should be used requires the use of legal judgment and could be UPL.[84] Shortly after the court ruled, the parties settled; the settlement required LegalZoom to pay the plaintiffs but allowed it to continue to offer services, although it had to make some modifications to its practices.[85]

Do-it-yourself manuals or computer programs can be helpful but may be less useful than the personal services of a good lawyer, although of course they cost far less. A *New York Times* writer tested four will-writing programs and also consulted an estate planning lawyer. She discovered that her will came out quite differently with each of the programs. After she used the programs, she "still needed a lawyer to help decode some seemingly standard clauses and their consequences." She noted that "a computer program

---

82. Tex. H.B. 1507, 76th Leg., Reg. Sess. (Feb. 16, 1999), enacted as Tex. Govt. Code Ann. § 81.101 (2005).

83. Unauth. Prac. L. Comm. v. Parsons Tech., 179 F.3d 956 (5th Cir. 1999).

84. Janson v. LegalZoom, Inc., Case No. 2:10-CV-04018-NKL (W.D. Mo., Aug. 2, 2011), 2011 U.S. Dist LEXIS 84839 (available at http://scholar.google.com/scholar_case?case= 2671645762556405280&hl=en&as_sdt=2&as_vis=1&oi=scholarr).

85. The settlement agreement is available at http://www.jansonsettlement.com/docs/sa.pdf (accessed Dec. 6, 2012).

can't ask you about your family relationships or tease out complex dynamics, like your daughter's rocky marriage."[86]

Are nonlawyers really prosecuted for helping individuals who can't afford to pay lawyers?

Hard data is difficult to obtain. However, in 2009, bar officials in a third of 39 states that responded to an ABA questionnaire reported that they anticipated "an uptick" in enforcement efforts, including the adoption of more rules and regulations, implementation of undercover "sting" operations, increased penalties, and larger budgets for enforcement.[87] The Virginia bar's ethics committee decided, at about the same time, that state bar investigators may use deception, notwithstanding the ethics rules discussed in Chapter 11, if necessary to catch nonlawyers who are giving legal advice and advertising only by word of mouth.[88]

May a lawyer provide guidance to a nonlawyer who helps people with their legal problems?

Suppose a community organizer who is not a lawyer but who is an expert on landlord-tenant problems advises poor people about their problems with their landlords. Suppose this person has a lawyer friend whom she calls for advice when questions come up that she can't answer. If she has the advice of her friend, is her assistance of tenants still UPL? Or does the lawyer's "on-call" assistance solve the problem?

If the lawyer employs the nonlawyer, takes and accepts responsibility for the quality of the work that is performed, and subjects herself to malpractice liability and bar discipline if the work is performed incompetently, the organizer's work is not unauthorized practice. But if the organizer is independent, either she or the lawyer could get into trouble. Rule 5.5(a) states that a lawyer may not practice law in any jurisdiction in violation of the laws regulating the practice of law in that jurisdiction or "assist another in doing so."

How can nonwealthy individuals obtain the legal help that they need?

Large corporations and wealthy individuals are able to foot the bill for legal services they need, but most poor and middle class individuals cannot afford to hire lawyers when they need them. Many lawyers would like to

---

86. Tara Siegel Bernard, In Using Software to Write a Will, a Lawyer Is Still Helpful, N.Y. Times (Sept. 11, 2010) (available at http://www.nytimes.com/2010/09/11/your-money/11money.html?pagewanted=all).

87. Latest ABA Review of UPL Enforcement Finds More Regulation, More Prosecution, 77 U.S. L.W. 2695 (May 19, 2009).

88. Va. St. B. Standing Comm. on Legal Ethics, Op. 1845 (2009) (available at http://www.vacle.org/opinions/1845.htm).

serve the needs of people in their communities, but the costs of running a law office—rent, utilities, staff, electronic subscriptions, malpractice insurance, advertising, and the like—are high, and lawyers must charge substantial legal fees as well as to support themselves and their families. Thorough investigation of a client's problem requires, at a minimum, an interview of the client and usually some additional investigation, counseling, and drafting. If the problem involves a potential adversary, some negotiation or litigation is required. Even if lawyers do not aspire to great wealth, costs associated with law practice often preclude offering low-cost services.

The solution to this problem may require greater efficiency in the operation of law firms. For example, even greater efforts may be required to take advantage of technology to avoid replication of effort and to delegate routine tasks to lower-cost paraprofessionals. Some lawyers might locate in less expensive areas of the country (or the world) and supply services over the Internet. Lawyers, bar associations, and state courts should loosen the monopoly that lawyers currently enjoy on providing what we think of as legal services. More states should license legal document technicians who have practical training but not law degrees. Retail stores rather than law offices may provide some of their overhead expenses. More government agencies should allow persons who come before them to be represented by lawyers or nonlawyers. The unauthorized practice rules should be relaxed to allow more advocacy and assistance by experienced laypersons. Companies like LegalZoom may also fill part of the yawning gap between lawyers and underserved clients.

The world of legal practice is changing. Will it change in ways that benefit ordinary people, or will it degenerate into a system in which too many lawyers are chasing the few clients who have wealth and power? Today's law students will help to decide the shape and scope of the legal profession of tomorrow.

About the Authors

 Lisa G. Lerman is Professor of Law at The Catholic University of America, Columbus School of Law, where she has taught since 1987. She attended Barnard College and NYU School of Law. She received an LL.M. from Georgetown University Law. Before joining the faculty at Catholic University, Lerman was a staff attorney at the Center for Women Policy Studies, a Clinical Fellow at Antioch and Georgetown law schools, a member of the law faculty at West Virginia University, and an associate in a small law firm. She also has taught at the law schools of American University, George Washington University, and Jagiellonian University (Krakow, Poland).

At Catholic University, in addition to her teaching responsibilities, Professor Lerman has served as Coordinator of Clinical Programs since 2006. She is responsible for development and administration of the externship program and oversees some clinical courses. From 1996 until 2007, Lerman was Director of the Law and Public Policy Program, an academic enrichment program for students seeking careers in public service. She has taught professional responsibility since 1984. She also has taught contracts, family law, public policy courses, and clinical and externship courses.

Professor Lerman is co-author of *Learning from Practice: A Professional Development Text for Legal Externs* (2d ed. West 2007). She has written many articles about lawyers, law firms, the legal profession, and legal education, including, for example, *Blue-Chip Bilking: Regulation of Billing and Expense Fraud by Lawyers,* 12 Geo. J. Leg. Ethics 205 (1999), and *Lying to Clients,* 138 U. Pa. L. Rev. 659 (1990). Lerman's earlier work focused on domestic violence law.

Professor Lerman has served as an expert witness on legal ethics issues in numerous legal malpractice cases and lawyer disciplinary matters. She has written, lectured, and consulted on legal ethics issues and on various aspects of legal education, including the teaching of professional responsibility, the structure of externship programs, and the use of interactive teaching in law school classes. Professor Lerman has served as a member of the AALS Standing Committee on Bar Admission and Lawyer Performance, as chair of the AALS section on Professional Responsibility, on the DC Bar Legal Ethics Committee, and on the planning committee for the ABA National Conference on Professional Responsibility.

Philip G. Schrag is the Delaney Family Professor of Public Interest Law at Georgetown University Law Center. He attended Harvard College and Yale Law School. Before he started a career in law teaching, he was Assistant Counsel of the NAACP Legal Defense and Educational Fund, Inc., and in 1970 he became the first Consumer Advocate of the City of New York. A member of the founding generation of clinical law teachers, he developed clinics at Columbia Law School and the West Virginia University College of Law, as well as at Georgetown. During the administration of President Jimmy Carter, he was the Deputy General Counsel of the United States Arms Control and Disarmament Agency.

At Georgetown, Professor Schrag directs the Center for Applied Legal Studies, an asylum and refugee clinic. He regularly teaches civil procedure and has also taught consumer protection, federal income taxation, legislation, administrative law, and professional responsibility. He has written fifteen books and many articles on public interest law and legal education including *Asylum Denied: A Refugee's Struggle for Safety in America* (with David Ngaruri Kenney) (Univ. of Cal. Press 2008). In 2007, he helped to persuade Congress to create the Public Service Loan Forgiveness Program, which provides partial student loan forgiveness for graduates who work for ten years in public interest jobs. He has been honored with the Association of American Law Schools' Deborah L. Rhode award for advancing public service opportunities in law schools through scholarship, service, and leadership; its William Pincus award for outstanding contributions to clinical legal education; Lexis/Nexis' Daniel Levy Memorial Award for Outstanding Achievement in Immigration Law; and the Outstanding Law School Faculty Award of Equal Justice Works, for leadership in nurturing a spirit of public service in legal education and beyond.

Professors Lerman and Schrag have two children, Samuel Schrag Lerman and Sarah Lerman Schrag. As this book goes to press, Sam is a Staff Sergeant in the United States Air Force and Sarah is teaching high school English with Teach for America in Louisiana. Professor Schrag has two adult sons, David and Zachary. The authors have three grandchildren, Leonard, Nora, and Thomas. Professors Lerman and Schrag live in Bethesda, Maryland, with their three cats.

TABLE OF ARTICLES, BOOKS, AND REPORTS

Works that are quoted at length in the text appear in bold italic type in this table. Works that are quoted briefly or summarized appear in italics.

TABLE OF CASES

Principal cases are in bold italics. Cases that have not been excerpted but have been quoted, discussed, or summarized in the text are in italics.

TABLE OF RULES, RESTATEMENTS, STATUTES, BAR OPINIONS, AND OTHER STANDARDS

ABA Model Rules of Professional Conduct and Delaware Rules of Professional Conduct

Note: As explained in the Introduction, rules of professional conduct quoted in the text are from the Delaware Rules of Professional Conduct. Except as indicated in the text, these quoted rules are identical to the ABA Model Rules of Professional Conduct. Therefore, the following list of Rules of Professional Conduct refers both to the Delaware Rules and to the Model Rules. Entries in bold refer to pages on which the language of a rule, a section of a rule, or a comment is set forth in the text.

U.S. Constitution

Federal Statutes and Regulations

Federal Rules of Civil Procedure

INDEX